PEN

LOWER TH

'Immensely broad in scope, inc
with no small measure of hu
time and again. The overarchin
of the subject is magisteria

'An erudite, judicious and often sympathetic account of Christian history, in all its complexity, by a historian and theologian with impeccable credentials ... *Lower than the Angels* is sweeping in its scope and expresses an amused tolerance for the oddities of religious life ... It is a work that cannot fail to command respect' Lucy Wooding, *LRB*

'This history takes us from early Jewish concepts of God and sex right up to the current Anglican rows about homosexuality ... the author [is] a genial, knowledgeable companion' Melanie McDonagh, *Spectator*

'Diarmaid MacCulloch explains in *Lower than the Angels* [how] many biblical pronouncements on sexuality are ambiguous, if not downright contradictory ... by showing us the bigger picture, MacCulloch allows the reader to fully appreciate the complexity and diversity of Christian experience, and to identify recurrent themes ... [a] thought-provoking and compassionate book' Katherine Harvey, *Engelsberg Ideas*

'An intricate history with a clear moral: Christians should think twice before casting the first stone ... a compelling book' Michael Ledger-Lomas, *History Today*

'I loved the interplay of learned theology with the experiences and voices of ordinary people across the ages as they tried to make sense of questions connected to sex. MacCulloch writes with eloquence and wit even as he addresses the most moving subjects that lie at the heart of being human' Hannah Skoda, *BBC History Magazine*, Books of the Year

'Wry and original ... As a compendious and rigorous guide to the histories that underlie current church debates on sex and gender, this work is invaluable' Penelope Cowell Doe, *Church Times*

ABOUT THE AUTHOR

Diarmaid MacCulloch is Emeritus Professor of the History of the Church at Oxford University. His *Thomas Cranmer* (1996) won the Whitbread Biography Prize, the James Tait Black Prize and the Duff Cooper Prize, and *Reformation: Europe's House Divided 1490–1700* (2004) won the Wolfson Prize and the British Academy Prize. *A History of Christianity* (2010), which was adapted into a six-part BBC television series, was awarded the Cundill and Hessel-Tiltman Prizes. He was knighted in 2012 and was awarded the Norton Medlicott Medal by the Historical Association in 2022.

DIARMAID MACCULLOCH

Lower than the Angels

A History of Sex and Christianity

PENGUIN BOOKS

PENGUIN BOOKS

UK | USA | Canada | Ireland | Australia
India | New Zealand | South Africa

Penguin Books is part of the Penguin Random House group of companies whose addresses can be found at global.penguinrandomhouse.com

Penguin Random House UK
One Embassy Gardens, 8 Viaduct Gardens, London SW11 7BW

penguin.co.uk

First published by Allen Lane 2024
Published in Penguin Books 2025
001

Typeset by Jouve (UK), Milton Keynes
Printed and bound in Great Britain by Clays Ltd, Elcograf S.p.A.

The authorized representative in the EEA is Penguin Random House Ireland, Morrison Chambers, 32 Nassau Street, Dublin D02 YH68

A CIP catalogue record for this book is available from the British Library

ISBN: 978-0-141-99095-8

Penguin Random House is committed to a sustainable future for our business, our readers and our planet. This book is made from Forest Stewardship Council® certified paper.

For Alex, Ben and Max, in memory of Felicity and Alice

Contents

PART FIVE
New Stories

List of Illustrations

Photographic acknowledgements are shown in italics.

ILLUSTRATIONS IN THE TEXT

COLOUR ILLUSTRATIONS

Acknowledgements

Hardly had my reading for this book begun in 2020 when the world was plunged into lockdown. It was a particular pleasure in those peculiar conditions to enjoy the virtual or carefully regulated face-to-face company of my colleagues and friends at Campion Hall Oxford, who in my retirement from the Oxford Theology and Religion Faculty had generously elected me to a Fellowship at the Hall, complete with study space. Their hospitality afforded pleasant hours contemplating angels proudly bearing rifles, in the delightful collection of Cuzco art donated to the Hall by Prof. Peter Davidson. I extend my thanks to all at Campion for their welcome and conversation, alongside my continuing happy association with St Cross College over three decades, now as Emeritus Fellow.

Although I take full responsibility for both the reading and research I have done and for the conclusions I have drawn, I was very lucky to have expert and enthusiastic assistance from Dr Anna Chrysostomides and Dr Rachel Dryden, specialists in Orthodox and Oriental Orthodox Christianity, who drew up bibliographies for me on some of the topics investigated in this book. What an unalloyed pleasure it was to work with them and enjoy their learning and friendship: it was a privilege to discuss this material with them, and they hugely enriched what I have been able to write. I am deeply grateful to the British Academy Small Grants Fund, supported by the Leverhulme Trust, for providing funding for that research assistance.

I am also grateful to friends and colleagues for fruitful conversations and advice, of whom these are especially to be thanked, while exempt from blame for remaining faults: Lindsay Allason-Jones, Sarah Apetrei, Nick Austin, Matthew Bemand-Qureshi, John Blair, Averil Cameron, Sarah Caro, Martin Carver, Mark Chapman, Sophie Grace Chappell, Sarah Coakley, Katy Cubitt, Brian Cummings, Peter Davidson, Bea Groves, Peter Groves, Helena Hamerow, Michael Harazin, Martin Henig, Judith Herrin, David Hilliard, Ronald Hutton, Isidoros Katsos, Jim Keenan, Tim Lavy, Philip Lindholm, Jack Mahoney, Noel Malcolm, Rachel

Rafael Neis, Nicholas Orme, Aristotle Papanikolaou, David Parker, Ken Parker, John Paton, Glyn Redworth, Malise Ruthven, Alison Salvesen, Josephine Seccombe, Gemma Simmonds, Michael Snape, Guy Stroumsa, Susan Walker, Robin Ward, William Whyte, Christopher Woods and Simon Yarrow. In addition, Sam Baddeley, John Barton, John Blair, Katy Cubitt, Sue Gillingham, Paula Gooder, Helen King and Judith Maltby kindly read all or part of my text and made invaluable suggestions. I learned much from the late John Boswell and the late Alan Bray, brave and pioneering scholars whom I would dearly love to have known longer.

As ever, I am hugely grateful to the support provided even for retired University staff by the Oxford library system and its heroic staff members, from Bodley's librarian onwards. What a luxury it is to enjoy this association. All through my three decades in Oxford, I have also luxuriated in the range of our graduate seminars and the welcome I received into their specialist deliberations. I co-edited the *Journal of Ecclesiastical History* for two decades from 1995. That journal, leader in its field worldwide, publishes around three hundred book reviews a year, commissioned by the editors from experts across the entire range of Church history: a superb resource of up-to-date discussion which I have found a sure guide in formulating the structure of my historical narratives. The present editorial team continues to be a source of friendship, fun and wisdom. Likewise, my fellow judges of the Wolfson Prize and our admirable support team have prompted both enjoyable discussions and a constant reminder to spread my sights across the whole field of historical publication beyond my own arbitrary interests. At Penguin Press, Stuart Proffitt's warm encouragement, expert editing and constant interest in the enterprise have remained essential to its completion, together with many Penguin colleagues, notably Richard Duguid. Cecilia Mackay has brought her usual energy and skill to enrich my choice of illustrations.

At an early stage in my preparation of this book came the death of my long-standing literary agent, Felicity Bryan: so much more than an agent, as friend, motivator and inspiration. Her zest for life in general, and for the writing and publishing of books in particular, will remain in the affectionate memory of all who knew her; this book itself owes much to her encouragement and spirited championship of my proposal, and it is a privilege to dedicate this book to her memory and for those who love her. Her colleague and successor, Catherine Clarke, has been a continuing source of support and friendship, and I am delighted by the continuing benevolent part that the fine folk at Felicity Bryan Associates play in my enterprises. Finally, those who have taught me what little I understand about human relationships will know who they are, and why they deserve my gratitude.

Diarmaid MacCulloch
St Cross College and Campion Hall Oxford,
February 2024

Conventions Used in the Text

In a work regarding the Christian faith, a first concern must be the most appropriate way to address the God who is the common object of worship for Jews, Christians and Muslims alike. In the past, like many modern Christian historians and biblical scholars, I have been in the habit of using the form 'Yahweh' to refer to God in a pre-Christian Judaistic context; so did a widely influential Roman Catholic English translation of the Bible, the Jerusalem Bible, until revised in 2019. This is potentially offensive to Jews, who for more than two millennia have refrained from pronouncing the Divine Name YHWH, to the extent that we do not really know how the name was pronounced before the ban on saying it arose. This is because Hebrew script originally registered only consonants. The addition of small dots and dashes, to ensure that the traditional pronunciation of Hebrew was not lost, came in only well into the Common Era, long after the ban was in place. The conjectural pronunciation 'Yahweh' rests on evidence in sources in Greek. Moreover, to use the 'Yahweh' form suggests that there is a difference between the God of the Hebrews and the God of Christians, a notion that mainstream Christianity vigorously rejected in the second century CE. For similar reasons, it is judicious in a work of history such as this not to distinguish 'God' in discussions of Islam by the use of his name in Arabic, *Allāh*, since the Qur'an makes a clear affirmation that God as proclaimed by the Prophet Muhammad is the same God as that of the Hebrews and of Christians.[1]

Readers should note that, for reasons of historical accuracy, I follow a recent trend in scholarship that translates the ancient Greek and Latin terms *Ioudaios* and *Judaeus* as 'Judaean', not 'Jew', when I refer to the long period of antiquity during which this description denoted not so much a religious identity as an ethnicity among the various ethnicities of the ancient world. The ethnicity included its own distinctive religious practice and, for some centuries, a political existence, in territories of Israel and Judah/Judaea. That period ended with the Romans' defeat of rebellions in Judaea during the second century CE, resulting in a major reconstruction of Judaistic tradition at that time, as well as accelerating dispersion of Judaean people from their historic lands.

I will speak of 'Jews' and 'Jewishness' first when talking about the various dispersed communities beyond Judah/Israel that were created by successive dispersals and exiles from the sixth century BCE. From the second century CE, 'Jews' and 'Jewishness' became a primarily religious identity without a territorial homeland, created both by an internal process of reframing that created rabbinic Judaism, and by the hostile discussion by Christians when they achieved increasing cultural and political ascendancy in the Mediterranean from the fourth century CE onwards. The chronological boundary is untidy but, in general, it is a safe principle to speak of Judaeans alongside Judaism when talking about the land of Judah and Israel, in which a distinctive religion was developing: otherwise to speak, alongside Judaism, simply of Jews and Jewishness.[2]

Equally, I have tried to avoid descriptions within Christian history that are offensive to those to whom they have been applied. That means that readers may encounter unfamiliar usages: so I speak of 'Miaphysites' and 'Dyophysites' rather than 'Monophysites' or 'Nestorians'. I hope that Jewish readers will forgive me if for simplicity's sake in some contexts, but not all, I call the Hebrew Bible/Scripture (in medieval and later Jewish usage often called the Tanakh) the Old Testament, in parallel to the Christian New Testament.

The terms 'polygamy' and 'polygyny' are commonly used interchangeably when marriage customs are under discussion, but it is almost always the case that what is being discussed is a marriage involving one man with more than one woman – that is, polygyny, a whole sub-category of polygamy. The strict opposite is polyandry, a social system enabling one woman to marry more than one man. That is much rarer in recorded human history and will feature little in this book, but it acts as a reminder that one should seek precision in discussing the whole topic. To avoid the common confusion of terminology, which looks suspiciously like a male assumption about norms, I do not often employ the widely used term polygamy and will normally speak of polygyny, when referring to a single male in a marriage to more than one woman; I retain the 'polygamy' usage where appropriate and in quotations from others. The term 'monogamy' does not present the same problems, so I use it throughout the text.

Most of my primary-source quotations in English are in modern spelling, but where I have quoted translations made by other people from other languages, I have not altered the gender-skewed language common in English usage up to the 1980s. I am more of a devotee of capital letters than is common today; in English convention, they are symbols of what is special, different and, in the context of this book, of what links the profane and the sacred world. The Mass and the Rood need capitals; both their devotees and those who hate them would agree on that. So do the Bible, the Eucharist, Saviour, the Blessed Virgin, and the Persons of the Trinity. The body of the faithful in a particular city in the early Church, or in a particular region, or the worldwide organization called the Church, all deserve a capital, although a building called a church does not. A similar distinction is worth making in capitalizing 'Gospel' when it refers to a sacred book, but not when 'gospel' means the 'good news' of the Christian message. The Bishop of Birmingham needs a capital, as does the Earl of Arran, but bishops and earls as a whole do not.

My general practice with place names has been to give the most helpful usage whether ancient or modern, sometimes with the alternative modern or ancient usage in brackets, and with alternatives given in the index. The common English versions of overseas place names (such as Jerusalem, Moscow, Milan or Munich) are also used. Readers will be aware that the islands embracing England, Ireland, Scotland and Wales have commonly been known as the British Isles. This title no longer pleases all their inhabitants, particularly those in the Republic of Ireland (a matter towards which this descendant of Scots Protestants is sensitive), and a more neutral, as well as more accurate, description is as the Atlantic Isles or Atlantic archipelago, which is used at various places throughout this book. I am aware that Portuguese-speakers have long used that phrase to describe entirely different islands, and indeed that Spaniards use it for yet a third collection; I hope that I may crave their joint indulgence for my arbitrary choice. Naturally the political entity called Great Britain which existed between 1707 and 1922, and which persists to the present in modified form, will be referred to as such where appropriate, and I use 'British Isles' in relation to that relatively brief period too.

I follow the same general practice with personal names, opting untidily for the most convenient form whether ancient or modern. That may be in the birth-language which they would have spoken, except in the case of major figures, such as those rulers or clergy (like the Emperors Justinian and Charles V, kings of the Polish-Lithuanian Commonwealth or John Calvin), who were addressed in several languages by various groups among their subjects or colleagues. Those familiar with much Western Latin writing of Christian history will have to put up with recognizing such Greek individuals as Athanasius or Epiphanius under the forms that they themselves would have used, that is Athanasios or Epiphanios. Many readers will be aware of the Dutch convention of writing down names such as 'Jan Beuckelszoon' as 'Jan Beuckelsz': I hope that they will forgive me if I extend these, to avoid confusion for others. Similarly, in regard to Hungarian names, I am not using the Magyar convention of putting first name after surname: so I will speak of Károly Mária Kertbeny, not Kertbeny Károly Mária. Otherwise, the usage of other cultures in their word-order for personal names is respected; so, Mao Zedong appears thus. In notes and bibliography, I generally try to cite the English translation of any work written originally in another language, where that is possible.

I avoid cluttering the main text too much with birth and death dates for people mentioned, except where it seems helpful; otherwise, the reader will find them in the index. I employ the 'Common Era' usage in dating since it avoids value-judgements about the status of Christianity relative to other systems of faith. Dates unless otherwise stated are 'Common Era' (CE), the system which Christians have customarily called 'Anno Domini' or AD. Dates before 1 CE are given as BCE ('Before Common Era'), which is equivalent to BC.

Readers will quickly notice the citations of the Bible that inelegantly but unavoidably litter my text. For convenience, I normally use the titles that Christians have commonly adopted for their ordering of the books of the Hebrew Bible as the 'Old Testament'. One has to make a decision as to whether to number the 150 Psalms by usage in the Hebrew or Greek scriptures, differently employed by different Christian traditions; I have arbitrarily decided on the Hebrew number pattern, which is for instance used by the King James version of the Bible and in Protestantism generally (though also in some Roman Catholic contexts). Biblical references are given in the chapter-and-verse form which Western Christians had evolved by the sixteenth century, abbreviated as in the appended tables: so the twentieth chapter of the first Book of Samuel at the forty-first verse becomes 1 Sam. 20.41; the third chapter of John's Gospel, at the fourteenth verse, becomes John 3.14, and the first of two letters written by Paul to the Corinthians, second chapter at the tenth verse, becomes 1 Cor. 2.10. My quotations of the Bible are generally either from K. Aland (ed.), *Synopsis of the Four Gospels, Greek–English edition of the Synopsis Quattuor Evangeliorum* (9th edn, Stuttgart, 1989), or from the Revised Standard Version.

After a long, loud noise, a sudden silence may seem deafening.

John Boswell, *Christianity, Social Tolerance and Homosexuality: Gay people in western Europe from the beginning of the Christian era to the fourteenth century* (Chicago, 1980), xvi

Humans are distinct and separated from each other, in countries and lands, peoples and languages, customs and laws. Each of them desires a way of life in accordance with the customs and laws in which they have been habituated and raised. Indeed, they never depart from something when they have been habituated and raised in it. They accept change from something when they have been established in it only with difficulty and thousands of dangers; for custom is second nature, as the saying goes . . . Who, then, can bring to a unity and gather together that which, a thousand times over, is separate and differentiated according to its [very] nature?

East Syrian Patriarch Timothy I (*c.*740–823), quoted and translated in L. E. Weitz, *Between Christ and Caliph: Law, marriage and Christian community in early Islam* (Philadelphia, Pa., 2018), 63

PART ONE
Foundations

I
Setting Out

'To other subjects it is expected that you sit down cool: but on this subject if you let it be seen that you have not sat down in a rage you have betrayed yourself at once.'[1] A characteristically sharp observation of the Georgian philosopher Jeremy Bentham: the display-case in University College London sheltering his handsomely clothed sedentary skeleton is a secular shrine to the man who talked more common sense about sex than has been customary in the history of Western culture.[2] Bentham was referring specifically only to what we now call homosexuality – although, when he wrote, that particular word did not yet exist. In our own time, his remark applies more broadly to almost any discussion of sex, marriage and gender, particularly when it touches on religious belief and practice.

Anyone sitting down to read a history of sex and Christianity in the twenty-first century is likely to have one reason or another for being in a rage. This book will serve as a receptacle for an impressively contradictory range of furies. It will displease those confident that they can find a consistent view on sex in a seamless and infallible text known as the Bible, or those who with equal confidence believe that a single true Church has preached a timeless message on the subject. Others will bring experiences leading them to hate Christianity as a vehicle of oppression and trauma in sexual matters, and they may be dissatisfied with a story that tries to avoid caricaturing the past.

We are all participant observers in matters of gender and sexuality, and few topics are more likely than sexual experiences or non-experiences to arouse intense personal memories, for good or ill. They shape our identities and self-esteem, so we are prone in moments of stress to dump this legacy beyond ourselves, often in curiously shaped guises. After a quarter-century and more of fielding the aggression of strangers, in media ranging from (literal) green ink to lengthy emails, I can ruefully second the comment from a fellow scholar analysing emotions in society, 'the historian's reminder of things forgotten is hardly ever welcome in the religious sphere.'[3] Historians should accept this gladly as our fate and our calling. A delightful remark survives from an Indian historian in the days of the British Raj, Sir Jadunath Sarkar, who while chairing a meeting of the India Historical Records Commission in 1937 drily observed that civil servants in the Imperial Record Department were worried that free access to archives would 'unsettle many settled facts'.[4] That is the inevitable, and welcome, consequence of examining the past properly.

Some may feel that the splendours and miseries of sex were ever thus; human nature has not changed in perhaps three hundred thousand years of recognizable *Homo sapiens*. Yet while I write on the assumption that this is likely to be true, in the last half-century sex and gender have rapidly become more instrumental in internal Church conflict than at virtually any time over the last two millennia of Christian life.[5] Some institutional Churches have recently split apart as a result; everywhere there is hurt and contention. Once upon a time, ecclesiastical explosions were fuelled by such matters as the nature of the Trinity or the Eucharist, the means of salvation or patterns of Church authority; now human genitalia overshadow most other organs of ill-will.

That sudden convulsion in religious thought reflects the extraordinary speed of societal changes centring on sex and gender over a period of, so far, little more than half a century. This transformation has been experienced right across the world, not just in societies with a Christian complexion. More than half a century ago as a young graduate student, I was exhilarated at my radicalism in being open about homosexuality, and in subsequent years I felt rather pleased with myself in being at the forefront of sexual liberation. Then I found that my assumptions had been completely outflanked by proclamation of trans identities hardly ever discussed in my youth, and equally by vituperative criticism of trans identities on feminist grounds; those opposing but passionately held convictions both shared roots in the sexual revolution of the 1960s and 1970s.

These confusing experiences have taught me a lesson about being more observant or empathetic about the differences of others. In such circumstances, we should not be surprised that those slow-moving conglomerations of myriad opinions known as Churches have found it agonizingly hard to react coherently to questions they had not previously asked, let alone answered. Church leaders feel obliged to bring some clarity or comfort to those whom they seek to guide, and they are right to be wary of embracing the latest primrose path to novelty. The story of eugenics in the nineteenth and twentieth centuries, which we shall visit in this book, is a salutary warning about that (below, Chapter 17).

Yet everyone confronting the unfamiliar, inside or outside a religious system, has a duty of enquiry and exploration, as a means of combating fear. Fear is generally fear of the unknown. Knowledge is like a medicine to soothe a fever; in particular, proper knowledge of the past is a medicine for intellectual fevers contracted from prejudiced views of history. Prejudice, like fear, generally bases itself on ignorance, and such ignorance breeds distorted perspectives that poison present-day lives. My aim for this book is to deal with some of that fear by chronicling and even celebrating the sheer complexity and creativity of past generations grappling with their most profound emotions and consequent deeds. Looking at past attitudes to sexuality, we will find that over centuries they have been startlingly varied.

A theme of this study is that after weighing the witness of history and gathering historical evidence over three thousand years, there is no such thing as a single Christian theology of sex. There is a plethora of Christian theologies of sex. Christian societies and Church bodies have at different times believed totally contrary things about sexuality, depending on the structure of their society and the individuals doing the thinking. We may be surprised by some of the matters that seemed vital to past generations, and we ought to be surprised that some of the matters apparently vital to the Jesus depicted in the Gospels do not seem to have so worried his followers over the centuries. Jesus, for instance, bitterly condemned hypocrisy, unlike that topic now so agitating Christianity, homosexuality, which he never mentions. Yet Christian powers have never put hypocrites to death for their hypocrisy, in contrast to the fate of 'sodomites' in medieval Europe and its offshoots worldwide.

The same is true if one moves beyond pronouncements from Jesus himself to letters ('epistles') from later community leaders now incorporated in the Christian New Testament. 'In the very same list which has been claimed to exclude from the kingdom of heaven those guilty of homosexual practices, the greedy are also excluded. And yet no medieval states burned the greedy at the stake' – a wry comment from the twentieth-century Catholic historian John Boswell on 1 Corinthians 6.9–10.[6] Accepting the glorious and inglorious difference of the past from the present may make it easier to see that our own beliefs about sexuality are our own creations, rather than something handed down on tablets of stone for all time. We may become less afraid of things that initially look strange and frightening.

WORDS AND THE WORD OF GOD

Christian readers may find it particularly unsettling to look afresh at the series of ancient religious texts on which Christian belief rests, collectively known as the Bible, but an essential part of our preparations in teasing out the history of sex must be to tackle the complex issues that the Bible raises. These writings are eternally inseparable from Christian practice and identity, as undeniable as the mothers and fathers who are bound into our lives by their presence or even their absence. This inescapable reality has encouraged some Christians to simplify the character of the Bible into the phrase 'the Word of God': an authority as unyielding on matters of sex as on any other concern of religion and, in that capacity, liable readily to be cited for simple solutions to complicated problems. Yet Christianity is one of three world religions, along with Judaism and Islam, that share a closer common relationship to each other than they do to any other faith system. All of them are more dependent than other religions on a sacred written text, leading their adherents often to be characterized collectively as 'People of the Book'. Another collective label that scholars in particular have found useful for the three faiths in recent decades is 'Abrahamic religions', since they all stress a common ancestor in their approach to God, Abraham, first encountered in Judaism's sacred writings – the oldest collection of the three.

Judaism's collection of sacred texts is now commonly known as the Hebrew Bible or Hebrew Scripture, though actually some small sections are written in another, related Semitic language, Aramaic. Since the medieval period, Jews have also often called it the 'Tanakh'. That immediately suggests its composite character, for the word is an acronym formed from the three initial Hebrew letters of three different category-names of books that Jews consider it to contain: Law, Prophets and Writings. Christians took this collective scripture to prophesy their proclaimed Messiah or 'Anointed One', Jesus, and in the course of time they created their own collection of texts about his life and significance: their 'New Testament'. This supplemented an 'Old Testament', which was the Hebrew Bible but with its constituent parts rearranged by Christians in a different order for their own purposes. So the Christian Bible is Old and New Testament: two collections of various texts, the second collection of which selectively affirms truths in the first. Despite the selectivity, Christians regard Old and New Testament as inseparable, after a painful row in the second century CE when a talented early theologian called Marcion asserted that the God of the Hebrew Bible was not the God who was the Father of Jesus. Marcion and his followers did not convince the mainstream body of the Mediterranean Church, and their movement has long since disappeared.

'Bible' is a word conjuring up an image of a single-volume book: in the last three centuries of Western Christianity, classically bound in bible-black. Historically that is not so; the word was first Greek, *Biblia*, which is in the plural, and had been used by Greek-speaking Jews to describe their sacred writings. It meant 'scrolls', because single 'books' or collections of shorter books from the Hebrew Bible occupied individual scrolls of papyrus or vellum (and in Jewish liturgy, they still do). Greek-speaking Christians borrowed the word *Biblia* from Jews, alongside so much else, and it passed into the Latin language unaltered, though Christians quickly replaced the scrolls with bundles of short strips of papyrus or vellum bound side by side like a modern book, the *codex*.[7] When, in the seventh century CE, Anglo-Saxons, a newly converted and energetic set of Christians, crafted a new set of technical religious words in their own language (and did so with considerable sophistication and linguistic awareness), their Old English translation of *Biblia* remained in the plural as 'biblioðece'. That will easily be recognized as the word still surviving in other modern European languages, meaning 'library'. The Bible is a library, not a book, despite the degeneration of *Biblia* in post-Latin speech into a singular form.

In a library, as in musical polyphony, books contain many different voices, and we will unpick many melodies from the mixture on the subject of sex. That is hardly surprising in a set of texts in which some fragments may date from the second millennium BCE, and which extend forward in date into the earlier part of the second century CE. Yet biblical complexity extends much further. An additional set of sacred writings loiters between the chronological boundaries of Old and New Testament – a gap of two or three centuries. Some of these books were actually added to the Hebrew Bible by Jews in Greek-speaking settings such as Alexandria, so early Christians who were also Greek-speaking regarded them as having the full status of God's Word. During the fourth century CE, some Christian commentators began to voice doubts and gave them the description *apocrypha* ('hidden things').

In the sixteenth-century Reformation of the Western Church, Protestants resolved to exclude the books defined as Apocrypha from what Christians term the 'canon' of recognized scripture. Roman Catholics did not, since they included some Catholic doctrines that were otherwise difficult to justify from scripture, such as the existence of Purgatory. Still further out than the Apocrypha in terms of biblical respectability are a great number of texts that mostly date between the second century BCE and the first century CE – in other words, during the period that the 'Second Temple' rebuilt by the Jews in the sixth century BCE still stood in Jerusalem as one of the Mediterranean's greater shrines. Often in the past Christian scholars gave these documents the loaded title of 'Inter-Testamental literature' – self-evidently not a term with any meaning within the Jewish tradition. A less value-laden though clumsy term would be 'non-canonical literature of the Second Temple'. Some of the texts have only been rediscovered in modern times, but all of them contributed to the thought-world of Judaism and the Christianity born out of it alongside the Hebrew Bible.[8]

Laying aside the considerable impact of these extra scriptures, the Hebrew Scripture and the Christian Old/New Testament themselves are not the straightforward authority that they might seem. We must heed the blunt warning of the biblical scholar John Barton that '[a]lmost everyone who reads the Bible today reads it in translation.' In a translated text, there is a constant danger of original meaning and context falling through the cracks, and the gap then being stopped up with our own preoccupations and interpretations; yet the call to understanding is inescapable, an act of faith regardless of whether or not we might hold that the Bible is the Word of God. Barton reminds us of Rabbi Judah's realistic comment on the dilemmas of translation, recorded in the Babylonian Talmud: 'One who translates a text literally is a liar; one who adds anything to it is a blasphemer.'[9]

This is not a new dilemma in sacred scripture, as is symbolized by the colloquial (*koine*) Greek in which the whole New Testament is written. That was not the native language of its chief subject, Jesus, though he would probably have had some working knowledge of it. Moreover, the everyday speech of Jesus would not have been the Hebrew of the Bible that he might read or hear read in the synagogue, but that different, though related, Semitic language, Aramaic. A few Aramaic words are embedded in phonetic Greek form in the text of the New Testament – sometimes an entire phrase, such as *talitha cumi*, which the author has to explain to his readers as 'little girl, get up'.[10] That reminds us that we can only see the life and teaching of Jesus through the filter of a different language and culture.

The complexities multiply in early Christianity. Those who created our present New Testament texts were reading the Hebrew Scripture not in its original Hebrew but in the form of the 'Septuagint'. This is the Latin name for a Greek translation of the Hebrew text, heroically created by Alexandrian Greek-speaking Jews two or three centuries before the time of Jesus, to ensure that they did not lose touch with their ancestral writings – the name comes from the legend that this was the achievement of seventy-two translators all working simultaneously without consulting each other. The present literary form of the Hebrew Bible actually postdates the Septuagint, being the outcome of extensive Jewish editing in later centuries (principally the second century CE). The editors rejected some variant readings in the Hebrew texts redeployed in the Septuagint, often precisely on the grounds that Christians now affirmed these variants for their own purposes.

Because of this, the Septuagint retains many earlier and more 'authentic' variants of the Hebrew text, which in turn have been lodged in Christian memory and literature when they are not present in the modern versions of the Hebrew Scripture. From the sixteenth century onwards Christian translations of the 'Old Testament' have sometimes followed the present unified, edited Jewish text and sometimes the Septuagint, and there is no way that the uninstructed reader of the Bible can tell what scholarly decisions have been made on that, unless that particular Bible edition is honest enough to put the alternatives in a footnote.[11]

When we read these sacred texts of Judaism and Christianity, therefore, we do so through a further set of filters, the honourable efforts of translators to convey the meaning of the original words. Naturally enough, they disguise the realities that sometimes biblical Hebrew is baffling because of textual corruption, and that sometimes the New Testament's Greek is not very competent, and there are instances where it is impossible to say what the original meaning was. In the New Testament, the Lord's Prayer, one of Christianity's most commonly used texts, contains a phrase in English that is usually translated 'Give us this day our daily bread.' The original Greek adjective *epiousios* cannot possibly mean 'daily', and its significance in its context remains mysterious: hence the long-established but technically unjustifiable substitution of that word 'daily'.[12]

The Book of Ezekiel is, notoriously, one example of a text of the Hebrew Bible containing serious textual difficulties. The author of a recent authoritative commentary on that work of prophecy remarks drily: 'It may often be that we do not have access to the original text, but the alternative can itself be exciting enough.'[13] The loss of the original may in this case be just as well, as even the existing text is alarming in its sexual fixations (discussed further in Chapter 2). Centuries after its composition, anxious rabbis (the religious 'teachers' of Judaism after the destruction of the Temple in 70 CE) banned public liturgical recitation of parts of Ezekiel.[14] Later Christians have faced the same embarrassment. In the sixteenth-century Protestant Reformation, the Church of England had the same instinct as Rabbi Eliezer in making very sparing use of Ezekiel in detailed regulations for public reading of the whole Bible over a year of its daily Offices of Morning and Evening Prayer. In the various versions of the Church's Book of Common Prayer between 1549 and 1604, the compilers made no bones about the parts of scripture that are 'least edifying, and might best be spared, and therefore are left unread'. The Prayer Book's revisers in 1662 felt that this instruction was a little too honest about the limitations of Holy Scripture, and replaced Archbishop Cranmer's forthright Tudor phrase with the more discreet thought that the 'most part' of the Old Testament 'will be read every year once'.[15]

We must also be alert for modes of translation that do not reflect the concerns of the original but, instead, some contemporary preoccupation of our own, or of some previous generation. An innovation with serious consequences occurred in translations of the Bible in the mid-twentieth century which first introduced the anachronistic word 'homosexual' into biblical moral denunciations, not just in English but in other languages. Some translations continue to sport this distortion of the text, though others have retreated from it, such as the anglophone Revised Standard Version widely esteemed by scholars. Significantly, 'heterosexual' has rarely, if ever, made a similar linguistic appearance in modern Bible versions.[16]

The biblical texts, Judaistic or Christian, also share a further filter on the worlds that they portray: an overwhelmingly male gaze. Whatever

THE ORDRE
howe the reste of holy Scripture
(beside the Psalter) is appoynted to bee redde.

[The olde Testament.] The olde Testament is appoynted for the first Lessons, at Matins and Euensong, and shal bee redde through euery yere once, except certain bokes and Chapiters, whiche bee least edifying, and might best be spared, and therfore are left unred.

[The newe Testament.] The newe Testament is appoynted for the second Lessons, at Matins and Euensong, and shalbe red ouer orderly euery yere thrise, beside the Epistles

The ORDER how the rest of holy Scripture is appointed to be read.

THE Old Testament is appointed for the first Lessons at Morning and Evening Prayer; so as the most part thereof will be read every year once, as in the Kalendar is appointed.

The New Testament is appointed for the second Lessons at Morning and Evening Prayer, and shall be read over orderly every year thrice, be-

1. Contrasting rubrics (instructions) for the lectionary (daily cycle of Bible readings) in the Book of Common Prayer, altered between the original 1549 version and the Prayer Book's recasting in 1662.

the realities of the society which created them, the writing was done by men. No whole book of the Bible claims authorship by a woman, although two books of the Hebrew Scripture (Ruth and Esther) are named from women. Suggestions have been made about some books or sections of text in the Hebrew Scripture which lack an authorial attribution, particularly convincingly about the very ancient Song of Deborah (Judg. 5.1–31), but we are at an early stage in investigating such possibilities.[17] The one other likely major exception is the book now called the Song of Songs, or Song of Solomon: this is a late work in the Hebrew Bible's evolution and highly unlikely to have any real connection with King Solomon.

The rabbis debated whether the Song was one of the books that 'defile the hands' in ritual contact, which probably meant the opposite to what we might assume about the defiling character of its erotic content. All the scrolls of the Hebrew Scripture ritually defile the hands, needing ritual attention. So to affirm the defilement was an affirmation of the Song's sacred character, stilling worries that it is among the very few biblical books that nowhere employs the Divine Name YHWH (Qoheleth/Ecclesiastes and perhaps Esther being the others). The Song of Songs is unlikely to be a single work but gathers together love-poems or songs in which around two-thirds of the texts are presented as the voices of women, very active in their pursuit and enjoyment of their male lovers. Majority opinion among modern scholars is that at least some of the anthology does indeed have female authorship, since the Bible itself more than once attests that singing and composing songs can be considered a female speciality, whether in joy or in sorrow.[18]

The authorial attributions of New Testament texts are all unequivocally male. The Evangelist Luke presents one important text as the words of a woman: Mary the God-Bearer, mother of Jesus (Luke 1.46–55). This hymn of praise for her miraculous pregnancy, 'My soul doth magnify the Lord . . .', commonly called the Magnificat from its opening word in Latin, lies at the heart of liturgy across the Christian world. As such, it might be an exception to prove the rule, but it is probably in reality a composition by a man, and possibly a man living a century or so before the time of Mary, though it also reflects a still earlier text, the Song of Hannah, which might indeed be a woman's composition (below, Chapter 4). Otherwise, as we will see, the importance of women in the New Testament and during the first generations of the Christian Church has to be read against the grain of the present text.

When the biblical scholar Elisabeth Schüssler Fiorenza wrote one of the first and most distinguished analyses of such matters, she chose a title for her book that elegantly draws attention to a paradox in a Gospel incident in which a woman spontaneously anointed Jesus, to the annoyance of the men present. Remarkably, this story appears in all four Gospels, and Mark reports Jesus as saying that 'wherever the gospel is preached in the whole world, what she has done will be told in memory of her.' Yet for all that, we are not told what the woman was called, though John the Evangelist makes one unconvincing suggestion. We may remember her, but we cannot name her. Fiorenza's book is in more than one sense '*In Memory of Her*'.[19] Even with the example of Fiorenza's rigorous historical criticism, a proper Christian history of sex and gender will always be an effort in outstaring the male perspective, not just in the Bible but in the centuries down to the present.

There is rarely any point or intellectual respectability in altering the biblical text itself to suit modern sensibilities, in the same way that there is no way of altering the Gospel of John's regrettable tendency to style the opponents of Jesus as 'the Jews', even though it is one of the springboards for later Christianity's dismal record of anti-Semitism. We need to be alert to the distance of early Christian literature from our own understanding of past and present and acknowledge that distance as part of Christianity's problematic inheritance. John Barton warns troubled readers of the Bible that '[t]o make a few texts less androcentric than they really are is to pick at a small loose thread, only to find that the whole garment starts to unravel.'[20] Instead of unhappy tinkerings, we might ask ourselves how to recover realities that the Bible does not openly acknowledge.

We need to be alert to the possibility that, when we read of women or their apparent words in past centuries, what we may be reading will have been the creation of a man 'thinking with women': using the image of the other to understand himself and his kind.[21] Men have done most of the writing, not least because historically more men than women were encouraged to master the technology of writing. For much of Christian history, a subset among males was doing most of this writing: male clergy, a high proportion of them professed celibates, with their own personal preoccupations in seeking holiness. Increasingly, once the Church was in a position to create legislation seeking to impose its will on society, many of these males also had interests and expertise in law. In law and legal prohibitions (and not just those stemming from the Church) it is always worth remembering that a command to cease some practice or behaviour generally indicates how common it is.[22]

We need some caution before we simplify this characteristic of Christianity's literary inheritance into describing Christian societies or their predecessors straightforwardly as 'patriarchies'. Clearly women did exercise power in their own sphere, which in most of the societies we will examine meant the private space of the household, the power being over children and servants. Additionally, domestic power might involve highly developed skills that men did not cultivate, in craft or cooking, and over which men had no real control thanks to their lack of skill or comprehension. Hierarchies in society may not be arranged in a single vertical pyramid but may exist side by side. Historians have coined the word 'heterarchy' for such arrangements; unattractive jargon though the word is, it usefully stops us reaching unthinkingly for the more familiar term and reminds us to look out for untidiness in gender power-relationships in all periods.[23]

The writings that have been preserved to us from earlier Christian eras might thus reflect the world only as the male authors wished it to be, rather than how it actually was. Equally, when women encountered male writings, they could be as capable as any modern scholar of hearing them and appropriating them against the grain. Not merely women: we do not have access to the thoughts in people's heads that, in their own time and culture, they felt it wise not to express. Even when a branch of the Christian Church was as powerful as the Western Church became in Europe between 1100 and 1500, we would be naïve in looking for one single outlook on sexual matters which was that of 'the medieval West' (below, Chapter 13).

As the printing-press became available as a means of rapidly reproducing and spreading ideas, one can begin to notice, amid the growing torrent of printed matter, expressions of ideas that are very difficult to register in the written witness of earlier centuries. The previous apparent silence is no guarantee that the thoughts had not been thought, or expressed in private. Often the hints come in ephemeral forms of print like that of sixteenth- and seventeenth-century single-sheet ballads. The production and sale price of ballads were inexpensive, but their survival as physical evidence may be unrepresentatively small, since they were read to death by a great many people and ended up as recycling (often no doubt as toilet paper). For those without access to the technology of writing but with the capacity to read text – a likely distinction for women in much of Christian history – such ballads were witnesses to the oral and aural culture in which they could express themselves more fully. In the England of the Reformation era, a reader could brood on the personal implications of cheap ballads as much as she or he did when reading or hearing more officially acceptable works of prayer or piety. Folk will have been as eager as we are ourselves for novelty or emotional stimulation.[24]

WORD COMPLEXITIES: SEX AND GENDER

Such are some of the problems in sifting evidence from the past in a general survey of history. The continuing sexual revolution of our present world offers another series of puzzles: how historians should talk about both past and present, what words to use. Bliss was it in that dawn of the 1970s to be alive, when one leading historian of sexuality could blithely assert that, 'for the first time in Western culture, we have the potential of coming to terms with human sexuality', including a language to describe it ready to hand, as in his own massively judicious survey.[25] The term 'heterosexuality', for instance, is now so commonly used as to seem a basic part of our vocabulary on sex, gender and the family. It is nevertheless logically secondary to another word-coinage in 1869 by the same German-Hungarian journalist (Karl Maria Benkert/ Károly Mária Kertbeny): his innovative term 'homosexuality' sought to describe same-sex behaviour, newly regarded in Kertbeny's time as arising from medically defined behavioural disorders. English language borrowed both words from medical/psychological German usage, and they have persisted to our own time when other nineteenth-century attempted word-inventions have fallen by the wayside.[26]

Like 'homosexuality', the early use of 'heterosexuality' described a medical pathology, an abnormal appetite for the opposite sex – an origin likely to surprise most of those who casually use the word today. Indeed, the etymology of 'heterosexual' is even more unsatisfactory than 'homosexual', for to the literal-minded pedant it should imply a sexual being who enjoys multiple potential means of enjoying sexual congress across a variety of genders. That possible form of 'heterosexuality' seems a far cry from what has been a dominant Christian model of sex: a binary system in which God initially created humankind 'male and female' (Gen. 1.27) and subsequently sanctioned only one set of sexual transactions between them, solely within marriage. Yet modern Christian arguments about sex commonly use the language of hetero- and homosexuality.

Given the brief and problematic history of this terminology about sex, in the later twentieth century those seeking sexual liberation in new perspectives defiantly repurposed other words such as 'gay' and then even 'queer' out of the pejorative language of mainstream anglophone Western society, to elbow aside 'homosexuality'. Yet that word still hangs around, in contexts both positive and negative. The eminently respectable and same-sex-positive academic *Journal of Homosexuality* has, albeit with some misgivings, retained its founding title, for reasons both of sentiment and of easy identification. Otherwise, language around sex and gender remains extremely unstable, and Christians and non-Christians alike need to be alert to this in their conversations.[27] An entertaining and instructive spat occurred some years ago in a British literary journal over the use of the word 'queer', which much offended a former activist in the Gay Liberation Front when freely deployed in a positive sense by a later generation of scholars. One of the latter ended his riposte to the complainant with the lapidary remark that 'Language moves quickly . . . Trying to nail it down to one particular moment in the 1970s is like standing in a river, yelling at it to stop.'[28]

Current fluidity of language is one reason for the wide contemporary use of the stopgap descriptive acronym LGBTQ (Lesbian/Gay/Bisexual/Transgender/Queer or Questioning), often with an extra initial, plus-sign or asterisk to signify further openness. Aware of the linguistic river's likely further eddies, I deploy this currently useful signifier fairly minimally; it does have a *faute de mieux* usefulness in the varied sexual identities that are emerging in our own time. I am also dissatisfied with the imprecision (and sometimes downright literary pretentiousness) of the signifier 'queer', and I likewise employ it minimally in this book. I am admittedly attracted to a shape given to its definition by the visual historian Elspeth H. Brown, as 'oppositional space to dominant norms', but that still seems to leave unanswered too many questions about the assumptions of the observer about dominance, opposition and norms to make 'queer' especially useful for historical purposes.[29]

The swamp becomes still more treacherous in the lively (and often angry) current debate on the distinction between sex and gender. Those terms themselves disrupt the traditional Judaeo-Christian mantra that 'male and female created He them', which is in any case not quite what it might at first sight seem: 'male and female' in the text is not as categorical a statement of differentiation as a more precise 'male or female' would be. In any case, the word 'gender' is an English borrowing from its strictly limited, originally linguistic usage in relation to grammar. There are many languages (not English) that have their nouns differentiated by 'gender', and sometimes in confusing ways, so that French speaks of *la sentinelle*, with 'feminine' gender endings, even though the person concerned, a military sentinel on duty, has traditionally been a male soldier. German gives 'neuter' gender in grammatical terms to a young lady who is definitely female in every other way: *das Mädchen.*

Beyond this extension of strictly technical terms into emotionally charged wider usage, we can no longer see 'sex' and 'gender' in everyday life as so easily distinguishable as they seemed a few decades ago. 'Sex' might seem more easily definable than 'gender': surely 'sex' is a matter of a few swift appraising glances at genitalia? That could be followed up by references to one of the functions of biological sex, which is to lead to procreation: a matter to which we will return repeatedly in this book. Yet the reality of sex includes physical/biological matters that are not at all easily observable to us, particularly in decorously well-organized social situations: chromosomes and hormones, for instance, are also involved.

By contrast, we read gender off a set of codes that we have educated ourselves to understand with apparent ease: dress, mannerisms, roles in conventional society. The historian Joan Wallach Scott pointed towards a definition of gender that shows its complicated and changing relationship to sex: gender is 'the knowledge that establishes meanings for bodily differences'.[30] At the moment, the reality alongside that observation is that most world societies are still largely male-dominated, and the codes have largely been determined by self-described males. Yet while we are construing gender codes, we encounter fellow humans who are passionately convinced that they have been allotted an inappropriate gender early in their earthly lives despite their visible genitals. The physical mismatch assaults a deeply felt sense of personal identity and may lead them to decisions for permanent bodily alteration. Gender and sex are not then easily untangled.[31]

Christians might feel that their doctrinal inheritance allows them to rise above such disputes: that they can afford to ignore the abundant evidence of flexible gender identities in innumerable human societies, throughout history and at the present day, since those lie beyond Christian theological constructions of reality. Yet current academic interest in looking at history through the lenses of gender and sex has proved immensely fruitful in understanding the history of sex and the Church. In particular, we will find many examples within Christian history of gender or sexual ambiguity, right up to a literal reconstruction of sex and identity. There is, for instance, the interesting category of eunuchs, once so powerful and influential a set of individuals in long-lasting Christian societies (see below, Chapter 8).[32]

These are not debates as abstract as those caricatures of medieval Western theologians counting the number of angels able to dance on the head of a pin – in fact angels perfectly illustrate how much questions of sex and gender must concern Christians. Angels, messengers of God between Heaven and Earth, make constant appearances in the Hebrew Bible, the New Testament and the literature created in the intervening period, which heavy presence in scripture makes angels as esteemed by Protestants as by Catholics or Orthodox Christians. The New Testament writer of the Epistle to the Hebrews (quoting the Greek version of Psalm 8) describes humankind as 'for a little while lower than the angels': how might we tell the difference between angels and humans, if the two created species are so close?[33] The difference might be about sex and sexual attributes, but angels take on many characteristics that make them seem quite like humans, such as, in some instances, their possession of personal names (Michael, Gabriel, Raphael).

Does that imply that, like humans, angels can be categorized by sex or gender? The general answer presumes a certain maleness in angels, as those primarily (though now not exclusively) masculine personal names imply; that is unambiguously the case in both the Hebrew Bible and New Testament. In fact, the Book of Jubilees, a Jewish text possibly of the second century BCE that did not make it into the Hebrew Bible but was widely influential in both 'Second Temple' Judaism and Christianity, even claimed that angels had been created with circumcised penises, just as Jewish men were circumcised as a sign of God's Covenant with Israel.[34] The self-congratulatory male gaze on angels has once more produced predictable results: in this case portraying heroic spiritual figures who could be seen as God's courtiers, bodyguards and heralds in cultures where monarchy was the prevailing form of political organization. It was a material consideration for Christians that an angel was the agent of God's announcement to Joseph, Mary's husband-to-be, that she was to bear a son, who would be called Emmanuel and was in life called Jesus (Matt. 1.20–24). In Luke's version of the same story, the angel (this time named as Gabriel) made the announcement to Mary herself (Luke 1.26–38). That role of agency, with Mary's conception of Jesus following on that announcement, sounds distinctly male.

Angelic maleness did tiptoe in later centuries towards androgyny, underlined in art by the quiet decision of Christian artists during the fourth century CE that angels should not sport beards, and by the general pretty-boy good looks of angels ever since.[35] John Milton, an English Puritan with a scholarly knowledge of the Christian past, was playful in dealing with angelic gendering in his great epic *Paradise Lost*:

For Spirits when they please
Can either Sex assume, or both; so soft
And uncompounded is their Essence pure,
Not ti'd or manacl'd with joynt or limb,
Nor founded on the brittle strength of bones,
Like cumbrous flesh; but in what shape they choose . . .[36]

After reversals of standard clichés about gender in the Western Enlightenment of the eighteenth and nineteenth centuries (below, Chapter 15), many modern angels have lurched towards outright femininity in appearance, but between the fourth century and the modern age, the androgyny still overwhelmingly tilted in a male direction. The concept of 'guardian angels', beloved of the late medieval and Renaissance Western Church, strengthened their tendency to male character – delightfully (or alarmingly) expressed in colonial South America by Peruvian painters, who revelled in depicting *ángeles arcabuceros*: angels in splendid dress shouldering a rifle, like some jaunty young noblemen in the honour-guard of the Spanish Viceroy (see Plates 1 and 2).[37] If we had been indecorous enough to have investigated under their fine Cuzco robes, what would we have found?

We might extend our curiosity into downright irreverence, to ask similar questions of the Christian Trinity, two of whose Persons are customarily given a precise male reference as Father and Son. Even to raise that thought shows how important it is for Christians to distinguish between sex and gender. The absurdity of discussing sexual organs in relation to Father and Son also reveals the absurdity of arguing from the male gender of Jesus in his earthly life that Christian priesthood (and therefore presidency at the liturgical act of Eucharist) is irretrievably male in character. It also raises questions about using gender references in relation to the Third Person of the Trinity, the Holy Spirit.

What clues there are about the Spirit do not concern genitals but grammar. The many references to the Spirit of God in the Hebrew Scripture are to *ruach*, a noun of feminine gender; the post-biblical Hebrew word *shekhinah*, signifying the presence of God, is also feminine, as is the allied concept of Wisdom (*hokmah*: see Chapter 2). That remained the case in Syriac, closely allied to the Aramaic language that Jesus himself spoke and productive of a wide variety of Eastern Christianities: in Syriac, 'Spirit' is likewise the feminine *rukha*. Some early Syriac texts suggest that in such a context, it was not considered at all shocking to think of a Divine Trinity composed of Father, Mother and Son.[38] As the Hebrew religion embraced Greek speakers, and later went on to shape the Greek-speaking Christianity of the Mediterranean, Spirit became the grammatically neutral Greek *pneuma*, but Wisdom remained strikingly female as *sophia*. Small wonder that after five centuries of argument after the time of Jesus, mainstream Christianity became insistent that believers should not confuse the Persons of the Trinity or regard them as mere aspects of the one Godhead, even though Christians should be conscious of their ultimate unity.[39]

We will repeatedly stumble over such worries through two millennia. Such awkwardnesses are natural outcomes of dealing with truths beyond the visible world, which humans find expressible only through simile and metaphor relating to the physical world. Theologians over the centuries, taking their cue from the statements in Gen. 1.26–27 that God made humanity in his own image and likeness, have sought to explore how human relationships might mirror divine realities. They have generally ignored or explained away the complication that this same passage goes on to tell us that 'male and female created he them': does that mean that God is likewise male and female? They ought to have considered more seriously the possibility that the process of manufacturing images may have worked the other way round: at particular periods of history and of human social constructions, Christians have made the Trinitarian God in their own image.

Here is an example of a further puzzle about God's gender: how does one square the circle that Jesus called himself 'the Son of Man' while his humanity came through a woman, Mary? The question is not just frivolously playing around with words: it seriously concerned a gathering of Latin-speaking bishops at Mâcon, in what is now eastern France, in the late sixth century. Faced with an obtuse colleague who maintained that the description 'woman' could not be included in the term 'man', they decided, on the basis of Gen. 1.26–27, that Mary's humanity as a woman (*mulier* in Latin) must be interchangeable with the 'Man' (*homo*) in 'Son of Man'.[40] The problem in Christian theology is always how far to push the figurative gendered language of biblical and theological discussion towards precision. Precision is a particularly besetting sin of Christian theology in the

Western tradition, which is based on Latin – a language whose exactness is heaven-sent for the theological filing-systems of tidy-minded bureaucrats, as the exasperated discussion at Mâcon reveals. Such questions go to the heart of what Christianity is, and how it functions.

There is thus plenty of fuel to ignite the varied bundles of anger that we all bring to thinking of sex, sexuality and gender. All the more reason to embark on a three-thousand-year voyage of exploration through the origins, developments, reversals and unexpected new directions that have brought the Christianities of the present day into their present turmoils. Often those expeditions have been characterized by self-righteous ecclesiastical interference in the happiness and freedom of others. Equally, on occasion, the struggles of Christians with the implications of their tangle of sacred scriptures have brought people genuine liberation and a sense of self-worth. Readers will be forced into their own judgements about the balance between these extremes in particular situations. I aim to provide some evidence for making decisions. As we set out on our travels, it is worth being armed with a quiet reminder from one of Greek Orthodoxy's greatest scholarly bishops of modern times, Metropolitan Kallistos Ware: 'Trying to gaze through the keyhole is never a dignified posture.'[41]

2

Greeks and Jews (*c.*1500–300 BCE)

A pair of contrasting cultural traditions have been woven together to create Christian faith: Greek and Judaic, crafted in distinctive ways before the time of the Saviour, and, after that, providing twin matrices for how early Christians went on to understand his life and death. With that in mind, a couple of decades ago I teasingly subtitled my large-scale history of Christianity 'The First Three Thousand Years'. We need to explore the thousand years or more before Jesus's birth to see why Christians have proclaimed their faith as they have done for the last two millennia, and what lies behind their tangle of opinions and precepts about sex. The first point to grasp is that this thousand-year-long background starts as two parallel stories. It is best to begin with the culture dominating the entire eastern Mediterranean during the earthly life of Jesus: Greeks and the Hellenistic monarchies that had spread Greek influence a vast way eastwards into Asia. Readers may feel frustrated that this chapter postpones much direct engagement with matters sexual. That is unavoidable, because a great deal needs to be understood about Greek thought and culture before its three millennia of influence on the shape of Christianity becomes apparent.

GREEK: A LANGUAGE AND ITS LEGACY

Introducing a stimulating recent book that also covers more than three thousand years, the historian Roderick Beaton defines Greeks simply as 'speakers of the Greek language'.[1] That is what makes Greece so fundamental to Christianity, since its New Testament was composed in a colloquial form of Greek. The linguistic choice was the dynamic legacy of a people originally scattered through an intricate complex of valleys, coastal areas and islands, now mostly represented by the modern Republic of Greece. They spoke many dialects across that patchwork of lands, but all were forms of Greek; by the time of Jesus and those who interpreted his life, Greeks had spread their speech and their outlook on life astonishingly widely across three continents.

Traces of Greek language retrieved by archaeology witness the first distinctively Greek society around 1500 BCE, which, through three centuries, built cities, palaces and monumental tombs across what is now southern Greece and south-west Turkey. These people appear never to have formed a single political unit, though the city of Mycenae and its rulers in central Greece wielded wide authority. After a general political and societal collapse occurred around 1200 BCE (for reasons still not clear), no single power ever again commanded the entire Greek-speaking world, not even the military phenomenon that was Alexander the Great nine centuries later.

Instead of empire, the Greeks experienced an ever-widening sense of unity through what they said and wrote, providing the identity of *Hellas* ('Greekdom'). Chief among their literature were two epics which were not sacred books like the Hebrew Bible or New Testament but performed the same unifying task: the *Iliad* and *Odyssey*. The first tells of a single military campaign, probably reflecting some real war of centuries before, in which Greeks besieged and destroyed the (non-Greek) city of Troy in north-west Anatolia (Asia Minor, today Turkey). The *Odyssey* chronicles journeys home to Ithaka from the siege by one Greek hero, Odysseus, over ten years.

The two epics took shape orally in recitation sometime in the eighth or seventh century BCE, attributed to a poet named Homer, of whom we know nothing for certain. They were written down in a form of script that the Greeks borrowed from the Phoenicians, another coastal Mediterranean people, and refined for their own purposes: the alphabet, ancestor of our own alphabet via its later adaptation by the Romans. The Israelites, neighbours (and frequently fractious neighbours) of the Phoenicians, took the technology of the alphabet in a different direction to record their own Hebrew language and write down their own sacred literature. In both cases, literature reinforced or created self-identification. For the Greeks identity was based on their shared knowledge of Homer's epics, together with certain religious sites, temples and ceremonies which they saw as common property in *Hellas* – especially the oracle of the god Apollo at Delphi and a shrine and associated pan-Hellenic games held at Olympia in the Peloponnese.

It is notable that the *Iliad* portrays the defeated Trojans as no different in culture from the Greeks besieging them. Greeks loftily told themselves that all non-Greeks were *barbaroi*, an expressive way of saying that non-Greek languages were as meaningless as a baby's 'ba-ba' babble. In reality they were keenly interested in other sophisticated cultures, particularly in two great empires impinging on their lives: Persia (Iran), which long dominated their eastern flank and actually ruled many of their cities; and Egypt, south across the Mediterranean. While Greeks were impressed by the antiquity of these civilizations, they were not enthused by the political organization of such giant powers, and they showed an emphatic preference for living in and identifying with small city-states. That made perfect geographical sense in the fragmented and mountainous heartlands of Greece and Anatolia, but Greeks deliberately replicated such independent city-states in flatlands when they founded colonies far dispersed round the Mediterranean coast. These colonies affectionately remembered their origins for centuries, and in time of trouble might draw on the link with an ancient Greek founder-city.[2]

The outlook that nurtured such long-term relationships reflected this sense that a city-state was the natural Greek way to live. The Greek word for city is *polis* (pl. *poleis*) – but Greek is a language where apparently simple words can have as many resonances as ripples from a stone thrown into a still pond, and with *polis* the resonances are rather like those of the English word 'home'. A *polis* was more than the cluster of houses and marketplaces around a temple which was universally its visible embodiment in *Hellas*. The *polis* included the surrounding mountains, fields, woods and shrines, as far as its borders; it was also the collective mind of the community that made it up, and whose daily interactions and efforts at making decisions came to constitute 'politics'. This sort of politics was fundamental to the creativity of Greek civilization and to the Mediterranean civilization that sprang from it; the memory of it has shaped the Eurasian world and the various versions of Christianity it created.

From *c.*1200 BCE, *poleis* in the Greek islands and Aegean archipelago experienced several centuries of political experiment, and often violent upheaval, before evolving distinctive forms of government. Simple monarchy, particularly in hereditary form, was rarely an option they chose. Should they then be ruled by noblemen whose claim came from family antiquity? Should they opt for a strong individual with no such respectability or aspirations to dynasty? From the mid-seventh century BCE, the

Greeks called such a ruler a *tyrannos*, a word that they had borrowed and misunderstood from a language of Asia Minor, indicating the novelty and anomalous nature of this political arrangement. A *tyrannos* could claim neither ancient lineage nor to have been chosen by some god, as was the norm in ancient society (and which, as we will see, was a long-term norm in Israel). Instead, the *tyrannos* was (at least in theory) bound by laws to which the *polis* had assented, and which bound him as much as the community.[3]

This was a momentous step, another Greek innovation: making a ruler dependent on decisions of those who lived in his territory, without requiring much divine intervention. In the sixth century BCE a further innovative move in many city-states, most famously in Athens in 508–7 BCE, gave birth to a system of government with little traditional precedent: rule in the *polis* not by an individual, but by the communal decision of the *dēmos*, all citizens meeting in assembly. 'All citizens' meant all freeborn males of the *polis* over the age of twenty – not women, not other Greeks from other *poleis*, still less imported slaves or other servile people. Thus, though we call this Greek system 'democracy', we need to remember its limited character by twenty-first-century Western standards. Greek democracy had many resonances for the future of Christian ethics and self-identity. Christians took up the word for the citizen decision-making assembly of a democratic *polis* and applied it to their own collective existence: *ekklēsia*, a word which has descended into many languages to denote 'Church'.

To govern a community in this way was an intimidating, perhaps terrifying, responsibility. Literally, it needed thinking about. Probably for that reason, two characteristic activities of Mediterranean society newly evolved in *Hellas*: drama and philosophy. Drama was the foundation of the Western tradition of theatre, which is still designed to help us contemplate and draw lessons from the world around us, in tragic or comic mode: a useful way of clarifying important life-decisions. Drama began as part of public religious ceremonies, and in time it infiltrated the thought and even the liturgy of Christianity, despite Christians ruthlessly abandoning the spectacular open-air theatres which had become one of the marks of a proper city in Greek and Roman antiquity. Through an astonishingly brief period of little more than a century, from the fifth to fourth centuries BCE, Athenian theatre created what survive as the classic works of this theatrical tradition. Aeschylus, Sophocles and Euripides explored the depths of human tragedy and folly; in the second half of the same period, the comedies of Aristophanes often mocked the very Athenian audiences watching and enjoying them. They may have reflected that they needed to laugh at themselves to remain sane.

In philosophy, Greeks did have precedents for their adventures. Across the world that they knew, from Mesopotamia to Shetland, people had long brooded on the movements of stars and planets which governed farming practice and shaped religious observances. Greeks considered that the learning of a race as ancient as the Egyptians must conceal wisdom needing to be shared more widely, and when they eventually encountered the Hebrew Scripture, they were likewise impressed by the antiquity of its texts. But they were not afraid to turn from the past to seek wisdom for themselves. They called those who did so 'lovers of wisdom': philosophers. Greek philosophy, compulsively questioning, classifying, speculating, was far more all-encompassing than anything now preserved from earlier intellectual explorations. Notable was Greek philosophy's willingness to detach itself, if it chose, from structures of traditional religion, just as theatres evolved an architecture separate from that of the temple.

Philosophers involved themselves intimately in the debate about what society should be like, and how it should govern itself. The most original and fruitful minds gathered circles of admirers in their lifetimes and afterwards. These became known as 'schools' – the word *scholē* means at root 'leisure', and what better use for leisure than disputation, or even the lecture-room in which the leisure activity takes place? Eccentricity might form part of the philosopher's instruction. The splendidly offensive behaviour of the vagrant Diogenes of Sinope in the late fifth and fourth centuries BCE was an enacted reminder that, although human beings were rational animals, they were still animals – he was nicknamed 'the dog', from which his school of admirers took the name Cynics ('those like dogs'). His lifestyle later provided one model for Christian ascetics and 'holy fools' who likewise wished to demonstrate their rejection of worldly values (below, Chapter 7).[4]

At the other extreme from Diogenes, philosophers might enter practical politics. During the late sixth and the fifth centuries, followers of the mystical mathematician Pythagoras seized power in various Greek cities in south Italy, but generally Pythagoreans do not seem to have made a great success of their activism, which included an alarming tendency to live by intricate, binding rules – fellow citizens who did not share their obsessions briskly ended Pythagorean ambitions.[5] Most philosophers instead restricted themselves to commenting on the society around them. In the fifth and fourth centuries, three philosophers successively taught in Athens: Socrates, Plato and Aristotle. This trio are foundational to the Western philosophical tradition, Christian as much as Greek or Roman.

As Socrates wrote nothing himself, we hear his voice mediated through writings of his pupil and admirer Plato, mostly in dialogue form: insisting on the necessity of constant questioning in human affairs. In Athens, Socrates' questions included searching criticism of the democracy which was then only a few decades old. In the midst of a dire political crisis for the city, his teaching goaded the Athenians into putting him on public trial and executing him for what was termed impiety and corrupting the young; Plato portrays Socrates as insisting in his speech of defence that '[t]he unexamined life is not worth living.'[6] Western religion and philosophy have remained in the shadow of these events and their consequences. Successor-cultures have repeatedly turned to the insistence of Socrates that priority should be given to logical argument and rational procession of thought, over received wisdom. The Western version of the Christian tradition is especially prone to this Socratic principle, which is one aspect of how Western Christians approach the sexual revolution of our own time.

The injustice of Socrates' fate shaped Plato's own contempt for the results of Athenian democracy when he explored for himself how human society should be shaped, and how politics links to justice and divine purpose: all in a very different style from the parallel discussions that were accumulating in the Judaic tradition. His dialogue on the character of the *polis* (known in Anglicized Latin as *The Republic*) presents an elite-dominated, authoritarian society. He directly confronts, indeed subverts, the Athenian democracy which he had contemptuously observed authorizing the execution of Socrates. No one sane has sought to replicate Plato's picture of government in the real world; one hopes that Plato did not intend it to be more than a mirror for earthly societies, including his own, to contemplate.[7]

Consistent with this, Plato regarded the visible world as a sad illusion, or delusion, in comparison with the deep realities or Forms that lay beyond it. He looked to ideals beyond the particular – so an ultimate Form of 'Treeness' was more real than any individual tree. Importantly, he applied this principle to divinity itself. Plato took his cue from Socrates' radical rethinking on the traditional Greek range of gods (the 'pantheon') and made ethics central to his discussion of divinity. The pantheon portrayed in Greek myth and literature can hardly be said to exemplify virtue: the origins of the gods are a particularly bizarre catalogue of violence, and their behaviour in Homer's epics is arbitrary to the point of self-centredness, rather than following any ethical principle. Greeks generally viewed with cheerful resignation this disconcerting lack of moral predictability among their divinities and did their best to secure the best bargain available from them by due ceremonial observances at home or in temples or shrines.

Plato was not the first Greek to feel that the gods of Olympus needed some rethinking; he could have read the poet and traveller Xenophanes (who died around the time that Socrates was born) observing that 'there is one god, greatest among gods and men, similar to mortals neither in shape nor in thought.'[8] In that spirit, Plato contemplated a supreme and single reality, whose character is both goodness and oneness. Although Plato nowhere explicitly draws the conclusion, oneness involves the proposition that God also represents perfection. Being perfect, the supreme God is without passions, since passions involve change from one mood to another, and it is in the nature of perfection that it cannot change. Inevitably Plato's God is distanced from compassion at human tragedy, because compassion is a passion or emotion.

It is difficult to see how this God could create the sort of changeable, imperfect material world in which we live – indeed, have any meaningful contact with it. Even the created wholeness of the Forms would most appropriately have been created by one other than the God who is the Supreme Soul: perhaps an image of the Supreme Soul, an image which Plato describes in one of the most influential of his dialogues, *Timaeus*, as a craftsman or artificer (*demiourgos*, from which comes the English term 'demiurge').[9] Creation was likely to extend away from God in a hierarchy of steadily more imperfect emanations from the supreme reality of the divine.

It will be apparent how different this account of creation is from the very personal account of God's creative work in the Hebrew Scripture's two creation narratives in Genesis 1–3. The *Timaeus* assumes that, at whatever remove, the individual human soul has clung to a tiny spark of the cosmic soul; the physical flesh that enfolds that soul is a tragic irrelevance, and the reality of human life is as a disembodied soul. Moreover, on Plato's reckoning, the soul is male; women are as unequal to men as animals are, both lower forms of being. Plato's discussion of

God fed into the commonplaces of discussion of divinity in the ancient world, and that, as we will see, became both an inspiration and a problem for Jews and Christians as they tried to talk about their faith.[10]

Aristotle's quest for truth led him in different directions to Plato. He looked to experience reality in individual and observable objects – seeking, therefore, to classify different sorts of tree rather than brood on Treeness. His path to knowledge lay in systematically analysing as much information and opinion about the objects and forms that exist and can be described in the world of human consciousness. He could apply the technique to all branches of knowledge, from subjects like biology and physics to theories of literature and rhetoric (the art of public speaking and debate). His discourses did include analyses of abstract matters such as logic, meaning and causation in texts which bear the functional label *ta meta ta physica*, 'After *The Physics*', simply because they were placed in his collected works following his treatise on physics and the natural world. So, the name of metaphysics, the study of the nature of reality, was born in an accident.

Aristotle's work resembles a gigantic classified filing system. The surviving texts (apparently most of what there was originally) are not polished dialogues like most of Plato's writings, but lecture notes taken down by his 'School', his pupils and assistants. What power over the future those listeners wielded. Two thousand years after his death, Aristotle set the framework in which Christians and Muslims alike shaped their thoughts about the best way to organize and think about the physical world, nature, the arts and the pursuit of virtue. He provided the basis for Christian contemplation of the created world and of the conduct of human society, in what Christians came to call natural law. Its competences included sex, the family and gender, as we will repeatedly discover.

The full flourishing of Greek democracy in genuine independence, the 'Classical' period of Greek culture, was short-lived: less than two centuries down to the late fourth century. Alliances of Greek city-states had triumphantly repelled repeated efforts at conquest by the Persian monarchy, but they fell to invasion by King Philip II of Macedon (a monarchy to the north of the Greek mainland), who won a close-run victory over combined Greek forces at Chaeronea in 338 BCE. Philip's assassination two years later did not end Macedon's triumph, thanks to the charisma and military genius of his twenty-year-old son Alexander III – 'the

Great', as posterity termed him. For once, that overused description is unchallengeable: Alexander's eastward triumphs overwhelmed both Egypt and the Persian Empire and propelled him and his armies as far as northern India, all before his death aged only thirty-two.[11]

Now *Hellas* found itself newly dominant across the Mediterranean and western Asia, in some compensation for the humiliation of Chaeronea. Macedonians had long resented the condescension of their southern neighbours who did not see them as nearly Greek enough; the reaction of Philip and his son had been to immerse themselves in Greek modes of thought and behaviour. The great Aristotle had travelled to Macedon to act as tutor to Alexander; now Greek identity would travel as far as Alexander's armies marched. Even though it was impossible to hold together his monstrously extended territories as a unit after his early death, the Macedonian and Greek generals who parcelled out his conquests set themselves up as the founders of dynasties, becoming the latest in the ancient sequence of semi-divine monarchs with armies and tax-collecting bureaucracies.

The distinctive feature of this sudden crop of new regimes was to bring an overlay of a Greek mode of life across the ancient cultures that they annexed. They followed Alexander's lead in founding new cities or refounding old ones, complete with temples in the Greek style and theatres where Greek drama was performed. These local imitations of the classical Greek *polis* sprouted as far away as the Himalayas in the east; thus in Afghanistan there is a city called 'Alexandria' (locally pronounced 'Kandahar'), a name which Alexander and his admirers gave to a scatter of cities across their territories. The greatest Alexandria of all arose in the Nile Delta in Egypt, a port-city founded by Alexander himself. Ptolemy, the Macedonian soldier who founded the latest and last in the long series of Pharaonic dynasties for Egypt, equipped the new city with an academy of higher learning – ancient precedent for the medieval and modern university – and the most splendid library in the ancient world, a symbol of how Aristotle and Plato took new root in an alien setting. Alexandria became one of the most important cultural exchange-points in the Mediterranean, a major catalyst in changing the nature of what it was to be Greek.[12]

Nineteenth-century scholars started calling the world created in the wake of Alexander's victories 'Hellenistic', to emphasize that it was Greek but not as Classical Greece had been in its days of independence.[13] Instead of democracy, Hellenistic monarchs took on god-like trappings, revived first by Philip II of Macedon, and extended by Alexander into personal identification with a variety of Greek and eastern divinities.[14] Even when the new rulers wore their Greek guises, they usurped forms of worship which the Greeks had reserved for the gods of Olympus. A much-enriched variety of encounters in religion and culture was paired with a steep decline in political choice for the inhabitants of Greek or Hellenistic *poleis*. What independence of action they now had was no more than administering their localities and their temples and organizing taxes for their royal masters.

When compared with the golden days of Classical Athens, there was a degree of sham in this Greek culture. Historians have detected in it a gradual lessening of the exuberant creativity so prominent in Classical Greece. When philosophers could no longer hope to steer the policies of cities, philosophy might as well concentrate on the inward life of the individual which no mighty ruler could tamper with: a proper cultivation of the self. At one extreme, some took up the label of 'Cynic', honouring the purposefully antisocial behaviour of Diogenes; others admired Pyrrho of Elis, a contemporary of King Philip and Alexander, who advised that it was best to refrain from making any judgements at all. Zeno, teaching in the *Stoa* ('Porch') in Athens, inspired 'Stoics' to strive to conquer their passions, so that life's inevitable miseries did as little as possible to hurt them. Another contemporary, Epicurus, saw life's goal as the pursuit of happiness: an affirmation echoed in the American Declaration of Independence in 1776, but without the original Epicurean qualification that happiness consists in attaining inner tranquillity. Overall, a strain of pessimism ran through Hellenistic culture, drawing on Plato's pessimism about everyday things, his sense of their unreality and worthlessness. That pessimism readily extended to one major source of human joy and misery, sex.[15]

Greek cities and their imitations across Asia and North Africa continued to stand side by side with ancient cultures conquered by Macedonian and Greek generals turned gods on earth. The different worlds made untidy and unstable accommodations in repulsion, incomprehension and mutual exploration and exploitation. Nowhere was the clash more bitter or more productive than in the land of Judaea, where the Hellenistic mixture of autocratic brute force and distinctively Greek construction of society ran up against a culture with just as high a sense of its unique destiny as any Greek. To understand the eventual encounter, the Judaeans, Jews and Judaism need an introduction.

ISRAEL: PLACING A PEOPLE IN THE LAND

The ethnic grouping into which Jesus was born, the Judaeans, had long lived in a small but geographically complex band of territory in southwest Asia behind the Mediterranean coast. The fate of this land was bound up with its inescapable position between long-standing power blocs with far greater resources at their disposal. To the south, in northeast Africa along the Nile, lay the Egyptian empire; to the north a sequence of empires emerged in the Anatolian peninsula, or in lands to the east shaped by two other great rivers, the Tigris and Euphrates (hence from those rivers, this latter area is called in Greek Mesopotamia, 'the between-rivers-lands').

People thus poised between Egypt and west Asian powers could never ignore these mightier neighbours, who were repeatedly inclined to occupy or devastate their territory. Equally, they could not agree among themselves as to who had the best claim on their tangled little tract of coastline, hills, valleys and plains – or even what to call the land: Canaan, Israel, Judah, Judaea, Phoenicia, Palestine, Promised Land and Holy Land were among the choices over two millennia. The lack of agreement continues. The Hebrew Scripture, reorganized by Christians as their 'Old Testament', is a bundle of documents setting out one answer to the answerless question. Yet it is far more than that: an astoundingly fertile and adaptable heritage of words and images of the divine with a capacity to shape human lives in countless different situations through three thousand years.

It would be a mistake to date the Christian Old Testament's sequence of books from Genesis to Malachi as if it were a linear historical accumulation from oldest to most recent. The various texts represent a cumulative meditation which manufactured as much as it documents the identity of its writers and readers: a patchwork of texts from different eras, organized on a principle that is not conventional history as practised today. For instance, the Hebrew Bible and Christian Old Testament both open with two different accounts of the creation of the world (Genesis 1–3), the second of which was written much earlier than the first, maybe by two or more centuries. The chronological difference was not apparent to any reader before the eighteenth century, and commentators have habitually smoothed over the contradictions or used them as the basis of ingenious speculation.[16] In considering the significance of texts like these for sex, gender and marriage, we must reconstruct what can be gleaned of the actual history of Israel. That involves sifting through the texts that constitute its literary and theological epic: an account of how the Jews discovered themselves through their relationship to their God, who increasingly became one God alone.[17]

The people of the Hebrew Scripture only gradually begin to emerge into the sort of history we can date and evaluate, aided by external sources, after 1200 BCE – the era echoed in the texts of Joshua and Judges, respectively the sixth and seventh books of the Hebrew Bible and the Old Testament. The people already had a presence in the wedge of Mediterranean territory that they went on to occupy for more than a millennium, 'the land', even 'Promised Land'. It was a time of general upheaval in the eastern Mediterranean, the same era that saw the collapse of institutions far to the north-west around Mycenae, and it may be that the disruption of many power structures gave these folk their opportunity. Behind them was a saga of four centuries of slave labour in Egypt followed by escape, told at length in the previous four biblical books, Exodus to Deuteronomy. This story must have a kernel of truth in it, since its hero, the man who led the people out of Egypt north-eastwards to the very verge of entering the land, is called Moses. This is an Egyptian name, which would have been an unnecessary complication to a purely fictional text; the people's escape had been a defeat and humiliation for the Egyptians.[18]

Even if not all the people gathered in the land had come from Egypt, in the thirteenth and twelfth centuries BCE they began coalescing into a single community. Maybe a newly forged religion was all they had to unite them, rather than ethnicity, common origins or a single settled territory of their own; it is interesting how many different names they have carried forward for themselves down to the present day. One of the names that stuck with them was 'Hebrews', which is a word that occurs with wider reference in non-biblical sources in forms such as 'Habiru'. The contexts suggest that 'Habiru' were on the fringe of various settled societies, and commonly something of a nuisance. From a territory in the southern part of the land called Judah, Hebrews eventually gained yet another collective name for their future: Judaeans. Another name for them was 'Israel', borrowed from one of their ancient legendary leaders or 'patriarchs'.

The name Israel is intriguing, for the Jews later explained it as meaning 'He who strives with God'. The man who bore it was previously called Jacob, and he is portrayed as a habitual trickster who gathered to himself comic tales of deceit. His change of name is a piece of folk-etymology derived from one particular story in Genesis: his all-night wrestling match with a mysterious stranger. In the end, this 'man' cast Jacob down with casual divine power, but then renamed him with a paradoxical promise: 'you have striven with God and with man, and have prevailed.' Jacob/Israel then exclaimed that he had seen God face to face (Gen. 32.22–32). It was not the first time that the God of the 'Children of Israel' had given a new name to a patriarch; he had renamed the trickster's grandfather Abram ('exalted father') as Abraham ('father of many peoples': Gen. 17.5). Abraham became the greatest hero in the people's foundation stories, from way before their four centuries in Egypt.

God himself possesses several names in the Hebrew Scripture's stories of origins, scattered through its first five books. This variety suggests the coming together of various understandings of personal and local loyalties to signify a single God. Just as he had done with the joker Jacob, the many-named God gave marginal folk who were among the 'Habiru' a new identity in the land that they sought to control; but he also gained a single generally used Hebrew name for himself. Its pronunciation is lost to us now because, over time, his people came reverently to refrain from speaking it out loud, but its consonants are YHWH, which may mean 'I AM WHO I AM', or 'I WILL BE WHO I WILL BE' – a name without a name. In its place, since liturgical reading of Scripture demands that something should be pronounced, Jews generally spoke the word *adonai*. That means 'my Lord', and so translates into Greek as *Kyrios* and Latin as *Dominus*. These became the words for 'God/Lord' that Christians used in their New Testament as well as in their reading of the Septuagint.[19]

Eventually, and in accordance with this verbal reticence, Jews came to avoid creating any image of their God: a most unusual practice in west Asia, and therefore one mark of the Jews' distinction from those round them. This was in complete contrast also to Greek custom, which created images of the gods as more beautiful versions of human beings and reproduced them wherever they went. Yet Judaism piled up the most detailed and elaborate verbal portraits or metaphors to describe God in the sacred literature that they steadily accumulated. For a Hebrew prophet in full ecstatic and intimidating flow, God might be pictured as a predatory bear or devouring lion; for a poet singing his praises in more reassuring mood, God might even become a mother hen.[20]

In other respects, this God was not at first much different from other gods of the peoples around the Children of Israel. His people were not monotheists, and would not be for some centuries, even though they gradually became more committed to the view that this God was the supreme deity in their lives. Most significantly, for centuries the God of Israel enjoyed a wife, Asherah, a fruitful deity who had long been paired with leading west Asian male gods. She emerges as an active consort and object of Hebrew devotion in, for instance, a series of inscriptions from different Judaean sites dateable to the eighth century BCE. A fragment of poetry has survived in the Hebrew Bible, embedded in later material, in which the divine couple bless the sons of Jacob/Israel.[21]

Unlike most of the peoples around them, the varied folk gathered in worship of their God – Hebrews, Children of Israel, Judaeans – did not in their early years look to a single monarch. In the historical books of the Hebrew Bible they are portrayed as living under a gathering of rulers referred to as 'Judges': as much military leaders as dispensers of justice

2. Iron Age glimpses of Asherah: (*left*) pottery fragment from Kuntillet Ajrud (north Sinai) with a trio of figures, two bovine; in the inscription above, 'I bless you by Yahveh our Guardian and his Asherah'; (*right*) figurine of Asherah in a common Judaean 'pillar figurine' type, with hands emphasizing her nursing breasts.

or law. Nevertheless, perhaps in the eleventh century BCE, the peoples of Israel yielded to the clamour for a single monarch. The process was controversial, as revealed by some negative perspectives on kingship in the narrative now known as 1 Samuel. In fact, the first incumbent of the throne, Saul, was eventually elbowed aside and his incipient dynasty destroyed by a courtier, David, who is depicted in the sources as a spectacular if ethically flawed hero.[22]

The subsequent narrative in the Hebrew Bible (which, it has to be said, is not much reflected in archaeological discoveries) portrays David as conquering most of the tract of territory in which the Children of Israel lived, though never subduing their main rivals in coastal cities. His son Solomon (reigned *c.*970–*c.*930) brought extra swagger to the resulting kingdom – though probably not nearly so much as the biblical sources claim. Solomon's most lasting achievement is undeniable: he built a new Temple for God on a hill beside Jerusalem, a spectacularly sited small city conquered by David a few decades before. There God reigned along with his consort Asherah, though she found herself unceremoniously ejected in later centuries.

This monumental Temple became increasingly an unchallenged symbol of Judaic faith and identity, and though its successor was finally destroyed by a Roman army in the early years of Christian emergence a thousand years later, it remains a potent presence in the imaginations of Jews, Christians and Muslims alike. It may have been in Solomon's time, the tenth century BCE, that the combination of monarchy and Temple priesthood spawned a bureaucracy of record-keepers. In turn they began producing what are probably the first large-scale fragments of text to remain in the Hebrew Bible: works of history chronicling and celebrating the monarchy, including a suitably edifying presentation of the rather awkward transition from Saul's to David's dynasty. Overladen with much long-term adaptations and preoccupations, these form the backbone of the books of Samuel, Kings and the later reworkings of them which Christian Bibles label the two books of Chronicles.[23]

Solomon's realm quickly split after his death into two kingdoms, southern Judah and northern Israel; their political union had probably never been robust despite their common worship of the God of Abraham. That political disaster led to constant nostalgia for the remembered and now much-exaggerated glories of David and Solomon, through two or three centuries of dual monarchical rule which the Hebrew Bible portrays as repeatedly falling short of earlier standards, not least in faithfulness to

God and his laws. Because of this, alongside complex narrative history the Hebrew Bible enshrines a remarkable genre of literature rarely surviving from other ancient cultures: passionate denunciations of the society around the divinely inspired speaker, who is known as a prophet. Centuries later, Christians ransacked the texts inherited from these prophetic performances for clues about the coming of Jesus and the radical change of direction for the Judaic tradition that it represented. Judaism has remained more conscious of the reality that prophets spoke primarily to their own times, pitilessly clarifying current crises and how these represented judgements of God on the backsliding of his chosen people.[24]

What is noticeable about the prophetic literature even in its earliest surviving phase is the emphatic connection it makes between sexual misconduct, more often than not on the part of women, and infidelity to the God of Israel. It is not surprising that this eventually led to the ejection of God's wife from her place of honour (though, of course, the causality might be the other way round). Hosea was a prophet of the eighth century whose diatribe is one of the earliest to survive in written form. He shaped his bitter denunciation of the people's betrayal of God around what he at least claimed was his own personal tragedy: a direct divine command to marry a woman he already knew to be promiscuous, and soon to be the mother of illegitimate sons and daughters – 'children of harlotry'. This extreme form of enacted prophecy was a mirror to the religious unfaithfulness of Israel, the dark reversal of God's promise of fatherhood to Abraham; Hosea interrupts even the promises of national restoration in his text's latter half with more sexual denunciation.[25] This theme of personal sexual humiliation mirroring a cosmic tragedy is extremely powerful: it has resonated with the fears and miseries of countless individuals through three millennia, as well as providing a dark but plausible explanation of communal misfortune.

Equally extravagant on the theme of promiscuous unfaithfulness was the later prophet Ezekiel, both prophet and sometime priest in the last years of the Jerusalem Temple at the beginning of the sixth century BCE. The sexual theme in the collection is not as all-consuming as in Hosea, but when the denunciation of sexual and religious faithlessness does emerge, it is startlingly and brutally uninhibited. At what is now Chapter 23, verse 20, for instance, a harlot is portrayed in nostalgic mood for her time back in Egypt, and 'her paramours there, whose members were like those of donkeys, and whose emission was like that of stallions'. That is the attempt of the New Revised Standard English translation to be relatively decorous while still faithful to the text; James Davidson's more full-throated recent rendering of it gives the male lovers 'cocks as big as donkeys'', and their sperm 'as copious as that of horses'. That passage ends (23.45–48) with God smacking his divine lips at the thought of the violent execution by stoning of such promiscuous women in Israel.[26] Small wonder that the text of Ezekiel that we now have is so damaged (see above, Chapter 1).

Thus an often-uneasy trio of monarchs, prophets and priests of the Jerusalem Temple lies behind the literature created while the twin monarchies survived. Between the eighth and sixth centuries BCE an accumulating series of disasters provided prophets with plenty of fresh material for warnings and denunciations. First, around 722 BCE, God allowed a new imperial northern power, Assyria, to overwhelm the kingdom of Israel, deporting many of its people northwards. That left the kingdom of Judah, less squarely in the normal path of invading armies sweeping through the land than Israel had been, to carry forward Judaic identity, bolstered by its continuing possession of the Temple in Jerusalem. The monarchy of Judah produced a remarkable convulsion of reform designed to stave off further wrath of God, in the reign of King Josiah (*c*.640–609). The young and energetic monarch became poster-boy for the new implementation of a codified divine law, conveniently discovered in the Temple.

Josiah's scroll of the law, resulting in some drastic changes to public life in Judah, was presented as something very old: a set of detailed regulations for worship and society attributed to the ancient hero Moses, long before the Temple had taken physical form. What may be presumed to be its contents are retrofitted into the account of the Exodus from Egypt in the book of Deuteronomy (or 'Second Law', so styled by Greek translators of the Hebrew Scripture, since this law continued other lawcodes presented in Exodus, Leviticus and Numbers). The Deuteronomic code, which we now read much elaborated in later generations from its original core, is full of prohibitions; as in lawcodes generally, these 'don'ts' are a sure guide to what ordinary people were actually doing that must now be prohibited. It is notable for its emphasis on purity: pure worship of God without rivals, and purity of life for the people and their land, enacted in minute regulation. Thus would God's chosen nation be distinguished from the faithless and idol-worshipping peoples around them. The sacred books contained an increasing number of fierce orders not to marry neighbouring peoples, particularly those still disputing the territories that the Judaeans considered their own. Marriage with other foreigners might be considered as permissible as long as they agreed to a thorough religious conversion.[27]

The Kingdom of Judah lasted down to 586 BCE, when the monarchy and the Temple itself were reduced to ruin by a new imperial power in Babylon. Once more there was large-scale deportation to Mesopotamia, including many elite figures, and it was not until 539 BCE that yet another empire, ruled by Cyrus of Persia, gave any of them the chance to return and fulfil their longing to rebuild the Temple in a modestly restored Jerusalem – for them, divine providence; for Cyrus a sensible measure to plant loyal allies as part of his strategy for conquering Egypt.[28] This 'Second Temple' was reconsecrated in 516 BCE, and for another half-millennium, including a magnificent enlargement by King Herod the Great not long before the birth of Jesus, the hill-top complex became one of the chief goals of pilgrimage in west Asia.

Now Judaean identity was spread wider than it had ever been, and we can begin to think of it as Jewish, as much as Judaean. Besides the Judaean exiles who returned to the Promised Land, many Judaeans continued to live in Mesopotamia, increasingly also in Egypt. These communities beyond Judaea came to refer to themselves as the *Diaspora*, a Greek word for 'the scattered' and originally used by Greeks with a negative meaning to describe misfortunes in their own history. It retained that tragic sense in its first extensive Jewish use in Egyptian Alexandria, in the Septuagint.[29] A strong urge towards keeping this dispersal within a single Judaic fold was the rich sacred literature that had built up in the two kingdoms from the time of Solomon onwards. It was now much expanded and edited, to aid restoration not simply of the Temple but of a Jewish sense of identity.

It proved impossible to restore a native monarchy, as one or two short-lived attempts starkly demonstrated.[30] Other Judaic cultic centres to rival the Jerusalem Temple no longer existed or had gone their own way – including as far away as Egypt. Judaean mercenary soldiers in the service of the Pharaohs built an alternative Temple far down the River Nile at Elephantine, apparently before the first Jerusalem Temple was destroyed. Possibly it was a statement against Josiah's Deuteronomic reforms in the seventh century BCE; remains suggest that it was an attempt at a faithful reproduction of biblical descriptions of Moses' travelling tabernacle in the Exodus years. It lasted around two centuries, but, after its destruction by hostile Egyptian authorities in 410 BCE, its restored successor was short-lived.[31] Jerusalem's now unchallenged role as the place for sacrifices to God was underlined over the next few centuries by the emergence of a different local institution to host Judaism's non-sacrificial communal worship, prayer and instruction. This needed a distinctive name for its purpose and, as a sign of changing times, it was known not by a Hebrew word but by a Greek one – *synagōgē*, 'assembly'. Synagogues, first as assemblies of devout Jews and, eventually, also as buildings to house them, became the centre of community life not merely in the Judaean land, but wherever a Jewish community developed in the *Diaspora*; with the Temple long gone, they still are.[32]

All this left the Second Temple much more central to Judaic identity than its Solomonic predecessor had been. This Second Temple period, its preoccupations and new experiences, permanently coloured and transformed the way Judaeans viewed past and present, and it is when the majority of texts in the Hebrew Bible took on their present form. The 150 psalms familiar to Christians and Jews alike are now a compilation of the songs sung liturgically in the Second Temple, though a great deal in them also goes back to the centuries before the Babylonian destruction of Jerusalem.[33] Much was now purged from Judaic religion that had once been acceptable, even in the Jerusalem Temple: notably Asherah, God's long-standing wife, now recast as one of the seductresses who had turned the people of God from the right path. She was the most prominent victim of Jerusalem's theological spring clean, which also involved reducing the status of lesser gods whom the Judaeans recognized as deities, albeit below the level of God himself. This was not yet Jewish monotheism, but what the biblical scholar Francesca Stavrakopoulou has deftly termed 'pantheon reduction'.[34]

Although Asherah had been thus rudely ejected from God's family, God was still not without female companionship in his divinity. She was a much more abstract figure than Asherah: the Lady Wisdom (*hokmah* in Hebrew, *Sophia* in Greek) and she emerged from a strand of discussion in the Hebrew Bible that modern scholarship has termed 'Wisdom literature'. The origins of these texts take us back to the early monarchy of Israel, for they frequently invoke the name of Solomon, himself repeatedly described in the Hebrew Bible by terms relating to wisdom. The Hebrew Bible also tells us that the chief of Solomon's wives was the Egyptian princess Naamah (his only wife named there, the mother of his heir); appropriately, a small section of Wisdom literature, now Proverbs

22.17–23.11, is linked to an older text of proverbial wisdom from Egypt rediscovered in the nineteenth century, the *Instruction of Amenemope*.[35]

The theme of such material is what the biblical scholar Eric Heaton termed 'the ability to cope' amid the everyday problems of a complex society: Wisdom literature has come from a sophisticated royal court that could have existed anywhere between Egypt and Mesopotamia.[36] Yet much of the content of Wisdom texts can be dated far later than the end of the Israelite monarchy and the monarchy in Judah, simply because of the language that they use, frequently peppered with Aramaic idioms and word-forms; some of the material actually lies beyond the bounds of Hebrew Scripture, in the texts known as Sirach or Ecclesiasticus and the Wisdom of Solomon (the latter actually written in Greek by Alexandrian Jews). It is clear that shorn of their original courtly or aristocratic setting, the themes of Wisdom literature continued to fascinate and delight Jewish readers. Amid the varied concerns and curiosity of the texts, the very form of Wisdom became a female companion of God, most notably at Proverbs Ch. 8, where Wisdom was with God 'before the beginning of the earth': 'when he marked out the foundations of the earth, then was I beside him, like a master-workman [or in some manuscripts, 'little child']; and I was daily his delight' (Prov. 8.23, 29–31).

In the course of time, Christians became very excited by this female Wisdom-figure *Sophia* as they puzzled how to relate Jesus to the Father; here was a personality accompanying God that had been with him before all worlds, and surely that must have been Jesus. Elisabeth Schüssler Fiorenza went so far as to maintain that 'the earliest Christian theology is sophialogy', though not every reader has seen that as the most convincing strand in her biblical analysis.[37] Prov. 8.30 was at the centre of the bitter fourth-century disputes between 'Arians' and 'Nicenes' as to whether the Son was subordinate to the Father: Arians could very reasonably argue that it supported their case for subordination, but that phrase 'begotten of his Father before all worlds' is embedded in one of the Creeds that marked the defeat of the Arian cause in the imperial and now Nicene Church. Equally, though, Wisdom could be identified not with the Son but with the Third Person of the Trinity, the Holy Spirit, since, as we have seen in Chapter 1, most of the words for the Spirit that Christians used were grammatically feminine in gender. The procreative female capacity of *Sophia* also appealed to various gnostic writers (below, Chapter 6) as they worked out their own solutions to the problem of God's nature and purpose in forming the world. These were creative redeployments of a Hebrew theme that had evolved for other reasons.

It is a tribute to the generous spirit of developed Judaism that it was able to accommodate the rich and inventive world of Wisdom alongside the concern with national identity and national sin that can frequently seem so wearing in the tradition of the Law and the Prophets. The idea of 'Covenant', already prominent in the Deuteronomic tradition, became increasingly central to other new sacred texts, as Judaeans brooded on their history of disasters and decided that an overarching explanation was God's anger at their failure to keep a sequence of covenants or agreements: divine requirements expressed in the various lawcodes recorded in the Hebrew Bible. Second Temple writers created a tidy narrative out of the bundle of legends they inherited from their remote past, and these backdated the successive covenants to God's promises in the time of such patriarchs as Abram/Abraham and Jacob/Israel. Covenants with God and leading figures of the biblical story are therefore repeatedly found in the Hebrew Bible, right back to God's command to Adam not to eat of the tree of the knowledge of good and evil, disobeyed with lasting consequences (Gen. 2.15–17).[38]

Our finished text of the Book of Genesis now tells us that Abram first journeyed to the Promised Land from Ur, a city then near the mouth of the Euphrates in Mesopotamia. He had done so, making his Covenant with God in the land, more than a millennium before the Children of Israel had suffered seventh- and sixth-century exile to Assyria and Babylon, and even before their supposed four centuries in Egypt. It is not hard to see this historical double-back as wishful thinking, a comforting assurance through an ancient link to Ur that recent Judaic exile in Mesopotamia was simply a return visit, part of God's plan for them; now God had given them back the land of Israel.[39] It was a way to cope with the very partial control that Judaeans now had over their own affairs; but it also placed the whole history of Israel in a covenantal framework that embraced all matters sexual in God's overall purposes. That would set patterns for Judaism as it encountered cultures with very different attitudes to sex and the family; we must now turn to this, often uncomfortable, cross-cultural conversation.

3
Hellenism Meets Judaism (300 BCE–100 CE)

After some two centuries of Persian rule in Judaea, Greeks and Judaeans were suddenly thrown into close contact in the 330s when Alexander the Great's generals divided up his conquests. It was in this period that Judaeans/Jews were first commonly described by the Greek noun *Ioudaioi*. To begin with, control of Judaea went to the new Egyptian/Macedonian Pharaoh Ptolemy I. This encouraged the flourishing of an Egyptian Jewish community in Alexandria; in that great and cosmopolitan city, the inclination of the Jewish *Diaspora* to appreciate Hellenistic cultural values and adopt the Greek language was at its most pronounced. During the third century BCE Alexandrian Jewish scholars, anxious to keep full access to their ancient sacred literature as Hebrew ceased to be their main everyday tongue, undertook the formidable task of creating the Greek Septuagint out of the Hebrew texts. This lasting achievement witnessed a sense throughout Judaism that there was now a recognizable repertoire of sacred texts of Hebrew Scripture that must be translated. The Hebrew Bible was becoming what would later be described as a 'canon' – yet another Greek word, meaning 'rule' or 'measure'. Christians later extended the concept of canonicity to their own scriptural additions, the New Testament.[1]

The new voice of the Hebrew Bible in Septuagintal form encouraged devout readers of Hellenistic outlook to view the text afresh. That provided new perspectives on matters relating to physicality, the body and sexual custom. Ancient as the Hebrew Bible was, and all the more impressive for that, it did present God in an immediate and physical fashion rather alarming to the philosophically minded. He walked in the garden of Eden talking, in increasing rage, with his first-created humans Adam and Eve; he was drawn into haggling with the patriarch Abraham as to how many righteous citizens of Sodom would qualify the city to avoid divine destruction; and Moses the deliverer from Egypt had on one occasion been afforded a reverent glimpse of his person, even if only in a rear view.[2] Such stories seemed indecorous if taken literally. Worse still were the wilder pronouncements of some of the prophets, particularly Hosea and Ezekiel.

Fortunately, the Greeks had provided a technique for dealing with this problem, arising from their centuries of esteem for the epics of Homer. Some Greek commentators had decided that there must be deeper meanings behind the violence and the voyaging in the *Iliad* and *Odyssey*, so a volume of commentary had grown up expounding them: looking for allegorical profundities of which the literal text was simply a surface. The same allegorical technique could easily be transferred to the Hebrew Bible or Septuagint. It could extract much more than an unpromising literal meaning, as could typology – that is, treating a theme or event in the Bible as symbolizing some wider or more profound meaning. The allegorical or typological approach to sacred text was best exemplified in the voluminous writings of an Alexandrian Jewish intellectual who was a rather older contemporary of Jesus, Philo. Philo's work was later more esteemed by Christians than by Jews, particularly because it enabled Christians to explore their whole Bible, 'Old' and 'New' Testaments together, using his method to reconcile their varied messages: to begin with, in Alexandria, but later throughout the Christian world.

There were, after all, already clear examples of allegorical meaning in the biblical text. For instance, Jesus told his disciples to beware of 'the leaven of the Pharisees', helpfully explaining that by 'leaven' he meant their teaching (Matt. 16.12). Noting that enabled the reader of Scripture to be alert to any use of the word 'leaven' anywhere in the biblical text, and then to explore it in the same way. The problem, of course, is that one may sift the biblical text with some particular agenda and come up with allegories to prove the correctness of that proposition. Commentators have frequently found allegory and typology a lifeline to boost some particular argument on sex and marriage, and we will be meeting with more than one example. Sixteenth-century Protestants, infuriated by what they considered absurd over-use of the method in biblical commentary from the Western Latin Church, compared the results to a 'nose of wax', a comic false nose such as people wore at carnival time, capable of being twisted in any shape to please the wearer. They might have a point, though they themselves were not above resorting to the allegorical method when all else failed.[3]

Both Jews and Christians reading the Septuagint through such Hellenistic lenses might be drawn to think of the God of Abraham rather as Greek admirers of Plato viewed the transcendence and perfection of the supreme deity of the Greek pantheon. Yet even in its Septuagintal form, the Hebrew Bible obstinately pulled its readers back to the physicality of their God. That problem was one of the perpetual fault lines between Judaism and Hellenism. It passed into Christianity and has never been resolved, especially since Christianity adds to the mix the audacious claim that in Jesus the Christ there is God. If that is so, then which God is it: Jewish or Greek? Christians spent the first five centuries after the life of Christ trying to find answers to the conundrum; they have never satisfied everyone.

The second century BCE witnessed a more violent and immediate confrontation between Judaism and Hellenism. In 198 BCE, the Hellenistic Seleucid dynasty of Syria wrested control of Judaea from the Ptolemies of Egypt. That led to open revolt in Judaea in 167 led by Judas Maccabeus, when the Seleucid king Antiochos IV grossly interfered with the cult at the Temple in Jerusalem. His religious aggression was most uncharacteristic in Mediterranean society, but all of a piece with the King's megalomaniac award to himself of the title *Epiphanēs* or 'God manifest'. The Maccabean rebels suffered terribly in fighting him, but they succeeded in returning Judaea to a native dynasty descended from heroes in the liberation struggle; known from an earlier ancestor as the Hasmoneans, they ruled as high priests for the Jerusalem Temple.

Though the Hasmonean monarchy proved to be the last Judaean experience of prolonged independence in the ancient world, it was an extraordinary achievement against a great power: a victory to cherish, reinforcing the sense of a unique Judaic destiny and distinctiveness in God's purpose. The Hasmoneans remained a significant regional force in the eastern Mediterranean for a century until conquered by a new imperial power arriving from far to the west of Judaea's previous overlords. When the Hasmoneans first encountered the Roman Republic in the second century BCE, Rome was still a far-away city, a potential ally against their threatening neighbours. By 63 BCE, the Roman army's invasion of Judaea was part of its mopping-up operations around Rome's real prizes, the Seleucid and Ptolemaic empires. Roman conquest led to a further Jewish *Diaspora* into the western Mediterranean: the Jewish community in Rome was one of the first to be affected by Christian activism in the first century CE.

In 37 BCE, looking for a compliant local ruler for Judaea but finding no convincing Hasmonean candidate, the Romans displaced the last Hasmonean and replaced him with a relative by marriage, who reigned for more than three decades. Their choice, an outsider from the land of Edom (which the Romans called Idumea) south of Judaea, was Herod I, 'the Great'. Herod rebuilt the Second Temple as one of the largest sacred complexes in the ancient world; its remnants still impress by their monumentality. Yet his subjects gave him little thanks, and self-conscious Judaean upholders of purity in God's Covenant were angered by Herod's Greek-style innovations such as public sporting contests (male nudity always a possibility), gladiatorial combats or horse-racing in newly built arenas.[4] After Herod's death in 4 BCE, his sons divided the extensive territories that the first Roman emperor Augustus had allowed the puppet king to build up. For more than a century thereafter, and during the life of Jesus, Rome experimented with a mixture of indirect rule through various members of the Herodian family and, for parts of Judaea, direct imperial control through a Roman official.

Rome's triumph in the eastern Mediterranean only reinforced the central cultural role of Hellenism. Remarkably for such an aggressively expansionist power, which by the time of Jesus had conquered the entire Mediterranean basin and had ruled the Greek heartland for two centuries, the Roman Empire did little to challenge Hellenistic cultural superiority: quite the reverse. The original city-state of Rome somewhat resembled a Greek *polis*, but, unlike Greek citizen status, the quality of being a Roman (*Romanitas*) was never restricted by racial or local exclusiveness. In their relentless drive to expand their territory, Romans were happy to confer Roman citizenship throughout their empire on deserving foreigners with something to offer in return, if only grateful collaboration; occasionally they granted whole areas citizenship. Even slaves might change from being non-persons to citizens, simply by a formal ceremony before a magistrate, or by gift in their owners' wills.[5]

It is puzzling that the Romans did not use the word *Hellas* and its derivatives when they made contact with Hellenism, but instead opted for the obscure word *Graeci*, a usage they have bequeathed to modern European languages. In any event, Greek culture, literature and philosophy fascinated the Romans beyond any obviously expedient consideration, perhaps because the model imperial conqueror – Alexander – had already so enthusiastically embraced it from outside in Macedon. Greek became an international language for the Roman Empire alongside Latin; it could be understood throughout the urban Mediterranean and beyond in something like the colloquial form in which the New Testament is written. Consequently, to speak of 'Classical' civilization is to describe more than half a millennium of linguistic partnership. Latin has a monumental precision that reinforces the Romans' highly developed skills in military affairs, administration and law. The flexibility and subtlety of Greek make it hospitable to argument both philosophical and theological. Greek society provided patterns for Roman public and private behaviour, though the fit was never perfect: Romans, for instance, long remained uncomfortable with the Greek enjoyment of young men publicly performing nude in athletic competitions.[6]

CULTURAL CONVERSATIONS: ATHENS, ROME, JERUSALEM

One great likeness between Hellenistic, Roman and Jewish society is hardly surprising, since it was the shared characteristic of their Mediterranean world. Public power was organized for the benefit of free adult males: Greek, Roman and Jewish women, whatever the realities of their everyday lives in which they might exercise informal power, could not fully represent the common cultural identity of their societies as could men.[7] Israelite identity was socially recognized by genital mutilation: male (and never female) circumcision, particularly remarkable in a society which otherwise fiercely condemned bodily modification, including tattoos.[8] Circumcision was an ancient attribute of some among the male gods in Mesopotamia who preceded Israel's recognition of its God: Judaeans probably originally intended the practice as a symbol of purity for priests alone, but during the Second Temple period they extended the obligation to all males, as contemporary commentators outside Judaism testify. By that time, circumcision had become inextricably linked to the concept of covenant now so prominent in Hebrew Scripture, and the practice was backdated to God's promises to the patriarch Abraham.[9]

When Judaeans brooded on the two creation accounts in the opening of Genesis (regarding them of course as a single unit, without considering any internal contradictions), they generally concluded that women could not be considered as in the 'likeness' of God; after all, the first woman Eve had encouraged the first man Adam into his fatal rebellion against God's command – the 'Fall' that resulted in their expulsion from the Garden of Eden. That was reflected in the architecture and ritual life of the Temple in Jerusalem. The hierarchy of six sacred spaces in the developed Temple complex only allowed women access to the sixth and outermost, the 'court of the women'. The gender of the animals sacrificed in Temple rituals (cattle, sheep and goats) was overwhelmingly male: the option of a female animal was only available in the cases of what were called sin-offerings and shared-offerings.[10]

Temple liturgy was here expressing theological prejudice. Women from Eve onwards were catalysts for male faithlessness and spiritual impurity: worse still if they were women from outside the nation.[11] The evident Judaic anxiety about women and purity was particularly concentrated on menstruation, that aspect of female physiology that has always puzzled and intimidated men, and which is treated with considerable care in the Book of Leviticus. The Jewish historian Josephus, writing about the Temple of his own times as rebuilt by Herod, observed that menstruant women were not even allowed in the outermost space; a prejudice which has long lingered in Christianity as well.[12]

Classical Greece formalized the same inequality in identity by making adult males the only people who were entitled to take part in government: the *polis* has been aptly described as 'a men's club'.[13] There was a distinct mismatch between everyday life and the mythology and literary portrayal of Greek or Roman goddesses. Female divinities were notably active in initiating events, breaking every gender stereotype in the normal range of classical clichés about women; evidently, they were not regarded as offering useful role models in the terrestrial world. At no stage in Greek or Roman history up to the time of the Roman emperors is there anything like the same level of direct political engagement by real women. In general, the only appearance of women in a public role was as priestesses in a variety of temples, though there are some signs that, as the political significance of the *polis* waned in the Hellenistic period, women gained small footholds in public office and greater property rights in public law.[14]

The philosophers and physicians of the ancient world provided what passed for intellectual justification in these commonplaces. Aristotle led the pack through his discussion of animal and human biology, discussion that later Christians came to see as authoritative. He spoke bluntly of a woman as a deficient male; five centuries later, the widely revered medical authority Galen of Pergamon could still echo him in speaking of the imperfection of women. Galen was also influential in choosing to emphasize one particular analysis of human bodies that he found in much older Hippocratic medical literature.[15] They were constituted by four fluids or 'humours' – phlegm, blood, yellow bile/choler and black bile: a notion that, thanks to Galen's continuing prestige in medical discussion, remained prominent in Christian discussions of sex and gender down to the seventeenth century. The four humours were associated with the four elements (earth was associated with black bile, fire with yellow bile, water with phlegm and blood with air) and determined a variety of personal temperaments via an amalgamation of the complex combinations derivable to decide the 'properties' of any individual. Since most of the writing on humoral theory was done by men, it is not surprising that most of the outcomes did not favour femininity. Thus, a major polarity within the system was between dryness and moisture, the general and observable moistness of women being another perennial male fear. Dryness (male) reflected fire and therefore heat; moisture (female) reflected water and coolness. Heat good, coolness not so good. Perfection versus imperfection.[16]

One key battleground concerned sexual intercourse, an occasion on which men do have intimate contact with women, and which often results in children. The experts did not agree here. Aristotle considered the production of children from intercourse to be primarily a male achievement: a man provides the seed; a woman is merely an inert incubator for the foetus. The extensive group of Greek medical writers whose collective literary efforts eventually passed down under the name of Hippocrates saw things differently. Many subsequent commentators (Galen included) followed this Hippocratic tradition rather than Aristotle: women did also produce seed, but their natural moisture made it weaker than that of a man. It was an intricate task to square the correct put-downs of women with the correct rhetorical polarity of temperature and liquidity, but there were plenty of alternative possibilities.

Masculinist biology converged with politics and philosophy. Self-control was a prime masculine characteristic in the Classical world; Greek tragedy is mostly concerned with the dismal fates of those who lack self-control (*enkrateia*) or moderation (*sophrōsynē*). Moderation was the mark of an ideal ruler, and so it was the model for every man who ruled wife, children and slaves in an individual household – in Latin, the *paterfamilias*. Women, by contrast, lacked self-control. The observable abundance of female moistness in the excitement of sexual intercourse revealed that women possessed a more intense sexual desire than men: a latent and potentially chaotic power that needed a proper masculine governor to rein it in.[17] In all this, males still came out on top, in every sense. There is a fascinating crossover between Hellenism and Judaism in a popular Greek commonplace, so common in fact that no one could quite decide who said it first: leading candidates were Plato or the earlier philosopher Thales of Miletus. In any case, Hellenistic men could quote it with cheerful satisfaction as comprising three reasons for gratitude: 'that I was born a human being and not a beast, next, a man not a woman, thirdly a Greek and not a barbarian'. Jewish men liked the thought as well and, suitably emended, it ended up as part of the synagogue liturgy, reattributed to the venerated Rabbi Judah: 'Three blessings one must say daily: Blessed [art thou] who did not make me a gentile; Blessed who did not make me a woman; Blessed who did not make me a boor.'[18]

The skewing of Classical society towards male privilege naturally expressed itself in conventions of sexual behaviour. The prime criterion was who should take the initiative in sex. To penetrate was a right and privilege, indicating superior social status. It was enjoyed by adult freeborn males: citizens, householders. Those penetrated might be women, teenage boys, or slaves of either gender. Conventionally there were controls on abusing male sexual privilege. Since a basic criterion of full maleness was self-mastery, that distinguished a man from all those available for his active sexual initiative and laid responsibilities on him. The struggle to control the passions and avoid excess included the fight against temptation to excessive penetrative sexual pleasure: this was a fight as 'manful' as any exploit on the battlefield.[19]

All this was a matter not so much of morality as of honour. The self-aware Greek or Roman householder must preserve himself from the multiple threats to his bundle of masculinities – a constant neurosis, needing vindication against the competitive scrutiny of other men. One symptom of this, remote from modern social taboos, was a deep horror of dishonourable indulgence in fellatio or cunnilingus, which was particularly pronounced in Roman society. These practices represented the ultimate denial of the male prerogative of penetration. The Roman satirist Martial even claimed that some who indulged in such perversion tried to disguise it by masquerading under the lesser stigma of being passive males in intercourse.[20] That indicates the general nervousness that clung to Classical society's permissible expression of same-sex relations: a major issue for the future of Christianity.

Research over an extraordinarily wide range of periods has converged on identifying a particular cultural form of same-sex behaviour in societies around the Mediterranean and the Middle East: a structurally unequal sexual partnership between older and younger males. Examples of this sexual system have been detected from the Bronze Age down to the nineteenth century CE, going forward from the Classical era to encompass both Christian and Islamic societies.[21] Although strikingly persistent, the custom has met with very different degrees of social acceptance or rejection. Historically most Christian regimes have reacted with denial or repression; at the opposite end of the spectrum lies its acceptance and institutionalization in ancient Greece and Rome. In the developed democracy of Classical Greece, the educational value of an intense and often sexual relationship between a young man and an older and wiser citizen was as much part of the preparation for active political life as was the cultivation of drama and philosophy.

Teenage boys were not yet fully males, as Aristotle observed in passing when he asserted (wrongly) that their sperm remains sterile till the age of twenty-one, after which time fully functioning men go on increasing in vigour, in sperm as in much else.[22] There was no biological justification for Aristotle's statement; it was about the politics of democracy. That age coincided with male eligibility to be a fully participating citizen in the *polis*. In Roman society, lacking such an urgent political justification, the acceptance of same-sex activity of this sort was much more provisional, playing in uneasy ways against the popular fantasy of an older, simpler Rome of martial virtue; sexual exploitation should in

3. Red-figure bell krater, *c.*500–490 BCE: Zeus pursues the beautiful young Ganymede with a spear. Ganymede clutches a hoop and a cock, customary presents in Athens from an older suitor to his younger potential lover.

theory be confined to slaves rather than young free Romans. Even in Greece, one should be aware of the boundaries. The younger, passive male partner was not supposed to enjoy any physical element of the relationship, just the esteem and the presents, and he would eventually have to negotiate an awkward and little-theorized transition from the passive junior to the active senior role.[23]

Neither Greeks nor Romans saw this same-sex activity as a lifelong identity. It was a life-cycle stage; such relationships proceeded alongside opposite-sex exploits by the active partner. A separate concept of a lifelong same-sex sexual identity certainly existed; such a person was termed in Greek a *kinaidos*, mercilessly mocked as a traitor to masculinity in the comedy of Aristophanes, in a fashion reminiscent of twentieth-century mockery of effeminate men.[24] Illogically, both identities ran alongside a literary tradition of the heroic same-sex coupling of equals, such as that of Achilles and Patroklos in the *Iliad*, and the undoubted existence of military units of same-sex lovers in certain *poleis*: most famously the 'Theban Band' eventually defeated by Alexander the Great at the battle of Chaeronea. By comparison, and predictably, Greek and Roman literary interest in any variant of same-sex activities among women was belated and limited.[25]

All this is in sharp contrast to the general deep negativity to same-sex relationships in Judaism (though in parallel fashion, Jewish attention was mostly on men and not women). At its root is an interpretation of passages in the laws of Leviticus (18.22, 20.13) which in later Judaism, and then in Christianity, were interpreted as strong condemnations of all male same-sex activity, right up to the point of punishing it by death. An increasing number of modern scholars point out that this centuries-long assumption ignored the actual grammatical construction of the Hebrew text, whose original meaning seems to have been more narrowly focused: Leviticus was outlawing same-sex intercourse involving married men, alongside a range of other activities defined as sexual deviance in relation to marriage.[26]

The Levitical laws reflected Judaism's strong rhetorical bond between faithfulness to God and the marriage of man and woman. Nevertheless, all same-sex activities were eventually caught up in a general condemnation of all sexual activity not contained in marriage for producing children to fulfil God's promise of fruitfulness to the patriarchs. It is possible that the negativity directed against male same-sex coupling (otherwise very unusual in west Asian cultures) was a reaction to male prostitution in temples of gods other than the God of Israel, but there is little actual evidence of that. In the Hebrew Bible, bestiality receives more severe and more frequent condemnations than same-sex activities; maybe Judaeans experienced bestiality more and found it more socially problematic?[27]

Ironically, an incident in Genesis 19 that has bequeathed Christian societies the word 'sodomy' was little used in ancient Judaism for condemnations of specifically same-sex activity (see Plate 26). Sodomy in any case long continued to refer to a much wider range of sexual activity not leading to procreation. The outrage committed in the ill-fated city of Sodom certainly had a sexual element in it, for the men of the city sought to humiliate a couple of travellers by male rape (Gen. 19). Nevertheless, the outrage is the rape, not the gender of the victim: God punished Sodom for an inexcusable breach of the hospitality conventionally to be offered to travellers in the ancient world. That is demonstrated by an incident in Judges 19, supposedly much later but evidently in reality the model for the Sodom narrative at Gen. 19: dwellers in the city of Gibeah rape a male visitor's 'concubine' as a substitute for raping the man himself. 'If Genesis 19 condemns homosexuality, then clearly Judges 19 condemns heterosexuality,' tartly observes one modern commentator.[28]

Jesus evidently considered the sin of Sodom to be inhospitality. Advising his disciples on how to treat houses or towns who rejected them and their message, he observed that it would be worse for such communities than for Sodom and Gomorrah on the Day of Judgement (Matt. 10.15). By contrast, his Jewish near-contemporaries Philo of Alexandria and Josephus did indeed identify Sodom's sin as same-sex activity. Their observations were part of a growing hostility in Jewish literature from the second century BCE and after, which denounced Graeco-Roman unequal same-sex relationships, a genre of relationship that is simply not mentioned in the Hebrew Bible itself. By now, Hasmonean Judaism had won its victories against the intervention of Hellenistic monarchs, and the abomination of Greek nude male gymnastics concentrated Judaean minds on the general Mediterranean sexual custom, which they rejected as symbolic of Hellenism.[29]

It is a further irony that one of the purest examples of the heroic same-sex love of equals from the ancient Mediterranean is to be found in the Hebrew Bible: the saga of David and Jonathan, told now in texts between 1 Samuel 18 and 2 Samuel 1. Jonathan was the eldest son of King Saul; David and Jonathan loved each other 'passing the love of women', in the words of a song which lamented Jonathan's admittedly well-timed subsequent death in battle (2 Sam. 1.26). At one particularly torrid moment in their relationship, 'they kissed one another, and wept with one another, until David *recovered himself*.' Thus runs the Revised Standard Version of 1 Sam. 20.41 in English, though it has the honesty to add the alternative reading of the verb, that David '*exceeded*'. That is the word that the English scholars creating the King James Version of 1611 had decided was closest to the Hebrew meaning in this passage.

The most obvious way to read 'exceeded' is physical and sexual: either as erection or orgasm. This reading of the original text nevertheless already worried later generations of Hebrew readers, which has resulted in a good deal of confusion in its transmission. The Greek of the Septuagint kept the final phrase candidly but awkwardly as 'until a (or the) great consummation', and one surviving early Latin translation followed suit.[30] By contrast, other alarmed early commentators moulded a new direction for the phrase, with David 'weeping the more' than Jonathan's tears; these included the early Christian Syriac translation known as the *Peshitta*, and later the Vulgate, the classic fourth-century Latin translation by Jerome of Stridon, who was no friend to sexual activity of any sort. That has been a lifeline for those modern translators embarrassed by any suggestion of physicality in the relationship of David and Jonathan; so on this matter, Evangelical Protestant scholars uncharacteristically side with the Pope's translator Jerome rather than those of Protestant King James. None of them can do much about a much less disputable text, 1 Sam. 20.30, where the relationship is said to be 'to the shame of your mother's nakedness'. That clearly implies something sexual.[31]

The shame implied in 1 Sam. 20.30 is not going to please modern advocates for gay rights, but it is not the overall tone of the David/Jonathan story, which lacks any other element of moralizing (and of course pairs it with multiple heterosexual exploits on David's part). In fact, its sexual element is secondary but significantly complementary to its political purpose. Whatever the original truth of the tale, if any, the elaborate exposition is clearly intended to deal with the embarrassment of David's usurpation and his murder of his king: the natural heir, Jonathan, passes his royal right over to the usurper by the intensity of his love.[32] As a piece of Solomonic royal propaganda, it comes from much the same chronological era as the Greek epic in which Achilles and Patroklos cemented their passion for each other. It did not have successors in the Hebrew Bible (see Plate 20).

When Jews turned with relief from problematic same-sex to male–female relationships, they could contemplate the Hebrew Bible's wholly extraordinary anthology of love-poems gathered with the formal title of Song of Songs or Song of Solomon (introduced above in Chapter 1). The collection is all the more strange because, despite the general Jewish insistence on the uniqueness of marriage and unthinking Christian assumptions often made about the text today, it does not concern itself at all with weddings or marriage. Its picture of male–female love is entirely the reverse of the obsessive theme of female betrayal in Hosea or Ezekiel: it consistently proclaims that the woman yearns desperately for her lover, who is quick to respond. For Jews in the catastrophic era of Roman conquest and destruction, the symbolism of these originally secular poems could usefully be turned into a poignant allegory of Israel's longing for her God; and so, the Song was launched into many allegorical and mystical adventures for both its Jewish and its Christian audience.[33]

Judaism was happy to allow the frank eroticism and sensuality of the Song to colour its view of marriage, but Jewish literature brooding on the whole message of the Hebrew Bible increasingly emphasized that marriage was the only permissible setting for such physical delights. The prophets and the Deuteronomistic tradition in biblical writing had inextricably linked fornication and adultery with spiritually equivalent behaviour towards God, particularly if God's people looked to any other god or any other temple than that of Jerusalem. All forms of sexual pleasure outside marriage were thus linked to the first commandment of the Ten that God had given Moses on Mount Sinai/Horeb to be the foundation of the elaborate structure of Law in the Hebrew Bible: 'You shall have no other gods before Me' (Deut. 5.7).

The tradition of Hellenistic Judaism that grew up around the Alexandrian achievement of the Septuagint translation further emphasized this horror of sexual crime. The Greek word *porneia* resounded through the text of the Septuagint. In Greek usage before contact with Judaism, *porneia* had simply signified prostitution. In the Septuagint it was given a spiritual dimension and extended in its meaning to include both fornication and adultery, because they constituted acts of prostitution which were rebellion against God. All other sexual behaviour outside marriage was collateral damage in the crafting of this metaphor – same-sex activity, masturbation, bestiality.

The writings of Philo of Alexandria hammered home these points. He melded with the Septuagintal message his deep reading in Plato and Pythagorean philosophers, who had their own reasons for condemning untrammelled sexual pleasure and for making disagreeable remarks about the entire female gender. Philo added a distinctive degree of misogyny all his own. His commentary on the Genesis Creation story is preoccupied with sexual difference, which he saw as a product of the Fall of Adam and Eve in their disobedience to God in Eden. Moreover, in Philo's eyes, only a sexually undifferentiated Adam, not yet bereft of the rib with which God created Eve, can be a true likeness of the divine.[34] It may be that there were alternative philosophical voices in Alexandria in his time, but their names and opinions are lost to us. It was primarily Philo's Christian readers rather than Jews who preserved his writings, while still acknowledging that he stood at one remove from their own faith by commonly calling him Philo *Judaeus* ('the Jew'). A century or two after his death, Christians particularly in Alexandria listened to Philo avidly on a wide range of sexual matters, notably his low view of women, and they elaborated their own conclusions from the directions that he had set (below, Chapter 7).[35]

MARRIAGE: GREEKS, ROMANS AND JEWS

The one common feature of marriage in the Mediterranean world, whether Hellenistic, Roman or Jewish, was that it was primarily a contract between two men: the fathers of a prospective bridegroom and bride. The contract was set up as between two families, with future practicalities in mind, and its setting was secular, without much or any reference to sacred ceremony. That is the form of marriage that through the Gospel of John we glimpse Jesus attending in Cana in Galilee (John 2.1–11): far from being a visit to the synagogue or the Temple in Jerusalem, the wedding at Cana was a big post-contract party in a convenient local house, where the main concern was the quality of the wine. After that, the similarities end: Judaism and Graeco-Roman society were at odds about the nature of marriage, and the Christian future lay not with Judaism, but with Hellenism.

The positive feature of sexual teaching in Judaism, from the Abrahamic covenantal promises onwards, has been its exuberant celebration of marriage and children, not to mention the generous catering that sustains large families in celebratory mood. It is a consequent duty for every man to marry, and Judaism shows strikingly little cultural approval of celibacy, that option which was eventually to become almost overwhelming in Christianity (below, Part Two). What Christians find less easy to deal with in their inheritance from Judaism is the fact that the Jewish emphasis on marriage and the family long included the option of polygyny – as, indeed, is the case in the great majority of human societies in history.[36] Husbands can find multiple wives expensive, and so polygyny is generally a practice for elites (or for those who regularly travel long distances between their centres of operation, like traders). The stand-out case in the Hebrew Bible is King Solomon, with his collection of seven hundred wives, plus three hundred concubines. These ladies are not portrayed with approval in 1 Kings 11.3, not because of their polygynous character, but because many of them were foreign and led the ageing monarch into spiritual faithlessness.

No such stigma attached to the earlier polygynous patriarchs such as Abraham, the most respected figures in Judaic history. This became a great difficulty in interpreting scripture for Christians, who inherited the patriarchs while deciding to reject polygyny (below, Chapter 4), but it was no problem for Jews, since polygyny continued to be a reality in the time of Jesus and for at least a millennium more. An exceptionally lucky archaeological find in Israel in the 1960s revealed, in a bag of papyri, the personal archive of a wealthy woman named Babatha, who lived about a century after Jesus, and may have died in the last Judaean stand against Rome in 135 CE. Included were legal papers relating to her remarriage after the death of her first husband to a man called Judah, who still had a living wife and daughter. Not all went smoothly thereafter, hence documents from lawsuits among Babatha's papers.[37] A thousand years more passed before rabbis prohibited polygyny, a ban first recorded in the German city of Mainz, and hence no doubt a defensive reaction to the unsympathetically monogamous eleventh-century Christian society surrounding European Jewish communities. Jewish polygyny could linger later still in Muslim-ruled territories.[38]

This is one of the starkest contrasts between Judaism and Graeco-Roman society. Jewish acceptance of polygyny needs little explaining, since it represents the norm in ancient west Asia. It is the insistence of the Greeks and the Romans on purely monogamous marriage that is the conundrum, not so far solved. The *Odyssey* may have helped to enshrine monogamy as standard among previous competing Greek models of marriage, since the whole point of the epic is Odysseus' determined efforts to return to his wife Penelope in Ithaka, and her equally determined faithfulness to him during his long absence. After that, monogamy may have been one of the factors in the Greek decision for democracy, since the equality of citizens in a *polis* is compromised by the likelihood that polygyny is most easily sustainable by the powerful and wealthy.

For whatever reason, monogamy became a cultural custom to distinguish Classical civilization. Christianity has sustained that through most of its expansion, though we will be repeatedly encountering exceptions to that rule. A notable stress in Roman monogamy is its emphasis on marital love. One might think this is at odds with the lack of formal ceremony to initiate Roman marriages and the relative ease with which either party might obtain a divorce (both were characteristics of Jewish marriages as well). It also sits untidily with the functional Graeco-Roman emphasis in sex on male penetrative privilege and initiative. The theme of marital love simply has to be seen as a different set of organizing beliefs about men and women; humans have always been capable of simultaneously holding together not wholly compatible beliefs about personal relationships.[39]

Love was monumentalized (literally) in countless gravestones throughout the Roman Empire, expressing grief and deep mutual affection, children included: sculptural images or epitaphs for husband, wife and children are touchingly numerous. Many may have been formal expressions of what the monument-reading public expected, but it is significant that this *is* what was expected. The theme also springs out of what romantic novels survive from the Roman imperial period, starting in the first century CE; the pattern in these is for a pair of young lovers to go through all sorts of adventures, generally of a chaste nature, before arriving safely at the goal of marriage. They found an eager readership.[40]

Graeco-Roman tomb sculpture and inscriptions also form part of the very widespread evidence that Graeco-Roman families (certainly elite families) were generally small, like the nuclear families of modern western Europe or America, with no more than one or two sons being considered a desirable norm. This is in sharp contrast to Judaism's emphasis on marital fertility and large families. After considering all the factors that might accelerate mortality such as war or disease, that can

4. A Roman sarcophagus (second century CE) for the boy Marcus Cornelius Statius shows in strip-cartoon fashion his parents gazing fondly on the infant Marcus, and then his father cuddling him. Later scenes show the older Marcus with pony and chariot and at his lessons.

only indicate a resort to methods of family limitation, including contraception and abortion. It needs to be remembered in all discussion of abortion across history that, before the arrival of modern surgery, methods of abortion were largely medical rather than surgical: various abortifacient concoctions, many of which clearly proved their efficacy by long usage.

Classical literary sources are less extensive on contraception than on abortifacients, of which many Graeco-Roman authors disapproved (the Hebrew Bible never discusses the issue), and there was still more discussion of what was, clearly, a widespread practice: the exposure of unwanted infants. Exposure was a father's legal right in most Graeco-Roman legal systems until the adoption of Christianity by Roman emperors in the fourth century. Its outlawing in Roman law at that period was a significant turning point. Nevertheless, whatever the legal and theological framework, Christian societies up to modern times have in practice been little different from others in turning to this desperate expedient where poverty is the norm, even if it is less obviously a simple favouring of male infants over female in feeding and general care. Such are the limits of the rhetoric of marital love and family, in the Roman Empire as much as in other eras.[41]

The Romans had the whole Mediterranean at their disposal by the late first century BCE, but more than two centuries went by before they made any official attempt to suppress polygyny and its supporting legal systems among their subject peoples. That was in accordance with the normal Roman strategy of not interfering with subject peoples unless absolutely necessary. A shift occurred in the early third century CE, as a necessary side-effect of the Emperor Caracalla granting Roman citizenship to all free imperial subjects in 212 (he took this sweeping initiative largely to extend his available revenue-raising base). Universal citizenship gave an incentive for a great many more people to settle marital disputes in the imperial law courts, where Roman law was of course based on the principle of monogamy. When Roman officialdom did actively intervene on questions of marriage law, the interventions were naturally aimed at safeguarding monogamy rather than paying much attention to polygyny; that meant dealing with incest.

The Romans had firm views about what they regarded as incest, particularly marriages between uncle and niece; the Emperor Claudius had caused great offence by doing precisely that, though the law grudgingly accommodated him. This imperial exception aside, Roman law contains repeated prohibitions on matters of incest. Romans had a particular prejudice against the widespread west Asian custom of close-kin marriage, and they would, for instance, have found abhorrent Judaism's provision for a brother to marry his deceased brother's widow, so-called levirate marriage.[42] They were especially horrified by one variant on close-kin marriage – the Egyptian custom of brother and sister marrying. It is mysterious why this ancient practice (rare in world history) spread so vigorously in Egypt during the early Roman imperial era. Previously it had been confined to the elite around the Pharaohs, but, far from disappearing with the Ptolemaic dynasty, it spread through society and comprised around a fifth of all Egyptian marriages in the first to third centuries CE.[43]

It is clear that Caracalla's decree did not do much to change west Asian marital customs among the multitudes of new Roman citizens, and eight decades later, in 295, the co-emperors Diocletian and Maximian tried to remedy that with a general imperial decree against incestuous marriages. Egyptian custom was prominent in their targets: they numbered among offenders those who married 'a sister on the father's side, or on the mother's side' in addition to straightforward marriages of siblings. These two emperors were historically among the greatest Roman foes of Christianity, but they presented their action with elaborate reference to morality, in the shape of the opinions likely to be held by the pantheon of Roman gods: 'even the immortal gods themselves will be favorable and gentle to the Roman name, as they always have been, if they have seen that all people living under our rule lead a wholly pious and religious and peaceful and chaste life in all respects.'[44]

In later years, Christianized Roman emperors did repeat incest bans, this time in the name of the Christian God, but, before Diocletian and Maximian, Christian writers had proved oddly silent about 'the Egyptian problem' amid other zestful attacks on examples of pagan immorality, including pagan incest.[45] Diocletian and Maximian were making their pronouncements in a period when imperial religion was acquiring a new moral aspect, in parallel to what was happening in Christian moral discourse. Yet their rhetoric was nothing like the overarching narrative tragedy shaping Israelite history from the prophets onwards, which threatened Judaism with extinction and underlay its praise of matrimony and its condemnation of every other sexual practice. We have seen how marriage in Judaism was not a mere social institution but a metaphor for the people's relationship to their God. That is very different from the rather formal sense in the imperial decree of 295 that there was a right way to behave in sexual matters, and that the gods were naturally aware of it. Roman disapproval of west Asian choices in matrimony derived from a sense of cultural superiority: what behaviour was fitting for Roman citizens. This was not exactly a matter of personal morality, more part of the self-image of any man of honour. It was linked to concepts like self-control or moderation, but as part of a much broader understanding of those terms than any regard for sexual morality or immorality.

Such were the cultural choices that surrounded a young man growing up in Galilee in what is now thought of as the first century of the Common Era. Galilee might be considered an obscure part of an obscure corner in the Roman Empire, but if provincial, it was provincial in the two parallel milieux, Judaean and Graeco-Roman. In everyday life, Jesus would have spoken Aramaic, and he is portrayed in the Gospels as expounding the Hebrew Scripture in synagogues. Yet in the other cultural direction, he probably also spoke some everyday Greek. For the son of a craftsman, it would be absolutely necessary to know even just a little: enough to do business in the marketplace only four miles from his Galilean home in Nazareth, in a predominantly Greek-style town called Sepphoris, capital city of the younger of two successive Hellenized (or, indeed, Romanized) King Herods.[46]

Both these Herods figure in the four Gospels, but, curiously, no Gospel says a word about Sepphoris. That is a symptom of the Evangelists' concentration on Jesus against his background in the culture of the Hebrew Bible, despite the fact that they themselves were writing in Greek. By the time that the Gospels were composed towards or even beyond 100 CE, the balance between the two cultures within Christianity had shifted decisively. The earliest surviving remnants of Christian literature are letters written by a Judaean called Saul or Paul from the Anatolian city of Tarsus, writing in the two or three decades of the first century following Jesus's relatively brief life. Paul's language of choice was not Aramaic, but that same colloquial Greek that had echoed in Jesus's ears in the marketplace of Sepphoris. To Jesus and Paul we must now turn, to see what they made of their joint legacy from Jerusalem and Athens.

4
Jesus the Christ

The energies released by the relatively short earthly life and execution of Jesus still fuel a world faith, currently engaging the loyalties of around a third of its inhabitants. A little over three decades in an identifiable period of history have resonated beyond historic time, transforming all around them. Yet the young man at the centre of it startles by having such an ordinary name. His parents, like many at the time, called him Jeshua, in memory of the liberator who led the Hebrews into the Promised Land after the death of Moses.[1] Christians do their best to disguise this relationship between the two Jeshuas, by differentiating their names, so the name of the original liberating hero is rendered for instance into English as Joshua. The later liberating Saviour is called Jesus, a Greek variant (*Jesous*) on the original Hebrew.[2] Christians have added a second descriptor for him which is a title, and which should not be mistaken for a surname like 'MacCulloch'. 'Christ' is another Greek word, translating the Hebrew word 'Messiah', or 'Anointed One', the future hope of Israel; it takes the ordinariness of the first name Jeshua and catapults it into the cosmos. The Saviour of the world has taken flesh (*carnis* in Latin), in what Western Christians call the 'Incarnation'.

This is the story set forth in four different accounts of the earthly life and resurrection of Jesus Christ, written for different communities now difficult to identify somewhere on the eastern Mediterranean seaboard. They form a literary genre with little Classical precedent, focusing on a level of ordinary society that biography normally ignored: the interactions of Jesus with ordinary people, often on the margins of their society. One modern scholar has described them as 'down-market' versions of biography.[3] It is therefore appropriate that they (and some later imitations of them) share a distinctive description, which is, in English, 'Gospel'. This is an Old English word meaning 'good news'; many languages have kept the same idea in forms of the preceding Latin word, deriving in turn from Greek: *Evangelium*. Three of the Gospels, written by 'Evangelists' identified as Mark, Matthew and Luke, are together known as the 'Synoptic' Gospels, to distinguish them from the Gospel of John, which was probably written a decade or two later than they were. The Synoptics present the basic story of Jesus in a similar way, quite differently from John's narrative: they even disagree with John on the length of Jesus's public ministry, John's account suggesting around three years, the others something over one. On this and other issues, the Synoptics 'see together', the root meaning of the Greek *synopsis*.[4]

INFANCY AND FAMILY

In the fourth century CE, the Mediterranean Christian Church created two summary statements of belief, now known as the Apostles' and the Nicene Creeds. These Creeds were constructed on the basis of the Gospels and those texts that follow them in the New Testament – often all collectively referred to as 'the Gospel'. The purpose of Creeds was to eliminate alternative lines of argument about the content of Christian faith, and to be easily taught to Christian believers. Amid many very complex theological statements about the nature of the Christian God, they incorporated two assertions of what sounds plausibly like historical or chronological fact, specifying the bounds of Jesus's life on earth: he was born of Mary and died during the rule of the Roman administrator Pontius Pilate. Thus, just as with the double name of the Saviour, the Creeds embed the fleshly ordinariness of the human Jesus within the cosmic reality of Christ.

Of these two biological turning points, all four Gospels contain elaborately detailed descriptions of his arrest and death, which may be the earliest written elements in their text. By contrast, only two of four Gospels concern themselves with Jesus's birth: Matthew and Luke. Mark, almost certainly the earliest Gospel, says nothing about it, but instead plunges straight into describing Jesus's short public ministry in Palestine, heralded by the ancient prophet Isaiah and the modern forerunner prophet called John the Baptist. John the Evangelist's Gospel, the outlier, bursts instead into a majestic cosmic hymn, a deliberate echo of the Creation stories in Genesis, which makes Jesus the eternal and pre-existing Word (*Logos*, a Greek term of divinity inherited from Plato and Philo Judaeus). This Word had been with God in the making of all things: John describes a beginning, not a birth.

By contrast, Matthew and Luke craft an elaborate sequence of stories generally described by Christian commentators as the 'Infancy Narratives', describing his birth from Mary in Bethlehem and his early childhood. Much of this material is very familiar to even occasional churchgoers from their own childhood onwards, through its regular rehearsal in candle-lit services during the Yuletide season, and the familiarity extends to anyone choosing Christmas cards with a religious flavour. Consequently, to cast a critical eye on these accounts in Matthew and Luke is to enter perhaps the most emotionally charged territory in all Christian discussion of sex. In the 1980s, Jane Schaberg, a biblical scholar who conscientiously took a scalpel to their texts, had her car firebombed in her university car park, amid other less dramatic harassment and cold-shouldering by her academic colleagues.[5]

Such extreme reactions may be reinforced by that deceptive familiarity of the Infancy Narratives, yet if one returns the excerpts commonly run together in Christmas services back into their actual places in their respective Gospels, it quickly becomes apparent how little overlap there is in the various incidents recorded in Matthew and Luke. Both Infancy Narratives contain linear genealogies for Jesus, but only some names occur in both (to the discreet puzzlement of Christian commentators from early times, resulting in much busyness in trying to reconcile them). Both genealogies end in a feature that makes no sense for a family tree, or for conventional accounts of the Incarnation: their genealogical goal is Joseph, who on any reading of the stories in the Infancy Narratives cannot be Jesus's biological father. Both genealogies rather lamely make that clear, Luke launching his version by speaking of Jesus as 'the son (as was supposed) of Joseph' (Luke 3.23).[6] Matthew has previously stated that Joseph 'knew [Mary] not' (that is, did not consummate their marriage) 'until she had borne a son': that is, Jesus (Matt. 1.25).

The peculiarity of Matthew's and Luke's genealogies, their biological pointlessness, is a clue to how and why they evolved. These genealogies share a purpose in linking Jesus as Messiah to the ancient hero King David, who features in both of them, via Joseph. That purpose links to the other shared feature in Matthew's and Luke's infancy stories: they locate the birth of Jesus in Bethlehem, 'the city of David', where the prophet Samuel had discovered the founder of the Davidic royal line (1 Sam. 16). Yet everywhere else in the Gospels, as well as in the New Testament book called the Acts of the Apostles, Jesus is described as coming from the villages of Nazareth or Capernaum in Galilee. In fact, not even Matthew and Luke mention Jesus's birth in Bethlehem outside their Infancy Narratives, and the single other reference to Bethlehem in the rest of the New Testament is a note of scepticism. John's Gospel describes an argument about whether or not Jesus was the Messiah; sceptics pointed out that Jesus was from Nazareth, while the Hebrew prophet Micah had foretold the birth of the Messiah in Bethlehem, about a hundred miles to the south.[7]

Luke solves this geographical difficulty (Luke 2.1–5) by claiming that Joseph and Mary had been forced to travel from Nazareth to Bethlehem by a Roman imperial tax decree. This necessitated that everyone should return to their birth city to be enrolled: so to the City of David the couple must return, on genealogical grounds. What at first sounds like an historical detail in fact reveals how unhistorical the Infancy Narratives are, before ever considering their more obviously challenging miraculous accounts of angels, heavenly choirs, a Star in the East and magi. A well-attested Roman imperial census did indeed happen, a first real taste of how direct Roman rule would affect Judaea and therefore long remembered there as a traumatic event. Yet this census was not until 6 CE, far too late for any possible birth date for Jesus – and there is no other evidence anywhere of a universal imperial tax levy at this time. More importantly, it is absurd to think that Roman officials would consider a thousand-year-old claim to Davidic kinship as relevant to their filing systems; whereas to pious Christian readers of the two Davidic Gospel genealogies converging on Joseph, not much concerned about the sort of analytical history that Livy or Tacitus wrote, it would make perfect devotional sense.

This is the key to expounding and appreciating the Infancy Narratives. The Gospel writers, following Jesus's own characteristic use of parables in teaching rather than abstract discourses, preferred telling stories to setting out bald theological propositions. The Narratives are not exercises in historical research, but early Christian explorations of the meaning and significance of Jesus. They seek to explain how an ordinary Judaean in historical time took a central place in the structure of the Hebrew Bible in its Septuagintal form. They are part of a debate among early Christians, and they offer a different solution of the problem to that presented by Paul of Tarsus. Writing to Christians in Rome in one of the earliest surviving Christian texts, half a century or so before the Gospel writers, Paul had asserted that Jesus 'was descended from David according to the Flesh and designated Son of God in power according to the Spirit of holiness by his resurrection from the dead', which locates his divinity in the culmination of his earthly life (Rom. 1. 3–4): that might be regarded as promotion from secular royal ancestry to the godhead. By contrast, the Infancy Narratives use their sequence of miniature stories around Jesus's birth to glorify the child from the outset beyond his own people to the whole world and to the cosmos. Given such an all-encompassing agenda, the Narratives demand multiple approaches to understanding, from which we must single out their future significance for the construction of family and sex.

Jesus grew up in the family of Joseph and Mary in Nazareth of Galilee, as sceptics observe in John's Gospel (John 6.41–42). All sources agree that his mother was Mary, *Miryam* in Hebrew and Aramaic (one of no fewer than seven different Marys in the New Testament narratives; Miryam was an even more common name than Jeshua). Yet Matthew and Luke separately face questions that had arisen around Jesus's birth; it was not in the regular pattern of families, and Joseph could not be said to have been Jesus's father. Amid Mark's general lack of comment on Jesus's parentage, there is one remarkable moment where he ventriloquizes the people of Jesus's home town as offensively calling Jesus 'the son of Mary' as well as brother of James, Joseph, Simon and Judas. This phrase 'son of Mary' would normally indicate that the addressee's father was unknown. Matthew, Luke and an echo of the story in John all briskly alter the alarming usage to highlight Joseph, only Matthew keeping any reference at all to Mary; but Matthew and Luke then provide two different accounts of the circumstances of Jesus's birth in their Infancy Narratives.[8]

In Matthew, Joseph is the main actor, and in Luke, Mary. Matthew tells the story of Joseph's initial horror at Mary's pregnancy; he has to be instructed by an angel in a dream not to follow his instinct to repudiate his young betrothed, for this child is the Messiah (Matt. 1.18–22). Matthew, of all the Gospel writers, is the most concerned to link Jesus's ministry to the Judaic past, and his narrative here is in dialogue with the terms of Judaic law in Deuteronomy (Deut. 22.20–29), which discusses what should happen when a betrothed virgin is seduced or raped. The penalty in Deuteronomy is execution by stoning: kindly Joseph instead resolves to end the betrothal quietly, even before the angelic intervention.

Luke seems more indirect than Matthew, but when in his story the angel Gabriel tells Mary of her pregnancy, she immediately asks him how that can be, since she has no husband (Luke 1.34). In fact, Luke goes much further than Matthew. Among the songs he incorporates into his Infancy Narratives are two hymns of victory, still commonly used in the various Christian regular daily rounds of worship called 'Offices'. One is attributed to John the Baptist's father Zacharias (the canticle 'Benedictus' used for instance in Anglican Morning Prayer), and the other to Mary herself (the 'Magnificat' of Anglican Evensong). Not all their content is relevant to their present context, and it has been plausibly suggested that they are martial songs borrowed from the Maccabean period more than a century before, but their general message of renewal and the overthrow of existing power suits Luke's purpose.[9]

Significant therefore is Mary's proclamation in the Magnificat that God 'has regarded *the low estate* of his *handmaiden*' (Luke 1.48). Those Revised Standard Version translations underplay the shock value of these words to their early Christian readers. 'Low estate' renders *tapeinōsis*, which in its many shades of meaning stretches to 'humiliation', 'disgrace' or 'baseness': 'handmaiden' hardly hits the essence of *doulē*, which starkly means 'female slave', and which would therefore immediately suggest someone available for the humiliation of sexual assault. It was thus perfectly appropriate for Jane Schaberg to suggest the possibility that, in his use of this vocabulary, Luke is portraying Mary as the victim of rape.[10]

Early readers of the Infancy Narratives were not slow to pick up the general implications of what they were saying. When Christians and Jews became increasingly at odds, some Jews hardened their perception into anti-Christian sexual polemic. John's Gospel records what sounds like an early example of this, in an angry argument presented as directly between Jesus and 'the Jews': they sneer 'We were not born of fornication, we have one Father, even God' (John 8.41). A story arose, first surviving from a literary attack on Christianity by the late second-century Greek writer Celsus, that Jesus was the son of a Roman soldier called Pantera. Pantera is indeed a surname attested from the period – the gravestone of a legionary with the name can now be viewed in Bad Kreuznach in Germany. The tale may be not so much a malicious fabrication as a confusion, based on a genuine surname of Pantera in Joseph's family; certainly, that was the contention of the occasionally reliable Christian polemicist Epiphanios in the fourth century, drawing as he claimed on an ancient tradition.[11]

Given the nature of the Infancy Narratives as theological exposition, there is no contradiction between their theological claims and the historical untidiness that is likely to lie behind them. Both Gospel writers have built their stories round illegitimacy, a difficult premise that no one is likely to have created just for the sake of it. The New Testament repeatedly refers to the sinlessness of Jesus, but nowhere does it associate that with the circumstances of his birth, whether from a virgin or not. The 'virgin' element comes from Matthew. He prefaces his Infancy Narratives by quoting a saying of the prophet Isaiah, nine centuries before, that 'a virgin shall conceive and bear a son' (Isa. 7.14; Matt. 1.23). In fact, Matthew was reading his Isaiah in the Greek of the Septuagint, which has translated the 'young woman' of Isaiah's Hebrew text (*'almah*) by the word which in Greek normally signifies a virgin (*parthenos*); he thus sparked a long and expanding Christian devotional tradition to Mary as virgin.[12] Yet is Matthew enunciating the doctrine of the virginal conception as understood by later Christians? He could equally well be seizing on the underlying idea of this Isaianic passage in the Septuagint that matches his overall message: in a time of crisis for the people of God, God chooses not a king or military genius to save a remnant, but the most vulnerable of young women and her infant son.[13]

How does God do this? In Matthew and Luke, an angel describes the pregnancy respectively to an astonished Joseph and to Mary as of or by the Holy Spirit (Matt. 1.20, Luke 1.35). This is that same Spirit that according to the Hebrew Bible had moved on the face of the primeval waters in creation – as the breath of God's mouth, the means by which he renews the earth.[14] The Spirit is divine restlessness: it manifests the apparent randomness of God's will to imperceptive humans. The Gospel genealogies go out of their way to feature marital unconventionality amid the apparent smoothness of their generations. In Matthew, the line specifically passes via four women in eyebrow-raising situations: Tamar, whose story and marriage are grotesquely mixed up with apparent prostitution; Rahab a harlot; Ruth a foreigner; and then the unnamed wife of Uriah the Hittite, a soldier of King David who had been effectively murdered so that the King could have her.[15] The God of surprises has in the Infancy Narratives thus set aside conventional expectations of family, ending with the 'son of Mary'.

This has never been an easy message for Christians. In my own sheltered youth in a rural corner of Western Christian society, illegitimacy still remained a lifelong taint for children born out of wedlock. Schaberg's sometime doctoral supervisor, the biblical scholar Raymond E. Brown (who became increasingly alarmed at the direction of her work), had earlier observed in his own distinguished commentary on the Infancy Narratives that, for the simple believer at least, 'illegitimacy may be an offense that would challenge the plausibility of the Christian mystery.'[16] Half a century after Brown wrote, Christians may be in a better position to think past that venerable opinion than at any time in the last 1,900 years. The alternative is to stop at the surface of the metaphors in the Infancy Narratives and, as is often the case with Christian metaphors, to end up in absurdity.

There was a centuries-long and risibly solemn Christian debate as to which of Mary's bodily members or orifices the Holy Spirit employed as physical agent in the Incarnation; which of the human senses did it involve? The discussion of orifices did not involve the vagina. An early suggestion from the (possibly second century) *Martyrdom and Ascension of Isaiah* identified the eyes and therefore sight: Mary was disturbed by seeing a small child and immediately conceived.[17] An anonymous Egyptian author (long confused with another writer, Demetrios of Antioch) suggested the nose, with Mary savouring the sweet smell of the angel Gabriel; others advocated the mouth, with analogous connotations of taste. Probably the most popular option was the ear, since in Luke's story of the angelic 'Annunciation', Mary learned of her conception through a conversation with Gabriel. This was a suggestion given authority from pioneering and influential Christmas sermons by Archbishop Proklos of Constantinople in the fifth century, and it had a long life in front of it, probably because the idea appeared more seemly than the alternatives, and was also easier to depict in art. None of the suggestions seem particularly edifying now. A society more attuned to modern genetics may ask, with equal clumsy literalness, how an incarnate Christ might be male, if his human chromosomes were entirely derived from Mary.[18]

After the Infancy Narratives, only Luke of all the Evangelists gives us any incident in Jesus's youth before his public mission in his thirties (Luke 2.41–51); this is his visit to the Temple aged twelve, and there is no reason to treat it as any more historical than what goes before it. Later Christians, hungry to learn more about these missing years, created a great many more childhood stories, some of which are downright bizarre, extending as far as little Jesus repeatedly inflicting multiple mayhem on his playmates. Several of them met unusual ends, such as falling to their deaths when sliding down a sunbeam; they were only miraculously resuscitated after the Holy Child had been given a good telling-off by his mother, following complaints from the neighbours (see Plate 5).[19]

Some of the reality is to be gleaned elsewhere in the Gospels, which make clear that Jesus had brothers and sisters. Once the Church began developing the idea of Mary as virgin, indeed as perpetual virgin, this scriptural testimony of a large family became an embarrassment. At the turn of the second and third centuries it was still not a problem for the North African theologian Tertullian, who looked at Matt. 13.55 and Mark 6.3 in matter-of-fact fashion to find four named brothers of Jesus (let alone at least a couple of unnamed sisters, whom he could also have encountered in some scribal versions of Mark 3.32). Tertullian, who was intent on combating contemporary Christians who were denying any true humanity in Jesus, as well as in his own fashion defending the value of family and marriage, viewed these as younger siblings to the Saviour, born of Mary by Joseph; and, rather startlingly to later ears, when he considered Matthew's use of Isaiah 7.14, he commented that, in bearing Jesus, Mary was 'a virgin as regards her husband, not a virgin as regards child-bearing'. He was not alone among his theologian contemporaries.[20]

One can see why later theologians were desperate to avoid such conclusions, many finding it impossible to stomach even the saving possibility (still the official view in Orthodox Christianity) that Joseph had had a wife before Mary to produce such a substantial family. It all involved just too much sexual intercourse, even for Joseph. In the fourth century, Jerome, the Latin theologian whom we will repeatedly encounter busily decoupling sex from holiness, suggested that 'brothers' really meant 'cousins', and that these had been interchangeable terms in Hebrew and Greek. This argument is still promulgated in conservative Christian circles. In the case of Greek, as Jerome surely knew, it was nonsense: Greek was a language with a very precise and extensive set of words to describe particular degrees of cousinage, and Greek-speakers would be unlikely to confuse any of it with 'brothers'. The Apostle Paul, who was writing plain down-to-earth Greek and not translating from some earlier Aramaic, unselfconsciously (and, in context, crossly) referred to his fellow Apostle James in Jerusalem as the brother of the Lord.[21]

Altogether, the Holy Family, so apparently familiar from Christmas cards, makes an uneasy fit with the many different views of family that Christian Churches have constructed over the centuries. Irreverently to adapt a famous remark of the late Princess Diana, there were three of them in that marriage, so it was a bit theologically crowded. From the matrix of this family in Nazareth, nevertheless, Jesus embarked on his public ministry throughout Galilee and Judaea. Amid these events, we move from dealing with purposeful and resonant myth to retrieving a number of the Lord's concrete propositions about sex, family and relationships.

THE TEACHING OF JESUS

Since Jesus left no writings himself, we hear his Aramaic voice through a Greek filter in texts written sixty to a hundred years after his execution sometime around 30 CE. Given such distancing, it is surprising how much a recognizable and charismatic individual emerges from the Gospels: preaching an urgent message in punchy phrases that resound with confident authority but are also full of comedy and irony. His discourses sparkle with stories that subvert normal expectations – sometimes puzzling the listeners, including the Evangelists who recorded them. Around him he gathered many disciples, messengers and admiring companions, but at the centre of them were the Twelve, a number signifying the long-dispersed Twelve Tribes of Israel: Twelveness was a sign that the tragic past and broken present were to be made perfect. All of this pounded home the proclamation of an imminent end to all things in 'the Kingdom of God', which would be very unlike the kingdoms and empires of the world around Judaea.[22]

Jesus came to his own decisions within his own understanding and practice of Judaism on how his followers should behave, and he struck out in directions which, as one might expect from someone from an unconventional background, were frequently distinctive, deliberately divisive and countercultural. Should Christians, then, take that pious modern American bumper-sticker 'What would Jesus do?' as a touchstone for discussing such matters as marriage? The problem about the bumper-sticker is that the sayings of Jesus on marriage and the family (or indeed on anything else) are a series of occasional illuminations that over the four Gospels and the other New Testament books light up like fireworks, and often as startlingly.

Jesus can be disconcerting, as in his careful interest in classifying eunuchs (Matt. 19.12): 'there are eunuchs who have been so from birth, and there are eunuchs who have been made eunuchs by men, and there are eunuchs who have made themselves for the sake of the kingdom of heaven.' The other Gospel writers, who do not record this thought, may have found it unhelpful; though not much discussed in modern Christian focuses on the family, it has in the past been of great interest to Christians for a variety of reasons (below, Chapter 8), and it may prove to be so again in an era of gender fluidity. Family values are far from being Jesus's main concern. In one saying echoed from Mark's Gospel by Matthew and Luke, he speaks of the extravagant reward for those who have left home and family for the sake of what is variously described as the kingdom of God, the Gospel, or Jesus himself.[23]

This repudiation of family is a strong theme in Jesus's sayings in the Synoptic Gospels, particularly those which Matthew and Luke derive from a further source beyond the material that they reinterpret from Mark (it is sometimes known by scholars as 'Q', from the German *Quelle*, meaning 'source'). They may reflect conflicts after Jesus's earthly life about authority among Christian leaders – family members versus others – but they are all of a piece with his urgent theme of the imminence of the last phase of earthly existence. He speaks shockingly of bringing not 'peace, but a sword' (Matt. 10.34), a saying in Matthew that is spelled out in pitiless relational detail in Luke (Luke 12.52–53): 'henceforth in one house there will be five divided, three against two and two against three . . . father against son and son against father, mother against daughter and daughter against her mother, mother-in-law against her daughter-in-law, and daughter-in-law against her mother-in-law.'

Overall, these are not comforting words for those seeking to make Christianity the religion of the modern nuclear family. In accordance with these thoughts, Jesus often seems frankly dismissive of his biological family, including his mother: when Mary and his brothers and sisters came to one of his public events asking to speak to him, his discouraging response was to point to the disciples around him as his mother and siblings.[24] The tug between family ties and one's own choice to construct a substitute family has been a constant tension within Christianity, with the balance swaying between them over the centuries. The transformation of Jewish familial norms relates once more to the theme of imminent cosmic changes, for instance in Jesus recalling the end of traditional family life when God flooded the whole earth in the time of Noah: 'they ate, they drank, they married, they were given in marriage, until the day when ... the flood came and destroyed them all' (Luke 17.27, echoed in Matt. 24.38–39).[25]

In the new end-time set of relationships that Jesus creates around him, we read of a mixture of male and female disciples and apostles, supplemented by a record of two sparky but positive conversational encounters between Jesus and resourceful foreign women, who both made a good account of themselves in the exchanges.[26] Among the disciples and apostles who followed Jesus, the Twelve had to be male, because they represented the male identities of the Twelve Tribes. Others did not bear this symbolism, and the biblical text may contain more females than are at first apparent – for instance, only unthinking assumptions about one important story lead the reader to identify as male both of the disciples who encountered the risen Christ on a road to Emmaus.[27]

Among the most important followers were sisters from a village called Bethany, Mary and Martha, along with their brother Lazarus, clearly a particular favourite of Jesus, though Lazarus says nothing recorded in the Gospels. Then there is the stand-out figure of Mary Magdalen; all four Gospels name her as among the first witnesses of the Resurrection. Mary Magdalen's role is particularly enhanced in John's dramatic presentation. She meets the risen Jesus alone – first in deep distress mistaking him for a gardener, and then in deep joy, recognizing the reality (John 20.11–18). For this reason, she has often been called 'Apostle to the Apostles', for she passes the astonishing news on to the wider disciple-group. In the course of later history, she has undergone almost as many transformations as her familial opposite number, Mary the Mother of the Lord.

John the Evangelist is responsible also for the theme that there was one special male disciple whom Jesus 'loved'. It sits untidily beside the motif recorded in the Synoptics that Jesus sternly rebuked some of the Twelve for seeking a special place in Heaven (Mark 10.35–45; Matt. 20.20–28; Luke 22.24–27). The beloved disciple is never named in John's Gospel, though it says that he provided its textual content (John 21.24); traditionally the character has been elided into the person of John the Evangelist himself. Other identifications have been suggested, such as Lazarus, but the indications are that the final editor wished the content of his Gospel to be seen as coming from John, son of Zebedee; John was one of the Twelve, and was actually one of those whom the Synoptic Jesus rebuked for seeking special treatment. This language of love and particular favour has inevitably aroused interest in those aware of Graeco-Roman institutions of same-sex relationships. Like the turbulence built into the picture of Mary Magdalen, the resonance passed down the centuries for those inclined to find it (see Plate 19). That irrepressibly witty monarch James VI of Scotland and I of England, for instance, astonished his Privy Councillors at Hampton Court in 1617 with a truculent defence of his undoubtedly erotic relationship with his favourite, George Villiers, Duke of Buckingham: Christ had his John, he said, and James had his George.[28]

Jesus's Synoptic snub to his visiting family coheres with the unexpectedly combative tone in some of the New Testament's scanty references to Mary outside the Infancy Narratives. Luke (11.27–28) records Jesus's direct put-down both of Mary and an over-enthusiastic female follower, who had cried 'Blessed is the womb that bore you, and the breasts that you sucked!' – to which he retorts: 'Blessed rather are those who hear the word of God and keep it!'[29] Given the rising tide of devotion to the Mother/Bearer of God over more than a millennium, Christians were not much inclined to explore that disturbing thought until the sixteenth century, in the European Protestant Reformation. Protestant Reformers then identified Mary as the chief culprit in a cult of saintly intercession which they regarded as a leading fault of the old Western Church, and they were infuriated by the claim that she was sinless. These theological considerations made them turn to a keenly literalist reappraisal of her presence in the Bible, aided by whatever less-than-positive comments about Mary that they could cull from early Christian writers (below, Chapter 14).

If Mary is an elusive figure in the New Testament outside the Infancy Narratives in Matthew and Luke, the same is even more true of her husband Joseph, who is otherwise only mentioned in a straightforward genealogical fashion as the father of Jesus (Luke 4.22; John 1.45, 6.42). Perhaps Joseph's lack of any active appearance indicates that he had died by the time that Jesus embarked on his mission. By contrast, Jesus is constantly portrayed as calling God his Father. Mark indeed portrays him as addressing God as *'abbā* (Mark 14.36), an Aramaic or Hebrew word never used to address God in the Hebrew Bible, which in any case rarely refers to God as father. The possible novelty of *'abbā* is attested by Mark preserving it in Jesus's own language amid the Greek, and before that, Paul's surviving writings deploy *'abbā* twice, in a rare conscious echo of Jesus's own words, likely to derive from prayers used by early Christians (Rom. 8.15, Gal. 4.6). The superficially attractive notion popular in the twentieth century that the word indicated an informal childlike relationship ('Daddy') should be discarded, on linguistic grounds; rather, it was a solemn, respectful address from son to father.[30] Even so, this concept of an intimate Fatherhood between God and humanity is a basic layer of Jesus's message. In the 'Lord's Prayer', still at the heart of Christian prayer, he tells his disciples to pray to *their* Father in heaven – using the ordinary Greek respectful word for 'father', *patēr*.[31] Not just Jesus himself, but all his followers can use it: they have become the family in place of the blood-relatives he snubbed.

The brutal and horrifying death of Jesus on the cross ordered by the Romans marks a reconciling end to such narrative ambiguities around family. Alone among the four Evangelists, John brings Mary to the foot of the cross to watch her son die – she is absent from the witnesses named by the Synoptics. The Evangelist builds still more on her presence (John 19.25–27): hanging half-alive on the cross, with Mary standing beside the disciple whom Jesus loves, he commands them to regard themselves as mother and son. 'From that hour, the disciple took her to his own home' (Plate 4). Thus were biological family and Jesus's chosen and beloved associates melded into one as he died.[32] Interestingly, John never gives Mary her name either, consistently calling her simply the mother of Jesus; she and the unnamed disciple have both become symbols, but paired and crucial symbols. If one reads back to the beginning of the story of Jesus in John's Gospel, the wedding at Cana, Jesus leaves for Capernaum straight afterwards 'with his mother and brothers *and* his disciples' (John 2.12; my italics). The motif seems to be that at both polarities of Jesus's public career, his first miracle and his crucifixion, the two relational polarities are united. John must be aware of the familial tensions in other narrative traditions.

The disruptive constructions of family and relationships in the Gospels are paired with some strong opinions from Jesus on marriage: crucial and individual statements on divorce and monogamy. Jesus condemns divorce, which under existing Jewish custom was easy to obtain. To justify his condemnation (Mark 10.10; Matt. 19.9; Luke 16.18), he quotes the Creation narratives in the book of Genesis (Gen. 2.24): 'a man leaves his father and his mother and clings to his wife, and they become one flesh.'[33] He uses this proof-text not simply to forbid divorce, but, by implication, polygyny as well. He thus significantly decouples this central Jewish text on marriage from Judaism's previous history and practice of marriage.

As we have seen, Genesis's 'one-flesh' theology did not deter the Jews from honouring patriarchally based polygyny, as much in Jesus's time as before or later. But in rejecting polygyny, Jesus injects the idea of a restrictive twoness into his version of the Genesis quotation, where it had not been before: 'the two shall become one flesh', he says, a modification of the original that is already present in the version quoted in the Gospel of Mark and repeated in Matthew's Gospel. In many modern Christian translations of Genesis, that 'two' word has leaked back from the Gospels into the Hebrew Scripture, where actually it makes no such appearance – rather as some modern Christian Bibles retrofit the word 'virgin' into Isaiah 7.14.

Why such strong and directive pronouncements on divorce and monogamy? Probably it relates to the apocalyptic theme that is such a marked feature of Jesus's teaching. Two of his parables telling his listeners about the Kingdom of God describe it in terms of a wedding feast. So if marriage is such a powerful metaphor for the glorious Last Things of Christian faith, one can see why it must happen only once in human life, as it will happen only once in the summing-up of all history that will usher in the Kingdom.[34] Jesus, then, was explicitly countercultural in contemporary mainstream Judaism both in his rejection of divorce and his coldness towards polygyny. His negativity on polygyny can otherwise be found in a different countercultural and apocalypse-minded community outside mainstream Judaism, whose theological archives (the 'Dead Sea Scrolls') emerged from around Khirbet Qumran in the decade after 1947.[35]

It remains controversial as to whether this group can be identified with the ascetic sect known as 'Essenes' who are described by Josephus, the Jewish historian and near contemporary of Jesus, for the apocalyptic impulse had seized more than one movement in Judaism around this time. The most authoritative recent study is content that the Qumran community that produced the Scrolls were indeed Essenes; they certainly originated before Jesus's time, but may still have existed then, despite not being mentioned in New Testament texts and themselves making no allusion to anything resembling early Christianity. Their literature indicates that some men among them adopted community celibacy; this was very rare in Judaism, and there is no evidence of it surviving from Qumran in parallel among the first few generations of Christians. So it is difficult to see any relationship between Jesus and the

Qumran or Essene development from the Jewish mainstream, or to judge whether his ideas were at all influenced by theirs.[36]

Jesus's prohibition on divorce caused serious embarrassment to his early followers, many of whom clearly wanted continuing provision for divorce. That remains the case, for instance among divorced Evangelical Protestants who would otherwise be very anxious to know what Jesus would do. The Gospel of Matthew already modifies the blanket prohibition of divorce to be found in Mark and Luke, to provide an exception in the case of a wife's unfaithfulness.[37] Even before that intervention, which was made some six or seven decades after Jesus's death, his early interpreter Paul of Tarsus had taken it upon himself to provide two different exceptions to Jesus's universal prohibition.

These remarkable testimonies to Paul's independence of thought occur in his densely constructed disquisition on marriage regulation now forming Chapter 7 of the first Epistle to the Corinthians: a fertile text indeed for Christian views of marriage, and one to which we will frequently return.[38] Paul specifically says that these exceptions were his idea, not the Lord's: he concedes that a wife might choose to separate from her husband, while a non-Christian husband might repudiate his Christian wife. Indeed, Paul's very contradiction of Jesus is a testimony to the authenticity of Jesus's original saying about divorce in its stark form; it is also a rare reference in Paul's writings to what Jesus actually said, rather than to what Paul thought Jesus signified to faith.

In contrast to their neuroses about divorce, Christians did not have nearly so much problem in following the Lord on monogamy. One good reason for that was that monogamy was already the exclusive marriage custom in Greek and Roman society, into which Mediterranean Christianity proceeded to expand, regardless of what Jews continued to believe and practise in relation to marriage. One should remember that the early Church came to ignore other major elements of Jesus's authentic pronouncements – for instance the shockingly cavalier 'leave the dead to bury their own dead' (Matt. 8.22), or his promise of imminent return. Monogamy might have been treated in the same fashion had there not been a powerful social impulse in the Roman Empire for Christians to stick with Jesus on this matter.[39]

That still left Jesus's followers with a biblical conundrum. Making monogamy the Christian norm left subsequent theologians having to explain away the polygyny of the Hebrew patriarchs; they have never fully succeeded.[40] Early commentators from the second to the fourth century CE considered that what they called the patriarchs' 'immorality' had been allowed by a special dispensation from God, although no such dispensation can actually be found in the text of the Hebrew Scripture. The Latin theologian Augustine of Hippo in the fifth century took a different and rather arbitrary line in defending the patriarchs against condemnation of them by Faustus, a formidable critic of Catholic Christianity from the parallel religion known as Manicheism. In the age of the patriarchs, Augustine said magisterially, 'a plurality of wives was no crime when it was the custom; and it is a crime now, because it is no longer the custom ... The only reason of its being a crime now to do this, is because custom and the laws forbid it.' Augustine did not elucidate when exactly in history this crucial transition had taken place, or what the theological arguments for it might be.[41]

Besides Jesus's two interventions on marriage, his voice has not much been preserved on matters sexual – notably he disappoints many conservative Christians by saying nothing whatsoever about homosexuality, about which they would especially love to know what Jesus would do.[42] There nevertheless exists one curious textual fragment from his sayings that has ended up in John's Gospel, though in narrative texture it feels more like the three Synoptic Gospels, and it does not appear in the earliest surviving manuscripts of John. Now it usually forms John 7.53–8.11. Its textual wanderings and the verbal variants in the manuscript testimonies to it probably indicate that many in the second-century Church found it disconcerting and were not sure what to do with it. Like Matthew's version of Joseph making his own decisions about the unexpected pregnancy of Mary in the Infancy Narratives, it confronts the punitive adultery provisions of Deuteronomy 22.20–29.

The story is presented as being a test by the conventional enemies of Jesus's preaching, 'the scribes and Pharisees', to see how he would deal with the Deuteronomic mandate for death by stoning for adulterous women. Jesus is teaching in the Temple when they drag before him a woman 'caught in adultery' (notably, not accompanied by the man who was presumably caught with her). What would Jesus do? they ask. His first reaction is to squat down on the ground and write with his finger. It is ironic that the only reference in the Gospels to Jesus writing is in their most textually insecure section, and what he might have written has been a source of inevitably fruitless speculation over the centuries.[43] Rather than disclosing the meaning of his doodles, Jesus observes, 'Let him who is without sin among you, be the first to throw a stone at her.' They will be forced to recognize that sin encompasses much more than sexual sins. When they have all shuffled off looking sheepish, Jesus is left alone with the woman. No one had condemned her; 'neither do I condemn you; go, and do not sin again.'

Jesus is proclaiming his own prerogative of forgiveness; yet this tiny biblical fragment has wider implications for his followers over two millennia and more. Like his pronouncements on divorce and monogamy, it subverts the ethical expectations and conventions of its age: part of a ferment of new possibilities while Christians began creating identities separate from parent Judaism in a Hellenistic Mediterranean society. Its troubled textual history and the equally troubled later commentary on it witness that its subversive role did not end in the first century CE. It has continued to challenge Christianity's constant reconstruction of Christian ethics up to our own time. We may be in the early stages of exploring its full implications.

5. For more than two centuries, the parishioners of St Margaret's (Herefordshire) have exited church beneath a disconcerting quotation of John 8.11, unusually painted above the medieval south door. Today a hand-sanitizer brings practical assistance to this stern Georgian admonition.

PART TWO

Families or Monasteries?

5
Paul and the First Christian Assemblies (30–60)

The earliest surviving Christian texts are seven or eight letters ('epistles') written by Paul, a Jew of the *Diaspora* from Tarsus in Asia Minor, writing to various Christian communities probably in the forties and fifties of the first century CE, so around one or two decades after the execution of Jesus.[1] In later decades, admirers of his produced further epistles in his name which need to be distinguished from those earlier letters; the vital difference is that the Christianity depicted in these latter texts mostly postdates the catastrophe in 70 CE for Judaism, the destruction of Jerusalem and its Temple, as well as the death of Paul sometime in the sixties.[2] We also have 'Acts of the Apostles', a composite account focusing on Paul's journeys and preaching missions as far around the Mediterranean as Rome. This was compiled in its final form apparently by the same author as the Gospel according to Luke – so around the turn of the second century. Acts has the feel of a historical novel, and its portrait of the Apostle is rather less abrasive than the authentic Paul whom one meets in his own letters (nor does Acts mention Paul's letter-writing activities). Nevertheless, used with caution, it can illuminate events during Paul's lifetime. Accordingly, we can reconstruct much of how the first Christians moved away from their Jewish origins, taking with them the already countercultural pronouncements of Jesus on marriage and sex.[3]

INCLUDING, EXCLUDING

Paul's letters testify that he and his sympathizers became severely at odds with other prominent followers of Jesus, including Peter (one of the Twelve) and James the brother of the Lord, over the nature of the Good News that was their common pursuit. The issue was how far the

Christian mission still lay within the bounds of existing Judaism and its wider contacts with sympathetic Gentiles already established through the *Diaspora*. Paul emphasizes his own chosen role by such self-identifications as 'an apostle to the Gentiles' or 'minister of Christ Jesus to the Gentiles' (Rom. 11.13; 15.16). Nevertheless, it is in fact clear from what he writes that he is still operating within the framework of the *Diaspora* synagogues around the Mediterranean. Such communities had long contained plenty of Gentiles who had made a personal decision to embrace the faith of Judaism. They were known in *Diaspora* communities as *theosebeis* ('God-fearers' or 'God-reverers'): a Greek word that is also used in the Book of Acts.

At stake between various leaders of the Christian initiative in the synagogues was how far to remould the long-established pairing of Jewish and 'God-fearer' relationships in such communities, in the light of the life, death and resurrection of Jesus. Paul, as he testifies himself, was a former persecutor of Christian believers in Jewish settings, who had never met Jesus in his earthly life. Instead, on a journey from Jerusalem to Damascus, he found himself exhilarated and traumatized in a shattering personal encounter with Jesus's power and forgiveness: he suffered a complete turnaround, or, as later Christianity would term it, a conversion. After that, Paul felt compelled to convey the same healing experience to a world in which the distinction between Jew and Gentile was now meaningless.

Paul brought to this task dynamic contradictions: a deep and proud knowledge of his Jewish heritage, alongside his pride in being a man who could claim Roman citizenship and whose natural first language was non-literary Greek. It is significant that when writing to *Diaspora* communities, he habitually uses the names of Roman imperial provinces. This cultural combination contrasted with the background and assumptions of Christian leaders in Judaea. They were still close to the Aramaic inheritance of Jesus's teaching, and they lived their new faith in close quarters to the ancient religious observance in the Temple of Jerusalem, proceeding as it had done uninterruptedly for six centuries, with all that meant for Jewish identity.

When Christian activists (whom we now see almost exclusively through Paul's eyes) erupted out of Jerusalem into the synagogues of towns on the fringes of the Mediterranean, conflict among them was particularly marked in two spheres: first, dietary restrictions founded on scriptural commands and elaborated in a variety of ways by later custom; then, more fundamentally, on the ancient mark of what it was to be a Jew – male circumcision. On dietary matters, Paul could be conciliatory, partly because his opponent Peter had apparently already reconsidered traditional dietary laws for himself (Acts 10). The toxic clash came around circumcision, and the bitterness is evident in Paul's letter to the Christian assemblies (*ekklēsiais*) in Galatia. This text is, among much else, an impassioned plea to these assemblies not to be bound by a rule of circumcision, but to identify with Christ Jesus through the new observance of baptism.

Baptism is now such a fundamental part of being a Christian that it is easy to overlook its curious origins, which are very late in Second Temple Judaism. Ritual washing had become essential for those approaching the Temple for worship, and the Qumran texts show how important similar ritual washings had become to that separatist community in the century or so before the life of Jesus; in neither case can the washing be identified as an initiation rite. The New Testament identifies a different specialized source for the baptismal rite. Christians borrowed it from a slightly older sect, for whom baptism was so fundamental that the sect's charismatic leader is known in the New Testament as John 'the Baptist'. This John is carefully positioned in the Gospels: given great honour but in a subsidiary role to Jesus, despite the fact that it was John who had baptized Jesus, not the other way round. John the Evangelist indeed takes the trouble to interrupt the majestic cadences of his opening Gospel hymn to let us know with a certain banality that the Baptist was 'not the light, but came to bear witness to the light' (John 1.8).[4] The movements may have started out in rivalry before their ostentatious reconciliation through Jesus's baptism in the River Jordan.

Jesus did not leave any clear line of development for baptism, and John the Evangelist further claims that the Lord did not himself perform the rite, leaving it to his disciples (John 4.2). This directly contrasts with Jesus's direct institution of the breaking of bread and distributing of wine in the 'Eucharist' (from the Greek for 'thanksgiving'), around which Christian life has been organized ever since. The institution of the Eucharist is one of the few parts of Jesus's teaching or practice that Paul thinks fit to record (1 Cor. 11.23–25), in a fashion later echoed by the Synoptic Gospels. By contrast, it is Paul who dwells on and spells out the crucial nature of baptism: 'as many of you as were baptized into Christ have put on Christ' (Gal. 3.27). More than that, he goes on to say that 'in Christ' (that is, among those that are baptized in the name of

Christ), 'there is neither Jew nor Greek . . . neither slave nor free . . . neither male nor female' (Gal. 3.28).

There is much to be read out of this profound statement about the relation of Saviour to believer, but, at one level, it is a startlingly simple statement of fact.[5] The basis of identity for the people of God has been overturned. Instead of the Covenant in the Hebrew Scripture witnessed by an outward sign of mutilation to male genitalia, the act of initiation for a Christian is a washing in water, baptism, which can make a full Christian out of a woman just as much as it does a man. Jesus himself said nothing that has survived about circumcision, positive or negative; he may well have taken it for granted in traditional Judaistic fashion. We first hear this fundamental change discussed by Paul, without any word from the Lord. In Acts (Ch. 15), a definitive rejection of circumcision for Gentile (non-Jewish) converts to Christianity is presented as being confirmed in Jerusalem through debate and a general resolution of assembled leaders, Paul, Peter and James included. Even the general emollience that characterizes the narrative of Acts cannot hide the acute polarization and continuing disagreement around that occasion.

To reject universal male circumcision for Christians was therefore to attack basic Jewish assumptions about masculinity, and the rejection had wider implications for Christianity in the Hellenistic world. As a theme in Paul's thought, it rides alongside a repeated rhetorical construction of himself that reverses the normal priorities of being a man in Hellenistic society. He tells us that he was physically weak (indeed suffering an unspecified 'thorn in the flesh'); lacking in rhetorical skill (an essential quality of a good citizen); willingly a labourer alongside women and even slaves; all this alongside a readiness to suffer ill-treatment and even imprisonment at the hands of worldly powers.[6] Moreover, Paul is only imitating the example of his Saviour and Lord, Jesus, who had surrendered all power in order to hang in weakness and humiliation on the cross. That reversed every aspiration of a successful Graeco-Roman man, and so was 'a stumbling block to Jews and folly to Gentiles' (1 Cor. 1.23). Such images of masculinity undermined and betrayed have remained a constant problem over two millennia for those Christians who want to construct their own version of Christian maleness, with Jesus as a latter-day Hercules (see Plates 6 and 7).

Paul did not single-handedly turn baptism into the initiation rite for Christianity. It is clear from his own extended and ill-tempered list of examples of baptism in the Corinthian *ekklēsia* (1 Cor. 1.11–17) that

Christian assemblies were already launched on that path before him, and the ringing statement of gender equality in Gal. 3.28 is likely to have formed part of a formula already used in baptism before Paul quoted it.[7] Nevertheless, at this turning point in the future of Christianity, Paul provided the crucial impassioned arguments for abandoning circumcision alongside baptism, particularly in his letter to the Galatians. The Christian mission could spread unimpeded beyond the bounds of Judaism, beyond even those Gentiles who had long formed the category of *theosebeis*.[8] And now women potentially had very much more opportunity in Christian life and practice to play an equal part alongside men than ever they had done in Judaism or in most forms of Graeco-Roman religion. They were not barred from any ceremonial observance. Maybe, to begin with, in some communities that might even have included their presidency at the Eucharist.

It is clear from Paul's authentic letters that he was writing to assemblies where Christian women exercised as much local leadership as men; locally, some of these women may have been seen as superior in authority and social position to the visitor Paul as he travelled round the Mediterranean. That was inherent in the way that these new communities were constituted; many converts to Christianity were no longer welcome in the synagogues or had never been associated with them. If they were to gather as an *ekklēsia*, it would have to be in a generously sized house, hosted by someone with the appropriate resources. The household was female space more than it was male; and it could indeed be headed by a woman, particularly if she were a widow.

All this puzzled and embarrassed later generations of Christians, who would have to face the fact that the courtesies in Paul's letters include greetings to a great many women, some clearly in positions of authority alongside men, and even given the same titles. Phoebe is one of these: Paul refers to her as a *diakonos* (in the Greek male form) of the assembly in Cenchreae, a little port near Corinth. Modern translations relegating her office or function to a specialized role of 'deaconess' tell us more about the translator than about the original text.[9] Most notorious and cavalier is the subsequent Christian treatment of the lady Junia in Rome, whom Paul describes as 'of note among the apostles' (Rom. 16.7), alongside another 'apostle' with the male name Andronicus. In later recopying of biblical manuscripts, Junia's name was frequently changed to a male form, or simply treated (without any justification) as a man's name. Early biblical commentators and liturgists, led by the highly respected fourth-century preaching Bishop of Constantinople John Chrysostom, were honourably prepared to acknowledge Junia's surprising femininity, but the thirteenth century saw a sudden turn in the writings of the Western theologian Giles of Rome, which was only rectified during the twentieth century.[10]

In all this we should see Paul as being descriptive rather than prescriptive; he was working within the situation he found. It is noticeable that, unlike the Gospel writers some decades later, he does not number any women among those who first bore witness to the risen Christ (1 Cor. 15.5–6). His own opinions on the place of women are revealed in 1 Cor. 11.2–16, where he creates a layered hierarchy of comparisons by gender: 'the head of every man is Christ, the head of every woman is her husband, and the head of Christ is God.'[11] One notices that Paul's hierarchical definition is innocent of the next four centuries of furious theological battles that would determine the Church's affirmation of co-equality of Father, Son and Holy Spirit within the Trinity, but it also bases its structure on a family model already prominent in the thought of Jesus, who so frequently referred to God as his Father (above, Chapter 4). And in traditional Jewish fashion, it also reaffirms that a woman's nature is not fully in the image of God, unlike a man's, and that she is dependent on her relationship to a man to define her relationship to God.

Assessing this central assertion of Paul on gender hierarchy is made more difficult by the nature of the texts that survive from his correspondence with the Corinthians: they are now presented as two letters but have possibly been stitched together from more. In any case, they react against particular conditions and assertions inside the Corinthian Christian community of which we know little, except as we glimpse them through Paul's words. The glimpses reveal women who have independent wealth; women who have converted when their husbands have not; women who have similar roles of authority to men, and who assert themselves in public worship as filled with the Holy Spirit. Much of this goes against the conventions of both Jewish and Graeco-Roman society; it is justified by the unpredictable and hardly controllable presence of the Spirit active in the everyday lives of the assembly, to the extent that the Spirit will lead women as much as men to speak in languages beyond ordinary understanding, *glossolalia*.[12]

The result in Paul's texts is downright incoherent. His hierarchical gender definitions in 1 Cor. 11 are followed by a long discussion condemning long hair in men ('degrading') and insisting that women should publicly pray or prophesy only when veiled, among the justifications being that this is 'because of the angels' – a cryptic argument, but dependent on the common assumption in Judaism of the propensity of angels to lust after mortal women. A few chapters further on (1 Cor. 14.34–35) comes an emphatic assertion that women should simply keep silent in worship, 'as in all the churches of the saints'. The inconsistency is so blatant that many commentators have seen the latter statement as a later insertion in the text, reflecting conflicts of a later generation; its placement in early manuscripts is significantly varied, perhaps indicating a degree of puzzlement about how to reconcile the two pronouncements.[13] The one unavoidable consistency between the two passages is their differential treatment of women and men, in line with the general tradition of Mediterranean society. That differential was then – and is now – in perpetual tension with the common inclusion of the sexes in baptism: a reflection of early Christianity's perpetual ambiguity between presenting a radically new message and trying to ensure an appeal in that message to all levels of surrounding society.

MARRIAGE AND BEYOND: A NEW DEPARTURE

As we have seen, Paul's hierarchy of relations between man and woman is crafted in a metaphor: a marriage relationship. In one letter to the Corinthians (now 2 Cor. 11.2) he daringly makes himself the *paterfamilias* who has 'betrothed [your assembly] to Christ to present you as a pure bride to her one husband'. This is in the face of the untidy fact that Paul personally finds marriage a distasteful prospect, and speaks to the married as if an outsider. One hundred and fifty or so years later, the theologian Clement of Alexandria would claim that Paul had been a married man, but whether true or not, that does not alter his extremely grudging comments about the married state, most famously in his concentrated essay on marriage for the Corinthians: 'because of the temptation to immorality [*porneia*], each man should have his own wife and each woman her own husband . . . it is better to marry than to be aflame with passion.'[14]

Despite Paul's apparent lack of enthusiasm for the realities of marriage, he made some markedly original contributions to later Christian views on the marriage relationship. We have already noticed his cavalier modification of the Lord's command on divorce (above, Chapter 4).

What is also apparent is that he was already constructing a dichotomy between marriages within the new Christian community whom he was addressing, and every other sort of marriage anywhere. That is actually tangled up with his qualifications modifying Jesus's prohibition on divorce in 1 Cor. 7, relating them to two different categories of married people, one simply referred to as the 'married' and the other as 'the rest'. He was passionate in urging Corinthian Christians to avoid confusing the two so as not to be '*mismated* with unbelievers', as the Revised Standard translation has it, softening the burdensome implications of *heterozygountes*, 'unequally yoked'.

One can see why Paul might feel he could be radical on this: the assemblies of people emerging as Christian Churches had already broken with a host of relational ties to the world around them, simply by constituting themselves Christians – particularly if they were Jews. If a married man and woman had both entered the new rite of baptism, then their marriage became 'marriage'. Yet what was the extent of novelty in this Christian marriage? How did it relate to God's general setting-up of marriage for Adam and Eve in the Garden of Eden and thereafter for all humans (the so-called 'creation ordinance'), or, in Paul's phrase, for 'the rest'? There is no trace of a Christian wedding ceremony in the New Testament, and there would be none in the Church for several centuries, as we shall see (below, Chapter 10). Since there was no Christian marriage ceremony for converts from beyond the faith to undertake, the Church simply recognized the 'creation ordinance' in their existing marriage – as long as it was monogamous, which in Graeco-Roman society it normally would be.[15]

The only difference between Paul's 'marriage' and those of 'the rest' was in the minds of married believers about their status 'in Christ', expressed in their liturgical place in the Christian community: they shared in a common heritage of baptism, and then, after instruction, received the Eucharist together. So to take an important example of biblical marriage, where did that leave the wedding at Cana, which John's Gospel (John 2. 1–12) marks as the occasion of Jesus performing the first of his miraculous signs? It was not a Christian marriage, but under the creation ordinance – on Paul's definition, the unnamed happy couple were unmistakably not among 'the married', but among 'the rest'. If this wedding could in some sense be considered as a forerunner of Christian marriage as being performed within Israel's 'household of faith', presumably that applied to all other Jewish weddings, which logically included weddings of polygynists, past, contemporary and future. Christian discussions of marriage through the centuries have tended to avoid such problems or allegorize them away: indeed the wedding at Cana, with its miracle of water turned into wine, has generally been given a special status in biblical exegesis as a metaphor for the Church's central liturgical act, the Eucharist.[16]

Paul injected another startling independent variable into Christian thinking about marriage in his rulings for the Corinthians: an idea for which it is difficult to find any exact precedent. He creatively developed the 'one flesh' theme that Jesus had emphasized in marriage. In the word of the Lord, we have seen that it had remained obstinately male-centred: 'a man leaves his father and his mother and clings to his wife, and they become one flesh.' But Paul expanded the fleshliness into a surprising reciprocity between marriage partners. More remarkable still, the reciprocity was grounded on marriage as based on sexual expression: 'the wife does not rule over her own body, but the husband does; likewise the husband does not rule over his own body, but the wife does' (1 Cor. 7.3–4). This sexual equity in moral expectations is completely at odds with common Mediterranean assumptions in Paul's time: in his assertion, a woman has as much right to expect faithfulness from her husband as the husband has from his wife.

Scholarship has come to term this reciprocity the 'marital debt'. The puzzle is how it relates to Paul's own personal distaste at the prospect of marriage – but as so often in his one-sided fragments of correspondence, we have little idea as to what extreme opinions on marriage and assertions of an overriding need for celibacy he was countering in the Christian community at Corinth. Moreover, there is one source within the Hebrew Bible that could direct Paul's thoughts in this direction: the Song of Songs. Paul would assume that the participants in its passionately erotic dialogues were husband and wife, and the whole tone of them suggests sexual reciprocity.

As an intervention into sexual morality, Paul's assertion of a marriage debt has had two thousand years of erratic consequences. It clashed with that major presumption within much Graeco-Roman discussion of human biology already noted from Aristotle: a woman was a mere incubator for male seed in the process of procreation, not, as Paul implied, an equal partner in some sense. Even though other ancient authorities likewise disagreed with Aristotle, notably Galen, it is Paul's mutual marital debt theory that has remained a reference-point, and not always a welcome one, when Christians have discussed marriage. It seems an obvious fit with modern Western views of companionate marriage, but in many other ages it has been a problem for the Church in the societies that it has sought to regulate.

The Pauline idea of a marital debt clashes not only with the assertions of male privilege in Hellenistic science, but also with the assumption widespread across many societies that marriages are constructed not so much by the decision of the couple embarking on matrimony but through alliances constructed by two families.[17] Furthermore, the marital debt's basis in sexual activity as an expression of the mutuality of marriage has always fitted uncomfortably with a pervasive ecclesiastical sense that even marital sex is shot through with sin. Physicality within marriage has often only escaped condemnation as long as the sexual act is intended, in utilitarian fashion, to produce children: what Ingsoc in George Orwell's *Nineteen Eighty-Four* called 'our duty to the Party'.

It is difficult to escape the general conclusion that centuries of Christian pronouncements making marriage a second-best to celibacy do originate in Paul – but not in any link to procreation. The necessity for procreation is not present at all in Paul's reluctant justifications for marriage. Later Christians often overlooked that, since they enthusiastically borrowed classic statements of procreative intention from non-Christian philosophical sources in both Greek culture and Hellenistic Judaism (below, Chapter 6). Paul's contemporaries would have found it obvious that his silence on procreation in marriage, let alone his warm commendation of celibacy or virginity, was radically out of line with both normal Jewish assumptions about marriage and official imperial encouragements to breed large families. The marriage legislation of Augustus and subsequent emperors was obsessively concerned to engineer citizen society in order to encourage childbearing: it tried to make marriage mandatory for women aged between twenty and fifty, and gave privileged status for freeborn women who had born three children, or for freedwomen with four.[18]

As a result, Pauline Christianity was a rare example of a religious culture which did not make the appropriate expression of sex a priority in marriage. Paul gives the overriding reason for this half-way through his essay on marriage, with a proclamation of the approaching Last Days echoing teachings of Jesus: 'the appointed time has grown very short; from now, let those who have wives live as though they had none . . . For the form of this world is passing away' (1 Cor. 7.29–31). This set Christianity off in a radically different direction from the traditional view of marriage in its parent Judaism. Yet still Paul was drawing on one ancient

Jewish theme as mediated in the thought of another Hellenized member of the Jewish *Diaspora*, Philo of Alexandria (above, Chapter 3).

The intellectual genealogy between Philo and Paul is clear from Paul's central justification for getting married: the avoidance of *porneia*, Philo's catch-all word for any form of impermissible sexual activity. The spiritual meaning that Philo had given this word tied it into the tragic metaphor crafted by the Hebrew prophets: faithlessness in the people of God was like the fornication committed by a bad wife. Had not Paul told the Corinthians that they were like a pure bride to their one husband, Christ? The most extreme extrusion of this line of thinking from Philo into Paul's writings is his opening salvo in what is now the first chapter of the Epistle to the Christian assembly in Rome. It is a blistering attack on idolatry: the universal propensity of humankind (Mediterranean humankind in particular) to exchange 'the glory of the immortal God for images resembling mortal man or birds or animals or reptiles' (Rom. 1.23). So far, so traditional Judaism; then Paul pulls out of his rhetorical storehouse a suitable punishment for idolatry, sent from God – a wholesale change of nature in the sexual behaviour of idolaters. 'Their women exchanged natural relations for unnatural, and the men likewise gave up natural relations with women and were consumed with passion for one another, men committing shameless acts with men and receiving in their own persons the due penalty for their error' (Rom. 1.26–27).

There is nothing in the Hebrew Bible quite like this diatribe, not least the very unusual inclusion of same-sex female relations. Perhaps we should see male and female idolaters' equal-opportunity fate as a nightmare mirror image of the sexual equity in Paul's concept of the 'marriage debt'. Paul's argument differs especially from the Hebrew Bible in deploying a concept of 'nature' which is simply not to be found there; instead, Paul has borrowed 'nature' from Greek philosophy via the theological conduit of Philo. For the rhetoric of his increasingly excitable argument to work, it has to presuppose a state of sexual nature completely reversed for both sexes, as an exemplary means of punishing idolatry. That also means that whatever Paul is denouncing in Romans 1 is distinct from the hierarchical and life-cycle-specific same-sex male activity which he would observe in Hellenistic society.

Unsurprisingly, nevertheless, Paul is ready with a condemnation of that too, in a fashion that links him to general Judaistic prejudice against Hellenism from the Maccabean period onwards. It is to be found in a prelude to his long discussion of fornication and marriage in 1 Corinthians 6–7, included in a list of those who will not 'inherit the kingdom of God' (the list was echoed elsewhere later by imitators of his epistles). Alongside the unsurprising inclusion of idolaters, adulterers and robbers, and the slightly wider catchment area of the greedy and the drunk, are two less obvious categories, *malakoi* and *arsenokoitai* (1 Cor. 6.9). They make an odd pairing, *malakoi* being a quite common Greek word with a central meaning of 'soft'. *Arsenokoitai* is much rarer and less easy to pin down; Paul's use of it is among the first surviving instances, which suggests that he was employing a fairly localized slang term. If one hazards an interpretation, Paul's pairing of the two words suggests the binary assumption of passive and active partners in same-sex male activity, which was so much part of Greek and Roman social mores.[19]

It will be apparent what an inexact fit that description is for modern understandings of male and female 'homosexuality'. Yet the passing mentions of same-sex activity in the New Testament have been made to

6. A Parisian de luxe pictorial *Bible Moralisée*, *c.*1220, depicts same-sex couples, a rare subject in Christian art, particularly both male and female, echoing Rom. 1.26–27. Punitive devils do not distract them unduly. The picture's peculiar placing between Adam and Eve's eating of the forbidden fruit and expulsion from Paradise is best explained as alluding to the recently coined Christmas legend that Christ would not enter the world to redeem humanity from its Fall and universal sin before all sodomites had been destroyed.

do a great deal of work on sexuality over the last 150 years. Besides the idolatry passage in Romans 1 and the list of the excluded in 1 Corinthians, there is an echo of the latter, rather vaguely classified, in another list of undesirables presented in a rather later New Testament text that purports to be a letter of Paul to his disciple Timothy (1 Tim. 1.9–10). In the Reformation of the sixteenth century, John Calvin had predictably made extensive use of Romans 1 in the *Institutes*, his monumental summary of Reformed Catholic theology, but he did not bother to mention the fact that the chapter said anything about sex. What interested him in it was its thorough treatment of his theological preoccupation: idolatry and the true knowledge of God.[20]

In Paul's writings, the secondary reference of Romans 1 to same-sex activity is unique amid his all-pervasive treatment of the general concept of sexual and theological fornication. In that respect, he is at one with Hosea and Ezekiel before him: faithlessness to the Lord is to be viewed primarily through the prophetic lens of heterosexual deviance, as men veer from their divinely destined life of purity under the influence of harlots. The construction of family in early Christianity is one defence against this encircling menace of *porneia*; the other is virginity or celibacy. As we move into the development of organized Christian Churches out of radically transformed Jewish assemblies, we will see these two possibilities contending with each other as Christians pondered on how best to meet their risen Lord.

6

From Jewish Sect to Christian Churches (*c.*70–*c.*200)

The imperial authorities executed Paul of Tarsus in Rome around 65 CE, and early though not conclusive tradition suggests that Peter, his fellow missionary and Apostle, died there about the same time.[1] This was on the eve of a catastrophe for Jerusalem and its Temple: the Roman repression of four years of rebellion in Judaea, culminating in 70 CE with massacres of those besieged and in the burning of the Temple, this time never to be rebuilt. Complementing that dark event in history was an equally important missing event for the infant Christian assemblies: by the end of the first century CE, it was apparent that their Lord Jesus had not returned in triumph from the heavens, to scroll up the passage of earthly time. That was the first Great Disappointment of many in Christian history, and we know very little about it because, historically, Christians have been much less inclined than Jews to speak of disappointment.

Set between event and non-event, conditions for the future of both Judaism and Christianity radically changed: a turning point in both their stories. Roman armies crushed further rebellions in Judaea in the 130s, and after more than a thousand years of dominance, Jewish presence in the Promised Land steadily declined. Out of previous entanglement, two separate new clusters of religious identity eventually emerged, each with its own sacred literature, devotional practice and structures of authority. The process of separation was hesitant, piecemeal and took much longer than the histories of either side cared to admit.[2] Perhaps it was only complete in the fourth century CE, and a single Christianity never emerged from the end of the process, more a family of identities that have continued to proliferate up to our own era, even while some have faded from history.

For a long time, developments within Judaism would have seemed more significant than those within the Christian groupings: they ensured the maintenance of Jewish life in a myriad of synagogue communities around the whole Mediterranean and west Asia. With the governing elite in Jerusalem eliminated along with the Temple, leadership was increasingly dependent on the rabbis: male teachers dedicated to the preservation, standardization and an industry of detailed interpretation of the Hebrew Bible as a basis for shared Jewish identity. Moreover, the rabbis concentrated on refining Hebrew versions of their sacred writings, and on instruction and commentary in Hebrew around the scriptural text. Greek-speaking Judaism took a long time to decline, but it was never part of the future dominated by the rabbis. As a result, the rich culture of the Septuagint and of Philo, the greatest representative of Alexandrian Jewish thinking, faded from Judaism; ironically their influence remained far stronger on Christians than on Jews. One could argue indeed that Mediterranean Christianity was essentially a rebranding of Hellenistic Judaism, and eventually so successful that it is not surprising that its parent culture atrophied.[3]

Roman attitudes to Jews followed the same pattern as towards early Christians, fluctuating between localized hostility (extending sometimes into pogroms) and an indifference that generally allowed Jewish life to flourish. The great exception was the complete refusal to allow the rebuilding of the Jerusalem Temple or revival of any Jewish presence in the city around it, renamed Aelia Capitolina in the mid-second century to hammer home its new status as a Roman colony. The imperial authorities nevertheless continued to treat Judaism as an officially recognized religion (*religio licita*), and one great puzzle is that, amid all this, the Romans adopted the Jewish division of the week into seven days, complete with rest-day, rather than the traditional Roman eight. This happened in much the same period that saw the destruction of Jerusalem.[4]

Christianity was by comparison statistically insignificant until the mid-third century CE, probably even in its first area of comparative strength in Asia Minor (modern Turkey), the corner of the Mediterranean that produced most of the literature found in the present New Testament, from the epistles of Paul of Tarsus onwards. The religion may have remained little-known among most of the Empire's subjects; early in the second century, it baffled a well-informed and conscientious Roman senior administrator, Pliny the Younger, who had the misfortune to encounter aggressive Christians as governor of the province of Bithynia in Asia Minor, and was uncertain about how to treat them.[5] Unlike Judaism, early Christianity had no public presence of its own – the earliest roughly dateable Christian building known, from Dura Europos in Syria, is a converted house no earlier than around 240 CE, and Christian adherents seem generally not to have taken legal refuge in the *religio licita* status of Judaism.

One careful estimate is that by 100 CE, there may have been around a hundred Christian *ekklēsiai* or assemblies around the eastern Mediterranean, few of which can have boasted more than seventy members, and another is that even by 300 CE, on the eve of gaining great power, Christians may have formed no more than 1 or 2 per cent of the Empire's population. An accumulation of evidence about mid-third-century Rome does indicate an exceptionally large community of several thousand there, but this was in a city which was also exceptionally large, numbering between 750,000 and a million people. Even if these estimates are minimalist, they are more realistic than listening to the triumphalism to be found in many early Christian texts and then constructing theories as to why such rapid success should have taken place. It is also useful to be reminded what a small number of people in these tiny communities took the decisions that created broad currents and shapes within Christian doctrine – on sex and on everything else – down to the present day: 'scarcely a few dozen, perhaps rising to two hundred, literate adult males, dispersed throughout the Mediterranean basin' in the century after Jesus's death.[6]

SHAPING CHRISTIAN FUTURES

In the background were the steadily looser ties of Christian assemblies to the synagogues, and resulting uncertainty about how much Christians should jettison or retain from their Jewish heritage. Some Christian answers to the problem moved very far from the Hebrew Bible towards different constructions of sacred 'knowledge' (*gnōsis*). Such *gnōsis* might present itself as of equal antiquity to the Hebrew Scripture, even if a particular system was in reality newly created by individuals brooding on their multiform religious inheritance. Much of the literature created outside the 'canonical' Hebrew Bible forming the common heritage of Christians and Jews (above, Chapter 1) already had that character long before the time of Jesus.

Historians used to write about 'Gnosticism' with a capital G. That usage consciously or unconsciously reflected a Christian polemical stance that anything beyond mainstream Christianity must be a sect or cult, its identity marked out under the 'Gnostic' umbrella, often with reference to some 'heresiarch' founder. Certainly, we can name various gnostic leaders and theologians, such as Valentinus or Harpocrates/Carpocrates; but it is more helpful to see the gnostic phenomenon as a series of strikingly varied personal explorations of religious frontiers, within Christianity as much as beyond it.[7] The initial fault line had been between Judaistic and Graeco-Roman culture, but the gradual separation of Christianity from Judaism created a three-way set of identities providing fertile thoughts about the nature of God and creation. Further influences might come from beyond the imperial frontiers, in contacts with the ancient religions of central and south Asia, Zoroastrianism, Buddhism and Hinduism: a fruitfully porous border for all varieties of Christianity, as we will see.

Amid the variety of Christian belief and practice and the shapeshifting gnostic constructions of religion, some Christian groups showed a remarkable determination to stay connected across very great distances, and to devise a common message about the risen Jesus. They summed up their emphasis on connection and common belief by a Greek term for 'general', 'whole' or 'universal': *katholikos/e*. This adjective does not appear in any New Testament text, but by the beginning of the second century it could be used unselfconsciously by Ignatios, leader of the *ekklēsia* in the Syrian city of Antioch, with an expectation that Christians far away to the west to whom he was writing would know what he meant, without further explanation. 'Catholicity' has remained a touchstone for Christian identity, albeit with a great many different meanings placed upon it.[8]

Various developments guarded Catholicity. Out of the proliferating texts on sacred matters written in Christian communities, a number were gradually recognized (by processes no longer clear to us) as having the same authoritative status as the Christian inheritance of Hebrew Scripture, extending its 'canon' into a 'New Testament'. In Christian worship, candidates for baptism were offered short formulae to recite, summing up their belief: early versions of creeds. Leaders emerged in established communities who (ideally) recognized each other's authority among those making these complex decisions or scrutinizing generally agreed teaching.

The male leaders binding this system together adopted one of the early Christian terms for leadership, *episkopos* or 'overseer', in much the same period as Judaism was regrouping under the leadership of learned males, the rabbis. By the end of the second century, *episkopoi* (bishops) formed a network binding together local Churches from one end of the Empire to another, eventually even beyond imperial frontiers. In general, they exercised authority from an assembly in a particular town or city, giving rise to the convention still general in episcopally led Christianity, that a bishop takes his title from an urban settlement. Such outcomes for the future of authority and doctrine in Catholic Christianity emerged from a constant internal conversation through a century and a half after the destruction of the Temple. During that period, in the dry observation of the historian Peter Brown, Christian writers 'made considerably more noise to each other than they ever did to outsiders'.[9]

We will observe a repeated pattern in Christian history that movements which start in enthusiasm and spontaneity gradually (or sometimes rapidly) conform to expectations in the societies around them. Even amid the fluidity of opinions visible in the surviving letters of Paul, from the age when Christians still cherished excited expectation of imminent Last Days, there is a perceptible tug between overturning conventions and accommodating the expectations of surrounding society. The balance there soon tilted, reflecting the preoccupations of communities settling down as generation began to succeed generation. New Testament literature generally says little about issues that might be considered public politics. The people whom we meet in the texts surviving from first-century Churches were not usually from the landed elites who wielded political power in cities and towns; what wealthy Christians there were, generally made their money from commerce or crafts.[10] There is a sharp contrast here with the detailed discussion of political matters in the Hebrew Bible, much of which was the creation of writers very much involved in wielding power in Judah or Israel.

Powerless or not, Christians would have to get used to living in a wider society if the Lord chose not to return to them imminently. Their conversation is reflected in a series of New Testament texts (mostly addressed to Churches in Asia Minor) that clothe their reformulations of Christian identity with the authority of Paul or some other leaders from the previous generation, and reveal a new set of priorities.[11] Only a decade or two later than Paul's writings, the writer of the Epistle 'to the Ephesians' spoke of 'the coming ages', apparently meaning a long time on this earth, during which the glory of God would be made manifest 'to all generations, for ever and ever' (Eph. 2.7; 3.21). The writer also repeated Paul's use of marriage as a figure of speech for the relationship of Christ to his Church, and on that theological basis he explicitly ordered wives to submit to their husbands ('the head of the wife as Christ is the head of the Church' (Eph. 5.23). Ephesians takes no account of Paul's innovative idea of a mutual sexual 'debt' in marriage, and its theology sanctifies the husband's control over his wife in marriage. The Hebrew Scripture had used marriage metaphors for theological purposes, and Christian imagery of marriage has built lavishly on the Ephesians precedent. But does metaphor govern the institution, or the institution the metaphor?[12]

A subordination of wife to husband is simply the male-centred pattern familiar in the ancient world. That increasing move towards domestic conformity infuses the remainder of the Ephesians passage, which is an example of a set of practical (though theologically infused) rules for conducting a human household in the New Testament; in the sixteenth century, Martin Luther termed them *Haustafeln*, 'tables of household duties'. The Ephesians' *Haustafel* was echoed elsewhere, maybe indeed anticipated in another Epistle 'to the Colossians' of much the same date which likewise asserts its Pauline authorship, and later they were imitated in the first of two epistles attributed to Peter.

Echoes of *Haustafeln* also recur throughout a trio of letters claiming to have been written by Paul to his assistants Timothy and Titus (conventionally grouped together since the eighteenth century as the 'Pastoral Epistles').[13] It is noticeable that all this post-Pauline literature elaborates commands of obedience for children, 'that you may live long on the earth', as Ephesians had loosely referenced a phrase from Deuteronomy. With the Last Days deferred, the Church now needed to consider the next generation and its earthly future: more than that, it needed to integrate children into its practice of marriage.[14] The 'Paul' of the Pastoral Epistles actually seems to create a three-generation sequence of a Christian family, starring his correspondent 'Timothy'. The writer reminds Timothy that having been taught by his mother Eunice and grandmother Lois, he has been acquainted 'from childhood . . . with the sacred writings' leading to 'faith in Christ Jesus'. The writer might simply have been referring to teaching from the Hebrew Bible before Christian conversion, but otherwise, the rather prolonged chronology that this statement implies increases doubts that the letters are genuinely by Paul.[15] The writer of the Pastoral Epistles also adds a significant extra element on

Christian marriage by telling women that their salvation will come from having children (1 Tim. 2.15). Thus procreation had arrived back at the centre of marriage where Judaism had placed it, despite Paul's original silence on that issue.

Children were not the only problem for the *Haustafeln* to regulate in Christian Churches. Equally in need of careful management were women who lacked the benefit of subordination to a husband, generally thanks to bereavement: widows. They presented a dual headache for developing Christian communities, either being dependent through poverty or age, or not being dependent enough. Some might enjoy financial resources and opinions of their own, not to mention the ability of grandmothers in most known human societies to intimidate the rest of their family, which an increasingly male clerical leadership might find difficult to control. A subsidiary issue, and a potential point of friction with surrounding society, was how to treat young widows: should they remarry or not? Crystallizing official Christianity was firmly of the opinion that they must remain faithful to one spouse, even if he were deceased; Roman legislation on marriage and procreation underlined imperial concern that they should remarry. The author of the Pastoral Epistles was torn between Christian theology, a desire for public respectability and a firm conviction that young widows were natural troublemakers: his eventual conclusion was that they should remarry, so as 'to give the enemy no occasion to revile us'. That contradicted Paul's earlier preference that all widows should stay unmarried, whatever their age.[16]

As a result, an air of anxiety hangs over New Testament references to widows. The Acts of the Apostles indeed backdates trouble even to before the time of Paul's ministry, when the surviving disciples of Jesus had to sort out accusations of preferential treatment between Greek- and Hebrew/Aramaic-speaking widows in the assembly in Jerusalem (Acts 6.1–7). After the Pastoral Epistles' detailed regulations for their behaviour and the scope of their activities within the Church, Churches developed formal associations for eligible widows, mostly centred on confining them as much as possible to private life. The most restrictive view comes from a Syrian order for the running of a Church community, probably of third-century date, the *Didascalia Apostolorum* ('Teaching of the Apostles'). In general, the *Didascalia* seeks to remove Christian laypeople from civic life, but it is particularly ingeniously eloquent about widows staying home: 'let a widow know that she is the altar of God', it says, adding unctuously that 'the altar of God indeed never wanders or runs about anywhere, but is fixed in one place.'[17]

In view of such a narrowing of options for senior women, it is rather charming to find that the earliest known epitaph anywhere for any member of the Christian Church's hierarchy, predating anything for bishops, priests or deacons, is for a formally enrolled widow from the second-century Church in Rome: Flavia Arcas, 'the sweetest of mothers' according to her daughter Flavia Theophila, who financed the inscription.[18] Moreover, it has to be said that a formal place for widows, and a warm and open welcome for the financial patronage that wealthy widows might offer a Church community, were a good deal more than the rabbis were offering women in the synagogue. Judaism also continued its relentless emphasis on marriage, whereas Christianity in the second century was on the verge of opening another possible choice for Christian women in developing institutional celibate communities, a matter which we will visit in Chapter 7.[19]

The *Haustafeln* also tell household slaves what to do: obey. That really is consistent with Paul. Just as Paul's proclamation of equality between men and women in Galatians 3.28 stood in tension with his pronouncements elsewhere affirming gender inequality, so 'neither slave nor free' in the same text did not affect his attitude to a slave called Onesimus, as revealed in a short letter to the slave's owner Philemon. Far from containing any plea for freedom for Onesimus, as is often asserted, this Epistle hints that Paul would appreciate continuing to enjoy the benefit of Onesimus' service, while he could be 'more than a slave' to Philemon – there is no indication that Onesimus was consulted about his own wishes.[20] The tendency of modern biblical translations to bowdlerize biblical words for slaves to 'servants' to lessen their impact is rather like the modern vogue for inserting the anachronistic word 'homosexual' into the biblical text. It is also sometimes said that it was a Christian innovation for Christian slave-owners to allow their slaves to marry, but there are also non-Christian examples of this in Roman society, despite prohibitions in Roman law.[21] Christian attitudes to any marriage of Christian household slaves remained as ambiguous as in the general slave-owning society around the Church. Bishop Ignatios of Antioch even forbade slaves to ask fellow Christians for charitable contributions to buy their freedom.[22]

The repetition of *Haustafeln* over at least two generations of texts reveals their importance to the steadily institutionalizing Christian assemblies in the later first century. Now the various gradations of status and authority to be found in the world, the family values of male Graeco-Romans, were to shape the way in which Christians conceived their faith, and they were justified as hierarchical theologically. Churches were concerned to show that they did not form a subversive organization threatening the well-being of society, particularly in the matter of enforcing submission on wives, 'that the word of God may not be discredited'.[23] The author of the Pastoral Epistles also insisted that Church leaders must be 'well thought of by outsiders' as well as inside the community.[24]

Nevertheless, Christianity did inherit some distinctive preoccupations to its construction of marriage, beyond public respectability. One problem no longer seems like a problem to many modern Christians, though it still does to some: could Christians enter a second marriage, for instance on the death of a partner? The Lord's ban on divorce might apply: if one took that to mean that marriage really was for ever despite death, then a second marriage after the death of a spouse was no different from adultery. Most Churches did give way on the issue of bereaved or even divorced spouses remarrying, though often very grudgingly and after some considerable time. Remarriage nevertheless long remained deeply controversial; in the fourth century we shall meet Jerome fiercely denouncing it (below, Chapter 9), while one anonymous contemporary of the theologian ventriloquized Jesus into the opinion that 'after a third wife, the sinner is unworthy of God'.[25] Remarriage is probably the issue at stake in the course of the Pastoral Epistles' discussion of desirable qualities for Church officers, bishops or deacons; among much else, such a man should be 'the husband of one wife' (1 Tim. 3.2, 12). That suggests that on occasion, just like young widows, bishops or deacons did indeed remarry as widowers and needed to be told not to, though there is a more radical possibility in the phrase 'husband of one wife': perhaps the communities addressed by the author still included polygynists as the synagogues did, and they needed to be ruled out of the running for the episcopate or diaconate.

ALTERNATIVE VOICES

The only major dissident voice in the New Testament against Catholic Christianity's frank quest for public respectability is the Book of Revelation, last both in terms of its placement in the Bible and its general acceptance as part of the biblical canon. Authored by a man named

John who writes as one with authority, it is an open letter addressed to a number of named Church communities. It is set in Asia Minor, like most of the New Testament epistles, but one mark of its difference from the other New Testament texts is its frank and unqualified attribution of the title 'King' for Christ. The New Testament elsewhere avoids this in any straightforwardly programmatic usage, in awareness that the Roman authorities crucified Jesus precisely because of his alleged claim to be 'King of the Jews'. Revelation is not afraid to challenge the worldly powers of its day; indeed, it revels in their forthcoming destruction, culminating in a vivid imaginative picture of Christ's triumph as cosmic ruler at the end of time, following epic battles with evil. Its flamboyantly victorious Christ is thus far more like the militant God habitually portrayed by the Hebrew Bible than the image elsewhere in the New Testament (see Plate 6). Such a character in effect seizes hold of the masculine ideal of Roman society, whose power Revelation sees overturned, and confers it on the Saviour.[26]

Beyond the canon, we can hear a further range of perspectives from second-century Christianity. Some of them have only re-emerged to historical view over the last hundred years, particularly thanks to a remarkable find in 1945 near the modern Egyptian city of Nag Hammadi: a labourer discovered a pottery jar containing fifty-two fourth-century texts in the Egyptian Coptic language which were versions of much older Greek works, mostly with a gnostic character. In natural excitement at encountering these and other newly available texts, it has been tempting to read gnostic Christianity as providing more open possible futures for Christian faith than what became the Catholic mainstream: less judgemental on sexual matters or less prone to patriarchalism.

There should be caution about this, or indeed the proposition that gnosticism contributed anything much to the lasting forms of Christianity (beyond an inclination to austerity that could have plenty of other sources). One of the most consistent themes within gnostic literature is indeed its prioritizing of the spiritual and the ultimate over the everyday and fleshly, in the manner that Plato had viewed reality. So the real nature of a gnostic believer has no solidarity with the flesh of the human body or the course of conventional human life. Even the Gospel of Thomas, which among several surviving Gospel-pastiches beyond the New Testament most resembles the four 'mainstream' Gospels in its content and may share their late first-century date, records a cry of Jesus to his followers to 'be passers-by!' That reverses the moral message of Jesus in Luke's presentation of his Parable of the Good Samaritan, who was good precisely because he did not pass by.[27]

Given the gnostic theme that mortal flesh is despicable, gnostics might treat the flesh in two ways. They could mortify the body with austerities – or, on the contrary, regard their souls as so independent of the body that the most wild earthly excesses would not imperil its salvation. Hostile 'mainstream' Christian commentators probably took much more relish in contemplating the latter luridness than was justified by real evidence about gnostic believers. In the fourth century, Epiphanios, a busily unlikeable Cypriot bishop and heresy-hunter, described gnostic rites that parodied the Eucharist using semen and menstrual blood.[28] Accordingly, one of very few supposedly gnostic texts of such a nature, involving Jesus deliberately indulging in illicit sex, now only survives in a deeply unpleasant small fragment preserved by Epiphanios himself, supposedly from 'The Greater Questions of Mary'.[29]

In fact, there is far more evidence for the austere, ascetic strain in gnosticism than for any licentiousness. It is unwise to rebrand gnostic belief as hospitable to modern liberalism in sexual outlook; still less plausible is a view of gnostic belief as a form of proto-feminism.[30] Gnostic hatred of the physical body matches very uneasily with some modern emphases on the liberating power of sexuality, or feminism's celebration of all that it is to be female. Gnostic writers were just as inclined as writers in contemporary mainstream Christianity to assert that females needed to become males in order to enter the kingdom of heaven, and they might turn to contemporary medical wisdom to assert that in procreation (human or cosmic), females only provide substance and males the form.[31] Given such themes, we should heed one modern commentator in contrasting much gnostic thought with the baptismal proclamation in Galatians (3.28), where 'Paul wanted to eliminate the *inequality* between the sexes, while the gnostics wanted to eliminate the *distinction* between the sexes.'[32]

Nevertheless, a gnostic emphasis on individual revelation rather than on hierarchical teaching might provide continuing opportunities in communities of gnostic inclination for women to assert their opinions or their active role alongside men. By the beginning of the third century, Catholic Christians were sneering at gnostics precisely because of this programmatic gender-blindness. The North African polemical theologian Tertullian exclaimed with outrage at practices many of which would have been commonplace in the Churches of Paul of Tarsus: 'The very women of these heretics, how wanton they are! For they are bold enough to teach, to dispute, to enact exorcisms, to undertake cures – it may be even to baptize.'[33]

Gnostic texts do include some significantly positive messages about women, particularly around the charismatic figure of Mary Magdalen. The Gospels' fourfold affirmation of Mary Magdalen's Resurrection experience can account for a good deal of the subsequent interest in her, but she clearly also became a symbol of resistance to the ways in which authority structures in Churches were beginning to crystallize exclusively in the hands of men. Feminist theologians have naturally taken an interest in this, but the literature also describes some men as supporting the status of Mary Magdalen in opposition to other men. The Gospel of Thomas describes a confrontation between her and the Apostle Peter, in which Jesus intervenes on her behalf and reproaches Peter, although this is also one example of a text where a favoured woman must renounce femininity: 'Now I will draw her to me to make her male . . . for every woman who makes herself male will enter the kingdom of heaven.'[34]

This theme of antagonism around the Magdalen occurs elsewhere. The 'Gospel of Mary', for instance, is a gnostic work probably of the second century. It represents a fairly even-tempered attempt at conversation with non-gnostic Christians, and Jesus's disciple Levi is presented as exclaiming to Peter 'if the Saviour made [Mary Magdalen] worthy, who are you then to reject her? Certainly the Saviour knows her very well. That is why he loved her more than us.'[35] More individual is a second- or third-century 'Gospel of Philip' now only preserved in a later Coptic translation. Here the Magdalen becomes one of three Marys who 'walked with the Lord continually', the others being his mother and a sister of his; she is distinguished as 'his partner', which is not without physical connotations. It must be emphasized that no ancient text, gnostic or otherwise, calls Mary Magdalen the wife of Jesus, unlike the recent forgery 'The Gospel of Jesus's Wife', which deserves to be placed alongside its rather more extended predecessor, the 'Hitler Diaries'.[36]

In the background was the gradual atrophy of itinerant prophecy in Catholic Christianity, in favour of the locally based ministry led by bishops, who had rarely been referred to as prophets. The Apostle Paul of Tarsus or the Apostle Junia would once have been numbered among the itinerants. Now where bishops established their authority in Churches which had accepted the hierarchical structure of *Haustafeln*, they were exclusively male, and they did their best (no doubt unsuccessfully) to stop women in their congregations saying anything at all. As the author of the Pastoral Epistles orders, with a certain pomposity and without any of Paul's confusion on the subject, 'Let a woman learn in silence with all submissiveness. I permit no woman to teach or to have authority over men; she is to keep silent' (1 Tim. 2.11–12). Here theological constructions combined with masculine convention, to the point of fearing social embarrassment. Given Graeco-Roman attitudes to the place of women in public life, Church leaders feared the sniggers of Mediterranean men at the incongruity and presumed ineffectiveness of female preaching: 'they will deride and mock, instead of praising the word of doctrine', as the third-century *Didascalia Apostolorum* put it, anticipating Dr Samuel Johnson's ungallant remarks about dogs walking on their hind legs.[37]

Such an attitude was in the course of time inevitably going to restrict the role of female deacons in the Catholic hierarchy of the local ministry. In the same way that widows were told to keep their opinions to themselves while doing circumscribed good works, those deacons who were women were increasingly confined in their duties strictly to matters involving women and children, where it might be indecorous or unconventional for men to exercise ministry – baptism in particular, which involved the candidate disrobing before entering the waters, but also much pastoral visiting.[38] Some historians do argue that rather than suffering a diminution in role, a female diaconate was promoted in the second and third centuries to curb the influence of formally enrolled widows in a Church, but this seems less plausible; at the very least, it does not take enough account of the New Testament evidence of common terminology applied to male and female deacons, especially at Rom. 16.1.[39]

In a contest between itinerant and local ministry, visiting itinerants were at an increasing disadvantage by the turn of the first and second centuries. Even if they were suitably male, they might bring with them any variety of doctrine, perhaps of a gnostic nature, which the resident leadership would feel their duty to listen to and evaluate for their flock. A tract known as *Didachē* ('Teaching') has been recovered from obscurity in the last 150 years; in the early Church, it occasionally sneaked into the canon of the New Testament and is probably contemporary with its last layers. The *Didachē* encourages the testing of prophets who might turn up in a community, with limits on the length of time they should be given entertainment, and it also reminds its readers that the local ministry should be honoured just as much as itinerants: 'despise them not: for these are they which are honoured of you with the prophets and teachers.'[40]

This rivalry among Christian authorities is also represented in the last texts that did permanently make it into the New Testament during the early second century. A short epistle written to an unnamed *ekklēsia* by a certain Jude (backdating his apostolic authority as 'brother of James') denounces 'ungodly persons' who 'reject authority and revile the glorious ones'; he completes an ancient circle of sexual denunciation in the same manner as Philo of Alexandria by comparing them to dwellers of Sodom, 'which likewise acted immorally and indulged in unnatural lust'. The Revelation of John in this respect sides with the settled ministry against 'the woman Jezebel, who calls herself a prophetess' in the Church of Thyatira in Asia Minor; he threatens her and encourages her local opponents in appropriately apocalyptic terms (Rev. 2.20–25). John has revived the name Jezebel from one of the Hebrew Bible's most picturesque villainesses. In either case, as with Epiphanios's pornographic musings on gnostics later on, sexual insult performs its habitual task of belittling opponents.

The eventual death blow to itinerant prophecy was a renewed surge of prophetic activity in mid-second-century Asia Minor, calling itself indeed 'The New Prophecy'. It is otherwise known as Montanism, after its early leader Montanus, who proclaimed new revelations of the Holy Spirit and stirred up mass enthusiasm for his message in his native Phrygia. That was a direct challenge to the guardians of the Spirit in local communities, the bishops, but it was made more pointed by the fact that Montanus' leading companions in authority were female prophets, Prisca and Maximilla, prominent in a ministry by now barely acceptable in the mainstream Church.

Phrygian bishops could draw on Catholic contacts across the Mediterranean, and already it was an asset for them and a blow to their opponents to secure a condemnation of Montanism from one of the leaders of the large Church in Rome, Eleutherius. A further gathering of bishops reinforced the condemnation, but the fervent rhetoric of renewal in Montanism appealed more widely through the Mediterranean world beyond Asia Minor; it gained the allegiance of Tertullian, the constitutionally emphatic North African theologian whom we shall meet again. An obstinate Montanist remnant survived in their home territory of

Phrygia for at least another four centuries, guarding the charisma that Montanus and his companions had conferred on their stronghold of Pepouza.[41]

Along with the Montanists departed for the time being a Christian enthusiasm for prophecy and prophetic performance. Characteristically it has re-emerged in Christian tradition whenever Christians want to challenge existing power structures – as has a linked possibility, inadvisably dismissed as remote by one Victorian Church historian: 'If Montanism had triumphed, Christian doctrine would have been developed, not under the superintendence of the church teachers most esteemed for wisdom, but usually of wild and excitable women.'[42] Amid stirrings of great change in Western Christianity some seven decades later, Monsignor Ronald Knox could still opine in his polemical but learned and entertaining study of Christian 'enthusiasm' that '[f]rom the Montanist movement onwards, the history of enthusiasm is largely a history of female emancipation, and it is not a reassuring one.'[43]

Such comments seem risible now, but there is a serious historical point to them in looking at the directions taken by the developing Christian Church during the second century. This was the age of the impressively competent and generally sane Antonine emperors. It witnessed a growing moral seriousness among the Graeco-Roman elite, exemplified by their fascinated disapproval of supposed sexual excesses among Roman rulers in the previous century; we may follow their prurience in Suetonius' lurid and still entertaining second-century account of the *Twelve Caesars* from Julius Caesar to Domitian.[44] So little did most outsiders know about this obscure, small-scale and often deliberately secretive religious organization that it was easy for them to project prurient sexual fantasies on to what they did know about unconventional Christian behaviour. What did the Eucharist signify, with its talk of eating flesh and drinking blood? Cannibalism? What happened in ceremonies of Baptism, when adults went nude into water? Was there incest involved?[45]

In this almost Victorian atmosphere, with public suspicion of obscure groupings like Christians easily turning to indignant fantasies about their licentiousness, when Christians defended their devotional practice and common life in literary 'apologies', many found it tempting to stress sexual renunciation, a theme of austerity that would appeal to many strands of Graeco-Roman philosophy. It was equally natural, though a little contradictory, to emphasize respectability and conformity to the norms of a society based on a male construction of family, and to make attack a form of defence by criticizing the immorality and promiscuity of Graeco-Roman society. Yet such defence was never a simple task, because even as the Church constructed its notion of Christian marriage, the enterprise was complicated by the obstinate persistence of other thoughts in its tangled inheritance from the past, in which both celibacy and a new place for women contended with the demands of family. It is to those complexities that we now turn.

7
Virgins, Celibates, Ascetics (*c.*100–*c.*300)

The writer of the Pastoral Epistles had told the women of his Church that their salvation came from childbearing. During the second century CE, Christianity experienced a powerful reaction against this thought, as both women and men sought salvation by a flight not just from general sexual activity, but even from Christian marriage: this was the beginning of the Christian monastic life. Increasingly, theological commentators were unmarried clerics even if they were not monks, and they praised marriage's virtues with a certain condescension, or worse. Indeed, over the next thousand years, from the second to the twelfth century, Christians wrote a very great deal more about celibacy than marriage. The two themes have stayed uncomfortably entwined right down to the present day, and so we must scrutinize developments in the second century with some care.

MONASTICISM: AN UNEXPECTED ARRIVAL

If we consider the impressive growth and role of monasticism in Christian history, it has always been a problem that the phenomenon of dedicated groups of celibates in settled communities is elusive or invisible in the Bible. Monks looking for a scriptural basis for their lifestyles have been frequently forced to resort to biblical allegory. In the extreme case of the Carmelite Order of friars ('Whitefriars'), the effort extended further into extravagant make-believe. Carmelites, who began in the late twelfth century as a gathering of Western Latin hermits living around Mount Carmel in the Latin Kingdom of Jerusalem, linked themselves right back to the Hebrew prophet Elijah, whose activities had also extended to Mount Carmel; thus they transformed themselves into the only religious Order claiming an origin before Christianity itself. Further Carmelite fictions carefully obscured the untidy reality of their early transfer from the wreck of Crusader Palestine back to Western Europe, but none of this unhistorical ingenuity has prevented Carmelites making a distinctive and fruitful contribution to Western Christian spirituality ever since.[1]

Unsurprisingly given the generally negative attitude of Judaism to celibacy, the Hebrew Bible provides little basis for or discussion of monasticism. In the decades before the life of Jesus there were (as we have seen) exceptions to the general Judaistic rule: Essenism and the community at Qumran. Alongside them is a further apparent exception: Philo of Alexandria's description in the treatise *On the Contemplative Life* of an ascetic community of philosophers – not attested in other sources – whom he calls the *Therapeutae*. They consisted of both male and female communities, the two sexes joining together in common worship, so one consideration in accepting Philo's story as genuine has been his generally low opinion of women's piety or spirituality: would he have invented such a positive account of female community life? There are nevertheless good reasons to doubt the reality of Philo's account – and there are indeed questions as to whether Philo actually wrote *On the Contemplative Life*. It could reflect an exegesis of various passages in the Septuagint, from which the writer constructed an ideal and imaginary philosophical community beyond contemporary society, fulfilling God's original purposes in creation before the Fall introduced distinctions of sex. As in the case of the Carmelites, fiction may have done its best work in shaping later reality, since various later Christian communities were impressed by what they read of the *Therapeutae* and structured their lives accordingly.[2]

The New Testament offers little extra help – notably its total silence about Essenes or Qumran. In fact, the only account in the New Testament dealing with communal sharing of resources is discouraging and ends in failure (Acts 4.32–5.11): a married couple called Ananias and Sapphira tried to cheat a system set up in the Jerusalem Church whereby the community held all possessions in common. God duly, one after the other, struck the greedy pair dead, but that is also the last that we hear of Christians in the apostolic age trying such an experiment. The tale is so out of line with the social reality that can be glimpsed in New Testament epistles (local Churches based on families) that like the Gospel Infancy Narratives, it may have been created to convey theological messages through a story. One point might be that the Jerusalem Church represented a New Israel; the old Israel had supposedly set up a system of 'Jubilee', a year in which all land returned to the family to which it had originally belonged, and during which all slaves were released (Lev. 25; maybe itself a fiction). Another more prosaic lesson to be taught, and perhaps referencing contemporary Christian arguments, might have been that marriage was not conducive to strenuous asceticism.[3]

Paul's authentic letters certainly suggest that there were influential Christians in the communities that he was addressing who privileged sexual renunciation over marriage, and who claimed to monopolize the revelations of the Spirit because of their ascetic state. That would hardly be unusual either in Hellenistic Judaism or beyond it among the many would-be philosophers seeking wisdom or *gnōsis* in the Graeco-Roman world. The convolutions in Paul's discussion of marriage in 1 Cor. 7 (above, Chapter 5) are probably caused by his determination to restrain such enthusiasm, despite his own inclinations to avoid the married state: he is forcefully insisting that all Christians, married or celibate, can have a part in the Spirit-filled salvation offered by Jesus.[4] Yet he and his opponents were arguing within a common tradition of asceticism, presented in its most thoroughgoing form to Hellenistic Jews or Christians by Philo of Alexandria. This radically narrowed the Greek term for self-control, *enkrateia*, into a preoccupation with sexual continence, to defend good Jews – and now good Christians – against the multiple temptations of sexual indulgence.

Mainstream Christianity went on to invent a heresy out of the *enkrateia* word: 'encratism', used to castigate various people as religious deviants, among whom was the combative Syrian biblical scholar of the second century known in the Graeco-Roman world as Tatian.[5] In reality, the heresy of encratites consisted in the degree of rigour in their advocacy of self-denial compared with that of official Christian leaders, including an emphasis on a variety of such self-denials as abstaining from meat or alcohol or modes of dress, but always with the main emphasis on sexual *enkrateia*. Attempts by some Christian leaders such as the tidy-minded Bishop Irenaeus of Lyons at the end of the second century to present encratite views as aligned with gnosticism were deliberately misleading.[6] Really the debate about asceticism and encratism was an angry conversation within Christianity between variants of enthusiasm for *enkrateia*, expressing different degrees of distaste for marriage.

Encratist rigour seems to have been at its most intense in that large area of the eastern Mediterranean and western Asia mostly represented by the Roman imperial provinces of Syria, though extending along the coast of Asia Minor; this was Tatian's home territory. Syrian ascetics were much more prone to look for potentially helpful references to their state in the New Testament than were other early Christians, and they were also inclined to adjust Gospel texts in their Syriac translations to suit their rigorist agenda. Luke, the favourite Evangelist among the Syrians (and the presumed editor of the story in Acts that included the downfall of Ananias and Sapphira), was especially handy for providing appropriate texts. For instance, Luke's Gospel made a stronger statement than Matthew or Mark in his version of Jesus's observation to the Sadducees about the afterlife, saying that his followers do not marry in the next world, for 'they are equal to angels.'[7] This is a hint with much future significance that angels, as genderless beings in heaven, were a useful rhetorical ally and inspiration for celibates. A few male enthusiasts did their best to imitate angels with uncompromising literalism, by surgically dispensing with their genitals.

To begin with, the developing Christian hierarchy was not certain how to react to this zeal for castration; should it be commended as demonstrating Christian self-control? Thus the Athenian convert and philosopher Athenagoras, addressing his *Plea for the Christians* to the Emperor Marcus Aurelius in the mid-170s, emphasized that 'remaining in virginity and in the state of a eunuch brings one nearer to God.'[8] At what point did rhetoric shade into practice? Justin Martyr, pioneer among the second-century literary defenders of Christianity now known as apologists, sympathetically described the disappointment of a young man in Alexandria who petitioned the Roman governor in the city for permission to seek castration from surgeons, to show to the world how far Christians were from indulging in free love. The governor rejected the proposal, leaving him to be 'satisfied with his own approving conscience, and the approval of those who thought as he did'.[9] The Emperor Antoninus Pius was the notional reader of this apology, so Justin must have believed that elite Romans would have found the tale impressive rather than risible. In a slightly later generation in Alexandria, the brilliant speculative theologian and biblical commentator Origen is said actually to have undergone castration through similar youthful enthusiasm. Yet during the course of the third century Christian official mood-music on voluntary castration changed, and the fourth-century Church historian Eusebios (Eusebius), author of an admiring biography of Origen, reports the story with a mixture of embarrassment and defiant commendation – a confusion that probably indicates its genuineness.[10]

Among Syrian ascetics, the loudest encratite voice was Tatian, who had been a student in Rome with Justin Martyr. His conversion to Christianity after an immersion in Hellenistic philosophy and thought involved his dismissing the Graeco-Roman divine pantheon not as fictional, but as active current enemies of the Christian God. The combat was most dramatically expressed in Tatian's rejection of the whole Graeco-Roman construction of sexuality that we have surveyed (above, Chapter 3), for among the worst of all the Gods of Olympus was Aphrodite, promoter of sexual attraction throughout creation. Caught up in Tatian's loathing of Aphrodite was the ancient Greek poet Sappho, not for any understanding of her as lesbian, but because of the general eroticism of her verse. 'Sappho, the sex-mad and cheap little whore, sings licentiousness about herself,' he snarled.[11] Accordingly, Tatian radically developed his reading of Paul of Tarsus into statements that all those indulging in sexual acts, even in marriage, are 'enslaved ... to sexual fornication and to the devil'. Adam's disobedience to God was a direct result of his sexual coupling with Eve.[12]

Tatian's influence was immense in Syria; his greatest scholarly achievement, his 'Harmony' or *Diatessaron* of the four Gospels, was used liturgically as Gospel text in the Syriac Church from the second down to the fifth century. Not surprisingly, therefore, his views on the literally Satanic nature of sexual intercourse had a considerable following in Christian west Asia. The Christianity that he and his missionary admirers

7. Adding later preoccupations to Origen's story, a late fifteenth-century French MS of the *Roman de la Rose* satirically depicts him emasculating himself to share a bed with nuns without arousing suspicion. In the background, the pre-Christian Greek philosopher Empedocles prepares to throw himself into flames in an unsuccessful effort to prove his immortality to his disciples.

created would necessarily be of a single generation – since his converts could not procreate – but they could sustain their life by drawing others to it. They could and did live in communities together, liberated from the normal expectations of sexuality in the ancient world, taking advantage of the many remote places of their region to practise their faith. In other words, this was the first known example of a pattern that has survived till our own time: the community life of Christian monasticism. The priority of Tatian has rarely been acknowledged in Christian history because of his eventual outcast status.[13]

This is the likely reason for one of the oddest displacements in Christian historical writing: the generally accepted idea that Christian monasticism and the life of hermits originated in Egypt. Not so. There is no chronological evidence for anything in Egypt as early as the undoubted presence of male and female ascetics (so both monks and nuns) in Syria during the second century. Nor did Syrian asceticism consist only of those communities who adhered to Tatian and put themselves beyond the pale of Catholic episcopal Christianity by retreating into solitude. There were also celibate ascetics who gathered in community among other Christians, happy to contribute their service to general community life and liturgy, both men and women: the 'Sons (or Daughters) of the Covenant'.

One of the chief ways in which this movement of the Covenant showed how embedded it was in the general life of the Church was its leading role in Syrian liturgical music. Syria was the first region to foster an increasing elaboration of Christian communal singing after a mainstream Church emerged from the communities of Paul's generation. The first known great composer of hymns (some of whose texts are still sung across the Christian world) lived his Christian life among the Sons of the Covenant: the fourth-century Syrian theologian Ephrem. The involvement of the Daughters as well as the Sons of the Covenant in this public musical activity radically infringed conventions in both Graeco-Roman and early Christian society about the need for women to be silent in public, but as Bishop Jacob of Serugh, one of the most outstanding of Ephrem's Syrian successors as poet and theologian, generously observed around 500 CE, Mary the mother of Jesus had by her prudent use of speech restored to women their right to speak, sing and praise. The Daughters of the Covenant were preserved from any hint of public scandal by the holiness of their celibate state.[14]

Quite apart from the role played by the maverick Tatian in the first monasticism traceable in the Christian Church, there is a further consideration to complicate the traditional story. It is not fanciful to point out that Syrians in the eastern frontier provinces of the Roman Empire had long been the leaders in a vast and flourishing commerce still further east with India, Central Asia and China; this brought a remarkable flow of luxury goods to the Mediterranean and (to the chagrin of Greek and Roman rulers) drained the Mediterranean of currency to pay for them.[15] Syrian Christians early on made their Christian faith part of the package in their eastward import–export business. Given their familiarity with India, they could not have failed to notice the importance of celibate communities in the Buddhist tradition as well as the solitary holy men of Hinduism, traditions long predating Christianity.

The trajectory of Christian monasticism therefore extends at least from Syria to Egypt, with maybe an earlier westward movement from non-Christian Asia. By the mid-third century Egypt provides firm evidence at least for solitaries, though Egyptian monastic communities would have to wait for the fourth century and the initiatives of the former soldier Pachomios. The Greek word for both a solitary or a member of a monastic community (a 'monk') is still *monachos*, which literally means 'solitary'; the idiom may have started out as a translation of *îhîdāyâ*, the Syriac word with the same meaning applied to the Sons and Daughters of the Covenant. The first known use of the word *monachos* is in an Egyptian administrative papyrus dateable to 324 CE. Whatever degree of holiness was in the life of this *monachos* did not prevent him strolling down a village street and thus having the opportunity to break up a fight among his neighbours.[16]

That coheres with what we know of Pachomios's first creation of monastic communities not in the Egyptian desert but in the setting of ordinary villages, as with the Sons and Daughters of the Covenant in Syria. The presence of this *monachos* among ordinary folk was clearly socially beneficial, but it was not such an obvious example of heroic spirituality as that of the long-lived desert solitary Antony (*c.*251–356). Antony was nevertheless not a pioneer, for the famous *Life* of him said to be by Athanasios of Alexandria speaks of him in his youth visiting a previous Egyptian ascetic, who would have been alive in the mid to late third century – so well after the Syrians had established the patterns of ascetic practice. What Antony, as presented by his biographer, did was to establish a pattern of strenuously separate life for hermits: the 'eremitical' or 'anchorite' tradition.

Anchoritism, unlike monasticism, could find some good precedent in the

New Testament from its central characters John the Baptist and Jesus himself, although in both cases their withdrawal to 'the Wilderness' had been strategic and temporary during the course of their ministries. Equally significant in the practice of lifelong anchoritism was a rather unexpected model in Greek culture from six centuries before: the magnificently self-sufficient and countercultural Diogenes of Sinope, the 'Cynic'. The fit is not complete; it is not surprising that, in the Christian climate of *enkrateia* we are examining, Diogenes' deliberately performative habit of masturbating in public did not feature in Antony's ascetic practice.[17] As for monasticism, there is in the end little that is scriptural in its origins, and much that lies beyond Christianity, from Greek philosophers to Philo Judaeus to Buddhist monks. The monastic tradition is none the worse for that.

MARRIAGE: AGAINST AND FOR

A very considerable Christian literature survives from the second century onwards discussing and praising celibacy; beside it there are distinctly fewer discussions of marriage, and, overall, in much less positive mood. Alongside the New Testament, two of the most influential fictions among many in early Christianity came from a second-century setting in Syria or Asia Minor: the intimidatingly named *Protevangelium* ['Prologue Gospel'] *of James*, and the *Acts of Paul and Thecla*. Both in their fashion promoted the cause of virginity, and, among their other legacies, some of the stories of the *Protevangelium* eventually resurfaced in the Qur'an. The *Protevangelium* tackles and materially reshapes that centre of early Christian contention, the birth of Jesus and the questions thereby raised about Mary's virgin state: it enriches the Gospel Infancy Narratives, smooths out their difficulties and significantly extends their message about virginity, all under the cover of authorship by Jesus's brother James.[18] It is the wild fiction of the *Protevangelium* that has bequeathed us a name for Mary's mother and Jesus's grandmother, Anna. Not only did Anna here lay the foundations of her future career as a saint, but she enjoyed a narrative of the birth of her daughter Mary that was as near as it could be to a virgin conception – certainly anticipating the story of Mary's own Annunciation from the angel Gabriel.

Unsurprisingly, therefore, the *Protevangelium* much elaborates Mary's own virginity in bearing Jesus; her midwife exclaims 'A virgin has given birth – something impossible for her to do!' The midwife's friend Salome, a feminine equivalent of a doubting Thomas, is suitably punished for scepticism that a virgin could thus have given birth, in view of Mary's still virginal appearance and the absence of normal postnatal physical mess. When Salome attempts a manual gynaecological investigation of the mother, her offending hands miraculously catch fire; an angel then equally miraculously heals her for her instant penitence. The *Protevangelium* has previously described Mary spending her childhood in the Jerusalem Temple from the age of three to the onset of marriageable or childbearing age at twelve: an appropriate home for a sinless human being, isolating her from the profane world's temptations, and providing her with suitable specialist cuisine provided by an angel. Mary's unusual upbringing was a theme much elaborated by Christian narratives over the next two centuries, as they discussed female virginity with ever-greater intensity.[19]

From these narrative beginnings emerged the doctrine of the perpetual

8. In this early sixteenth-century French Book of Hours, Mary the Mother of Jesus forgives Salome, whose hands were burned away (according to the *Protevangelium of James*) to punish her gynaecological investigations of Mary's virginity. An angel proffers a pair of hands for reattachment.

virginity of Mary and, later still, in the West her 'Immaculate Conception', free from the original sin of Adam like her son; the *Protevangelium* has been called 'the ultimate source of almost all later Marian doctrine'.[20] Around it, Syria's precocious development of hymnody only swelled the chorus of praise of Mary as virgin Mother. For instance, Ode 19 of Christianity's earliest known hymn book, *The Odes of Solomon*, from much the same era as the *Protevangelium*, uses strikingly physical metaphors to celebrate her virginity. They reflect the view common in antiquity that milk and blood were different forms of the same fluid:

The Holy Spirit opened Her bosom,
And mixed the milk of the two breasts of the Father.
Then She gave the mixture to the generation without their knowing,
And those who have received [it] are in the perfection of the right hand.
The womb of the Virgin took [it],
And she received conception and gave birth.
So the Virgin became a mother with great mercies.
And she labored and bore the Son but without pain,
Because it did not occur without purpose.
And she did not require a midwife,
Because He caused her to give life.[21]

Justin Martyr was a product of the same eastern Mediterranean Christianity as these writers and singers of the second century, and he insisted on the importance of Mary's virgin conception (although not yet of a virgin birth); he did admit that not all Christians agreed with him on this.[22] Justin was a pioneer in linking his argument to the Evangelist Matthew's quotation of the prophecy in Isaiah 7.14 about a virgin who conceived. He was apparently also first in crafting a powerful rhetorical contrast between the first woman Eve who had brought the Fall of humankind through sexual attraction, and this second Eve who had reversed it by her virginal purity. A snappy, easily remembered phrase is often the best way to cement a doctrine in popular consciousness, and as this trope spread from Greek-speaking theologians to Latin-speaking Christians, Latin provided a satisfyingly simple word-reversal expressing the contrast between the two archetypal women: EVA turned to become AVE, the greeting 'Hail' that the angel Gabriel had addressed to Mary in the Annunciation.[23]

To our second great fiction of the period: Thecla was supposedly a disciple of Paul of Tarsus. The popularity of her second-century *Acts* kept her memory green, and in the fourth century it stimulated one of Christianity's first cults of a female saint, even before Mary or Anna (below, Chapter 8). The *Acts of Paul and Thecla* resembles a contemporary Graeco-Roman novel even more than does the canonical Acts of the Apostles, but here boy and girl are not happily united at the end of their adventures, since the part of the romantic lead is taken by a grittily celibate Paul, and part of his contribution to the story is to persuade Thecla against agreeing to marriage and sexual relations with her family's choice of husband. Nevertheless, amid her adventures Thecla takes an active role in transforming herself from dutiful daughter to defiant standard-bearer of Christianity, explicitly defying her mother in her determination to keep her virginity. As a woman, she openly teaches her faith, and she may even presume to administer baptism: she certainly baptizes herself.[24]

Lurking in the background of Thecla's *Acts* is a confrontation with the family-centred and hierarchical message of the Pastoral Epistles, whose supporting cast of characters actually features some of the same names to be found in the *Acts of Paul and Thecla*.[25] Like the *Protevangelium*, with its obsessive exploration of Mary's purity, the *Acts* is a text to make those of encratite inclination cheer. Significantly its exciting portrayal of obstinate virginity had a far greater immediate effect on early Christianity than a more plausibly circumstantial Latin account of female heroism from much the same period, the *Passion of Perpetua and Felicitas*, which culminates in their ghastly and pornographic martyrdom in a civic arena in North Africa, possibly in 202 CE.

The *Passion* includes accounts of Perpetua's visions and other experiences during imprisonment before her very public execution; these passages are one of the very few surviving pieces of extended text from the Roman world likely to have been composed by a woman.[26] One obstacle to any wider influence was that it was composed in Latin, which was not at that stage the Church's main language, but the fact that its Greek translation made little impact is in itself significant. More of a handicap was that for all Perpetua's heroism in representing her faith against Roman authority and her own family, she was a married woman, whose memoir pours out her anguished longing for her baby son, as well as for a younger brother who had earlier died of cancer. The fairly safely historical Perpetua and Felicity (a pregnant enslaved woman imprisoned and then killed alongside her) picked up a joint cult of modest proportions in later centuries, particularly in their native North Africa, but this was nothing like the eastern Mediterranean enthusiasm for the almost certainly fictional but reassuringly virginal Thecla.[27]

Supporting the varied texts of second-century encratism stands the remarkable appropriation of a New Testament parable from Jesus specifically for sexual themes, even though the parable itself gives no encouragement to such an interpretation. This was the Parable of the Sower: shared by all three Synoptic Gospels (Matt. 13.1–23, Mark 4. 1–20, a shorter version in Luke 8.4–15) and also present in the Gospel of Thomas, it was clearly a widely popular saying from the Lord. The main burden of the story was the different fates of seed sown by the sower on the path or amid rocks or amid thorns; no grain grew from any of these, but only that sown into good ground. It was this latter productive crop that interested later commentators, since Jesus or his editor had differentiated its results into varied yields, 'thirty and sixty and a hundredfold'. What was that about? Jesus had changed the subject at this point, so he was no help.

At first, theologians with other preoccupations had not aligned the yields in the parable with sex. Tertullian and Bishop Irenaeus of Lyons had gone for an ascending classification between 'material', 'psychic' and 'spiritual' Christians, reflecting second-century debates between Catholics and gnostics about degrees of Christian maturity. But then in the early third century, a now anonymous North African contemporary of Tertullian's had created a sermon on the classification which turned it towards encratite debates; so the hundredfold yield was from martyrs, sixtyfold from virginal ascetics, and thirtyfold from married persons who had renounced sexual activity. A North African in the next generation, Bishop Cyprian of Carthage, repeated the hundredfold and sixtyfold classification in a pioneering treatise dedicated to Christian virgins, and thus from the mid-third century, the parable was launched on a long career as a way of classifying Christians based on their sexual austerity, particularly women. The general consensus, right into the medieval period, was to divide the differential yields up between virgins, widows and the married, to the distinct disadvantage of the married, down at the thirtyfold mark.[28]

Amid this growing assertiveness by encratites in the Church, what other voices might be heard? Forming a polar opposite to the strident polemic against sex in Tatian, and enterprisingly reversing the priorities of monastic life, was the work of a mysterious young man called Epiphanes. We now know his writings only through scandalized quotations of them by the late second-century Alexandrian philosopher and teacher Clement, who was a Christian admirer of Philo Judaeus and also one of the first theologians to devise an extended framework for Christian ethics and morality. Epiphanes is reputed to have died aged seventeen, so it is easy to dismiss his literary efforts as the sort of over-clever essay that a bright sixth-former produces in the midst of teenage sexual turmoil – that is precisely how they were treated by his modern editor, Henry Chadwick, discussing the fragments of Epiphanes's *On Righteousness* preserved by Clement.[29]

At the time, some of Epiphanes's Christian contemporaries reached for their standard marginalizing ploy by writing him off simply as one more gnostic. Kathy Gaca, a refreshingly original genealogist of Hellenistic Jewish and then Christian rhetoric on fornication, sees him rather as a serious Christian, reading Plato and early Stoic philosophers alongside what he knew of New Testament texts, and doing so without the filter provided by Philo of Alexandria. Other commentators have pointed out that his reading must have included Cynic admirers of the outrageous ascetic Diogenes.[30] Epiphanes saw conventional marriage as a confidence trick designed to protect property rights: it should be replaced by arrangements for communal sexual activity alongside a general communalism. His blueprint for a just society, 'sharing in common on the basis of equity', might be seen as a logical, if unusual, deduction from the picture of community sharing in the Jerusalem Church in the Acts of the Apostles, as much as an expression of Platonism or Cynicism. Epiphanes does explicitly echo Paul's cry in Galatians 3.28, urging Christians to end the division between 'female and male, slaves and free persons'. His extension of that into a ban on marriage and the conventional household nevertheless makes a rather radical leap beyond Paul – not to mention his ridicule of the tenth of the Ten Commandments that forbids coveting one's neighbour's wife.

Nothing in the history of the second-century Church suggests that Epiphanes's line of argument was ever going to rally Christians against celibacy in favour of uninhibited sexual enjoyment. He forms a contrasting pair with his young near-contemporary in Alexandria whom Justin Martyr had praised for seeking castration. Was there a middle way between these two teenage extremes? It might have been the warm defence of marital sexuality written around 180 by Theophilus, Bishop of Antioch. In his one surviving treatise, justifying Christianity to a well-read non-Christian friend, Autolycus, Theophilus could speak of the exclusive passion of married love in terms more reminiscent of Graeco-Roman romanticism than of contemporary Christian writings, but he still related it squarely to the first biblical marriage:

> God made woman by taking her from his side so that man's love for her might be greater . . . what man who marries lawfully does not disregard his mother and father and his whole family and all his relatives, while he cleaves to his own wife and unites with her, loving her more than them?[31]

Alas, Theophilus's emotional literacy did not find many committed successors in early Christianity. Closest to him was Tertullian, his contemporary in North Africa. Tertullian devoted a significant part of his writings on Christian conduct to texts specifically written for women, intended for courses of instruction in Christian faith (*catechēsis*). His Latin prose did incline towards untrammelled vigour, and he has rather unfairly been remembered for one extreme verbal sally that women were 'the Devil's gateway', for which he has earned reproof from no less a patristic authority than Simone de Beauvoir.[32] In fact Tertullian never repeated this remark anywhere else; it occurred in the course of a discussion of modest female clothing, referring back to Eve's part in the Fall, and if anything, it was a criticism of men for their lustful efforts to enter the vagina, that gateway of female desirability.

In the same spirit, Tertullian's treatment of Adam and Eve is not nearly so insistent on Eve's special guilt as Justin Martyr had been (see Plate 13). Rather, he emphasized the joint responsibility of Adam and Eve: in another delightfully brutal phrase, he said of Adam's eating the forbidden fruit that 'he sold salvation for his gullet'. Elsewhere, in emphasizing Adam's culpability Tertullian observed that 'the whole human race, infected with his seed, were also made the carrier of his condemnation.'[33] This is consistent with Aristotle's views on biological reproduction, in which male seed is the essential agent in procreation, but it also reflects a conviction common in North African theology about the fatal legacy of Adam's sin. By the fifth century this was to develop into what in theological jargon is termed 'traducianism': Augustine of Hippo's conviction that this inheritance of sin from Adam via procreation is the source of a universal sinfulness in humanity – 'original sin' (below, Chapter 9).[34]

Consistent with Tertullian's equal apportionment of blame for the

Fall between Adam and Eve was his exceptional emphasis on equality in marriage, hearkening to Paul's idea of the 'marriage debt'. In his treatise addressed to his own wife (*Ad Uxorem*), his usual eloquence turns to this startlingly positive thought:

> What kind of yoke is that of two believers, sharing one hope, one desire, one discipline, one and the same service? Both are brethren, both fellow-servants; there is no difference of spirit or of flesh . . . Together they pray, together prostrate themselves, together perform their fasts; mutually teaching, mutually exhorting, mutually sustaining. Equally are both in the Church of God; equally at the banquet of God; equally in straits, in persecutions, in refreshments.[35]

Admittedly, in that quotation one does not hear anything directly about the physical dimension of marriage, though Tertullian was insistent on the virtue of marriage for the bringing up of Christian children. He could remind a follower of the revisionist theologian Marcion that 'if there be no marriage, there is no sanctity.'[36] The North African was caught between his strong desire to defend marriage against gnostics, Marcionites or any other Christian who denigrated human physicality, and his equally strong sympathy with Paul of Tarsus's gloomy thoughts on fornication.

In the course of his career, Tertullian's conversion to the rigour of Montanist Christianity darkened his view of marital sex. '[Marriage] too, in the shameful act which constitutes its essence, is the same as fornication,' he said; and he underlined that this applied even to a Christian's first marriage. It is significant that 150 years later, Jerome was able to quarry Tertullian's writings, often without acknowledgement, for his own relentless denigration of marriage in general (below, Chapter 9).[37] Moreover, all through his career, Tertullian was one of the loudest Christian voices opposing any second marriage after bereavement, let alone divorce. On more than one occasion he commended the legendary (and of course pre-Christian) Queen Dido, who in the version of her story told in Tertullian's native North Africa chose to cast herself on a funeral pyre rather than remarry – so much for Paul of Tarsus's remark that it was better to marry than burn with lust.[38]

Tertullian was an increasingly rare and marginalized figure in Christian theology as a married man writing about marriage. Moreover, he had the disadvantage of writing in Latin, which in his time was still the third language of Christianity after Greek and Syriac. What proved really decisive was the contribution of teachers and writers in Christian groups around Alexandria's thriving and venerable schools of Greek higher education – at the turn of the second and third centuries, the greatest fount of long-lasting theological discussion in mainstream Christianity. Clement of Alexandria's extended consideration of marriage was certainly not short on informed detail: Peter Brown notes that Clement's early twentieth-century editors felt that his discussion of married sexual intercourse was embarrassingly frank, and that he ought to have known better.[39] Nevertheless the line that Clement took on marriage was to defend it by faint praise; not as far from encratite condemnation of the fleshliness of sex as one might expect.

In one sense Clement exalted the institution of marriage, by picking up the metaphor from the letter to the Ephesians in seeing it as reflecting the monogamous relationship that the Church enjoys with Christ. The idea of a woman remarrying after the death of her partner infringed the simplicity of the trope; grudgingly Clement allowed that it might happen. However, remarriage after divorce was unthinkable, a collapse into 'fornication' or adultery against Christ.[40] This was a very different melding of the New Testament and the Greek philosophical tradition from the broodings of young Epiphanes. Looming behind Clement was Philo Judaeus, whose prose often reappears in Clement's writings, unreferenced.

Unsurprisingly amid Clement's borrowings from Philo came the familiar Hellenistic Jewish circumscribing of what was approved sex even within marriage: heterosexual sexual acts should be solely for the purposes of procreation. In turn Philo had borrowed that principle from a particular strand in Greek philosophy already four centuries old by his own time, since it derived from Pythagoras.[41] Clement followed Philo, also explicitly noting that Pythagoreans make love 'only for procreation, not for pleasure' with their wives; it is significant that Clement even called Philo 'the Pythagorean'. Yet Clement still advanced the Pythagorean and Philonic procreational rule on sex as if it was to be found in Paul's epistles and the New Testament generally, which it is not.[42]

What might be seen as the 'Alexandrian rule' of procreationism in marriage, beginning with Clement, has had a long afterlife in Christian thought. It still lies embedded in official Roman Catholic marriage doctrine, particularly in opposition to contraception. Other Alexandrians echoed Clement, perhaps via alternative theological and philosophical routes. Justin Martyr for instance had been taught by Pythagoreans in Alexandria and may not have needed Philo to link him to their conclusions that there was no middle way between sexual intercourse for pleasure or complete continence. Justin's negative views on sexual pleasure also align with the rhetorical contrast that we have already noted him pioneering on the roles of Eve and Mary in losing and regaining salvation.[43]

Like Justin, Origen did not share his teacher Clement's preoccupation with Philo, but in line with what may have been his personal physical enactment of negativity on sex, Origen made a remarkable extension to a comment by Paul of Tarsus. Paul had suggested that married couples might agree to suspend their 'marital debt' to each other for a while to devote themselves to prayer (1 Cor. 7.5). If prayer was thus incompatible with sex, Origen suggested that 'perhaps the same consideration should apply, if possible, to the place'; in other words, people should not pray in a building where sexual activity had taken place. It is worth speculating that if others in the third century hearkened to Origen's squeamishness about this, it could be the origin of Christians embarking on a programme of constructing separate buildings called churches: spaces for prayer free of any possible sexual taint.[44]

Logically following from Alexandrian procreationism was a statement that may sound chilling today, but which still lurks behind some self-styled Christian theologies of marriage: 'Every man who is sexually unrestrained in his interaction with his wife commits adultery with her.'[45] Its origins were once more Pythagorean. Philo had said something similar, but this version was transmitted by early Christians, probably Alexandrians, who around the end of the second century edited writings of the pre-Christian Sextus the Pythagorean, otherwise now mostly lost.[46] It was enthusiastically repeated in the fourth century by Jerome amid his general negativity about sexual expression, even though in other respects Jerome rubbished the work of Sextus as worthless paganism. Medieval Western readers could still find an elaborated form of it in the writings of one of their most widely copied and prolific thirteenth-century commentators on morality, the Dominican Vincent of Beauvais, citing Jerome.[47]

At the end of it all, after two centuries of argument first attested in the Corinthian Church visited by Paul, there were still Christian families, worshipping increasingly in buildings exclusively devoted to Christian liturgy and thus observing Origen's insistence on keeping sex and worship ritually separate. There was another allied separation relating to female purity, rarely discussed by theologians over many subsequent centuries for the good reason that very many Christians regarded it as such a given as not to be worth discussing: the exclusion of menstruating women from church buildings. Clearly this related to the elaborate discussion of menstruation in the Levitical laws of the Hebrew Bible (above, Chapter 3), though that raised the usual question of how far Christians were bound by these laws, and there were disagreements as to how far they should be deployed in the life of the Church. Notably, there was rarely much inclination to exclude recently ejaculant men from Christian liturgy on Levitical lines, even while exclusions were being imposed on menstruant women.[48]

Some early Christian commentators extended the ban on menstruant women to Baptism, saying that the rite should be postponed till after a woman's period was past: this was the case with the third- or fourth-century manual of Church practice known as the *Apostolic Tradition*, and in the third century the *Didascalia Apostolorum* described Syrian women as absenting themselves from prayer or scriptural study as well, on the same grounds. Central was the ban on attendance at the Eucharist.

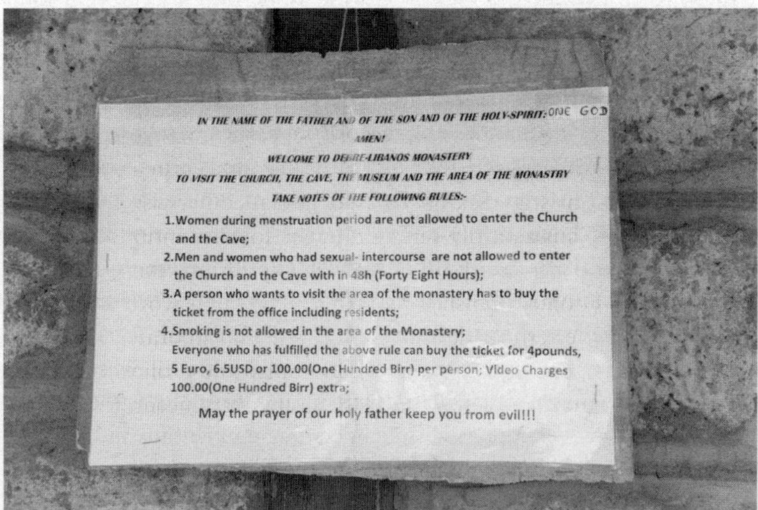

9. Modern tourists visiting the Ethiopian monastery of Debre Libanos are provided with a laminated set of instructions covering both admission charges and decorum, including a ban on menstruant women.

The first actual evidence for this is a pastoral letter circulated by Dionysios, Bishop of Alexandria in the mid third century, but he was already taking the exclusion for granted; 'I think it unnecessary even to enquire' about its enforcement, he said, for women, 'being faithful and pious, would not dare in such a condition either to approach the holy table or to touch the body and blood of Christ'. Thereafter, just occasionally over many centuries commentators refer to the ban, but generally it was similarly not felt to be a matter of comment, simply practised. There are places, notably the Orthodox Church of Ethiopia, where that is still the case.[49]

It was no accident that a chorus of deeply restrictive views of marriage first appeared in Christianity in the second century. For Christians in the imperial world, monastic and eremitic lives provided a sharp reminder that early Christianity could be a counterculture, which the married state was not. Monastic communities paid no respect to any of the traditional hierarchies of the Mediterranean: maleness, ancient lineage, wealth. For women opting into monasticism, it provided an honourable escape route from both marital life and perhaps unwelcome sexual expectations. It is wise not to elevate this into the still often-advanced claim that early Christianity had an especial appeal to women, a thesis for which there is very little evidence beyond assertions in some early Christian polemical writings.[50]

There was a much wider reason for monasticism developing as a fruitful outgrowth of Christian institutions: for all those without power amid the massive inequalities of Graeco-Roman society, it gave an unparalleled opportunity to seize one's own fate and exercise personal choice. In that respect, monasticism was like martyrdom, which has been neatly described as an 'equal opportunity employer', guaranteeing immediate admission to heaven.[51] Martyrdom at the hands of Christianity's enemies in government and society was not nearly as frequent in Christian experience during the first three centuries CE as later Christian legend would have it, whereas the option of monastic or anchoritic life was a choice increasingly available to devout and strenuous Christians as the Church expanded. Moreover, monasticism gained new momentum and purpose from the profound change in Christianity's fortunes that quite unexpectedly appeared in the opening years of the fourth century: its sudden acquisition of power in wider society. Our story will now be told in this new context for a further millennium and a half.

PART THREE

The Coming of Christendom

8

Suddenly in Power (300–600)

When at the beginning of the fourth century the aspiring Emperor Constantine I abruptly decided to show especial favour to the Christian God, it produced one of the most surprising and enduring turns in the course of Mediterranean history, comparable to the much less enduring campaign for religious transformation by the Egyptian Pharaoh Akhnaten sixteen hundred years before. There was nothing else like this moment in the previous history of the Roman Empire: the special favour shown from the 190s by Septimius Severus and his sons to the North African god Serapis, and the later cult of the Sun-God embraced by the eccentric young Emperor Elagabalus (Akhnaten replayed as farce), were merely adjustments within the Classical pantheon.

The steady march of Christian power during the fourth century was fragile and might have been reversed, as was demonstrated by Constantine's nephew the Emperor Julian, who, after a Christian upbringing, was shrewdly aware of the Church's potential weaknesses. Yet Julian's rather effective moves against Christian ascendancy were ended with his death in battle in 363, after only two years on the imperial throne. Following that, emperors resumed Constantine's alliance with the Church hierarchy, and by the beginning of the fifth century, a new project was in train in Mediterranean society: 'Christendom' – an integrated, monopolistic, hierarchical Christian society that endured for centuries, in some places to within living memory.[1]

Christendom was never equivalent to Christianity, for it was a child of empire, and it did not embrace the Churches spreading beyond the Roman imperial frontiers eastward and southward into Asia and Africa. Those Christians refused to let Roman emperors dictate the shape of their faith, considering their own practice and belief as preserving older versions of the Christian message uncorrupted by an alliance with secular power; they had a point. Christendom even in its heyday never represented more than a substantial regional chunk of the Christian faith, and one can ponder which Christianities it included. Did Christendom later extend to the successive empires of Orthodox Christianity based in Constantinople and Moscow? Arguably Christendom in its purest form was only to be found in western and central Europe, and that between about 1000 and 1530. In this area, it signified a single though intricate structure of power and devotional practice, united in a 'Western Latin Church' and taking as its spiritual head the Bishop of Rome, now commonly known, like the far-away Bishop of Alexandria, as the 'Pope' (below, Chapters 12 and 13).

IN THE MIND OF EMPERORS

Thus from the 300s, the constructions of sex made in the mainstream Church over the three centuries from the death of Jesus suddenly ceased to be the private concern of a relatively small set of inward-looking groupings around the Mediterranean and west Asia. Through the first three centuries of Christianity, its sacred, theological and pastoral writings generally (let alone their treatment of sex) were the work of people who regarded themselves as an elite, who nevertheless lacked any worldly or coercive power. From the fourth century, Christian beliefs and practices affected the whole population of the Roman Empire and became the basis for norms that still shape the lives of millions around the world, although to call these 'norms' is a little misleading because the variety and clashes of Christian opinions and customs in sex and non-sex continued to proliferate and shape-shift, and still do. Behind that cacophony of voices, the arguments of pre-Constantinian Christians echo down to the present day.[2]

The transformed status of Christianity in the Mediterranean contains mysteries now incapable of solution, because they lay in the minds of a trio of energetic emperors: Diocletian, Galerius and Constantine. The first two came to make it their business as imperial colleagues to renew the Empire not merely in administration but in observance of traditional religion and morality, as we have seen in the decree against incestuous marriages issued by Diocletian and his co-Emperor Maximian in 295 (above, Chapter 3). In this task, they identified Christianity as a major enemy, launching a systematic persecution of clergy and laity. This action did build on previous occasional bouts of official hostility towards

Christian practice over the previous century, but its intensity remains surprising, perhaps reflecting a new moral seriousness in traditional Roman religion.

Even more difficult to explain is Constantine's extreme reaction against their policy of persecution. That was rapidly visible after his initial bid for power in 306, when the army in Britannia at Eboracum (York) proclaimed him as successor to his father Constantius, to join the imperial team of four co-emperors that Diocletian had created. Over the next two decades, Constantine came to be at odds with his co-Emperor Licinius, who as their alliance broke down in mutual suspicion turned against Christians in his entourage. In 324, now sole Emperor with Licinius murdered, Constantine reaffirmed the promises of 'peace and undisturbed concord' to his subjects that the two emperors had made at Milan (*Mediolanum*) in 313. For the moment that continued to mean toleration for both traditional religion and a newly favoured Christian episcopal organization, but Constantine was already deeply involved in the internal business of the Christian Church.[3]

Constantine had in fact made unmistakeable his alliance with the Christian faith only six years from his accession, when in 312 he crushingly defeated and killed another rival imperial claimant, Maxentius, meeting him on the northward road from Rome at the Milvian Bridge. Before the armies clashed, Constantine ordered his soldiers to pray to the Christian God, and decisive victory followed. That is about as much as we can say to account for his embrace of Christian faith, which on any rational political calculation would seem bizarre: Christianity was simply not that important in the Empire, and Christians would have been delighted merely not to be persecuted. Jesus, who had died on a cross at the hands of Roman imperial administrators and soldiers, now blessed the military success of a universal ruler of the Mediterranean world; it is unsurprising that none of Constantine's new breed of courtier-bishops stirred themselves to point out the incongruity.

Among the many consequences of Christianity's new status was Constantine's founding of a second imperial capital for the eastern part of the Empire, far from the starting point of his imperial venture in York: he chose the city of Byzantium with its superb strategic site at the meeting of Mediterranean and Black Seas. Constantine followed the precedent of rulers back to Alexander the Great in renaming Byzantium after himself: 'Constantinople', though its old name bequeathed an identity to later eastern Mediterranean Roman rule and to eastern imperial Christianity as 'Byzantine'. The new capital became such a dominant feature of eastern Roman identity that for centuries it was frequently known simply as 'The City'. Constantine furnished it with a suitable array of traditional symbols of Roman power, but what was new was its growing series of magnificent Christian churches in close relationship to imperial palaces. That contrasted with the ancient and outwardly non-Christian character of the ancient urban heartland of the empire in Rome. Constantine had no reason to esteem the city of Rome, the former base of his enemy Maxentius. In any case, during the third century Rome had already become increasingly a symbolic rather than actual base for imperial rule, since emperors had based themselves in a series of strategically more convenient cities throughout the Empire.

Paradoxically the imperial desertion of Rome benefited the Christian Church there, because as the role of secular power diminished in the city, its Christian bishop gained in status. The Church in Rome had indeed long been numerically one of the largest Christian communities in any imperial city, let alone in the Western Empire (where Christianity was at that stage otherwise statistically insignificant), but the fourth century witnessed a new prominence for its bishop within Mediterranean Christianity. In the later fourth century, Bishop Damasus of Rome newly claimed that the Apostle Peter had been his first episcopal predecessor, rather than simply one in the pair of prominent early martyrs in the city's Christian history (the other being Paul of Tarsus). By this time the bishops of Rome had become informally known as *papa*: 'Father', or 'Pope'.[4]

The consequence was the rise of a Western Christian identity using the old imperial language of Latin, rather than the Greek that had previously dominated Church life even in Rome. This was a contrast to Constantinople, where the Church naturally continued to use Greek in its life and liturgy, and Latin became increasingly confined to formal, official secular use. By the end of the sixth century, it was increasingly apparent that this linguistic separation was encouraging a steadily more significant split in identity within the Mediterranean Christian Church and its various offshoots; the Latin West sought to arrogate to itself the ancient universal term 'Catholic', while the Greek, Syriac and Coptic East characterized their construction of Christian theology as 'Orthodox'. That still leaves a period of six centuries – from the fourth to the ninth – where the life and thought of imperial and post-imperial Christianity were still closely involved in mutual conversation around the Mediterranean.

Their common inheritance was Roman imperial power. In the west the last titular Western Emperor, Romulus, nicknamed in derision *Augustulus* ('little Augustus'), lost his evanescent throne in 476, but both Empire and Rome remained as potent symbols, as we will see. In much of the east, imperial Rome remained for centuries a present reality. Bishops even took up a word to describe their jurisdictions that Christianity's enemy Diocletian had first deployed in his drastic administrative reforms of the Empire in the 280s: even now in episcopally governed Churches, bishops each preside over a 'diocese'. In their increasingly elaborated liturgies, the clerical hierarchy wore the best clothes of imperial courtiers, since the worship of God was an entrance to the divine Court of an Emperor greater than any occupant of a worldly throne. Eastern and Western clergy still wear versions of these courtly costumes in their liturgical vestments.

Constantine could not yet make his Empire into a Christian society, even if he had been able to formulate that thought. The structures of Christianity were not at the time well adapted to the possibility: Christian leaders did not in general belong to the social elite experienced in running the Empire, and they did not have the legal training to make effective interventions in the ancient and sophisticated Roman practice of law and justice. The Emperor did make provision for a system of Christian courts presided over by bishops, with powers to intervene in any of the usual legal matters in parallel to existing judicial institutions, but they did not prove very effective, and their activity became confined to minor matters and dispute resolution. In fact, in 399 the Emperor Honorius ordered the bishops not to interfere in civil cases unless they involved purely religious disputes. Those would not include legal proceedings relating to sex that in later centuries very much concerned the Church, such as marriage. When a pope did try intervening in a problem of marriage law for the first time, at the beginning of the fifth century, his effort was not immediately effective.[5]

Nor do Constantine's own interventions in lawmaking reveal much knowledge of or interest in Christian moral standards, whatever excited Christian leaders may have thought at the time. In one or two token respects of law one can see Constantine making reference to Christianity; for instance, he does seem to have abolished crucifixion as an imperial penalty. In 315, he prohibited the branding of criminals on the face (notably only on the face), 'which is shaped in the likeness of the celestial beauty' – a nod, perhaps at second hand, to the Creation story in Genesis 1.26–27. Overall, his legislation followed the busy moralizing and heightened interference in people's ordinary lives that had characterized lawmaking by Diocletian, Maximian and Galerius; if anything, Constantine added to the brutality of criminal penalties and diminished the legal rights of women. In 320, for instance, his prohibition of elopement carried the penalty of execution for both the young people involved, while any female servant who helped them would have molten lead poured down her throat.[6]

For more than a century, Roman legal enactments made very little reference to Christian Scripture. A more characteristic moral attitude was that of a constitution of Constantine's issued in 326, which, with very traditional Roman priorities, observed that a case of adultery by a high-status woman deserved punishment as it affected all society, while the same conduct by a woman of low social standing was merely private in character.[7] Gradually change in legislation did reflect more Christian preoccupations: for instance, in 374 the Emperors Valentinian, Valens and Gratian condemned the ancient Roman acceptance of exposing unwanted infants, stipulating death for those who did, and said that everyone must bring up their own children.[8] Yet it was only in the 390s, under the extended rule of the Emperor Theodosius I, that a Christianization of Roman power became decisive. In 378 the Western Emperor Gratian sent Theodosius, a senior army officer from what is now Spain, eastwards as co-Emperor to restore order after a usurpation. Theodosius proved himself energetic in enforcing not merely Christianity, but its theological form agreed at the general ecclesiastical Council of Nicaea back in 325; he therefore eliminated remaining 'Arian' leaders from the Church hierarchy of the Empire.

After further political confusion in the Western Empire, Theodosius also seized power there in 392, and he had no hesitation in confronting the last resource of traditional strength in the senatorial aristocracy of the ancient capital Rome. That continued his previous policy in the East of ending all privileges for ancient priesthoods and closing temples wherever he could. Theodosius's determination to tip the scales of society in favour of Christians had been startlingly witnessed in 388, when he forbade Christians and Jews to marry together, making it a crime on a par with adultery (which in theory carried the death penalty). This was the first time that Roman law had yoked marriage to confessional identity. 'Christian marriage', glimpsed in the writings of the Apostle Paul, was now an enforceable legal reality, subject to coercion.[9]

*

Among Theodosius's other actions against previously sacrosanct customs was the ending of the Olympic Games in 393, after which celebration of the traditional divine pantheon, the Emperor closed them down for good. In Antioch, similar games lingered till 520, but by then the Greek custom of male athletes exercising naked had long ceased.[10] This end to the Classical cult of the male body was a fitting symbol of one of the most significant changes to Graeco-Roman society when the Empire officially turned Christian. Church leaders now had a chance to criminalize the centuries-old practice of male same-sex relations, condemned in New Testament Epistles from Paul of Tarsus and a successor-writer, and attacked thereafter (somewhat repetitively) by later generations of Christian writers.[11]

Theodosius's edict on the subject, issued jointly with his pliable co-emperors in 390, is first preserved in the contemporary writings of an anonymous Latin Christian author who was anxious to demonstrate how the Law of Moses in the Hebrew Bible agreed with Roman law – this eccentric project influenced Western Christian attitudes to law for centuries, including on sexual matters.[12] The Emperor made clear his revulsion that a soul enshrined in a body of male sexual characteristics should turn that masculine body to female sexual positions. This was taking traditional Roman disapproval of passive male intercourse and giving it a new spiritual dimension. In its condemnation of 'the poison of shameful effeminacy' enfeebling Roman society, Theodosius's decree left far behind the assumptions about masculinity that once had constituted the rationale behind the heroic same-sex Theban Band.

As a result, the imperial authorities rounded up male prostitutes in Rome's same-sex brothels. It may be that those arrested suffered the penalty of being burned alive in public; certainly that was enacted in a revised version of Theodosius's decree incorporated in a comprehensive codification of Roman law by his fifth-century namesake Theodosius II, which also extended the punishment to all passive males. The imperial court was thus orchestrating a new public mood of hatred of homosexuality; a symbol of the radical shift in official attitudes to same-sex relationships survives in a stone portrait bust of Antinous, archetype of male beauty and famously the lover of the Emperor Hadrian back in the second century CE, which at some point in this era was recut to resemble a respectable upper-class Roman matron.[13] Those aware of modern conservative myth-making about sexual degeneracy might appreciate the irony that this puritanism was followed within decades by the fall of the Western Roman Empire.

10. A late Roman female bust reveals its recutting from a second-century portrait of Hadrian's lover Antinous, recognizable by his distinctive hairstyle surviving at the rear of the head.

At the same time, one of the early Church's most significant churchmen and preachers was devoting his considerable powers of oratory to sermons and treatises vehemently denouncing same-sex activity. John Chrysostom ('Golden-Mouth') was Bishop first of Antioch and later of Constantinople, though that proved not to be his finest hour. Sexual relations between men were indeed quite an obsession with him; John Boswell comments that Chrysostom 'probably wrote more about the subject of same-sex sexuality than any other pre-Freudian writer except [the eleventh-century] Peter Damian'. In his angry addresses to city and Church, the Bishop was consciously campaigning against a still-flourishing contemporary culture of Mediterranean older–younger male relationships, even (he claimed) within Antioch's large Christian community.[14]

Chrysostom's picture of same-sex relations was quite traditional: not an exclusive lifetime sexual identity, but as part of a generalized sexuality that might make adolescents lust after the beauty of women or young men alike. What was not traditional was that Chrysostom was campaigning at all; in doing so he pointed to the sea-change in official mood, as well as to the Bible. He specifically contrasted the customary (and deplorable) Graeco-Roman treatment of the practice 'not as a vice but something honourable' with Paul's strong condemnation of it in Romans 1, but in the same passage he also abruptly shifted his argument away from Paul to parallel the punitive actions taken in Rome in 390: 'A dog at least is useful, but a male prostitute is good for nothing.'[15]

With such denunciation in the background, emperors in Constantinople successively tidied up inconsistencies in the repression of same-sex activity, one remarkable inconsistency being that the imperial government continued to benefit financially from a tax on male prostitutes, until it was abolished by the Emperor Anastasios (reigned 491–518).[16] During the reign of Anastasios's soldier-successor Justin, real imperial power passed to a nephew of Justin's, Justinian. Even before Justinian began his long, hyperactive and transformative reign (527–65), the regime in 521 unleashed a set-piece punitive action against various prominent men accused of same-sex activity; they included two bishops from widely dispersed parts of the Eastern Empire. These were changed times in more than one sense, for such bishops were now part of the political establishment: one of them, Isaiah, Bishop of Rhodes, had previously been the imperial official in charge of security in the city of Constantinople.

Whatever the truth of their activities, and whatever political element there was in scapegoating these significant public figures, their fate spelled out Justinian's Christian values on sex. Bishop Alexander of Diospolis in Thrace and a number of other offenders were taken to Constantinople, sexually humiliated in public with exceptional sadism and then castrated, although Bishop Isaiah merely suffered torture and exile for life.[17] What motivated this brutal political theatre in the name of morality? The answer may be found in texts incorporated in the huge collection of centuries of Roman law undertaken during Justinian's long reign: the *Corpus juris civilis*, which shaped the future of Byzantine law and was to have a similar effect in the West when Western scholars rediscovered it in the eleventh century.

On homosexual acts, the *Corpus* consolidated the legislative beginnings made under the two Emperors Theodosius. Justinian amplified the Emperor Augustus's harsh legislation on adultery and divorce to extend the death penalty from adultery to those 'who give themselves up to works of lewdness with their own sex' (we have already seen Theodosius I adding Jewish–Christian marriages to the original Augustan provisions). To that remodelling of a central pre-Christian text, Justinian added newly created legislation, gathered in his *Novellae* or *Novels*, which displayed Christian reference and which reflected the natural crises blighting the Empire in Justinian's time: a concentration of unusually catastrophic earthquakes on the Empire's Mediterranean tectonic fault lines, and then, beginning in 541, one of the most severe known plague pandemics in human history.

Accordingly, the Emperor admonished same-sex offenders in Novel 77 'to take to heart the fear of God . . . that they may not be visited by the just wrath of God . . . because of such crimes there are famines, earthquakes, and pestilences'. The Antiochene chronicler John Malalas, who had recorded the fate of the bishops of Rhodes and Diospolis with relish, habitually used the same phrase 'the wrath of God' to describe earthquakes. Justinian completed the circle of references in Novel 141 'against the defilement of males', after Constantinople suffered a second episode of plague in 544; he made an archetype of the fate of Sodom, where 'to this very day the land burns with inextinguishable fire.' This became a recurring cliché as the Byzantine Empire suffered fresh outbreaks of plague through the next two centuries to 750: despite a long Classical tradition of viewing plague as a physiological or medical problem, Byzantine analysis was now primarily couched in terms of morality. As far as same-sex offenders were concerned, accounts of Justinian's reign show that the general fate of those accused under such legislation imitated that in the pogrom of 521: castration rather than immediate death (though the latter often followed the former).[18]

ASCETIC CHRISTIANITY IN IMPERIAL SOCIETY

This was not the only way in which Christians twisted the ancient structures of the Empire to accommodate their bundle of social and theological suppositions; society now had to accommodate a growing institutional celibacy and asceticism. Mainstream Christianity had already tilted the balance between, on the one hand, marriage and the family, and on the other the practice of celibacy for both men and women. Christian bias towards celibacy was accompanied by a general negativity about sexual activity inherited from Philo of Alexandria's variety of Hellenistic Judaism; by contrast, traditional Roman society took marriage to be the foundation of civic and imperial order, regarded sex as for recreation as well as for love and relationships, and found little cultural space for celibacy. At most celibacy had been an aspiration for a tiny minority of would-be philosophers, and, with vanishingly rare and partial institutional exceptions like the Vestal Virgins of Rome, Graeco-Roman culture produced nothing like a monastic community, any more than did mainstream Judaism.[19]

Within the fourth-century Christian Church, the network of monastic life spread steadily outwards from its beginnings in Syria and Egypt. In early fourth-century Egypt, a former soldier called Pachomios imitated the Syrians in steering most Egyptian ascetics towards life in communities (above, Chapter 7). Far to the west, probably in the early 360s, Martin (another ex-soldier, from what is now Hungary) drastically reshaped a pre-Christian sacred site in Gaul; he created the first known Christian monastery in the western Mediterranean at a place now called Ligugé, near the Gaulish city of Pictavia (the modern Poitiers, in west-central France).[20] It is probably significant that these two charismatic pioneers emerged from the regulated single-sex life of the imperial army. Originally the Church had frowned on Christian men joining the imperial army, largely because of the regular religious rituals involved in swearing loyalty to the Emperor. That consideration no longer applied now that emperors were Christians.

Effectively Pachomios and Martin were redeploying and remodelling military discipline for their communities, although their campaigns were now waged by prayer against the Satanic spiritual powers surrounding Christians. Supportive of that main end was an often spectacularly strenuous physical asceticism exceeding anything demanded of a legionary. Among the most picturesque examples of such feats were those 'stylite' hermits in Syria and Asia Minor, some 120 over seven centuries from the early fifth, who built themselves a stone pillar on which to live and preach, generally in positions frequented by travellers that would become public landmarks for devotion and instruction.[21] Even without such spiritual athleticism, monastic or eremitical life offered the chance for individuals to approach union with God by embracing a sort of living martyrdom: actual martyrdom was no longer a possibility at the hands of a Roman imperial power that had inconveniently replaced persecution with financial subsidies.

All this was invitingly heroic, and not only the stylites aloft their strategically placed columns experienced the complicated enjoyment of a good deal of public admiration and even political influence. They were unmistakably a spiritual elite, when once all Christians could have been regarded as an elite. Just as the early Syrian phase of monasticism had overlapped with so-called 'encratism' and rebellion against Church authority, these monastic communities posed potential problems of authority for a Christian Church now firmly committed to government by monarchical male bishops. Very few hermits or monks were also priests, so if they were in some remote desert place, they had little connection with the Eucharistic life of a church congregation over which a bishop presided. Equally seriously, the manifest and strenuous holiness of spiritual leaders like Antony of Egypt, Pachomios or Martin of Tours offered a charismatic alternative to the episcopal hierarchy which based itself on cities of the Empire, and which owed its legitimacy to recognition and consecration by fellow bishops.

There proved to be ways of neutralizing the clash. The bishops were more or less reconciled to fourth-century monasticism by the evident loyalty that the major figures displayed to episcopal Christianity. Antony was an outspoken supporter of a grateful Bishop Athanasios of Alexandria in mid-fourth-century battles to uphold the Nicene theological agreement on the Christian Trinity against 'Arian' Christians. Indeed, Athanasios is credited with writing the definitive biography of Antony. It became one of Christianity's bestsellers over the centuries: a highly edited and enriched version of the reality, and perhaps indeed modelling itself on the Lives of pre-Christian philosophers, but all the more important for its literary fashioning in setting patterns for the future in the ascetic life. In the delicious phrase of Peter Brown, its eager readers from Beirut to Bangor saw 'an Egypt dressed in its Sunday best'.[22] The work was the beginning of an Egyptian ascetic literature, portraying both 'Desert Fathers' and 'Desert Mothers'.

In the Latin West, Martin actually became bishop himself in the Gaulish city of Civitas Turonum (Tours), still leading a monastic community alongside his energetic shepherding of his diocese. Such was his reputation that, as the cult of saints blossomed throughout the Mediterranean in the next generation, he rapidly became one of the most popular saints of the West, a powerful symbol in death for communion with the Pope in Rome. It is likely that over two centuries and more, the cult of Martin was decisive in rallying Catholics in western Europe against an alternative Christian theological future offered by the followers of Arius.[23] Besides these happy historical contingencies, a useful policing measure for the monastic life developed. Against independent-minded ascetics, the authorities deployed a concept of 'messalianism', vague but negative; like 'encratism' before it, messalianism signified ascetic devotional practices and attitudes going beyond what was considered seemly or reasonable. Of course, in both cases it was the bishops who defined what was acceptable or unacceptable.[24]

The monasticism of Egyptian desert or Syrian wilderness expanded and flourished in forms that would have been familiar to Christians before the time of Constantine: a 'silent rebellion' against Graeco-Roman society that reflected the general character of early Christianity as marginal in relation to the powerful and wealthy.[25] A monastic family was a direct challenge to the biological family that was the foundation of mainstream society: the leader of such a community was, after all, known as an abbot, *Abba*, that very title for father that Jesus had applied to God himself. Part of an abbot's duty was to cut off his monks from the distraction of their previous worldly relationships. Christ himself had spoken approvingly of his followers leaving family behind, so one could not say that this was going against the Saviour's demands. Here ancient Christianity can often seem at its most remote from modern Christian assumptions, though there are still forms of Christianity that might not see it as a problem.

That problem is encapsulated by a horrible tale told by one of the chief writers in early monasticism, John Cassian, a fourth-century ascetic from the Eastern Empire whose writings brought eastern monastic discipline to the attention of ascetic communities in the western Mediterranean. In his book of community instruction, the *Institutes*, Cassian reminisces about a wealthy man whom he calls Patermutus, who, when he became a monk, brought his eight-year-old son with him. The abbot now assumed the role of *paterfamilias*: he deliberately broke them up to sever the biological bond, and sent them to separate communities. Patermutus was then sadistically tested: his little son was 'purposely neglected', 'clothed in rags' and left filthy, even randomly beaten until he cried, just to emphasize that the natural father should not intervene in this cruelty. The tale shockingly culminates in a ritually enacted parody of the Old Testament patriarch Abraham's offering his son Isaac for a sacrificial death: the abbot ordered Patermutus to throw his son into the river, and the pair were actually at the water's edge before a couple of strategically placed monks intervened to tell the father that he had passed the test of loyalty to his new vocation. The boy did not die, any more than Isaac had done, but now Patermutus had lost everything from the past; he was no longer even a parent.[26]

Yet not all Christians submitted as Patermutus did to this twisted version of the 'silent rebellion'. The growing establishment of the Church brought in many converts who were no less aspiring Christians because they were powerful and wealthy, and who did not choose to reject their existing place in the society of their day. They too could be swept up in the movement to asceticism, but accommodating their power and wealth alongside its flat rejection by other ascetics was not straightforward. One wealthy and spiritually distinguished Christian family set useful patterns providing an answer. With an honourable ancestry among senators and urban magistrates, they lived in rural respectability in Asia Minor. Even before the fourth century, it was not so unusual in Asia Minor to encounter a Christian family among the local landed elite, but one fourth-century generation of the children of Basil and Emmelia made a remarkable joint contribution to Christian life and theology.

Basil the son of Basil became Bishop of Caesarea Mazaca (now Kayseri in eastern inland Turkey). Having become a monk, he is known as 'the Great' both for his writings about structuring monastic life and general pastoral discipline, and for his strong support of the anti-Arian cause in the Church. Basil's brother Gregory became Bishop of Nyssa in Asia Minor and was likewise a great Nicene theologian and spiritual writer. They both revered their older sister Macrina ('the younger' to distinguish her from a saintly grandmother), who played a major part in educating and bringing up her various brothers. A significant feature of this family history is that its considerable joint wealth ended up in the hands of the Church, because so many of the siblings embraced ecclesiastical careers or celibacy; that became a recurrent theme in later Christianity.[27]

Gregory paid his own emotional debt to his sister by writing an affectionate though highly crafted biography of her. The story of Macrina lacked the lively incident of Antony's, but the useful lesson of her life for many others was how to pursue lifelong Christian celibacy in a respectable if unexciting Graeco-Roman household, latterly presiding over her own monastic female community. Gregory's account is a major pioneering text in the fourth- and fifth-century enterprise of picturing upper-class women to be as much of a model for holiness as any of the Desert Fathers or Mothers: a flagship in a growing literature which admiringly described women of particularly outstanding holiness in everyday (generally prosperous) society. The accounts were written by men, but at least took seriously the possibility of female holiness.[28] That was an encouragement for various wives, widows and heiresses who now sought to combine often staggering personal wealth with Christian seriousness. Most notable representatives were in the elite senatorial families of Rome, who with the arrival of Theodosius

I in the 390s realized that the game was up for traditional religion and briskly embraced Christian practice.

Clergy were on hand to offer a rigorously controlled version of Christian life for the outstandingly rich. One such mentor was the tetchy but brilliant scholar Jerome of Stridon, though he was incommoded by his hasty departure from Rome in 385, in the wake of some intensive direction in asceticism to a young noble lady called Blesilla. She died aged twenty after indulging in an excess of fasting and general spiritual rigour, which would no doubt now be diagnosed as anorexia; and there was talk. Moreover, the unkind gossip extended to Jerome's close relations with Blesilla's mother, Paula, a situation that has remained a constant problem for celebrity spiritual advisors. Jerome's subsequent defensiveness, which included angry criticism of Paula, is not much more edifying.[29] He has already appeared in our story and will do so again in Chapter 9.

What united these varied forms of asceticism? It may seem a statement of the obvious that their shared characteristic was the renunciation of sexual activity. That did not mean banishing sex from the consciousness of the ascetic: temptation needed to be confronted. Athanasios's classic life of Antony set the pattern by detailing the various alluring guises by which Satan sought to distract the holy man: principally two standard objects of sexual recreation in the Classical world, a seductive young woman and then a black boy (the Devil's second try when the woman had proved unsuccessful – see Plates 17 and 18). Stories of hermits over the generations chronicle Satan's continuing and largely futile efforts along these lines – for Egyptian hermits, the black boy (or sometimes girl) often became specifically Ethiopian, a familiar but still exotic other, who might even be won over to the right side given particular holiness on the part of a prayerful ascetic.[30]

The increasingly rich corpus of devotional stories about ascetics furnished how-to manuals in resisting what were very real psychological dangers in the celibate's life. Resistance needed careful thought, and indeed prayer. It is noticeable that a major concern of early ascetic literature is how to cope with nocturnal emissions: depressing symbols of the uncontrollable nature of the human body to which the celibate is particularly liable despite the best spiritual intentions. Likewise, Christian texts do not seem to have discussed masturbation at all before the time of John Cassian in the late fourth century.[31] Not all would have followed the fifth-century monk Pachon's desperate technique for resisting demonic spiritual temptation, by applying a small desert snake to his genitals, but it was worth being aware that this was potentially an item in a hermit's spiritual toolkit.[32] More common would be the effect of intensifying the routine observance of fasting by early Christians; a side-effect of extreme hunger would be loss of sexual appetite. In turn that led to another preoccupation in early ascetic texts: food, how to get it in a desert environment, and how to resist its excesses. Success in that respect would signify a further triumph over that constant worry of most people in ancient society, how to eat well, or even just how to get anything to eat.[33]

A further distinctive regulatory device evolved in Eastern monasticism as a liturgical mechanism to form a framework for close monastic relationships: *adelphopoiēsis*, or 'brother-making'. The earliest manuscript evidence for this rite is as early as the first surviving Byzantine prayer books, from the eighth century, which indicates a well-established existing custom (and in fact there are papyrus fragments possibly attesting early forms of the ceremony from an Egyptian monastery site dateable to around 600 CE). From then on, down to the nineteenth century, around seventy manuscripts from Orthodox Christian contexts preserve versions of the rite.[34] The pioneering historian of sexuality John Boswell became over-excited by his rediscovery of this institution (and he excited many others too), describing it as a ceremony for same-sex union – shifted by less subtle commentators towards 'gay marriage'. Something like that thought might earlier have occurred uncomfortably to modern Orthodox theologians, which could explain the obscurity into which the rite has fallen in recent times, despite its continuing formal presence in liturgical books.[35]

It has taken later historians, notably the careful work of Claudia Rapp, to restore a still-significant context to *adelphopoiēsis*, while gently detaching it from some of Boswell's wishful thinking and exaggeration of its similarities to later Orthodox forms of marriage liturgy for men and women.[36] Rapp demonstrates that *adelphopoiēsis* relates to the once very common practice in Egyptian and Byzantine monasticism of two or three monks sharing a common life. That might be seen as a development of traditional Mediterranean same-sex relationships with older and younger partners, in counterpoint to the imperial legislation seeking to drive that institution out of society. In such circumstances, for both practical and emotional reasons, it was eminently sensible to frame such a relationship with agreements before God accompanied by set prayers, recognized by the wider monastic world as a fictive or sacred making of brothers. That is what *adelphopoiēsis* originally was and long continued to be in the Orthodox tradition, but never in the West: only one surviving medieval Latin manuscript of the rite has been located, significantly deriving from the boundary of Greek East and Latin West in what is now Croatia.[37]

The likely reason that *adelphopoiēsis* remained exclusively an Orthodox custom is that Western Latin monasticism quite early on set its face against such pairs or small groups of monks. This was much encouraged by the authority of John Cassian in his presentation of Eastern monastic custom to a fascinated West at the beginning of the fifth century: he sneered at this type of monastic life, which he darkly and indeed obscurely termed as 'of the *Sarabaites*'. As a third variety of monasticism, standing midway between the hermit tradition of Antony and the community tradition of Pachomios, it was 'a poor sort of thing and by all means to be avoided'. The sixth-century Italian monk Benedict, creator of a distinctive Western approach to monastic discipline, emphatically agreed with Cassian, and he made that clear in what is now known as the Benedictine Rule, basic to shaping Latin monastic life in later centuries.[38]

It was perhaps in defensive reaction to this Western hostility that *adelphopoiēsis* remained important and widely practised in Eastern Orthodoxy. Yet in the course of time, such paired monastic life became rarer in Orthodoxy as well, and even Easterners might forget the origins of the ceremony. No doubt some couples of men, monastic and secular, did decide to use it for their own emotional purposes. There have been some quiet modern efforts in Orthodox contexts as widely separated as Jerusalem and Serbia to redeploy 'brother-making' to structure a variety of relationships, and also predictably, in the face of modern developments in sexuality, the Serbian Orthodox Church nervously suspended use of the ritual in 1975. Whatever its future, it is important to return it to its appropriate place in the past.[39]

ANGELS, EUNUCHS, SAINTS

The ascetic conquest of sex by whatever means, if successful, was a means of liberating constructions of gender from the traditional constraints of Graeco-Roman society. In fact, did the ascetic life create a third gender? There was a possible answer, or analogy, in the esteem accorded to angels. They were powerful sacred personalities close to God, who might be considered models for human behaviour, but this involved some radical rethinking about them. In both pre-Christian Jewish and Christian tradition, angels were frequently characterized by aggressively masculine sexual activity, as a perusal of Genesis 6 in the Septuagint's Greek would inform any curious reader. A long scriptural and extra-scriptural tradition led forward from Genesis, with its lustful and fruitful angelic couplings with mortal women, right up to Paul of Tarsus's now obscure warning to Christian women (1 Cor. 11.10) to veil their hair 'because of the angels'.[40]

Suddenly, from the fourth century, Christian commentators busily backtracked on this long-standing view of angels. Their change of perspective is revealed in Christian art, which had been developing from the third century, particularly to enrich the carved stone coffins of elite Christians: sarcophagi. In the fourth century, Christian angels remained visually just like adult males: one sarcophagus shows several of them with beards, and at least one of them is balding. From the end of the century came a dramatic shift: not only were later angels invariably clean-shaven, but for the first time they virtually all sprouted wings, and they have done so ever since. We are so familiar with this convention that it comes as a surprise to learn that there is no scriptural or ancient Jewish basis for it; in the Hebrew Bible, cherubim and seraphim have wings, but they are a different class of celestial being. The winged models for angels were from non-Christian Classical art; moreover, those models were specifically female, particularly the winged figure of Victory (*Nike*). Angels were henceforth a good deal less masculine than they had ever been. Already ranked between divinity and humanity as dwellers in the heavens, they were now neatly positioned between distinctive gender identities.[41]

The initial prompt to the concept of a genderless angel came from Jesus himself when, in answer to a provocative question about marriage in the afterlife, he had observed that at the resurrection men and women 'neither marry nor are given in marriage' but are 'equal to angels' (Luke 20.34–36). Various commentators brooded on this pronouncement: Syria, cradle both of Christian monastic life and of angelic hymns sung in church by Daughters and Sons of the Covenant, was particularly precocious in developing the theme.[42] Alternative Christianities, some of gnostic inclination, also took readily to the idea: for instance, the biblical commentator Marcion, expelled from the Church in the mid-second century for his drastic reinterpretations of the biblical text, observed of the Lukan passage that Christians who practised sexual abstinence in this life might become 'already equal to the angels'.[43] The brilliant third-century scholar Origen, who did not suffer such a complete disgrace as Marcion but who was still widely condemned for his venturesome theological propositions, asserted flatly that, like angels, humans who attained salvation would lose their earthbound sexual differentiation in heaven. Even as clouds gathered over Origen's reputation, this idea kept its attraction; when asceticism gained hold in the Church in the fourth century, it was repeated from Origen by the combative champion of celibacy Jerome, admittedly not without fierce criticism from others.[44]

Theologian contemporaries of Jerome who lacked his talent for making enemies were nevertheless prepared to echo Marcion in seeing angelic celibacy as an achievable goal in the present age. Gregory of Nyssa's biography of his sister Macrina portrays her life as angelic: she provided the perfect example of Gregory's insistence that prayer-filled and ascetic Christians can already ascend to participate in the reality of heaven. In a fashion which Philo Judaeus and a succession of his Christian admirers through Clement of Alexandria would have applauded, Gregory insists that, before the Fall of Adam and Eve, human beings would have procreated without sexual intercourse, as angels did – a process (he had to admit) 'unspeakable and inconceivable by human conjectures, except that it assuredly exists'.[45] In the seventh century the same thoughts, and the same readiness to deny gender difference in the interest of union with God, remained central to the ascetic theology of the former Byzantine imperial civil servant Maximos the Confessor; any theme championed by the hugely respected Maximos was going to keep its place in Byzantine spirituality.[46]

There was, however, one problem of rhetoric with sustaining the notion of angels as a genderless model for ascetics: another influential group of Eastern Christians was equally anxious to apply the angelic analogy to their own situation. These were eunuchs, males who had undergone what can only be described as drastic gender-modification surgery. Eunuchs were an ancient presence in the Mediterranean world: many were slaves who had not been given any choice in the matter, but some had been deprived of their genitalia by their own or their family's decision – castrated priests of the Phrygian goddess Cybele were one celebrated example of a religious tradition dating back for at least a millennium.[47] During the second and third centuries Christians had debated the rights and wrongs of voluntary castration, and with some hesitancy had decided against approving it (above, Chapter 7). Yet a fascinating feature of the imperial establishment of the Church in the fourth century is that, far from continuing to reject 'pagan' or idolatrous precedents, it greatly enhanced the role of the eunuch in imperial society. By the fifth century, when 'barbarian' kingdoms were replacing the crumbling Western Roman Empire, Vandal and Ostrogoth rulers clearly thought that employing eunuchs at their royal courts was part of the package in their adopting Roman ways, alongside their adoption of Christianity.[48]

There was obvious political usefulness in giving eunuchs important roles in the administration. They were not going to seek to supplant the ruling dynasty with their own, and they could be considered as less of a risk in close proximity to female empresses or princesses. Traditional Graeco-Roman discussion of the eunuch state had nevertheless long found it perplexing. Aristotle frankly found it difficult to classify eunuchs satisfactorily in terms of gender, with castration in their youth prolonging their high voices and beardlessness into adult life. Later Romans, preoccupied as they were with masculinity, were equally nervous and often hostile to the point of crafting laws against castration. Nevertheless, in the Roman imperial period, Galen was content to go beyond Aristotle to embrace the concept of eunuchs as constituting a third state in humanity.[49]

That is how eunuchs might go on to find a niche in Christian theological vocabulary. Were they not like the angels in heaven, genderless servants of the supreme ruler? And, in a remarkable development during the age of Justinian, did they not number among their ranks some of the Empire's most successful generals? That was reminiscent of the heroic military achievements of the angels Michael and Raphael in the divine cause, and it was a fine riposte to long-standing Roman ridicule of the eunuch as effeminate. Accordingly, eunuchs featured in Byzantine society not merely as generals or court officials, but increasingly as time went on also as senior Churchmen, despite official ecclesiastical bans on castrated men taking clerical office dating back to the landmark Council of Nicaea in 325.

Nicaea had actually left convenient legal loopholes when it ordered all eunuch clergy to be deposed. Not only did it exempt those who had been castrated against their will, but also eunuchs who had undergone the operation for medical reasons (not the last time that this would be a provision in ecclesiastical legislation on various moral issues). Because of this, eunuchs regularly appeared among the Church hierarchy, right up to the Patriarchate of Constantinople: there were five eunuch patriarchs between the ninth and the eleventh centuries, and maybe others. Certain monasteries in the eastern Mediterranean from Greece to Judaea were established exclusively for eunuch monks, but eunuchs were also commonly to be found in 'mixed' communities of male monks. It therefore made sense for families, perhaps in some poverty-stricken village in the Balkans, to arrange castration for a promising son, which would set him up for high imperial or ecclesiastical office as much as did a decent education.[50]

Since eunuchs often wielded significant political power, it is not surprising that helpful theologians might draw attention to their resemblance to genderless angels. Moreover, Jesus had bequeathed posterity a comment distinguishing three categories of eunuchs that was certainly not negative about them, albeit a little puzzling (Matt. 19.12; above, Chapter 4). One might even regard a decision for castration as a lesser imitation of an emperor's liturgical inauguration for public service; by comparison, the eunuch's bearded colleagues among Court attendants lacked any such formal ceremony anticipating their future career. The doyenne of Byzantine scholars Judith Herrin directs our gaze to the famous mosaics flanking the altar in San Vitale, Justinian I's great church in Ravenna, where, in defiance of normal Byzantine iconographical convention, secular courtiers accompany the imperial couple in procession to the altar. Contrasting with Justinian's largely bearded entourage, the Empress Theodora is accompanied to the altar (a space officially forbidden to women) by two beardless attendants who assist in making her gift of a chalice (see Plate 12). Probably we are viewing eunuchs at the very heart of imperial liturgy, helping to mediate between earth and heaven alongside the angelic host.[51]

The very success of this association of eunuchs with genderless angels rendered the analogy problematic for late imperial ascetics, despite its continuing place in the thought of ascetic theologians like Maximos the Confessor. Not everyone in Byzantium bought into the angelic image of eunuchs, and there were plenty of scandalous stories – either genuine or efforts to discredit them – not to mention some pointed and disapproving theological reflections from major authorities such as the fourth-century writer Basil, Bishop of Ancyra: 'the removal of parts denounces the adultery of the one who mutilates himself', he commented acerbically.[52] As a result, it was only in Western Christendom, where for the time being eunuchs quickly lost any accepted niche in society, that ascetics went on being uninhibitedly compared to angels. Yet when almost a millennium later in the sixteenth-century Counter-Reformation, the Western Catholic

Church gave a surprising renewed welcome to eunuchs (*castrati*), the image of castrato as angel was to experience a bizarre revival.[53]

More securely and straightforwardly directed towards the ascetic life was a sexual theology which, as usual in the ancient world, prioritized the moral worth of men over women. Asceticism, whether of hermit, monk or nun, could be construed and gendered as a new form of martial masculine virtue, as it had been in the lives of Pachomios and Martin, so that interpretation offered a similar life to biological women in their own separate communities, albeit usually under exceptionally rigorous conditions. Certainly women could face simple misogynistic hostility from male ascetics worried about their own feelings: so one Egyptian monk turned aside from the road to avoid meeting some travelling nuns, and was suitably rebuked by their abbess – 'if you had been a perfect monk, you would not have looked at us, and you would not have known that we *were* women.'[54]

Yet the point of recording this majestic put-down was to curb thoughtless misogyny, and there were more positive answers to such emotional issues. Beginning in the fifth century there is a peculiar genre of ascetic literature from Egypt and Palestine devoted to religious women who disguised themselves as men, often spending their entire ascetic lives in reverent disguise and being revealed at their deaths, to general astonishment. Their holiness contradicted the ban on transvestism in the Book of Deuteronomy (22.5), but, despite considerable worries from the Church hierarchy, the disparity was not allowed to stand in the way of an edifying theme.[55]

Just occasionally amid this literature, a woman was allowed to be a woman, as long as she lived in extreme penance and contradiction of normal female attractions. Hugely popular was the story of Mary of Egypt, who spent her ascetic career as a woman, but in a most extreme form: completely naked, physically withered and tanned black by the sun. This reversal of her former seductive beauty was a symbol of repentance for her frank enjoyment of prostitution in younger days; the effectiveness of her transformation was affirmed at her death when her confidant, the holy and virginal priest Zosimas, reverently buried her, having to his chagrin arrived too late to give her the Eucharist. In most other respects, Mary's story resembled that of the female transvestites, and likewise it originated in the fifth century.[56] Soon it was influencing devotional views of that always fascinating companion of Christ bearing the same name, Mary Magdalen, who by the sixth century was regularly being identified with another New Testament female, a forebear of Mary of Egypt, the anonymous sinful woman who had washed Christ's feet with her hair.[57] With that biblical prompt, this concatenation of saintly figures gained a great deal of hair in illustrations, often covering their whole bodies (see Plates 14 and 16).

The less dramatic reality of most early female monastic life is witnessed, like the first known mention of a *monachos*, by a legal document from the Nile Delta: around 400 CE, two *monachai apotaktikai*, 'female renouncers', granted a Jewish man a sixth-month lease of an apartment that they jointly owned in the city of Oxyrhynchus.[58] Some of the colourful transvestite ascetic stories may have contained a kernel of truth, but the majority are likely to be further examples of male storytellers 'thinking with women' to organize their own emotional worlds. It is telling that there are no complementary stories of male ascetics passing as women. We are back with that trope of early Christianity that, to achieve perfection, a woman must become male, albeit a virginal male. It is the only way of transcending that natural characteristic of women, their subjection to ungovernable passions.

11. The early thirteenth-century portal depicting the parable of the Wise and Foolish Virgins at Hovhannavank monastery (Aragatsotn province, Armenia) shows the Wise Virgins as monks with beards.

Examples of this thought are frequent in contemporary Christian literary texts that are far more obviously based on reality than the transvestite legends. It could be regarded as one of the organizing principles in Gregory of Nyssa's biography of Macrina, who practised her asceticism in a very different social setting from that of Mary of Egypt. Gregory begins his account of his sister with the observation that, 'A woman is the start of the narrative, if indeed a woman, for I do not know if it is proper to name her who is above nature [out of the terms] of nature.'[59] Genderless or male, certainly not female: this was the best way of expressing Macrina's extraordinary closeness to heaven beyond normal feminine capacity. 'According to nature I am a woman, but not according to my thoughts,' said the fifth-century Egyptian 'Desert Mother' Amma Sarah, a saying preserved when very few of her pronouncements attracted the attention of male scribes, and a fine definition of 'gendering'.[60] Some of the iconography of the Church in Armenia goes further than most Christian art by expressing the idea in a sculptural motif. Jesus's parable of the Wise and Foolish Virgins (Matt. 25.1–13) is pictured with the wise among the virgins lighting their lamps for the bridegroom, but not as the young women of the original story: they are monks with beards.[61]

One major witness to the way in which early Christianity skewed the balance between virginity and marriage is that asceticism commonly annexed marriage as a metaphor. This had two chief biblical sources, though many others were creatively added as scriptural ballast. The first was a wholesale allegorical reading of the Song of Songs, based on the textually unwarranted assumption that the relationships celebrated in it were those of husband and wife. Given that initial false premise and a good deal of imagination, its startlingly erotic imagery could illuminate the inner life of the ascetic. The second was the metaphor of marriage to Christ that Paul of Tarsus had first developed (for instance 1 Cor. 11. 2–16), and which Ephesians 5.23 took further. Early commentators on these sources commonly identified the bride with the Church rather than with any individual Christian, but, in the third century, some theologians of the Latin Western Church, notably the two North Africans Tertullian and Cyprian, Bishop of Carthage, began extending the thought to individual professed virgins.

The writings of the late third-century Methodios (probably Bishop of Olympus) moved that theme into Greek-speaking Christianity. The only work of his surviving intact is the first systematic treatment of Christian virginity, structured adventurously as a conversation among ten virginal women, and entitled *The Banquet of the Ten Virgins* in allusion to Plato's *Symposium*.[62] Methodios otherwise earned his place in Church history by his relentless opposition to the theology of Origen, but, on the matter of virginity, the two were in thorough agreement. One striking feature of the *Banquet* is that it gives the history of sex and marriage a framework of dynamic development from Creation to Methodios's own time: incest in the early days (necessary for Adam and Eve and their offspring), then the Old Testament's polygyny, which was now forbidden, alongside various previously permitted forms of adultery. Finally in the Christian era came the triumph of the virgin state.

In this happy age, the Church is certainly still the Bride of Christ, but, in Methodios's account, so is every individual Christian soul, inseminated by Christ, so that Paul of Tarsus himself is the very example of one receiving 'into his womb the seeds of life'. That outdoes the Song of Songs in its audaciously positive view of femininity, naturally in the interests of virginity, although the product of the union of Christ with both Church and individual is predictably male: 'the enlightened receive the features, and the image, and the manliness of Christ, the likeness of the form of the Word being stamped upon them, and begotten in them by a true knowledge and faith, so that in each one Christ is spiritually born.'[63]

The great expansion of professed virginity over the following century gave Methodios's arguments increasingly wide purchase. His references to the Song of Songs were repeatedly echoed, for instance by Bishop Athanasios in various letters addressed to particular professed virgins, and inevitably by Jerome too, who was capable of referencing the Song of Songs around thirty times in just one letter out of his intense correspondence with the ascetic Eustochium, a hugely wealthy senatorial widow turned monastic leader in Palestine. Jerome, so unenthusiastic for actual marriage, was very free with sensuous borrowings from the Song in his frequent spiritual addresses to Eustochium: 'Let the seclusion of your chamber ever guard you; ever let the bridegroom sport with you within. If you pray, you are speaking with your spouse.'[64]

Equally profligate with scriptural bridal imagery was the celebrated Ambrose, Bishop of Milan at the end of the fourth century. He was the chief exemplar of the new style of political bishop, having enjoyed a previous secular career governing the province of which Milan was the capital (at a time when the city was also the effective capital of the whole Western Empire). Ambrose's background in the most exalted Roman nobility might have propelled him on to the imperial throne, and during his quarter-century as bishop of the capital from 374, he was the only person who could publicly overawe Theodosius I. Yet Ambrose's power was also based on his outstanding ability as a theological author and preacher, as well as being the first major writer of hymns in the Latin West. He directed his talents to strong support for the ascetic movement, not least among the imperial elite, writing a whole series of treatises on virginity between 377 and 395. They are honest enough to concede that a significant number of parents were not at all enthusiastic about their daughters wilfully withdrawing themselves from the upper-class Roman marriage market. That is not the only evidence of unease among many elite men, Christian and non-Christian, about the radical rejection of their traditional values that the monastic life represented.[65]

Ambrose, an astute judge of how to thrive in complicated political situations, made attack the best form of defence.[66] He enlisted the Mother of God as an ally, insisting repeatedly that she had been ever-Virgin, her womb and hymen physically inviolate even in the birth of Jesus (*virginitas in partu*). There was theological innovation here, based on a new Roman understanding of gynaecology: very few ancient doctors before the third century had believed that women possessed a hymenal barricade that must be broken to end their virginity. Now this idea was becoming common, and it has persisted into modern medicine. Equally uncommon before Ambrose's time was the doctrine of Mary's perpetual virginity, first asserted two centuries before in the lone and eccentric voice of the *Protevangelium of James*, but in the 390s the Bishop contrived to give it its first official status through an ecclesiastical Synod held at Milan, which condemned those who opposed the idea.[67] Ambrose extended the theme of virgin marriage and the closed, defended womb both to the Church as a whole and to his prospective consecrated virgins. He spoke eloquently of the contrast between the marital fecundity that every *paterfamilias* expected of a wife, and the spiritual fertility of the committed virgin: her womb might be closed biologically, but that opened her whole energy to embrace alike Holy Scripture, Christ the Saviour and the poor who begged for Christian charity.[68]

Ambrose gave this package of theological novelties a public liturgical expression. The Bishop used his cathedral as a theatrical stage, giving a new dramatic prominence to an existing liturgical rite previously only observed in private: the solemn consecration of virgins. Ambrose and his Roman contemporary Jerome provide the first surviving accounts of its use; in the Western Latin Church it is the ancestor of the modern liturgical consecration of nuns, but the Orthodox East did not take it up at all. It became commonly known as the *velatio* (veiling), because it borrowed from the traditional marriage custom (not simply for Christians) of a bride being veiled before entering the bridal chamber. To judge from the oldest surviving version, it resounded with quotations from the Song of Songs, which Christians regarded as the poetry of bride and groom. Thus, when a bishop like Ambrose presided over this rite, he took the place of the Roman *paterfamilias* introducing his daughter to her new marital relationship. That was an important claim for bishops in a world where marital alliance and the interest of the family structured all society, and one can see why many biological fathers would not be best pleased by the usurpation. There could be no better example of a metaphor being transformed into liturgical reality, or of the Church inserting itself into the traditional structures of power within the Empire.[69]

Yet, in elite families, the female ascetic normally remained a continuing presence in the household. The form of the *velatio* with its allusions to marriage reinforced a widespread assumption from the fourth century onwards that a professed virgin woman, like any good Roman wife, was best kept from the public gaze in an ordinary domestic setting.[70] After all, that was the pattern demonstrated by the archetype of the devout well-born celibate, Gregory of Nyssa's sister Macrina. There remained a fruitful tension between such domestic assumptions and the heroic lives of those women who ventured into the world unsupervised in the colourful fashion of 'Desert Mothers' like Amma Sarah or Mary of Egypt, let alone the flurry of transvestite ascetics who graced eastern Mediterranean hagiography.[71]

Both these extremes of the celibate life had a future throughout the Christian Church: for men as well as women. The crucial figure in enriching the options within asceticism was Jerome, who in terms of Eastern Christian asceticism can be described as a failed monk: after a couple of solitary years in the mid-370s, he fled his effort at eremitical life in a rural area south of Antioch (not quite so much of a wilderness as he later liked to make out) and returned to Rome and to what proved a much more congenial role as secretary to Pope Damasus and chaplain to the ultra-rich.[72] As we have seen, his career in Rome also came to an abrupt, unplanned end, at which point he relocated to Jerusalem, alongside a number of Roman self-exiles in Palestine led by such exalted figures as his friend the Lady Paula (mother of the late Blesilla), who now presided over a distinctly aristocratic Latin-speaking monastery in Bethlehem. Jerome joined Paula's community (despite his rudeness towards her); it was a perfect setting for continuing the biblical research that had already begun to fascinate him during his unhappy Syrian venture.

Jerome was a pioneer in suggesting that the demands that scholarship made on him and like-minded monks – those congenial hours spent in his chamber sifting words to craft his great new version of the Bible – were just as much a sacrifice of self as the spiritual athleticism of a pillar-saint. This self-serving thought was the spark and justification for subsequent centuries of monastic scholarship that had not previously been a significant part of ascetic life. Henceforth the monastery was a vital conduit for conveying the imperial knowledge and culture of the Mediterranean forward to transformed societies. The sheer variety of ascetic experience that so proliferated between the fourth and sixth centuries has continued to give it vitality and appeal amid the choices available to Christians in the expression and regulation of their sexuality.[73]

In the background was a devotional revolution based on various forms of sainthood, through which the now vastly enlarged congregations of Christians sought out places associated with martyrs and the godly dead that offered an especially close proximity to holiness. Saints had successfully negotiated the perils of death to enter the presence of God; many had been aided by a martyr's death at the hands of the Roman authorities before the Constantinian revolution, and devout imagination manufactured many more pre-Constantinian martyrs in the same mould. Now asceticism, as a variety of living martyrdom, provided new routes to sanctity both for its practitioners and its admirers.

There had long been some shrine centres among Christian communities – archaeology suggests pilgrimage to the tombs of Peter and Paul in Rome from the end of the second century – but the fourth century was the vital growth period. Star attraction was Jerusalem, newly reorganized as a Christian city showcasing the site of Christ's crucifixion and burial in the decades following a formal visit by the Emperor Constantine's mother, Helena, in 327. Not all Church leaders were delighted by this development, particularly because the Bishop of Jerusalem became a new player among the Mediterranean's senior bishops, but by the end of the fourth century the Holy City had already devised an elaborately developed liturgy for a growing stream of pilgrims from right across the Empire.[74]

It is noticeable though unsurprising that the front-runners among the saints who were goals of pilgrimage were largely celibates. An exception to prove the rule was Peter in Rome, who the Synoptic Gospels attest was married (his mother-in-law benefited from one of Jesus's healing miracles), but that could not be helped. Squarely in the ascetic frame

12. St Thecla accumulated a formidable array of legend and symbol: this late sixteenth-century Dutch engraving shows her surrounded by wild animals, while, in the distance, Roman soldiers try in vain to burn her alive, echoed in the text caption from the Apocrypha, Sirach Ch. 51.

was the first major international saint's cult, celebrating Paul of Tarsus's perhaps fictional friend Thecla (above, Chapter 7). Thecla's final resting place was specified in her second-century Life as Seleucia (now Silifke) in Asia Minor, which by the end of the fourth century had acquired an Empire-wide pilgrimage clientele and stately buildings, and, over the next century, archaeology furnishes an astonishing range of witnesses to her esteem, as far away as Italy, Gaul and Germany. Most prominent was Egypt. Here Bishop Athanasios had contributed his own enthusiasm for her, making her the star exhibit for virginity in his treatise on that subject; but she also acquired an association with an ascetic and ex-soldier Menas, hugely popular in Egypt, which is all the more mysterious since this almost equally shadowy figure flourished around two centuries later than her.[75]

The literature around Thecla duly expanded in the fifth century, and for the first time did not shrink from calling her an 'apostle'. She was also commonly styled the first female martyr, even though most versions of her story did not actually end with a martyr's death; the general though not uncontested view was that she had simply disappeared miraculously into the earth. Surprisingly, there were no relics of her body even at Seleucia. That helped her insert herself into many different saintly settings around the Empire. Thecla's new 'apostle' title might itself be evidence of these widespread contacts, because it is shared by (and perhaps borrowed from) a heroic ascetic woman of the early fourth century whose story culminated across the Black Sea in Georgia: Nino.

The Georgian hagiography of Nino seems to originate in the fourth century, for her core story is briefly summarized by Jerome's sometime friend Rufinus around 400. She is very specifically pictured as an itinerant apostle and evangelist, as Thecla had been in her earliest *Acts*; appropriately for an evangelist, Nino herself tells the core stories, so they also recall the first-person narrative in the second-century *Passion of Perpetua* (above, Chapter 7). There was much loving Georgian elaboration of Nino's exploits later, but the Georgians had no hesitation in maintaining her apostolic status, hailing her as a missionary who had travelled from other lands to become prime agent in converting the Georgian royal house. If Thecla's devotees did indeed borrow a title from the Apostle of Georgia, the influences may have passed in both directions, for Nino follows a precedent set up by second-century versions of Thecla's story at odds with Christian norms in the fourth and fifth centuries: she herself baptizes an entire household.[76]

The most remarkable aspect of Thecla's and Nino's lively cults is that they seem to predate the rise of one saintly devotion that could provide an obvious model of virginity, a virgin who interestingly, like Thecla, left no bodily relics on earth by the manner of her death: Mary, the Bearer of God. It is significant that when that third-century pioneer of literature on virginity Methodios of Olympus had prepared his *Banquet of Ten Virgins*, the virginal guests did not include Mary, and chief in honour among them was Thecla. Naturally Mary has already frequently appeared as an essential theological presence in our story. Her role as mother of Jesus was the cornerstone of the Nicene theological case for the co-equality and co-eternality of Jesus with the Father in the Trinity that over the course of the fourth century defeated the 'Arian' party in the imperial Church; it encouraged pious meditation on her place in God's plan for human salvation ('he who is not a Marian, is an Arian' according to a later English aphorism). In the 380s and 390s, Ambrose, as we have seen, enlisted her as an ally in his championing of virginity.

At the beginning of the fifth century, Mary was equally central to the dispute that engulfed all Christianity within and without the Empire over the relationship between the divinity and the humanity of Christ. The poison in the row centred on whether one should call Mary 'Bearer of God' (*Theotokos*), a description strongly contested by Bishop Nestorios of Constantinople, a theologian in the tradition of Antioch who had a strong sense of the distinctness of these divine and human natures in the Second Person of the Trinity. He argued that a more precise description of Mary to do her proper honour would be *Christotokos*, 'Bearer of Christ'; by doing so, he stirred up a formidable combination of enemies.

This theological dispute was so bitter that it became a matter of imperial security to solve it. In 451, a major Council of bishops was summoned by the Emperor Marcian (and his rather more imperious wife Pulcheria) to Chalcedon near Constantinople: strategically near enough to the capital for imperial troops to reach it quickly if necessary, yet far enough away to prevent angry mobs coming from the city to intimidate the bishops. The Council not only condemned Nestorios and deposed him from office but produced a lengthy compromise 'Definition' of the natures of Christ. At the heart of it is contradictory language about those two natures – 'without confusion, without change, without division, without separation' – designed to get on board as many of the contenders as possible. Yet, as is often the way with compromises, Pulcheria and Marcian's 'solution' left Nicene Christianity split three ways between imperial defenders of the Chalcedonian Definition and those standouts on either side who refused to accept it: 'Miaphysite' (or Monophysite) believers in Christ's full divinity and full humanity in 'one nature'; and 'Dyophysites' (or Nestorians), who affirmed Christ's one substance, but in 'two natures'. Such terminology may baffle Western Christians now; however, it still represents passionate belief among the successor-communities of these ancient disputes.[77]

Despite the lack of agreement at the Council of Chalcedon, it was in no one's interest amid these schisms to dishonour Mary as Mother and Virgin, and she was embarked on the spiritual journey that would make her 'Our Lady' to countless generations of Christians. While the dispute that led to Chalcedon ran its course, there were signs that pilgrims were seeking her out as well as theologians; that strengthened the hand of those opposing Nestorios. An important stage on the way to Chalcedon had been an earlier Council of bishops, held in 431 in turbulent circumstances in the city of Ephesus; Ephesus had a strong claim to be the place where Mary had died, and the bishops (who referred to that tradition in a letter to Constantinople) appear initially to have met in Ephesus's 'Church of Mary', which sounds like the first known church dedication to a saint anywhere.[78]

Only a few years later, mid-century, around the time of the Council of Chalcedon, Pope Sixtus III (an outspoken enemy of Nestorios) built a church in Rome also dedicated to Mary; it was so monumental that in essence his building survives as the magnificent S. Maria Maggiore. Mosaics which Pope Sixtus commissioned survive in the church, so their representation of Mary is a pioneering effort to portray her in a public fashion, with little apparent precedent. She appears as a stately Roman matron, such as Jerome might have bullied into refraining from a second marriage, and, although occupying a prominent place in the mosaics, she is notably without the halo sported by her son and attendant angels (see Plate 11). Yet, in less than a century, the familiar haloed mother holding her infant son had become a standard motif in both the Latin Western Church and in the East.[79]

Mary's consolidation in official and popular devotion gathered momentum, but curiously slowly. Liturgy is always usefully both an expression of communal mood and a way to stimulate it. The great Akathistos hymn of Orthodoxy, which praises Mary as *Theotokos* and portrays a sequence of episodes in her life, is now considered to have been composed fairly soon after the Council of Ephesus, a good deal earlier than was long thought.[80] Preaching is as important as liturgy; we have already noted the importance of the various sermons preached by Archbishop Proklos in Constantinople in the early fifth century, expounding the doctrine of *Theotokos* (above, Chapter 4).[81] A liturgical feast of her Assumption or Dormition, affirming her direct reception into heaven (and thus accounting for the lack of bodily relics of her), was promulgated by the end of the sixth century. More gradual alongside these actions of the clerical elite is the accumulation of evidence for popular devotion: dateable stories of miraculous intervention, for instance. A crucial moment was Mary's part in ending sieges of Constantinople, repeatedly imperilled by the Avars and the Persians between 619 and 626; this involved the faithful parading in solemn procession a robe of hers allegedly acquired from Jerusalem. Around those saving events for 'the City' there accumulated in the next three or four centuries a great body of legend and further relic-objects associated with Mary, backdated to the period.[82]

Essential to the eventual success of these developments, which the Iconoclastic Controversies of the eighth and ninth centuries much encouraged (below, Chapter 10), was the ability of Mary to appeal to a wide range of Christians at all levels of society for a variety of reasons. In the fourth to sixth century, the concentration was on her virginity and the encouragement that it provided for ascetics: a mother and virgin whose sexual identity was removed from normal expectations, just like theirs. Yet even early on, there could be a simple (though not necessarily simple-minded) identification with her as Mother. The fourth-century pioneer of heresy-hunting, Bishop Epiphanios of Salamis, can often be suspected of making up heresies for the sake of completeness, but sometimes he denounces beliefs so delightfully banal that they could have been real: he was furious about the popular custom in such widely dispersed regions as Thrace and Arabia for women to bake loaves to tickle Mary's palate on certain feast days.[83] What was a heretical perversion for Epiphanios might a millennium later be seen as a pleasing folk custom in honour of Our Lady.

One important aspect of the new cult of the saints was the honouring of people who would once have been outcasts amid the pacifism of early Christianity – soldiers. We have already met some of them: Martin of Tours, Pachomios, Menas of Egypt. Now Roman martial virtues were celebrated, and the saints involved came to be lovingly portrayed in their imperial military costumes, even though the early examples of the genre had gained their sanctity by being killed by the military authorities. One of the first great Christian cults to range alongside that of Thecla was that of the saintly soldier-partnership of Sergius and Bacchus, victims of persecution under Galerius. On the eastern margins of fifth-century Byzantium lay the territory of an Arab people called the Ghassanids, who preserved their freedom of action by their formidable military skills, and they were early enthusiasts for this warrior pair, who had been martyred on that same eastern frontier.

The sway of Sergius and Bacchus was thereafter far-reaching and prolonged, for instance winning devotion from eleventh-century Mongol nomad rulers who otherwise remained unimpressed by the overall Christian package. One element in the soldier-saints' popularity must have been their intense same-sex bonding, a constant background theme in their joint portrayal in icons. Although obviously that was presented in the cult as a bond of asceticism, their martyr-legend included the interesting detail that they had been humiliated before their deaths by being paraded in women's clothing. Their defiantly masculine holiness might appeal to soldiers such as the Ghassanids or a Mongol Khan of the Keraits, but it could be equally inspirational for a pair of monks who had expressed their special relationship in the form of *adelphopoiēsis*. And in all these cases, mothers anxious about their sons' military adventures might have found equal comfort from the heavenly intercessions of Sergius and Bacchus.[84]

It is ironic but also telling that, in the era we have visited, the Church evolved two different liturgical procedures for celibates in East and West, *adelphopoiēsis* and the *velatio* respectively, before it showed any great interest in creating liturgies for marriage in church, or even exerting much energy in getting the faithful to come to church for their weddings. That was a much more long-drawn-out process: the late arrival of the church wedding on the Christian scene is one of the chief forgotten facts about the Church and sex. It remains to see when, where and how this happened, so we may place developments in marriage after the fourth century into the wider Christian story.

9
Marriage: Survival and Variety (300–600)

By the fourth and fifth centuries CE, celibacy, virginity and the ascetic life had won a privileged position over against marriage in the theology and devotional practice of Christian Churches. The general message was that it was simply easier to obtain salvation as a celibate than as a sexually active married person. Yet the reality was that even as Christianity became ever more dominant in the Roman Empire, and most of the population became at least nominally Christian, most people also went on marrying and having children as they had always done. Both realism and a wish to offer pastoral care to this rapidly expanding flock demanded answers as to what that fact of life meant for them in a Christian framework. Moreover, the exaltation of celibacy raised major questions about clergy who were not monks and who were married – they were by far the majority at the beginning of the period. What would happen to their clerical successors over the next centuries?

FROM JOVINIAN TO AUGUSTINE

Some of the greatest names in fourth-century Western Christianity were impresarios of the newly intensified celebration of celibacy: who were the voices on the other side? Most notorious is Jovinian, a monk from Asia Minor, who, though a celibate himself, nevertheless took it on himself to stand up to Jerome's relentless denigration of marriage and the developments in doctrine encouraged by Bishop Ambrose. Jovinian's reward was to be condemned as a heretic in 393, both in a Synod at Milan dominated by Ambrose and by a similar assembly in Rome under Pope Siricius. We only know what Jovinian thought in detail because in the course of bitterly refuting his writings Jerome reproduced large portions of his text (throughout Christian history a frequently employed but self-defeating tactic, for which historians should be grateful). Jerome's opponent was portrayed in the Church's later narrative as an eccentric deviant justly condemned; even Protestants in the Reformation who were pursuing similar arguments to his were cautious about commending Jovinian by name, such was the vilification of him (below, Chapter 14). It is clear that actually Jovinian spoke for a great many sincere and well-informed Christian contemporaries, and that if anything, it was he who was fighting theological innovation, not his opponents.[1]

Jovinian chose his battleground astutely (forcing Jerome to answer him on the same issues), by beginning not with marriage but with the basic Christian sacrament of baptism. We should remember that, in that era, baptism was conferred not on infants but on adults, conscious of what a choice it was to enter fully on the path of Christian faith. Accordingly, Jovinian emphasized that there was a single, undifferentiated reward in heaven for those making that choice; the Devil could never overthrow a baptized Christian. There was therefore no difference in merit or status between baptized virgins, widows or married women; despite anyone's misuse of the Parable of the Sower, one condition did not automatically yield a better harvest than the other. Jovinian compared decisions for marriage or for celibacy with another basic Christian custom, fasting: commendable though fasting might be, there was no difference in the eyes of God between abstaining from food and enjoying it with devout thanks for divine providence.[2]

Where Jovinian was most theologically vulnerable was in rejecting a doctrine that with some justice he regarded as eccentric, the perpetual virginity of Mary, especially when it was made a springboard for viewing virginity as superior to marriage. As a result he made enemies of three clerical leaders – Jerome, Bishop Ambrose and Pope Siricius – who could unite in fury on this, despite considerable other disagreements and mutual animosities. Jerome had already bitterly attacked another writer, Helvidius, whose work like Jovinian's is only preserved through Jerome's reproduction of it, framed by abuse that cannot be dignified by calling it argument. Helvidius pointed in common-sense fashion to the New Testament's evidence of Jesus's brothers and sisters. They witnessed that Mary had at least not remained a virgin after the birth of Jesus, and so she had a normal married life; thus, she honoured all married life as part of God's creation. In opposing Helvidius and Jovinian, Jerome forged an increasingly extreme polemic against sex *within* marriage, let alone outside it.[3]

From Jerome's treatises and many letters, even in some measure in phrases of his supreme achievement, the 'Vulgate' version of the Latin Bible, there emerges a tangle of personal loathings coupled with fascinations: notably about the nauseating physicality of marital sex and the general physicality of women (who are also among his closest correspondents). One attentive modern reading of his Vulgate admires the care and accuracy of his translation of ancient Semitic texts, with one exception: irregularities and mistranslations cluster round passages relating to women.[4] Jerome's tirades against women marshal previous misogynist rants right back to pre-Christian antiquity, notably those of Aristotle's philosopher-colleague in Athens Theophrastus, who was mostly known thereafter because Jerome quoted him. Jerome's literary war-chest for denigrating women echoed down the centuries; in fourteenth-century England the poet Geoffrey Chaucer made fun of it in his *Canterbury Tales*, ventriloquizing his satire via the splendid fiction of the Wife of Bath, a much-married lady whom Jerome would have detested.[5] Jerome was also one of the chief conduits to a later age of that unpleasant remark imported from the Pythagoreans into Christianity, that a man who loves his wife excessively is an adulterer.

Jerome particularly hated the prospect of widows entering a second marriage, especially women in his intimate circle – second marriage had always been a controversial matter in Christianity (above, Chapter 6). Unsurprisingly his visceral reaction spawned some hilarious efforts at biblically based argument: for instance, his typological contention to Jovinian that since Jesus only attended one wedding (at Cana, in John's Gospel) the Saviour had taught that people should only marry once.[6] Faced with an uncongenial contrary opinion from what he would have regarded as Paul's first letter to Timothy (5.14), which strongly advises widows to remarry, Jerome countered it with an appeal to Genesis: just as Noah's Ark had contained animals both clean and unclean, a remarried widow would have to make do with being an unclean person within the Christian ark. Besides – in a rapid improvisation on one of his favourite tropes – the Parable of the Sower only included in its grain harvest the three categories of virgins, widows and the married, so anyone twice-married would be left merely as an anomalous tare lurking in the wheat.[7] Naturally the Book of Ruth, that charming Old Testament story of a young widow who finds happiness in a second marriage, not to mention a son who was among the ancestors of David and Jesus, did not feature prominently in Jerome's recommended reading on the subject.

Jerome wrote to at least three widows in his circle of admirers pleading with (or hectoring) them not to remarry. In 394 he addressed the young widow Furia: inevitably hugely wealthy, and actually sister-in-law to his unfortunate protégée Blesilla. His scatological remarks to Furia on wedlock bear repetition in Jane Barr's translation, brusquely improving on the delicacy of some standard versions:

> You've already learned the miseries of marriage . . . It's like unwholesome food, and now that you have relieved your heaving stomach of its bile, why should you return to it again . . . 'like a dog to its vomit'? . . . Perhaps you are afraid that your noble race will die out, and your father will not have a brat to crawl about his shoulders and smear his neck with filth.

The image of excrement dripping down Grandpa's neck effortlessly outshines Cyril Connolly's pram in the hallway as a symbol of marriage's threat to the life of the spirit. It has to be said that, whatever one thinks of Jerome's opinions and character, the virtuoso of the Vulgate could craft knockabout Latin prose as enjoyable as that of his irascible theological predecessor Tertullian.[8]

Jerome's emphatic feelings about sex and marriage led him into an interesting logical trap around the always tangled theological status of Jesus's family. He was drawn into the question of what constitutes a Christian marriage, already a matter of contention in his time. Is it defined by an act of consent, or by the beginning of sexual relations? The case of Mary the Mother of God, in which the decisive moment was her 'Be it unto me according to thy word', suggested a solution based solely on consent, but Jerome's obsessions had led him to insist that sexual activity was an integral part of marriage. Logic then drove him to argue that if this was the case, since Mary was ever-virgin, Joseph and Mary had only been betrothed, not actually married.

This created an entertaining complication for Jerome in his parallel insistence that Christ's union with the Church was the model for Christian marriage; one presumes that such union is based on consent, not sexual intercourse.[9] Generally, in late antiquity, the anomalous model of marriage provided by Joseph and Mary became more obviously at odds with Paul's proposition of a mutual sexual debt between husband and wife. Significantly Joseph was customarily portrayed as an old man, which would (alas) diminish his chances of sexual activity of any sort.

Far from being regarded as a good Roman *paterfamilias*, Joseph's devotional stock went down in the Church of late antiquity, even as Mary's rose, and took around a millennium to recover (below, Chapter 13).[10] Contention about defining marriage, and the place of the Holy Family in that contention, raged on into medieval and Western Reformation Christianity, as we will see; moreover, the question marks remain.

Straight away, many even among Jerome's friends (a moving target) felt that his bitter rhetoric went too far. Always lurking around any praise of celibacy and denigration of marriage were those two vague menaces, encratism and messalianism, and the rather more concrete present reality of a rival Mediterranean faith, Manicheism, which strenuously and consistently classified matters of the flesh as evil. Jerome had accused Jovinian of Manicheism, but the charge could more convincingly be levelled at his own writings. It was that uncomfortable thought that led to the writing of one of the most influential early Christian texts on marriage: *De bono coniugali*, 'On the good of marriage'. Probably written in 401 and deliberately paired with a consideration of virginity (*De sancta virginitate*, 'On holy virginity'), it dominated Western Latin Christianity's thinking on marriage for a millennium and more, because it was the work of the key theologian in the Western tradition: Augustine, Bishop of Hippo Regius in North Africa and a celibate presiding over celibate communities in his diocese.[11]

In writing his autobiographical *Confessions* over the five years or so prior to his treatise on marriage, Augustine of Hippo has provided us with the most rounded picture we have of any individual in the ancient world. No autobiography is entirely trustworthy, and his is couched as a giant prayer to God, with the connected underlying purpose of winning the reader to the life of Christian continence that Augustine had embraced for himself, after many emotional and sexual adventures. Nevertheless, *Confessions* is extraordinarily revealing about one of the most fascinating leaders in the history of Christianity. It retails the youthful affairs of a brilliant student and teacher in higher education; successive monogamous relationships with two women, the first of whom bore him his son; his psychological fencing with his strong-minded mother Monica about his marital future – but also his intense bond with a teenage male friend who died young, and his deep feelings for his long-term friend Alypius. Inevitably the same-sex friendships have in modern times attracted both excessive excitement and contrary, embarrassed efforts to deny physicality in them.

They should simply be regarded as an unusually well-documented example of emotions that were commonplace in late antiquity, and any physical component to them (perfectly plausible) is of secondary importance.[12]

Overall, Augustine's account of himself suggests an interesting complexity of experience, reflected in his treatises on marriage and virginity. By the time he wrote in 401, his son was dead: a promising and much-loved young man called Adeodatus ('Given by God'), a name that suggests that the pregnancy had not been planned. Also part of Augustine's past history was his flirtation with Manicheism. Manichee views were now among his chief objects of attack, but he remained vulnerable to unsympathetic accusations that his theology was still not totally distanced from their dismissal of the flesh. Around him was the North African diocesan flock whose care he had dutifully, though initially unenthusiastically, taken up; his sermons (of which an extraordinary and recently augmented number remain) reveal his frequent impatience not just with their inattention in church but their general sexual laxity, especially the men. Additionally, Augustine brought to his task a deep admiration for Bishop Ambrose of Milan, a great influence on him at an important moment of change, so he embraced Ambrose's view of Mary as pure virgin as well as perfect mother. All this created a difficult balance to maintain in his paired treatises on marriage and virginity – it is noticeable that around half of Augustine's treatment of consecrated virginity consists of a pointed commendation of humility, which is not an automatic virtue among ascetics.[13]

Augustine's exploration of marriage is a conscientious attempt to do justice to the often-contradictory elements of biblical pronouncements on the subject and to create from them a distinct pattern of 'Christian marriage', against the background of all marriages since the Garden of Eden. He draws on pre-Christian philosophy to maintain that there is good in marriage, both Christian and non-Christian, since marriage and the union of man and woman are the foundations of all society. Yet he must show – against ascetic extremists (Jerome is in his sights) – that marital sex is not a consequence of the Fall, but part of God's original purpose in creating Adam and Eve. Here, and elsewhere, this leads him into speculations that are not without their comic aspect: what must their sexual congress have been like in Eden, he wondered, when their wills were not disordered, and their reproductive organs under perfect control? Every Roman *paterfamilias* would be aware of the prime importance of masculine self-control and would sympathize.

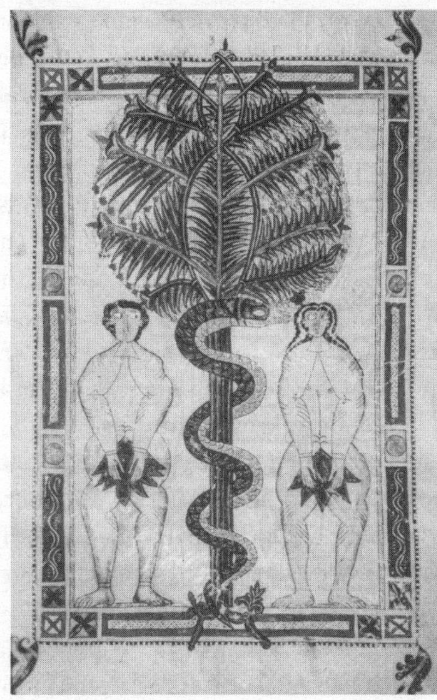

13. In this tenth-century Spanish *Beatus* (commentary on the Book of Revelation), Adam and Eve look especially embarrassed by their discovery of shame in the Fall.

In his great work *The City of God*, Augustine is prepared to associate the Fall directly with the embarrassment of losing this sexual self-control: 'the punishment which was a kind of evidence of their disobedience', including Adam's first experience of an erection. As Genesis 3.7 tells us, their shame led to their making themselves loincloths (*campestria*) – Augustine used the Latin word that signified the covering for the genitals worn by Roman athletes.[14] The Western Church was thus launched on an inescapable association between shame and sex, not excluding marital sexuality, and for many commentators over the last three centuries that has earned Augustine a dark reputation for shaping Western Christianity's variety of the ancient Christian negativity on sex.[15]

Yet it is important to note that alongside Augustine's gingerly discussion of sex in the Garden of Eden, before and after, he returns to that theme of Paul's so often neglected in later Christianity: the mutual sexual debt of husband and wife (1 Cor. 7.3). Sex is fundamental to marriage. He does read on from there to Paul's evident personal distaste for the implications of the marital debt, and Paul's observation (1 Cor. 7.6) that God's tolerance for the enjoyment of marital sex is 'by way of concession' – in Augustine's Latin '*per veniam*', which has the implication of 'indulgence towards a fault'. A sin, in other words, but not a fatal one: the later Western concept of 'venial sin' is struggling to be born, making marital intercourse inherently sinful, particularly if it is entered with no purpose of procreation, yet not beyond redemption.

Then Augustine must turn to Ephesians 5.32 and draw on its description of marriage as a *mystērion*, especially as a *mystērion* of the relationship between Christ and his Church. Translating that word with its typically Greek broad raft of reference, which might just signify 'hidden meaning', Latin-speakers had opted for *sacramentum*. Augustine rightly noted its etymology: *sacramentum* had started life as the unbreakable oath that Roman soldiers swore to the Emperor. The Latin word was not yet blossoming into the full Western notion of 'sacrament', but it did give ballast to the common opinion in the Church that marriage was as indissoluble as a military oath. Augustine enlarged on its oneness, without generally descending in his biblical exegesis as far as Jerome's absurdities: thus, as a relationship of unity, a lifelong marriage reflected the heavenly Jerusalem, where (as Psalm 133 reminds us) brethren dwell together in unity. So when affirming that marriage should not be subject to normal Roman or Jewish customs of divorce, Augustine specifically ruled out the exception that Matthew's Gospel had made to Christ's command against divorce (Matt. 5.32). The Western Church took note.

Out of all his discussion, Augustine crafted his celebrated threefold description of Christian marriage as exhibiting *fides, proles, sacramentum* – faithfulness, offspring, a lifelong allegiance. In his last years he collected a set of *Retractationes* ('Revisions'), an engaging collection of matters on which he felt regret for some of his earlier statements, and among them was an admission that 'I think that I did not reach a perfect solution of this question'.[16] That did not prevent the Western Church setting out on a road to a complete ban on divorce and remarriage on the basis of his discussion. That course has meant that the Western Church has fundamentally differed from the Churches of the East on the practicalities of marital separations. In the Byzantine dominions and those areas of the eastern Mediterranean influenced by them, the civil law of the Empire continued to govern marriage, which meant allowance for divorce. Even the Emperor Justinian, who in many respects consciously drew on Christian theology to shape his new legislation, and who did make divorce much more difficult before his successors reversed his efforts, was still able bluntly to say that, 'of those things that occur between human beings, whatever is bound is soluble'.[17]

Besides such imperial pronouncements, one of the most respected authorities of the Eastern Churches had already encouraged the possibility of reconciling civil marriage with Church practice, even before Augustine had begun to take the West in an opposing direction. Basil 'the Great' as Bishop of Caesarea from 370 made a series of provisions on pastoral matters in sermons, in letters and in moral treatises that later generations and Church Councils regarded as collectively 'the Rule of St Basil': a foundation for later codifications of canon law throughout the Orthodox world. Basil exemplified an attitude to sexuality that shaped Orthodoxy into being both morally rigorous and practically permissive. Eastern theologians have always said a great deal in praise of marriage, drawing not merely on the Song of Songs, but also on Jesus's parable of the Kingdom of God as like a wedding feast: so marriage can be seen as a metaphor for the end of time, and therefore necessarily not to be repeated (above, Chapter 4). Yet this is coupled with an interpretation of the Fall in Eden that sharply contrasts with Augustine's.

Orthodox theologians have generally opted to view sexual intercourse of any description as a result of the Fall; that would necessarily include marital sex. Early on, this led them into a problem with that idiosyncratic pronouncement of Paul in 1 Corinthians 3.5 that we have so often encountered: the sexual 'marital debt'. Western commentators right through to their great enterprise of constructing canon law for the Church in the twelfth century recognized what that passage of Paul was saying about sex in marriage, and they took the idea very seriously, but Basil the Great's younger contemporary John Chrysostom had already led the way for Easterners in redirecting Paul's notion away from sexual expression. In his homilies on the passage, Chrysostom reinterpreted the debt as one of mutual 'due honour' or 'due favour', which primarily meant observation of mutual chastity, plus an obligation to financial support. Anything, really, but a sexual debt. In this Chrysostom was followed by later Byzantine ecclesiastical lawyers.[18]

Any marriage whatsoever is a concession to human sin, therefore, and as a result it is vulnerable to being repeated, as is the way of sin in this life – Eastern theologians have never had any time for petty Western distinctions between mortal and venial sin. Sin is sin, but it can be atoned for by penance. Accordingly, Basil the Great cited a different though adjacent opinion of Paul's, that it was better for a young widow to marry to avoid more sin (1 Cor. 7.8–9), and that therefore a second marriage might take place with due observance of penance – for divorce or bereavement alike, perhaps a one- or two-year bar from receiving the Eucharist. Even a third marriage might be permitted, with likewise more considerable penalties, though Basil did draw the line at allowing fourth marriages.

When in later centuries Orthodox marriages acquired specific liturgical occasions in church (see below), their character was then noticeably different between first and subsequent marriages: the festive crowning ceremony that was available for a first marriage was not at first permitted for a second. In the later medieval period, Orthodoxy did concede a crowning to second weddings, but the general liturgical atmosphere of the ceremonies remained stripped-down and penitential. There is a dour flexibility about this bundle of attitudes that contrasts with various later Western efforts to find legalistic ways round the Latin West's strict ban on ending a first marriage, such as deciding retrospectively that it had never properly happened – the procedure known as annulment.[19]

A remarkable might-have-been on divorce in Western Christianity, an exception proving the rule in the developing gulf between East and West, occurred during the seventh century in the recently constituted Anglo-Saxon Church (below, Chapter 11). In 668, Pope Vitalian consecrated as Archbishop of Canterbury a Greek-speaking refugee scholar originating from the same eastern Mediterranean city as the Apostle Paul: Theodore of Tarsus. It looks like an emergency stopgap appointment, and it may be that Vitalian wanted to distance such an exotic figure from Rome; nevertheless, Theodore remained an energetic leader for his remote province for a quarter of a century. When he was chosen for the post, there had been fears lest he should, 'according to the custom of the Greeks, introduce [to Canterbury] anything contrary to the true faith into the Church where he presided'. Indeed so: Theodore's penitential provisions for his English flock, carefully setting out circumstances in which second marriages were allowable, contrast starkly with any other contemporary or future Western regulations. It is significant that, despite Theodore's golden long-term reputation in Anglo-Saxon memory and the lasting effect of many of his legal provisions, his views on marriage were thrust aside in the general hardening of Western Latin attitudes against divorce.[20]

The contrast between traditions on marriage stemming respectively from Augustine and Basil underlines the fact that, otherwise, our marital journey from Jovinian via Ambrose and Jerome on to Augustine has been our first sexual adventure experienced almost exclusively within Latin Western Christianity. Augustine, so crucial in shaping the life and thought of the West, himself spoke little Greek and was not greatly aware of what his distinguished Greek theological contemporaries were saying. Even his knowledge of ancient Greek philosophy, the ocean in which Greek theologians unselfconsciously swam, was mostly at one remove, through the writings of 'Neo-Platonist' philosophers of the second and third centuries CE. That did not stop Augustine praising Plato and commenting in his mammoth discussion of God's purposes in *The City of God* that Platonists were esteemed among Christians 'above the rest of the philosophers'. Perhaps surprisingly, it was his Platonism that opened another gulf between West and East.[21]

Augustine's affirmation of Plato was part of his classically Platonic description of God: utterly transcendent, perfect and remote from contact with his human creation, despite the puzzling biblical contrary that we are created in God's image. That view of God alone might have propelled Augustine towards his proposition that God's perfection could never be swayed into changing the divine purpose for every individual human, which therefore encompassed not merely salvation but eternal damnation: a 'double' predestination, therefore. Yet, in the latter half of Augustine's career, theological conflicts further propelled him into peculiarly pitiless versions of that thought, just as Jovinian's bold statements on baptism had weaponized Jerome's attitude to sex. The result was a distinctively Western insistence on predestination as a framework for human destiny, coupled with a connection between sex and sin which was peculiarly North African in origin, and which Eastern theology did not make.

As in the case of Jovinian, the cockpit of conflict was in Rome. Jerome's abrupt and enforced leave-taking of the city in 385 (above, Chapter 8) left opportunities for other aspiring spiritual consultants to the Roman aristocracy, notably the British monk Pelagius. Pelagius's campaign to instil a strenuous genuine devotional practice in his wealthy clientele led to a theology emphasizing individual human responsibility in striving for salvation. This is what provoked Augustine's fury, especially because Pelagius had rashly taken his name in vain, criticizing a prayer in *Confessions*: 'you command me to be continent. Give me the grace to do as you command, and command me to do what you will!'[22] Pelagius interpreted this cry as surrendering all personal moral responsibility to God: the reverse of the fear of sin that he was trying to instil into his flock amid all the temptations to sin that their wealth offered them. Often Pelagius is seen as a generous-minded opponent of a harsh and judgemental Augustine – the reverse is true. Pelagius was by temperament a puritan, determined to frighten Christians into anxiously examining every deed and thought to check for sin.

Augustine was as much infuriated by what he saw as Pelagius's lack of realism, not taking seriously enough the irredeemably confused and fallen state of humanity, as by the apparent Pelagian rejection of the need for God's grace and mercy. His confrontation with Pelagius and a considerable body of supporters grew bitter, generating a literary war that became ever more extreme in its statements and enlisted Latin Christian leaders from as far away as the community around Jerome in the Holy Land. It took a long time for Augustine to secure the condemnation of his opponents that he sought. Meanwhile he became ever more extreme in expounding the idea of humankind as utterly damned by the Fall in the Garden of Eden, only capable of winning salvation through a merciful but arbitrary decision of God. The Fall was a taint of sin transmitted onwards from Adam and Eve in the act of procreating later generations. That association of guilt and sex (the 'traducianism' which had been part of North African theology for at least two centuries) produced in all humanity an inescapable 'original sin', before any specific act by any individual human.[23] However virtuous the actions of a non-Christian might appear, all human actions that lacked faith in God had the character of vices, because they displayed the same arrogant self-belief and rejection of God's commands that had caused Adam and Eve first to sin.[24]

Augustine sharpened his thoughts on these matters especially thanks to the critical intervention of Julian, Bishop of Aeclanum in southern Italy. Julian was himself the son of a bishop: an aristocrat with as good an education as Augustine, and perhaps a wider knowledge of the Christian world, backed by a compassionately humorous understanding of humanity. As Pelagius's most able defender, Julian has suffered the same sort of denigration in Latin Christianity as Helvidius and Jovinian, and, just like them, till recent years he was heard mostly through the quotation of his works by his opponent. Now in addition to those, two works of biblical commentary can be attributed to his pen, and a broader assessment of his significance is possible.[25] Julian had read his Augustine, notably *Confessions*, and in its narrative he discerned not only personal experience that led his opponent into a negative view of sexuality, but a lurking Manicheism, denying the goodness of creation and seeing evil as a substance created by the Fall. That may seem unfair to Augustine, whose writings resound with fascinated reference to the Creation stories in Genesis, but Julian pointed to his insistence that original sin stemmed from the Fall, of which sexual desire appears one of the chief symptoms (Julian had some fun with Augustine's speculations about Edenic sexual intercourse).

Augustine draws a nightmare contrast between humanity's state before and after the Fall. He repeatedly uses the terrible word 'lump' (*massa*) to describe humanity in its state of loss. It is a word to which he often returned, associating it with Latin words for 'loss', 'sin' and 'filth'.[26] By contrast, Julian emphasized not only that God's creation was good, but that all humanity was born into the state in which God created Adam: full of virtue yet mortal (doomed to die). He insisted that pain had already been part of Adam and Eve's experience in Eden, an idea that especially shocked Augustine. The human man Jesus of Nazareth suffered as other humans do, and yet, because he was divine, he transferred that burden and equally expressed it in his divine as much as his human nature. Crucial in the debate was a flat contradiction in the way that Julian and Augustine understood both sex and the saving work of Christ. Julian believed that a truly human Jesus Christ would also experience sexual desire as part of the totality of his humanity; otherwise, he observed, if one followed Augustine's arguments, Christ was no better than a eunuch.

In Julian's view, therefore, Augustine did not take the struggles of Christ seriously, and such a Christ could not fully save the human race. Julian pictured the Saviour's life and death as an example to all humanity of how to live in a Christlike way. It has become apparent from modern research that Julian was a close reader of the formidable Eastern theologian Theodore of Mopsuestia (who was also a theological inspiration to the unfortunate Nestorios); Julian translated some of Theodore's work from Greek into Latin, and it is likely that he knew him personally. So Julian was echoing a very different theological tradition to that of the North African Latins: he knew the Greek East, with its confidence in the possibility of ascetic life approaching union with God, or *theōsis*.[27] This is one symptom of the divisions that over the next centuries would become chasms between Eastern and Western Christianity.

VARIATIONS ON A MARITAL THEME

During the fourth and fifth centuries, Christianity avoided the extreme possibility of rendering itself a giant monastic community in which marriage was outlawed. Augustine, in his nuanced defence of marriage, would have been aware of statements by more than one extremist admirer of his opponent Pelagius maintaining that the married state was incompatible with being a true disciple of Jesus.[28] Nevertheless the tide of opinion against sexual marital expression had some strange outcomes. The fact that asceticism trumped the married state is evident from the fact that normal Christian prejudices against divorce were set aside if a husband decided to take up the monastic life, leading to careful provisions for the two parties involved, up to and including chaste conjugal visits. In the Eastern Churches, the Church's legal system eventually went so far as to say that if a wife went to enter a nunnery on her own initiative, her husband had no right to demand that she return; if she refused, he could go no further than persuasion or flattery, certainly not 'using violence or laying hands upon her'.[29]

In the background was the long-standing and often acrimonious debate about what constituted a marriage: sex or consent? Many saw Jerome's opting for a definition based on sexual intercourse as awkward, which indeed theologically it was. Consequently they privileged assent, in which case a Christian man and woman might not go to the drastic extreme of divorce as the gateway to celibate life, but, either from the beginning of their marriage or at some point during it, they could agree between themselves to enter an exclusive valid union whose exclusions extended to sexual intercourse. A vow of celibacy spilled sideways into matrimony. Reflecting male priorities as usual, the custom of marriage without sex was described in relation to the women involved: in the Western Latin Church *virgines* (or *mulieres*) *subintroductae*, in the Greek East *gynaikes syneisaktoi*, from which comes the English word (admittedly not now frequently on anglophone lips) 'syneisactism'.[30]

There is very early evidence for this practice from the days when Christians were a small and self-consciously separate elite, demonstrating their holiness by defying common human impulses. The *Shepherd of Hermas*, a work not much later than portions of the New Testament and once often accepted as part of it, encouraged the idea, with the female companions of the eponymous Hermas telling him, 'You will sleep with us as a brother, not as a spouse. You are our brother, we intend to live with you, for we love you dearly.' That exemplifies the problem: whatever Hermas's housemates were claiming, were such relationships some sort of marriage, or a show-off form of asceticism?

Various unimpressed bishops posed that question. One of the most influential among them, the second-century martyr-bishop Irenaeus of Lyons, supplied a killer anecdote about a group of devotees around the gnostic leader Valentinus: when they put the idea of a mixed celibate life into practice, they had not been successful in eschewing sex, with predictable practical consequences. Even without resorting to such routine smears against heretics, bishops could point to one of their own in the third century who was generally agreed to have gone to the bad: Bishop Paul of Samosata, accused, among much else both heterodox and financially dubious, of living with various young female followers.[31]

There are consequent repeated condemnations of syneisactism by the Church hierarchy, which condemnations nevertheless also witness by their repetition how much prestige the practice enjoyed among early Christians. Even before the alliance with Constantine, the Synod summoned to Antioch in 267/8, while in the course of ousting Bishop Paul of Samosata, had begun the official efforts at outlawing syneisactism. In the fourth century, a variety of leading theologians wrote angrily against it. They saw it as playing with fire: recklessly showing off one's continence in a situation of extreme temptation, and in all likelihood not succeeding. Their attacks on syneisactism made great play with a biblical passage precisely (though more generally) on the theme of men tempted by women: 'can a man carry fire in his bosom and his clothes not be burned?' (Prov. 6.27). Unsurprisingly, Jerome was one of those seizing on this rhetorical question and answering in the negative. In one of his most sexually charged letters to the Lady Eustochium, he coined another of his horridly memorable phrases, in describing the women involved as one-man whores (*meretrices univirae*).[32]

Leading the pack of opponents in the Greek East was John Chrysostom, who wrote more on the subject than anyone else in the early Church, just as he did on male same-sex relationships. Chrysostom may indeed have found syneisactism even more disturbing and dangerous than same-sex activity, because relationships of syneisactism were avowedly for life. Like many of his contemporaries, he picked up one of the dangers of confusing asceticism and matrimony: asceticism dissolved all the normal conventions of wifely subservience, and characteristically put male and female on the same spiritual level. Chrysostom's argument teetered dangerously close to common Classical assumptions that close relationships between males were more 'natural' than those between males and females, but his trump card was to ridicule men embarking on syneisactism as feminizing themselves: sitting beside women as they spun and wove, absorbing their various little feminine ways, running errands for them. All that was a Graeco-Roman man's worst nightmare.[33]

Yet not everyone listened even to Chrysostom. From his own time, and so two generations after Macrina, comes the vivid literary life-story of the Roman aristocrat Melania the Younger; the work of a fifth-century ascetic, it has been described as 'the most vivid and animated biography of a woman to have survived from antiquity'.[34] Melania was married as a teenager to the slightly older teenager Pinian, who was sympathetic to her pleas on their wedding night to live as brother and sister, but felt a sense of duty to produce heirs for his consular family. After two successive children died in infancy, Pinian decided that he had done his best, and the relationship was free to develop as they wished, far away from family pressures back in Rome. Inherited wealth financed a life of suitably austere comfort in Jerusalem, and Pinian was buried in the grounds of the community of monks and nuns that Melania had devoted her energies to creating.[35]

This tradition continued to fascinate couples in the eastern Mediterranean; at least three saints' Lives variously dating between the sixth and the tenth centuries discuss outright celibate marriages with warm approval. The most complicated was that of Andronikos and Athanasia, where a sadly recognizable family tragedy expands into a miniature Greek romantic novel with echoes of the story of Melania and Pinian: the husband and wife, a golden couple from wealthy families in Antioch, separate in grief over the deaths of their two children. Later they are reunited in twelve years of monastic companionship, but without Andronikos recognizing his lost wife, for (in classic transvestite ascetic style) she is disguised as a man – as an Ethiopian, no less – and she does not enlighten him about her real identity before their edifying deaths. The other two stories are from Syria and Egypt, backdated to the time of pre-Constantinian persecution: from the outset of their marriages the couples portrayed pledge to live together without any sexual contact.[36] If it is argued that Lives of saints are just Lives of saints, literary constructions, one has to reckon with an extraordinary fifth-century tomb inscription to a couple at Aosta in Italy, which claims that, in the course of a long marriage, 'the wife relinquished her husband and lived for more than twenty years in perpetual chastity.'[37]

Structurally chaste marriages lasted in the minds and conversation of Christians and were esteemed and practised for more than a millennium. At the end of the tenth century, the English Benedictine monk Ælfric was still lovingly retelling by then venerable tales of Julian/Basilissa, Cecilia/Valerian and Chrysanthus/Daria in his major cycle of Lives of the saints in Latin and Anglo-Saxon; the English were also very fond of the seventh-century local heroine Æthelthryth (Etheldreda), who had sabotaged the marital expectations of two successive royal husbands by her flinty choice of chastity (below, Chapter 11).[38] From the twelfth century, Western Christians began to have second thoughts, as we will discover, but Eastern Christians remained much more enthusiastic for marriages without sex. It was a remarkably long-lived rejection of the procreational principle for marriage that Clement had imported into Christianity from Pythagoreanism and which lurks amid much modern theology about marriage, Catholic and Protestant.

Embedded in these debates on syneisactism was a complicated conversation straddling the boundaries of clergy, ascetics and laity, marriage and celibacy. Much of it, though not all, was closely linked to the status and role of clergy. Was sexual intercourse a taint on the episcopal or priestly role in presiding at the celebration of the Eucharist? Back in the third century, Origen had suggested that prayer and sexual activity were practices to be kept strictly apart (above, Chapter 7), as indeed they were in the lives of ascetics; should that principle apply to all clergy? By Origen's time, the main clerical orders of bishop, priest and deacon had become universal in the Church, though debate remained as to how far women could be part of these structures as well as men. By then, too, celibate asceticism had emerged in the eastern Mediterranean: but asceticism was a separate phenomenon to clerical orders. Should the rule of celibacy apply to both? If it did, that would involve a great deal of social engineering in the middle of the Constantinian revolution after 306. Nearly all Christian clergy of the third century for whom it has been possible to establish whether they were married or not, turn out in fact to have been married: that may seem a startling conclusion, but it is consistent with the regulations set out in the Pastoral Epistles in the later first century, which had assumed that both bishops and deacons should have a wife.[39]

One significant moment was the Council of Nicaea, presided over by the Emperor Constantine himself in 325, which did so much for both the future direction of theology and the organization of the Church in both East and West. The third of its canons, much copied by Councils thereafter, 'altogether forbids any bishop, presbyter or deacon, or any of the clergy, to have a woman dwelling with him, excepting a mother, or sister, or aunt, or such persons only as are above all suspicion'. That sounds comprehensive, but there could be plenty of argument about what woman was 'above all suspicion': did that define or exclude a wife? The ambiguity had been absent from the pronouncements of a Council of bishops held at Elvira in Spain around twenty years before, which among much rigorist regulation had declared that clergy should 'entirely keep themselves from their wives and not have children', on pain of dismissal from their clerical orders. On Elvira's reckoning, if clerical marriage were to continue it must strictly be without sex, in the syneisactic manner.[40]

There was a strong movement at Nicaea to go down this same route, perhaps not surprisingly since Hosius, the chief ecclesiastical advisor of the Emperor at the Council, was himself a bishop from Spain. Supposedly it was defeated by the dramatic intervention of Paphnutius, an avowedly celibate Egyptian bishop and heroic survivor of persecution, 'roaring at the top of his voice' that his choice of continence should not be arbitrarily imposed by others. This story comes from a century later, in the writings of the Church historian Socrates of Constantinople, and may itself be a fiction that was part of an ongoing and unresolved argument.[41] At one extreme of that debate was a logical extension of the newly emerging role of the Church within Roman imperial structures: encouragement of clerical dynasties. It was a natural assumption among the Roman upper classes that son should follow father in the same honourable position. In 349 that led the Emperor Constantius II to propose legislation that the Christian priesthood should become a hereditary caste, like some levels of imperial officialdom. Although this met too much opposition from bishops to become a reality, the idea, and versions of it in practice, did not die away, as we will see in different settings and centuries.[42] At the other extreme was the effort of Bishop Eustathius of Sebaste in Armenia, who allegedly encouraged people to boycott liturgies performed by married priests; Eustathius faced condemnation at a Synod at Gangra in Asia Minor around 340, and his historian admirer Sozomen later sought to excuse him, clearly embarrassed.[43]

Between these two polarities was the effort of Ambrose of Milan to make ordination the moment to separate sexual activity from marriage, so that clergy previously could 'have had sons, [but] not continue to have sons'.[44] This concession was not so authoritative as to prevent bishops having wives and more children, as mindful as any other Roman *paterfamilias* of their dynastic duties. Thus, Ambrose's contemporary the wealthy and cultured Synesius of Cyrene in Libya was not going to resort to subterfuge. He made it clear to the Patriarch of Alexandria that he would only become Bishop of the Libyan city of Ptolemais if it did not interfere with his marriage; his prayers would continue to include his firm wish 'to have virtuous children'. He was not alone.[45]

Far to the west, one contrasts a continuing and repeated hard line from Spanish bishops against clerical marriage generally with gravestones dateable to the fifth and sixth centuries in the western fringe of the former Roman Britannia, what is now north Wales: one specifically refers to a bishop's wife, and another to a cleric's wife, which emphasizes that she was 'a most holy woman'.[46] Generally, no doubt, as the decades rolled on in a marriage, most senior clergy and their wives were reasonably content to leave sex behind, and in the life and practice of the Church that joint decision was not something that required public discussion. Enough had been said along those lines by Pope Leo I ('the Great') in the 440s or 450s: 'so that from a carnal marriage a spiritual marriage might be made, they must both keep their wives with them, and have them as if they did not have them, by which the charity of marriages may be kept safe, and marital sex cease.'[47]

Christian late Latin even evolved words with feminine endings to describe the wives of bishops, priests and deacons, respectively *episcopae*, *presbyterae* and *diaconissae*. These usages can be found into the seventh century, mostly in Francia (the former Gaul), and emphasized the public profile of and presumably general respect for such wives – like the US presidential 'First Lady' in the White House. In one celebrated ninth-century mosaic in Rome in the church of S. Prassede, the title *episcopa* is applied to the honoured mother of a pope, Paschal I (reigned 817–24). It is not surprising that, amid the modern reconstitution of the ordination of women, this vocabulary has aroused interest and the suggestion that these women were performing episcopal functions, but the case has never been strong, and the testimony to the persistence of marriage in the Western episcopal hierarchy is more convincing and just as interesting.[48]

In the Eastern Churches, there was a completely different trajectory on these matters, both in the Churches that accepted the Chalcedonian compromise of 451 (above, Chapter 8) and those that did not. One striking symptom of the difference was the prolonged survival of a functioning diaconate for women, complete with rites of ordination in a similar fashion to male clergy. This puzzled, and indeed disconcerted, Western Catholic scholars when, in the late seventeenth century, the study of manuscripts revealed these diaconal ordinations. The standard way of writing off the phenomenon was to confuse these female deacons with the Western Latin usage of *diaconissa* for the wife of a deacon. That ignored the evidence of the ordination rite and the abundant reality of their liturgical presence in the Byzantine Church until at least the ninth century.[49] One outstanding and much-celebrated fourth-century example was Olympias of Constantinople, who turned her lavish palace adjacent to the church of Hagia Sophia into a centre of charity and female community; her charitable energy (not to mention her exceptional wealth and property portfolio) led the Patriarch Nectarios to bend the rules and ordain her deacon at the age of thirty, thirty years before the normal accepted age. The leading theologian Gregory of Nyssa indeed dedicated a biblical commentary to her, significantly on the Song of Songs.[50]

The Eastern Churches in general also came to a different solution to the West in the disputes over whether clergy should marry. They took their cue from an imperial *novella* (law) of the Emperor Justinian in the sixth century forbidding the consecration of married men with children to the episcopate, though he said that married men without children could be eligible if they separated from their wives. This provision was repeated more than a century later by a general Council of 691–92 (having met in the *Trullum*, a domed hall in the imperial palace, it is generally called the Council *In Trullo*). Its main purpose was to gather together for the first time a general code of discipline for the Orthodox Church, so its legislation was much repeated.[51]

From then on, Orthodox and non-Chalcedonian Eastern Churches alike have come over time to observe a two-track convention for clerical careers: bishops are customarily chosen from among monks, while those opting for pastoral ministry in local churches are almost invariably married. The process was slow and untidy, and particularly belated for the politically sensitive position of the Patriarchate in Constantinople, but the groundwork was laid in the sixth and seventh centuries. The monastic episcopate was becoming the norm long before 1200, after which it was almost unquestioned in the Orthodox world. One good reason was that when ancient, pre-Christian institutions of learning atrophied or were closed down by Christian emperors in the fourth and fifth centuries, the only places that continued to shelter scholarship – and thus equip Church leaders with some ability to discuss or assess theology – were monasteries. This was a far cry from those early days of monasticism in the second to fourth centuries when monasteries were not places for scholarship, and when monk and bishop might have seemed to be two dangerously opposed sources of authority in the Church.[52]

Beyond the old eastern frontiers of the Roman Empire there had flourished from the fifth century an increasingly widely dispersed and numerous non-Chalcedonian Church, primarily Syriac-speaking. It came to despise the Greek-speaking Church of Byzantium, whose theology it regarded as tainted by imperial interference, especially at Chalcedon in 451; it proudly adhered to the 'Dyophysite' theology of the displaced Patriarch of Constantinople Nestorios and his older theological inspiration Theodore of Mopsuestia (whom we have also met as the mentor of Julian of Aeclanum, gadfly against Augustine in the Pelagian Controversy). Courtesy, and indeed theological accuracy, demands that this Church should be called not 'Nestorian', as Chalcedonians in West and East have tended to do, but Dyophysite, or simply 'the Church of the East'. It may seem surprising that both the Church of the East and the other non-Chalcedonian Eastern Churches of diametrically opposed 'Miaphysite' theology (as they would prefer, the 'Oriental Orthodox') seem eventually to have concurred with their imperial rivals on clerical marriage and celibacy, but their particular circumstances encouraged this.

In the case of the Church of the East, the fundamental contrast with the imperial Churches of the Mediterranean is that it never enjoyed the alliance with power that led to 'Christendom' in Byzantine Orthodoxy and Catholicism. The eastern frontier of the Empire swayed over time, but, from the third century to the seventh, the great power was the Sasanian Shah (king) in Iran (Persia), self-consciously heir to Iranian monarchies that had fought Mediterranean empires all the way back to the time of Athenian democratic greatness. Their religion was Zoroastrian, a far older monotheistic faith than Judaism, and indeed an influence on it. The establishment of Christianity in the Roman Empire encouraged Zoroastrian Sasanians in pogroms against what they saw as a Christian fifth column in their midst. Though these bouts of persecution in the fourth and fifth centuries were savage, they were intermittent, while the Church of the East's own quarrel with the Byzantine Chalcedonian Church gave it every incentive to come to an understanding with the Iranian monarchy.

The high level of scholarship in the Dyophysite Christian elite was an advantage for integration. A Christian school of higher education established in Gondeshapur in south-west Iran was a repository of Graeco-Roman learning which included medicine, and Christian physicians proved very useful to the Sasanian rulers.[53] Nevertheless, reconciliation with a Zoroastrian monarchy posed even greater problems for Christians than the Roman imperial system. At the centre of the difficulty was marriage and celibacy, one of the major issues in Sasanian persecution: the Shahs could detest Manichees and Christians equally because they both belittled the institution of marriage through the programmatic celibacy of their clergy. Sexual abstention offended the Zoroastrian principle that humanity had a moral obligation to have children and to work the land: Zoroastrians saw the monastic vocation of prayer and abstention as an insult to this divine command, and such an offence to the divinity deserved to be punished by death.

To counter this, a Synod of the Church of the East held at Seleucia-Ctesiphon (the Sasanian capital) resolved in 486 that all clergy should be married and beget children; the presiding Patriarch Akakios (Aqaq or Acacius, reigned 485–96) echoed Paul of Tarsus in pronouncing that 'it is much better to take a wife than to burn with desire.' That did present the problem that, despite Sasanian hostility, the Church contained many monastic communities, and, as the Church expanded through Central Asia, its expansion was driven by missionaries who tended to be monks. In such circumstances, the leadership bent the rules: whereas in the heartland of the Church, bishops were elected by the local clergy and laity, both of course mainly married, in these more remote regions, the Patriarch himself chose bishops for the local episcopal hierarchy.

Thus monastic leadership survived in the Church of the East, aided by a resolution of the energetically reforming Patriarch Aba I at a moment of favourable relations with the Sasanian regime in 544 that henceforth the Patriarch himself should be a celibate. Other bishops were forbidden marriage only as late as the twelfth century.[54] It is worth noting how remote much of the argument in these disputes was from the discourse of holiness and virginity in the Mediterranean Churches. There were severe practicalities to consider in a Church dominated by external power: survival and distinct identity. Patriarch Yosep presented his Synod in 554 with a canon on the marriage of bishops, which pointed out that a married episcopate was liable to lead to corrupt appropriation of Church land for the benefit of the family: worse still, a female descendant of the erring bishop might marry a Zoroastrian, and so former Church property might be lost to the 'entire community of Christianity'.[55]

Despite the central importance of marriage for Zoroastrians, their practice of it was disconcertingly at odds with Christian custom. The Church did not have the advantage it had enjoyed in entering Graeco-Roman society where the dominant culture was monogamous; Zoroastrians allowed polygyny, and they also made close-kin marriage not merely an honourable custom but a religious duty, whereas as we have seen the Romans particularly detested it (above, Chapter 3). One can sample Syrian Christians wrestling with the resulting difficulties in their relations with the Zoroastrian authorities through an extraordinary Syriac text entitled *The Cave of Treasures*, probably composed in the sixth century. This once popular and widely circulated book is nothing less than a retelling of the whole biblical story from Creation to the coming of the Holy Spirit to the disciples after Jesus's Ascension, with special reference to the Sasanian world; it includes extra material, but also omits much biblical content that did not suit the author's purposes.[56]

The agendas within the *Cave* are multiform, but overall are intended not merely to glorify Syriac Christianity over against that of the Roman Empire, but to conciliate the Sasanian dynasty and disarm potential hostility to the Church. One symptom of that, for instance, is that the three 'wise men' who came from the East to worship the baby Jesus are here not actually magi (magicians or astronomers, who might be taken to be Zoroastrian priests), but kings, bearing the names of three late fifth-century Sasanian shahs.[57] On marriage, the *Cave* devotes some energy to distancing the practice of close-kin marriage from the founders of the Zoroastrian religion, including Zoroaster himself, implying that it is an illegitimate and undesirable innovation. Having demonstrated that to his own satisfaction, the author feels free to criticize the custom, emphasizing its close link to the Zoroastrian priesthood in particular, and associating it with demonic forces; all of which is a sure sign that some of his Christian readers were perfectly happy with it.[58]

Accordingly, the Church of the East's hierarchy set its face firmly against kin marriage, treating it, like the issue of married bishops alienating Church lands, as a matter of survival for the Christian community securing its identity against the surrounding culture. Mar Aba I's ruling on Patriarchal celibacy in 544 was twinned with a battery of regulations that has been described as 'the first substantial body of Christian family law'. They were aimed at both close-kin marriage and polygyny, and they were only the centrepiece of repeated condemnations of these practices by Church synods under the Sasanians, especially in 410, 484 and 585.[59] That meant that the bishops made powerful lay enemies within the Church itself. As we have repeatedly noticed, polygyny is generally an elite activity, and, for many wealthy Christians in the Church of the East, to enter into polygynous marriage was simply one of the marks that they had found a place in the elite of the Sasanian Empire.

Such exalted figures were not going to let the tidy-mindedness of patriarchs threaten their hard-won positions. Thus, at the turn of the sixth and seventh centuries, the leading campaigners against the practice, Patriarch Sabrisho' I and Bishop Gregory of the city of Nisibis (now Nusaybin in Kurdish Turkey), found themselves facing the fury of polygynous Christians, particularly royal physicians, at the Court of Shah Khusrau II (reigned 590–628). Khusrau was a cultivated if ruthless monarch, and naturally a polygynist, whose most influential wife was Shirin, a Christian; he showed a sporadically generous attitude to her faith while also listening to the less-than-positive things that she said about the bishops of the Church of the East. Gregory of Nisibis was abruptly sidelined and forced to retire from his diocese to a monastery, and his hopes of succeeding as Patriarch on the death of Sabrisho' in 604 were dashed.

Yet this was not merely a clash within high politics; there are signs that the fault line descended through the ranks of Iranian Christians. This was not surprising in view of the association of Syriac Christianity with international trade right across Asia; it was very convenient for travelling merchants to base more than one wife in commercial locations that might be as far apart as Damascus and the Chinese coast. One remarkable documentary survival is a collection of ordinances for an association of artisans, probably of late sixth- or seventh-century date, but not now attributable to any particular town or city or craft. Among its various provisions for administrative and communal activity is the stipulation that members 'shall obey without dispute all the holy laws laid down by the leaders of the Church', which included the ban on 'the foul practice of having two wives'. Clearly, alas, many Syriac Christians were doing just that.[60]

The first few decades of the seventh century mark turning points in

Christian history at either extreme of the Christian world, Asian and Atlantic. We have not heard the last of tribulations for Dyophysite patriarchs, but they would now be enacted under new circumstances impossible to have predicted when Khusrau II came to the Sasanian throne in 590: the sudden emergence of a new religion and world power that eliminated the Sasanians and came close to repeating that success against Byzantium. In Western Christianity, an unusual initiative of the Pope in Rome began a great expansion of Latin Christianity beyond the bounds of the old Empire, when in 597 Gregory I sent the Roman monk Augustine to a small coastal kingdom in the former Britannia, with its capital at Canterbury. Both these widely separated histories were to result in further twists in the story of Christian marriage and the family.

10

Eastern Christianity: Enter Islam (600–1200)

We must now take up a story of the Eastern Churches that will take them far from the Western Christian experience. The usual assumption in reading history from a Western viewpoint is that the Roman imperial adventure finally ended in 1453 with the death of the last Palaeologos Emperor in Constantinople, just as the Western Roman Empire had been snuffed out in Italy with the deposition of young Romulus Augustulus in 476. This associates Rome's imperial identity too closely with Christianity, which was as much a religious interloper in the Empire as the new variety of west Asian monotheism proclaimed in the seventh century by the Prophet Muhammad: *Islam* ('submission to the Will of God'). Following the extraordinary expansion of Islam thereafter, it would be more accurate to see an imperial succession to Rome in Constantinople as lasting until 1924. In that year, the secularizing National Assembly of the Turkish Republic finally deprived the former Ottoman Sultan of the title of *Caliph*, or representative of the Prophet. Since then, there has been no consensus in Islam on a successor, or indeed as to whether there should be a successor.

Abdulmejid II, deposed as Sultan by the new regime of Kemal Atatürk a year or two earlier, had been the last monarch of the Ottoman imperial family, who had made a claim to the Caliphate a century before they conquered 'The City' of Constantine. Several previous dynasties claiming the title of Caliph had sought what the Ottoman Sultan Mehmet II actually achieved in 1453: the establishment of Islamic imperial power in Constantinople. As Sultan Mehmet's counsellor the Greek philosopher Georgios Amiroutzes observed to him in later years, with understandable hyperbole, 'No one doubts you are the Emperor of the Romans. Whoever holds by right the centre of the Empire is the Emperor.'[1] Islamic rule never actually made it to the First Rome as it did to the Second, but it did swallow up the lands where Christianity began, and it came to dominate swathes of the ancient Mediterranean Empire, as far as the Atlantic Ocean for centuries in parts of Europe, as well as in Africa to the present day. The civilization that Islam created relied on what had gone before in the Graeco-Roman world, especially in scholarship, science and philosophy, but in turn Islamic learning enriched Christian culture with its own developments of this ancient legacy.

Much remains mysterious about the coming of Islam, its prehistory and its astonishingly rapid conquests, but at the centre of it is what has always been recognized by Muslims ('those who submit' to God): the poetic inspiration of the Prophet Muhammad in crafting the message and forms of the *Qur'an*. That title means 'that which is to be recited', even though the Qur'an is now a carefully curated written text; in similar fashion, it is likely that the foundation narratives about Jesus's Passion in the New Testament were originally created for liturgical recital before being incorporated in what we call the four Gospels. The recitation of the Qur'an is a communal bond within the *ummah*, the worldwide Islamic community, whatever else divides it. Far more than the Judaeo-Christian Bible, the Qur'anic text is associated with the language of its original composition, Arabic, and it has often been remarked that the relationship of this book to the divine is close to that of Jesus Christ in Christianity, as a final revelation of God: an 'inlibration', rather than an 'incarnation'.

Muhammad was from a family of western Arabia long prominent in defending and promoting the ancient shrine in their city of Mecca (Makkah), the Ka'ba, and the sacred black stone that it sheltered. Thanks to the phenomenon of the Prophet's visionary composition, which began around 610 CE when he was already middle-aged, Mecca was destined to rival in world significance the west Asian cultic centre of Jerusalem, and provided another worldwide bond for Muslims in the command to journey to Arabia on pilgrimage. Yet Jerusalem too held an important place in Muhammad's thinking for its role in the previous revelations of Judaism and Christianity, 'the people who were given the Scripture before you'. It is the Qur'an that also gives us the phrase 'the People of the Book' to embrace the three south-west Asian monotheisms; the context is a pronouncement that it is perfectly permissible for Muslim men to take wives in due form from among those of the two other faiths.[2]

Evidently that is another example of the 'male gaze' in a sacred text, but the Qur'anic message on sex, gender and the family should not be caricatured or simplified any more than that in Hebrew and Christian Bibles. In the same manner as those collections of sacred texts, from its very early days Islam built up a formidable battery of commentary on the meaning of the Qur'an, partly in order to remedy what the faithful perceived as gaps in the matters on which it pronounces. Post-Qur'anic interventions, beginning with the early explanatory instructions known as *hadith*, propel the Qur'anic message in as many varied directions as Christianity has taken its foundation documents. The variety has been enhanced, as in Christianity, by proliferating divisions within Islam, from the foundational clash between Sunni and Shi'a onwards, and, even within those divisions, variety of opinion has been encouraged by the general absence of any class of professional theologian to attempt definitive rulings on doctrine.

It is worth looking past all that, as modern Christian and Jewish biblical critics have done for their sacred texts, to hear what the Qur'an actually says in its treatment of both women and men. In the same fashion as in Christianity, there may be messages that have rarely been heard, and so may be listened to afresh; for instance, the Qur'anic observation that God 'created spouses from among yourselves for you to live with in tranquillity'. Here 'spouses' has commonly been translated as 'wives', and 'you' as having a male reference, but there is no necessary male bias in the Arabic word *azwāj* for 'spouse', and there is every reason to read this passage in the light of the theme of reciprocity in marriage and sexual enjoyment by both partners that is to be found elsewhere in the Qur'anic text.[3] That reciprocity is reminiscent of Paul of Tarsus's distinctive concept of the 'marital debt'.

Nevertheless, the Qur'an maintains a resounding and surely deliberate silence on the subject of Paul, who would have been a familiar figure to Muhammad through his lifelong contacts with Christians and their literature. That contrasts with the singular honour that the Qur'an gives to Mary the mother of Jesus. Her role in it is a point of contact with the special place that by the seventh century she held in Christian devotion; in fact, she appears in the Qur'anic text more frequently and with more intense contemplation of her significance than she does in the New Testament, and an entire *sūrah* (chapter) of it takes her name, the only *sūrah* to bear the name of a woman.[4] It is one of the Qur'an's curious features that it never refers to any other woman by a personal name, but amid its portrayals of women in sacred history, from Adam's spouse through Mary up to Muhammad's own time, the text frequently celebrates their resourcefulness and spiritual excellence, and it depicts God intervening in circumstances where women are oppressed or at risk.

In his pioneering analysis of attitudes to sex across the great world faiths, Vern Bullough was prepared to classify Islam as a 'sex-positive religion', unlike the Judaeo-Christian tradition or the ascetic tradition in Greek philosophy on which Christianity had drawn. Muhammad 'regarded sex as a good rather than an evil aspect of life', for both men and women, and indeed marriage was the highest good, including the traditional Arabian institution of polygyny.[5] In symmetry with this, the Qur'an is not positive towards the ascetic celibacy that we have seen become so central to Christianity; it veers between denouncing monks as greedy charlatans and admiring the piety of some Christian ascetics, so accordingly the relationship of Muslims with celibate communities remained uncomfortable and untidy.[6] Besides that ambivalence, over centuries Islam allowed considerable cultural space for same-sex relations both male and female, via a generously creative perspective on the Qur'an's criticisms of same-sex activity, which are in any case a good deal more tepid than the denunciations to be found in Hebrew Scripture or New Testament.

It is important not to allow the accidents of modern history to obscure those historical characteristics of the Muslim world. The loudest current noise in Islam comes from its Wahhabist or Salafist variant, a revivalist movement created in eighteenth-century Arabia. That is no more representative of Islamic tradition than it would be to consider Christianity as solely embodied in contemporary American Southern Baptists: a Christian variant that likewise happens ultimately to be a product of eighteenth-century revival.

UNINTENDED CONSEQUENCES: ISLAMICATE LANDS AND CHURCH WEDDINGS

None of this would have mattered greatly for Christian futures had the impact of Muhammad's revelations been confined to the Arabian Peninsula, or had Muslim expansion been as gradual and peaceful as that over the first three and a half centuries of Christianity. Muhammad is generally agreed to have died in 632 CE, leaving a flourishing community for

Islam in Mecca. It had survived much conflict, not least with local Jews and Christians, but nothing in those skirmishes would have provided a clue to what happened next: within no more than five years of Muhammad's death, Islamic forces had headed out of Arabia into the Mediterranean seaboard and what are now Syria, Iraq and Iran, repeatedly defeating major armies of Byzantium and the Sasanians. In 638 the Caliph Umar entered Jerusalem as conqueror, restoring to sacred uses the site of the Temple that Christians had so long left desecrated as a rubbish dump. The Sasanian Empire collapsed, and the last heir of the dynasty spent his days in exile as far away as China – ironically in view of his ancestors' persecution of Christianity, he died as a devout member and benefactor of the Church of the East.[7] The Byzantines seemed in just as much peril as the Sasanians.

Byzantine Alexandria and Egypt fell to Muslim armies within a year or two of the capture of Jerusalem, and then over a century Muslims remorselessly fought their way along the North African coast, into the Iberian Peninsula and on into central Francia (France), only being checked in battle at Poitiers in 733, a century after the death of Muhammad.[8] That belated Islamic defeat spared Christian Rome and the remaining Latin West, and during the seventh and eighth centuries, Christian Constantinople also survived repeated Muslim sieges. Yet much of the Christian world, including the land of Jesus's life and ministry, was now under the control of the new monotheism. It was a remaking of global power as rapid as that of Alexander the Great, while far surpassing the range and long-term impact of Alexander's conquests in both Asia and Europe.

Now Christian Churches that over three centuries had become accustomed to wielding power in their territories had to become reacquainted with the experience of their rulers espousing a different religion. Not all Christians would have found this a trauma, since the imperial Church had done its best to make life difficult for both Miaphysites and Dyophysites, and non-Chalcedonians generally may not have been displeased to have new masters professing what initially may have seemed no more than an eccentric variant on their own creed. Early Islam remained the religion of a small military elite in its wide new dominions, and it was not a proselytizing faith, following the Qur'anic precept that 'there is no compulsion in religion'.[9] Muslims were usually content to avoid trouble among their subjects by letting Christianity go its own way, on the understanding that it should accept a co-operative second-class status in society. That left Christians as the most numerous of the early Caliphate's subjects in west Asia until at least the tenth or eleventh centuries: until then, this was an 'Islamicate' rather than a predominantly 'Islamic' society.

Above all, for Dyophysite Christianity, the new dispensation was a change from often downright hostile Zoroastrian monarchs to a rather more congenial form of monotheism. If Dyophysites read what the Qur'an said about Mary – chief among examples of believers, into whom God breathed his Spirit – they might have been reminded of Patriarch Nestorios's effort to give Mary an appropriate honour that avoided the title *Theotokos*.[10] Indeed, the Church of the East found it easier to find a cultural niche alongside Islam than it had done under the Sasanians. It is remarkable to read the relieved words of the Dyophysite Patriarch Isho'yahb III in 649, soon after the Muslim conquest: 'Not only do they not oppose Christianity, but they praise our faith, honour the priests and saints of our Lord, and give aid to churches and monasteries.'[11] When the Abbasid dynasty overthrew the Umayyads as Caliphs in 750, they moved the centre of power eastwards from Damascus into Mesopotamia and in 762 created a new capital, Baghdad. This move east particularly favoured the Dyophysite Church hierarchy over its more westerly Miaphysite or Byzantine rivals.

The Abbasids granted the Dyophysite Patriarch a newly enhanced authority which really did create a Church of the East. His writ extended over all Christians in the Caliphate, which now extended from Cairo into Central Asia, and he was in charge of Christian missions beyond the Caliphate's eastern frontiers as far as China. It is no exaggeration to say that, in the eighth and ninth centuries, the great and long-lived Patriarch Timothy I (reigned 780–823), who supervised bishops from Tibet to the Mediterranean and saw some of his Christian layfolk well-placed among the Baghdad governing class, looked out on a flock as numerous and certainly far more extended than that of the Bishop of Rome in the far west.[12]

Nevertheless, the patriarchs of the Church of the East and the other religious leaders of west Asia faced some very porous boundaries between Christians, Jews, Muslims and Zoroastrians. This was an age when many people had an interest in not declaring a definite religious identity. Rabbinic Judaism was still in the process of formation across a varied and widespread set of Jewish communities, while among Christians the partisan bitterness left by the Council of Chalcedon in 451 did not necessarily percolate downwards from the leadership to the relaxed practice of local churches. Out in the countryside the faithful might just regard their liturgy as something that Christians did, without bothering too much about the dismal history of Christological debates that had created rival episcopal hierarchies. Muslims would certainly sympathize, and might value personal relationships above confessional ones. The scholarly Bishop Jacob in the course of his pastoral duties in late seventh-century Edessa (modern Urfa) had to write to a subordinate about the tricky case of a Christian woman married to a Muslim who was threatening to kill their local priest for banning her from the Eucharist; she was disobeying Church rules by her mixed marriage, but if the Church enforced the ban, murder might follow.[13]

In this situation, Christian teaching on sex and the family presented both a challenge and an opportunity for episcopal authority and religious identity. As in Sasanian days, Islam accepted polygyny as one of the options of marriage, though, unlike Zoroastrians, Muslims did not make a point of close-kin unions. Marriage could provide an essential point of difference for Dyophysite Church leaders to clarify for the putatively faithful; in an Islamicate society, monogamy would be a mark of Christian distinctiveness, whereas, in the areas of the Graeco-Roman Mediterranean not under the control of Islam, it was simply everyone's traditional form of marriage. Accordingly, the bishops re-emphasized their ban on polygyny for their flocks.

Just as in the Sasanian era, elite lay figures in the Church of the East were outraged that bishops should thus try to infringe their privileged perquisite of polygyny as part of their positions of influence in the Caliphate. More than one anecdote of their hostility to moral instruction on marriage survives in patriarchal chronicles, some with edifying repentance attached to the story, which may or may not represent the real outcome. One court physician of the great Caliph Hārūn al-Rashīd (reigned 786–809) furiously confronted his Patriarch Timothy and appalled that austere celibate by shouting that he was a pederast; another court physician (who additionally served as a deacon of the Church) applied an epithet to a subsequent Patriarch best left in the decent obscurity of a monograph.[14] This was two centuries after the humbling of Patriarch Sabrisho' and Bishop Gregory of Nisibis at the hands of Christian laity on the same issue, in the time of the Sasanians (above, Chapter 9).

The bishops acted early in the era of the Caliphate to assert themselves against such independence of mind. As we have seen, even before the Chalcedonian schism, as early as the fifth century the Church of the East had been a pioneer among Christians in creating 'canon law', ecclesiastical legislation, including on the subject of the family (Chapter 9). In 676, by which time the Umayyads were ruling as an Islamic military caste in Damascus, Patriarch Giwargis (George) I convened a Synod on the little island of Dayrin in what we now call the Persian or Arabian Gulf, to consolidate his authority among recalcitrant local Christian communities around the Gulf – not least by enacting a number of ground-breaking canons. Among them was the stipulation that henceforth any marriage of the faithful would absolutely require the agreement of priests and a Christian ritual:

> Women who have not [yet] been married or given in betrothal by their fathers shall be betrothed to men through Christian law, according to the custom of the faithful . . . through the consent of their parents, the mediation of the holy cross of our Saviour, and a priestly blessing.[15]

This was an emphatic statement of marriage primarily as a transaction between one *paterfamilias* and another, according to the general custom in west Asia, but it was also an unequivocal bid for the Church to insert itself in the process: a startlingly radical move in the history of Christianity. Indeed, it is perhaps only after 676 that we can speak unequivocally of a thing called Christian marriage affirmed by the Church, even after the pioneering thoughts from Paul in 1 Corinthians 7. Patriarch George was seizing a crucial moment: his opportunity occurred between the disintegration of ancient Sasanian and Byzantine elites and the full consolidation of Umayyad power at a local level. George usefully filled this vacuum with ecclesiastical power, which his successors did not relinquish – indeed, they extended their canonical oversight and law-making to the whole structure of the family, and their Islamic rulers were happy to see the Christian community thus governed. Soon Miaphysite Western Syrians also saw the usefulness of this move by the Church of the East, and they began creating their own marriage legislation. These were anticipations of, or maybe inspirations for, the development of canon law still further west, in the Chalcedonian Churches of the Mediterranean.[16]

It is worth setting these moves in a wider context to see what an important turning point 676 CE represents in the history of Christian marriage.

It is one of the greatest forgotten realities of Christian history that for centuries, from the first years of the Church, there was no such thing as a church wedding, and when church weddings did start appearing, patchily, in the fourth century, the Church did not offer them to all the faithful. When in 2020 the Church of England, after great effort and community discussion, published a study of sexuality entitled *Living in Love and Faith*, in none of its 482 pages and its eightfold-repeated assertion that there is a 'Christian understanding of marriage' did it get round to mentioning this really rather important historical fact.[17] In part this is because modern churchgoers are shaped by the assumptions of the long years of 'Christendom', in which the local church has presided over rites of passage to mark human life: birth (baptism), marriage and death. That was not so in the centuries before Constantine and other Mediterranean monarchs entered their alliance with the Church hierarchy.

Obviously, from early decades Christians had taken a good deal of trouble over Christian burial. Dedicated burial areas remain among the first surviving archaeological traces of the new religion, for instance in the elaborate maze of catacombs in Rome from the late second century onwards, encouraged in their construction by the peculiar geology of the city, and (more generally) in the distinctive Christian custom of burying corpses aligned east and west. Oddly, that Christian practice is nowhere laid down in Church law, and, odder still, early funeral liturgy has left puzzlingly meagre traces in surviving texts. Baptism was for at least the first five centuries generally conferred on adults, not children; so, there was little if any presumption of a liturgical connection between baptism and birth.[18]

Above all, before the fifth century, the Church had remarkably little to do with the ceremonies of marriage. Obviously from early days, Church communities took benevolent notice of newly wedded couples. At the beginning of the second century, Bishop Ignatios of Antioch urged couples to marry with the knowledge and blessing of the bishop, so that marriage should be according to the Lord and not by human desire, but he did say this in the course of a careful programme of defining and probably pushing the boundaries of power for bishops like himself, at a time when episcopal authority such as his was not universal in the Church.[19] There is no reason to disbelieve that such blessing did indeed become common, but all that it meant was that the couple went to the community Eucharist as they would have done anyway as single persons, rather than in any separate ecclesiastical ceremony. If that was in fact the case, it was a rather less emphatic marker of marriage than the non-Christian practice in some Hellenistic cities, notably Alexandria, of some city official or priest adding formal recognition to the usual agreement made by the two fathers of the couple.[20]

It is remarkable amid the cornucopia of various liturgical forms for all sorts of purpose set out in Church orders from the second to the fourth century, and in most later collections into the sixth century, none concern weddings – not even to change the status of married couples who had embraced Christianity after their marriage.[21] Particularly after the coming of the Constantinian era, some leading Churchmen grew restive at this situation. Among his various other furies, John Chrysostom denounced the secularity of marriages in fourth-century Antioch, further complaining that priests were rarely invited and then told to leave early. Not all his contemporaries took his point of view: his predecessor-but-one as Archbishop of Constantinople, the theologian Gregory of Nazianzus, noted that some Christian families did ask their priest to perform the traditional ceremony of crowning newlyweds, but he himself preferred that it should be done by the father of the bridegroom. Jerome, always at the extreme end of any polarity, in a much-cited letter to one of his clerical protégés went so far as to opine that 'a preacher of continence should not be a maker of marriages,' which was not much of an incentive to complete the proceedings liturgically.[22]

The dispute did herald the beginning of change, and from the fifth century it was becoming more common for clergy to bless at least the uncontroversial first marriages of their flock. Nevertheless, this was not as yet a coherent view of marriage as something that was done in church. The contours of what can only be called a social stratification in marriage were created in 537 CE by *Novella* 74 of the imperial legislator Justinian. This defined marriage under three categories, to be marked in different ways: 'glorious', for the imperial elite, 'middle' for imperial officials, merchants and the like, and 'vile' for the rest. The 'glorious' needed merely a careful legal contract, the 'middle' should be witnessed by clergy and Church lawyers in some fashion, while the legislation did not concern itself as to how the generously wide category of the 'vile' marked their unions. Justinian had no doubt been describing existing practice in Constantinople, and his threefold provision was echoed as late as the 880s, when a massive Byzantine legal compilation known as the *Epanagōgē* or *Eisagōgē* observed that marriage could be completed by 'a blessing, or by a crowning, or by an agreement'.[23]

From the Latin Church in the former Western Empire, prayers for blessing marriage in the context of a Eucharist appear in the oldest surviving liturgical compilations to guide priests ('sacramentaries'). Their content cannot definitely be pushed further back in date than the sixth century, in the Verona (or 'Leonine') and 'Gelasian' sacramentaries, originating in Italy and Francia. Yet the blessings that these provide are only for the bride, a peculiarity that would disappear from later liturgical forms, and it hardly suggests a very developed view of how to structure marriage in church; it actually reflects traditional non-Christian marriage ceremonies, just as does the crowning of couples in the East.[24] What is not clear in any case is how widely such ceremonies would be used; probably not much beyond elite circles. A perfect exception to prove that likely rule is the earliest known attestation of a wedding ceremony in church, which is from the early fifth century. On this occasion both bride and groom could hardly be more part of the Christian elite, both being the children of bishops. Very appropriately, the groom in this young pair of enthusiasts for the holiness of marriage was the critic of Augustine of Hippo on matters sexual and himself a future bishop, Julian of Aeclanum (above, Chapter 9).[25]

The silences continued. In the East, the energetic legislation of the Synod *In Trullo* in Constantinople in 691–92 dealt with various matters around marriage, but a wedding ceremony in church was not one of them.[26] There is also a significant omission in a text that is roughly contemporary with those early Western sacramentaries in the late fifth or sixth century. This is the anonymous collection of Syrian theological and mystical treatises and letters whose author is only known under a pseudonym, masquerading as the first-century convert of Paul mentioned in the Acts of the Apostles, Dionysios (Dionysius) the Areopagite. Even though this *Corpus Dionysiacum* may have been written by a non-Chalcedonian ascetic, it became influential on theology and Church practice throughout both Eastern and Western Christianity for many centuries, right up to and beyond the sixteenth-century Reformation.[27] The *Corpus* discusses as sacraments Baptism, Eucharist, Ordination, entry to the monastic life and funerals, with descriptions of the liturgy attached to them – but not marriage.

The omission of marriage from among the sacraments continued as a silence in the theological commentary of such greatly respected Eastern Christian authorities as John of Damascus in the eighth century. It is the same a century later with the writings of a monk from the Stoudios monastery in Constantinople who hence is known as Theodore the Stoudite, a major reformer of Byzantine monastic life.[28] Lurking behind this general reluctance in such a wide variety of commentators was that quiet anxiety about the nature of marriage that we have now traced through so many Christian centuries: should something so universally practised by humankind, and so inextricably involved with the physicality of sex (plus the raucous fun of the marriage celebrations on the day), enter the sacred mysteries of God? Nevertheless, the Church of Byzantium moved on, to comply with a drastic change in imperial law not long after Theodore the Stoudite had repeated much of the text of Pseudo-Dionysios. Sometime around 900 a new law (*Novella*) of the Emperor Leo VI (reigned 886–912) laid down that, for free citizens (slaves hardly mattered), the only form of union recognized would be one blessed by a priest – anything else would be 'illegitimate concubinage'.[29]

Leo's *Novella* decided the shape of marriage in the Orthodox world thereafter; from the tenth century, Orthodoxy finally developed its own wedding ritual to the full. One awkward consequence that the Church of the Mediterranean had up to now avoided was that Orthodox clergy became responsible for all marriages within their jurisdiction. The untidiness of marriage in human society, perhaps tolerable in the 'creation ordinance' face of marriage, was hardly the model for the believer's eternal relationship with Christ, as set out by Paul of Tarsus and the writer to the Ephesians. Previously any discrepancy, such as divorce or remarriage, could simply be left outside the bounds of the Church in the hands of civil law. The fact that this was no longer the case was embarrassingly demonstrated by Emperor Leo VI himself when, in 906, he compelled the Church authorities to recognize his fourth marriage, way beyond anything that the Church authorities ought to have considered theologically acceptable, following the principles of Basil the Great (Chapter 9). It took the Emperor's forceful replacement of Patriarch Nicholas Mystikos by a marginally more compliant Patriarch to bring the Church reluctantly to heel.[30]

The *Novella* of Leo VI appeared two centuries after the Dyophysite Patriarch George had launched his bid for monopoly of marriages among his own flock at the Synod of Dayrin. Why now? Imperial politics was one factor. An earlier sensational crisis over an imperial marriage in 796 had centred on the Emperor Constantine VI's ruthless insistence on gaining the blessing of the Church for his own eccentric marital arrangements, after he had divorced his wife and married a lady of the Court, thereby jeopardizing the imperial succession. The Patriarch Tarasios's inept though understandable lenience in imposing a light penance led to a crisis in the Church, and eventually to a political coup in which Constantine's own mother, Irene, removed the Emperor from power by having him blinded. This messy affair was certainly an incentive for clarity in marital legislation. The very determination of Constantine VI to get ecclesiastical approval was witness to the fact that, by the late eighth century, the Byzantine elite were coming to expect the security provided by the Church blessing marriages.[31] Yet to sum up a complicated story, it was the tenth century before this became the norm in the Byzantine East, much later in northern Orthodoxy, and, as we will see, in the West no earlier than the twelfth century (below, Chapter 12).

ICONS AND THE 'TRIUMPH OF ORTHODOXY'

Running in parallel to these momentous developments in marriage practice was the prolonged 'Iconoclastic Controversy' in Eastern Christianity. The 'icon', a sacred image normally presented as a painting on a wooden panel, is now so much an essential part of Orthodox Christian identity that it may come as a surprise that in the eighth and ninth centuries icons were at the centre of a deeply divisive conflict in the Orthodox world about their place in its worship life. The issue was an old one in Christianity. Which of its two inherited cultural impulses should it follow: the Jewish tradition with its strong prejudice against sacred imagery, or that of the Hellenistic world, which delighted in creating images of the divine? The coming of Islam in the seventh century posed the problem once more in a new and more acute form, for the Prophet and his successors were determined foes of any image in a sacred context. And Islam had been horrifyingly successful: did that mean that God favoured Muslim iconophobia?

That was certainly the conclusion of the Byzantine military commander who in 717 became Emperor Leo III (known as 'the Isaurian', coming from a frontier province of Asia Minor). Shocked by another apparent sign of God's displeasure in a massive volcanic eruption in the

Aegean archipelago of Santorini in 726, Leo implemented what was at first a fairly restricted programme of removing prominent icons from imperial buildings and whitewashing over church mosaics.[32] His son Constantine V (reigned 741–75), another successful soldier, extended the iconoclastic campaign into persecuting 'iconophiles', the defenders of sacred imagery: he had one of them whipped to death in the Hippodrome of Constantinople.[33] Images were destroyed in huge numbers, as is proved by how few icons dating to before this era survive to us outside the remote haven of the monastery of St Catherine in Sinai, which the iconoclasts never reached. Archaeology has revealed the systematic removal of images from mosaics on both sides of the frontier between Byzantium and the Caliphate.[34] Both Church and imperial government were deeply damaged by this bitterness.

One feature of the long-drawn-out dispute, finally only settled by an imperial decision in 843, was that the turning points in favour of icons were the work of two successive empresses. Constantine V's daughter-in-law Irene, whose blinding of her son Constantine VI left her as the only reigning Empress in Byzantine history (sole reign 797–802), had gone so far as to summon an Oecumenical Council in the name of that unfortunate teenager, at that stage still in possession of his eyes, and this second Council of Nicaea (787) systematically reversed iconoclast policies. For the time being the shift was temporary, since Irene's unmaternal behaviour, combined with the alarming diplomatic prospect that she might make a second marriage, to the Western Latin monarch Charlemagne, led to her deposition and exile in 802.

The issue remained in play for another half-century, before the later Empress Theodora was freed by the death of her iconoclast husband Theophilos in 842 to emerge as a second female champion of icons. A run of military victories for iconoclast emperors had abruptly and humiliatingly ended in the 830s: God's favour seemed to have deserted the iconoclast cause. As regent for her son Michael III, toddler as well as Emperor, Theodora ordered a new Patriarch hand-picked for his iconophile sympathies to restore the icons to public worship. The occasion of their joyful formal reintroduction to the great church of Hagia Sophia, 11 March 843, was a decision never reversed, and it has always subsequently been celebrated in successor-Churches as the 'Triumph of Orthodoxy'.

It is possible to read this sequence of events simply as a matter of high politics and of the doctrinal statements produced by successive ecclesiastical councils and distinguished theologians (now much weighted to the iconophilic side, thanks to later censorship by the victors). Yet it is no accident that a succession of military men as emperors with strategic considerations in mind favoured the iconoclastic cause, and that two (admittedly ambitious and ruthless) women should successfully defy them and alter the future of Eastern Orthodoxy. It has been plausibly argued that the two sides represent contrasting ways of approaching the mystery of God at the heart of Christian faith, appealing to different constituencies in Byzantine society. Iconophilia became an alliance between women and monks, and the debate was about how to find holiness in this world.[35]

It was a theme among iconoclasts that Christians met holiness in the particular situations where the clergy represented the Church to God, primarily in public performance of the Church's liturgy. No one on either side was going to deny the place of the liturgy in the life of the Church, but it could perfectly well continue in its magnificence in churches without artistic representation of sacred figures. One reason for iconoclasts to reject the holiness of icons was that there was no official provision for a cleric to say a prayer of blessing over them (in the centuries since the Triumph of Orthodoxy, that has been remedied).[36] In terms of art, iconoclasts were content with rich depictions of a plain cross in their churches, some of which survive, and which might call to a soldier's mind the humiliation brought to Christians by the Muslim seizure of Jerusalem, site of the crucifixion of Jesus and shrine to the miraculously preserved True Cross.

Yet the churches and their liturgy were public space, and, by definition, they were therefore primarily male space, both for clergy and for laymen. Iconoclasts laying claim to that public space in their years of success had nothing else to offer those for whom the liturgy might have become impossibly splendid and too remote to satisfy every spiritual need, in churches that might be too crowded for quiet private devotion. That could include men: the traditional story of the Iconoclastic Controversy has been built around male iconophile theologians, of whom the most influential was the much-revered John of Damascus (*c.*675–*c.*745). John, an unusually privileged subject of the Caliph in the Caliph's chief city, knew Islam intimately, and deeply considered his reasons for rejecting their iconophobia; he contended that true Christianity demanded the place of icons in the life of the faithful, 'so that we might glorify God and be filled with wonder and zeal'.[37] Advocates of the icon asserted that God's glory does not need some clerical initiative to welcome it into human life: everyone can freely encounter the sacred, because all that God has created is by nature sacred. In this meeting, the chief intermediary in holiness, gateway from the everyday to the eternal, is the icon, and the icon can live anywhere, not simply in a church.

That is why icons could especially appeal to women, in the private world of the household. They saved icons through the years when they were torn down in churches: little wooden painted tablets could migrate from public space to the home. In a domestic setting, mothers and grandmothers could exercise their customary prerogative of giving hospitality to a guest, in this case a sacred guest, and also impress their love for this private source of divine power on their children. It is worth noting the story in a biography of one contemporary saint that the very first act of iconoclasm in Constantinople by Leo III was met by a furious crowd in which the women led the lynching of one of the workmen sent to remove a prominent public image of Christ.[38]

In particular, the image of Mary with her child Jesus was something that every mother could make her own. By bearing and nursing the Saviour, Mary showed how essential it was for the physical to be the vehicle of the divine: she was an icon among icons. John of Damascus was the first Greek theologian routinely to refer to her as the Mother of God, a more straightforward term than the *Theotokos* affirmed at the Council of Chalcedon, though 'Mother of God' never achieved the universal usage among the Orthodox that it did in the Latin West.[39] Of course, Mary could hardly be kept out of public preaching or liturgy even when her images were taken down, and the eighth century, while the iconoclastic dispute raged, produced a great crop of sermons and hymns in her honour; it was a major moment in developing her place in Byzantine Orthodox devotion. Perhaps that was a deliberate move to protect her in case iconoclasts extended their aggression from images to the very cult of the Virgin – but that is difficult to prove, since our knowledge of what the iconoclasts actually believed is now so patchy.[40]

Certainly, it was a riposte to iconoclast denigration of icons that, in the wake of the Triumph of Orthodoxy in 843, miracle stories proliferated around icons of Mary. One of her icons performed the exceptional feat of swimming to Rome from the eastern Mediterranean coast (doing the last celebratory lap up the Tiber in a standing position); the deposed iconophile Patriarch Germanos I had thrown her for safety into the sea at the port of Lydda, the modern Lod or Al-Ludd.[41] If women and children became defenders of icons, so did holy men who might owe little to the Church hierarchy and its compromises with the Emperor's wishes. Monks and nuns who loved icons as much as John of Damascus could ally with a movement rooted among laypeople to save images from the consequences of high clericalism and imperial policy. The iconophile empresses listened to that impulse rather than caring for the grand strategy preoccupying their menfolk. Everyone, male or female or eunuch, could reach God through the contemplation of icons whenever they sensed God calling them to it. Devotion to icons wherever they may be found remains a form of sacred democracy in Orthodoxy, undergirding it against the powerful who would like to monopolize Christian allegiance.

The ninth century witnessed a momentous development for the Orthodox Church as the iconophiles emerged triumphant from a century of savage conflict. Photios, an especially energetic and creative Patriarch of Constantinople (reigned 858–67, 877–86), launched missions westward and northward beyond Byzantine frontiers, first into the territories of Khan Boris of the Bulgars (reigned 853–89). Boris was a shrewd and successful monarch who had been weighing up whether to entrust his proposed conversion to Christianity to the guidance of Latin Western or of Greek Eastern Christians. Pope Nicholas I (reigned 858–67) was exceptionally assertive in advancing the Roman Papacy's historic claims, and he was furious that Boris eventually opted for Constantinople. A war of words escalated into full-blown schism between East and West and anticipated later unhappy divisions. One of the issues on which the Pope seized was that the Byzantine missionaries were insisting that their converts among Boris's people should receive ecclesiastical blessing for their marriages to be valid: a reflection of the distinctive developments on marriage in Orthodoxy over the previous century. Interestingly, when in 867 Patriarch Photios penned a comprehensive counter-attack on Rome that spelled out many of the future contentious theological issues between Orthodoxy and Catholicism, he failed to make any riposte to this particular charge in Nicholas's battery of complaints. Photios must have been aware that in this era before Emperor Leo VI's *Novella*, his missionaries were on shaky legal ground.[42]

The ninth-century initiatives in mission launched by Photios to Slavic peoples north and west beyond the Byzantine frontier were one symptom of the recovery in the Church and secular commonwealth. Partly that was because there was now an exceptionally capable 'Macedonian' dynasty of emperors, named from the origins of the first in the line, Basil I (reigned 867–86), and continuing thereafter for almost two centuries. Beyond immediate politics, in the wake of the Triumph of Orthodoxy during the later ninth century there was a new coherence in the theology of the Byzantine missions. A mark of Orthodox self-confidence was that the missionaries encouraged their Slavic converts to celebrate the Orthodox liturgy in their own language, not in Greek: a flexibility that stands in contrast to the Western Church's insistence on the continued use of Latin, and piquant in view of modern Orthodoxy's frequent insistence on its never-changing character. Photios's missionaries even devised new alphabets to suit the sounds of these Slavic languages, and when a first effort, the Glagolitic alphabet created by the priest-brothers Constantine and Methodius, proved not to be a great success, a Bulgarian scholar created another system. It has entirely supplanted Glagolitic, though it has become tactfully known as 'Cyrillic' – Cyril was the monastic name adopted by the pioneer Constantine – and it has seen off later northern Orthodox efforts to supplant it.[43]

What the general acceptance of Cyrillic script for the Slavonic languages meant was that the Orthodox mission was strengthened to expand northward into very different lands from the sunny shores of the Mediterranean that were the setting for Byzantine Christianity.[44] A century after the Patriarchate of Photios, the Byzantine emperors concluded a fruitful diplomatic deal with a northern European settler-people who, in migrations beginning in the ninth century, had established their capital at a strategic settlement on the River Dnipro (Dnieper), in what is now Ukraine: Kyiv. There they were called by a Scandinavian name, Rhos or Rus'.[45] The Rus' formed part of an extraordinarily dispersed population movement southward and westward from Scandinavia. Western Christians, initially terrified by the violence of their invasions, took up another Scandinavian name for them: Vikings. The first contacts of the Rus' with Constantinople in the era of Photios had been equally alarming, but, over time, the Kyivan dynasty known as the Rurikids (after a supposed ancestor) became more integrated into Slav society, as well as increasingly fascinated by the imperial City.

The year 988 was a turning point, when the Rurikid Prince Volodymyr (Vladimir) chose Byzantine Orthodoxy over Latin Christianity or Islam, reputedly after being impressed by ecstatic reports from his envoys about the heavenly magnificence of Hagia Sophia in Constantinople. In fact, by that time political and military circumstances did not make the choice especially difficult, particularly given the cultural links to the Slavic peoples of Balkan and central Europe created in the previous missions inspired by Photios. Thereafter, the Christianity of Constantinople remained the model for the newly converted Christians of Rus' and of later political entities such as Muscovy and eventually Russia. In 1039 the Patriarch of Constantinople granted the Bishop of Kyiv the title of Metropolitan, as he had done elsewhere in eastern Europe; this Metropolitan remained the leader of all the northern Orthodox Churches, though further convulsions were to take his successors far away from Kyiv to that later political entity called Russia. Church architecture imitated Byzantine forms; so did the liturgy (though using an increasingly formal ecclesiastical language, Church Slavonic) and Church organization generally, including the increasingly elaborate system of canon law that the Byzantine Church was developing in the ninth and tenth centuries to regulate a Christian society.

Nevertheless, all this imitation of Byzantium took place in a very different setting, which meant that imitation often became creative divergence.[46] It was not merely that snow was more common than sun for northern Orthodoxy: this new Christianity had no cultural memory of what had gone before in Mediterranean society, and it was liable to see Western Christianity (whose formal language of Latin was another barrier) through the increasingly hostile perspective of Byzantium. Social organization took a different form from that developing in the West; rather than any sort of layered hierarchy of landowners emerging as in Carolingian Europe (below, Chapters 11 and 12), society below the level of the ruler and his courtiers was based on ancestral landholding in partible inheritance. That created its own framework for understanding marriage and sexual activity outside it, with a priority for rightly defining inheritance from one generation to another.

Without any tradition of civil law as in the former Roman Empire, the regulation of sexuality was entirely in the hands of the Orthodox Church. It remained so right down to the revolution in government and society engineered by Peter I 'the Great' that at the end of the seventeenth century created a Russian Empire. In creating a moral code, northern Orthodoxy drew selectively on Christian traditions, with an inevitable bias towards its Eastern ascetic tradition. Totally unknown was Augustine of Hippo's nuanced defence of marriage, or (of course) any inheritance from Graeco-Roman secular literature on the theme of romantic love, which in the West would begin to affect thoughts about love and sex once more in the twelfth century (Chapters 12 and 13).

Marriage in northern Orthodoxy therefore had nothing to do with love – nor indeed had sexual desire much to do with marriage. There is a grim realism in an anecdote about the celebrated thirteenth-century royal couple of the Kyivan principality of Murom, David and Euphrosyne; in later years they both entered the religious life and took monastic names as Peter and Fevronia, after which they showed their mutual devotion by dying on the same Easter day, 1228. Fevronia once contemptuously rejected the adulterous sexual advances of a married nobleman by ordering him to draw two buckets of water and taste samples of both: was there any difference, she asked? When he admitted that there was not, she commented that, in the same way, all women are sexually alike, so a husband should stick to the wife he had married.[47]

Northern Orthodoxy's view of sexuality and marriage drew on the Greek Orthodox tradition stemming from Basil the Great and pursued through the most authoritative Eastern theologians up to and beyond Maximos the Confessor (above, Chapters 8 and 9): sexual reproduction, even sexual difference, was the product of humanity's Fall engineered by Satan. Within the bounds of the fallen world, marriage was more unequivocally than elsewhere something for families to agree on, rather than an individual's choice to make. In that respect, it reflected the assumption that sexual misbehaviour, like behaviour in general, was the business of all society, not simply of the individuals involved. The Church's task was to keep sex as tightly controlled as possible within the ecclesiastical regulations of canon law.

The system had its own logic. It could not have worked if the laity had not accepted it and come to see it as a badge of their own identity. Just as the Church of the East had with eventual success made a particular form of marriage the token of being a Christian in the face of Islamic acceptance of polygyny, so northern Orthodoxy survived amid the devastating invasions of animist and Muslim Mongols from the 1220s by preserving an identity built up over three previous centuries of Christian society, much of which was structured around the Church's regulation of sex. Popular Slavic culture might seize on a feature of that regulation and internalize it to an alarming extent. Thus, despite cautionary words from theologians and pastors about the continuing goodness of marriage after the Fall of Adam and Eve, Slavic laypeople could view even marital sex as sinful, to the extent that epic literature in Serbian might use the phrase 'by sin' (*po grehu*) to identify a parent or child by birth, while the child's godparent was its 'parent without sin' (*roditelj bezgrešni*).

Such unromantic beliefs would be encouraged by the usage employed in some Church legal texts for the one sexual position allowed to a married couple: what has flippantly been termed by Westerners 'the missionary position' was known in Church Slavonic as sexual congress 'on a horse' (*na koně*), in reference to its demonstration of the male's dominance over the female.[48] Predictably, Jerome's principle derived from the Pythagoreans that too much marital affection was as bad as adultery continued to flourish amid the general Orthodox pessimism about marriage. One thirteenth-century text of moral instruction advised men to 'separate from your wife, so you don't become attached to her'. It was common to find in Russian Orthodox guides to what confessors should ask of their penitents that the questions grouped excessive sexual intercourse between married partners alongside serious sexual offences like anal intercourse or association with prostitutes.[49]

The northern Orthodox Church faced daunting problems of scale; centuries passed before there was a network of parishes and their priests, such as was created in Mediterranean and western Europe, which could ensure that Orthodox marriage customarily began in a ceremony in church.[50] Yet the same informal alliance that had proved so fruitful to Constantinople in the Iconoclastic Controversy sustained northern Orthodoxy and the Russian Orthodoxy that grew out of it. Monks and mothers, ignoring the whims of monarchs and, indeed, of the Church hierarchy, centred their devotional life on the icon, away from the public sphere. Taking a cue from Mediterranean Orthodox practice, the Russian category of monk was a good deal more capacious than in the increasingly regulated Church of the Latin West. So it was a common experience to meet wandering individual monks, 'Holy Fools' even, who were a good deal more like Diogenes of Sinope than they were like Pachomios. In their wild sanctity, they could be lively sustainers of remote communities far from the tidy-mindedness of a bishop.[51]

All this was the saviour of Russian Orthodoxy when, after 1917, imperial rule disappeared and the powers of the state were turned viciously on the Church. Over many previous centuries, Orthodoxy had never completely melted into the alliance with power that official Christianity had entered back in the time of Constantine the Great, and that quality endures to the present day, despite what patriarchs might say in Moscow cathedrals.

11

The Latin West: A Landscape of Monasteries (500–1000)

The theological and diplomatic confrontations between Rome and Constantinople in the period of the Iconoclastic Controversy and the missions launched by Patriarch Photios reveal how far the sympathies of Latin West and Greek East were diverging by the ninth century, and how much Christian society would continue to differ in West and East. The reasons for the contrast become clear if we trace back the story of Western Christianity from the collapse of the Western Roman Empire in the fifth century. Just as in the far east of the Christian world, the Latin Church in expanding west and north met new societies in which the forms of family and marriage, polygyny included, posed a challenge to its inherited bundle of beliefs.

While the Western Empire decayed through the fifth century, there was no certain future for Catholic Christianity and for the Bishop of Rome. The Western Church's strength had lain in the episcopal system that, as much as in the East, was based on imperial towns and cities, so the Catholic Church's character was urban and in many areas of the disintegrating Empire largely a religion of the social elite. The two provinces of Britannia were an extreme example, for archaeology suggests a late Roman minority Christian culture based on towns (three of them named as sending bishops to the Council of Western bishops at Arles in 314) and on the country villas of prosperous landowners.[1] Gaul and the Mediterranean basin had experienced greater growth in rural Christian practice, especially encouraged by the charisma and continuing golden memory of the fourth-century Martin of Tours, but demography and politics still suggested another possible future for the West: a different variety of Christianity, identified with the Germanic peoples who had been drifting westward across the Roman frontiers since the third century, prompted in turn by population movements to their east in Asia. Their arrival became unstoppable as the legions retreated or disbanded.

During the fifth century a whole series of Germanic kingdoms emerged in place of imperial power, and, although most were Christian, theirs was an Arian Christianity, rejecting the conclusions dictated by Constantine I at Nicaea.[2] The now largely overlooked hero of Arian triumph in converting Germanic peoples to Christianity is Bishop Ulfila. He pioneered the missionary strategy later adopted by Patriarch Photios in creating a Christian literature and script for a vernacular language. Coming from an Eastern Christian family but raised across the northern imperial frontier, he devised a Bible text in the Gothic language, complete with a new alphabet to convey its particular sounds. Ulfila was consecrated bishop at a time in the 330s when Arian styles of belief championed by the skilful politician Eusebios, Bishop of Nicomedia (now İzmit in Turkey), had become dominant at the Roman imperial Court. When Arianism was ousted from imperial Christianity by 'Catholics' such as Bishop Ambrose of Milan, the Germanic peoples moving into the Empire continued proudly to wear their version of Christian faith as a badge of cultural identity over against Romans.

Right up to the end of the sixth century, the Germanic successor-kingdoms to the Western Empire, from Spain to the Alps and the Adriatic, were primarily Arian in leadership. Gaul, the modern region of France, proved the crucial exception. Clovis, King of the Franks from 481, certainly dallied with Arian Christianity, and members of his family opted for Arianism.[3] Nevertheless, Clovis married a Catholic wife, and, besides that incentive, his beliefs were focused by his military victories, like the Emperor Constantine before him. Clovis attributed his success in battle to the charismatic saint of the West who had been first a soldier like himself and then a wonder-working (and Catholic) bishop, Martin of Tours.

A fascination with both the Roman imperial heritage around him and its local saintly champion tilted Clovis's Christian beliefs towards the faith of his wife and of the Bishop of Rome. Later popes have been duly grateful ever since; Francia under the 'Merovingian' dynasty of Clovis set patterns in reshaping Western Christian monarchy into a Catholic mould, from the Mediterranean to Europe's furthest north. Until then, Germanic and surviving Roman cultures had uneasily coexisted side by side in much of the former Western Empire, Catholic Christians acknowledging the dominance of their Germanic masters rather as Eastern Christians acquiesced in the Caliphate.[4] When Western Roman imperial institutions had collapsed, what was left of its administrative and social

1. After early Christian angels became beardless: a detail from Abraham's meeting with three angels at Mamre (Gen. 18), mosaic in San Vitale, Ravenna, 6th century.

2. A late 17th-century vision of an angel with an arquebus by an unknown Bolivian artist of the Cuzco school.

3. The classic Orthodox Virgin and Child as icon: Our Lady of the Don, possibly by Theophanes the Greek, *c.*1385.

4. The medieval Western group of the Rood (Christ on the Cross flanked by his mother and John the Beloved Disciple) here, as so often, surmount a 'rood screen' and 'roodloft': parish church of Saint-Yves, La Roche-Maurice, Brittany, *c.*1560–80.

5. From the apocryphal Infancy stories, young Jesus rather sulkily obeys his mother's command to bring a dead playmate back to life, after remonstrations from the neighbours (Italian, 13th century).

6. The mounted warrior-Christ of Revelation 19.11–16: fresco, Auxerre Cathedral, Burgundy, now dated *c.*1100.

7. The MAGA Christ, as seen on a rally and march for Donald Trump, New York, 25 October 2020.

8 & 9. Female mystics inspired distinctively maternal images of spirituality: in the early 14th-century *Schwesternbuch* (Nuns' Book or Chronicle) from the Swiss Dominican nunnery of Töss, Margarethe of Zürich bathes the Christ child (*left*) and Adelheid of Frauenburg is suckled by Our Lady (*right*).

10. A liturgical *Graduale* from the south German Cistercian nunnery of Wonnental (1340s) unusually portrays the unborn Jesus and John the Baptist 'leaping' in their mothers' wombs on the Visitation of Our Lady to her cousin Elizabeth (Luke 1.39–56).

11. The mosaic on the triumphal arch of Santa Maria Maggiore, Rome (*c.*450) shows Mary as a dominant imperial figure beside her enthroned Son, but she is not afforded a halo, unlike Jesus or his angels.

12. In the sanctuary mosaics of San Vitale, Ravenna (*c.*550) Empress Theodora stretches convention by her presence within the altar enclosure accompanied by her Court ladies and eunuchs (beardless, unlike most of her husband Justinian's attendants).

13 & 14. Two aspects of multifaceted Mary Magdalen in Western art, 'before' and 'after' her conversion: *left*, as elegant lady of pleasure ready to anoint Jesus's feet (by the Venetian Carlo Crivelli, *c.*1480); *right*, as emaciated penitent (carved with startling realism by Donatello probably for Florence's Duomo Baptistery, *c.*1440), taking its cue from Eastern images of Mary of Egypt covered in her own hair.

15. Mary Magdalen made safe for Georgian Protestant bachelor dons; a *Noli me tangere* ('Touch me not', John 20.17), commissioned by All Souls College Oxford from the fashionable artist Anton Raphael Mengs in Rome, 1769.

16. A Western use of Eastern prototypes (Parisian 'Master of the *Hours* of Jean de Dunois', *c*.1436–50): in the desert, the priest Zosimas offers Mary of Egypt his mantle, supplementing her characteristic clothing of her own hair.

17 & 18. Demonic desert temptations for the long-suffering 4th-century ascetic Antony of Egypt: by an Ethiopian boy and – more dramatically – by some enthusiastic ladies. As envisaged in a Parisian volume of the *Golden Legend*, 1404 (*above*) and by the Parisian artist Hippolyte Delaroche, *c.*1832 (*below*).

functions was in the hands of the Catholic Church. That included the conservation of the Classical literary and philosophical heritage, which from the mid sixth century survived in a perilously fragile condition: survival was a matter of copying and recopying perishable manuscripts, and alarmingly few manuscripts can be dated as the work of copyists over the next two hundred years.

The surviving literature was largely in the care of monks and nuns. Thanks to Jerome's rhetorical sleight of hand in adding scholarship to the rigours of monastic life (above, Chapter 8), enough monastic libraries and readers remained to carry forward what portions of Classical knowledge they cared to preserve, when the libraries of villas, towns and schools crumbled into dust. Fortunately for Western civilization, the next half-millennium revealed the vigour of its monastic life. Much came eventually to be structured by the Rule devised in the sixth century for Italian monasteries, the work of Benedict of Nursia and monastic predecessors going back to the much-travelled Easterner John Cassian a century earlier. Benedict's Rule itself might be contained on a single skin of parchment, and its brevity was the key to its eventual success, because it could be creatively developed, particularly when its commands to 'labour and pray' extended to embrace a monastic vocation to study and preserve past wisdom. Central to any development of the Rule remained the principle of an autonomous community established in one place, in obedience to its abbot, part of a constellation of similar communities wherever they might be set up. Yet its adoption was a protracted process: for some centuries to come, Western monasticism was marked by its variety in societies embracing a Christian Catholic identity.[5]

BRITANNIA EXTENDED: IRELAND

Unexpectedly, the only significant expansion of Western Latin Christianity in the fifth and sixth centuries came from its most marginal Christian communities, in the island provinces of the former Empire called Britannia. In these lands that are now England and Wales, a Christian presence did endure, but, though it never disappeared, much of it was progressively hollowed out as the population abandoned Roman ways and even Celtic languages. In Britannia the Germanic arrivals, 'Saxons' as the Romans knew them, were from northern European lands that had not taken up even Arian Christianity, and Arianism was never a feature of the Atlantic archipelago. Yet from the fifth century, archaeology and surviving monuments in Wales and Cornwall all chart intensified Christian activity, spilling also into Scotland north of the old Roman frontier. Maybe this was through Celtic migration westward away from Germanic culture; emigration certainly did also propel British Christians and their language overseas to what is now Brittany.

Scotland's first known episcopal centre, at Whithorn in its extreme south-west, significantly had Martin of Tours as its patron saint. This reminiscence of Catholic Gaul highlights the connections of British Christianity to the Gaulish or Frankish Catholic Church, as part of a seaborne Celtic circle of trade and social exchange that extended to Brittany. The links to the Catholic south are underlined by the continuing use of Latin in British monumental inscriptions, and various borrowings into Celtic languages from Latin dealing with ecclesiastical topics. This British Christian culture inevitably affected the second major island of the Atlantic archipelago, Ireland, which the Romans had never made any effort to conquer. Modern simplification of the story of Ireland's Christian conversion down to the name Patrick has been aided by how little we know of how it happened; certainly, he did not initiate the process, but came into something already establishing itself.[6]

There is startling illumination in two authentic fragments of Patrick's own Latin writings, rediscovered in the seventeenth century by his Protestant successor in the see of Armagh, the formidable scholar-archbishop James Ussher (1581–1656). Among much other often puzzling detail, Patrick's autobiographical *Confessio* places his British origins with fair certainty at a small settlement on Hadrian's Wall called *Banna*, now known as Birdoswald, before he had been kidnapped by Irish slave raiders. Other scraps of near-contemporary information suggest that Patrick's activities should be placed in the fifth century, which is more certain in the case of a slightly earlier and unconnected Christian emissary to Ireland from Rome called Palladius.[7]

Amid the wisps of fact swirling in much later partisan or self-congratulatory Irish myth-making, Patrick's own distinctly emotional and defensive texts include the interesting nugget that he met much hostility to his success in persuading suggestible young Irish aristocrats (both male and female) to embrace vocations as monks and 'virgins of Christ'. Significantly, recruitment from powerful families had also been characteristic of Martin of Tours' ministry in Gaul, but in Ireland the context was of an outsider intervening in a culture where Christianity was a recent arrival, and with complex social arrangements of its own, into which Christian leaders were suddenly introducing new and disruptive financial and personal demands in the interest of building a pioneer Church. Patrick testifies that such professions of virginity were 'not with the consent of their fathers' and were met with 'persecution and reproaches from their kindred'. Despite the very different social context, this sounds remarkably like the less-than-enthusiastic reaction of fourth-century Roman nobility to the initiatives of Ambrose of Milan on professions of virginity: all part of various other indications in the Latin West that elites often resented the growth of the ascetic life (above, Chapter 8).

Patrick's virgin-followers would be part of the entourage of a bishop, as Martin's had been at first; this does not suggest communities of monks or nuns living separately. Throughout the Atlantic Isles, that development of monasteries and nunneries is more plausibly placed in the sixth century, and in Ireland in particular it became vigorously and fruitfully tangled with the distinctive social and political structure of the island.[8] There was much to puzzle a missionary Roman bishop here: apart from the financial conundrum, there was nothing like a town from which to launch a bishop's activities or to provide a territorial title for his diocese. Moreover, there was no central monarchical authority in the island, and never had been, but instead a large collection of groupings (*tuatha*) headed by dynastic leaders, whose power over kin and clients was based on their capacity both to provide defence against other dynasties and to obtain favour from supernatural powers for prosperity in crops and cattle. To call these leaders kings is misleading, since there may have been anything between one hundred and fifty and two hundred of them in Ireland at any one time.

Bishops had not previously met with anything like this social organization since the Church had first allied with the powerful. A profitable solution was to root the Church in Irish society in close alignment with dynasties of the *tuatha*. Irish legal custom made it impossible to provide monasteries with independent estates for their maintenance, as was the norm in the Mediterranean world, which suggests why Patrick had run into trouble. Instead, monasteries and nunneries became part of the joint estate of great families, intimately involved in the life of each local dynastic grouping and all the more powerful for it because monasteries became so enmeshed in the pride and pre-Christian traditions of each *tuath*. While patterns of connections between particular monasteries and their local noble dynasties can also be detected in contemporary England and Francia, here they provided the norm for centuries.[9]

There was nothing fixed or enduring about many *tuatha*, and, reflecting the itinerant character of much of Irish society, the Church developed a peculiar phenomenon of roving ecclesiastical families, in whom priesthood and care of churches descended from one generation to another; they carried with them in their migrations the stories of their founding saints, spreading the same cult to widely separated parts of the island.[10] The boundaries of hereditary priesthood and celibate monasticism were distinctly fluid; it was all very different from the monastic rule of Benedict, with its emphasis on a settled monastic life and its hostility to wandering ascetics.

Equally fluid was the frontier between ascetic life and the married lives of laypeople. One instance of that sounds like a prolonged version of the retreats hosted by modern religious communities: the ninth-century romance about Liadain and Curithir, lovers and poets of the seventh century, who were set up in adjacent cells at Clonfert (Co. Galway) under the spiritual direction of Abbot Cummean Fota ('the Long'). He set up a careful rota of solitary walks in the graveyard so that they never actually saw each other. Given such creative arrangements for the religious life, it is not surprising to find evidence of male and female ascetics housed in the same sacred precincts, or even apparent nuns being described as the 'wife' of a local priest.[11]

It would only be in tenth-century Ireland that first signs of pressures for uniformity of monastic observance arrived from central Europe and began to disturb these long-hallowed arrangements, provoking a new Irish debate about how to organize monastic life that was not resolved for another couple of centuries. There is a remarkable tenth- or eleventh-century narrative of the holy though not easily dateable Scothíne of Tisscoffin (Co. Kilkenny), who, in order to demonstrate his continence, habitually shared his bed with 'two maidens with pointed breasts'. Equally pointed was the ladies' allusion to the burning coals of Proverbs 6.28, when in indignant response to the celebrated St Brendan, who had queried these arrangements, they accosted Brendan in his chamber with 'lapfuls of glowing embers in their chasubles', emptied out the embers in front of him from their ostentatiously unsinged robes and then joined him under the bedcovers. They eventually told him to go and have a cold bath, since his evident longing for them was keeping everybody awake. It is clear that this splendid tall tale was part of a continuing conversation in Irish Catholicism, on the eve of major eleventh-century transformations in the Western Church (below, Chapter 12).[12]

The local peculiarities of early Irish monasticism might suggest insularity in more than one sense, but in fact the contacts revealed by surviving Celtic art are astonishingly wide, right as far away as Egypt and the eastern Mediterranean. What is true of artistic motifs and design equally applies to theology. In two respects, Irish borrowings from the East precociously anticipated their adoption elsewhere in the Western Latin Church: the cult of Mary, and a distinctive moral theology. Both probably relate to the rapid flourishing of monasteries and nunneries in Ireland. In Byzantium, Mary could be modelled in the imagination alongside powerful empresses such as Pulcheria or Theodora. That comparison did not resonate in the dispersed political structures of seventh-century Ireland, but it was easy for the Irish to recognize the role of most favoured mother interceding with the most powerful male, her womanly virtues a model for all femininity. That was a special power worth annexing in prayer, a power enhanced for celibates by Mary's virgin purity.[13]

Alongside Marian devotion, Irish monastic spirituality was inspired by the moral instruction and rules for monastic living provided by the Eastern monk John Cassian when his writings and example travelled westward through Gaul and beyond. Cassian represented an ascetic outlook discreetly unsympathetic to the campaigns of Augustine of Hippo against the British theologian and pastor Pelagius (above, Chapter 9), and Irish monks were as anxious as Pelagius had been to take responsibility for the individual's struggle against being overwhelmed by sin. It was also through Cassian, mediating earlier Eastern ascetic discussion of the spiritual life, that Western views of sin became structured around specified sins that were eventually clarified into a sevenfold set of definitions. This may have taken its cue from the 'seven devils' that Christ cast out of Mary Magdalen, according to the Gospel of Luke, though seven is always an attractive number for those seeking conceptual schemes. It provided a tidy and comprehensive basis for a new Western scheme of moral regulation, so that sin could now be sorted out as pride, greed, wrath, envy, lust, gluttony and sloth. It is worth observing that only one of these seven directly concerns sex and sexuality.[14]

Irish ascetics fighting demons in their windswept stone cells, as well as laypeople in their everyday lives, were set the task of identifying and dealing with the sins they committed. Their spiritual progress was a constant series of little setbacks, laboriously compensated for before the next little lapse; each time the Church would help its flock find an appropriate degree of sorrow and penitence. Out of this theology of moral struggle came a new practice of individual penance. Public penance as practised in the early Church had been a daunting, once-in-a-lifetime act witnessed by a congregation, and connected with adult baptism.[15] From the sixth century, clergy in Ireland and Wales pioneered a penitential practice of individual confession, based on the compilation of 'tariff books' or 'penitentials' to guide confessors in dealing with their flocks, whether monastic or lay. The penitentials were structured around the idea not only that sin could be atoned for through penance, but also that it was possible to work out exact scales of what penance matched which sin: tariffs of forgiveness. Clergy were armed with their books when they presided over 'auricular confession', a face-to-face personal encounter between two people, priestly confessor and penitent; it enabled the confessor to seek out and deal with any manifestations of the sins that the Church had defined.[16]

When in the seventh and eighth centuries Irish monks launched missions within and beyond the boundaries of Latin Christianity in mainland Europe, they continued to practise individual confession based on tariff books. So did missionaries from the Anglo-Saxon Church, which enthusiastically took over the custom from the Celts – interestingly, on the initiative of the Archbishop of Canterbury who came from the eastern Mediterranean, Theodore of Tarsus. By contrast, bishops in Francia put up some initial resistance to this innovation, notably in the hostile comments of a major episcopal Synod at Chalon-sur-Saône in 813 – 'the errors are obvious, the authors undetermined', the Council observed sniffily about Irish penitentials.[17] Itinerant missionaries of any sort, not merely Irish missionaries, did arouse suspicion in the hierarchy of mainstream Latin Christianity, which had already consciously set its face against wandering monks.

Nevertheless, this was a temporary setback, no doubt overcome by the deep impression made by the missionaries in their determination to spread their version of the Christian faith; it was a notable act of self-sacrifice for Irish monks to have left their own society and its all-embracing network of kinship support to venture into an unfamiliar world across the seas.[18] The harsh words of the Synod of Chalon about tariff books were actually part of a growing movement of the Frankish bishops to take control of the system and produce a more uniform version of it. As a result, a system of individual penance became a feature of the whole Western Church, and then beyond into Orthodoxy.

The penances laid down in the penitentials centred typically on rigorous fasting for set periods, but also common were repeated recitation of sets of psalms (maybe even having to sing them, more daunting for some than others), and a variety of extravagant ways of keeping still for set periods, such as lying in a grave with a corpse. Punishment might overlap with traditional pre-Christian law systems, so it could include flogging or almsgiving or compensation to an injured party; a sentence to travel as an exile as punishment might now be given a Christian focus as a pilgrimage to a suitably cleansing holy place. Self-evidently such penitential results of confession were unlikely to be secret even if the initial formal conversation was in private. They directed the penitent's spiritual rehabilitation back into the whole community, lay or monastic.

One of the first surviving Irish penitentials, from the early seventh century, plausibly claims to have been compiled by Abbot Cummean Fota of Clonfert. The level of detail in this pioneering effort is impressive and is echoed in later compilations. It opens with a good deal of specificity around drunkenness or gluttony, particularly coping with the distressing possibility of vomiting up a consecrated host (forty days' fasting penance, or a hundred if a dog gobbles up the vomit). Cummean's swift transition on to sex enumerates penitential payback for an array of carefully specified sexual activities: for instance, a year's penance for bestiality; for a layperson masturbating, penance throughout the three forty-day annual penitential seasons (only one season for young teenagers) or, for clergy, a whole year of penance. 'Those who befoul their lips', that is indulge in oral sex, earn four years of penance, or if they persist, seven years, which is also the penalty for acts of 'sodomy'. 'Femoral' (intercrural or maybe lesbian) intercourse only merits two years' penance. Among other punishments there is a good deal of banning conjugal relations for set periods, but Cummean also specifies those liturgical and medical days on which any husband and wife should not have sex at all, amounting to around two-thirds of a calendar year.

After enumerating some thirty-three different sexual and sinful possibilities (including subdivisions, mostly with male perpetrators in mind), Cummean turns no doubt with relief to avarice, but once he has covered all John Cassian's eight (rather than the later seven) 'Deadly

Sins', it is back to coping with a range of mostly sexual offences for boys and men living together in monastic communities. The Abbot displays a gloomy awareness of what might be possible, for instance in single or mutual masturbation, sexual activity between older and younger boys (worse if the younger boy enjoys it), intercrural sex, bestiality, and even youthful simulation of heterosexual intercourse (on this, twenty days of penance, forty for recidivists). Unpleasant personal habits are folded into these regulations, which overall give the appearance of being just as interested in curbing bad behaviour and lack of consideration for others as in denouncing sin.[19]

Tariff books were thus from the outset remarkably comprehensive, as well as providing a fascinating index of official opinion about the relative seriousness of particular transgressions in the penances specified. They guided pastoral advice in both Western and Eastern Christianity into modern times, forming new common ground between Catholicism and Orthodoxy when so much else in Christian practice was diverging between the two communions.[20] No doubt penitentials represented a clerical ideal difficult to enforce, and maybe their detailed case law was a tribute to the vivid imaginations of priestly confessors anxious to provide cover for any situation. It would be unwise to have given potential penitents ideas by asking them too many leading questions, so a sensible priest would have been selective in confession.

Nevertheless, the penitentials do suggest the rich variety of potential sin available to early medieval Irish folk and their successors, in sexual matters as in much else. They also offer to a violent and unpoliced society a good deal of common-sense regulation of cruelty and general public misbehaviour, seen through the prism of the seven Deadly Sins: a new framework for organizing human affairs that transcended the intricacies of Ireland's existing structures of power and lawmaking, reassuringly entrusting the anxious to the care of a universal Church. If this Irish/Welsh innovation had not proved to have wide appeal as part of the package of Irish Christian mission in mainland Europe, the institution of private confession would not have enjoyed such power over the following millennium, for good or ill. It has to be recognized, nevertheless, that in all eras from the earliest days a major part of that power was directed towards the regulation of sexual behaviour, even though it constituted only one-seventh of the quota of deadly sin.[21]

BRITANNIA SUPPLANTED: ANGLO-SAXON CHRISTIANITY

In 597, the Christianity flourishing in the west of the Atlantic archipelago was confronted by a remarkable initiative from one of the most significant popes in Latin Christian history, Gregory I ('the Great'). He commissioned Augustine, a monk of the monastery of St Andrew that Gregory himself had founded in Rome, to lead a group of Italian monks and priests into the former Roman province of Britannia Superior. The province's south-east corner was now ruled by the Jutish Kings of Kent, and that kingdom became the base for a wider mission across territories now culturally dominated by a patchwork of Germanic kingdoms of Jutes, Angles and Saxons. These peoples were now generally known to Latin-speakers as *Angli*; their lands would later be called England.

It was not at all normal for a Bishop of Rome to launch a project of conversion like this. Maybe it emerged from a sudden decision on Gregory's part, which might account for signs of haste and lack of up-to-date information in Augustine's venture.[22] The English themselves nevertheless soon advanced a more long-term explanation, a story incorporated in the very first surviving biography of Pope Gregory, probably written by his admirers in the monastery of Whitby in Yorkshire around 700, and retold by the foremost Anglo-Saxon historian of the same period, Bede (*c.*672–735). Before Gregory became Pope, he was struck by the good looks of some English boys or youths who, Bede says, were being sold as slaves in Rome. Enquiring where they came from and being told that they were *Angli*, Gregory commented that the name was appropriate to those with angelic faces, and he varied that cheerful thought in a clutch of further devout Latin puns. Traditionally Gregory's reported literary playfulness has been summed up in a misquotation as '*Non Angli sed angeli*': 'Not Angles, but angels.' Perhaps the agreeable neatness of the pun has allowed the survival of a story which, if reframed as 'Pope, impressed by beauty of young enslaved males, launches mission', might not meet modern safeguarding standards in methods of evangelism.[23]

Regardless of the truth of the tale, which has certainly pleased the English down to modern times, it is possible to suggest a contemporary background in European-wide ecclesiastical politics. There is only one candidate as a possible papal precedent for Gregory's initiative in Kent:

Palladius's now shadowy mission from Rome to Ireland in 431. In both cases, the suspicion arises that the Pope was chiefly concerned to bring existing Christian activity closer into line with Roman authority; in Palladius's fifth-century venture, the worry may have been British interest in Pelagianism via the monastic theology promoted in the writings of John Cassian.[24] In the Canterbury mission of 597, the background was not Pelagianism but an obvious ebbing in the Europe-wide Arian threat to Catholic Christianity, which would make it opportune to consolidate Catholic theology and practice in the Atlantic archipelago. This was the era when Arianism lost its power in western monarchies, with the Byzantine Emperor ending Ostrogoth rule in Ravenna in the 550s and the Visigothic king in the Iberian Peninsula converting from Arianism to Catholicism in 589, right on the eve of Augustine's mission.

Pope Gregory was not enthusiastic for Byzantium's renewed assertiveness in the Adriatic, and he saw a more attractive western ally in the now well-established Catholic Merovingian dynasty of Francia. Well before Augustine's arrival the Frankish princess Bertha had married King Æthelberht (Ethelbert) of Kent, installing a Catholic bishop as her chaplain in the royal capital at Canterbury. Archaeology reveals the Anglo-Saxon mood-music around these events: an abrupt shift in the artistic style of objects found in elite graves from Germanic to Frankish types, first perceptible in Kent around 580. The *Angli* were already enthusiastically looking south, regardless of whether or not that inclined them to Christianity.[25] Augustine was coming to a land prepared, but he brought a programmatically Roman style of Christianity which he signalled with various prominent church foundations in Kent: a monastery in Canterbury named after Rome's cult saints Peter and Paul, plus a cathedral there dedicated as Christ Church like the Pope's own cathedral in Rome, and eventually a second monastery/cathedral at Rochester which took as its patron St Andrew, like Pope Gregory's monastery in Rome from which Augustine had come.

Most of what we have traditionally known about these events comes via the brilliantly presented and absorbing *Ecclesiastical History* of Bede, writing just over a century after Augustine's mission to Canterbury. His story celebrates a steadily more united Church originating with Augustine and as a consequence exceptionally loyal to the Roman Papacy. England and its Church certainly became just that – it consistently honoured Pope Gregory, rather than Augustine himself, as 'Apostle of the English'.[26] Bede's home territory was the joint monastery of Monkwearmouth–Jarrow in

Northumbria, more than three hundred miles north of Kent, but his vision of a Christianity embracing all Anglo-Saxon lands enabled him to draw on friendship, reminiscence and surviving archival resources in Canterbury; this inevitably distorted his richly detailed narrative in favour of the Augustinian mission. His account of the pre-existing British Church is minimalist and generally unsympathetic, and probably underplays its role in Christianizing the *Angli*.

Nevertheless, such is the excellence of Bede's writing and research that it is possible to read his text against the grain, particularly because archaeology has steadily enriched and realigned the wider picture. For instance, a princely burial discovered in 2003 at Prittlewell in a kingdom beyond Kent, the land of the East Saxons (Essex), produced an enjoyable complication when analysed. Archaeological technology made possible quite precise dating of its rich grave contents, demonstrating that the royal Saxon occupant probably died in the decade before Augustine arrived in Kent, yet he had already been given an unambiguously Christian burial with characteristics linking it to Italy.[27] Pope Gregory himself had earlier revealed that he was perfectly well aware of a Church already operating in the lands soon to be visited by Augustine when, in 596, he wrote to the Frankish Queen Brunhild; he criticized its clergy for neglecting the *Angli* and for being 'remiss in handling their desires [for conversion] by their own exhortations'.[28]

One curious preoccupation leaps out from letters of advice from the Pope to Augustine that Bede preserved from Canterbury archives. A large proportion of Gregory's attention is taken up in brooding about sex – to be more specific, ritual impurity. Gregory argues at great length against people who have been perplexing Augustine in Kent because of their strong opinions about what constituted sexual uncleanness. These rigorists want to borrow Old Testament exclusions from participation in Temple worship and apply them to pregnant women and the sexual relations of married couples; moreover, the restrictions include one of those rare sightings of the centuries-long Christian prejudice against menstruating women being allowed to receive Communion. Clearly such people were Christians, since non-Christians would have no interest in or knowledge of the Old Testament. The Roman missionaries were coming up against a significant body of well-informed local Christians with different and stricter moral proscriptions from themselves.[29]

Gregory's thoughts on female ritual impurity may have been so generously permissive out of irritation at the independent-mindedness of the existing Kentish congregations, and, as it turned out, his liberality did not impress subsequent English Christians any more than it did their predecessors, or indeed later Christians in Orthodox lands. Perhaps the British Church in the lands of the *Angli* had self-consciously maintained rigid moral standards to maintain its distinctiveness in the face of a majority Germanic non-Christian culture: the same impulse had led the Dyophysite Church of the East to champion monogamy in Sasanian and Islamicate lands.

Bede did not trouble to highlight features of the Anglo-Saxon Church that mark it out as distinctive in Western Latin Christianity during its 'conversion' era. The most important of these was that for about two centuries beginning around the 580s, elite women took leading roles and independent initiatives in the Anglo-Saxon Church, before this faded away into a more normal pattern of male dominance. The phenomenon still needs investigation and explanation; the only parallels are in northern Francia, which was already linked directly to Kent and East Anglia by royal marriages when Augustine arrived. Behind it may lie attitudes inherited from non-Christian Germanic culture, where certain women were honoured with richly furnished graves, such as a sixth-century lady excavated at Bidford-on-Avon in Warwickshire. Her two bags of amulets suggest that she enjoyed the status of a wise woman, and her bucket-pendants would have jingled on her clothing as she danced; this looks like the costume of a shaman. Amulets as emblems of magic power were especially associated with pre-Christian female graves in England, but they were succeeded in Christian interments with a new crop of amulets with cross designs, or little bags likely to have contained sacred relics.

These graves are another notable feature of Anglo-Saxon Christianity; contrary to the general custom in most Christian societies, richly furnished burials continued after Augustine's arrival and even revived around 660, and the majority are female.[30] This local individuality overlaps with other special features of the early Anglo-Saxon 'conversion' that reflect the reality that Christianity spread through the decisions of Christianized monarchs: having opted for the new religion, they ordered their people to accept it in place of previous polytheistic cults. First came a brief vogue for male royal holiness: some kings deserted their realms to undertake long pilgrimages to Rome from which they did not return. At least four Anglo-Saxon Christian monarchs even voluntarily renounced their thrones and retired to monasteries, beginning with King Sigebert of the East Angles sometime after his accession as king in 630/31.

This was a most unusual impulse among the Germanic kingdoms of Europe, and it was accompanied by the promotion of saintly cults for further monarchs who died defending their Christian faith, such as King Oswald of Northumbria, killed in battle against the non-Christian King Penda of Mercia in 642. Associated with particular royal families, these were the first native Christian cults created by the Anglo-Saxons. There may be a connection with local pre-Christian traditions of honouring kings who sacrificially defended their people in battle; later monarchs who died violently, such as young Edmund of East Anglia butchered by non-Christian Danes in 869, also joined the saintly club of royal martyrs.[31]

The seventh century nevertheless saw a change of direction for royal activity in the Anglo-Saxon Church. Elsewhere, in both Latin and Byzantine Christianity, when monarchs became monks it was done under duress and was a sign of personal failure. Perhaps with that in mind, and maybe accompanied by a certain restiveness among their subjects at what might be viewed as royal malingering, the Anglo-Saxons swiftly reconfigured their own thoughts on royal holiness. In place of kings becoming ascetics, female members of the various royal dynasties acted on recent precedents that they might have noted among their relatives in northern Francia. Royal ladies founded lavishly funded monastic communities and presided over them as abbesses, ruling over both men and women; over several generations an appropriate female member of the dynasty would then succeed as abbess.

The women involved were princesses or queens who were either widowed or had effectively made a decision to declare themselves single, such as the celebrated Æthelthryth, who insisted on guarding her virginity through two royal marriages. After twelve years as Northumbrian Queen Consort, Æthelthryth finally separated from her unfortunate second husband in 673 and returned to her East Anglian homeland to found and govern her own abbey on its fenland border; it still flourishes in modified form as Ely's Anglican Cathedral. Various royal relatives followed Æthelthryth in ruling over this powerful Fenland community; after her interred corpse had been revealed as miraculously incorrupt when her successor had it moved to a new tomb in the abbey church, she became one of the most popular among native Anglo-Saxon saints. Pilgrims also became enthusiastic about her saintly royal siblings from the

East Anglian dynasty, Seaxburh, Æthelburh and Sæthryth, and devotional demand appears to have later added an extra princess-sister, Wihtburh, for good measure. The ladies' confusingly named father King Anna received further pious attention, though on a smaller scale. One notes that, as in early monasticism in the Christian East, Æthelthryth's deliberate abandonment of a marriage for something better was no obstacle to sainthood.[32]

The establishing of such royal monasteries led by women started in the mid-seventh century kingdom by kingdom whenever Christianity came to monopolize the practice of religion, and the custom greatly expanded in the last three decades. The twenty-five or thirty such royal foundations that we know about in the Anglo-Saxon monarchies between the sixth and eighth centuries are unquestionably only a fraction of the original total. Clearly this division of royal labour well suited the dynasties orchestrating Christian conversion. It left male monarchs to do what they were expected to do – wield worldly authority and wage war on behalf of their people – while women embodied the dynasty's spiritual power: evidently a much more congenial prospect for many of them than marriage. John Blair has identified more than fifty female Anglo-Saxon saints as either royal or from the highest aristocracy.[33] Around them, the leaders of royal war-bands who had sustained armed aggression between kingdoms settled down to a more peaceful existence as 'thegns', courtier-administrators with royal grants of land for life. Endowment of family monasteries (or 'minsters', as Old English developed the Latin word *monasteria*) multiplied well beyond royal patronage.

There was a problem in this lively development: in the seventh century, northern Europe had no generally agreed model for a monastic community, for the Italian Benedictine Rule was not yet generally imitated elsewhere. Just as Irish monasticism and mission had shaped itself to the society in which it found itself, enthusiastic Anglo-Saxon Christians creatively improvised: as ready to define monastic life for themselves as they were fertile in devising new Anglo-Saxon words for Christian concepts they found expressed in Latin. The word 'minster' had a generous breadth of meaning, covering both communities of celibates and large churches offering liturgy and pastoral care to a wide area, staffed largely by married clergy, in which sons succeeded fathers in their clerical duties.[34] Whatever a particular minster's place on that spectrum, it was endowed with land formally conveyed from the king by the novelty of a charter written on parchment. That might seem a good way to stabilize and protect the assets of a family which was itself newly settled down around a former warlord, as well as offering a pleasantly pious Christian way to live.

While this suited lay dynasties very well, the male hierarchy of Catholic bishops created on the basis of Augustine's mission was not so enthusiastic. What appeared a seemly and comfortable arrangement to eighth-century Anglo-Saxon aristocrats both male and female outraged Bede, as spokesman and chronicler of Roman clerical obedience and initiative. In the course of a long letter of avuncular but splenetic advice to a former pupil who had become Bishop of York, Bede expressed his fury at what he observed in the minsters of his own Northumbria. He was outraged by the spiritual untidiness of these institutions: their self-interested confusion of lay and clerical roles. It was especially disgraceful that thegns

> even go so far as to ask for places to build monasteries, as they themselves put it, for their wives, who in equal foolishness, although they are laywomen, allow themselves to be abbesses of the maidservants of Christ. That saying of the common folk suits them well: 'wasps may well build combs but they store up poison in them, not honey.'[35]

Expressing similar sentiments, Bede's *Ecclesiastical History* recounts the sad destruction by fire in 683 of Coldingham Abbey, blaming the wicked ways of the inmates – both women and men – presided over by the Northumbrian princess Æbba. A censorious passing angel submitted a critical report on Coldingham to a particularly austere male member of the community; the specific wickedness seems to have consisted of accomplished weaving and oversleeping, plus 'feasting, drinking, gossip, and other delights'. Bede's rhetoric of denunciation is so dramatic that the reader may forget his initial rather lame admission that the fire was the result of carelessness. Evidently two different visions of life in a royal monastic community were the real issue at Coldingham.[36]

By the end of the eighth century, these remarkable and individual Anglo-Saxon arrangements were coming to an end. Partly this was the result of a calamity for the whole island that began in the 790s: a sequence of destructive raids escalating to prolonged invasion by Scandinavians, who in their eruption into eastern Europe had been called Rus' and here were known as Vikings or Danes. At first they were non-Christians with no sympathy for the religion that they found. Monasteries as comfortable and prosperous as Whitby or (the rebuilt) Coldingham were obvious targets for plunder and worse. The impact was greater in the east and north which bore the brunt of Viking attack and of which the Scandinavians eventually took territorial control, but everywhere there was disruption and demoralization. A painful recovery followed, particularly when the Scandinavians themselves made a spiritual U-turn and adopted Christianity; but there was no going back to the past.[37]

Quite apart from the destructive impact of the Vikings, there were strong pressures for change from within the Anglo-Saxon Church that were given opportunity by the need for reconstruction, but which did not involve reconstructing exactly what was there before. The echoes of Bede's accusing voice remained strong: his firm views on what monastic life should be like were echoed by monastic reformers of the ninth and tenth centuries. That was aided by the pride of Anglo-Saxons in being part of a greater sacred unity than their own land; that might trump ecclesiastical arrangements which had served dynasties well in the conversion years. This concept of unity was encapsulated in the Anglo-Saxon word 'Christendom', a ninth-century coinage by one of their own scholars, now anonymous, in the course of translating into Old English a four-century-old Latin Christian history. The translator was probably associated with the court of King Ælfred (Alfred) of Wessex: successful military leader against the Vikings and an enthusiast and participant in both English and Latin scholarship in his effort to rebuild his kingdom.[38]

Alfred's military triumph was the basis for uniting the multiple Anglo-Saxon monarchies under the royal house of Wessex by the later Kings Æthelstan and Eadgar (reigned 924–39 and 959–75 respectively). Æthelstan, prompted by Bede's history, boldly reached back to the lost Roman provinces when he styled himself on his coinage *rex totius Britanniae* (king of all Britain), but the more realistic title that endured among his successors was kingship of a people now simply called the English, in a realm of 'England'.[39] This triumph of a national identity was actually reinforced by the wider concept of 'Christendom' centred on the Papacy, for the new political unity of the Anglo-Saxon lands had been anticipated for three centuries by the united organization of their Church, fruit of Gregory's mission in 597. English pride in this alliance of universal and national was expressed in a development unparalleled elsewhere in the contemporary West, a lively vernacular English literature alongside local scholarship in Latin; encouraged by King Alfred, it lent vigour and confidence to efforts to reform Church institutions under royal patronage.

The focus of this programme was to press for the adoption of the Benedictine Rule in English monasteries, in imitation of an already expanding programme of monastic renewal to the south across the Channel. The Rule itself was translated from Latin into Old English by the leader among the clerical reformers, Æthelwold. Like many reform-minded Anglo-Saxon clergy, he was in close and admiring contact with the Frankish monastery of Fleury in the Loire valley, perhaps the largest monastery of its era and renowned for possessing the actual body of Benedict (which the monks had hijacked from its original Italian home at Monte Cassino). Indeed, Æthelwold is said to have sent to Fleury to get his copy of the Benedictine Rule.[40] In England, he enjoyed the esteem of both Kings Æthelstan and Eadgar, so that his career climaxed as Bishop in the royal capital of Winchester. From the same circle of energetic ecclesiastical reformers, Eadgar promoted Oswald and Dunstan as Archbishops respectively of York and Canterbury. A junior member of the same group, Ælfheah (Alphege), who likewise went on to be Archbishop of Canterbury, was given the nickname 'the Bald', which probably refers to the fact that, as a monk originally professed in Gloucestershire, he displayed a full monastic tonsure, at the time a novelty among senior English clergy.[41]

The tenth-century reforms asserted one single form of male power in the Church, with two targets in sight: radically adjusting the role of royal women, and launching an attack on married clergy. Queens went on endowing monasteries for women in the tenth century, but no longer did their abbesses rule over men as well, and generally religious life for women was much diminished, with far fewer and less well-endowed foundations than for monks.[42] The radical change was symbolized when Æthelthryth/Etheldreda's monastery at Ely was refounded in 970 after Viking destruction. Now it became an all-male monastic community, and so it remained thereafter, with the unspoken historical embarrassment that its flourishing and profitable pilgrimage cult was focused on royal holy women of previous centuries. Later monks in the magnificently rebuilt Romanesque Ely Cathedral even balanced that inescapable femininity by carefully creating a shrine to seven worthy Anglo-Saxon and Scandinavian males from more recent times, so that pilgrims might pay them devotion before they made their way onwards to the main attraction of Etheldreda's grave.[43]

Etheldreda did have a continuing usefulness for tenth-century reformers because of her emphatic defence of her virginity through her two marriages. Beyond her was the ultimate example of the divine favour offered to virginity, in Mary. There is previous evidence of the cult of Mary from the seventh century, but that evidence mainly comes from the north and west Midlands, the kingdoms of Northumbria and Mercia, suggesting that it may have been an overspill from devotion in Irish or Welsh Christianity. A new phase in the tenth century has a different distribution in southern England, with its central energy in Winchester, just at the period and in the area most involved in monastic reform.[44]

There was more to Mary than simply a symbol of virginity. Prominent in the lively literature that Marian devotion generated was the theme of Mary as Queen of Heaven, which chimed with the long-standing Anglo-Saxon devotion to queens who were saints. Even if their royal successors had lost much of their actual power in the Church, a turn to

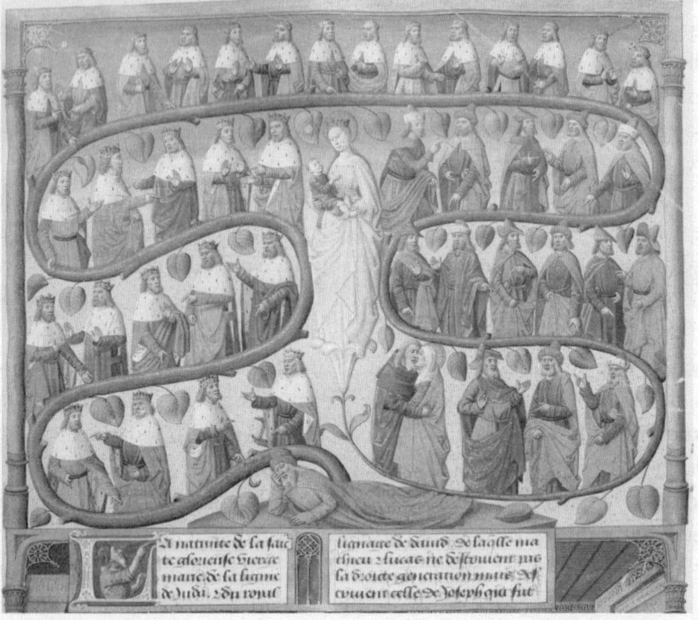

14. This late fifteenth-century French translation of the *Golden Legend* puts Mary emphatically at the centre of the family tree back to Jesse, father of David, though the caption below hints at the complications of genealogy in Matthew and Luke's Gospels.

Mary was perhaps a way of squaring that rhetorical circle. In the same fashion as the links of the whole monastic reform movement with Francia, English Marian devotion could draw on a century or more of Frankish Marian literature. Such literature had grown increasingly fascinated by Mary's genealogy that made her Queen of Heaven: she now became the pinnacle of the genealogical line of Jesus set out in Matthew's Gospel, regardless of the complications of that genealogy which we have already observed as leading not to Mary but to Joseph (above, Chapter 4). The Marian family tree was a development that well suited an age of royal families struggling to retain or reclaim their power.[45]

Church reform in England created a second set of victims, this time male. Contemptuous of what remained of the former Anglo-Saxon system of religious foundations organized with families and dynasties in mind, the reformers bitterly attacked the supposed sinfulness and debauchery of clergy living as 'canons' of English minsters, whether married or professedly celibate – the distinction was not always clear. Bishop Æthelwold led the way in expelling the existing clerical staff of two adjacent minsters in his cathedral city of Winchester, all with the backing of King Eadgar and the King's thegns. Such reformers as Æthelwold were reading Bede's diatribes against those monasteries of which he had disapproved, and behind Bede was the 'Apostle of the English' Gregory the Great. Both these venerated authorities reached back to the writings of the mysterious Easterner Pseudo-Dionysios the Areopagite, and they confronted their readers with Dionysios's resonant identification of true ascetics as angels: remember the investigative journalism of Bede's angel at Coldingham.[46]

Conversely, Bishop Æthelwold (ventriloquizing King Eadgar in a royal charter to the refounded New Minster in Winchester) compared his clerical victims to the angel companions of Satan/Lucifer/the Devil whom God had expelled from Paradise, 'cast[ing] out the filth of the rebel angels with their puffed-up haughtiness'. The Wessex campaigners for purity were in the same way 'clearing away the filth of evil deeds'.[47] In the Byzantine world, eunuchs had seized on the image of the angel for their own purposes (above, Chapter 8), but eunuchs hardly impinged on the consciousness of Latin Westerners, and so the angelic metaphor was now left in the sole possession of monks. Nuns rather fell out of this comparison, in keeping with the unexamined assumption that the genderlessness of angels was still vaguely male: as vague as the maleness of a monk should be. Therefore nunneries were not going to share much of the benefit of this literary construction. Nor could a nun celebrate the Eucharist, unlike an ordained monk, who upstaged her virginity by his resemblance to an angel.

Prolonged and serious resistance from married clergy no doubt encouraged the violence of the reformers' rhetoric, who might have had to recognize that in the Atlantic islands, as in the coastal regions of Francia facing England, most clergy were in fact the sons of clergy right into the eleventh century, if not beyond. One defiant marginal comment on a reformist sermon from a now anonymous eleventh-century English priest probably speaks for many: 'It is right that a priest love a decent woman as a bedmate.'[48] One lasting result of reform did mark out England as distinctive in Europe: several of its cathedrals now doubled as Benedictine monasteries, something hardly known elsewhere except under English influence, and continued thus over the next half-millennium. Otherwise, the goals of the reform movement had not been fully achieved when Anglo-Saxon England disintegrated in 1066, particularly in regard to clerical celibacy. On a continent-wide scale the English reform was nevertheless influential in creating a direction of travel for the whole Latin Church.[49] It was a lively part of a wider western European movement that also gained momentum through dramatic changes in the lands of Francia from the end of the eighth century, when the Frankish King Charles created a new imperial ideal to rival the Old Rome of Byzantium.

THE CAROLINGIAN MOMENT: MONASTIC CITIES OF GOD

The monarch who became known as Charles the Great or *Carolus Magnus* ('Charlemagne') was descended from Charles Martel, a court official of the Frankish Merovingian monarchy who had turned back the Islamic advance at Poitiers in 733. Martel's family elbowed aside their increasingly ineffective masters, dispatching the last Merovingian king into enforced monastic retirement in 751 and claiming the throne themselves. Like the usurping dynasty of David in Israel long before when eliminating the House of Saul, Martel's son King Pippin III and his successors made sure that their chroniclers demonstrated how emphatically God favoured the new dispensation.[50] Essential to this process was courting the most energetic and influential Churchmen in

Francia and, beyond them, the Pope in Rome. Quite apart from their own political position, these abbots and bishops guarded the shrines of powerful saints headed by St Peter in Rome, whose celestial approval would be a prize for the new regime.

An alliance with the Pope was of mutual benefit, for it gave a vulnerable Papacy a powerful source of support in the West against the Byzantine Emperor and his Patriarch in Constantinople. The bargain was emphasized when Pippin III captured former Byzantine lands in Italy from yet another Germanic immigrant people, the Lombards; he did not restore these territories to the Emperor but gifted them to Pope Stephen II (752–57) – the origin of that long-lived political unit, the Papal States. In return, a few years later Pope Hadrian I (772–95) ceased to date documents from his administration by the Emperor's regnal year, and instead used the year of his own period in office and the regnal year of the King of the Franks.

This was a double blow to the fading power of the Byzantine Empire in the West; Pippin's son Charlemagne sealed it with an extraordinary symbolic gesture. Having succeeded to the Frankish throne in 768, on Christmas Day 800 he celebrated his steadily expanding conquests with a ceremony in Rome in which Pope Leo III crowned him Emperor 'of the Romans'. More than that, Leo knelt in homage before the newly minted Emperor. That was an understandable gesture from an insecure ruler whom Charlemagne had helped rescue from a murderous attempted coup in the previous year, but subsequent popes regretted it, never repeated it, and began making strenuous attempts to bolster their own authority with a series of supposedly historical documents: these forgeries became highly important in the Papacy's future claims to universal authority.

Thus, during the ninth century twin sources of political legitimacy emerged in the Latin West: an aspiring papal monarchy and the Carolingian imperial project that later became known as the 'Holy Roman Empire'. The emperors' expansion of that title from the imperial original during the High Middle Ages was a clear bid for sacred authority against the Pope. With goodwill the two powers might complement each other, but frequently they became bitterly opposed. Both were created through the eighth and ninth centuries against a wider background of steadily more bitter tensions between Western and Eastern Christianity (see Chapter 10); that gulf remained when the issues moved on.[51]

The Emperor was fascinated by the Roman imperial heritage he had annexed. He filched columns from imperial Ravenna to decorate his stately new Palace chapel at Aachen (from which its French name, Aix-la-Chapelle, is derived); he bathed nude in the hot springs of Aachen as a good Roman gentleman would have done, and in his last years he issued a most remarkable coinage, meticulously imitating Roman coins from more than half a millennium earlier, bearing a portrait bust of himself depicted in a thoroughly un-Frankish manner, laurel-wreathed and clean-shaven.[52] Yet this was a Christian Roman Empire; among Charlemagne's favourite books (read aloud to him for relaxation) were Augustine's great meditation on the divine shaping of world history, *The City of God*, and the writings of Bede on history, angels and much more. The Emperor's energetic programme of codifying law for his empire compared him with God's ancient ministers Moses and King Josiah of Judah. This enterprise of rediscovering the Graeco-Roman world and interpreting it for a new age is just as worthy of being termed a 'Renaissance' as later convulsions of cultural excitement in the twelfth century and in fourteenth-century Italy; it was the recovery of a culture and a language that were in severe decay through most of Europe.[53]

Annexing the Classical and Christian past like this demanded that the Empire should conserve what remained of its literature, and then expand on it with new explorations. A vital part of the multiform programme that Charlemagne launched was the copying of manuscripts, so alarmingly neglected since the mid-sixth century. He even sponsored a new Latin script to produce easily readable texts reproduced with relative speed; it is now known as 'Carolingian minuscule', a direct ancestor of the typeface employed in modern printed books such as this.[54] This mammoth task, which saved the collective memory of the Latin West from further loss, would absorb the time of countless professional scribes, and the most readily available source of such specialist labour was the monastery, or indeed the nunnery. Anglo-Saxon monastic life as created by 700 was at the height of its self-confidence and creativity and provided a model for the new monastic culture in mainland Europe. It is remarkable that such a latecomer to Latinity as the Anglo-Saxon Church should become one of the chief energies behind the recovery of idiomatic high-level Latin for speaking and writing, and one of the most honoured scholars of the Carolingian court was a late product of that energy, Alcuin of York (*c.*735–804), who is likely to have been the source of the Emperor's interest in Bede.

With initiatives from Pippin and Charlemagne, duly imitated by their leading noblemen, monasteries were founded or expanded with generous new endowments to spread across the growing imperial dominions; the Emperor followed the recommendation of his officials that these institutions adopt the Rule of St Benedict. That decision was clearly encouraged by the benevolent presence of the saint himself at the heart of Francia, having put up no apparent resistance to his kidnapping from Monte Cassino by the monks of Fleury. The appropriation of his Rule might seem almost as surprising, because, instead of the simple communities of ascetics for which it had been written, the artful and flexible simplicity of its provisions now governed Carolingian monasteries that were more like contemporary towns, though a good deal better administered.[55]

Carolingian monks followed their increasingly elaborate monastic observance in worship, prayer and scholarship amid a bustle of lay servants, craftsmen, labourers and guests, in stately architectural settings which could outdo most of the secular palaces of Western Christendom. These were indeed cities of God on earth: the ordered splendour of their life was an awe-inspiring image of heaven in a world distressingly short of order or regulation. To see their monks as like the angelic courtiers of God was a natural embodiment of those potent metaphors drawn from Augustine and Pseudo-Dionysios (whose voice was suddenly directly available, since a copy of his writings arrived in ninth-century Francia from the East).[56] A striking feature of these holy cities was that among the swarm of inhabitants were a great many children: products of a newly popular pious custom known as oblation, by which parents gifted their young offspring to the monastic life.

Oblation was not a complete novelty. In the eastern Mediterranean and Egypt, the tradition of Pachomian monasticism had produced communities of similar elaboration supported by lavish endowments, like later Carolingian practice. From early in the development of Egyptian monasticism, children had been present in such monasteries; placed there by their relatives for protection, as a gesture of gratitude to the community, or accompanying their fathers into monastic life, like the unfortunate little son of 'Patermutus' recorded for us by John Cassian. The amount of concern for them in early monastic regulation and in anecdotes about the spirituality of monks, particularly moral temptations, also reveals that such children needed careful provision against sexual abuse.[57] The evidence from Egypt in the fourth and fifth centuries leads on to the close regulation of children in sixth-century Irish monasteries that we have already encountered in the penitential of Abbot Cummean Fota (above, p. 221), but in the West, oblation took a decisive turn away from earlier Eastern practice, thanks to the Benedictine Rule.

The general consensus among Eastern monastic authorities was that it was not suitable to demand an early decision in life on something as important as chastity. Basil the Great sensibly observed that 'it is not proper to consider children's words entirely final in such matters' and suggested the mid to late teens as an appropriate age, for girls at least. By contrast, Benedict's Rule provided that parents might offer their children for life to a particular monastery, making it a solemn liturgical moment in the context of the Eucharist, and with none of the provisions for probation or second thoughts that the Rule allowed for older entrants to monastic life. From that moment, the young oblate, in theory at least, ended all contacts outside the community. It is interesting that various adaptations of Benedict's Rule over the next hundred years often omitted this provision on oblation, which suggests that it was controversial, but after explicit support from the Papacy in the eighth century lifelong oblation became standard in the West for the next three centuries; there were, after all, distinguished examples of the practice as precedents, including none other than Bede at Monkwearmouth–Jarrow.[58]

From what had apparently been a minor provision of Benedict's Rule, oblation became a major feature of Carolingian life between the ninth and the eleventh centuries, both for boys and girls (though we know a great deal less about the custom in nunneries). It is likely that the majority of inhabitants in monasteries and nunneries were now products of oblation in early childhood, and thus they formed a category of European Christians who spent their whole lives in celibacy, thanks to a decision made for them by their family. In the modern West this seems bizarre, and it is possible to interpret it with cynicism as an efficient way of providing unwanted offspring with security for life; yet it could also be considered a sensible division of family labour in which few people expected personal choice. Moreover, because oblation was a conscious sacrifice to God, just as much as any donation of money or land, it was logical that it should be irrevocable. As its historian comments, oblation 'was the opposite of abandonment'.[59]

Oblates made a lifelong contribution to their family and community economy by their prayers: a duty as important as (if not more than) helping with seed time and harvest, because prayer was the road

15. A late thirteenth-century French MS for Gratian's legal treatise the *Decretum* looks back on the custom of monastic oblation, by then much diminished. The parents hand the abbot a bag of money: equivalent of a dowry.

to individual and collective salvation. The highest and most powerful form of prayer was the Eucharist (or 'Mass', as it was styled in Latin): the more Masses the better, Westerners considered, especially if they were celebrated near the tomb of some influential and attentive saint.[60] Society's demand for Masses therefore multiplied in the Carolingian West, to be celebrated in return for large donations provided by royal and noble benefactors and countless lesser offerings. Amid increasing arguments about whether clergy should be part of the sexual economy at all, oblation supplied the Latin Church with a reliable supply of pure males to celebrate these Masses, so more and more monks were ordained priests. In fact, between the oblation of children to monasteries and the training of sons for ordination by their clerical fathers, it was now very unlikely that an adult layman would consider getting ordained to the priesthood: there was just too much specialist education involved. It is not surprising that, on the basis of these two streams of clerical identity, the medieval Western Church proceeded to create a version of Christianity with an exceptionally strong separation between clergy and laity.[61]

Thus, from being the exception in monastic life, by the tenth century priestly ordination of monks became the norm, and this change went hand in hand with the more general assumption that a priest should celebrate his own Mass every day. Charlemagne's abbey churches accordingly adopted an architectural layout that made provision for many side-altars, at which priests could celebrate their daily 'Low Mass': a less elaborate Eucharist than that sung for the whole community at the high altar, and simply performed as a spoken rite with a token congregation perhaps of one server.[62] Eastern Christianity did not experience these developments, any more than it promoted lifelong oblation. In the East a single altar in each church has continued to serve the celebration of a sung Eucharist, as a glance at their church buildings will still confirm: another respect in which the Western Latin Church, its church buildings and its monasteries were now permanently parting company with Orthodoxy.

Naturally monasteries made provision for oblates in schooling, not just to educate them in liturgy, literacy or even scholarship, but to instil in them the whole ethos of monastic life, including the regulation of that inherently spirited self-expression of the young, noise. Monasteries were not silent communities, for they resounded with bells, sacred chant and the collective sound of murmuring from the reading of books, not customarily then a silent activity. The point was that all this noise must be framed and orchestrated as the community directed. The inevitable din also produced by guest hospitality and farming was increasingly segregated by the new development of a particular formal architectural layout for Western monastic buildings, now familiar to any historically minded tourist: a monastic central grouping of church, dining-hall, dormitory and chapter house around a cloister, with everything else and its resultant racket relegated to the margins.[63]

Within that sacred enclosure, permissible sound was complemented by developing a silence that was also language, because it was a system of hand-signs so everyone might communicate information and thoughts that absolutely needed to be passed on within the chief settings of common life: church, library and kitchen. Moreover, the signs incorporated forceful reminders to those who learned it of how monastic society worked: so the common sign for 'angel' was the same as for 'Alleluia', since that is what angels sing, and so do monks in their church services. In the unusually elaborate sign-system developed for the eleventh-century Cluniac house of Hirsau in the Black Forest, the sign for 'laughter' was classified as part of a group of signs relating to sickness, including nose-bleeding and vomiting: these were all unfortunate and undesirable phenomena, especially if they punctured monastic silence.[64]

The unity of the Carolingian empire did not long survive the death of Charlemagne in 814, and various later versions of western Latin empire, Holy and Roman though they eventually might claim to be, represented a different assembly of territories as time went on. Over the next two centuries, the various lords, princes and emperors struggling to benefit from the political confusion continued to look to the various great Benedictine monasteries to bolster their own positions; the abbots were more convincing spiritual allies than a dismal succession of tenth-century popes, who collectively represent an all-time low in papal prestige. Alongside various recent Benedictine imperial foundations in the eastern portion of the Empire (now southern Germany, Austria and Switzerland), in Francia Fleury remained the leader, together with a newly established abbey at Cluny, whose foundation in 909–10 paralleled the new enthusiasm for Benedictine monasticism in England, and which in the eleventh century was to reframe Benedictine monasticism for a later age (below, Chapter 12).

Even if the Empire fragmented, the society that Charlemagne created represented a lasting new departure for the formation of Christendom. For its noblemen, wealth increasingly came from the exploitation of landed estates rather than from warfare and plunder. That process was accelerated by Charlemagne's deliberate and determined campaign of legislation from the 780s, in which he sought to frame aristocratic behaviour within Christian constraints. That included public rituals of shaming offenders against good order – pilgrimages to distant shrines, even carrying a saddle on their backs at royal pleasure. All of this was combined with a concerted official effort to create a uniform system of penitentials out of the various versions imported by Irish or Anglo-Saxon missionaries.[65] Nobles faced with such coercion also saw the positive advantage of interesting themselves in agricultural improvement and bringing more land under cultivation, all of which encouraged them in tying down the obligations of the labour force needed to achieve this.

The population of Christian Europe thus became both more settled and more subject to systematic control than it had ever been. The Western

Church modified its institutions accordingly, to create a system of pastoral care for the whole population throughout its range with no exact precedent: the parishes. The word *parochia* had long existed in Christian usage, and before the ninth century it meant an area of Church jurisdiction smaller than a bishop's diocese; but just as the word 'diocese' diminished from describing something very large indeed, so gradually over the next two hundred years *parochia* came to define a particular fairly small neighbourhood with a single church building.

To begin with, most of such churches were the property and personal chapels of particular lords, but in an intricate and regionally uneven fashion they evolved to be a unified system that effectively covered the whole continent, spreading ultimately (in very similar form) to the parts of Eastern Christianity still ruled by Christians. In effect, allowing for the usual anomalies of geography, the parish system completely parcelled up the map of Europe. In my East Anglian childhood in the 1960s, I was still very conscious of living in such a parish, because my father was its Rector, surveying the village and church from his parsonage house on the hill; for the previous millennium or so, this parish had been a very pure example of the type, where within an hour or two a single priest might walk the bounds of his parish end to end, doing his duty by his parochial flock. No doubt Wetherden, with its tidily rectangular parish boundaries, had started life as one of those single lordship estates out of which the system had been born.

Archaeology portrays the process better than surviving documents, as between the ninth and eleventh centuries parishes gradually evolved to become the accepted administrative norm, and a parish church building with its graveyard arrived in virtually every European settlement of consequence. Born primarily in relation to a settled agricultural society, the system was financed through farm produce, on a principle derived from the Old Testament: a tenth for the parish priest ('tithe' in Old English) levied on yearly production. When I was a boy, fragments of that system had endured in England to within living memory, though contentiously and with extreme historical untidiness. There was a pastoral consequence to this. Churchmen, conscious that the source of their maintenance was ultimately the work of all the folk to whom they ministered in their church, felt constrained to take more notice of the spiritual condition of everyone in Christendom.

It would have been a natural assumption in the age of first conversion in central and northern Europe, when the work of Christianization depended so much on the decisions and inclinations of monarchs and nobility, that the Church should concern itself primarily with the salvation of the ruling elite. No longer. The parish system developed alongside the huge growth in the industry of prayer represented by Benedictine monastic life and power; indeed, monasteries were among the lords and landowners creating that parish system. Benedictine elaboration or enriching of the liturgical round could percolate down to the humblest parish church, encouraging Latin literacy in the clergy to a level competent enough to offer the spiritual power of the Mass to all people. Parishes were also components of episcopal dioceses, whose bishops (who might or might not be themselves monks) were increasingly galvanized by Carolingian insistence on regulation and enquiry: they were beginning to make a regular system of visitations to check that the faithful were observing such basic Christian observances as the penitential and fasting season of Lent in the later winter months.[66]

Inevitably, such a detailed scrutiny of the spiritual condition of all Europe ran up against pre-existing customs in northern European society. Just as in the northern expansion of Orthodoxy, these lands did not share ancient Mediterranean social assumptions, and they had well-developed social systems of their own which the elites making decisions to adopt Christianity might be reluctant to jettison when adopting their new faith. For dynastically organized societies, marriage was a central consideration. There were various ways in which the existing northern marriage systems differed from those defined by the Western Church. Early Irish lawcodes (which are from the Christian period, and so post-dating the conversion era of Patrick) provide for divorce by either husband or wife, and they make careful provision for dividing property between the separating parties; contradictory Church provisions in other contemporary documents probably reflect clerical efforts to intervene that were impossible to enforce in Irish conditions.[67] Germanic legal systems also allowed for divorce, though less generously than the Roman law with which Church hierarchies had already contended; they generally included fewer provisions for women to divorce men than in the Roman system.[68]

Above all, northern Europe did not partake in the Mediterranean custom of exclusive monogamy. The evidence is lacking for Anglo-Saxon society even before its Christianization, but elsewhere it is clear that those who mattered in society, while opting for Christian faith and practice, showed as little sympathy for the Christian principles of monogamy as they did for the idea of indissoluble marriage. Existing northern European practices of elite polygyny blended with the presence in Roman law of an institution of concubinage alongside marriage – a stable relationship, but one where the female partner was of lower status than the man, often indeed a slave. The Mediterranean Church had not liked this, but it was a long time before it was in a position to challenge established reality. It will be remembered that after a good Christian upbringing, Augustine of Hippo had opted for concubinage, an evidently satisfying thirteen-year-long relationship that produced that greatly loved young man Adeodatus (above, Chapter 9).[69]

Similarly, in Francia, Merovingian monarchs (Catholic Christians from 481) did not opt for either strict monogamy or outright polygyny, but consistently maintained concubines and had children by them, alongside whoever they had married as queen. Naturally, reform-minded Churchmen loathed this long-lived expedient, but the Merovingians ignored the fulminations already prominent in the writings of their great sixth-century historian Gregory, Bishop of Tours. It was a rational strategy to widen the choices for royal succession in the event of some biological misfortune, so that, if necessary, a widowed monarch without legitimate offspring could elevate a long-standing concubine to queenly status, and their son might succeed as heir. That had the added advantage that, in her lowly social status, the concubine was probably outside the factional struggles of the higher nobility. The example would not be lost on other monarchs; some modern historians have termed this system in early medieval Europe 'resource polygyny'.[70]

In Irish society both before and after its adoption of Christianity, marital strategies more obviously tipped into polygyny, though the early legal texts do not in any case seem as preoccupied as those elsewhere by what constituted a legal marriage.[71] Nevertheless, the Irish recognized clear gradations of marital status, so an institution equivalent to concubinage was widespread: alongside marriage to a principal wife (*cétmuinter*), a prominent man might sustain relationships with an *adaltrach* (spouse), or maybe more than one, who would benefit from his financial support and protection, while he could enjoy the same potential genealogical benefits as in Merovingian practice.[72] Similar systems can be recognized in pre-Christian Viking-age Scandinavia, though here concubinage was linked to slavery, which became such a feature of Scandinavian raids right across Europe, and it was coupled with a much more flexible attitude to inheritance than elsewhere, including children from casual liaisons.[73]

The Scandinavian conversion to Christianity was piecemeal and late – a process gradually extending from the ninth century – and most of the literature that describes these arrangements, both sagas and law-codes, postdates official Christian arrival. Nevertheless, it shows that polygyny effectively survived. Looking northward from the German coast, the eleventh-century clerical chronicler Adam of Bremen observed that in contemporary Sweden men had several women each, and that all their children were treated as legitimate.[74] Twelfth-century Norwegian laws drafted under the influence of the Church prohibit plural marriages, a sure indication that they were still common at the time. It is significant that the lawcode also lays down differential fines to be paid to the local bishop for keeping a slave woman or concubine, or for having plural wives: the latter fine was twice the former.[75] The further out the territory in a society that had adopted Christian faith, the later was the survival of a discrepancy between official Christian views on marriage, divorce and clerical celibacy and the actual practice: in the case of Iceland, it was right into the thirteenth century, regardless of the personal esteem in which Icelanders held those among their bishops who were attempting reform.[76]

For Churchmen at the end of the Carolingian age, amid many initiatives of reform, there was therefore much to ponder and deplore. One can savour the frustration and anger of Lanfranc, Archbishop of Canterbury, writing around 1074 to the most prominent Irish king of his day, Toirdelbach Úa Briain of Munster. He raged against various disgraceful and improper practices in Ireland, including Irish customs around marriage, divorce and concubinage contrary to canon law; around the same time he also badgered Guthric, subordinate king to Toirdelbach in Dublin, on that theme. It would have been frustrating to Lanfranc that he had little power to interfere across the water on an island where Christians might cheerfully turn to the Old Testament, as alert polygynists have always been able to do. As an eighth-century Irish lawcode commented, 'there is a dispute in Irish law as to which is more proper, whether many sexual unions or a single one: for the chosen people of God [that is, the Israelites] lived in a plurality of unions, so that it is not easier to condemn it than to praise it.'[77]

It would take both time and thought to persuade the rulers of western Europe to conform to what the Church hierarchy wanted – indeed, first the Church had to decide exactly what it did want. Lanfranc was a voice from a new world, which from the eleventh century onwards built on what we have surveyed, but which also represented a new and unprecedented formation of a Christian society. From the previous five or six centuries, the new programme inherited campaigns to impose Benedictine standards on monastic life, to move even non-monastic clergy away from marriage and towards celibacy, and to persuade the laity that their marriages should reflect the form of monogamy that the Church had set as the sole standard in marital partnership. None of these campaigns remained anywhere near completion in 1000, but the developing parochial structure and the growing practice of individual penance provided a framework in which they could continue. Additionally, Western Christians had meditated on a new place for Mary in the Christian dispensation and had come to a new understanding of what they were doing when they came to the Eucharist. Around these existing elements, eleventh-century Latin Churchmen promoted what can only be described as a revolution in sexuality.

PART FOUR

Two Western Revolutions

12
Gregory VII and a First Sexual Revolution (1000–1200)

The story of Western Christendom between the eleventh and seventeenth centuries begins and ends with ideological revolutions, the second forming a destructive reaction to the first; we will explore them both in the following three chapters. The second upheaval, in the sixteenth century, is generally termed 'the Reformation' without reference to what happened before, but either event could be styled either a Reformation or a revolution: Martin Luther undid what had been built up by successive popes five centuries before. Just as the Bolshevik Revolution of 1917 cannot be reduced to the personalities of Lenin or Trotsky, the eleventh- and twelfth-century reorganization of Western Latin Christendom often summed up as 'Gregorian' means much more than the exploits of the Italian monk Hildebrand, Pope Gregory VII from 1073 to 1085.

We have already seen how many components were already in place by the turn of the millennium in 1000; fresh convergences followed around a new and exalted view of the universal authority of the Papacy promoted by Gregory and his circle. One monastery has an exceptional significance in what happened: the Benedictine Abbey of Cluny, founded in Francia in 909–10 as a late product of Carolingian-era monasticism, later flourished under a sequence of exceptionally shrewd and capable abbots. They exploited the happy chance that the original aristocratic founder, Duke William of Aquitaine, had been lavish in his endowment but unusually modest in demanding returns for his family; that offered a freedom of manoeuvre which Cluny exploited in imitation of its far older sister-abbey of Fleury.

In 1024, Cluny followed Fleury in gaining special exemptions and privileges from the Pope: these provided a springboard for further distinctiveness, not least expressed in stone. Successive rebuildings of Cluny's conventual church made it between the eleventh and sixteenth centuries the largest church building in the Latin West, a true rival in splendour and prestige to Hagia Sophia in Constantinople. Many will view its ruthless and prolonged demolition from 1798 as one of the worst tragedies of the French Revolution; only a remnant survives, a small fraction of the whole. The oddity of this vast Romanesque structure was that, exceptionally amid the major monastic churches of its age, it did not house the shrine of a major saint. Instead, Cluny used its geographically strategic siting in Francia to mastermind a continent-wide network of pilgrimage routes to a shrine on the far western edge of Europe, on the Atlantic coast of Iberia at Compostela: the reputed tomb of James, one of the Twelve Apostles.

Essential to this enterprise was that the European lay elite willingly founded satellite monasteries for Cluny right across the continent. Kings and nobles, anxious to benefit from the power of prayer that the monks offered in their intensified observance of Masses and Offices, were eager to oblige. Many such foundations were scarcely less magnificent or wealthy than Cluny itself, but, in a radical innovation, from Spain to Scotland, they were only 'priories', all dependent on their mother house, which became a centre of what was for the first time called a monastic 'Order'. The Cluniac Order was Christianity's pioneering international corporation. That gave a particular usefulness to its elaboration of the monastic silent sign-system (above, Chapter 11), since often Cluniac monks recruited from across the continent would not have understood each other's birth-language.[1] Cluny's European-wide vision lay behind a variety of new initiatives in Western Christian life whose connections might otherwise seem puzzling.

PILGRIMAGES, CRUSADES, A MILITANT SOCIETY

The Compostela route was only part of a growing Western enterprise of mass pilgrimage, new not in character but in scale; it became one of the defining features of Western Latin devotion right up to the sixteenth-century Reformation. This search for holy places and the route to salvation that they might offer was enticingly open to anyone who chose to undertake it (that might include the growing proportion of Europeans who were serfs, or other unfree people, if they could seize or were granted the opportunity). Choice, it is true, was not always part of the package: we have already noted in Chapter 11 that, from the beginning of the new penitential discipline in Ireland or Wales, one penitential possibility was an order to go on pilgrimage to seek the forgiving power of a saint. That became standard in medieval Europe's repertoire of penance, an early spiritual variant on the modern proposition that travel broadens the mind.[2] Pilgrimage afforded the same opportunities to women as to men, and, despite all the problems that medieval women might face in travel, they took full advantage of it; one estimate of Western pilgrim activity in the fourteenth and fifteenth centuries considers that women were almost as numerous as men among those known to have undertaken pilgrimages. Naturally all this activity created its own economy of service industries for support, entertainment and accommodation, besides very considerable financial benefit for the shrine churches themselves.[3]

Unusually, the devotional activism of pilgrimage put laypeople on the same footing as clergy during a devotional revolution that in so many ways gave clergy a privileged position in society. Indeed, holy travelling gave laity the advantage over monks and nuns who observed their commitment to sacred enclosure. In the fourteenth century, Geoffrey Chaucer's pilgrim Prioress did exploit seniority to exempt herself from enclosure for her cheerful journey to Canterbury, but her sisters would have had to make do with journeys of the mind. Accordingly, some late medieval nunneries resourcefully equipped themselves with a series of pictures of goals of pilgrimage for pleasantly profitable contemplation amid their other spiritual amenities. The Poor Clares of Villingen in south Germany outclassed most others by enriching their precinct with no fewer than 210 representations of places to visit in Rome and Jerusalem, and a generous papal grant gave them all benefits of indulgences just like a 'real' visit to these shrines (they all burst into tears with dutiful pleasure when this grant was read out to them). This was the ultimate tribute to the power of the pilgrimage.[4]

Those travelling to the actual scenes of Christ's life, death and resurrection in Jerusalem and the Holy Land had to face the reality of Muslim rule. From the beginning of the eleventh century, the growing numbers of Western pilgrims provoked rising tension, fuelled by the development of a new land-route through Hungary especially useful for northern Europeans. An unusual flashpoint occurred in 1009 when, in the course of steadily more deranged general behaviour, the Fatimid Caliph al-Hākim ordered the complete destruction of the magnificent Church of the Holy Sepulchre in Jerusalem, built long before in the time of the Emperor Constantine I. Even after Byzantine reconstruction in the 1030s and 1040s, the evidence of al-Ḥākim's demolition was still obvious to travellers, and memories of it fed into an increasingly vocal call for revenge and for the Christian sites to be liberated from Muslim rule.[5]

Loudest among those voices were monk-historians associated with Cluny's rebranding of Benedictine life in its own image, Rodolph Glaber ('the Bald') and Adémar of Chabannes. They also banged the drum for the cosmic significance of the world turning its millennium of 1000 CE, a chronological detail that may not have excited those beyond Cluny's influence quite so much.[6] The link of these themes to Cluny was no accident, given its management of pilgrimages to the westernmost extreme of Christendom at Compostela. The shrine of St James the Apostle, now safe from Muslim expansion as Christian armies successfully pushed back Muslim territory in Iberia, was itself a proof that God approved of warfare directed against the Church's enemies. (In the Americas, where Spain and Portugal forcibly established new empires in the sixteenth century, a thousand years later James the Apostle still doubles as a symbol of the defeat of 'Moors' by Iberian Christians, as I have myself observed as a festal processional float passed me in rural Mexico: there was James on horseback, constructed entirely out of multicoloured peppers, triumphantly trampling a Muslim, equally vegetable though inevitably supine.)

Accordingly, one of the many interconnected features of the Gregorian revolution was that, by the end of the eleventh century, pilgrimage was linked to the Church hierarchy's radical rethinking on armed conflict: defining what violence was forbidden to Christians and what was actually holy warfare, blessed by God. Both definitions had dramatic effects on the Western Church. The first practical results stemmed from the more obvious and traditional proposition: fellow Christians should not fight each other, at least within Western Latin Christendom. The development of the parochial system had directed the attention of Church leaders to aristocratic violence that harmed all society, not least themselves and their own landed estates. In the late tenth century, Carolingian abbots and bishops began appealing to the consciences of their communities to secure peace. They convened large gatherings of laity and clergy; the Bishop of Le Puy in southern Francia provided the first known precedent in 975, threatening violent wrongdoers with excommunication and demanding that the crowds in front of him swear an oath to keep the peace. Other bishops imitated his initiative, drawing on their churches' various collections of relics to reinforce their threats with the wrath of the saints. Eventually they even brokered formal agreements defining on which days fighting might legitimately take place.

This 'Peace of God' movement spread through much of western Europe; Odilo, the renowned and energetic Abbot of Cluny for more than half a century from 994, was among its leading advocates. Soon both monarchs and popes were involved in regulating these councils and agreements. In the same way that the parochial system was embracing everyone in society beyond religious houses, the Peace of God movement was a practical demonstration of how the Church could appeal to consciences beyond social elites; the crowds who witnessed the proceedings were as much part of the pressure put on recalcitrant magnates as the bones of the saints and the clergy who guarded them. There was a clear general benefit from the Church offering an institutional setting to resolve disputes, and the success of the Peace of God movement suggested that the nobility of Europe might be persuaded that it was in their own interests to modify their way of life in other ways.

Many such councils accordingly extended their activities into all sorts of regulation affecting the lives of both laity and clergy, since the resolution of violence necessarily involved adjudicating in disputes which could involve any aspect of society – for instance, questions of disputed inheritance that might turn on whether or not a marriage was valid in the eyes of the Church, or whether a local scandal had been made worse by clerical misbehaviour (however defined). Establishing peace on earth was, after all, the heart of the Church's pastoral task; it meant that a council of bishops that was not formally a 'peace' council might turn out to have a rather similar agenda. The Papacy's role in all this eleventh-century decision-making was particularly significant for the future, because it pointed towards an inexorable conclusion: if the same sort of problem occurred all over Europe, it was best dealt with by one authority.[7]

When should Christians legitimately take up arms, if peace was God's will for Christendom? Christian leaders since Constantine had looked to God to justify their success in war, but an ideal of holy war was effectively a novelty in Christianity, and a far cry from the pacifism of the Church in its first three centuries of existence. The defeat of Muslims, first in Iberia and then in Sicily in the 1060s, suggested that not just earthly victory in battle but salvation might follow from violence blessed by the Church: a 'Crusade', taking its name from the cross of Christ whose especial shrine alongside Christ's tomb Caliph al-Hākim had violated in Jerusalem.[8] The author of the Epistle to the Ephesians had used a tangle of Roman military imagery to urge his readers to 'put on the whole armour of God' (Eph. 6.11–17), but the great Crusader preacher Bernard of Clairvaux in preaching the Second Crusade reversed the direction of that theme away from metaphor to practical military exhortation:

> The knight who puts the breastplate of faith on his soul in the same way as he puts a breastplate of iron in his body is truly intrepid and safe from everything . . . so forward in safety, knights, and with undaunted souls drive off the enemies of the Cross of Christ.[9]

In 1074, Gregory VII tried but failed to launch a Crusade to recapture the Holy Land. It was actually a monk of Cluny in the generation after Gregory, becoming Pope Urban II in 1088, who successfully launched the First Crusade, after an appeal for help against Islam from the Byzantine Emperor Alexios Komnenos. Alexios, an astute and capable ruler, would not have anticipated the dire long-term consequence of his request for Byzantium as well as for Islam. When Pope Urban launched his project in 1095, he proclaimed that to die on Crusade in a state of repentance and confession would guarantee immediate entry to heaven, doing away with any necessity of penance in purgatory after death. The papal grants associated with this promise were the origins of a system of 'indulgences' claiming to structure human salvation; many later Western Christians were to find the institution problematic (below, Chapter 14), but for the moment indulgences sparked huge enthusiasm and the mustering of armies from across the continent.

The remarkable feature of the Crusade that followed in 1096–99 was that it worked. In their brief window of opportunity, western Europeans set up a Latin Kingdom in a Jerusalem devastated by Crusader massacres in 1099; the invaders targeted its Muslim, Jewish and even Eastern Christian inhabitants with a ferocity that Christian commentators did not deny. Yet the reality was that Crusaders had hit unawares on a moment of peculiar weakness and disarray in Islamic states, which was not repeated, and none of western Europe's herculean efforts over the next centuries equalled that first fluke.[10] The Latin territorial presence in the eastern Mediterranean was only finally snuffed out by the Ottoman Turks who took the island of Crete from the Republic of Venice in 1669, but by then the Latin hold on the Holy Land itself had long been extinguished – in Jerusalem, since 1244.

The saga of the Crusades had many consequences, but one of the most lasting was newly to associate Western Christianity with a masculine gender stereotype that it has still not entirely rejected: the holy warrior. We have already encountered military saints in the early Church – Sergius and Bacchus, Martin, George – but, whatever their popularity had been in the past among soldiers, their stories were constructed on the assumption that they gained their sanctity by renouncing earthly warfare. Right into the eleventh century, waging war still triggered heavy penances for those involved: that had been one major consideration when Europe's monarchs and lords founded monasteries and nunneries, in order to construct a reservoir of grateful religious ready to take on the burden of penance vicariously in their prayers. Now the very act of being a soldier and killing Christ's enemies could earn holiness.

At the time, this was a specifically Western development: a Greek traveller who made it all the way to Compostela in the early twelfth century was apparently taken aback to hear St James admiringly called 'a knight of Christ'.[11] Not just saints, but God himself: it is an equal surprise to enter the crypt of Auxerre Cathedral in Burgundy, where the vault is dominated by a fresco of Christ himself at the end of time, riding a white horse in knightly fashion and leading a warrior-band of mounted angels (see Plate 6). The motif is rare in the New Testament, but here it directly illustrates a scene from that exceptional text, the Book of Revelation (19.11–16).[12] The thought had an immediate resonance for the cleric commissioning the fresco: almost certainly Humbaud, Bishop of Auxerre, protégé of Pope Urban II and himself an active promoter of the First Crusade. Humbaud actually died on his return journey from a Jerusalem pilgrimage in 1115.[13]

In the background was a new rhetoric of classifying Christian society three ways: those who prayed, those who fought and those who laboured (*oratores, bellatores, laboratores* was a common summary of these categories). Two sets of fighters emerge from the scheme: clergy fighting Satan with their prayers, and soldiers fighting God's enemies on earth (for instance, in contemporary Anglo-Saxon England, the 'pagan' Danes). The lay *laboratores* would be expected to get on with providing resources for the other two groups. The threefold classification occurs quite suddenly around the year 1000, to be found in the devotional and pastoral writings of one of the Anglo-Saxon monastic reformers, Ælfric of Eynsham Abbey, and very soon also in Francia, influentially in a popular satirical poem by the eleventh-century Bishop Adalbero of Laon. The neatness of it is probably why it appealed to a western European society that was in reality becoming much more complex than that, and where it might be possible to change one's social position; where, for instance, did the increasing commercial life of towns fit into it? Even within its unrealistic simplicity, it was primarily a man's effort to categorize men, saying nothing useful about the role of women but providing a convenient way of discussing why secular men should keep away from appropriating Church lands – and, increasingly also, why priests should not take wives, a practice only suitable for the two categories of laypeople. That was about to become a major issue in Western society, as we will see.[14]

The inadequacy of this much-employed social cliché is revealed by the emergence, amid many new varieties of monasticism appearing in the Latin Church, of a peculiar and paradoxical form of monastic life blurring the threefold boundaries: Orders of celibate warriors dedicated to fighting and killing on behalf of Christianity. The Knights Templar and Knights Hospitaller were the first, spelling out their agenda by their names: the Hospitallers were so called from their Hospital headquarters in Jerusalem, and the Templars from the monumental sacred building that they annexed in the city under the mistaken impression that it was the Temple as built by Herod – it was in fact the seventh-century Muslim Dome of the Rock. The military Orders became wealthy from being endowed with estates right across Europe, on which they established administrative communities of knights (preceptories or commanderies), frequently reproducing the centrally planned Dome of the Rock or the Church of the Holy Sepulchre in the plan of their church buildings – a symbol in stone of the new acceptance of warfare as part of God's purpose.

At the end of the twelfth century an Order of 'Teutonic Knights' from German and north European lands joined the same work of defending Crusader conquests in the Holy Land, just in time to witness them disintegrate; that forced them to turn back to northern Europe to fight other enemies. Not all contemporary commentators were blind to how incongruous the military Orders looked in the light of Christian tradition, and failure made them vulnerable. The loss of any foothold in the Holy Land in the thirteenth century forced all the Orders to rethink their mission, and it also made the secular rulers and nobility of Europe regret their forebears' generosity in furnishing the landed endowments. In the case of the Templars, the wealthiest of the trio, the consequence was disgrace and destruction at the hands of the French monarchy in 1307–12.[15]

Throughout the medieval period, Crusades continued on the frontiers of Latin Christianity in Europe, and Crusader rhetoric was still useful when European Catholic powers began expanding beyond Europe's boundaries in the fifteenth century. One curious little symptom of it in later medieval Europe is the use of a popular song, 'The Armed Man' (*L'Homme armé*), as the thematic basis for choral settings of the Mass. It seems bizarre that this warlike tune should have so fascinated Western musicians writing for choirs singing the nodal points of Christianity's central devotional act, but for three centuries beginning with the much-revered Guillaume Dufay (*c.*1398–1474), the Mass *L'Homme armé* became something like a proof of proficiency for choral composers. Perhaps Christ could be seen as the Armed Man, just as Bishop Humbaud had seen him at Auxerre, or perhaps it was the militant Archangel Michael, on whose feast day such Masses were often performed. The tradition finally slipped from the interest of composers in the seventeenth century along with the fading of any practicality in the Crusader ideal.[16] The ignominious failure of monastic knights to defend the Crusader conquests up to the final loss of Crete has nevertheless not extinguished Western Christian fascination with Holy War, including much modern muddle-headed conspiracy theory inspired by the messily brutal dénouement of the Templars' story.[17]

Both the phenomenal growth of pilgrimage and the herculean, if eventually doomed, enterprises of Crusades witnessed the new ability of the Western Church to harness the energies of a whole continent around a single cause. That success was dependent on an overarching view of papal power in the Church previously inconceivable, although it was based on the energy of earlier documentary forgers in the eighth and ninth centuries: they had created a supposed 'Donation' of the entire Western Roman Empire by Constantine I to Pope Sylvester I, and a series of legal 'Decretals' amalgamating carefully edited older documents with some newly minted confections. These gave plausibility to the claim that a pope could construct law himself, without reference to a wider gathering of bishops in a 'General Council', let alone the authorities in the Byzantine Empire.[18]

The self-confidence of eleventh-century popes is evident from their clash with the Patriarch of Constantinople: ostensibly a disagreement about what variety of bread should be used for the Eucharist, which was in reality only a symptom of an increasing lack of sympathetic communication between East and West. This culminated in 1054 when Pope Leo IX dispatched his close associate Cardinal Humbert (a former monk of Cluny) to Constantinople; Humbert personally excommunicated Patriarch Michael Keroularios during the liturgy in Hagia Sophia itself. Such crises of excommunication had happened before, but this 'Great Schism' was not formally reversed for nine hundred years, and its effects on Christian identity are still with us.[19]

In 1073 came the papacy of Gregory VII, another member of the papal entourage around Leo IX, and, once he was Pope, determined to formalize the claims made for a universal papal monarchy and to use it for what he saw as the correction of error and the fulfilment of God's purposes for the world. The list of pronouncements known as the *Dictatus Papae* entered into his papal register in 1075 make remarkable reading, including the claim that 'the Roman pontiff alone can with right be called universal' and that 'for him alone is it lawful, according to the needs of the time, to make new laws'. Many of the propositions might have been found individually in previous documents, but the assertion of universality was among the real novelties, providing a justification for schism with the East.[20] Moreover, between the eleventh and the thirteenth centuries, amid repeated clashes with the Western Emperor, popes made a significant modification of their title. Gregory still thought of himself as 'Vicar [representative] of Peter', reckoned as the first Pope; by the time of Innocent III (1198–1216) the description was amplified to be 'Vicar of Christ', a priest in charge of God's providential plan to mould all society to his commands.[21]

Many secular rulers joined successive Holy Roman Emperors in resisting papal claims to universal authority, and the Papacy never wholly fulfilled the vision of Gregory and his circle, but, from the eleventh century, Western society was united by an unprecedented expansion of ecclesiastical lawmaking, based on a growing papal bureaucracy in Rome. The stimulus to the legal innovations of the Gregorian revolution was a series of Italian manuscript rediscoveries: encounters with the *Digest* of Roman imperial law compiled in the systematizing efforts of Justinian half a millennium before. Much else in the imperial legal corpus had not been completely forgotten, but now this rich resource of previously unknown material stimulated a newly intensive study of the imperial system, which came to be known as 'civil law'. Alongside the recovery of civil law was the development of a legal code to suit the needs of a universal and papal Church: 'canon law'. This was a fusion of much from the Western Church's own tradition with borrowings from civil law, and it depended on a compilation of material created in stages through the first half of the twelfth century in Italy's chief centre of legal study, the university in the city of Bologna.

Universities were another new feature of eleventh-century Europe, and one of the institutions that united Western Christendom, providing universally recognized opportunities for advanced study and teaching. Paradoxically they modelled themselves closely on institutions of higher education developed by Muslims, especially the school of Al-Azhar in Cairo – even borrowing customary institutions like lectures, professors, qualifications called degrees marked by formal customs of dress, and methods of pursuing enquiry. It is ironic that one of the expressions of cultural unity in the Latin West was rooted in the culture which the West was trying to destroy. Western Christendom found itself in a position of inferiority in relation to a much more developed and sophisticated Muslim culture, just as once it had been the poor relation to Byzantium. This provoked a complicated mixture of envy, hostility and fascinated emulation which is part of the background to the Crusades. The reason for borrowing the idea of a university is clear: a shared interest in dealing with an explosion of ancient knowledge rediscovered in manuscripts, posing a problem faced by all three 'Religions of the Book', Islam, Christianity and Judaism. How did truths revealed by sacred scripture relate to the undoubted wisdom of the Classical past?

At the centre of that newly illuminated wisdom was the master of categorization and analysis, Aristotle, hardly known in the West before the eleventh century.[22] First through Muslim libraries looted after the Christian capture of Toledo in 1085, his writings gradually became available, soon in a widening flood of Latin translations from the Greek. Their interpretation became a three-way conversation with Arab and Jewish commentators on the texts and their relevance to Christendom, and the setting of that conversation was the university. The main task of exploration for Christians was how to speak of the Christian God, a task summed up as 'theology', a Latin neologism meaning the systematic analysis of belief about God. It was the title given in the 1120s by the teacher and philosopher Peter Abelard to a treatise that steadily expanded in successive versions: *Theologia Christiana*. Theology was a new discipline, different from the contemplative doctrinal task long practised in the monasteries of Latin Christendom. It culminated in the thirteenth century in a magisterial synthesis produced by the Dominican theologian Thomas Aquinas, *Summa Theologiae* (or *Summa Theologica*).[23]

Dealing with the rapidly expanding knowledge of ancient philosophy and law and constructing systems of theology required a distinctive educational and analytical method that has become known as 'scholasticism', simply because it was practised in the *scholae*, the new university schools. In essence it was a way of building up knowledge through discussion on a question: after *quaestiones* came assertion, denial, counter-assertion, and a final effort to harmonize the debate. Scholasticism respected learned authorities but recognized how alarmingly unpredictable and contradictory they might be. Scholastic method was therefore disputatious, sceptical, analytical, and that has remained the characteristic of Western intellectual exploration long after most Western intellectuals parted company with scholasticism itself. Western scholars in universities might see themselves in the service of the Church, but universities were from the beginning largely institutionally independent of the Church authorities, even when the Pope came to license new foundations. That was as true of canon law studies as it was of theology.

Traditionally the greatest collection of canon law created in the twelfth century goes under the name of one of those chiefly involved in its formulation, a shadowy Italian named Gratian, of whom virtually nothing is known. Given the new importance of canon law in the Western Church, it was no coincidence that every Pope of significance between 1159 and 1303 was trained primarily as a canon lawyer. Popes were, after all, now monarchs with universal claims, presiding over the administration of a law that was the only remedy available to everyone in Western Christendom.[24] Lawyers have traditionally lacked a reputation for human sympathy, but it is important to see that this body of law, the most comprehensive since the end of the Western Roman Empire, was intended to be pastoral, a way of healing the wounds of society through definition and instruction.

Nevertheless, there was a binary character to the medieval canon lawyer's view of the society that he served, more fundamental and more realistic in reflecting Gregorian Christendom than the threefold rhetoric of *oratores, bellatores, laboratores*. Canon law embodied the underlying principle for Gregory VII and his circle that there are two classes of Christians: clerical celibates and laypeople. In the twentieth century this could still be pithily spelled out in an official pronouncement of Pope Pius X (1903–14): 'The Church is essentially an unequal society, that is, a society comprising two categories of persons, the pastors and the flock, those who occupy a rank in the different degrees of the hierarchy and the multitude of the faithful.'[25] Making this assumption, canon lawyers put into formal terms a programme of marriage and celibacy that depended on winning the hearts and minds of the laity to a revolution that the Church had devised.

LAY MARRIAGE OR CLERICAL CELIBACY: THE GREGORIAN CHOICE

The most original element in the Gregorian scheme for society was unique in Christian history, and has never been attempted by any other branch of the Christian Church before or since: to make the two major orders of clerical ministry (priests and bishops) entirely celibate. Consequently, this was an effort to identify together (or confuse) two separate Christian vocations, one to celibate life and the other to priesthood. It was a formidable task, since, outside monasteries, the vast majority of clergy in eleventh-century Europe were still married men with families, and indeed themselves likely to be the sons of clergy. The growth of the parish system was fanning them out across the continent, often alone in charge of a rural community, contrasting for instance with the community life of an Anglo-Saxon minster church. In the past, the general understanding had been that married clergy would go on living with their wives after they progressed from minor orders to become a priest, even though they now abstained from sex; in a minster the convention could be quietly policed by colleagueship. That was not so easy in rural isolation, in a village where the neighbours would take for granted marriage of whatever status. The centralizing Church bureaucracy was determined to change all this.[26]

There was more than one level of ecclesiastical anxiety at work in the Gregorian move to ban clerical marriage. One practical motive was to defend clerical property: clerical marriage and the ties of paternal love expected of any family might disperse land and goods given to the Church. Reformers of monasteries in the Anglo-Saxon and Carolingian

Churches had shown the same concern, tidying up tangles of family and monastic property that had resulted in much appropriation by the secular aristocracy (above, Chapter 11). Neurosis on this matter explains the extraordinary level of hostility to clerical children among the eleventh-century reformers. The Synod of Pavia convened by Pope Benedict VIII in 1022 started a long effort by the Church authorities to have these unfortunates declared as serfs belonging to the Church, which among other consequences meant that they could not be ordained. The programme took a crazy though logical step in the order of the Synod of Bourges in 1031 to ban clerical children from getting married at all. Although that particular proposal went nowhere, all this was an obvious hit at the ancient institution of clerical dynasties, and it was allied to a general prohibition on illegitimate men becoming priests that lasted in Roman Catholic canon law until the twentieth century; part of a general stigmatization of illegitimacy in Western Christianity that has rarely been equalled in intensity in any other culture.[27]

A yet more potent fear was theological. In a pattern that will be familiar by now, the stimulus came particularly from Cluny, through exhortations of Abbot Odilo that united Augustine's reservations about all sexual activity with Cluny's promotion of a high theology of Eucharistic presence. If even marital sex was by its nature impure, the ritual purity or impurity of a priest was a threat to his proper celebration of the Mass. Latin theologians emphasized with increasing precision that in this liturgical drama, bread and wine become the body and blood of Christ. The notion of a 'real presence' of Christ in the Eucharist, common to Eastern and Western Christianity, was soon to crystallize for Westerners into definitions of a 'transubstantiation' of the Eucharistic elements in the Mass. This reflected Western scholars' rediscovery of philosophical texts by Aristotle, with their discussions of categories of 'substance'. Although transubstantiation was as yet a doctrine without exact boundaries, theologians who expressed doubts about such reframing of Eucharistic theology were firmly silenced: in the case of Berengar, Canon of Tours Cathedral, that included a humiliating recantation in front of a Council presided over by the future Gregory VII. Clerical reformers passionately believed that the Mass needed protection from married priests, and from their wives, who must be relabelled without equivocation as 'concubines'.[28]

The same people who pressed for clerical celibacy might also espouse a new Western theological or devotional impulse to make Christ's mother even better fortified against the impurities of the flesh: the proposition of her 'Immaculate Conception'. The tangled connection is exemplified by an English collection of Marian miracles which included a reminiscence associated with Anselm, early twelfth-century Abbot of St Edmundsbury in Suffolk: in his Italian youth, he had accidentally spilled consecrated wine while serving at Mass, and, appalled by the spillage and the dark stain on the altar cloth, he prayed to the Mother of God for help. The stain miraculously vanished.[29]

Anselm was prominent among a number of English Benedictine abbots who in their enthusiasm for the Mother of God, and anxious to commemorate that all the more splendidly in their already splendid liturgical round, began promoting the idea that she had been conceived without the normal human correlation of concupiscence (lust). Because (like Anselm's immaculate altar cloth) her conception was unspotted by sin, so was her flesh.[30] The doctrine spread far beyond England, but it remained controversial: the Cistercian Bernard of Clairvaux, one of the loudest advocates of devotion to Mary in his preaching, said flatly that the idea of Immaculate Conception was a novelty which Mary would not enjoy, and that no conception, not even hers, could be separated from carnal pleasure. It was the nineteenth century before the Church officially made up its mind on the matter (below, Chapter 16).[31]

A tangle of themes around sexual purity, Mary and the power of the Mass proved to be a cause for which reformers could annex the moral excitement of the crowds already involved in the Peace of God movement. Here the harshest voices from pulpits (and perhaps therefore the most exciting) were those of the austere Italian Benedictine Peter Damian and that agent of East–West schism Cardinal Humbert; they were cheerleaders for a campaign to get the laity to boycott any sacraments celebrated by married clergy that culminated under Gregory VII. As we have noted (above, Chapter 8) Damian shared with the fourth-century preacher John Chrysostom some distinctive and eloquently expressed personal obsessions about sex, although it is not certain that Chrysostom's version of them would have been available in Damian's time. One of these was a fanatical hatred of same-sex activity, about which he wrote and preached to an exceptional extent; the other was the association of priests with women. Both reflected Damian's passionate concern for clerical purity: same-sex acts by an abbot or bishop with his monks or clerics were spiritual incest with his 'sons', while Damian pointed out that any unchaste bishop who ordained a priest would be using the same hand 'to touch the private parts of harlots'. Since Christ was born of a virgin, he required the service of virgin hands at the altar.[32]

Various biblical themes were pressed into service to champion priestly celibacy. A formidable apparent obstacle was the statement in the Pastoral Epistles that a bishop should have only one wife, but, back in the fifth century, Pope Leo I in his discussion of clerical marriage had found an effective way of neutralizing it via allegorical interpretation: 'one wife' was a reference to Christ, with whom a bishop had a spiritual marriage. That thought might seem riskily misgendered, but it conveniently dispatched any of the myriad of positive references in early Christian theological writing to clergy wives, and it also had a more general usefulness in defending the already-well-established Western bias towards seeing all true marriages as by their nature indissoluble: every Christian husband was similarly allegorically married to Christ.[33]

Damian and Cardinal Humbert also adroitly added to their polemical armoury by redeploying for their own purposes an obscure biblical term of abuse: the sinister-sounding 'Nicolaitans' denounced in the Book of Revelation (Rev. 2.6, 15) as being hated by both the writer, St John the Divine, and his readers. St John had not specified what was particularly hateful in Nicolaitan teaching, but it could as well have been their advocacy of clerical marriage as anything else, and so it became in reformist denunciations. The 'Nicolaitan' smear fed into Humbert's abuse of Eastern Orthodoxy, in this case because the Orthodox continued to allow marriage to many clergy, so that polemic became part of the events leading to the schism of 1054. From the Church's past, the reformers also creatively misunderstood the diatribes of Chrysostom, Jerome and their contemporaries against *virgines subintroductae*, women chastely living with clergy in syneisactism (above, Chapter 9); they reapplied this hostile rhetoric to the case of any priest living with a woman.[34]

Laypeople began hearkening to such insistent voices, particularly in the increasing number of cities emerging as centres of economic power around the Mediterranean: these were expanding, restless communities where people uprooted from their rural world had to redefine their place in society, and equally might wish for a say in defining what that society might be. A crisis of Church reform erupted in one such Italian city, Milan, where from the 1050s a movement known as the *Pataria* (for now unclear but originally hostile reasons) emerged as among the first such convulsions of mass activism in medieval Europe. The *Pataria* looked remarkably like one of the morally charged crowds summoned by bishops in the contemporary Peace of God movement, complete with the regular swearing of communal oaths to defend the cause. Galvanized by charismatic local preachers, it developed a rhetoric of fighting against clerical corruption that anticipated the excitement of Crusaders against Muslims in later decades, hardly coincidentally. The purity argument had an obvious appeal to a laity expecting the best of their clergy. Arialdo, one of the chief 'Patarine' spokesmen, phrased it as a lay consumer's demand for quality assurance in prayer: 'Who is so stupid as not to be able to consider lucidly that the life of those I call upon to bless my house ought to be different and more elevated than mine?'[35]

The religious was also the political: the fury of the Patarines was directed towards their Archbishop, Guido da Velate, and his senior clergy, who were classic representatives of the old assumptions about the rightness of clerical marriage and dynastic succession in the Church. This won the insurgents sympathy from reforming clergy in Rome who also resented the Milanese clerical establishment's pride in its autonomy dating back to the fourth-century Bishop Ambrose, but now uncongenial to the likes of the future Pope Gregory or Peter Damian. Pope Alexander II went so far as to excommunicate Archbishop Guido in 1066, sparking violence in Milan that revealed the dangers of fusing an alliance of popular zeal with Rome's centralizing agenda. The Patarines thought for themselves and acted upon their vision of change and purification. Arialdo enunciated his own distinctive view of God's threefold ordering of society: one order of 'preachers, another of continent [clergy], a third of spouses' – two clerical orders and one of married laity. Pursuing such principles, crowds broke into houses of married clergy to separate them from their wives; resistant clergy were thrown out of their churches. In turn, Patarine leaders were murdered, Arialdo among them. Milan descended into chaos: the first experience for Gregorian reformers that revolutions have a way of devouring themselves.[36]

That was one end of the scale in lay indignation about clerical marriage. In general, over the next four or five centuries, the effort to stigmatize clerical families always faced the obstacle of reality, even down to the observation of Gratian, the authority on canon law, that more than one pope had been the son of a previous pope. In practice the whole system needed to be softened by the readiness of papal lawyers to grant dispensations in particular cases, for instance to allow the son of a priest or other illegitimate person to be ordained.[37] Beyond that, sheer inertia in effecting such a profound change meant that it was not at all complete when the sixteenth-century Reformation reversed it in much of Europe. There was a regional spectrum on this. Medieval England was generally always more ready to put all aspects of papal policy into effect than other areas of Europe, clerical celibacy as much as anything else. Perhaps this was because its monarchy was generally more efficient and centralized than elsewhere, and it is noticeable that the enforcement of clerical celibacy continued to be minimal in the English Crown's more miscellaneous jurisdictions in medieval Wales, let alone Ireland.[38]

That patchiness under a single European monarchy is significant. While much of our impressions of the imposition of clerical celibacy have previously derived from relatively 'well-behaved' parts of the Church such as England and France, the picture is remarkably different elsewhere, and everywhere the parishes continued to provide a different perspective than the view from a bureaucrat's window in Rome. Right up to the Reformation, bishops in Switzerland appreciated a steady and reliable income stream from fines on their parish clergy for keeping what were officially defined as concubines.[39] Parishioners in rural Iberia were as a rule perfectly happy with clerical families flourishing in the priest's house. It was not in response to Martin Luther's far-away Reformation that in 1533 the Synod of the diocese of Sigüenza in northern Spain forbade diocesan clergy from coming to church accompanied by a woman, or told them irritably that if they had children, not to flaunt them around the place. Practical-minded villagers across Europe would be content with a parish priest who did his job and whose female live-in partner, however defined, constrained his interest in everyone else's wives, while busying herself with baking bread for the Mass.[40]

The clerical family lives that the Gregorian sexual revolution did nevertheless succeed in ruining during the eleventh and twelfth centuries have left small traces in the historical record. What does remain is a substantial contemporary literature of argument in favour of clerical marriage, the flagship being 'A Letter on the Continence of the Clergy' (*Epistola de continentia clericorum*). This short treatise predated itself in authorship to the tenth-century Bishop Udalric (Ulrich) of Augsburg, in the usual manner of texts seeking respectably ancient authority, but it is now generally reckoned to have been written at the height of the Gregorian campaign, around 1074–75. Its arguments were straightforwardly biblical, with no need to resort to typology or allegory, unlike the proponents of clerical celibacy. The author was also aware of a supposed intervention in favour of clerical marriage from the celibate Bishop Paphnutius at the Council of Nicaea in 325: another historical embarrassment to Gregorian reformers, though it was probably itself an invention created in the fourth- and fifth-century explosions of debate on married clergy (above, Chapter 9).

There is little precedent between the fifth and eleventh centuries for such a text as the *Epistola*, but, significantly, of sixteen surviving manuscript copies of it, six date from the fourteenth to sixteenth century: this defiant voice from the past went on being read. Undoubtedly its most influential reader was a German friar called Martin Luther, in the fraught year 1520 (below, Chapter 14). Among other works, one poem of about 1090 explicitly written by a married priest anticipated a different argument, much revived in the sixteenth century by Reformers attacking Catholic clerical celibacy: it maintained that priests no longer allowed the joys of heterosexual sex would inevitably be driven into sex with other men.[41]

The Patarine crisis in Milan had revealed both the challenges and the opportunities for the reforming Papacy in extending its programme of reform of marriage across clergy and laity. The biggest prize to win was a grand bargain with rulers and aristocrats to eliminate the 'resource polygyny' that northern European elites regarded as the natural way to live and persuade them to accept the Church's control and regulation of marriage. The Church could offer a new stability for landowners in a new economic situation: if landed estates were to survive as economic units, it was important not to break them up by the old custom of letting all members of the family take their share (partible inheritance). A new inheritance custom of 'eldest takes all' (primogeniture) became widely established by the twelfth century. Now an aristocrat could view the Church, its concern for legitimate marriage and its rapidly developing legal system as helpfully identifying a true heir under primogeniture. Nobility might also be drawn to see allied advantages for dynastic succession in the celibacy imposed on those members of their families who were senior Churchmen, limiting claims on their lands. They might even consider all this a more cost-effective way to control inheritance than the alarmingly frequent aristocratic custom of forcibly castrating or blinding rival claimants to estates.[42]

Thus by 1139, when the second of a series of Councils of bishops to be called at the Lateran Palace (the main papal residence in Rome) declared all clerical marriages not only unlawful but invalid, the other half of the Gregorian sexual revolution was also fully launched. It hinged on a stark symmetry of opposites, emphasizing the gulf between clergy and laity. Lineage and inheritance were being eliminated from the Church (at least in legal theory), while for laymen and women, they were being stabilized, defined and enshrined within canon law. An essential part of this process was to refine a system of prohibitions on whom a layperson could not marry without committing the sin of incest. This was naturally something that had concerned ancient Judaeans, so the Old Testament gave some useful guidance, but the interesting feature of Gregorian Christianity was how far it extended the biblical system of proscriptions to mesh with primogeniture and to police the possibilities of marriage.

Before the eleventh century, the Western Church had allowed marriage between anyone who lay outside a range of personal memory of blood ties within families – roughly four degrees of kinship either by blood or marriage. Bishop Burchard of Worms (1000–1025) brought both precision and extended scrutiny to the genealogical grid with a more elaborate scheme that the Carolingian Church had favoured since the ninth century: six or seven degrees of relationship by blood to a common ancestor or to cousins related by blood or family marriages. This was widely adopted during the Gregorian upheavals, with particular encouragement from Peter Damian. It took a couple of centuries to see the flaws in Burchard's extension, though it proved mightily convenient for nobles who suddenly found good reason to rid themselves of an unwanted spouse by scrutinizing their pedigrees more closely. The major reforming fourth Lateran Council of 1215, which consolidated so much in the Gregorian changes, actually took a course of moderation: it returned to forbidding relationships within third-cousinage (the fourth degree).[43]

Yet that was only half of the Church's incest-related restrictions on lay marriage. A further dimension, entirely foreign to Judaism, was created by the institution of godparenthood. This developed in Christianity at the same time that adult baptism went into decline and the Church began baptizing infants: in the fifth and sixth centuries. Since babies cannot say the words of assent that are an essential part of the baptismal rite, adults were appointed to do it for them: sponsors or godparents, no doubt friends or patrons of the parents. Their duties did not end with the baptismal service but extended to helping the father and mother bring up children in Christian faith and practice. Attached to their role were the same prohibitions on incestuous degrees in marriages as between biological relatives, and naturally the scope of those prohibitions on 'spiritual kinship' extended in step with the Church's extensions of affinity. It would be wise for parents to make careful choices of godparents from among their friends and allies if they were not to limit their children's future marriage options; conversely, a betrothed couple having second thoughts might contrive a handy way out of a looming marital nightmare by acting as co-sponsors at a baptism.[44]

There was another important novelty in the Christian practice of marriage in the Gregorian revolution. In the snappy phrase of the historian Dyan Elliott, 'a clerical celibate elite requires a copulating laity' – the emphasis is on the word 'requires'.[45] This new syllogism would be a severe blow to several centuries of structurally chaste marriages: now the Church would expect marriages to produce children. That is a remarkable turnaround, and it is hardly surprising that a

16. In this mid-twelfth-century Psalter written in St Albans Abbey probably for Christina of Markyate herself, Christina poses with Christ in an historiated initial – poised for a sainthood that she never achieved.

continuing if diminished practice of celibate marriage survived in Western Europe. The case of the visionary Christina of Markyate in twelfth-century Hertfordshire illustrates both that persistence and the complications that made it increasingly problematic for the Church hierarchy. We read her story against the grain of the text of an effort to write up her life as the *Vita* of a saint, which exists in a single surviving manuscript in a significantly unfinished state.

As a girl, Christina invented for herself ceremonies to express her marriage to the Church, but, later, her family married her off against her will, under pressure from Ranulf Flambard, Bishop of Durham, who had himself shown a less than episcopal interest in her. She eventually ran away from her husband (a protégé of the Bishop) and entered spiritual living arrangements with successive celibates, one of whom was the formidable figure of Abbot Geoffrey de Gorron of St Albans. Out of the huge resources of one of England's wealthiest Benedictine abbeys, Geoffrey lavished gifts on Christina which included founding a whole nunnery for her at Markyate, over which she presided as prioress (plus male hermit companions). Evidently possessed of considerable sexual or emotional charisma, she sparked deep divisions between admirers and scandalized detractors in the Abbey. Abbot Geoffrey's death broke her power at St Albans; under the more discreet leadership of Geoffrey's nephew Abbot Robert, the Abbey began to recover. His successor wrote Christina out of St Albans' history and fostered a new cultic enthusiasm for an ancient and safely male companion of the Abbey's martyr-saint Alban, Amphibalus by name and probably fictional by nature. A syneisactic prioress had failed to make it through to sainthood.[46]

The general official change of mood in the twelfth century about marriage is patent, with much more concern to make sure that the sexual activity now assumed to be a normal part of marriage was directly concerned with conception. By the fourteenth century, confessional practice in England was including questions to make sure that couples were not making efforts to impede conception during marital sex.[47] More than that, the medieval Western Church embarked on a policy (widening in scope into the period of the Reformation and beyond) of dissolving marriages that had not been sexually consummated – at least when the parties wished that to happen. Cases of spiritual marriage continued to be found in the medieval Latin West; but by effectively making marriage dependent on sexual consummation, the Church hierarchy swung the balance decisively back towards sex in the old debate as to whether sexual intercourse or assent was the essence of marriage. The teaching of the Roman Catholic Church on marriage has made this explicit right down to modern times, with consequences that we will follow (below, Chapter 19).[48]

The new emphasis on the centrality of marital and procreational sex naturally gave a new currency to Paul's theological insistence on the marital debt of husband and wife in 1 Corinthians 7, which has so often proved an embarrassment to Christian societies with other social priorities. It is not a coincidence that the majority of canon lawyers in the medieval Western Church from Gratian onwards championed the Pauline marital debt within marriage. Just as in the time of Augustine and Jerome, such emphases left untidy questions about the status of the Virgin Mary's marriage to Joseph, as they always must, but canon lawyers were doing their best to be faithful to the Pauline principle in

17. A late thirteenth-century MS of Gratian's *Decretum* shows the importance of sexual performance (or lack of it) as one route to annulling a marriage: a canon lawyer listens to a wife's case, while two matrons (likely midwives) briskly investigate the humiliated husband for evidence of impotence.

the face of opposition both from landed nobility and many of their theological colleagues.[49]

All this is in contrast to the tradition sustained by Eastern Orthodoxy. It is noticeable that Byzantine canon lawyers were much less interested in the Pauline marital debt than their Latin counterparts; it hardly enters their thinking.[50] They were, after all, serving a Church that had not created a great lay–clerical divide or imposed universal celibacy on its clergy, but which on the other hand also maintained a more fundamentally negative attitude towards all heterosexual sex than did the Western tradition deriving from Augustine. Love, as we observed in Chapter 10, had no necessary connection with marriage for them. Moreover, non-consummation did not become a ground for annulment in the Orthodox tradition.

More remarkable still, there was a distinct reluctance, particularly among northern or Slavic Orthodox medieval theologians, even to admit to a direct relationship between sexual intercourse and procreation, despite evidence to the contrary in front of their eyes. Medieval Orthodox biblical commentaries or Lives of saints often slid away from making that physical connection; a theme of miraculous birth, in which sexual activity is not mentioned, spreads from discussion of biblical patriarchal couples such as Abraham and Sarah, or the parents of John the Baptist (Orthodox texts often described him like Christ as 'born of a virgin'), through to venerated saints of the Eastern Church, right up to the Byzantine Empress Theophano, tenth-century ally of the pioneering Christian Prince Volodymyr of Kyiv, or to Nifont, first Bishop of Novgorod in the twelfth century. Moreover, particularly esteemed female saints were liable to become virgins in Orthodox devotional manuscripts despite their stock-in-trade in saintliness being the fact that they were not virgins: Mary Magdalen and the reformed prostitute Pelagia of Antioch are cases in point.[51]

The novelties of eleventh- and twelfth-century Gregorian Christendom accumulate. Canon law was both their expression and their structure, offering good reasons why various different interests among the laity of the newly regulated Church should welcome fresh possibilities and opportunities. If the restructured marriage regime offered practical benefits to elite figures seeking to hand on their accumulations of land and wealth through primogeniture, canon law's emphasis on the couple's mutual consent might also appeal to those who saw their marriage as something more than a dynastic arrangement between two fathers. Young women and men wanting to make their own marital decision could and did feel benefits in accepting the principles of canon law. It also provided more flexibility than at first sight amid the general rigour of Western prohibitions on divorce and second marriages, by providing a range of ways in which a marriage might be considered never to have properly happened and therefore to be null: annulment could arise from the growing precision of prohibited degrees, but equally by sexual non-consummation. That did something to mitigate the disappearance of traditional forms of divorce.[52]

There were thus good grounds for even the furthest corners of the medieval West capitulating to the new marital standards by the end of the thirteenth century. The system survived without serious challenge down to the sixteenth-century Reformation, while the system of ecclesiastical courts became ever more elaborate and geographically all-embracing. Yet this ecclesiastical revolution went further in seeking to make the whole world a sacred society under the Pope. The chief stages of life and death, including marriage, must be framed within the rituals and jurisdiction of the Church: a contrast to the Christianity of the first five centuries. Now lay marriage, in which a man and a woman announced their assent to marrying one another, must become just as sacralized as clerical celibacy. The way to achieve this was to re-envisage or newly define marriage as a sacrament of the Church. This could be based on Augustine of Hippo's rather vague description of marriage as a *sacramentum*, by which he had meant little more than the Classical pre-Christian sense of that word as a solemn oath (above, Chapter 9).

The *sacramentum* of marriage had gained extra theological freight among some Western writers from the ninth century in the course of their determined assault on aristocratic 'resource polygyny' and on customary law allowing for a marriage to be dissolved.[53] Now the Gregorian revolution embraced marriage within a theological framework of seven sacraments, expanding the scriptural duo of Baptism and Eucharist. Peculiarities remained in this nuptial sacrament. Alone among the sacraments, it was now not available to priests, only laypeople. Moreover, a priest did not perform it: unlike the other six sacraments, it was a work performed by two laypeople – the couple – whose vows the priest merely witnessed and then blessed. The efforts of some theologians to alter that balance towards clerical authority were not successful: there was probably an awareness among clergy that the move would be unpopular. Many laity approaching marriage, particularly women, might relish the thought that their own consent was the crucial element in what they were doing.[54]

A sacrament being an outward and visible sign of an inward or spiritual reality, this new reality encouraged a formal ecclesiastical ritual in church for all, for the first time in the Western Church. Western clergy had previously only been involved in negotiating or presiding over royal or noble marriages, but from the eleventh century a long campaign sought to make this requirement universal.[55] This was a marked shift even from the new devotional activism of the Carolingian Church. Carolingian monarchs or high nobility might have considered a church ceremony as bonus legitimation for dynastic turning points, but it had still been optional. In an analogous liturgical situation, the Emperor Charlemagne did not consider giving an active role to the senior clergy present in his chapel in Aachen when he granted his imperial title to his son Louis in 813; the younger man simply took his crown from the altar while everyone present looked on as witnesses.[56] An institution of marriage carefully constructed on the basis of family negotiations had not felt itself needing much confirmation in Christian liturgy. As late as the end of the eleventh century, the German romantic poem *Ruodlieb* included a prolonged description of decorously cheerful wedding ceremonial in a knightly family. It was still entirely domestic and did not involve a priest at all – all the more remarkable since the poet-author was a monk of the stately Benedictine house of Tegernsee in Bavaria.[57]

A significant liturgical symbol of the anomaly in the marriage sacrament now constructed by liturgists was that at first it remained slightly distanced from the interior of the church building. The most prominent liturgical pattern-book in medieval England was the 'Use' of Sarum, designed to specify the elaborate round of services in a brand-new cathedral, under construction from 1220 on a virgin site at Salisbury (*Sarum*). Its wedding rite placed the bulk of the ceremony '*ante ostium ecclesiae*', in front of the entrance to the church. At Salisbury, what that meant was that the actual marriage took place in the new Cathedral's extremely large north porch. Only after the couple had taken their vows, exchanged rings and been blessed by the priest, did they get the chance to process into the church itself for a nuptial Mass. On the one hand, the Church wanted to take charge of the event, which after all had been declared to be one of the seven sacraments, but, on the other, it could not bring itself to do so inside the church building.

Architecturally one can see a response to Sarum in a distinctive thirteenth- and fourteenth-century development of church porches, right across England. Significantly, many of the earliest surviving porches contrast in architectural style with the main body of the building, for instance being built of wood rather than stone: that was a statement that they were part of a church, but also not part of a church. Yet the elaboration of Sarum or other cathedral Uses could only be a guide to what was possible in less well-resourced church buildings. It is noticeable that the architectural distinctiveness of church porches gradually faded, probably reflecting a changing reality in practice and their lessening role in weddings. Very few porches were as capacious as Salisbury's; northern European weather would not be kind to the overflow of guests, and a sensible parish priest who loved his people would have seen the point that it was no way to welcome a couple on what should be the happiest day of their lives. Accordingly, during the three centuries preceding the Reformation the performance of weddings increasingly

18. The earliest English church porches, provided to shelter weddings using the Sarum Rite, look architecturally distinct from their church building: often they were constructed of timber, not stone like the church itself, as at Offton (Suffolk), *c.*1300.

moved into the church building itself, without troubling to inform the liturgists.[58]

Considering how instrumental Cluny Abbey had been in all the new developments of the Gregorian revolution, it is an irony that by 1100 the very reformism Cluny had stimulated was beginning to sideline the Cluniac Order. It is a characteristic of Western monasticism that its communities exhibit a recurrent dissatisfaction with existing standards of community life and make an effort to renew and do better. The Cluniacs went on expanding, not least in their control of the Compostela pilgrimage, but increasing numbers of those attracted to the monastic life felt that Cluny's extreme elaboration of liturgy and architecture, and the extensive landed estates that underpinned Cluniac and Benedictine observance, were inappropriate for a life of self-denial and personal austerity.

It was actually a Benedictine abbot, Robert of Molesme in Burgundy, who looked afresh at the Benedictine Rule and determined on a newly austere observance of it. When most of his community disagreed with him, he left with a handful of followers to create a new foundation at Cîteaux (*Cistercium*). Cîteaux gave its name to a connected organization that was a deliberate rejection of Cluny, but did take its cue from the Cluniacs in forming itself as head of an independent, centralized and international Order: Cistercians, a huge success story in the twelfth-century Church. The preacher of the Crusades, Bernard of Clairvaux, was a Cistercian, and, by 1143, one of his monks had been elected Pope as Eugenius III.

A different initiative was to concentrate on reforming or founding communities of clergy who were not Benedictine monks, creating a structured communal life for them on a different pattern: an ancient series of statements and simple rules made by or attributed to Augustine of Hippo, for various newly founded religious communities under his control.[59] This was a useful way forward for some of the large churches that would have been known in Anglo-Saxon England as minsters, and occasionally for some cathedrals. Such clergy would not be enclosed monks but would continue going out from their communities into general pastoral ministry as 'canons' of their corporation. Because they nevertheless followed a Rule, not Benedictine but 'Augustinian', they emphasized their communal vocation by calling themselves 'regular canons'; that was an implicit criticism of 'secular' clergy, who were more obviously placed out in the world.

Such multiple discontents interacted with the passionate public preaching that was producing many different outcomes, from the Peace of God movement to the Patarine crisis in Milan to the Crusades. One such itinerant preacher was a former canon of a Rhineland church, Norbert of Xanten, who was more or less forced by the Church hierarchy in 1119 into structuring his most vocal followers as a monastic community at Prémontré in northern Francia – hence yet another monastic Order of austere Benedictine character, the Premonstratensians. Distinctively, it welcomed both monks and nuns (who were often the ex-wives of the monks), so a highly unusual feature of the early Norbertine communities as they untidily evolved was a close proximity of men and women, living chaste lives and enjoying more or less equal status; this earned them considerable suspicion and enmity from the Cistercians. Premonstratensian double communities of monks and nuns ended up being separated, and most of the nunneries withered away for lack of resources or endowments to support even the most ascetic of lives. Only a few similar, parallel-gender foundations survived the twelfth century: one was the wealthy Abbey of Fontevraud in central France, which had the advantage of royal patronage when preserving female leadership for itself and its various offshoots, and another (after some difficult early years) was a small Order confined to the kingdom of England, the Gilbertines, which took the precaution of making its leadership male.[60]

These new Orders multiplied during the twelfth century, each with its own charismatic founder and inspiration. The one common factor in their variety, and their great contrast with Carolingian Benedictines and the Cluniacs, was that they all galvanized adult enthusiasts into turning to a new monastic life; no longer would young children be sent to spend the rest of their lives in a monastery. The communities would be composed of those who had made a conscious choice, already knowing what it was to live in the world. Even illiterate adults could be included, just as they were recruited to the armies of the Crusaders: the Cistercians developed a system of 'lay brothers' who did not have to acquire the learning necessary to undertake liturgical action or the discipline of scholarship.

Thus, entering a monastery or nunnery in the new Orders was as much a statement of informed consent as canon law required of couples entering marriage. It was a conscious sidelining of that long-standing institution, childhood oblation, now increasingly treated as an obsolete institution. That was a remarkable U-turn in the official attitude of the Western Church, and it was capped by pronouncements from successive late twelfth-century popes. Clement III (1187–91) demanded that oblates re-examine their consent when twelve if female, or fourteen if male, just as they were now required to do in betrothal contracts, and his successor, Celestine III, spelled out that all oblates should make their own choice at the age of discretion, even if as a child they had agreed with their parents' decision. This was only catching up with the practice of the new religious Orders; the exceptionally rigorous new Order of monk-hermits, the Carthusians, had already fixed twenty as the age at which they would accept monks. Those who restructured the monastic world on such lines were perfectly aware that they were rejecting a past with a very different character. The Gregorian revolution had indeed remoulded Europe.[61]

Two sermons embodied in church architecture serve to illuminate this revolution. The first is a tale of petty clerical misogyny still enshrined in stone at Durham Cathedral. After 1081 its new reforming Norman Bishop, William de Saint-Calais, expelled the existing married cathedral clergy with their families and replaced them with Benedictine monks, splendidly rebuilding the whole precinct for the new male celibate community. Those visiting the Cathedral's Romanesque glories are likely to enter through its monumental north porch; once inside the Cathedral door, they may then observe a line that the monks laid in marble into the church floor across the nave and aisles. This marks the point beyond which women could not pass: now half the population of the diocese were no longer welcome in their mother church.[62]

Durham Cathedral's new ban on women received unexpected support from one of the most revered of Anglo-Saxon saints, the Cathedral's patron St Cuthbert. He had been dead for nearly half a millennium and was now buried behind the church's high altar, but a twelfth-century chronicler reports that the great man made a surprise intervention from beyond the grave. One day the Cathedral was visited by a noblewoman travelling in the retinue of the Queen of Scotland; she had decided to go sight-seeing in the magnificent new church. That night the senior monk charged with looking after the building had a vision: a visit from a very angry St Cuthbert, who did not mince his words about this female pollution of his beloved Cathedral: 'Get that bitch out of here!' roared the apparition. The poor lady was so mortified on hearing of the saintly wrath that she went off to be a nun at Elstow near Bedford.[63]

19. A line installed in 1189 in the stone floor of Durham Cathedral's nave and aisles marks the area beyond which women were not allowed – virtually the whole cathedral interior.

A more edifying architectural experience became universal through Western Christendom during this time: the visual impact of the crucifixion scene described in John's Gospel (19.25–27). Those primarily familiar with Western church buildings may not realize that it is a leading theme only in Latin Christian art; after some Anglo-Saxon beginnings in the ninth century, from the twelfth century depictions of Mary and John the Beloved Disciple standing flanking the cross swelled into a mighty visual flood. Up to the sixteenth-century Reformation, no Western church interior felt complete without this trio, raised specifically as carved images at the entrance to the chancel area of a church usually over a screen, and known as the 'Rood group' ('Rood' is the Anglo-Saxon word for 'Cross').[64] Amid the painted flat surfaces of Orthodox art, the theme is far less frequent in Eastern Christianity: the leading presence among Orthodox icons is the pairing of Mary and Jesus, biological mother and infant divine son (see Plates 3 and 4).

Why the contrast? It is surely no coincidence that the Europe-wide proliferation of Roods began in the chief era of Crusading enthusiasm for 'taking the Cross' in the West, which would be an equally good reason why Eastern Christians did not warm to the idea, given their experiences at the hands of Crusaders. Moreover, the Orthodox had probably not forgotten that a plain, unadorned cross had been a dominant visual theme in the church art of the disgraced Iconoclasts. Yet there is another dimension to the Rood group, as became apparent when we surveyed the Gospel material on the family (above, Chapter 4). John the Evangelist's portrait of the crucifixion scene unites and reconciles the biological mother Mary with the chosen and beloved disciple John, after all the tensions between these poles of relationship displayed in the Synoptic Gospel material.

This sacred binary of the Rood group was a powerful symbol of the new binary of family and priestly vocation set up in the Gregorian revolution. Yet it also preserves and embodies that complication that runs through all Christian views of sex and the family: on a medieval reckoning, both the watchers at the cross are virgins. Like all the most effective symbolism, the message of the Rood spools out in a complex mixture of tragedy, horror, love and reconciliation, taking it in a multitude of directions. Over centuries, in the end Mary and John and their crucified Saviour subverted the tidiness of Gregory VII's vision, both enriching and splitting apart the Latin Christianity that he and his circle had created.

13
Western Christendom Established (1100–1500)

The achievements of the Gregorian revolution were consolidated in a major Council of the Western Church summoned by Pope Innocent III in 1215 to his Lateran Palace in Rome. Among a range of canonical provisions, this fourth Lateran Council embodied the aim of imposing regulated holiness on the laity and ensuring their uniform belief and devotional practice. Priests were now expected to instruct their flocks in the essentials of Christian belief: manuals of instruction for pastoral care and preaching multiplied. The Council ordered every Catholic Christian beyond early childhood to receive the Eucharistic elements at Mass at least once a year (in practice usually only bread rather than both bread and wine, perhaps in case of spillages), and to prepare for that encounter through confession. There was nothing novel in the Council's stipulation that confession should be to one's own priest, or that both sides should preserve secrecy in what was said, but what was new was the universality of the demand; everyone was now obliged regularly to scrutinize their lives, assisted by expert help. Back in the ninth century a Council of Frankish bishops at Chalon-sur-Saône had voiced their suspicion of the institution of penitential manuals guiding individual confession (above, Chapter 11); this was a complete official turnaround.

Canon 13 among the decisions of the Council was an equally notable reversal of past Western Christian practice: it allowed a firm standing for a new form of communal but not enclosed celibate life, Orders of 'friars' (an English version of the Latin *fratres*, meaning 'brothers'). This was an important moment in regulating the extraordinary proliferation of religious Orders in the eleventh and twelfth centuries, crystallizing into a comprehensive ban on further creations in a Western Church Council at Lyons in 1274. Since 1215, Innocent III and his papal successors had formalized and put careful boundaries round various 'fraternal' Orders with centralized organizations.[1] Two charismatic leaders of very different character, Francis of Assisi and the Castilian Dominic de Guzmán, created the largest and most influential Orders ('Franciscans' and 'Dominicans'), but during the thirteenth century others also gained papal recognition.

The novelty of these Orders of friars, which were only taking shape as the fourth Lateran Council met, was that they overturned the long-standing Western Christian prejudice against wandering ascetics, dating as far back as John Cassian and Benedict. We have noted various exceptions to that general principle, including the Irish and Anglo-Saxon monastic missionaries across Europe and the proliferation of public Cistercian preaching through the Crusades, but now the fraternal Orders institutionally breached the principle in more respects than one. They rejected not merely the requirement for enclosed 'stability' in Western monasticism but also any financial reliance on great estates, by the simple structural device of forbidding their communities to hold property.

Friars consequently could only survive by begging for their living from the laity (hence they were also known as 'mendicants', from the Latin verb 'to beg'). That would necessarily bring them into everyday contact with European lay society, or they would perish. Laypeople would only go on funding friars if there were benefits in return: the spiritual consumer services on offer were principally preaching the Christian message to the laity and hearing their confessions. Since such services won the friars much esteem, friary churches also became greatly in demand for intercessory Masses in the developing sacred industry of prayer to speed souls through purgatory towards heaven.

The friars rapidly became the Western Church's specialists in preaching, so they needed to be intellectually alert and well informed; they quickly gravitated to university towns to get the best intellectual training that they could. Soon they had displaced the Benedictines as the most active scholars and teachers within the Western Church, after more than half a millennium. The Orders organized their preaching systematically on a continent-wide basis through a cornucopia of model sermon texts for all occasions, in Latin and so ready to be translated into any local language. As a result, the laity were presented with an unprecedented level of mass instruction in the Catholic version of Christian doctrine.[2]

A 'PERSECUTING SOCIETY'

A distinctive characteristic of medieval Latin Christendom, never equalled in Orthodox polities even at their most assertive, was its successful elimination of all rival religious systems. The one very qualified and often grudging exception to prove the rule was for Jews, afforded very bounded and separated lives, often wrecked by harassment or forced expulsion. Otherwise, European non-Christians ('pagans', as Christians have condescendingly termed them) lost their last foothold in the continent when in 1386 Grand Duke Jogaila of Lithuania, gaining the kingdom of Poland through a dynastic marriage, decided to join Europe's winners and embrace Christian practice in its Western Latin form. Within the half-millennium from 1000, with conversion to Judaism not a permitted option, most dwellers in European Christendom knew no other way of living or believing. Unless they lived on Christendom's frontiers in Spain, the Baltic or the Balkans, or ventured beyond on Crusade or pilgrimage to Jerusalem, their chances of meeting someone from outside their world (whether Muslim or that other variety of Christian self-styled as 'Orthodox') were vanishingly slender.

The Catholicism of Lateran IV was a deliberately tidy-minded version of Christian faith, intended to police both behaviour and ideas. Peter Abelard's *Theologia Christiana*, whose title had given currency to the word 'theology' as the chief object of study in universities, had proved a controversial work, revealing the difficulties in discussing what 'theology' should comprise and what its acceptable boundaries might be.[3] From the eleventh century this problem provoked active official persecution of heresy – defined as those propositions that led the faithful into persistently mistaken theological belief. At worst, those questioning the Church's defined teaching now faced being burned at the stake. The medieval historian R. I. Moore has popularized the description 'a persecuting society' for post-Gregorian Christendom.[4] The truth in the term can hardly be denied, but the extent of what it meant is still the subject of often heated debate among scholars expert in the period. This chapter will explore the limits of what the authorities in both Church and secular commonwealth could achieve, even when they were determined to impose a religious uniformity on Catholic Europe. There were always other voices.

The authorities in the Frankish Church and its royal allies first introduced the drastic penalty of burning for intellectual or theological adventurousness in the 1020s, amid some murky political manoeuvring. Ironically the origin of burning heretics was not Christian but began with burnings of Manichean believers by Christianity's last great imperial foe, the Emperor Diocletian, back in the late third century. The Latin West probably revived burning now because it neatly sidestepped ancient prohibitions stopping Churchmen from shedding blood.[5] It was a distinctively Western Latin development. In the Byzantine Empire there had been previous burnings at the stake but they ceased soon after the West took up the practice. In later centuries burnings resumed in Orthodox Muscovy – apparently, thanks to a prompting in 1490 from Western envoys of the Holy Roman Emperor.[6]

One new heretical movement in particular now emerged as a major challenge to the Western Church; apparently it resembled ancient Manicheism in its dualist view that material things were evil, sexual activity among them, so that true believers must transcend the physical in order to achieve spiritual purity. It became known as Catharism, from a Greek word meaning 'the pure' (*Katharoi*). This name was actually borrowed by Catholic commentators from a long-vanished deviant group in the first Christian centuries, but for many years it has been taken as a clue linking twelfth- and thirteenth-century Cathars to various recurrent forms of dualist belief in the Greek East, represented by 'Paulicians', a presence in the Byzantine Empire since the eighth century and, later, 'Bogomils' in the Balkans. So one way of accounting for a 'Cathar' presence in the Gregorian Church was to see a westward infiltration of dualist heresy encouraged by the upheavals of the Crusades. Certainly, contemporaries made this connection with the East: the English word 'bugger' and its French cognate are derived from 'Bulgarian', and reflect the usual canard of mainstream Christians against their opponents as far back as the New Testament that heresy, by its essentially unnatural character, leads to deviant sexuality.[7]

The Catholic Church identified Catharism in different settings in France and Italy. Cathar condemnations of the material world included the newly defined clerical hierarchy, with its all-too-material power and wealth. Over time, Cathars developed their own celibate hierarchy of 'the Perfect' – mostly male, and exclusively so at higher levels of authority and activity; female *Perfectae* were more like the nuns of Catholic Christianity.[8] The Church's defence against Cathar heresy turned to aggression and, from the late twelfth century, to a new Crusading enterprise – an 'Albigensian Crusade' (the city of Albi in south-west France was a Cathar centre, with its own Cathar leadership). This was not the Western Church's finest hour; the Crusade became a two-decade war of conquest in southern France on behalf of the French king and northern European nobility. Mass burnings at the stake were a regular feature of the Crusaders' retribution against their enemies, who were by no means all identified as Cathars.

This warfare was also the first significant laboratory for 'inquisitions': from the end of the twelfth century, a new institution of ecclesiastical enquiry and discipline authorized by the Catholic Church. Inquisitions with various regional jurisdictions remained a constant part of the Church's structure of regulation throughout European society into the eighteenth century. Their residual formal presence still endures in Roman Catholic bureaucracy under another name, as the Vatican's 'Dicastery for the Doctrine of the Faith'. The new Orders of friars, now the Western Church's leading intellectuals, were prominent among inquisitors, particularly the Dominicans.[9] Rich evidence on 'Catharism' survives, as inquisitions built up detailed records of their examinations of suspects. From the early fourteenth century comes an exceptional example: investigations by an inquisitor who later became Pope Benedict XII into a community in the Pyrenees called Montaillou. These are so informative that they have become the basis for a classic modern microstudy of medieval society.

Among a flood of detail on Montaillou, there is the statement of a Cathar village holy man Bélibaste that 'the sin is the same, to know one's own wife carnally or to do the same with a concubine', from which he deduced in decidedly pragmatic fashion that this sin was best contained in a monogamous marriage, avoiding a whole set of practical social pitfalls and undesirabilities. No theological issues were involved in this argument, because of Bélibaste's underlying theological rejection of the physical.[10] One has to allow for the nature of such inquisitorial sources, but cumulatively it is clear that in Cathar lands there were people with a profoundly negative view of sex – not just clerical sex, in the manner of Gregorian reformers, but all sexual activity. At least one treatise survives written by an avowed dualist, the mid-thirteenth-century *Book of Two Principles*: actually a debate internal to the movement, between moderate and hard-line dualists, and so not tainted by the coercive conditions of inquisitorial records. In the argument that it creates, both sides assume that all marriage is evil, being part of the visible, material world. That immediately suggests a link to the sexual negativity of Eastern Christianity generally, whether in Orthodox or heretical form, and indeed there is strong evidence of links eastward towards Byzantium among Cathar dissidents, especially in Italy.[11]

Given the Church's careful negotiation around love and marriage resulting from the Gregorian revolution of the eleventh and twelfth centuries, Catharism's far more thoroughgoing principled aversion to physicality and fleshliness is likely to have provoked a reaction within Catholic Christianity. Objection to minimalist Cathar views on marriage may have encouraged thirteenth-century Western preachers and theologians to drop the idea that marital sex always partook of the character of sin (below, p. 315). Beyond sex, Cathar negativity on physical creation extended to the fleshly humanity of Jesus Christ, born of a woman, thus threatening the increasing Western devotion to the Virgin Mary, biological mother of Jesus. More than that, it denied divine presence within the bread and wine of the Mass, as well as God's institution of hierarchy in the visible Church. There was much to persecute.

Puzzles remain amid the huge variety of evidence on Cathar heresy. It would be a strange dualist opponent of Catholicism whose chief heretical crime (in the eyes of a clerical heresy-hunting chronicler in twelfth-century Orvieto) was to show excessive concern for repairing the roof of the city's cathedral; such was the chronicler's accusation against Milita of Monte-Meato, 'daughter of iniquity'.[12] Equally odd is the case of a fourteenth-century Cathar woman of Montaillou on her deathbed, who, when alerted that the Catholic priest was on the way to give her the last rites, shrieked 'Holy Mary! Holy Mary! The Devil is coming!' It is possible to see Guillemette Belot's cry as reflecting a dualist affirmation that Mary was no more human than her son Jesus, and that is how many thirteenth-century Catholic commentators did explain the devout interest in Mary which many puzzled inquisitors encountered among Albigensians. Maybe, however, it was just that Guillemette viewed Mary as the Mother of God, just as her Catholic contemporaries did.[13]

The undoubted complications in the Cathar story have led some historians fundamentally to query the traditionally understood account of them: the British historian R. I. Moore leads other leading scholarly sceptics.[14] Such questioning returns to the eleventh-century Gregorian reforms. The very success in arousing Europe to a programme of renewal provoked energies that official restructuring could not contain: witness the Papacy's flirtation with the 'Patarine' disturbances in Milan in the mid-eleventh century (above, Chapter 12). The problem was that Patarines did not stop seeking reform when popes felt that there had been enough of it: they wanted a contemporary Church really worthy of the Apostles. In the mid-twelfth century, Lambert le Bègue ('the Stammerer'), a Patarine-style reformer in Liège far to the north of Milan, narrowly escaped a heretic's death for revivalist activities that included composing a metrical vernacular version of the Book of Acts for his followers, and the dynamic of official disapproval only intensified after that.[15]

Le Bègue was accused of starting a 'sect': a standard term in twelfth-century official accounts of religious movements of which the Church did not approve. Another grouping really did become a sect, the 'Waldensians', a movement started around 1170 in Lyons by a wealthy man called Valdes, who gave away all his wealth to the poor and ministered to a group who also valued poverty as the basis for Christian life. Church authorities were not prepared to make a distinction between this affirmation of poverty and that of any dualist Cathars in the same region, and, from 1184, a solemn papal pronouncement (a 'bull') condemned them both. The Waldensians persevered in clandestine expansion but were increasingly estranged from the episcopate of the Church on one vital issue: they were convinced that every Christian had a vocation to preach. That fatally clashed with the clerical priorities of the Gregorian reform.[16]

Particularly interesting are reforming movements that, unlike Waldensianism, split between groupings accepted and condemned by the authorities. We have already noted one case (above, Chapter 12): the movement begun by Norbert of Xanten, much of which was moulded into the Premonstratensian monastic Order, with its early commitment to communities of chaste men and women. Such joint communities did not survive, and, in general, female monasticism suffered constrictions during the twelfth century. The problem was the conviction of twelfth-century men, particularly those learned men trained in medicine, canon law and theology in the new universities, that females had greater sexual energy and urges than males, needing the protection of strict segregation within convent walls, even when they were consecrated celibates.[17] That was coupled with a suspicion of female celibacy inappropriately practised in the world: a dark irony followed. Since Cathars were accused of rejecting physicality, and therefore sexuality, in their dualism, it was possible to be burned at the stake accused of Cathar-style heresy merely for protecting one's chastity. Twelfth-century chroniclers report a couple of cases where women suffered this fate after male clergy tried unsuccessfully to seduce them.[18]

This background lends plausibility to the argument that a significant proportion of those labelled 'heretics' in twelfth-century Europe were disappointed reformers like Premonstratensians, still seeking to live a life of poverty and purity away from increasing official institutionalization.[19] It is noticeable how much of the twelfth-century hostile chronicling of heresy was done by Cistercian monks, the most energetic figures in the fully established Gregorian version of the Catholic Church, as well as chief rivals of the Premonstratensians. Cardinal Henri de Marci, for instance, was a Cistercian who rose to be Abbot of Clairvaux in the generation after the saintly Bernard; he was appointed papal legate to raise a Crusading army in 1181 in the early stages of the campaign against heresy in southern France (the Midi). The name 'Albigensian' was first used pejoratively in connection with this campaign, and it was at this time that heresy in the Midi was first linked to theological dualism.[20] The Cistercians also led the developing cult of Mary as they explored new ways of bringing the adults who joined their Order to a discipline of celibacy, of which Mary was the perfect earthly example: dualism was an offence to devout Marians.

Thereafter, dualism became a trope of Cistercian accounts of heretics throughout Europe, not merely in the Midi, and the thirteenth-century inquisitions had little to add; they just needed to ask the right questions to terrified people, dualists or not. By now they were regularly melding present heresy with the past movement of reform that had once been the ally of Pope Gregory VII and calling 'Cathars' 'Patarines'.[21] The movements that developed into the Orders of friars and the Beguines (below, p. 308) might have ended up in the same way. In the end, indeed, those mendicants who could not be contained in official structures created by thirteenth-century popes did end up, like the Cathars, being labelled as heretics and facing death by fire – often at the hands of inquisitors who were themselves Dominican friars.[22]

Why would so many dissenters in the twelfth-century West be given a dualist label if they were not? One answer is that descriptions of dualism were handily on display in textbooks used by students in the universities. It was routine for budding theologians to prove their prowess by refuting Manicheism as portrayed by such giants of early theology as Augustine of Hippo. There was also a contemporary geopolitical motive. The nadir in centuries of growing bitterness between Western and Eastern Christianity was the Fourth Crusade in 1204, which, far from defending Christendom, sacked Constantinople and set up a Latin carpetbagger Emperor and Patriarch in the wrecked city. Westerners had every reason to seek to justify such unjustifiable conduct by portraying the East as the nursery of heresy, and one thing that Westerners knew about heresy in the East was that it was dualist.

Once dissenters of various descriptions were formally defined as heretics, and persecution became systematized, it would encourage a defensive development of a formal hierarchical leadership in Catharism, united from a melange of dissidence by Catholic reaction, but there is no good reason to push back such leadership far into the twelfth century. A learned forgery by two seventeenth-century French historians put into print an account of a supposed pan-Cathar council in 1167, creating an impression of Cathar organization far earlier than any demonstrable reality, and the forgery has only recently been debunked. Add to that the repetition of chronicle narratives by later historians, and it has been difficult to see past the official narrative of Catharism; even many Cathars, under merciless attack by institutional Catholicism, may have come to embrace it.[23]

It has been worth examining the Cathar problem at length because it casts so much light on the 'persecuting society'. Regardless of how much one accepts from R. I. Moore's thesis about Catharism, Western Christianity was now intensely bounded, even paranoid. Not only 'heretics' were its victims; so were Jews. They first suffered systematic murderous violence from Christians while armed crowds were gathering in Germany for the First Crusade; they have never been entirely free of it thereafter. England, in the twelfth century the leading component in a transmarine empire under the French Angevin dynasty, has some unenviable firsts in the persecuting society: the first European example of the infamous 'blood libel' against Jews, in a Norwich Cathedral cult following the supposed ritual murder of a local boy in 1144; the first mass victimization of accused Christian heretics in 1165–66; a particularly ghastly massacre by fire of the whole Jewish community at York as a 'flagship' of nationwide massacres in 1190, and finally, exactly a century later, official expulsion of the kingdom's entire Jewish population, the first such expulsion in the whole continent.[24]

Paranoia in the Iberian Peninsula about the large-scale survival of Jewish populations as Christians reconquered regions from their Muslim rulers produced one lasting Catholic peculiarity: a rebranding of an inescapable part of Jesus's Jewish identity, his circumcision. From early centuries this was a liturgical Christian feast in East and West, to be celebrated around the turn of the year in January, but the Western growth in anti-Semitism stimulated the idea that it represented a Jewish physical assault on the infant Christ, the first shedding of his blood in anticipation of his crucifixion – to be blamed on the Jews just like their supposed murder of contemporary children. There resulted some disturbingly binary depictions of the Circumcision particularly in Iberian church art, ranging Mary and her Son against an ill-intentioned collection of Jews, with Joseph as a helpless spectator. In certain sections of the modern Roman Catholic Church, this is still perpetuated by the notion that the Circumcision is one of the Sorrows of Joseph, in parallel with the more long-standing devotion of the Sorrows of Mary, rather than the reality that it would have constituted a high point in any Jewish father's life.[25]

Victims of suspicion of the 'Other' varied over time. A particular moment of social panic throughout France in 1321 drew in all levels of society up to King Philip V himself, in the belief that lepers and Jews had combined together with the external enemy, Islam, to overthrow all good order in Christendom by poisoning wells. Lepers, normally the subject of institutional charity in medieval Europe, were victimized, tortured into confessions and burned at the stake, and the pogroms against Jews were no less horrific. Muslims had the good fortune at this time to be out of reach of French malice.[26] As the association of heretical Catharism with 'buggery' demonstrates, it was a very small step to bring same-sex activity defined as 'sodomy' into this circle of repression, although curiously, in the panic of 1321 mass hysteria passed the sodomites by.

The word *sodomia* was popularized in the eleventh century by Peter Damian in his polemic 'Book of Gomorrah' (*Liber Gomorrhianus*). It was an inescapably negative theological term, on the analogy of the older Latin word *blasphemia*; thus Peter paired 'sodomy' with the sin of denying God, in the process 'thinning and condensing' the wrongdoing of the biblical city of Sodom from malpractices that were originally much more various.[27] Ivo, Bishop of Chartres, Damian's contemporary and the major influence on canon law before 'Gratian', evolved the concept of 'sins against nature', in which same-sex acts were 'always unlawful and beyond doubt more shameful than to sin by a natural use in fornication and adultery'; at least fornication and adultery were not active obstacles to the continuation of the species. All this marched in step with the developing doctrine that marriage must necessarily involve the potential for reproductive sex. It was the obstacle to reproduction that was 'against nature', so the same acts committed between men and women, or solo masturbation, fell into the same category.[28]

This cluster of theoretical opinions already began crystallizing into legislation during the twelfth century. In 1120 a Church Council at Nablus in the Latin Kingdom of Jerusalem pioneered punitive enactments with provision for burning sodomites, just like heretics, perhaps with the ancient provisions of Justinian's Christianized civil code in mind (above, Chapter 8). The issue of male sexuality may have seemed particularly fraught in a militarized enclave surrounded by the ultimate Other, Islam, so often accused by Christians of harbouring sodomites, but the paranoia spread back across the Mediterranean into Western society.[29] A papal Council at the Lateran in 1179, which also took the first measures against Cathars, made enactments against clergy sinning 'against nature' with direct reference to the city of Sodom. From the thirteenth century this was increasingly echoed in the legal processes being developed by monarchs beyond canon law, as well as in ecclesiastical legislation.[30]

An incentive was the most bizarre and extra-biblical of Western Christian claims about 'sodomy': that at the birth of Christ all the 'sodomites' in the world died, before he would condescend to enter this sinful world, since they committed sins against nature. This malevolent Christmas fable involved distorted citations of Jerome and Augustine, good evidence that it started life in learned and clerical circles before moving out to instruct the wider public. After surfacing in an anonymous poem of around 1200 in honour of Mary, it has an early association with the Orders of friars as they began their task of preaching and instruction in the thirteenth century, and they went on plugging away at it for centuries; it appears in a Christmas sermon by one of Francis of Assisi's leading disciples, Bonaventure. It gained further currency through a standard text read, heard or recycled by the devout: the thirteenth-century Dominican Archbishop Jacobus de Voragine's anthology of saints' Lives known as *The Golden Legend*.[31] When in fourteenth-century England the Augustinian Canon John Mirk created his *Festial*, a massive round of vernacular sermons for parish priests to emulate the friars in preaching throughout the year, he drew much of his material from de Voragine; once more the story appeared in his sermon for Christmas Day.[32]

In the fifteenth century, the star Franciscan preacher Bernardino of Siena drew on the legend to solve a problem that still embarrasses some conservative Christians: why did Jesus say nothing about homosexuality? Bernardino triumphantly pointed out that Jesus would have no reason to speak of sodomy, since all the sodomites had just died. No one will assert that the universal cull of sodomites was an indispensable topic in Christmas preaching, but it remained widespread background noise across medieval Catholic Europe, particularly in Marian devotional literature.[33] Evidently, alas, the mass Christmas extinction proved less than a final solution, needing continuing vigilance from all right-thinking people. The more unpleasant corners of the internet persist in reminding the right-thinking of its contemporary relevance, though anachronistically relating it to 'homosexuals'.

All this is a contrast with Byzantine Christianity (and therefore with northern Orthodoxy as well). Since the Orthodox retained marriage for parish clergy, their religious culture did not share Peter Damian's pioneering linkage of hating sodomites and hating married priests. The main concern of the Orthodox Church was therefore to regulate inappropriate same-sex relationships in monasteries. Same-sex behaviour was disciplined within the Church's penitential system – for instance exclusion from Communion – and the priorities in punishment are interesting reflections of strong boundaries on male identity. Shaving one's beard off and thus resembling a woman carried harsher penalties than a man soliciting another man for sex, and mutual masturbation was regarded in Byzantine and northern Orthodox canon law as a good deal less serious than violating gender roles by anal intercourse with either sex.[34] Lesbian activities did not greatly concern the Orthodox, since they did not offend against gender boundaries; in Russia a greater worry was their possible link to widely surviving pre-Christian religious practices. So the common term for lesbians was the same as for female leaders in such cults: *baby bogomerzskie*, which may be translated delightfully and not inaccurately as 'God-insulting grannies'.[35]

Medieval Europe being medieval Europe, persecution of sodomites in the end produced a miracle story. In 1320 a man was caught in *al fresco* sex with a thirteen-year-old boy in the papal city of Avignon; the two of them were sentenced to be burned at the stake. As the flames consumed the adult, the boy was about to suffer the same fate when his anguished prayers aroused the pity not just of the watching crowd but of Our Lady herself, who loosened his bonds and released him (see Plate

27). The Pope, John XXII, was so impressed by Mary's intervention that he built a votive chapel in her honour on the site of the burning, and the boy was also given an honourable tomb in Avignon's Cathedral at his death fourteen years later.[36]

The contrasting fates of this pair, fiery oblivion and near-canonization, reflect the ambiguity around those participating in same-sex acts and how penalties should apply to them. Were they, like Jews, condemned as sinners simply by their birth (cursed by an unnatural nature), or was their crime a conscious choice, like heresy, something capable of recantation? Perhaps they were doubly damned by simultaneously though illogically being like both Jews and heretics.[37] Yet Our Lady's discrimination between the Avignon participants (no doubt conveniently harmonizing with that of many onlookers by the stake) is likely to have been an acknowledgement that a younger participant could be led on. It is a reminder that the reforming aspirations of a Gregorian persecuting society were complicated by the irrepressibly multiple voices of medieval Western Christendom.

PLURAL VOICES IN A UNITED WEST

The imaginative hold that the post-Gregorian Papacy and its focused authority enjoyed over Europe was based on its custodianship of the body of the Apostle Peter in Rome in the monumental basilica built by Constantine I, but also on the Church's custodianship of the memory of Rome and its Empire. A genuinely Roman Emperor still ruled in the known world, but his throne was in the New Rome of Constantinople, and the language of his Church was Greek. The West was united by its use of the Latin language, all the more powerful and all-embracing because nowhere was it now anyone's birth-tongue. It had to be taught, or absorbed through the Church's conduct of worship, as much a common language overcoming cultural barriers as English is in modern India. Just because Latin was a language to be learned did not mean that it was not lively and creative, with a range of registers from liturgical to cheerfully scatological and lewd. It was hugely useful, but also hugely entertaining. Possession of it liberated the speaker into joining a wider world of shared experience and memory, which must be one reason why it was embraced with such enthusiasm by both Irish and Anglo-Saxons, whose own languages bore very little relation to its grammar and vocabulary.

Fuelling this continent-wide conversation was the increasing circulation and range of ancient Latin texts and Latin translations of Greek texts, throwing European society open to the culture of a Mediterranean world centuries older than Christendom or Christianity itself. Like Carolingian society before it, twelfth-century Europe has been painted in colours borrowed from later centuries, as fostering a 'Renaissance' of Classical literature. There was no extensive equivalent in the Greek East, where, at precisely the same time, insecure imperial and ecclesiastical authorities reacted with hostility and repression towards scholars seeking to explore afresh the legacy of Aristotle and Plato in efforts to renew Byzantine society. The contrast between Western and Eastern Christianity thus deepened still further.[38]

Western Latin culture was imparted through surprisingly risky teaching materials. Impressionable schoolchildren learned their Latin through that most erotic of Roman poets, Ovid: already in the tenth century the reforming Anglo-Saxon Archbishop of Canterbury Dunstan relaxed from his ecclesiastical labours by annotating his ancient manuscript copy of Ovid's verse in his own distinctive hand. From the early thirteenth century, one of the most popular school texts in Europe (to judge by surviving manuscripts and vernacular translations) was a brief, newly written, pseudo-Ovidian comedy effectively about rape, entitled *Pamphilus, de Amore*: were texts like this intended to teach boys how to be men, and girls to be aware of male charm turning into male violence?[39] From an early age, therefore, those exploring literature were exposed to ancient assumptions some of which were familiar from Christian redeployment of them (such as monogamous marriage), but some very different (such as life-stage same-sex love). However hard schoolmasters might try to channel such reading, their efforts were likely to be frustrated by the perennial energy of the young in seeking out pages fascinatingly beyond the recommended range.

The tenor of Classical literature was to inject into Western culture a concern with human free will and moral responsibility, exploring how this might fit into a Christian view of heaven and earth in the control of Almighty God. This twelfth-century preoccupation can be labelled 'humanist' as much as the Renaissance of the fourteenth to sixteenth century, and its use in these contexts should not be confused with the common modern meaning of 'humanism' as the rejection of religion: it referred to those in universities who studied the *humanae litterae* of Classical learning, rather than the *divinae litterae* of theological texts.

Scholarship has even extended this as far as to describe the period as witnessing 'the discovery of the individual' – the title of a deservedly celebrated book by the British medievalist Colin Morris – though it would have been difficult in the twelfth century to gather the vocabulary by which modern Westerners express the concept of individualism. Nevertheless, the fourth Lateran Council's imposition of universal auricular confession made the examination of the individual self a central part of Western Christian identity.[40]

Individual self-examination implies awareness of others as individuals, not least as objects of personal love. The readers of Ovid could readily make that connection, and a growing contemporary literature applied the idea of love in a remarkable variety of contexts. The most famous love story of the period is the thwarted marriage of the theologian Peter Abelard to the intellectually gifted Heloïse: mutual love arising out of his tuition of her, which led to the birth of a son, a short-lived marriage and his forcible castration by her furious relatives before both parties were sent to monastic houses. After experiencing traumatic suffering for mutual passion, Abelard broke with the general Christian tradition since the second century CE and proclaimed the moral rightness of sexual emotions: 'It is clear, I think, from all this that no natural pleasures of the flesh should be counted as sin nor should it be considered a fault for us to have pleasure in something in which when it happened the feeling of pleasure is unavoidable.' Abelard said this as a married priest, so for the moment it looked as if history was not on his side. The Western world, let alone Western Christianity, would take a great many centuries fully to catch up with his opinion – or indeed his passionate defence of the ordination of women.[41]

Meanwhile, the rediscovery of a vocabulary of sexual love bore an uncertain relationship to the institution of marriage as newly recast by the Western Church. One of its early expressions was the peculiar genre of 'courtly love', part of a literature mainly composed, sung and then written in a number of languages beyond Latin; the lead here was taken by speakers of Anglo-Norman and Provençal versions of tongues used in Francia. Such texts were both entertainment and instruction: part of a glorification of the image of the knightly soldier, born in the age of Crusading. The word 'nobility' early acquired the double strands of meaning which it still possesses; it might overlap with noble birth, but it could also have origins in male character and military skill.

The soldier's deal with the authorities of the Western Church for blessing his activity in killing people included establishing ground rules for public and private conduct. There were the obvious military and feudal virtues of duty and loyalty to companions or superiors; yet also wisdom, generosity, even on occasion mercy towards the powerless – and appropriate relationships with women. Notions of appropriateness in courtly love rarely included marriage. The woman who was the object of male adoration was generally unattainable, on grounds of social rank or simply marriage to someone else. Or she was all too attainable: not simply in the school textbook sexual assault by Pamphilus, but in the adulterous tales of Tristan and Iseult or Lancelot and Guinevere – both first emerging in twelfth-century francophone texts.

Still more unexpected was the emergence in the eleventh and twelfth centuries of a literature of same-sex love. It is a prominent feature in classical Arabic poetry over many centuries, and in medieval Muslim-ruled Iberia the genre spilled over into Jewish literature, then closely bound into elite Islamic culture – in both religions, that was despite much official condemnation of same-sex activity.[42] Western Christian texts on same-sex love do not seem to relate to Muslim or Jewish writing, and the genre petered out during the thirteenth century, no doubt now seeming too risky in a more intolerant official climate. Unsurprisingly it picked up themes and conventions from Roman literature; a frequent reference was the figure of Ganymede, the youthful male lover (or victim) of Jupiter, but there were also straightforwardly biblical references to David and Jonathan, a rather more equal partnership. Abelard, so terribly maltreated in the course of heterosexual love, could nevertheless explore the feelings of the biblical lovers in paraphrasing their story as a prolonged lament for Jonathan's death. For the first time since the Classical period, some twelfth-century authors penned dialogues which are debates over the relative superiority of heterosexual versus same-sex love.[43]

The prominence of officially celibate clergy and monks among the writers is not accidental. Archbishop Baldric of Dol (?1046–1130) wrote a great deal of Latin verse (as well as the first major account of the First Crusade), mostly while Benedictine Abbot of Bourgeuil in west-central France. He delighted in exploring Classical poetic genres, Ovid especially, and some of his poetry addressed to men is remarkably prone to turn to physical expression. The monk Ralph he called his 'Other self, or myself, if two spirits may be one / And if two bodies may actually become one'. This was no random thought, but a purposeful reference to Ovid (predictably), and the poet's treatment of the legend of Hermaphroditus, the beautiful son of the god Hermes and goddess Aphrodite, forced by the gods into bodily and spiritual androgyny with an amorous water-nymph. To another monk Peter (whose comb Baldric always carried as a keepsake), he cheerfully wrote: 'If you can, keep your deeds above reproach, but if you cannot, at least keep your confidences to yourself.'[44]

Behind this literary efflorescence among clerical authors was a practical consideration: how to make emotional sense of the twelfth-century transformation in monastic formation. Rejecting the Carolingian Benedictine oblation of children, these were communities built up from adults who had made a free, informed choice to enter monastic life, and brought with them adult emotional and sexual experience.[45] They needed to explore how they might shape a new emotional life among other men for the rest of their lives. In literature that would mean moving on from the unequal-age, life-cycle model which was the accepted convention of ancient same-sex activity. Among the texts that they would draw on would be another biblical text about love between equals, even though the participants were male and female, the Song of Songs. From the glory-days of Cluny onwards, this book of the Bible was the most frequently read and written about of all biblical books in commentaries produced in male monasteries, while there are very few texts discussing it surviving from any medieval woman: it was a literary text in a man's literary world. For a monk, the Song of Songs was a meditation on divine love, but its vocabulary remained that of undisguised and mostly fulfilled adult sexual desire.[46]

The monastery was a safe space for even extravagant outpourings of same-sex expression, as long as one observed very careful delimits and a carapace of literary and biblical allusion. When those limits were understood, it could lead to remarkable emotional frankness – for instance in a series of treatises on friendship created in a major specimen of the new monasticism, the Cistercian Abbey of Rievaulx in Yorkshire. The author was one of its monks and later celebrated Abbot, Aelred, prolific in writing on spirituality and how it should be practised. In writing these texts on friendship, he was directly and successfully challenging his Order's original prohibition on particular personal friendships in a monastic community. Once more a celibate looked back to a pre-Christian Classical model, in this case Cicero's text *De Amicitia* ('On Friendship'), to illuminate urgent personal questions: how permeable was the boundary between friendship and love, the physical and the spiritual?[47]

Aelred was not prepared to define that frontier when writing of his grief for a dead friend, and neither can we: 'some may judge by my tears that my love was too carnal. Let them interpret them as they want; you, however, Lord, see them and consider them.'[48] Aelred's distinguished Cistercian contemporary, Bernard of Clairvaux, gave vent to agonies of deep loss like that of Aelred's over the death of his fellow monk Gerard, the cellarer of Clairvaux Abbey, in a sermon preached to the brethren there in 1138 (inevitably on the Song of Songs). Bernard spoke of struggling with expressing such individual personal emotion and, having resolved that problem for himself and his audience, he was able to say of his bereavement from the pulpit: 'All by myself I experience the sufferings that are shared equally by lovers when compelled to remain apart.'[49]

Various other all-male settings offered possibilities. A surviving witness is a small but significant number of memorializations of close same-sex relationships in tombs: images of two men sharing the monument. Academics are unsurprising among them: the remaining medieval college chapels of Oxford University have several examples. There is also the extraordinary survival in Istanbul of a tomb-slab for two fourteenth-century crusader knights, one of whom reputedly refused food and died a few days after the death of the other – the slab depicts a stylized kiss in heraldry marshalled as if for husband and wife. This is likely to be an example of 'sworn brotherhood': a formal agreement between two males for support in war or for power-sharing that escaped the punitive definitions of sodomy in the medieval West.[50] Sworn brotherhood pacts could be regarded as imagined, spiritual versions of biological relationships, in the manner of those who became godparents.

Aelred's works, probably little circulated in his own time, have found a new resonance and popularity in the very different setting of modern Western culture, just as Abelard's praise of physical sexual expression has done. Amid contemporary admiration of these voices from the past, one vital difference between then and now needs remembering: in the twelfth century this was a male literature for men. The background was the creation of those all-male institutions, universities, providing for men to do male things: study and create systematic theology against the background of Classical philosophy, or prepare for legal and medical studies. This shifted the academic and intellectual centre of Latin Christendom away from the Benedictine centres of scholarship that had included nunneries as well as monasteries, in a world where abbesses had often been as powerful as their male counterparts.

There was a last twelfth-century flourishing of the old tradition in the person of the now famous aristocratic polymath Hildegard, Benedictine Abbess of Rupertsberg near Bingen on the Rhine. She was a mystic and visionary, but her literary creativity embraced cosmology, medicine and musical composition as well as theology. She was among the last generations of the tradition of Benedictine oblation, and a proof of what that lifelong monastic identity might produce. After her time, the Gregorian insistence on a celibate priesthood characterized by its vocational commission to celebrate the Mass thinned down the conception of female vocation. No longer could abbesses like Hildegard be considered as being 'ordained' to their office; ordination, previously signifying entry to a new ministerial or vocational status, was now defined as something that could only apply to clerical males, charged with duties controlling the seven sacraments now defined by the Church.[51]

An amusing symbol of what nunneries now became is to be found in one distinctive feature of the single-sex female communities newly founded and endowed by Anglo-Norman noblemen and senior clerics in the twelfth century; this was at the same time that the authorities were curbing and bounding the reforming enthusiasm of the Premonstratensians and such other joint male and female foundations (above, Chapter 12). Now founders provided the nuns with statutes for their daily life and organization, but not in Latin, because women would not be expected to know it. Being for the most part well-born ladies, the nuns spoke Norman-French, and that was the language of their statutes. In later centuries, their successors in England went on conscientiously learning this archaic tongue solely to understand and follow their founding ordinances, as one of Thomas Cromwell's staff noted with fascination in 1535 at the admirably well-run nunnery of Lacock in Wiltshire, during the early stages of Henry VIII's dissolution of English monasteries. The Lacock nuns 'understand well and are very perfect in the same, albeit that it varieth from the vulgar French that is now used, and is much like the French that the [English] Common Law is written in'.[52]

One hundred and fifty years earlier, the same phenomenon had been gently satirized by Geoffrey Chaucer in his portrait of the Prioress in his General Prologue to *The Canterbury Tales*: she spoke French 'full fair and fetisly [elegantly], / after the school of Stratford atte Bowe / for French of

Paris was to her unknow[n]'.[53] Scholars and literary critics have puzzled over and usually misunderstood Chaucer's phrase. It was clearly a London joke of the 1380s that posh nuns such as those in the twelfth-century foundation of St Leonard's at Stratford-at-Bow had no knowledge of the French language beyond their weird-sounding private archaic Norman-French. How symbolic that is: refined ladies conscientiously observing intellectual limits laid on them by a long-dead man. It is not to be expected that any such restrictions could constrain the mental energies of women who sought God, but they would have to express themselves in other ways. They were distanced from formal Latin intellectual training in doctrinal propositions or in the argumentative clashes of scholasticism, but they could still use their imaginations to enter divine hiddenness, in the free explorations of the human mind that stretch across world religions in the form of mysticism.

Of course, in this as in every period, there were male mystics as well as female, but the preponderance of women is striking. A man might draw on a library of previous texts going back centuries; the texture of what the mystic says does not depend on such learning. The same themes to describe the indescribable – water, fire, light, silence – recur unsourced over millennia in the thoughts of mystics even if semi-literate or technically illiterate. Often in medieval Europe this would result in texts written in the vernacular language that a woman used. A female mystic might often pair with a male cleric to record what she wanted to say in Latin, but that was in order to spread her message more widely, and she had no automatic need of a priest to let her imagination range freely.

Such messages, unrestricted by professional theological training and detached from the clerical authority of the Gregorian revolution, ranged riskily beyond the structures of the institutional Church; it was easy to step into the realm that inquisitors labelled heresy. Two associated mystics of early fourteenth-century France and Germany, Marguerite Porete and Meister Eckhart, experienced this to their cost: Porete, who wrote of her experiences in a work in French entitled *The Mirror of Simple Souls*, was burned as a 'Free Spirit' heretic in France in 1310, and Eckhart, whose texts reveal scant respect for monks and clergy, died during inquisition proceedings against him. Yet even these victims of official suspicion might in the end be recognized as speaking profitable wisdom; eventually Rome partially atoned for its inquisitorial treatment of Marguerite when, in 1927, the first modern edition of her *Mirouer des simples âmes* was given official approval with a papal *imprimatur*.

Reading the mystics of this period allows us to hear the thoughts of medieval individuals in a relatively unfiltered state, compared with virtually any other text: variants on otherwise lost private conversations, gossip or the equivalent of the modern newspaper problem page. Hardly surprisingly, this often resulted in startlingly sexually charged broodings which elsewhere would have remained silent, gaining relative immunity by the holiness of purpose acknowledged by at least some readers. Not all is sex; the mystic may make a surprising choice of random physical objects and deepen their significance. Well known is the contemplation of a hazelnut by the fourteenth-century Norwich hermit Mother Julian, 'a simple creature unlettered': in the course of the Lord Jesus's pleasantly informal conversations with her, he showed her that the nut was 'all that is made' despite its littleness, for 'it lasteth, and ever shall, for that God loveth it. And so All-thing hath the Being by the love of God.'[54]

Nevertheless, women mystics were far more ready than men to seize on themes of marriage and motherhood in articulating what they felt about the divine relationship; it was an audacious transformation of the dependency to which medieval society assigned women (see Plates 8–10). As a result, visionaries recounted experiences that men would uncomfortably regard as female business, like changing babies' nappies. Adelheid of Frauenberg, a fourteenth-century Dominican nun at Töss in northern Switzerland, thought much about that, being reported as wishing to 'remove her skin so it could serve as a diaper for Our Lord, her veins to be made into a skirt [for him]'. Balancing her own self-recycling, she also envisioned Our Lady suckling her as her own child.[55]

Deliberately forgotten over the centuries was the disconcerting mystical output of Agnes Blannbekin, a celibate laywoman from Vienna. Her revelations, a form of spiritual diary created between 1291 and 1294, were recorded in Latin by her confessor, a male Franciscan friar (who prudently did not perpetuate his name). When first put into print in the eighteenth century their content was found so shocking that the scholarly edition was suppressed. A great deal of nudity cavorts through Agnes's more than two hundred visions of heaven, embracing both herself and Christ. Boldest of all, even through the filter of Latin, is her especial devotion to one feast of the Church's year, the Circumcision of the infant Jesus, innocent of the Catholic anti-Semitism then developing. 'About a hundred times' at the Mass of that feast day, she would feel a sweetness on her tongue, and described herself as swallowing the foreskin ('prepuce') of Christ.[56]

Such figures as Adelheid and Agnes may seem outliers among mystics, but as respected a figure as Catherine of Siena, a Dominican contemporary of Adelheid, is celebrated for envisioning her own mystical marriage to Christ: as a wedding ring she used that same sacred prepuce of Agnes's devotion. Sometimes such exuberant female constructions sound suspiciously as if they were testing out the embarrassment thresholds of senior male clergy. It is noticeable how few women achieved official recognition as saints in the two centuries after 1300. Catherine was exceptional in making it through against some sturdy resistance from Roman cardinals, aided by *campanilismo* from her fellow Sienese Pope Pius II in 1461; nevertheless, papal recognition that she had authentically borne stigmata like the charismatic St Francis had to wait till the seventeenth century.[57] The canonization of her fellow visionary Bridget of Sweden, who had

20. The Sienese artist Michelino da Besozzo (*c.*1370–*c.*1455) depicted St Catherine mystically wedding Christ, with the two desert saints John the Baptist and Antony of Egypt looking on. In this spiritual and ascetic ceremony, no one, including Our Lady and the Christ Child handing over his sacred prepuce as wedding ring, exudes jollity.

the advantage of an aristocratic background and of having successfully founded a new religious Order, began remarkably swiftly in 1391, within two decades of Bridget's death, but it became enmired in political controversy and had to be twice repeated.

THE CITY; THE FAMILY

The variety of conversations beyond the power or inclination of the Western Church authorities to control them was encouraged by the steady expansion of towns and cities across Europe. This was catch-up with a far more developed urban network in the Islamic Mediterranean – Islamic Cordoba in Spain may have already had a population of 450,000 around 1000 CE.[58] The new development was based on the growth of long-distance commercial networks and a monetary economy, exposing the artificiality and limitations of the theoretical convention of three orders in society – *oratores, bellatores, laboratores* (above, Chapter 12). The greatest cities grew around the commerce of Italy, the Rhine valley and the Low Countries, but significant outliers were Paris and London.

Everywhere, such gatherings of people were characterized by a high turnover of population, rarely self-sustaining in unhealthy urban conditions and relying on a constant inflow of newcomers escaping the settled ways and inquisitive eyes of rural communities to seek better opportunities and less restricted lives. Urban populations were therefore younger than elsewhere, with a particularly visible and audible proportion of young men expecting excitement. The Gregorian Church hierarchy had been able to draw on Patarine urban energy for its reforms (Chapter 12), but cities remained a challenge for ecclesiastical structures developed to serve and control a rural and agricultural world. Clergy did their best to control religious and social urban life through the parish system – medieval London, for instance, uniquely large in England though a pygmy by Italian urban standards, developed a staggering hundred-plus parishes in little more than a square mile of territory, each with its parish church, besides an array of monasteries, nunneries and friaries. Yet all London's provision would still struggle to cope pastorally with a population that numbered around 33,000 by 1500.[59]

The imperfect control of urban society encouraged various forms of male group cultures that Church and secular government needed to contain or neutralize. One symptom of aggressive male self-assertion in late medieval Europe was a matter of fashion: in a sudden turn of fourteenth-century taste, the clothing of young males (and therefore of older males trying to hang on to their youth) came to emphasize their genitals, culminating in the risible sixteenth-century fashion for the 'codpiece', revealing while pretending to conceal.[60] It was a depressingly easy move from there to a culture of male sexual violence against women. An extreme example is provided in fifteenth-century Dijon in eastern France, where a custom of gang rapes (*chasses joyeuses*) by groups of young men claimed around twenty victims a year, sometimes on the pretext of disciplining prostitutes or servant girls suspected of 'fornication'.

Equally depressing is the attitude of secular urban legal systems to such behaviour. The Dijon courts only imposed penalties if the rapists had misjudged a victim who was actually a young woman of some social standing or a child. On the principle that prevention was better than cure, the city authorities there allowed the creation of recreational societies known as *abbayes de jeunesse* ('abbeys of youth'), whose function was to organize carnival events as well as to indulge in more controlled carnivalesque mayhem, up to but no further than public displays of shaming those women of whom there was general social disapproval.[61] The same cluster of attitudes is revealed in fourteenth- to sixteenth-century Venice, where most rape trials were increasingly relegated to become the business of minor courts in the Republic's legal system, and where it is plain that authorities accepted rape as one way to begin a long-term sexual relationship, even as a preliminary to marriage.[62]

It was a very different matter in reactions to a quite open revival of the already ancient Mediterranean mode of same-sex behaviour last seen so prominently in the Classical world: the hierarchical sexual activity of an older and younger participant as a phase in a fundamentally heterosexual mode of life (as usual, the overwhelming focus is on males). This became a surprising reality in late medieval Italian cities, the standout case being Florence over two centuries from the early fourteenth century. Legal records and contemporary perceptions both agree on this, while evidence of court records from Venice and its Adriatic satellite Ragusa (Dubrovnik), a boom town rapidly growing during the fifteenth century, are parallel examples.[63] A late medieval German slang word for same-sex intercourse was *florentzen*, and detailed denunciations of sodomy, particularly of the Florentine variety, were a regular flesh-creeping theme in Bernardino of Siena's preaching, so much so that, on one occasion in 1427, outraged matrons frogmarched their daughters away from his open-air preaching to preserve their modesty, to his great chagrin.[64]

The legal statistics from Florence during this same period are exceptionally rich, thanks to the detailed archives of a city court set up with a specific brief on sodomy in 1432. This system actually represented an easing of the savagely punitive systems developed in southern Europe over the previous two centuries, suggesting a situation that had become too frequent for excessive repression. Offenders in Florence numbered in the thousands over a century, and it has been estimated that between 1459 and 1502, one in every two young Florentine males between twelve and twenty years old had been named before the 'Officers of the Night', characteristically as passive partners of older men.[65] It was testimony to the strength of a male-bonding culture in a Renaissance city, and was linked to the unusual sexual constraints on marriage arising from social custom. Male marriage-age was remarkably late in Florence in this period, early thirties on average, and connected to severe restrictions on available young women. Indeed, throughout the Italian cities of the period an astonishing and steadily increasing number of young elite women were sent off to nunneries, to save the rising cost of marriage dowries – in Renaissance and Counter-Reformation Milan it would eventually comprise three-quarters of their number. The picture was similar in other southern Mediterranean societies concerned to stop family resources being dissipated in marriages; that often resulted in a great many reluctant and discontented young nuns, as well as many frustrated young men.[66]

Corroborating Bernardino's splenetic but well-informed observations, this suggests a classic case of life-cycle behaviour on the part of unmarried youth, for few of them occur in later records as offenders, but it is combined with the fact that a high proportion of the older men involved remained unmarried, in a city which in any case exhibited an unusually high proportion of permanently unmarried men. That was a move away from the Classical model of same-sex activity. It might suggest (as Bernardino indeed maintained, in agreement with Peter Damian) that 'sodomy' could be both innate and learned behaviour. The new abundance of documentary evidence also suggests a contrary development with great significance for the future (below, Chapter 15): the 'Mediterranean' pattern of unequal-age sexual activity is not nearly so apparent in fifteenth-century northern European cities, where the cases revealed (in what is also a much smaller overall number of prosecutions) were more a matter of partners of equal age, many of whom returned repeatedly to their desires.[67]

One answer to such realities was for authorities in Church and society to find an accommodation with another phenomenon emerging from the medieval West's urban, monetized culture: women offering transactional sex. That covers a multitude of sexual activities, summed up in an unavoidably judgemental word as prostitution, even though they were not all necessarily straightforwardly in return for money. Florence explicitly saw a cure for its exceptional concerns for sodomy and its low birth rate when it set up a municipal brothel in 1403, regulated by 'Officials of Honesty' (*Ufficiali dell'Onesta*) and recruiting women from beyond the city to staff it.[68] This was a long way down Latin Christianity's road in finding theological justifications for prostitution, which had begun with Augustine of Hippo observing that 'if you remove harlots from society, you will disrupt everything because of lust'. Ptolemy (birth name Bartholomew) of Lucca, a Dominican writer who extended writings by his master Thomas Aquinas on government, amplified this into the well-known aphorism often attributed to Aquinas himself, adding a contemporary concern with same-sex activities: 'remove the sewer, and you will fill the palace with a stench ... take away whores from the world, and you will fill it with sodomy.'[69]

In *De bono coniugali*, Augustine had additionally remarked that all non-reproductive sex (even heterosexual sex) was abominable, but it was especially abominable in marriage. That was an attractive underpinning for the medieval Western insistence on linking marital sex to procreation, but it also suggested that outside marriage, in the form of prostitution, non-reproductive sex might be just a little more tolerable.[70] A brothel became a necessary evil, just as Jews could be tolerated to practise usury (lending money at interest), a service to the public that Christians were officially forbidden to provide. Indeed, the non-reproductive character of a prostitute's sexual services resembled the Christian moral view of usury as non-productive.[71] Moreover, like Jews, prostitutes were best confined to particular areas of a city, in brothels, which were increasingly licensed and run by municipal authorities. Florence's initiative in prophylactic brothel-keeping was quite late on the scene, for the first known creation was by the authorities in Montpellier near the French Mediterranean coast, in 1285.

The life of the brothel overlapped with another new civic amenity primarily to be found in francophone Europe: public bathhouses, known as *estuves* from the impressive stoves that heated them. These could be quite respectable places of communal recreation and entertainment, but many shaded in function towards sex work. Indeed, as England steadily slipped away from francophone society during the fourteenth century, *estuves* simply became 'the Stews', an area of Southwark reserved for regulated prostitution and ultimately under the authority of the chief landholder there, the Bishop of Winchester. Paris did not set up a publicly run brothel, but the strong *esprit de corps* among prostitutes coalesced into nothing less than a trade guild. This led to an embarrassing dilemma for the Cathedral canons of Notre Dame when the prostitutes' guild offered to pay for a stained-glass window or a chalice for their mother church. A counter-suggestion was made that the gift should simply be made privately, and the Bishop is said in the end to have refused their offer, as it would imply too open an acceptance of their profession.[72]

Equally potentially ambiguous was the inclusion of prostitutes in public festivities in Italian cities: was their public place in a procession or carnival a sign of acceptance or a deliberate public humiliation? Those towns that created a system of municipal brothels often complemented it with routines of reproof: compulsory attendance at admonitory sermons, for example. More easy to define, and a partial justification for giving a certain official shape to institutionalized prostitution, was a network of welfare for those who renounced their activities. The Papacy tried (in normal Gregorian fashion) to organize various local initiatives into a religious Order, named by Gregory IX in 1227 from the supposed converted prostitute Mary Magdalen. 'Magdalen houses' extended beyond those formally defined convents to provide what were in effect retirement homes for poverty-stricken elderly women, and, beyond the Reformation, the utility of these places later earned them imitation in Protestant cities.[73]

It became one of the chief vocations of the various Orders of friars as they were formally constituted in the thirteenth century to address their mendicant ministry to these problematic urban societies, besides targeting those specialist institutions to be found in cities, the growing tally of universities. Towns and cities became so central to the work of friars that the foundation of a friary in the thirteenth or fourteenth century is a useful testimony to the urban vigour of a particular settlement in that period. Yet the distinctive ministry of the friars remained obstinately male; parallel female Orders of Franciscan and Dominican nuns were set up at the same time as the male Orders, but it was not for them to leave their convents to preach in the roads and marketplaces of Europe like their male counterparts. Instead, the sisters had to agree to enclosure like the older Orders of nuns, with male friars doing the begging for them, and their recruitment took on much the same slightly elevated social status as in other convents.[74]

This development was sealed from Rome in 1298 by Pope Boniface VIII enforcing strict enclosure on all consecrated women by a bull with the significant opening word *Periculoso* ('dangerous') – as usual with the declarations of papal bureaucrats, the effect was not as all-embracing as they would wish, but it set a general framework.[75] Enclosed nuns had a worthy ministry of prayer, spiritual advice and contemplation, fostering such original mystical voices as Adelheid of Frauenberg and Catherine of Siena (a close associate beyond the cloister), but they could not fully absorb the energies of women out in the urban world. That gap was substantially filled by a remarkable spontaneous movement of celibate women committed to living out in the world and flourishing in urban settings from the northern Low Countries (Netherlands) to Italy: the Beguines.

The Beguine movement emerged as a phenomenon in what are now the Belgian provinces of Brabant and Liège around 1200, around the same time that the movements of friars were coalescing in Mediterranean Europe. Brabant was an already relatively urbanized area of northern Europe, wealthy especially from clothmaking, and on the cultural frontiers of the languages that were becoming French, Dutch and German. Levels of literacy in the region were only equalled at the time by the cities of northern Italy, but distinctive here was that women had unusual levels of access to formal education and a freedom of action that startled southern Europeans and did not please all local males.[76] Despite later hagiography designed to give the Beguine movement a conventional place in monastic history, there is no evidence that it had a male founder, or even a single origin; behind it lay the amorphous energies of twelfth-century popular religious discontents that had experienced varied fortunes at the hands of the Church authorities.

The odd name 'Beguine' still defies certain explanation, but it seems to be a term of ridicule verging on hostility, like the later description of English heretics as 'Lollard', meaning mumbler of possibly dubious prayers. That says something about the obscurity of the movement's origins, and possibly about male suspicion and surprise that it should exist at all. Its recent historian has commented that it is 'the only movement in medieval monastic history that was created by women and for women – and not affiliated with, or supervised by, a male order'. He points out some of the Beguines' unusual characteristics: 'a lack of overarching governmental structures, a low level of internal hierarchy, a tendency toward the sacralization of routine work, the use of dance and ecstasy in worship, and an emphasis on the continuity between female existence before and after entrance into the community'.[77]

Despite all this informality, the Beguines won papal approval during the thirteenth century, in step with the various Orders of friars, while keeping their distinctiveness. It was a remarkable exemption from the effects of *Periculoso*, which must have been the result of benevolent and deliberately untidy thinking by some senior clergy, aware of the sheer usefulness of the Beguines in their urban settings. Not least among their oddities was the size of some of the communities ('Beguinages'): several hundred strong in some places, and thus little female towns within a town, often surrounded by their own moat and walls, but readily welcoming visitors. One can still enjoyably tour some of the surviving examples and notice how different their informal clusters of cosy domestic buildings are from the classic monastery layout.

Beguinages were home to the range of craft skills deployed by women, especially textile production on an almost industrial scale: very different from the delicate embroidery that became the speciality of many nunneries in the wake of their isolation from higher education. The Beguines nevertheless also provided education for both girls and boys in surroundings permeated with worship and spiritual exploration. Among the ranks of the Beguines in their expansion across central Europe was the excitable Viennese mystic Agnes Blannbekin, joyfully contemplating her celestial nudity. Their communal life went on to inspire further female initiatives in celibate life during the Renaissance and Counter-Reformation (below, Chapter 14). Without having to think much about it, the institutional Church had discovered one civilizing force amid the streets of its great cities – although not everywhere in Europe since, rather puzzlingly, the Atlantic Isles showed little interest in the Beguine movement, despite England's close involvement with the Low Countries' textile trade, and southern Europeans may have found the Beguines' female assertiveness too much to handle.

More universal was the adoption of a new mode of conceiving the Christian family in Western Christianity, so that the copulating laity could take a decorous place alongside a well-regulated celibate clergy. Moreover, from the thirteenth century, more or less for the first time in the history of the Church, the clergy frequently told the laity what they should be thinking about marriage: that was part of the new work of preaching undertaken especially by the Franciscans and Dominicans.[78] The construction of the message was based on some theological innovations. One was a gradual shift of opinion among Western theologians, and then among clergy extracting advice from their writings to conduct confessions: Adam and Eve had found sex a pleasure. What was good enough for the first married couple surely provided guidelines for their successors.[79]

Just as important, even though not such an exact fit for the circumstances of present-day lay households as Adam and Eve, was a new presentation of the Holy Family as a model for all Christian families. It was created in text and in art. Writers, preachers and many of the artists were celibate clergy, who had (in theory at least) left their last intimate contact with a real woman in childhood, before they left home for their institutional home in the Church. Such talented men, set aside for sacred ministry, felt safer with women who did not flaunt their sexuality but who rejoiced in their motherhood, or in a commitment to a celibacy which paralleled that of the male priesthood. That was the model of life in Nazareth around the Holy Mother Mary that was now pieced together for Catholic Europe. It was dependent on a devotional exploration of the human life of Christ, as part of the general humanist and personal turn of Western devotion (see Plate 21).

Anselm, Archbishop of Canterbury in the eleventh century, was one of the first to create this form of meditation, but a century later it became a theme of Cistercian piety with their Order's particular dedication to Our Lady, universal patron of their monastic houses. That was paired with a new genre of writing about the person of Jesus. Aelred of Rievaulx was a pioneer in this, for instance writing a meditation on the passage in Luke's Gospel (2.42) describing Jesus straying in the Temple 'when he was twelve years old'. This was a literary present for Yvo, a Cistercian of Warden Abbey, remembered after his death in Aelred's treatise on friendship as the 'beloved' monk whose 'charming eyes' had smiled on the writer. Burrowing into the various layers of meaning of Luke's text in traditional fashion from 'literal' to 'moral', Aelred began by using his imagination to ponder on the boy lost in Jerusalem without a mother to feed him, make up his bed and tend his 'boyish limbs with oil and baths'. One has to say that Jesus sounds a rather molly-coddled twelve-year-old.[80]

The theme blossomed into the Christ-centred devotion preached by the Orders of friars. From the time of Francis onwards, that was a Franciscan speciality. In the early fourteenth century, the Italian Franciscan John de Caulibus penned a famous and much-imitated *Meditations on the Life of Christ* (the author is still often referred to as 'Pseudo-Bonaventure' as the work was long credited to the earlier Franciscan Bonaventure). It was written to help an enclosed sister of the Franciscans' associated Order of Poor Clares in her contemplation of Christ's earthly life, presenting her with a series of eyewitness accounts interlaced with commentary that imaginatively extended the Gospel narratives, inspiring the reader to imitate Christ in her or his own daily life. Like writers of early apocryphal Gospels, John exploited the fact that the Gospel narratives had not aspired to exhaustive accounts of Jesus and filled the gaps with further picturesque detail: the evocative words were commonly enriched with further illustrations in the manuscripts.

De Caulibus's embroidered version of Jesus's life clustered incidents around his birth and death. The Nativity had inspired another novelty created by Francis himself, the popularity of which has never dimmed in Western Christianity: the construction of a Christmas crib with a manger and live (though apocryphal) ox and ass. Later cribs, encouraged by reports of baby Jesus's miraculous appearance to grace Francis's manger, expanded to include the mother and *paterfamilias* in the now familiar fashion. At the other extreme of Jesus's life, there was much to say about his sufferings for humanity on the cross, which Francis himself had approached by spontaneously exhibiting in his own body the bleeding wounds suffered by the crucified Saviour, his *stigmata*. Some over-enthusiastic admirers called Francis *alter Christus*, a second Christ.

The new focus on the life and death of Jesus, and the consequent sufferings of his mother, had an unhappy side-effect, since it concentrated attention on those held responsible for his death: the Jews. The Gregorian 'persecuting society' had already launched a new active hatred of Jews in Western society, but the Franciscans only added to it, and they were not alone among preachers. It is particularly depressing that when some outrage against Jewish communities occurred, often involving massacre and vandalism, a destroyed synagogue might be replaced by a devotional chapel to Mary, whom the Jews were presumed to have blasphemed: Prague and Regensburg are two of the cities to have hosted these egregious buildings. That is the dark shadow of the enhanced devotion to the person of Christ that now structured the Western Church's view of the family.[81]

We noted in Chapter 12 how the binary pairing in the images flanking the crucified Christ on the beam at the chancel entrance were his mother and his beloved disciple. The creation of the Holy Family was another incentive for this Rood group to proliferate in churches across Europe. Alongside it, there flourished a new iconography of mother and child. In the first age of the friars, Mary commonly moved far from the serene Mother of God in Eastern icons or in the majestic figure of Romanesque sculpture, a Queen of Heaven to outdo any imperial or royal portrayal. Now she was commonly the bereaved mother, 'Our Lady of Pity' or *Pietà*, cradling her dead son in her arms after his body had been taken down from the cross.[82] In Mary's grief, she was also prone to fainting away: an interestingly popular if unbiblical novelty in lay devotion and in ecclesiastical art, transforming ancient clichés about uncontrollable female emotion into a positive quality of piety. It was too popular for some male theologians, notably Thomas de Vio ('Cajetan' or 'Gaetano'), Dominican champion of a revived interest in the writings of Thomas Aquinas, who in 1506 successfully discouraged Pope Julius II from instituting a new feast of the Sufferings of Our Lady. He bleakly remarked that the idea of her swooning was the glorification of a 'morbid state', implying some bodily defect in Mary, when it was plain that at the Passion, the Queen of Heaven could suffer only mental anguish.[83]

The mother of Jesus needed a more assertive earthly spouse than Joseph had been through most of Christian history. He needed rescuing from the frailty or comedy of old age, from being identified with the caricature of Jewishness, or even from being portrayed as angrily considering himself a cuckolded husband; all these themes can be found in plays in popular drama.[84] A major figure in rehabilitating him was the fifteenth-century French theologian Jean Gerson, long-term Rector of the University of Paris, who was particularly concerned to promote or construct a devotion for the Holy Family and composed *Reflections on St Joseph* (1413/14); moreover, when a major Council of the Western Church convened in Konstanz invited Gerson to preach in 1416, he devoted his sermon to commending Joseph, hoping to establish a feast day for him.

That proposal was for the time being defeated, only coming to fruition in 1487, by which time Joseph had emerged, with the aid of

Gerson's reassessment, as a good deal more noble and caring as husband and father than he had ever been before, and rather less geriatric. Gerson did hasten to say that Joseph was 'immune to womanly touch' and, along with the undeniably Jewish character of family life in Nazareth, Joseph's chastity would always remain a problem in constructing a Holy Family analogous with the everyday families that the Church was doing its best to regulate. Yet Joseph undoubtedly became a success with the devout public; by the early sixteenth century, artists could even portray him in cheerfully indulgent play with his infant divine stepson, and parents began naming their sons after him. His stock rose still higher through the Counter-Reformation, especially in the Spanish Empire, where he became patron saint of Mexico in 1555 and in 1679 the official protector of the realm of Spain (see Plate 23): an inconceivable role for him before the late medieval period.[85]

Even a nuclear family needs a wider reference than the parental trio, so added to the mix was a grandmother for Jesus, Mary's mother, conveniently provided with a name by the *Protevangelium of James*: St Anne. Perhaps as the cult of Mary became ever more elevated, some of those wishing to approach her or her Son might have felt that that was best done via a doting granny. Anne's sudden arrival on the devotional scene in the fifteenth century is remarkable: a study of a single late medieval English county, Devon, reveals at least a dozen dedications of new chapels in that and the next century (she had arrived too late to insinuate herself in the dedications of the parish church network).[86] Equally interesting is Anne's characteristic iconography, for she is generally shown as teaching her daughter to read, or at least as armed with a book, a motif unknown to the apocryphal Gospels and apparently first attested in the ninth century in a Byzantine source unlikely to have been on the radar of English theologians or artists (see Plate 22). Evidently the pious fifteenth-century Western public regarded it as perfectly natural for a girl to be instructed in basic literacy, enough at least for her to be able to say her prayers.[87]

Problem aunts are also a feature of family cliché, and that role was filled for Mary and the Holy Family by a reconstructed Mary Magdalen. The reconstruction had begun quite early for the Latin West by Pope Gregory I, who, in 591, preached an unusually influential sermon that audaciously gathered into a single person three of the spare Marys in the New Testament, all as Mary Magdalen. As a result, she became a sinner from whom seven devils had been cast out, but also penitential in washing Jesus's feet with her tears and listening to him rapt in her home in Bethany while her sister Martha bustled around with practical tasks, plus in the end becoming 'Apostle to the Apostles' as the first witness to the Resurrection. It was a rich mixture that in the next few centuries also annexed to itself the story of that hugely popular Eastern ex-prostitute Mary of Egypt. It also produced two successive and never wholly reconciled sets of relics of Mary Magdalen in eastern France, first at Vézelay, where they became a major prop of the Cluniac pilgrimage industry, and later at Saint-Maximin near Aix-en-Provence, watched over by the Dominicans.[88]

The Magdalen was thus readily available to take her place in the construction of the Holy Family, aided by the fascinated speculations of celibate authors who added to her backstory. Jacobus de Voragine's *Golden Legend* dismissed the idea that she had embraced her life of excess after being left abandoned on her wedding day, but evidently some readers felt that he was being a spoilsport. England's early printer William Caxton expanded the story without qualification in his English translation of Voragine's work, adding for good measure that some laid the finger of blame on no less a figure than John the Evangelist, who had jilted her to go off and become Jesus's Beloved Disciple. At least she had been a well-born *demi-mondaine*, and thus a worthy patron of all those Magdalen homes for the prostitutes of Europe's cities. In any case, it was comforting to know that within Jesus's inner circle there was a spectacular but beloved sinner who had suitably repented, a model for all those feeling wretched about their own sins and a little wary of Our Lady's sinlessness. Accordingly, the Magdalen's iconography varied between showing her in her alluring finery to extreme gaunt misery worthy of the desert years of Mary of Egypt (see Plates 13–15). In mid-fifteenth-century Italy, the sculptor Donatello famously chose the latter option.[89]

And, of course, a family needs a home. It is a phenomenon of the late Middle Ages that the Holy House of Nazareth, scene of Jesus's childhood with Mary and Joseph, decided miraculously to reproduce itself in locations more convenient to Catholic Europe than Galilee: in England at Walsingham and in Italy at Loreto. Walsingham's story dates to the eleventh century – a rebuilding of the Holy House in Norfolk inspired by a dream or vision – but it is clear from an accumulation of royal visits there that the devotion is actually two centuries later in date, from much the same time that Francis of Assisi was inventing the Nativity Crib. Loreto is a more miraculous transaction involving angels: its story of angelic transportation from Galilee dates it to the 1290s. That suggests a relationship to the European humiliation of the loss of the last Crusader footholds in the Holy Land, but references to Loreto multiply in the fifteenth century, when both Holy Houses had their first major glory-days.[90]

By the late Middle Ages, therefore, the Holy Family was in place, gathering together many strands of the Gregorian revolution to provide a more or less symmetrical model for lay sexual activity paired with clerical celibacy: a Catholic family for Western Christendom, though one where Jesus's brothers and sisters seem discreetly to have absented themselves. Canon lawyers, having in the eleventh and twelfth centuries obstinately revived the assent theory of St Paul's 'marital debt' in the face of unenthusiastic marriage-broking parents, helped the ideal relationship between husband and wife monopolize and legitimize all the strands of sexual love that had emerged alarmingly undisciplined into the consciousness of twelfth-century Europe. Marital sexual love, in contrast to all those untrammelled emotions, was not always sinful, though often previous writers during the Gregorian revolution had asserted that it was. This striking development was well summarized in a sermon by the star Franciscan preacher of the thirteenth century, Guibert de Tournai, quoting both Genesis and Christ himself: '"Man will leave [his father and mother]" by the privilege of love, for that love by which husband and wife love one another is more vehement than all carnal loves.'[91]

This was a flat contradiction of that ancient Pythagorean cliché beloved of Jerome and still being peddled by some writers (including friars) in the thirteenth century, that the husband who loves his wife too ardently is an adulterer. Friars in their pastoral contacts with the laity would see Guibert's view as a better fit for the realities of medieval Western society, where it was no less possible for parents to love each other and their children than it is in our own age. Some twentieth-century historians, notably in France Philippe Ariès and in the Anglosphere Lawrence Stone, developed the argument that there was little mutual affection in medieval or Reformation-era families, and so for instance parents invested little grief in early deaths of their children. Much of such claims was based on the particularly abundant evidence from elite families in England, where the peculiarities of English inheritance law distorted norms and were likely to exaggerate the constant temptation among landed elites to turn marriage into a commercial transaction.

More representative investigation has led to a blunt comment from one contemporary authority on medieval children: 'it cannot be overemphasised that there is nothing to be said for Ariès's view of childhood in the middle ages.'[92]

The late medieval Catholic family was a monogamous formation that ancient Romans or Greeks would have recognized, but they would also have noted the general absence of concubines and (for the time being at least) slaves, institutions which had both continued into the early Christian centuries as features of family structures in East and West. Pious fourth-century Melania and Macrina would also have found it familiar, but rather than their quietly luxurious villas providing a backdrop it was now to be the character of every Christian household in town or country. Moreover, with a novelty that would have surprised them, it began liturgically in church, followed by regular one-to-one clerical check-ups on its progress via sacramental confession.

The Western Church was exuberantly varied in the paths to God it offered: the life of the priest, the monk, the friar, the nun, and the devout layman and laywoman and their children. The proof of Western Christendom's vitality was its constant reinvention, way beyond the authority of the Papacy, which was in fact embarrassingly divided between claimants during the fourteenth century: the Western Church only achieved reunion under a single universally recognized Pope in 1417, after a great deal of negotiation at the Council of Konstanz much facilitated by Jean Gerson. Meanwhile, northern Europe had created its own new expression of Catholic piety, springing from the same region that had presented the Church with the gifts of celibate life offered by the Beguines. In the late fourteenth century there emerged in the Low Countries an intense, introspective and creatively imaginative mode of reaching out to God, known as the 'modern devotion' (*Devotio Moderna*).

The significant feature of the *Devotio* was that, just as with the now ancient activity of pilgrimage, laity as well as clergy, women as well as men, could aspire to the heights and depths of experience within it. Its earliest great name, the fourteenth-century Dutch theologian Gerard (Geert) Groote, was never ordained beyond the order of deacon; after spending some time in a Carthusian monastery near Arnhem, Groote conducted a roving ministry of preaching in the Netherlands and founded an informal community of friends in his native Deventer. After Groote's death this group did take on the character of a formal religious order, the Brethren of the Common Life; it spread through central

Europe and enrolled members of the calibre of the mystical writer Thomas à Kempis, the philosopher and theologian Gabriel Biel and the future Pope Adrian VI.

Nevertheless, the *Devotio Moderna* was never a purely clerical movement. Even the formally organized Brethren discouraged members from becoming ordained clergy (by then considered the norm in monastic Orders). They put their houses of Sisters and some of their male communities under the control of local urban corporations rather than the Church authorities.[93] Notably, married couples and their children might be involved on an equal basis in this devotional lifestyle. The *Devotio* ethos was diffused widely among the serious-minded. Its promise was that laity could aspire to the high personal standards, including literacy, previously thought more easily attainable by the clergy: its programme of practical action and organization of one's thoughts and life was summed up in the title of Kempis's famous devotional treatise, *The Imitation of Christ*.

Such imitation sounds a more than daunting agenda, but all sorts of expressions of pious activism might contribute to this earnest quest to come closer to Christ: it was not a quest only for the clever or the articulate, but, above all, it was a faith where the clergy did not have any particular advantage. The *Devotio Moderna* re-established the idea in northern Europe that married couples could experience as close and loving a relationship with God as any monk. That was implicit in the sexual binary created by the Gregorian revolution between celibate clergy and married laity, but out of it arose a new revolution, which consciously and angrily reversed so much that had been achieved by Gregory VII and his successors five centuries before.

14
The Second Revolution: The Reformation Chasm (1500–1700)

Statistically, throughout the world the great majority of modern Christians are spiritual descendants of Western Latin Christianity, which has a double effect on them. Western Christianity today, whether Catholic or Protestant, still lives in the slipstream of the eleventh-century Gregorian revolution; yet the sixteenth-century Protestant Reformation determinedly reversed many aspects of that revolution, in no respect more fundamentally than in marriage and the family. It is ironic that Martin Luther, the friar who sparked that spectacularly successful assault on the Gregorian binary system, was actually a member of the only male monastic Order ever to have been founded by a Pope, the Augustinian Eremites or Austin Friars. The Order was very conscious of that unique distinction and was still making use of it to gain papal favours in the decade leading up to Luther's confrontation with the Church hierarchy in 1517. The element of parricide has been underestimated in Luther's Reformation thinking, as he turned the private fury of a university lecturer in the small and undistinguished north German town of Wittenberg into an explosive public defiance of papal authority.[1]

Luther the Austin friar was an extreme case of the paradox of early Protestantism: nearly all its leaders were clergy of the old Church. Among them was a high proportion of friars, unsurprisingly since friars were the preachers and ideologues of the late medieval Western Latin Church.[2] They were highly principled, highly educated men, who were now furious to discover not only that they themselves had been cheated by the common and erroneous account of salvation provided by the Western Church, but also that, through their own teaching and preaching, they had shamingly been part of the deception. Anger and a sense of betrayal energized the Reformation and repeatedly made it a violent event, provoking in return violence from angry and frightened Catholic authorities. Naturally secular politics became quickly entangled in the ever-widening disputes – so the word 'Protestants' originally described the small group of princes of the Holy Roman Empire who 'protested' a majority decision to outlaw all Luther's adherents, taken at the imperial Diet meeting at Speyer in 1529. It was not a word that Protestants initially embraced – they would have seen themselves as the true Catholics, sweeping aside medieval corruption – but the coinage has endured.

The trigger issue for Luther in 1517 was a quite minor part of the late medieval Catholic scheme of salvation: the developed sales industry of money-raising indulgences. An indulgence (free, admittedly, to the very poor) detailed how much its purchase reduced an individual's time spent in purgatory before the penitential requirements for earthly sin were fulfilled and the purged soul could enter heaven. That suggested a power in the institutional Church to alter God's purposes in salvation which offended Luther's immersion in the predestinarian writings of that other patron of his Order, Augustine of Hippo (above, Chapter 9). It also contradicted his reading of the Bible, which he saw as the only touchstone for true belief – *sola scriptura*, by Scripture alone. The theology of indulgences was presented in peculiarly crass form in 1517 by a Dominican indulgence salesman, Johann Tetzel, backed by Pope Leo X and by Luther's own Bishop, Albrecht of Brandenburg, for their own revenue-raising purposes.

The issue then became one of authority: were the Church authorities justified in ordering Luther to keep quiet on the matter? He thought not, and, with a hitherto undiscovered talent for arousing popular passions through publishing his case in print, he turned this into a rebellion that convulsed all northern Europe, spreading far from Wittenberg and increasingly polarizing the political leaders of the Holy Roman Empire and beyond.[3] Ever more extreme in his defiance of the Pope, theatrically burning the papal bull excommunicating him in 1520, Luther soon proclaimed all the power of the existing clerical order to be a fraud. That included the priesthood's claim to be an especially holy category of human being, marked out by abstention from marital sex. This was to trigger a new historical departure: the reversal of the Western Church's unique insistence on universal clerical celibacy, and a reassertion of the primacy of the Christian family.

THE FAMILY: TRIUMPH AND TRANSFORMATION

Protestantism's account of its origins has prioritized Martin Luther's restating of an Augustinian theology of salvation, 'justification by faith alone', but more permanently momentous was his repudiation of compulsory clerical celibacy. He untangled clerical ministry from the ascetic vocation to abstain from sex, and that led to the subsequent elimination of the monastic life from Protestant Churches, with a few exceptions in Lutheran Germany that were the result of string-pulling by powerful local families.[4] Otherwise, the long reign of celibacy as the default option for Christian perfection was over. Protestant unity fractured straight away in its first decade, as many leaders of the Reformation considered Luther not radical or clear-headed enough in the work of reform; hence a permanent split developed between 'Lutherans' and the rest, who eventually found a constructive label for themselves as 'Reformed' Protestants.[5] Yet amid these often bitter theological disputes, and amid the constant splintering of Protestant identities that has continued right up to the present day, no branch of the Protestant religious revolution has ever questioned the rejection of universal celibacy for clergy. For the first time in centuries, the overwhelming majority of clergy became married men. And, therefore, virtually for the first time, theological discussion of marriage and the family was conducted by those with practical experience of marriage: even by some women.

An important preparatory contribution to this radical turn away from more than a millennium of monastic triumph in Christianity was from one who never himself became a Protestant: the doyen of Renaissance humanist writers and scholars, Desiderius Erasmus. His name was a belated Graeco-Latin self-coinage: as we will discover, this was a common affectation among humanists in university or school appointments, but in Erasmus's case it reinvented a young man who should not have existed at all under the Gregorian vision of the Church, for the boy Herasmus was the illegitimate son of a priest.[6] After what seems to have been an unhappy and insecure childhood in the fifteenth-century northern Netherlands, Erasmus (additionally styling himself *Roterodamus*, 'of Rotterdam', which may or may not obscure his actual birthplace) took the obvious route out of such marginality by seeking clerical orders; in the end he needed a couple of papal dispensations for illegitimacy to make his priestly ordination possible. Not merely ordination as a secular priest: around 1487 Erasmus entered a monastery of Augustinian canons at Steyn, a house marked by austere observance in an ecclesiastical landscape soaked in the piety of the *Devotio Moderna*. The experience of monastic life was formative for him: he hated it.

Erasmus's misery was compounded by falling in love with one of the other young men at Steyn, Servatius Roger.[7] The relationship is attested by his passionate and anguished letters to Roger in the late 1480s. They are among the earliest letters preserved in a massive and carefully curated lifetime of correspondence, too well-written to discard from the literary output of this arbiter of humanist Latin style, though only one of them was published during Erasmus's lifetime. Afterwards, they might feasibly be explained away as exercises in the expression of friendship in the monastic tradition going back to Aelred in the twelfth-century Renaissance. That has been a constant explanatory route for admirers of Erasmus embarrassed by the plain evidence of his same-sex affections, and equally uncomfortable with the continuing undercurrent of such emotions throughout his later correspondence, often obliquely inserted to entertain acquaintances who were in on what he was saying.[8]

The relationship with Roger subsided into elegant epistolary friendship, and Erasmus would never again venture into such uninhibited self-disclosure – certainly not to declare himself an adherent of the Reformation. He concentrated on enjoying his extraordinary literary curiosity and cultivating charming young men who additionally possessed brains and preferably also money, in the course of devising a means of surviving in lifelong financial comfort for himself. The conventional way of doing that was to find some pleasant and well-paid niches in ecclesiastical office, but Erasmus did not do that; he virtually invented the vocation of independent freelance writer, supported by financial agreements with publishers and subventions from admiring rich patrons (two of whom, Archbishop Thomas Cranmer and Johannes à Lasco, became prominent early adopters of the Reformation).[9] Erasmus's extraordinary literary accomplishments had provided the escape route from Steyn, when in 1492 he became secretary to the Bishop of Cambrai, and he never looked back, in any sense: particularly not to monastic life, nor, after a little time, to the Bishop either.

This interestingly complicated man may not seem the most obvious potential champion of marriage and the family, but what Erasmus wrote praising marriage should really be construed as an attack on monasticism. In the background was his radical undercutting of monastic life, when he remarked to a friend (an abbot of reforming and humanist sympathies, who later became a Lutheran) that a secular commonwealth ruled by a godly prince was 'a great monastery': everybody, laity just as much as clergy, should aspire to the same self-restraint as was demanded in the ideal of monasticism.[10] Music to the ears of princes was the additional implication that they themselves should play the role of abbot in their great monastery, plus the corollary that revenues of existing monasteries might be better diverted into their own hands.

In 1518, Erasmus published the first version of what proved a very popular and influential essay in praise of marriage (*Encomium matrimonii*).[11] In its introduction he claimed to have written it twenty years earlier as a rhetorical exercise for the young Englishman Lord Mountjoy, first in his series of glamorous aristocratic patrons; that would take its composition back to the years immediately after Erasmus escaped his misery at Steyn. Much of his enthusiasm for marriage (not something of which he ever had direct experience) will have been motivated by those memories. He tackled Gregorian clerical assumptions head-on, bluntly stating that the single state is 'a barren way of life hardly becoming to a man ... let us leave celibacy for bishops ... the holiest kind of life is wedlock, purely and chastely observed.' That 'chastity' did not equate with celibacy.[12]

In 1518, only a year after Martin Luther's first confrontation with the Church hierarchy, it might still have been possible to present such statements as theologically uncontroversial (and at least the Eastern Orthodox would have agreed that celibacy was best left for bishops). Yet in the manic pace of events over the next two or three years, Erasmus's assertions about marriage proved as much of a hand-grenade lobbed into Europe's controversies as his growing number of biblical commentaries. Josse Clichthove, a leading theologian in that bastion of traditional theological orthodoxy the University of Paris, went into print in 1522 to reproach him for undermining chastity by his praise of marriage. Erasmus's reply to Clichthove was pugnacious, and he felt strongly enough to repeat what he had said about marriage and celibacy in a second work of 1526, the *Institutio Christiani matrimonii*.[13]

This was the background conversation behind a swelling tide of clergy marriages, drawing reassuringly not merely on Erasmus's weaponized arguments, but on the late medieval construction of loving and companionate marriage that tried to model itself on the Holy Family. There were also clerical voices to hear from a more distant past: it was while Luther was rapidly rethinking his former loyalty to Pope and Emperor in the crowded year of 1520 that he rediscovered and realized the importance of the animated little pamphlet of the late eleventh century, *Epistola de continentia clericorum* (above, Chapter 12). Almost from the moment that Luther's Wittenberg protest became public in 1517, a handful of northern European priests began taking a momentous step into marriage. The first big name to cross this line in what was becoming the Reformation was a priest far to the south of Wittenberg, Huldrych Zwingli, leading a parallel reformation in the Swiss city of Zürich that was the first component of 'Reformed', non-Lutheran, Protestantism.

Zwingli's marriage in 1522 came as relief for his conscience, for he freely admitted that he had never succeeded in remaining celibate in his previous clerical appointments. His wife, Anna Reinhart, remained more in the background of Zwingli's public ministry than Katharina von Bora, the spirited ex-nun who married Martin Luther three years later, but Anna still deserves honour for her pioneering role in overturning the special status and privilege of clergy upheld by the medieval Western rule on clerical celibacy.[14] It is also interesting that two of Zwingli's reforming colleagues in Zürich, both important players in his variety of Reformation and also early entrants into marriage, were like Erasmus the illegitimate sons of priests: Leo Jud and Heinrich Bullinger. In the course of their wider work as Reformation leaders, they were righting personal injustices.[15]

Clergy who had been more continent than Zwingli compounded their excitement at combating theological untruth in discovering the physical pleasure of marriage: in the case of the forty-two-year-old Martin Luther, with the glee of delayed adolescence, despite the fact that his marriage to the twenty-six-year-old Katharina had at first been a practical expedient to shelter her after her previous marriage arrangement had fallen through. In the very first year of his marriage, Luther wrote a letter to his old friend Georg 'Spalatinus' (Burkhardt), secretary to the Elector of Saxony, apologizing for not coming to his wedding to another Katharina, but assuring him that he and von Bora would have a private marital celebration: 'On the night that I calculate you will receive this letter, I assure you that I'll make love to my wife, in your honour, while you're making love to yours – a joint effort!'[16]

In rather less toe-curling vein, in later years Luther's former convent in Wittenberg blossomed into a large family home, six children in all, enjoying a stream of guests plus student lodgers taken in to balance the domestic budget. At dinner, the guests and lodgers eagerly absorbed and jotted down unbuttoned bons mots from the great man, trivial and profound alike, and within a few years of his death anthologies were being published as Luther's 'Table Talk' (*Tischreden*). Historians have gratefully quarried that engaging heap of vivid details, though they have not always assessed them judiciously, taking too seriously the stereotyped misogyny of such laddish remarks as 'Men have broad chests and narrow hips; hence they possess wisdom. Women have narrow chests and broad hips. A woman ought to look after the house: creation itself declares (with the broad bum and hips) they should sit still.' Luther's beloved Katie was presiding over the well-furnished table, and her responses to this admittedly annoying teasing have not been recorded.[17]

Beyond this frivolity was Luther's gradual recasting of Augustine of Hippo's theology of sin, sex and marriage; the framework was still that of the fifth century, and his understanding of female biology was still unthinkingly that of Aristotle, but his own happy experience of the married state brought him a warmer picture of the family in Eden and through the Fall and expulsion from Paradise. Edenic marriage involved the conception of children in sexual pleasure that was chaste and without shame, just as was the hospitality of the Luther household. Child-rearing would then have been easy and joyful. Of course, none of this had time to happen in Eden, and the Fall had reduced it all to a shadow of its potential self, but there was no radical break in sexuality, or a hint that sex had taken on the Satanic character ascribed to it by Basil the Great. In the second generation of the Reformation, John Calvin is often seen as a more thoroughgoing Augustinian as well as a more joyless character than Luther, but he was more explicitly positive about sexual intercourse: it remained a gift of God despite the Fall, and husband and wife should enjoy it, observing of course due modesty and propriety.[18]

Who were the women whom these clergy married in the course of their personal liberation? Hardly surprisingly, to begin with, the majority were the partners with whom they were already living, contemptuously termed 'concubines' by the old Church. In the small Hessian town of Hersfeld, the town council took it on itself in 1523 to order that anyone living with a 'concubine' should marry her, which consciously encroached on the legal authority of their overlord, the Abbot of Hersfeld, and was really aimed at clergy who had not taken the course of marriage. Properly constituted clerical marriages were the symbol of Reformation in Hersfeld; angry crowds harassed the houses of offenders whom the Abbot was not disciplining, thus simultaneously defying Church authority and declaring official clerical celibacy to be a sham. What proved to be an indecisive stand-off in Hersfeld between Abbot and townsfolk did not stop other town councils in the Holy Roman Empire successfully passing similar ordinances.[19]

The image of clergy wife as concubine was not easy to shake off in the Reformation's first generation as clerical marriage spread through Germany. It was linked to the fact that a significant number of new partners not already in a relationship with their clerical husband seem to have been women otherwise marginalized: a high proportion of nuns and widows, who might be making a principled decision to signify their allegiance to the Reformation, but who might also have been seeking stability amid new social uncertainties. A tenth of clerical marriages in the 1520s were to former nuns, Luther's bride von Bora being the most famous. This sent mixed messages out to the public, for concubines were liable to come from a very different social stratum than the generally more socially elevated nuns (who often socially outranked their newly acquired clerical partners as well).[20]

An extreme version of how to resolve these puzzles was the phenomenal Wibrandis Rosenblatt, a one-woman Reformation on tour: daughter of an imperial official in Basel, she was first widow to the Basel humanist artist Ludwig Keller (Cellarius) before wedding in succession three prominent clerical Reformers: the former monk Johannes Oecolampadius (Hussgen), the first Protestant pastor of Basel; another former monk Wolfgang Capito (Köpfel), pastor in Strassburg; and finally one of the Reformation's most eloquent propagandists for happy companionate marriage, the former friar Martin Bucer, chief pastor of Strassburg and finally Regius Professor in Cambridge. Wibrandis had been recommended to Bucer by his dying first wife Elisabeth. Oecolampadius gave her a rave review: 'what I always wanted . . . She is not contentious, garrulous, or a gadabout, but looks after the household.' Bucer wanted a little more pepper – 'My first wife felt somewhat more free to admonish me and now I realize that that freedom of hers was not only useful but necessary.' Many clergy were to discover that a frank but affectionate wifely perspective was helpful preparation for the inevitable critics outside the parsonage door.[21]

Only gradually, as in the 1530s and 1540s Protestantism began winning the allegiance of more and more territories in and beyond the Empire, did the clergy wife begin to reflect what the new emerging Church authorities wanted in the marriages of pastors, in the manner of Fräulein Rosenblatt: a solidly respectable background in families among the middle layers of urban society. It took time for social attitudes to reflect changing realities beyond the ranks of men and women who championed clerical marriage as an ideological statement (Plate 24). In the Holy Roman Empire, it was not till 1555 that military defeat of the Habsburg Emperor and his Catholic allies and the resulting Peace of Augsburg forced the Habsburgs grudgingly to grant secure legal status to Lutheran clergy marriages and their children within the Empire.[22]

In England, where a truly Protestant Reformation rapidly gained in momentum after 1547 through a regime acting in the name of the young Edward VI, the one part of their legislative programme that met prolonged obstruction from conservative nobility and bishops in Parliament was the full legalization of clerical marriage; that legislation did not finally pass till 1549. Then when a version of the Edwardian Protestant Church was restored in 1559 after the death of Catholic Queen Mary, her half-sister Queen Elizabeth showed herself untypical of Protestants in her lack of enthusiasm for clerical wives (but then Elizabeth had problems with most people's wives). This personal idiosyncrasy could not withstand the Protestant tide even for the Supreme Governor of the Church of England, but it had one curious long-term effect that outlasted Elizabeth's own capacity to choose her bishops; after the death of her happily married first Archbishop of Canterbury Matthew Parker in 1575, no occupant of the see of Canterbury had a wife until John Tillotson in 1691.[23]

It is not surprising that an initially uncertain place in Western society encouraged clergy and their children to stick together socially, resulting in a great deal of intermarriage among clergy families. The pioneer – a veritable English male counterpart to Wibrandis Rosenblatt – was Thomas Cranmer's episcopal colleague William Barlow, who, like the Archbishop and his brother Edmund Cranmer, was a priest who married in the 1530s when it was still illegal to do so in England. Bishop Barlow fathered five daughters, all of whom wedded clergy in the Elizabethan and Jacobean Church who then became bishops (in one case eventually Archbishop of York). He was thus a father-in-God in more than one sense; he had many imitators. In the parish of Buxhall in rural Suffolk, four or five miles from my own childhood Rectory home, over an extraordinary chronological span of 1569 to 1948, the clerical and gentry family of Copinger (and then Hill, latterly Copinger-Hill) managed to find an almost uninterrupted succession of male family members capable of ordination and therefore of residence in their increasingly stately Rectory beside the church.[24] This was a triumphant re-creation of those clergy dynasties that the Gregorian reforms had sought to eliminate. Its ultimate expression was in the Principality of Transylvania, where in 1629 the militantly Reformed Protestant Prince Gábor Bethlen took to a new level the already high prestige of the ministry throughout Reformed Europe by ennobling the entire clerical order in his principality. Later political changes in the region did not diminish the social prominence of Reformed Transylvanian pastors.[25]

Now that Protestants had closed monasteries, together with chantries and most devotional guilds, Christian life concentrated on the parish; far fewer clergy than before ministered within the parish and they became very different in character. All of them would be expected to preach, essential to conveying a new formulation of the Christian message in the early Reformation but persisting as the main public duty of the Protestant pastor: a constant renewal of God's Word in spoken words. With the Orders of friars dispersed, preaching required far more professional education than before for local ministry. The change can be expressed in statistics. In 1500 the pre-Reformation diocese of Utrecht, comprising most of the northern Netherlands, boasted around 18,000 clergy; by the early seventeenth century that had been remodelled in the same area into an educated and Reformed Protestant parochial ministry only 1,524 strong, mostly married with families.[26]

The clerical *paterfamilias* even looked different from his priestly predecessors: commonly he would boast a generous beard, proof of masculine potency as well as conveniently like everyone's mental image of an Old Testament prophet. The beard also deliberately countered the smooth chins of Catholic clergy. Cleanshavenness had been a product of the eleventh-century Gregorian revolution, when Pope Gregory VII himself had threatened punitive action against obstinately bearded clergy in Sardinia. Ironically that reflected his antagonism to the Eastern Churches; they may have mandated clerical beards so that clergy might resemble Graeco-Roman philosophers – or possibly so that they did not resemble eunuchs.[27] Luther led the new bearded fashion in 1521 during his stay in Wartburg Castle while pretending to be a secular gentleman,

'Junker Jörg'. Although he made a personal decision thereafter to restore his shaven chin even after he got married, others ignored his change of heart, and most Reformers were bearded by the 1540s, led by the impressively hirsute Heinrich Bullinger in Zürich.

In England, Archbishop Cranmer similarly commemorated Henry VIII's death in 1547, which gave him the opportunity to come out as a married man: he grew a full-length beard and thus contributed his own authority to the fashion. Catholics, furious at Protestant innuendo that the celibacy of clergy inclined them to sodomy, sneered at Cranmer and his Protestant colleagues who had got married as 'bishops effeminate'; that adjective meant the opposite of what it means now. A thousand years before, John Chrysostom had sneered at clergy in chaste 'syneisactic' relationships with women as sacrificing their maleness to their partners' feminine whims, thus these bishops of Edward VI were so in thrall to their women that it robbed them of their masculinity.[28] Trollope's Mrs Proudie does indeed come to mind.

Thus, after shaky beginnings in the 1520s, the clergy family became a cornerstone of European Protestant society. The ideal was a companionate loving marriage, modestly productive of children within the limits of an income which must also provide for wider hospitality and for more books than neighbouring houses possessed: all under the generally respectful but appraising eyes of the whole community, like a miniature royal family. More important, the clergy marriage became a role model for every marriage, not a binary clerical opposite. Once Lutheranism settled into being the familiar traditional religion of much of northern Europe in the seventeenth century, with a strong sense of historic pride in its Reformation, the Luther family apartments in the former friary became something of a goal for pious Protestant tourism, or indeed pilgrimage. Engravings of the notoriously stout *paterfamilias* that was the later Luther, paired with his redoubtable wife, were more readily identifiable and realistic models for pious married couples than Joseph and the Blessed Virgin Mary. Such pictures for fixing or framing on the wall of a family home would have been an answer to prayer for the unimaginative Lutheran wondering what to give for a wedding present.

In effect, the image of the pastor's family supplanted that of the medieval Holy Family in Protestant Europe. Humanist Protestants were gleefully aware of the pious fictions that had gone into the Holy Family's construction, not least Pope Gregory I's portmanteau Mary Magdalen.

21. A German engraving of 1706 furnishes a group portrait to ornament a pious Lutheran family parlour: Martin Luther, his parents, wife and much-loved daughter Magdalena, who died in Luther's arms aged only thirteen in 1542.

Her disassembly into her various scriptural and extra-scriptural component parts was prompted by a humanist who, like Erasmus, never himself became a Protestant, the distinguished Paris polymath Jacques Lefèvre d'Étaples; his work aroused righteous indignation in distinguished defenders of the old faith such as the English theologian Bishop John Fisher which in the end proved injudicious.[29] Yet a far greater target than the Magdalen was the Virgin Mary, whose cult had so mushroomed in the previous centuries. Marian devotion could be seen as the flagship of the cult of saints and their shrines and associated pilgrimages;

Protestants now dismantled all that, alongside the monastic life in which it was entangled.

Negativity towards Mary emerged as early as 1520, in Martin Luther's anger at one recent manifestation of Marian pilgrimage enthusiasm at Regensburg. In winter 1519 the cathedral preacher (Balthasar Hubmaier, ironically a future radical Protestant) incited an anti-Jewish pogrom in Regensburg, after which Our Lady was drafted in to cure a workman badly injured while his team demolished the city synagogue. Fifty thousand pilgrims were reputed to have visited a makeshift shrine chapel to her on the site within a month of its completion on the Feast of her Assumption 1519. Hubmaier's combination of anti-Semitism and Marian fervour (both of which he later regretted) had a dire effect on Mary's place in Protestant Europe. Luther saw it as like Johann Tetzel's indulgence campaign; the year-old 'Beautiful Mary' formed the climax in his list of offensive shrines that should be 'levelled' as he launched a bitter diatribe against pilgrimage in his *Address to the German Nobility*, one of his key declarations of war on the old devotional world.[30]

As Protestants looked at the Bible with new eyes, seeking its meaning in humanist fashion as an historical text, the curiously negative elements in the Gospel portrayal of Mary became apparent to them after centuries of discreet neglect. The English celebrity preacher Hugh Latimer was a pioneer: during his brief stint as Bishop of Worcester in the 1530s, he relished destroying images of Mary in his diocese, including a cult statue in his own cathedral. Amid quite a few less than rapturous remarks about Mary in sermons, Latimer considered the arrival of Jesus's family in Matthew 12, and criticized her for 'interrupting [Jesus's] sermon, which was not good manners'. Preaching on Luke's account of twelve-year-old Jesus deserting his parents for three days while visiting the Temple, Latimer further told off Mary for failing to keep an eye on Jesus and then for quarrelling with him for wandering away, 'like a mother'.[31]

That remark might suggest some old personal grievances in Latimer; these did not affect John Calvin, certainly otherwise no friend to Marian devotion. With more human sympathy than he often displayed, Calvin defended Mary's rebuke to her son in the Temple: 'The weariness of three days was in that complaint.' Nevertheless, this was a remark born of attention to the biblical text rather than pious reflection. The ultimate put-down came from the Elizabethan Bishop of Salisbury and noted Protestant apologist John Jewel, writing in the 1560s: 'to be the child of God it is a great deal greater grace than to be the mother of God.'[32]

Yet early on in the Reformation, mainstream Protestants uncomfortably realized that there must be strict limits on such debunking. Both Lutherans and Reformed theologians tried to draw such boundaries, signalling a gulf between these Reformers who followed theological 'Masters' (*Magistri*) like Luther, Zwingli or Calvin into the 'Magisterial' Reformation, and various more radical thinkers who were prepared to make brutal breaks with pre-Reformation theology. One symptom was the surprisingly vehement defence by Magisterial Protestants of the doctrine of Mary's perpetual virginity. It ought to have been an easy target for all Protestants, for it was a teaching plainly not found in the Bible – its earliest formulation being in that apocryphal though very influential second-century text, the *Protevangelium of James* (above, Chapter 7). Far from it: to a man, the Magisterial Reformers assumed that in the major row over the matter in the time of Jerome and Ambrose, Jerome had won the argument and Helvidius had been roundly defeated (above, Chapter 9). They embraced the feeble traditional attempts to defend the doctrine on biblical grounds, which relied on allegorical interpretations of Isaiah and Ezekiel that in other circumstances Protestants would scorn as popish attempts to avoid *sola scriptura*.[33]

The motive for all this was not so much Mary herself, but an entirely different issue raised by defences of Mary's perpetual virginity. Erasmus had commented on the doctrine with a characteristic mixture of candour and prudence: 'we believe in the perpetual virginity of Mary, although it is not expounded in the sacred books.'[34] In other words, the only reason for accepting the perpetual virginity of Mary was because the Church said so, in its tradition. For Protestants, the real problem then became something much more central to the Christian life: the long-standing custom of infant baptism. Protestant Magisterial Churches were insistent on preserving this because, just like their Catholic predecessors, they directed their ministry to all society, and infant baptism signified that all society was contained within the Church. Yet the increasing understanding of Church history fostered by humanist scholarship made it clear that baptizing infants had not been the custom of the Church for its first four or five centuries; it could only be justified from the Bible on the most strained of readings. How else, then, but by the tradition of the Church?

Many adherents of the Reformation more radical than the Magisterial Reformers drew an obvious conclusion: infant baptism should be abolished and only believing adults should be baptized. They saw Christianity not as coterminous with worldly society, but as a fellowship of believers. Their Magisterial opponents angrily called these radicals 'Anabaptists', 'Rebaptizers' – misleadingly, for the radicals themselves would not have seen their adult 'believers' baptisms' as rebaptizing. The danger that Anabaptists represented to the Magisterial Reformation was their clear-sighted return to the biblical message. The only defence that the Magisterial Reformers could make against them was the long tradition of the Church in favour of infant baptism: the very tradition that in many respects their own Magisterial Reformations were overturning. Anabaptists also rejected the perpetual virginity of Mary, on the same scriptural grounds and rejection of Church tradition. So, for the Magisterial Reformers to preserve infant baptism, the perpetual virginity must be preserved and defended too.[35]

In the same fashion, Protestants learned very quickly that any revisions of marriage and Christian family life in the name of faithfulness to Holy Scripture had serious limits. The most consequential road not taken was predictable: the option of polygamy. Luther was open to the possibility: as a good 'scripture alone' man aware of Old Testament precedent, he was prepared to say of polygamy that 'I cannot forbid it, nor is it opposed to the holy scriptures.'[36] After 1540, he and his colleague in Wittenberg Philipp Melanchthon (Schwartzerdt) were badly affected by association with a marital scandal: together with the Strassburg reformer Martin Bucer, they had secretly condoned a resort to bigamy by their important princely supporter in the Empire, Landgraf Philipp of Hessen, in his effort to resolve his marital difficulties. Melanchthon and Bucer were actually guests at the bigamous wedding.

Landgraf Philipp was in fact the second prince whom Luther had encouraged to bigamy. When in the 1520s Henry VIII of England had been thrashing around for a way out of his long-standing marriage to the infuriatingly loyal and rightly affronted Katherine of Aragon, Luther had given King Henry the same advice, which that prudish monarch indignantly rejected (the Pope had already taken the same pragmatic line on bigamy as Luther). Even earlier in that decade, Luther was advising clergy whose adventures into marriage proved less fortunate than his own choice of Katharina von Bora that bigamy was much to be preferred to divorce. Later Lutherans were not aware of these radical opinions, for the simple reason that they were not presented in the published versions of Luther's correspondence until modern times.

In particular, Luther's permissive opinion on Philipp of Hessen's bigamy remained concealed for more than a century, to 1679, when the relevant documents were published by a prince of the Empire, Elector Palatine Karl I Ludwig, who like Philipp was in a bigamous marriage and was delighted to find support from the founder of Lutheranism. Their exposure was a blow to Lutheran theologians (that being the intention of the documents' actual owner, Philipp's descendant but convert to Catholicism Ernst of Hessen-Rheinfels, who had mischievously passed them on to the Elector Palatine).[37] Even after that, it did not yet become apparent that the Hessen scandal was not simply an isolated aberration in Luther's thought, but part of a consistent pattern dating right back to the beginning of his Reformation. By contrast, by the end of the sixteenth century, developed Lutheran theology had taken the hardest line possible against polygamy, declaring it to be against natural law as well as against the law of the Church.[38]

There was good reason for this Lutheran U-turn, after the most alarming demonstration of both polygyny and Anabaptism in a horrific episode in the western German city of Münster. In the early 1530s, groups of excited radicals began converging on Münster, convinced that it was the New Jerusalem. Arriving in their thousands, in 1534 they seized control of the city's Reformation, which had begun in conventionally Lutheran mode. A joint expeditionary force of Lutherans and Catholics besieged Münster, and under pressure, with the city running short of food, the radicals' revolution became ever more bizarre in its biblicism. In July 1534 they instituted polygyny on the basis of the Old Testament, provoking horror and opposition in the city that needed savage armed force to suppress. Girls as young as eleven were forced into polygynous marriages. The final Anabaptist leader, a charismatic young Dutchman Jan Beuckelszoon (known to generations thereafter as 'John of Leyden'), announced that he was the biblical King David reborn. His personal harem, living in bizarre luxury as the citizens starved, eventually numbered fifteen, although when hunger eventually reached even his Court, Beuckelszoon sent fourteen of them to seek refuge outside the city. When in June 1535 the besiegers burst into Münster after eighteen months, their revenge on the Anabaptist leadership was as grotesque as the events they were punishing. The iron cages in which the tortured bodies of Jan and his companions rotted are still displayed high up on the belfry of the parish church of St Lambert.[39]

The trauma of Münster put paid to open Magisterial Protestant consideration of polygamy. Ironically, nevertheless, a favourite role model in

Protestant sermons became the Old Testament Patriarch Abraham: a reassuringly fecund literal patriarch blessed in his fecundity by God, thus a better model for husbands than Joseph, and a symbol of faithfulness less liable to idolatry than Mary. Those definite plusses enabled preachers to ignore his undoubted polygyny.[40] Otherwise, when the former Capuchin friar turned respected Reformed Protestant preacher Bernardino Ochino published a dialogue on polygamy in 1563, it ended his career, even though in the text he spoke in his own character in defence of monogamy. Ochino left his latest adopted city, Zürich, in disgrace, and eventually found a refuge in a radical community in Moravia at Slavkov (Austerlitz). They welcomed him on the principle of sheltering a victim of Magisterial intolerance and honouring his daring speculations about the nature of the Trinity, rather than out of any sympathy for polygamy. Printed copies of his dialogue are vanishingly rare.[41]

By the time of Ochino's obscure death in 1564, memories of Münster had turned away even radicals from such experiments; like Luther, they had travelled a long way from their first excitements. Radical Reformation in northern Switzerland in the 1520s had included ecstatic sexual promiscuity beyond even any polygamous framework: women who felt liberated from all popish restrictions on gospel freedom offered themselves sexually to the men in their devotional circle. 'Why do you judge?' they replied to appalled townsfolk in St Gallen. 'We have passed through death. What we now do is against our will in the spirit.'[42] Their language of spiritual resignation has continuities with what female mystics had been saying in Catholic Europe over previous centuries; the speed with which male Anabaptist leaders reacted to reject it is a sign of the limits on radicalism even among radicals, particularly towards female self-assertion.

The Swiss 'Schleitheim Confession' setting out radical belief and principles in 1527 was in part a reaction to that crisis. It set Swiss and central European radicals on a different trajectory to the Münsterites: pacifist; resigned to suffering at the hands of mainstream Christianity; committed to a decorous construction of a common life. Within that framework, many radicals created communities where resources were shared, but on the basis of monogamous families – the sort of Hutterite village that sheltered the dying Ochino in Moravia. Their leadership remained male: a Hutterite community was called the Court of Brothers (*Bruderhof*). The radical Peter Riedemann, in drawing up one of the most prominent Hutterite confessional statements in 1540, set the tone of his discussion of the role of women by sounding an utterly traditional note: 'We say, first, that since woman was taken from man, and not man from woman, man hath lordship but woman weakness, humility and submission, therefore she should be under the yoke of man and obedient to him.'[43]

Hutterite communities nevertheless boasted one distinctive feature: a reversal of the medieval Western trend to emphasize a couple's initiative in marriage. Arrangements were taken out of the hands of a prospective couple and given to the community elders (men, naturally), so it broadened out from the ancient dynastic principle that marriages should be arranged by the fathers of bride and groom. The elders would choose a small group of eligible young people from among those of suitable age and bring together those selected; thus suitably supervised they then chose their partner, avoiding 'the inclinations of the flesh'. Hutterite marriage custom proved one of the greatest points of internal contention in their determinedly peaceable communities. In the seventeenth century, one of their most distinguished bishops had to put a stop to widespread blatant fraud, as young lovers schemed to gerrymander the chosen group for particular wedding occasions. The dispute rumbled on until the mid-nineteenth century, when the Church authorities finally admitted defeat and gave up their prerogatives.[44]

Matters were different in the Magisterial Protestant Churches, which hearkened to the Pauline epistles in emphasizing a couple's individual choice. No doubt a consideration in this was the aspiration of clerical families to heroic marital partnerships, together with early Reformation uncertainties for Protestants in dealing with unsympathetic Catholic parents. The Reformed Protestant Church of Scotland has seldom boasted a reputation for sentimentality, but right away during the revolutionary birth of 'the Kirk' in 1560, when making official provision for marriage in the *First Book of Discipline*, it emphatically declared that the attraction between young people was 'a work of God' which trumped the admitted desirability of parental consent. If parents stood in the way of their children's happiness for 'no other cause than the common sort of men have, to wit lack of goods and because they are not so high-born as they require', then the minister should try to win the parents round – but if that did not work, he should overrule them and go ahead with a marriage. 'For the work of God ought not to be hindered by the corrupt affections of worldly men': one in the eye for patriarchy, echoed elsewhere in the Reformed Protestant world.[45]

The Reformation universally rejected the Gregorian revolution's formulation of seven sacraments; marriage as sacrament was an inevitable casualty. That had an important consequence. If marriage was not a sacrament, its original character returned to being a contract, as in the ancient world and in early Christianity. A contract by its nature could be put aside, even if God and the Church had blessed it. The theology and practice were carefully and cautiously discussed in treatises on marriage by two major Reformers, Martin Bucer of Strassburg and Heinrich Bullinger of Zürich, with a wide influence throughout the Reformed Protestant world.[46] Divorce, a virtual impossibility in medieval Western society, thus emerged unequivocally from behind various medieval ecclesiastical constructions of annulment.

This was encouraged on the basis of biblical time-bombs left by Paul: not only did he tentatively suggest in 1 Cor. 7.12 that Christians married to an unbeliever might well decide to leave their existing spouse, but elsewhere he more forthrightly advised Corinthians not to be mismated with unbelievers (2 Cor. 6.14–18). Some prominent Reformation examples of an end to mismating with Catholics followed – among them the revered early Tudor Protestant martyr Anne Askew and Elizabeth Bowes, close friend and eventual mother-in-law of the Scottish Reformer John Knox: in both cases the wife took the initiative in separation.[47] As a result, many people now felt that they had the best of reasons to bring unhappy relationships to an end: far from their divorce or separation being a source of shame, they would be doing God's will, while gaining release from spiritual as well as emotional bonds. Divorce was not desirable, and remained rare, but it was at least possible: John Calvin's own brother Antoine divorced his wife in Geneva in 1557, citing repeated adultery.[48]

The only national Protestant Church not to introduce a divorce law was the Church of England. A comprehensive reform of medieval canon law chaired by Archbishop Cranmer made full provision for divorce; the scheme was ready in 1553 but was derailed by entirely irrelevant political antagonisms within Edward VI's government. When Queen Elizabeth revived her brother's Protestant Church structure after the brief Catholic interval under Queen Mary, the proposed canon law reform was the one major aspect to which Elizabeth did not return. So the Church of England remained without divorce provision, and through sheer historical accident, rather than any basic theological conviction, it kept the strictest canon law on marriage in all Western Christendom right up to the end of the twentieth century, not even much mitigated by annulments that oiled the wheels of Roman Catholic marriage practice. The repeated eloquence of John Milton promoting divorce through pamphleteering in the 1640s and 1650s after the failure of his first marriage had no subsequent legal effect, even in the venturesome years of Commonwealth and Protectorate. It was only in the nineteenth century that the stranglehold of the Church of England's divorce prohibition was loosened for England and Wales, and the law of the Victorian state began to diverge from that of the Church – to the horror of Anglican Churchmen.[49]

Ending marriage's sacramental status naturally had liturgical consequences: an extreme one would be the abandonment of church weddings. So, the initially small number of English Protestant 'Separatists' who rebelled against Queen Elizabeth's imperfect Reformation sneered at its 'especial liturgy' of weddings in church – 'liturgy' as an English word began its career with disapproving Protestant overtones. Separatists ostentatiously held weddings in the entirely secular setting of private houses or even in prison if necessary, an offence that contributed to Elizabeth's Protestant government executing three of them for sedition.[50] Their austere practice continued in the seventeenth-century Puritan colonies in New England, which in their enthusiasm for pure biblical Reformation at first kept clergy out of weddings to avoid superstitious notions of marriage as a sacrament; they excluded clergy from burials as well on similar grounds. After half a century or so, however, these colonies began conforming to a more general Reformed Protestant pattern, and the pastors' diaries filled up with weddings and funerals.[51]

As the Elizabethan government's furious reaction to Separatist weddings indicates, most Magisterial Protestants eventually decided that a wedding needed a public character in church; it was an important testimony to society's interest in individual marriage arrangements and would reinforce efforts to eliminate clandestine or perfunctory wedding contracts. Marriage might not be a sacrament, but it was still sacred – 'a work of God' indeed, as the Scottish Kirk had declared it. Protestants found ample biblical basis for exalting marriage over celibacy: ordination had also been demoted from the seven sacraments, but that did not stop Protestants valuing an ordained ministry. In consequence, even if the emphasis in marriage returned to the civil contract as in the early Church, the expectation remained that it should be marked by some church ceremony.

Protestants adopted a significant variety of liturgical markers of marriage, with more or less clergy involvement according to region. Lutheran practice was remarkably varied, but the emphasis was on the civil aspect of the marriage, generally supplemented by a sermon in church.[52] The Dutch Reformed Church commonly devoted a special area of its often over-large church buildings to weddings on Sunday afternoons, which, to the chagrin of its ministers, left a golden opportunity for Dutch newly-weds to enjoy lavish secular fun afterwards on Sunday evening. The Reformed Church of Scotland, with coercive community powers to curtail such festivity not available to the Dutch Church, likewise kept the clerical flavour in the form of preaching on a Sunday afternoon, so that the congregation could stay on after the main sermon of the morning. It was characteristic of the Kirk to see marriage as an opportunity for theological education: apart from the actual afternoon, prospective newly-weds were expected to have attended special catechism sessions, just as were parents bringing their children for baptism.[53]

At an extreme of Protestant wedding formality was England, where in 1549 the twice-married Archbishop Thomas Cranmer crafted a remarkably conservative marriage liturgy, and did not greatly alter it in his much more unequivocally Protestant rebranding of the Book of Common Prayer in 1552. Not only did Cranmer preserve a service carefully choreographed within the existing church building broadly following late medieval liturgical practice, but he stipulated that the happy couple must receive Holy Communion afterwards. It would be easy to mistake this for a traditional nuptial Mass, and English Puritans way beyond Separatists hated the wedding Communion provision for undermining the Reformed character of the English Church. When the opportunity arose in 1661–2 to revise Cranmer's Prayer Book after Charles II's restoration to the throne and the return of an episcopal Church of England, it is noticeable that one of the few wins that the triumphant bishops allowed Puritans in revising the Prayer Book was to make wedding Communion so optional as to become a dead letter; bishops were clearly not that concerned to defend it. The custom then more or less disappeared, but by then it had produced a cheering architectural consequence in the widespread preservation of medieval chancels in English parish churches, screened off as spaces for wedding Communions as well as Communions for the whole parish two or three times a year (see Plate 25).[54]

Out of all this variety came the universal Protestant celebration of marriage and the family as nuanced by the progress of Reformation. Archbishop Cranmer did make one interesting innovation when he put into liturgical form a common sentiment in late medieval discussion of the family, taking it beyond Augustine's bleak justifications of marriage as *fides, proles, sacramentum* (above, Chapter 9). From 1549 onwards, England's wedding service affirmed that a major purpose of marriage was 'for the mutual society, help, and comfort, that the one ought to have of the other' – the Scottish *First Book of Discipline* was clearly in the same frame of mind. Contemporary Catholic sources would not have disagreed, and indeed echoed the idea without giving it liturgical expression. What was different with Protestants was that theologians who overwhelmingly were married were saying this, and not only without a balancing exaltation of celibacy but with every evidence of personal delight.[55]

One of the most charming examples comes from mid-seventeenth-century England: Jeremy Taylor, a bishop in the Church of Ireland in the latter years of his ministry. Taylor was one of the first English Protestant theologians whose work represented that distinctive Church of England evolution of a theology consciously negotiating between Protestantism and Catholicism, what would later be called 'Anglicanism'. Repeatedly the twice-married Taylor revealed his delight in family life:

> no man can tell but he that loves children, how many delicious accents make a man's heart dance in the pretty conversation of those dear pledges; their childishness, their stammering, their little angers, their innocence, their imperfections, their necessities, are so many little emanations of joy and comfort to him that delights in their persons and society.

On another occasion early in his career, Taylor preached a sermon that may have startled a dozing congregation by enthusiastically urging mothers to offer their own 'exuberant fontinels' to breastfeed their infants rather than relying on wet-nurses. This was not a sentiment to have enthused St Jerome.[56]

THE PAPAL CHURCH: DEFENCE AND RECOVERY

The hierarchy of the Western Latin Church took some time to react coherently to the explosion of protest in northern and central Europe following 1517. Part of the problem was that much Protestant energy sprang from various currents of renewal already active and familiar within the late medieval Church. Those wishing to change Catholic Christianity for the better would now have to recognize that Luther and his fellow leaders were not just challenging the Church to live up to its own standards, a frequent theme among reformers over the centuries, but saying that the standards were wrong – the Catholic paradigm must fundamentally change. One needed then to choose between adopting the Protestant analysis or deciding that loyalty to the existing Catholic structure was more important, as representing the authentic Body of Christ whatever its faults might be.

A 'Catholic Reformation' was perceptible well before 1500, in movements such as the *Devotio Moderna* of the North Sea region, or a succession of refounded versions of monastic and fraternal Orders, especially among the perpetually restless and self-critical Franciscans. This momentum continued to unfold alongside Protestant advances, not least because it was travelling right across the world along with the empires of Catholic Portugal and Spain. The Portuguese mostly clung to trading-posts around continental coastlines, while the King of Spain gained potentially vast new mainland territories in the newly contacted continents of America. This was Western Christianity's first major venture beyond its medieval bounds, and the beginning of its dominance among world Christianities that has persisted to the present day. By the mid-sixteenth century, the returning self-confidence of Roman Catholicism could be recognized as a 'Counter-Reformation' to stand against the Protestant movements now formalizing into new Western Churches back in Europe.

Some of this Catholic fightback was inevitably institutional and centralizing, relying on decisions in a Council of bishops and supporting experts that the Papacy eventually summoned to the northern Italian city of Trent; it met episodically between 1545 and 1563. The Council of Trent's work made Catholic Reformation into 'Tridentine' Counter-Reformation. Those at the Council recognized that any defence of papal Catholicism would have to counter Protestantism's wholesale rejection of ascetic celibacy in favour of the family: they must reaffirm a millennium of tradition that had relegated marriage to a second-best status and had, in the end, outlawed clerical marriage.

In the very last stages of the Council, the bishops declared the inviolability of vows for nuns and male clergy and pronounced anathema (the most solemn curse possible) on anyone claiming that 'the married state excels the state of virginity or celibacy, and that it is better and happier to be united in matrimony than to remain in virginity or celibacy'.[57] This became a Counter-Reformation theme, for instance as set out in starkly traditional form in Cardinal Roberto Bellarmino's influential 'larger' catechism of 1598: 'Marriage is a thing human, Virginity is angelical. Marriage is according to nature, Virginity is above nature.' It was probably that observation that provoked Bishop Jeremy Taylor to a mild but definite Anglican rebuttal in his own praise of the family: 'Single life makes men *in one instance* to be like angels, but marriage *in very many things* makes the chaste pair to be like Christ.'[58]

The Catholic Holy Roman Emperor Ferdinand I was displeased at Trent's resolution on clerical celibacy, which complicated his aim of conciliating his Protestant subjects after the hard-fought negotiations for the Peace of Augsburg within the Empire in 1555. Yet Ferdinand's understandable preoccupations and those of Protestants hostile to Tridentine Catholicism overlooked the subtlety of what the Council had said. Protestant Europe was not the only dimension in Rome's sights at Trent. During the medieval period, the Latin Church had entered arrangements with various segments of Greek and Oriental or Armenian Churches, which had agreed to accept papal obedience while still keeping their distinctive liturgies in their own languages, and which crucially also kept their custom of allowing or indeed expecting marriage for their parish clergy.[59] In the forty years after Trent's conclusion, the Papacy scored further spectacular successes in coming to similar deals with large swathes of the northern Orthodox Church on the frontiers of Catholicism and Orthodoxy, in the Catholic-ruled Commonwealth of Poland-Lithuania. This culminated in the Union of Brest in 1596; 'Uniate' or 'Greek Catholic' Orthodox Churches have continued in those regions till the present day.[60]

There was therefore every reason for the Tridentine bishops to soft-pedal on clerical marriage, while stoutly affirming the priority of celibate vows. That same set of canons on marriage in 1563 was notably carefully worded in relation to clergy who were indeed married; it only anathematized any statement that marriages were valid for clerics and 'regulars' (monks and nuns) who had 'made solemn profession of chastity'. This of course did not cover clergy who had not made any such profession: that is, secular clergy in Churches of Eastern Rites. Naturally the Council was equally cautious in what it said about the use of vernacular languages in worship – it had 'not been deemed advisable by the Fathers that it should be celebrated everywhere in the vernacular tongue'.[61]

Diplomatically fruitful though this prudence proved in relation to Eastern Christianity, the limited nature of the concession on clerical celibacy represented a lost opportunity for the Roman Catholic Church in the middle of its huge expansion through other areas of the world. Greater flexibility and imagination in implementing the celibacy requirement would greatly have helped the Church's world mission in the many societies where an insistence on celibacy has always remained countercultural and baffling. Nevertheless, the precedents set proved very useful four centuries later when a number of Anglican priests, dissatisfied with Anglicanism over various theological issues, sought a place in Roman Catholicism; with reordination, they could resume their priestly ministry even if they brought their wives with them.

Back in sixteenth-century Europe, a central component of the Counter-Reformation programme was to make a reality of the universal clerical celibacy established in the twelfth century, thus distancing itself from Protestantism's reconstruction of clerical identity, especially on the frontiers of conflict in central Europe and France. Since the laity had tolerated so much sidestepping of celibacy in medieval Europe, it would be important to co-opt them in enforcing the system. It was a slow process, not always helped by foot-dragging from local bishops who might themselves keep a concubine, and by local admiration for what the lay faithful could observe in Protestant clergy marriages, but, by the end of the sixteenth century, not only were leading laypeople in Catholic villages much more inclined to denounce clergy who kept concubines, but in France lay judges were prepared to see adulterous clerics and their female lovers hanged. As late as 1676, in an extreme case, a priest was burned alive by order of the Parlement of Burgundy, convicted of having had sex with a nun.[62]

Renewal of celibate community life was equally important. It proceeded from individual initiatives rather than any plan in Rome – quite the opposite. Leaders in the changes were the Society of Jesus and a cluster of female congregations collectively known as the Ursulines; both predated the Counter-Reformation, and both provoked suspicion in the Catholic Church by their unconventionality. The Society of Jesus emerged in the 1530s under the leadership of a charismatic student from the Basque Country in the far north-east of the Iberian Peninsula, Íñigo López de Loyola. He had been an aspiring courtier in royal Spanish service until a serious wound sustained in the course of war with France in 1521 led to a prolonged convalescence and a radical redirection. Íñigo's conversion and/or personal trauma led him in the opposite direction to Luther's: he broke through his conventional family piety to a deeper passion for encountering God through the tradition and authority of the Catholic Church. Through a series of intense personal experiences, apparent setbacks among them, he noted down what was happening to him, and turned the results into a systematically organized practical guide to prayer, self-examination and surrender to divine power which others might follow. In its eventual shape as the *Spiritual Exercises*, it became one of the most influential spiritual guides in Western Christianity.[63]

Enrolling at the University of Paris in 1528, Íñigo signalled a change of direction by the new Christian name that he took: Ignatius, resonant of the ancient martyr of Antioch. Around him gathered a group of friends with a collective though as yet undefined religious enthusiasm. Their efforts to find out what to do with their fervour in the service of the Church led to some initial fiascos: an abandoned joint pilgrimage to Jerusalem to convert Muslims, and a mission of salvation to the prostitutes of Italian cities, which provoked unsympathetic questions. It was easy to see them as brilliant mavericks, and powerful clerics in both Spain and Rome were further inclined to see them as potential heretics; Ignatius's circle certainly did have more contacts with some of the more independent-minded leaders of Mediterranean heterodoxy than later accounts admitted.[64] Nevertheless, Ignatius was able to advance his cause with the authorities by deploying his particular gifts: not merely his exceptional pastoral skill but a courtier's ability to charm influential women in the greatest palaces of Catholic Europe. Great ladies proved the essential support for the new venture in its precarious early years.

Most significant in these contacts was Loyola's pastoral care for Margaret of Austria, illegitimate daughter of the Emperor Charles V, who had the misfortune to be married to one of the loutish grandsons of Pope Paul III. Loyola's concern for Margaret in her misery saved her blighted marriage, which had important diplomatic as well as personal significance, and this was the main reason for the surprising papal readiness to grant a generous Bull of Foundation in 1540 to a new organization that still lacked a clear agenda.[65] The Society's constitution, deftly crafted by Ignatius, gave its General (the first being himself) life powers over a meticulously centralized organization: those powers were not shared with the Pope, despite the conspicuous loyalty of the Society's leadership. That made for significant freedom of manoeuvre during its astonishingly rapid expansion across Europe and the world.

The name of the group was distinctive; it was in Latin a *Societas*, originally in Italian *Compagnia*, relating it not to the monastic life but to the lay-dominated guilds or 'confraternities' characteristic of late medieval Europe. They could have many purposes from trade association to particular religious devotion, but in late fifteenth-century Italy they had produced a number of elite 'Oratories' with a variety of penitential or charitable purposes. Dominicans, the Order of Preachers, did note with irritation similarities to their own vocation in the Jesuits' commitment to communal life and public preaching, together with the centralized organization that Ignatius created: these characteristics also annoyed a choleric future Pope (as Paul IV), Giampietro Carafa, who had founded a somewhat similar austere company of priests, known as Theatines after his then diocese (*Teate* in Latin, Chieti in Italian). In 1545, Ignatius adroitly sidestepped an offer of amalgamation from the Theatines, who remained a much smaller company, but Carafa was not a good enemy to make.[66]

The Society of Jesus has remained a Society of celibates, not a religious Order, without an obligation to the regular round of daily liturgical offices observed by monks, friars or nuns (nor even a distinctive form of dress, a 'habit'). That has freed its members to pursue their particular callings in the world. It would take a little time and some trial and error to discover what those callings might be. One emerged from the early success of the Society in establishing advanced schools for the rigorous and prolonged training that Ignatius demanded for Jesuits. Influential people in Italy took an interest and demanded that their sons be allowed to take advantage of this; Jesuit schools became a worldwide brand, advancing Catholic comeback in parts of Europe inclining to Protestantism such as Poland. Then experience of the confused religious situation in central Europe, with Protestantism rapidly expanding particularly among local elites, shocked Ignatius's assistant Jerónimo Nadal into launching the Society into a new strategy of positive action against Protestants. In the general tidying-up of early Jesuit history that took place in the 1560s and after, Nadal made sure that this appeared to have been one of the Society's original purposes. The Jesuits joined and now indeed exemplified the 'Counter-Reformation', yet always on the Society's own terms. Notably, they have nearly always remained aloof from the work of inquisitions, and, until the twenty-first century, there had never been a Jesuit Pope.[67]

Given the Society's initial fluidity of purpose and character, why should it not include women in its ranks? After all, energetic elite female supporters were crucial to steering it past male suspicions, and particularly in making it acceptable to the governments crucial to its world expansion, those of the kingdoms of Portugal and Spain. Some of these women saw no reason why they should not be enrolled in the membership; their efforts included lobbying Pope Paul III. Ignatius's resistance to these moves against contrary enthusiasm from some of his colleagues is significant. In the early years he was unable to block one or two especially influential ladies, culminating with Joanna of Portugal, sister of King Philip II of Spain, but he swore her to silence on her membership and made sure that no woman ever again became a Jesuit.[68]

In the early seventeenth century a remarkable Englishwoman, Mary Ward, took a different approach, devoting her life to creating an organization for women that would parallel the Society, working in the world and living by the Jesuit constitution. She had some strong and impressive supporters among the Jesuits, but the Society's opinions were divided, and her programme was simply too much for the male clerical leadership of the Church that she wished to serve. Pope Urban VIII banned her 'Institute' in 1639, but in a remarkable act of quiet disobedience, she and her colleagues found ways of working around the ban, and successors continued in their calling to the present day; we will meet them again in central Europe a century after the papal ban (below, Chapter 16).

As recently as 2002, Pope John Paul II officially recognized Mary Ward's continuing community under a name that she had wished for them, the 'Congregation of Jesus'; he even began the process towards Ward's sanctification. That belated vindication is a welcome act of restitution, but it could hardly reshape events in the sixteenth- or seventeenth-century Church. There was no similar initiative at that time anywhere else in Europe, with the significant exception of an earlier though short-lived community in western Ireland. The rare inspiration of Mary Ward and her predecessor in Limerick, Helen Stackpole, must link to the peculiar conditions of Catholicism under Protestant government persecution in Elizabethan England and Ireland: the whole Catholic community was often sustained by devoted laywomen because it was easier for women than men to escape official punishment, but also because circumstances meant that access to male priestly ministry might be infrequent.[69]

Alongside the Society of Jesus there did develop a loosely joined association of women that had begun in parallel to them though completely separately: the Ursulines. Their Italian founder, Angela Merici, companion to a widowed noblewoman in Brescia, naturally lacked the university education of Loyola and his companions. She drew on her experience of activism as a Third Order Franciscan and a member of the local Oratory of the Divine Love when she set up a society of unmarried women and widows; they would live a celibate life of charitable works and teaching the poor while still living in their own homes, in a style reminiscent of the Beguine communities of northern Europe.[70] The community that Merici formally organized in 1535 took its title from the popular late medieval cult of the supposed third- or fourth-century British martyr St Ursula, who in the course of legend-making had acquired eleven thousand virgin companions, massacred by the Huns at Cologne. The likelihood of scribal error in copying stories of the saints, plus a wish to account for a mass grave discovered in eleventh-century Cologne, probably explains Ursula's crowd of butchered ladies, but more important was the framework that this pious fiction created for Merici's reality.[71] A host of inspired celibate women did indeed mushroom out of her initial idea: again like the Beguines, a gift to the Western Church that its male leadership had not sought.[72]

The Ursulines began working among the poor and teaching children in settings which men either did not want to or should not enter. In 1544, Pope Paul III supplied a Rule moulding them into something more like a traditional religious Order, but its model was still the free-form adaptability of the Augustinian Canons in the twelfth century. Crucially, the Ursulines made no provision for central direction, so it was difficult for the Church authorities to enforce a single pattern on Ursuline groups. The official Counter-Reformation attitude to the female religious life ran on the same lines as its enforcement of universal clerical celibacy: it sought to bring reality to medieval directives, in this case the papal decree *Periculoso* of 1298 ordering enclosure for all monastic women, which the Council of Trent reaffirmed in 1563. Where the hierarchy could enforce this, it did, for instance in the jurisdiction of the classic episcopal micromanager Carlo Borromeo, Archbishop of Milan, where Ursulines became yet another Order of enclosed nuns. Elsewhere matters were not so straightforward, and, in the discreetly orchestrated confusion that continued in Ursuline history, the Society of Jesus was a crucial ally.

The Jesuits could see the potential of such an energetic movement as a complementary partner in their own very varied enterprises, especially work among women that they had decided compromised their own mission. In the late sixteenth century, they took on spiritual direction of the Ursulines; they both fostered Ursuline expansion and took a major voice in how that expansion could operate. They encouraged choices among the originally varied aims of the Ursulines, steering them away from their work among the sick and the poor and promoting their interest in education, for which the sisters need not move around so much in the ordinary world. Ursulines had in the early decades normally been humble women and girls with little education: that began to change, as the Jesuits encouraged their aristocratic patronesses to send their daughters into the work, and in turn to educate daughters of the wealthy and powerful, just as the Society did for their sons. That usually did indeed mean building convents to house the ladies (predictably, usually paid for by a wealthy woman), but that had the appearance of chiming with the purpose of the Council of Trent, and the Society was as ready to adapt in this as in everything else.

Yet in other circumstances, still in partnership with the Jesuits, foundations in an Ursuline style took other forms. On the frontiers of the French colony of Canada (New France) in north America, Jesuits contrived to further their work with colonists and indigenous people in co-operation with two aristocratic French ladies, Marie Martin (who took the name in religion of Marie de l'Incarnation) and Marie-Madeleine de la Peltrie. Their extensive dowries could fund missionary enterprise – in de la Peltrie's case, through nothing less than a fake (or spiritual?) marriage contrived by the Society, to the impotent rage of her family back in France. Mère Marie learned the languages of Algonquin and Iroquois peoples and wrote them dictionaries and devotional tracts, at a time when the efforts of Protestants in English colonies to the south to bring Christianity to indigenous neighbours were unimpressive. Once more, as in the Protestant Church of Scotland's vigorous defence of a young couple's choice against parental pressure, the Jesuits and Ursulines clearly felt that patriarchal society was a lesser priority than a spiritual goal.[73]

The history of the Ursulines, and the parallel work of the Daughters of Charity, begun in seventeenth-century France with spectacular growth and success, illustrate a recurrent Counter-Reformation pattern, rarely made explicit in traditional narratives. Energetic and talented women, often freed from demands of family life by the opportune death of a more-or-less lamented husband, started an organization maximizing and perhaps enlarging skills customarily regarded as a mother's responsibility and therefore allowable for women: nurture, nursing, passing-on of domestic skills, elementary education for little children and even advanced education for girls. If such enterprises flourished, men stepped in, aiming to turn them into a monastic Order on medieval lines. The more ingenious women then used the language of deference and subservience to subvert this assault, either finding allies among sympathetic men, playing off rival male authorities against each other to postpone irrevocable decisions, or gravitating towards emergency situations such as that in the Canadian mission, where the Church waived the normal rules in order to get things done. If one female initiative became frozen within the religious Orders, another took its place, and the best chance of avoiding cloister walls was to shelter under the authority of a charismatic male sponsor.[74]

It was not only Jesuits or Ursulines who were preoccupied with education: it is one of the achievements of the Tridentine Church greatly to have extended opportunities for acquiring literacy, and all that could follow from it, far down the social scale. Yet that brought problems that have persisted to the present day, exemplified in yet another new religious foundation, an Italian religious teaching order called the Order of Poor Clerics Regular of the Mother of God of the Pious Schools: 'Piarists'. Joseph Calasanz, a Spanish priest, spent a quarter of a century developing a network of free schools for the poor before in old age he secured papal approval for a Piarist Order in 1621. Piarist foundations spread as far as Poland, showed a pleasing interest in new mathematical advances and in the research of Galileo, and were characterized in their early years by their relentless holy poverty. Calasanz was a deeply austere man and was never himself accused of any sexual misbehaviour; his twin weaknesses were poor judgement of character and indulging particular favourites among his brethren. The Piarists then became the theatre of a classic child-abuse scandal, complete with cover-ups and perpetrators being promoted out of the way.[75]

Sexual scandal began to gain publicity only six years after the Order's formal papal approval, but the real trouble awaited the rise within its ranks of a rich Roman lawyer's son, Stefano Cherubini, a pleasure-loving young man whom Calasanz quickly over-promoted. Cherubini soon set out drastically to modify the Order's strict mode of life; then in 1629 Calasanz was urgently informed of far more serious sexual offences involving pupils of Cherubini's school in Naples. The old man, browbeaten by Cherubini and fearful for the future of his Order, took no action, despite a raft of explicit evidence from furious Piarist colleagues. He wrote to Cherubini:

> There is no one in the world today that wishes more than I that this rumour would disappear . . . because I have at heart the honour of the Order and of the individual people in it more than anyone else . . . The Lord make everything disappear as I wish and pray to his divine Majesty.[76]

Repeatedly in Calasanz's letters comes a preferred way forward: 'it seems best to me, that if we are allowed to be the judges of this case, we will not permit it to come into the hands of outsiders.' In later years, Calasanz added another reason for the cover-up: respect for Cherubini's distinguished family. In a pattern later all too familiar, Cherubini was promoted to Visitor General to get him away from the scene of his misdeeds. In the end the outraged chorus from the majority of conscientious Piarists across Europe was too great to ignore, but Pope Innocent X's Gordian-Knot-style solution in 1646 was simply to dissolve the Order. Several decades passed, and it was only refounded after all the principal actors were dead. The Piarists survived to educate an array of European great names from Mozart to Goya to Pope Pius IX to Egon Ronay. In 1948, Pope Pius XII named Joseph Calasanz as patron saint of Christian schools; it took a conscientious modern researcher to find the scandal still buried in Piarist archives, despite earlier efforts at archival weeding.[77]

The sorry tale is worth setting out at length because it illuminates two separate Catholic ideals intertwining with toxic results: the enforcement of clerical celibacy, and the provision of education for all. There was nothing new about child abuse in a clerical context as we have seen in Egypt and early medieval Ireland, but the Counter-Reformation brought a new structural problem without precedent in the Church. Catholic priests faced a new reality of celibacy, leaving many struggling to cope with the emotional consequences in their own lives. Some took out their frustrations and anguish on vulnerable young people. Piarist expansion of schools for the poor offered the opportunities – far more than ever before. Power over the young was there for clergy to misuse, filling emotional chasms. In the background was the ongoing din of the Reformation struggle between Catholics and Protestants. Catholic layfolk were being taught anew to revere priests as a caste apart, marked out by celibacy; when some clergy misused this special status, Catholic

Church authorities naturally felt defensive under Protestant attacks. They had little sense of their own structural problem, and no developed procedure to deal with it. So the poisonous silence of unintended consequences persisted through embarrassment and shame, but also for lack of any right analysis. It was easy to blame just a few bad apples, and so it has long remained.

COMMON CONCERNS: THE REFORMATION OF MANNERS

Amid the bitter divisions of the Reformation, a surprising amount remained shared across the confessional divide. Protestant and Catholics were, after all, at root arguing about the best way to understand a shared inheritance: the complex theological legacy of the single most important theologian in Western Christianity, Augustine of Hippo. In a bon mot of the American Presbyterian historian B. B. Warfield (oft-remembered among historians at least), 'The Reformation, inwardly considered, was just the ultimate triumph of Augustine's doctrine of grace over Augustine's doctrine of the Church.'[78] That useful definition sidesteps the question of marriage, over which, as we have seen, there emerged much agreement between both sides against more radical proposals for modification: principally that marriage should remain the business of all society and of Church institutions. Amid the general wish to consolidate the public control of marriage that had begun in the eleventh and twelfth centuries, Protestants and Catholics were determined to outdo their religious opponents in the most efficient regulation.

That was a centrepiece to what has been termed a European 'Reformation of Manners', affecting both sides of the religious divide. It related to Erasmus's gift to secular authorities of that useful notion that all society was their 'great monastery', to be subject to their regulation just like the rule of an abbot. Rulers battled for the honour of imposing the strictest morality on their subjects, and did so using Erasmian humanist clichés. When the Jesuits became widely influential in Catholic Europe, they encouraged monarchs who were often former students of theirs to become moral regulators, conscious that many Protestant rulers were earnest readers not simply of Erasmus but of that noted scholarly instructor of German society, Luther's colleague Philipp Melanchthon, who had many positive things to say about the moral role of the godly prince. Thus, one of the first acts of the Jesuit-educated Duke Maximilian I of Bavaria on his accession was to draw up a Law for Morality and Religion (1598), equally severe on sin and on Protestantism.[79]

The confessions were engaged in a public relations battle for who could best control society in both public and private life. We may forget that in a world without extensive police and with a population whose age-structure was far more weighted towards the young and unruly than in the modern West, rigid moral standards and control of public behaviour were generally prized. There is an interesting case of failed wedding negotiations in Languedoc, an area of contention between Catholics and Reformed Protestants: in 1602 a Catholic girl, Arnouze de Beaucaire, refused a dynastic marriage with the son of a local Protestant seigneur because it would mean changing her religion. She detested Protestant Bible-reading and sermons not because she was a flighty young thing, but because she had far more esteem for the Catholic penitential exercise of self-denial, especially abstaining from meat on Fridays. One form of religious austerity trumped its rival.[80]

The Council of Trent likewise did better than the disunited Protestants in establishing a uniform standard to define what a marriage might be, through one of its last decisions in 1563, the decree *Tametsi* ('Although'). This laid down stringent conditions on valid marriage: now it must demonstrate a declaration of consent in front of a clergyman together with two witnesses, thus drastically simplifying the complicated possibilities of couples privately exchanging vows either with immediate or future intentions. Protestant England only caught up with *Tametsi* in 1753 when Parliament passed Lord Hardwicke's Marriage Act, which, in its definitions, gave the established Church of England similar power over marriage, despite the existence of significant minority populations of both Roman Catholics and Protestant Dissenters.

Also significant and in accordance with the Gregorian revolution was the explicit stipulation of *Tametsi* that a marriage must be sexually consummated, so that the couple became 'one flesh'. This was honouring the Pauline principle of the 'marital debt': one standard work of advice published in 1609 by one of the leading Counter-Reformation spiritual directors, Bishop François de Sales, further advised that a couple were entitled to pay this crucial sexual debt to each other the night before or even on the morning of receiving the Eucharist. Henry Dodwell, a theological writer adapting de Sales's work for the Protestant Churches of England and Ireland in 1673, clearly found this permission embarrassing, so left it out of his English translation.[81]

Above all, just as in Reformed Protestant Scotland, *Tametsi* did not make parental consent a requirement for marriage. This restated a standard Western canon law principle that had never pleased those seeing marriage as a dynastic transaction, and it emphatically did not please the very Catholic King of France, who refused to implement the Decrees of the Council perhaps because of this issue; on his own authority he restored the requirement for parental consent for valid marriages within his realm.[82] Few conciliar decisions met with immediate or universal observance in Catholic countries, but generally the close regulation of marriage through *Tametsi* suited secular rulers, particularly in Spain, where the authorities were alarmed at a perceptible decline in peninsular population.[83] Equally well-disposed to greater definition of marriage in Church courts were those seeking legal ways out of it via the annulment process. In Venice in the century after *Tametsi*, the principal ecclesiastical court was hearing around one request for separation every month, and around four petitions for outright annulment every year. This provoked the Republic's Council of Ten (always jealous of independent Church authority) into increasing scrutiny of cases in the court, to correct what they regarded as its excessive lenience towards disobedient wives intent on humiliating husbands and winning back their dowries.[84]

Part of the shared regulation of marriage was the successful cross-confessional curbing of medieval lay assumptions that a marriage started when the couple consented in 'espousal', with a wedding in church as an optional extra. Protestants and Catholics both relabelled as 'fornication' sexual activities previously seen as the first stage of marriage after espousal; they re-educated populations to see this activity and any resulting pre-nuptial births as sinful. In Protestant Europe this was enforced by new courts replacing what Protestants considered the inadequate treatment of marital matters by the old Church; yet equally in areas where Protestantism never had a chance of success, like the Spanish Kingdom of Aragon in Catalonia, the continuing Catholic diocesan courts showed the same new preoccupations.[85] Even in England, where the Protestant Church remained saddled with a barely reformed medieval system of ecclesiastical courts, from around 1580 judges were prosecuting as fornication sexual congress that would generally have previously been seen as justified within espousal custom, and there was a corresponding rise in the proportion and number of weddings in church. The Protestant Elizabethan Church of England succeeded in this regard where its medieval predecessor had failed.[86]

The ultimate but largely ineffective effort at regulating marriage in either Reformation or Counter-Reformation was to introduce into secular law the Hebrew Bible's penalty for adultery: death. Pope Sixtus V, a zealous reformer, tried to introduce it in Rome in 1586, and we have noted its arrival in the legal processes of Counter-Reformation France for adulterous clergy, but Reformed Protestantism, with its emphasis on the positive value of Old Testament law, was more commonly the setting for such efforts. Calvin's Geneva led the way and Scotland was not far behind; in both cases, the admittedly small number of those executed were persistent offenders. In such legislation for Protestant laity there was a patriarchal double standard which demanded harsher penalties of an adulterous married woman. Men (except those committing adultery with another man's wife) were generally punished on the same level as fornicators, with gaol and fines, but a woman had offended against the obedience due her husband, and thus she had approached the crime of a sodomite in transgressing on the natural order; death was therefore appropriate. There is a significant contrast with the reverse double standard for priests involved with women in Counter-Reformation Burgundy, where the man was treated with greater harshness: Catholic clerical status trumped masculine values as the greater violation.[87]

English Puritans in their years of precarious triumph after their military victories in the 1640s also tried to bring into England proper Reformed discipline at last. The flagship of their policy was parliamentary legislation in 1650 allowing the death penalty for incest and adultery, but virtually no cases were even tried. It is true that in the 1650s the recorded percentage of illegitimate births in England fell to its lowest level since reliable records had begun a century before, but this is probably more a statistical illusion because of a breakdown in Church record-keeping in the 1650s than a reflection of reality. The Puritan attempt to impose biblical discipline was a resounding failure, and it seems to have left a permanent memory of the resentment it caused; the legislation was all repealed (with the significant exception of penalties against sodomy) after Charles II was restored to the throne in 1660.[88]

In one small but enjoyably paradoxical respect, both pre-Reformation and Protestant England quietly co-operated in departing from the

Western Church's normally punitive and marginalizing treatment of illegitimacy. This was in order to eliminate piecemeal another social institution: serfdom or villeinage, the state of personal unfreedom created as part of the feudal manorial system after the Norman Conquest of 1066. Feudalism treated villein families as economic units to exploit: they were tied to the land of a particular manor, their lives regulated by the lord, including the choice of marriage partners. The system was disintegrating in the late medieval period thanks to social change, but not fast enough for many serfs, some of whom had become prosperous on their tied property, resented the restrictions on their families and found their status shaming. Accordingly, some ingenious fifteenth-century lawyer invented a legal process to guarantee serfs freedom, dependent on the principle that serfdom passes through the male line, and that therefore someone whose father is unknown cannot be a serf: *bastardia contra villenagium*, 'bastardy against villeinage', as an anonymous clerk once gleefully commented in the margin of his legal register.

This charade was dependent on co-operation between the bishop of a diocese and the royal courts of the 'common law' in Westminster (the Court of Common Pleas took the business on): it produced a neat legal fiction. The serf began a legal action about a more-or-less fictional piece of land against his lord. The lord generally replied that the case could not be heard since the plaintiff was his serf and therefore had no legal identity – to which the serf riposted that he was illegitimate and could not be the lord's serf (sometimes it was the lord as defendant who claimed that the plaintiff was illegitimate and so had no legal title). In consternation the judges in Common Pleas turned to the bishop of the diocese containing the relevant manor, who obligingly confirmed this rural scandal. So the legal action ended with a judgment in Common Pleas: the plaintiff lost his case, and he was declared a bastard – but he was not a serf. The whole business, of course, involved a good deal of money changing hands all round, including set legal fees. The diocese of Norwich in particular made some tidy little sums out of it, all in the name of personal freedom – the lawsuits spanned the Reformation, between around 1440 and 1580, by which time English serfdom was more or less extinct. By then, in tragic irony, Protestant England was being drawn into a different and much more inhuman institution of slavery, the Atlantic traffic between Africa and the growing colonial empires of both Catholic and Protestant European powers in the Americas.[89]

It is unlikely that the 'Reformation of Manners' would have succeeded without the general population feeling sympathetic to a change in sexual standards, and being prepared to see those standards enforced in various forms of public shaming for fornication or adultery, such as the elaborate rituals of penance retained in the Church of Scotland, not otherwise a friend to formal liturgy. Scotland was only one example of a Reformed Protestant society where the laity were directly involved in administering this system, not merely as spectators in church, but as lay 'elders' who dominated the new Reformed disciplinary court known as the Consistory. Elders were likely to be prominent local men, but still they were likely to represent a wider section of the community than nobility or gentry who were frequently the cause of lawlessness or disruptive behaviour. The system would seem repressive to us; for people in Reformed Protestant territories, it might seem levelling and liberating.[90] We have noted how Catholic laity in France were persuaded into endorsing the new strictness of clerical celibacy (above, p. 342), and figures for illegitimate births and pre-nuptial pregnancies are likewise very low in France. Baptism registers appeared in both Catholic and Protestant regions in the sixteenth century, no doubt partly to keep an eye on Anabaptists who would not bring their babies to church for christening. The statistics that they reveal on illegitimacy are striking: in England between the 1540s and 1700s, rates are nearly always below 3 per cent of the total, less than half the rate in the Victorian period.[91]

There were encouragements to sexual discipline. In the 1590s serious economic stress and bad farming conditions across Europe disrupted many wedding plans; in this decade England was probably typical in registering the one noticeable spike in its bastardy rate (and consequent need for parishes to support illegitimate children), which probably frightened the tax-paying population. It was the beginning of a period of cooler weather in the northern hemisphere that lasted till the mid-nineteenth century, the 'little Ice Age', during which agricultural shortages always threatened social cohesion. A further background alarm had emerged a century before: an apparently brand-new disease that spread frighteningly quickly across Europe from south to north and which was soon observed as connected to sexual intercourse. The coincidence of Europe's first contacts with the Caribbean and the Americas by the expeditions of Christopher Columbus after 1492 has suggested an origin, but we have experienced a recent example of a killer disease suddenly emerging from insignificance through some accidental change of behaviour; the origins of this fifteenth–sixteenth century epidemic remain controversial. Certainly it had not figured in the consciousness of Graeco-Roman doctors, so inconveniently it lacked a widely recognized name until taking the title of a Latin poem of 1531 by an Italian doctor, Girolamo Fracastoro: *Syphilis*.

Syphilis caused distressingly visible symptoms and was no respecter of social boundaries, particularly not apparent celibacy in clergy (it may or may not be coincidental that Fracastoro was later official physician to the Council of Trent).[92] One reaction to the pandemic therefore was for social elites, both lay and clerical, to rally to help sufferers. Like the religious renewal movements of the period, syphilis was at its most intense in urban settings: the disease was one major stimulus for the emergence in various Italian cities of the devotional and charitable activism of Oratories and Confraternities that were such an important part of the prehistory of the Italian Counter-Reformation. A fleet of new purpose-built hospitals was set up, often dedicated to that boil-stricken Old Testament hero Job, now turned into an honorary Christian saint and patron of syphilis cures: with heartening inaccuracy, the hospitals were termed *Incurabili*. A treatment which was at least a palliative did emerge in the form of preparations from a wood known as *guaiacum* discovered in the Spanish colonies of America. Its origin and distribution through Catholic institutions made Protestants suspicious of *guaiacum* until experience did suggest its effectiveness.[93]

Fear of syphilis was also a major motive behind one of the more remarkable ecumenical phenomena of the sixteenth century: the large-scale closure of the licensed brothels which were such a feature of medieval city life (above, Chapter 13). Luther had already called for this in his manifesto of 1520, *Address to the German Nobility*, and such closures became an invariable feature of urban Protestant Reformations. Nuremberg, usually more conservative than most Lutheran cities, was unusually late in waiting till 1562, while Henry VIII of England also belatedly imitated mainland European Protestants in 1546 by closing the 'Stews', the Bishop of Winchester's licensed brothels in Southwark. Roman Catholics belatedly joined the stampede – the King of France in Paris in 1561, with successive Popes making two attempts in Rome, in 1555 and 1566, before getting their way, and Spain as late as 1623, following pressure on the monarchy from the Jesuits.[94]

Few public statements about such closures admitted the connection with disease: Henry VIII for instance gave moral rather than medical reasons in his proclamation closing down the Southwark brothels. But at the same time public bathhouses also disappeared across Europe, outside Finland and the eastern areas dominated by the Ottoman Turks. Not all baths had the dubious sexual reputation that is their prevailing memory and there was no plausible religious justification for closures: general fear of close contact must have been paramount.[95] Ironically, their disappearance must have produced generally lower standards of personal hygiene. Anxieties about catching syphilis did affect people's sexual behaviour, for instance keeping the future Jesuit missionary Francis Xavier a virgin at university. There is also evidence that personal codes of manners and gestures, encouraged by prescriptive literature on the subject, changed so as to avoid too much physical contact with other people.

Given this justified worry about sex, it is unsurprising that Europe showed an equally ecumenical hatred of 'sodomy'. Admittedly, Protestants allowed the medieval Catholic myth about a Christmas cull of the world's sodomites to fall into oblivion, but that will have been the result of their general contempt for friars and pious legends. There were complications: even more than in the twelfth-century 'Renaissance', the intense Renaissance humanist admiration for Graeco-Roman literature could not ignore literary encounters with same-sex activity. Once more, the ramifications were cross-confessional. The young French humanist Théodore de Bèze (Beza), future colleague and successor of John Calvin in Geneva, got his fingers burned by including among his elegant attempts at classical Latin verse a poem debating in Ovidian fashion the relative merits of his male and female lovers, and deciding in favour of the young man: later Catholic enemies did not let him forget this indiscretion.[96]

From the fifteenth century, a better acquaintance with classical texts had brought to the West a rediscovery of most of the works of Plato, which, among other homoerotic revelations, disconcertingly revealed the same-sex relations of Socrates with some of his students, previously censored from the available literature. Since Socrates was so widely praised in early Christian Greek writings, with his execution seen as a prefiguring of Christian martyrdom, this was an embarrassment. Not, however, for one Sienese humanist, Antonio Vignali, who was inspired by classical precedent in 1525 to publish *La Cazzaria* ('The Book of the Prick'), a Platonic-style Italian dialogue featuring 'Arsiccio' and his pupil 'Sodo'. It went through several editions, virtually all copies of which have disappeared.[97] Equally unbuttoned was the gleeful literary celebration of sexual activity between older and younger males by a Conventual Franciscan friar of Venice, Antonio Rocco, who vaunted its superiority to heterosexuality in Platonic vein around the theme of Socrates' charming though unreliable boyfriend in *Alcibiades the Schoolboy* (1652). Given the Venetian authorities' sensitivity on such matters, and after investigations of him extending as far as the Roman Inquisition, it is astonishing that Rocco died uncondemned.[98]

The Classics continued to make matters complicated as Westerners encountered other world cultures, some of which they came to respect, particularly through the heroic missions of the Society of Jesus to the empires of Asia. Matteo Ricci, a Jesuit pioneer of missions within China, pondered what text might illustrate for a Confucian culture the best and most congenial Western wisdom before the revelation of Christ. He came up with the *Enchiridion*, a collection of aphorisms on conduct from the Greek Stoic philosopher Epictetus, which Ricci translated and abridged first into Latin and then into Mandarin. In both those translations, he omitted remarks of Epictetus on emotional and physical moderation which would have been thoroughly congenial in their sentiment, if the subject of the urges to moderation had not been relationships with boys – their inclusion would have been routine for a Classical author but was now deeply unhelpful.[99]

In other writings, Ricci observed open same-sex activity in China with great unease and disapproval, not admitting to himself or his correspondents that he could have seen very similar phenomena back in Florence, Venice or his native Papal States if he had decided to look. What was offensive to him was how the Chinese cheerfully accepted such behaviour as part of the way their society worked.[100] As we have already observed, Christians have had a long-standing impulse to ascribe sodomy to the Other. That label could be applied to Muslims and aboriginal peoples overseas: it provided a handy reason for seizing their lands and possessions and enslaving them, just as did frequent accusations that such peoples were cannibals. That did not stop the contrasting sexual mores being a reality.[101]

In Reformation Europe, Catholics and Protestants could 'other' each other in the same fashion about sodomy. This was an easier rhetorical stance for Protestants than for Catholics, given the obvious available innuendo about priestly celibacy, and the reality of same-sex activity in Italy.[102] One of the earliest manifestations of Reformation attention to same-sex activity came from Henry VIII's England, when in 1534 Parliament passed a statute against 'buggery', to be punished with death. We do not know enough about its context, or even which member of the House of Lords introduced the draft legislation; it came amid King Henry's campaign to intimidate the Church authorities into accepting his forthcoming marriage to Anne Boleyn, so it is likely to be a further effort to discredit and demoralize clergy. The Act was too early in the English Reformation to have a Protestant motive, but it formed the first instance of Parliament taking to itself moral regulation previously the responsibility of the Church, and so it was a perfect instance of a monarch following Erasmus's advice to become 'abbot' or moral guardian in his own kingdom. As Henry's break with Rome morphed into a Protestant Reformation, the buggery statute endured, and it governed national legislation on the subject down to the nineteenth century.[103]

The cross-confessional unanimity was unmistakable. The scholarly Jesuit analyst of witchcraft and magic Martin del Rio recorded with fury in his memoirs that, when Dutch Protestants seized the city of Ghent in 1578, they forced four young friars to confess under torture to acts of sodomy with older brethren; the four were burned alive, one chosen from each of the four fraternal Orders.[104] Witnesses later confessed to the falsity of the confessions; but true or not, this was (perhaps consciously) the same penalty that the Spanish Inquisition inflicted on convicted sodomites in its Castilian jurisdiction, in fact around 150 of them between 1570 and 1630. In Rome, Pope Sixtus V burned a priest and a boy together for sodomy in 1586: on this occasion Our Lady did not intervene to save the younger participant as she had in Avignon in 1320 (above, Chapter 13).[105]

When Europeans took their 'culture' into conquests in other continents, they were equally unforgiving of unfamiliar social customs that they defined as sodomy. In the 1580s, after Spain acquired political power in the East Indies in what are now called the Philippines, the Spanish Inquisition burned alive Chinese men convicted of same-sex acts that were part of Chinese culture, just as it would have done in Iberia; Ricci would approve.[106] When the Spanish conquistador Vasco Núñez de Balboa reached what is now California, in 1513, he encountered *'aqi*, people assigned as male at birth now living as females, who might today be termed 'Two-Spirit' people. He ordered their execution, seeing to it that they were torn apart alive by hunting dogs. A handful of survivors were forced to dress in what Balboa considered male attire, but quickly fled from the scene of the atrocity.[107] Such cultural clashes continued, as is witnessed by the fourteen men burned together at the stake in Mexico City in 1658. They were selected from 123 individuals ranging from indigenous people to African slaves to Spaniards and Portuguese, rounded up from networks of males some of whom confessed to living as women.[108]

Such brutalities are especially ironic because the Counter-Reformation was responsible for reviving one particular form of gender modification in a Christian context when it employed eunuchs, not now as courtiers, generals or archbishops as in Byzantium, but as liturgical singers, castrated in boyhood to serve the increasingly varied and dramatic musical repertoire of the Church without the indecorum of allowing women to sing in the liturgy. The choral castrati began in Italy as a Catholic ecclesiastical speciality, but later expanded their clientele to Protestant Europe. When the continent-wide fascination with opera burgeoned in the eighteenth century, they became a major feature of the Western classical

22. Domenico Mustafà, Chapel Master of the Sistine Chapel and one of the last castrati, photographed in avuncular mode with St Peter's Basilica portrayed in the background, 1898.

musical tradition, arousing a variety of sexual frissons in polite society, together with a certain long-term evasiveness among Catholic Church authorities about how exactly they had arrived at their condition. The last castrato of the Pope's choral foundation survived long enough into the twentieth century for a perhaps underwhelming recording of his voice to be made for the gramophone; further castrati were forbidden in the Sistine Chapel only as late as 1903.[109]

One of the aspects of Reformation revealing the most puzzling parallels between Catholic and Protestant is in the widespread activity that has become known as the 'witch craze'.[110] Both confessional groupings, with honourable exceptions such as Martin Luther and the Spanish Inquisition (an unexpected combination), moved on from the general medieval belief in witches to active pursuit, persecution and execution of people thought to be witches and agents of the Devil. It is remarkable how seriously Protestants fearful of witchcraft took a rambling and misogynistic pre-Reformation inquisitors' textbook on the subject, the *Malleus Maleficarum* ('Hammer of Witches'), first published in Speyer in 1486 complete with a bull that the Dominican writers had obtained from the Pope endorsing their work. It provided most of the stereotypes to fear and act upon. Jacobus Sprenger, one of its two authors, structured his world around female polarities, for he was also instrumental in promoting the Marian devotion of the Rosary.[111] The *Malleus* was one of the most effective conspiracy-theory texts of all time, appealing to a fatal pot-pourri of muddle-headedness, pedantry, prurience and half-formed fears. Perhaps Westerners in the early twenty-first century are better equipped than previous recent generations to understand how that momentum can accelerate.

Maybe forty or fifty thousand people died in Europe and colonial north America on witchcraft charges between 1400 and 1800, most noticeably from around 1560, just about the time when large-scale Catholic execution of heretics was coming to an end. The activity showed curiously different peaks and troughs in different parts of Europe, but the majority of victims were female. The common stereotype of the witch as a gnarled old woman does not reflect the reality that the accused were characteristically prosperous or significant figures in their community, though commonly not the most peaceable. If they were indeed elderly women, there was often a long history of accusations against them – and a sudden lack of male protection when their husbands died.[112]

A high incidence of witchcraft prosecutions was often found in western European regions, both Protestant and Catholic, that had effective systems of court discipline which people living under them would find it difficult to challenge. Individual powerful personalities might then make all the difference. Some of the worst persecutions were in the Archbishopric of Cologne after it was secured for the Catholic ducal family of Bavaria, the House of Wittelsbach. Ferdinand, Archbishop of Cologne from 1612, was a typical product of the radical Counter-Reformation self-discipline characterizing both the Wittelsbachs and their allies the Habsburgs. It has been plausibly suggested that these devoutly Catholic rulers were fighting more than the Protestantism that certainly obsessed them: their Jesuit mentors gave them a preoccupation with sin and judgement, now strengthened for the clergy among them by the new demands of a clerical celibacy much more conscientiously maintained than in the pre-Reformation Church. As an array of conscientious Counter-Reformation bishops struggled with their own temptations, witches became symbols of the general temptations that Satan used to torment society.

Among Protestants, the mid-seventeenth-century Church of Scotland distinguished itself by one of the most statistically intense persecutions in Europe, which was not unconnected to the Scottish clergy's constant struggle to assert their authority against secular authority in the kingdom. The Scots Kirk had the distinction of inventing that form of torture still popular in the contemporary world, sleep deprivation, in order to extract confessions.[113] Curiously neither here nor in other jurisdictions that employed torture did interrogator or putative witch make much effort to link witchcraft to that other work of the Devil, sodomy: clearly the satanic had agreed on a division of labour.[114]

In both Protestantism and Catholicism, the impulse to encourage popular fear of witches began to fade in elite circles in the late seventeenth century, and so deprived persecutors of public legal backing. An oddity was the curiously late transatlantic outcrop around Salem in Massachusetts in 1692, leading to nineteen executions. Less frequently remembered by ghoulish modern tourists is the exactly contemporary hysteria in Stamford, Connecticut: it petered out without eventual fatalities after careful probing by its courts under English common law procedure, and some conscientious reconsideration by the pastors.[115] Back in Europe, an independent-minded Dutch Reformed minister, Balthasar Bekker, denounced witch-hunting in an influential book,

Bewitched World (1691). His Church did not thank him for it, but after a sequence of sceptical literary treatments of witch-hunting over the previous 150 years, this was the one that finally shamed many Protestant authorities in north-west Europe into giving up witch trials.

The pattern in eastern Europe was different: the paranoia started later, lasted longer and climaxed in the eighteenth century. By then, in now strongly Catholic Poland, half of those charged with witchcraft ended up being burned, whereas the proportion had been around 4 per cent in the sixteenth century. Poland was increasingly belying its reputation as a tolerant 'state without stakes', in parallel to the decline in its embrace of religious diversity. Executions ended only with a Polish royal decree in 1776, by which time perhaps around a thousand people had died, a similar figure to Hungary and Transylvania over the same period. The eastern persecutions took place amid new political crises and social tensions in the lands where Habsburgs, Romanovs and Hohenzollerns were remaking the map; as in Poland it was imperial Enlightenment scepticism in Habsburg territories that eventually ended the alliance between popular fear and the law. It is notable that in eastern Europe the gender balance was reversed between male and female witches as western witchcraft beliefs interacted with regional fears of vampires, or the charismatic activity of males such as the northern shaman or the Hungarian *táltos*.[116]

From witches to Ursulines, via the pastor's wife: a spectrum of new roles opened up for sixteenth-century women. How far could they extend? One might expect that the more generous or pluralist impulses of humanist scholarship would widen the possibilities open to all human beings: there was, after all, a strain of humanist opinion, following Erasmus, that exceptional women should be given access to all-round education. Humanists might also have recommended an end to the double standard in morality that punished female sexual transgressions more than male. Yet the problem was that humanist scholars were mostly men, and that the powerful lay and ecclesiastical rulers who picked and chose what they wanted to hear from their humanist clients were also mostly men.

One female scholar of the 1970s having asked 'Did women have a Renaissance?' therefore came up with a resounding negative.[117] The same could be said of the Protestant Reformation, which deprived women of multiple possibilities offered by the celibate monastic life and the lives beyond it in Beguine or Ursuline communities. Crucially, women both Catholic and Protestant normally remained barred from that key to power, a classical education. Exceptions were found among women whom accidents of genealogy destined to hold positions of power, like the two daughters of Henry VIII of England; likewise in the early years of the Reformation, some gifted Protestant women with affectionate humanist fathers. But insofar as the Reformation was a war of ideas fought out in Latin books, it remained male.

Otherwise, in both the Protestant Reformation and the Counter-Reformation, women typically experienced a period of self-assertion, followed by male reassertion and renewed traditional discipline. Female self-assertion was possible in periods of uncertainty and crisis. It was accepted for the time being by men partly because any help in the struggle was welcome, and also because the male-centred conventions of the time had a paradoxical side-effect: women were less likely than men to be punished for breaking rules, especially in matters of conscience, because their opinions did not matter as much as those of men. So women might defy repressive religious authorities and sustain their cause with rather more chance of avoiding death than if they were male. In Elizabethan England, for example, widows and matriarchs sustained Catholic recusant family life when men could not: a situation that produced the exceptional enterprises of the would-be missionary foundresses Helen Stackpole and Mary Ward. When times quietened, there was a gradual reining-in of possibilities for women, together with a rewriting of history. Yet regardless, history was moving the Church on.

From the beginning of the Reformation there were patterns of Protestant devotion which were predominantly female: one scholar familiar with Germany in the first turbulent decade after Luther's defiance suggests that already in that excitable decade one can see different religious texts lighting up for men and women, with men preferring to collect published books of sermons and favouring hymns spelling out doctrine, while women read general works of piety and showed especial affection for more personally expressed hymns.[118] What was less predictable was the beginning of a great change in the seventeenth century, now one of the distinctive features of modern Western religion. The devotional practice of Christianity was becoming an activity in which more women than men participated. The spectacular growth of female religious communities in Counter-Reformation Catholicism was one symptom: not simply the Ursulines in their various guises and the Daughters of Charity in France, but the many and growing number of nunneries that did conform to the requirements of Trent on enclosure. It was a significant moment in seventeenth-century France when for the first time female religious outnumbered men.[119]

Protestantism experienced a parallel phenomenon. In various settings, church attendance was becoming skewed, so congregations contained more women than men. The first signs so far detected are in parts of western Europe where voluntary religion became possible despite an established Protestant Church: the United Provinces of the Netherlands and England. In the Netherlands, even the officially established Dutch Reformed Church had the character of a voluntary organization: people chose whether or not to go to their parish churches, and, as early as the 1570s, 60 per cent of congregations were female. In the province of Friesland, the most northerly of the United Provinces, between a tenth and a fifth of the population had opted to join radical post-Anabaptist groups like the Mennonites; by the early seventeenth century those churches also show that majority membership of women.[120]

The pattern appeared in England when the coercive structures of the episcopal Church collapsed amid the Civil War of the 1640s: in membership lists of the growing number of voluntary Churches – Independents, Baptists, Quakers and more – women often outnumbered men by two to one. This extraordinary proportion lessened later, but still over three centuries of English Dissenting or Free Church life, from the seventeenth to the twentieth century, the predominance of women's membership over men's was rarely less than three-fifths of the total. When Methodism arrived in the eighteenth century, it showed a similar profile. The disparity was less in the Church of England and English Roman Catholicism, but still perceptible.[121]

On the other side of the Atlantic, the authorities in the established Congregational Church in Massachusetts also began to notice the phenomenon of gender-skewed church attendance during the seventeenth century. Why was this happening? One of the most perceptive modern commentators on religion in the early English colonies of north America has noted that this mismatch between male and female church attendance does not appear in the seventeenth or eighteenth centuries in the colonies from Virginia southward, where the Church of England was the dominant religious body. She suggests that this is related to the resolutely non-clerical but male character of Church leadership there.

The Church of England in north America lacked a bishop or hierarchy that side of the Atlantic; consequently, laymen ran the parish system in their parish vestries, and the clergy had little power. By contrast, to the north, Congregationalist Massachusetts was dominated by a self-confident and well-trained ministry emerging out of the most effective seminary in America, Harvard College: lay male leadership was atrophying, leaving the Congregational Church in the hands of male ministers and devout women.[122]

This idea would be worth testing out in other circumstances, but probably no single explanation will do. It would hardly apply in the official Reformed Church of Friesland in the northern Netherlands, which had a strong Genevan-style structure of consistories and elders involving laymen, though it may make more sense amid the sects of Civil War England. In the major disruption of English religious life in the 1640s and 1650s, a disproportionate number of women probably were indeed motivated to join independent congregations because they found more scope to express themselves than in the established Church. Some broke convention to preach a gospel of transformation as they saw it – way beyond the mainstream theology of the Reformation, but taking encouragement from the scholarly radical Puritan Henry Ainsworth, who, in his commentary of 1617, pointed out that when Psalm 68.11 spoke of a great army or company of preachers, the original Hebrew text was specific in calling them 'she-preachers'. Others founded their own new congregations of men and women. The charismatic Dorothy Hassard of Bristol set up a meeting separate from the nearby parish church at which her Puritan clerical husband ministered: hers survives to the present day as Broadmead Baptist Church, while his church has long vanished. It is clear that such activism had begun in the decades before the Civil War broke out, but now it was able to flourish freely.[123]

All this culminated in the radicalism of Spirit-inspired groups such as the early Society of Friends, who began gathering in the early 1650s: opponents called them 'Quakers', and, as often in Christian history, they defiantly borrowed the sneer as a self-identification. Quaker women in this period followed Psalm 68.11 to enjoy prophetic roles reminiscent of women in the early days of radicalism in central Europe during the 1520s and 1530s. Often as a result they met horrified repression from males in mainstream religion, particularly when they crossed to the Puritan English colonies across the Atlantic; a woman was among the four Quakers executed in Massachusetts between 1659 and 1661.[124] Just as in the sixteenth-century radical groups, over subsequent decades male Quaker leadership steadily moved to restrict women's activism, but that was part of a general disciplining of life in the Society away from its first inclination noisily to shock wider society into listening to the message; now Quaker gatherings were programmatically quiet but still obstinately distinctive. The Friends preserved an itinerant ministry whose members were as often female as male. When Dr Johnson made his famous sneer against a woman preaching as being 'like a dog's walking on his hinder legs', it was about a Quaker preacher that he was trying to be funny.[125] By the early eighteenth century, much of the appeal of the Friends to women may have become the way in which Quaker worship resonated with that more traditional and distinctively female form of spirituality, the outwardly silent waiting on the Lord.

At the same time as the consolidation of the Quakers in the 1670s, there developed within the official Lutheran Churches of northern Europe an intimately devotional renewal movement that came to be known (again at first abusively by its opponents) as Pietism: small private groups developed a spirituality which likewise emphasized an inner personal encounter with the divine, although in that case, the devotional group took its place alongside the public worship of the Lutheran Church. It is interesting that these Pietists were among the few people to interest themselves in the writings of women activists from the earliest days of the Lutheran Reformation.[126] Thus were emerging various female challenges to the male Reformation noise of polemical texts, sermons and massed congregational singing.

Some Protestant women took notice of their Catholic counterparts who had chosen monastic enclosure and contemplation in its many Counter-Reformation variants, and they considered that their own Reformation had suffered significant losses. Mary Astell was an English gentlewoman whose life spanned the Stuart and Georgian eras: a Church of England Tory of 'High Church' or sacramental outlook. Witty as well as devout, she was satirical about the liberal Whig politicians who had spearheaded the 'Glorious Revolution' that had brought William and Mary to the thrones of the Atlantic Isles; they talked loudly of freedom, but ignored women's rights just as much as they ignored the rights of slaves. Choosing to remain unmarried (an unexpectedly common state in late seventeenth-century England, embracing around one in four of all adults), Astell published in 1694 *A serious proposal to the Ladies*, a programme for a Church of England community of celibate women – a convent, no less. Mansplaining gentlemen, Whig and Tory alike, were scathing: the journalist Daniel Defoe sneered that 'nothing but the height of bigotry can keep up a nunnery: women are extravagantly desirous of going to heaven, and will punish their pretty bodies to get thither.' Others, including some thoughtful men, sympathized with Astell's perception that the celibate life of a convent was not confining, but liberating.[127]

A welter of different circumstances was converging on a single phenomenon, that of female religiosity. It is worth noting one contemporary explanation of the high proportion of women in Massachusetts churches provided by the leading late seventeenth-century Massachusetts minister Cotton Mather: he felt that women had a greater moral seriousness than men because of their constant consciousness of death in childbirth.[128] Right or not, Mather was expressing a radical turnaround in the ancient Christian stereotype of women as naturally more disordered than men and more open to Satan's temptations. Back in England, the Oxford don Richard Allestree anticipated Mather's remarks by observing in 1673 that, amid his devotional publishing (he was the anonymous author of the wildly successful *Whole Duty of Man*), he considered that women had hearkened to his message far more than men, and that 'the reputation of Religion is more kept up by women than men'. Like Astell a few decades later, Allestree regretted Protestantism's rejection of the 'angelical' state of celibacy – as a result some suspected that, behind the anonymity of his prolific works, a female author was concealed.[129]

By the seventeenth century, even Counter-Reformation clergy began to look past the misogynistic clichés of the past and notice that women were easier to teach than men – and might even shame men into behaving better.[130] As women appeared to show themselves more devout than their menfolk (and, gratifyingly to ministers and priests, often more appreciative of the clergy's toil), centuries of disparaging theological comments based on medical discussion of humours and a continuous spectrum of gender began to look less convincing. So, in quiet ways, a radical reconstruction of the relationship of the sexes was unfolding, although in the process it opened up a more precise divide between male and female identity.

The joint story of Reformation and Counter-Reformation embraces successful female subversions of patriarchy and discreet adaptations of public ideals to reality. It is a dialogue between theology and circumstance:

sometimes Christian theory transformed situations, while sometimes theologians found ways of dealing with and explaining situations in danger of escaping their control. At the end of it, around 1700, Western Christianity was becoming a worldwide religion in both its confessional forms, thanks to the expansion of colonial empires. It was discovering how disconcertingly different other long-successful societies might be throughout the world. Christianity was also about to find itself much less able to set agendas in matters of sexuality, gender and marriage.

PART FIVE

New Stories

15
Enlightenment and Choice (1700–1800)

The eighteenth century saw the beginning of a gradual but decisive split between sexual morality in Western society and what Churches had traditionally taught about sex. For the first time in a thousand years, Christian authorities lost control of the agenda in a series of unprecedented challenges, and have never regained it. The first of these challenges was a new balance between public and private at all levels of society. The seventeenth century witnessed a shift in Western values in dealing with what was defined as sexual misbehaviour: what would have routinely been seen as a threat to the whole community became a matter of private misdemeanour. The change was exemplified in Protestant England: in 1600, it would have been widely accepted that such matters as fornication and adultery should be punished publicly and exemplarily by corporal punishment. By 1700 that would have seemed unnecessary; and by 1800, any public punishment of such misdemeanours was almost inconceivable, particularly in urban settings, and instances of it provoked special comment.[1] Ducking-stools, village stocks and scolds' bridles became quaint objects of antiquarian interest by the nineteenth century. This was not for want of efforts to impose public discipline, but they were increasingly hampered by the diminishing power and scope of the legal structures that Western Christianity had put in place: Church courts and consistories in England and elsewhere in Protestant Europe, supplemented in Catholic lands by inquisitions.

All over Europe and beyond, ecclesiastical institutions of government and discipline (Catholic, Protestant and Orthodox) became less effective than they had been for centuries, yielding social control to increasingly powerful and well-funded secular administrations. In eighteenth-century Russia, the Church found itself under the thumb of the tsars, who from the reign of Peter I 'the Great' onwards deprived it of oversight from a patriarch and placed it under a system of royal government that was a more restrictive version of what some Lutheran princely states of the Holy Roman Empire had known for the previous two centuries.[2] In the Catholic world, monarchs brought pressure to bear on the Pope to suppress the most effective agent of independent Church power across the world, the Society of Jesus – a relentless campaign to eliminate one of the chief clerical challenges to temporal monarchy which culminated in the Society's papal suppression in 1773. It was ironic that the Society could only survive in parts of the world where papal authority did not cut any ice: the European territories of the Tsar (many newly acquired) and Protestant northern Europe and its offshoots in what was soon to be the United States of America.

When people formed organizations to campaign for public discipline in eighteenth-century Europe, that was itself a sign both that the official systems were losing their effectiveness and that there was no longer an agreed moral consensus about what social discipline should be. England's voluntary 'Societies for the Reformation of Manners' had a half-century of activism from the 1690s, including the recruitment of paid informers, but their own internal squabbles combined with widespread public hostility at their interference in what was now considered private life; their work withered away. In 1787 the British Parliament abolished the right of Church courts to prosecute pre-marital fornication. Simultaneously, advocates of moral discipline tried to make Parliament do what the Church no longer could, but many in the governing elite were not prepared to see new meddling in their lives when the old interference had atrophied: successive parliamentary bills against adultery foundered, albeit usually by small margins of votes, and efforts ceased after 1800.[3]

WHAT WAS ENLIGHTENMENT?

These momentous changes in Christendom played out against a background of equally profound change concerning consciousness of self and attitudes to traditional authority. By the 1780s, when the philosopher Immanuel Kant of Königsberg (the modern Kaliningrad) looked back over more than a century of this process to define the phenomenon of *Aufklärung*, 'Enlightenment', he was using a word already a cliché deployed in the many vernaculars of the European continent, rather than in its once universal language of Latin. Kant's famous essay answering the question 'What is Enlightenment?' encapsulates a central feature of the movement that seems radically opposed to the traditional Judaeo-Christian story of human decay and impotence after the Fall in Eden, particularly as formulated by Augustine of Hippo: 'Enlightenment is man's emergence from his self-incurred immaturity. Immaturity is the inability to use one's own understanding without the guidance of another.' Around that organizing thought circled the Enlightenment's emphases on happiness, reason and human passions: all familiar concepts in traditional religion, but now promoted into a new Trinity as a framework for secular society, past the preoccupations of Augustinian Latin Christianity.[4]

This might suggest Enlightenment as enemy to Christian life and belief or even religion as a whole; many among both the Enlightenment's proponents and its enemies have been anxious to see it in that light. Yet any examination of the varied sources of Enlightenment's intellectual energy will reveal how much it reflected eddies within Western Christianity itself, from Renaissance Christian humanism to Protestant rebellion against medieval Catholicism. To Christianity's original cross-cultural encounters with Graeco-Roman or Jewish literature, worldwide expansion of Western power added texts first from Islam and, in the eighteenth century, also from the great faiths of the Indian subcontinent and east Asia. As for 'reason', many roots of Enlightenment have little to do with what now seems rational: astrology, hermeticism, the newly constructed myths of Freemasonry, or the completely mythical organization of the Rosicrucians.[5]

Many strands within what is now called 'science' (and in that period 'natural philosophy') celebrated fresh currents of apocalyptic thought about the Last Days long-awaited by Christians: the end-time was now revealing new knowledge that was also lost ancient knowledge. That was what 'enlightenment' meant to Sir Isaac Newton, classic pioneer of a 'Scientific Revolution' who invested a large part of his intellectual powers in exploring the Book of Revelation.[6] The displacement of Graeco-Roman authority in scientific investigation left the Enlightenment world deliciously open to new discovery, which inevitably involved some embarrassing false starts. It is telling, for instance, that so many in Georgian England took seriously a bizarre hoax fostered in more than one sense by Mary Toft, a humble woman of Godalming in Surrey, who announced in 1726 that she had given birth to rabbits. In the fluid state of gynaecological knowledge even among Enlightenment doctors it was perfectly possible to argue, in a centuries-old fashion, that this was a case of maternal imagination producing an unusual but plausible result, and physicians of the Royal Household were among the experts hastening to examine Toft. Her imprisonment and conviction for fraud did not end her celebrity; controversy remained at her death nearly four decades later.[7]

It is no exaggeration to say that the early Enlightenment was an enterprise of serious-minded Christians and Jews troubled by the uses traditionally made of their sacred scriptures. In a multitude of personal choices, they assessed their heritage of belief for what could be remoulded and what was too toxic to save. Much inspiration came from experiencing religious persecution. At the forefront of Europe's religious refugees were Jews, Reformed Protestants and radical Anabaptist or anti-Trinitarian Christians, with a deep distrust of repressive dogmatism. Seeking personal and intellectual safety, many of them met in the northern Netherlands after it won independence from the Habsburgs over the half-century from the 1560s. The outcome of the Dutch Revolt had produced an unusual degree of religious untidiness and pluralism in the United Provinces; in the background was the fragrant memory of Erasmus of Rotterdam, who, in a Low Countries as yet undivided by Reformation and Counter-Reformation, had spoken much of spiritual religion and of tolerance, and had also discreetly questioned the way that Augustine of Hippo had shaped Western Christianity. Radical Christianity learned a great deal from Erasmus.[8]

In cosmopolitan and commercial Amsterdam, émigré Jewish communities from mass expulsions in Iberia prospered alongside a spectrum of Christians who were also refugees from less-hospitable territories, ranging from the Catholic southern Netherlands to regions of eastern Europe where Catholicism had reasserted its control. After 1685 the Reformed Protestant element was much reinforced when Louis XIV of France betrayed his grandfather's promises to tolerate his Protestant subjects ('Huguenots') and expelled them all after half a century of increasing harassment. The Netherlands also enjoyed ancient trading links with England, where the Stuart dynasty's attempt at creating an episcopal Protestant religious monopoly in its three Atlantic kingdoms collapsed into war in the 1640s and never recovered. That encouraged a conversation of doubt and religious radicalism spanning the North Sea.[9]

In this pluralist setting emerged some creatively disruptive views of biblical authority that interconnected and have never died away in the Judaeo-Christian tradition: the Jewish radicalism of Baruch Spinoza, the grimly physical rationalism of the English philosopher Thomas Hobbes, and a variety of biblical scepticism among early English Quakers who have only recently been given the recognition that they deserve. The distinctive witness of the Friends was to encounter divine authority in experiencing the light of the Spirit within them, rather than from the Word of God in Scripture. Quakers were inclined to demonstrate this by denigrating biblical authority. Protestants had already given a paradoxical prompt to this by their very attempt to stress the authority of *sola scriptura*, because they stressed the Bible's literal meaning as an historical text. In the process they had largely discarded more than a millennium of allegorical or poetic interpretation that had long unravelled or even celebrated the Bible's more baffling aspects.

Reading the Bible as history carried with it the problem that historical scrutiny of a sacred text is liable to reveal how similar to other texts it is in nature and construction. Martin Luther had tried to demarcate a Bible that was the revealed Word of God but was still set in the sort of historical time that humanist scholarship was defining. In doing so, he had narrowed the boundaries of the biblical texts by creating a category of Apocrypha, cordoned off from the Old Testament, though neither Jews nor the pre-Reformation Christian Church had made such a categorical distinction. Now Quakers noted the growing rediscovery of manuscripts containing new Jewish and Christian apocrypha, much of which reads remarkably like the Bible. The gifted Hebrew scholar and Quaker Samuel Fisher became familiar with the Amsterdam synagogues while trying to convert Dutch Jews; he may have used the young Spinoza to translate Quaker tracts into Hebrew. He correctly pointed out in 1660 that Paul's Epistle to the Laodiceans (which Paul or his ventriloquist in the Epistle to the Colossians had demanded be read in community worship, and so should be considered canonical) had gone missing altogether from the Bible – though it did exist in a text extant but not acknowledged by official Christianity. Fisher also drew attention to Jesus Christ's supposed correspondence with the historically elusive King Abgar of Edessa – why were such texts outside the Bible, when a trivial letter of Paul's to Philemon was inside?[10]

Fisher was not alone in his questioning, which spread far beyond the Friends through the eighteenth and nineteenth centuries and has become a major academic discipline, first in Protestantism, but then also in the last hundred years within Roman Catholicism. Now it also begins to affect the Churches of Orthodoxy as they enter dialogue with Western society. This enterprise of treating the Bible with all the skills of critical textual scholarship, which this book tries to honour, is one of the chief intellectual and devotional gifts of Western Christianity to the wider Church. It is in itself part of the Enlightenment's wider gift to humanity: a commitment to treating one's own culture with the same critical curiosity and detachment that most societies have found easier to exercise in scrutinizing other cultures. The heirs of the Enlightenment have often observed such relativism more in the breach than the observance, but it is still an ideal to which to aspire.

THE CHANCE TO CHOOSE: SEXUALITY IN SOCIETY

The Enlightenment era saw more than a transformation in attitudes to authority. It bore a complex but inescapable relationship to social and economic changes first apparent in two allied regions of Europe – once more, the Netherlands and England. In the 1690s these Protestant and pluralist polities were linked under a common monarch who had been *Stadhouder* in the Netherlands, and who after the 'Glorious Revolution' of 1688 also held the thrones of England, Scotland and Ireland, styled as William III, jointly with his Stuart wife Mary II. Quite suddenly in that same decade, in the cities of Amsterdam and London, Europeans began remodelling Christian assumptions about sexual morality. So, when moralizing alarmists blame the permissive society for modern Western attitudes to sexuality and gender, they should look to the permissive 1690s, not the 1960s.

Behind this revolution lay a large-scale extension of life-choices in society that no one had planned or theorized about. In seventeenth-century Europe, only England and the Netherlands achieved the ability to feed all their own people and more.[11] Their farming had become so efficient that no longer did these regions face starvation in a bad year; they had escaped subsistence agriculture and banished famine. When there was food to spare, that released money for other commodities, right across society: England and the Netherlands also became Europe's most advanced economies in manufacture and trade, their towns and cities expanding accordingly. Even quite poor people could enjoy the sensation of being able to buy more goods than they strictly needed: they experienced consumer choice, the English word 'consumption' itself taking on a meaning both economic and positive in this period.[12]

Such leisure, spare money and the nature of consumer durables on offer might seem trivial by modern standards of prosperity, but previously these commodities had been restricted to a tiny, privileged elite. Now choice was becoming democratized in society, long before democracy customarily extended into politics. Elites were not generally pleased by the implications of this popular phenomenon beyond their control, but they were among those making money from it, and the eighteenth century saw it spread across Europe, penetrating beyond urban centres of commerce into the countryside. A consumer culture was not merely a matter of a new ability to purchase goods beyond the minimum for survival: it awakened a wider psychological awareness of making choices, ultimately about one's own personal identity. Like consumption of goods, that choice had been a luxury in previous ages, reserved for the likes of monarchs and aristocrats. Now a much wider social range of individuals began to decide how to live and who they wanted to be, rather than accepting the role that their Prince or their Church told them they must take.[13]

Half the human race might indeed choose to draw their own conclusions about their place in society: that is, women might consider whether the patriarchy of traditional societies was justified in restricting their life-choices. Over the next three centuries, that produced successive waves of what is now called 'feminism'. The roots of feminism are unmistakably pre-Enlightenment, firmly planted as we have seen in female self-assertions independent of male initiative in both Reformation and Counter-Reformation, from Ursulines to women prophets to the perceptible skewing of religiosity towards women during the seventeenth century. Much of it continued to be expressed in religious change during the age of Enlightenment, as will become apparent; little of it owed anything to the male-centred construction of the world in Enlightenment thought. Articulate and self-confident women echoed what Mary Astell had said at the end of the seventeenth century. The English philosopher Mary Wollstonecraft in her *Vindication of the Rights of Woman* (1792) acerbically nailed the shortcomings of male *philosophes*: 'Who made man the exclusive judge, if woman partake with him of the gift of reason?'[14]

What the Enlightenment did do was shift medical theory on gender boundaries, based on the advance of natural philosophy at the expense of Graeco-Roman medicine. Classical doctors had evolved a rich variety of views on the nature of human bodies, debating whether one could see men and women as mirror images in the constitution of their sexual organs, against the background of even more widely ranging discussion about how 'humours' constituted human nature (above, Chapter 3). The debate was complicated in Renaissance Europe by the wider range of ancient texts now available, which only demonstrated how divided the rhetoric was in Classical medicine on whether men and women were fundamentally different or expressions of a physical continuum in humanity. From around 1700, the system tilted towards difference: humanity was increasingly conceived in terms of rigidly divided opposites – maleness and femininity, assessed by differences in physical bodies. Concepts of sex and of gender drew more closely together, so that sexual differentiation was seen as differentially reflected in the functions of gender. This was of course theory, and primarily male theory; in everyday life, far less may have changed in the way that women ran their own lives when they could, or in the sorts of work that they undertook.[15]

Nevertheless, these gender stereotypes spread into the clichés that organized everyday society. As always, clichés represented ideas already present in popular thinking, but they were now rearranged. Women might always have been seen as pure and virtuous, as well as being sexually voracious and aggressive, but from the eighteenth century it was purity and high moral qualities that society viewed as the natural female state. Now men were viewed as more in need of curbing their aggression, both sexual and otherwise. One remarkable turnaround in English popular culture in the eighteenth century exemplifies this – the popular rituals of shaming socially disruptive married couples known as 'charivaris' or 'rough music', which were designed to enforce what people commonly considered natural or the norm in marriages. In earlier centuries, these were aimed primarily at wives who beat their husbands; now charivaris targeted husbands who beat their wives.[16]

The most surprising symptom of personal choice, unprecedented in any society where Christian Churches had been in charge, was the open emergence of one particular minority variant of sexual behaviour. It was now possible to observe the formation of structured sexual partnerships between people of the same sex in an effort consciously to express who they perceived themselves to be, defying extreme public disapproval of the choice that they had made. Especially notable is that such partnerships were commonly characterized by emotional or generational equality. They were exhibiting a lifestyle that has endured to the present day and can be given that label of the nineteenth century of 'homosexuality' or gay identity without complication. It represented a coherent self-recognition, rather than the miscellaneous collection of deviant acts that Western Christianity labelled sodomy. That was soon reflected in official punitive reaction: homosexuality was increasingly prosecuted not just as behaviour but as an identity. It was also conceptualized as such by doctors, but, contrary to the assertions of some modern historians, doctors did not invent the identity, merely putting their own (generally negative) description on an existing psychological reality to make it a pathology. None of the negativities stopped individual human beings deciding to be who they thought they were.[17]

It will be no surprise that this modern form of homosexual identity first gained a public profile in the Netherlands and England; in previous centuries it had been in northern Europe rather than the Mediterranean that a similar formation was most noticeable. We have already glimpsed the distinctiveness of northern European same-sex relationships back in the fifteenth century, and what happened from the 1690s represents a continuum with that.[18] The possible outcome of lifelong homosexual companionship is similar to the ideal of companionate marriage that had emerged in the West in the Gregorian revolution and had endured in modified form in Protestantism. It obviously differs from the age-unequal and life-cycle-dependent pairings which were the basis of acceptable male same-sex relationships in the Graeco-Roman world, and which remained a persistent feature of Mediterranean society, both Christian and Muslim.

Is it coincidental that the same region of northern Europe also showed a different general family structure to that of the Mediterranean? Geographical distribution of European family types is not absolute or rigid, but there are clear historical dominances. In eastern and in Mediterranean Europe, together with the Celtic far west of the Atlantic Isles (Ireland and western Scotland), the dominant type was that of multi-generational households which included extended patterns of kinship. By contrast, north-western European society – Scandinavia, the Holy Roman Empire and the Netherlands, northern France, England and English-speaking Scotland – was (and is) dominated by the nuclear family model: households of two generations only, parents and children. This basic pattern of continuity seems unaffected by the divisions of the Reformation, and Europe's eventual religious formations straddled the divide.[19]

Homosexuality's connections with family structures remain to be explored, but it is surely significant that when Mediterranean family formations were not found in northern Europe, neither was the distinctive pattern of life-cycle same-sex relationships that was part of them. The era of choice brought a new continuous visibility for homosexuality, both male and female. Around 1700, Amsterdam and London witnessed amid their burgeoning public cultures of sociability and piety the emergence of a modern gay sub-culture that has never since been successfully suppressed: clubs and pubs, a distinctive argot and shared jokes shaping a semi-public lifestyle shot through with parody and irony – often with reference to its Christian matrix, for instance in ceremonies of marriage, veering between parody and serious statement. In turn this provoked periodic purges and moral panics targeted specifically on homosexual males. Such panics had not previously featured in early modern London or Amsterdam because there had been no such visible social phenomena to panic about; so what is now called 'homophobia', an unlovely verbal coinage for an unlovely fearful hatred, emerged almost as soon as what is now called homosexuality.[20]

The boundaries and possibilities of deciding a homosexual identity were still determined by the Enlightenment's evolving ideas about gender in society at large. When male and female identities drew increasingly further apart, it has been suggested the homosexual man in such environments commonly took on what amounted to a third sexual identity: a man who expressed exclusive attraction to other men, but who represented this 'unmasculine' preference by acting in a highly feminized way – like the *kinaidos* of the Graeco-Roman world (Chapter 3). Symmetrically in this scheme, a fourth sex would be the 'mannish' lesbian – a descriptive word invented during the eighteenth century, and so predating the word 'homosexual' by about a century. The idea has a tempting symmetry, but few actual people will have defined themselves in this way amid the multiple confusions resulting from the breakdown of Classical medical theories on humours in gender identity.[21]

There is nevertheless no doubt that 'effeminacy' also completely reversed its meaning as a description; previously, Catholics had mocked Tudor Protestant bishops as 'effeminate' for their excessive interest in women, rather as John Chrysostom had mocked male partners in chaste heterosexual relationships. A century after the Reformation, the same mockery was applied for the same reason to England's Charles II, that most ebulliently heterosexual of monarchs, so the subsequent switch in meanings after 1700 was very sudden. The new eighteenth-century stereotype of the theatrically effeminate homosexual has had a long life; it remains a source both of mockery and of proud gay self-assertion in masculinized heterosexual cultures.

As gender roles hardened into new forms, eighteenth-century society found an additional new fascination in those who deliberately transgressed them: principally females who decided to take advantage of the greater life-opportunities offered to men, and to present themselves as males. One can point to previous individual examples in medieval and early modern Europe. As we have seen (above, Chapter 8), early Christianity had developed a hagiography around the idea. It was revived and extended in the medieval West with the bizarre legend and devotional iconography of St Wilgefortis (Uncumber), who had grown a beard in order to escape the threat of a non-Christian marriage and as a punishment had been crucified (see Plate 28). She/they developed a cult among unhappy wives, and, despite official unsainting by Rome in 1969, Wilgefortis has attracted a new constituency of non-binary interest today.[22]

The eighteenth-century literature on trans issues played more towards titillation or entertainment, alongside the sudden growth in printed pornography from 1700. Male sexual fantasy interacted with the widespread reality of women adopting male guise to work in labour-heavy trades or even to enlist in the growing armies marshalled by European powers. An appreciable number of real marriages can be traced in which one partner was a woman presenting as a man. Equally complex was the public reaction to all this, ranging from punishment in court to a good deal of popular collusion and sympathy, with sensational journalism in a middle position (see Plate 29).[23]

These sexual transformations certainly accompanied the transformations of European mentality that constituted the Enlightenment, but the largely male spokesmen of the movement contributed little to them, even when they were personally bitterly opposed to the oppressiveness of traditional Christian institutions (particularly the case with French *philosophes*). The Enlightenment's fearless tearing-down of old tyrannies tended to come to a screeching halt when confronted with same-sex relations. *Philosophes* were as embarrassed as their Reformation precursors by the acceptance of such activity by admired Classical authors, and their suggestions for modifying existing treatment of same-sex activity usually extended no further than reducing it from a criminal offence meriting death into something marginalized by social disapproval. Among the major Enlightenment voices, only the English rationalist Jeremy Bentham properly applied Enlightenment principles of happiness, rationality and passion to the question, and 'sat down cool' to make the acerbic observation with which I opened this book. It has to be admitted that, in life, Bentham did not extend his thoughts into publication.[24]

Equally difficult for Enlightenment writers was the universal and ancient human activity of masturbation. It is intriguing that masturbation should suddenly seem a huge and threatening problem in eighteenth-century Europe. It had not been a particular concern for Graeco-Roman medicine or society generally; we have noted Diogenes the Cynic deploying it as a mild form of social satire (above, Chapter 7). Traditional Christian condemnation of masturbation was generally part of wider preoccupations about monastic discipline, and even Peter Damian did not let it distract him overmuch from his more energetic diatribes on sexual deviations. That remained the general pattern, for Protestant theologians as much as for Thomas Aquinas: any exceptional emphasis on masturbation suggests personal furies or insecurities in particular Christian commentators. Orthodox penitential practice was similarly low-key. Most Orthodox discussion was in relation to clergy misbehaviour, particularly in imposing different scales of penance on those clergy who properly understood that what they were doing was sinful. Now the laity of Christendom were going to have to experience a more general neurosis.[25]

A significant feature of the masturbation panic is that it began in the same places and at much the same time as the public emergence of homosexuality and the furious reaction to that phenomenon. In a similar fashion, it united Church and Enlightenment society in outrage, together with a third, distinctly less horrified, constituency in pornographic publication. First, in 1676, the Church of England was represented by *Letters of Advice from Two Reverend Divines, to a Young Gentleman*, published in London. In 1698, Hadriaan Beverland, a rackety Dutchman with an Oxford education, published a Latin tract that spent thirty pages denouncing masturbation. Three years later a vernacular work appeared in England from the prolific pen of Josiah Woodward, clergyman of the established Church and one of the leaders of the Societies for the Reformation of Manners: *A Rebuke to the Sin of Uncleanness*. This gained a popularity Beverland had failed to achieve, running to five more editions. Woodward followed it up with two further treatments of the theme, one of them in the much republished though incautiously titled *The Seaman's Monitor* (1705).[26] Woodward's efforts laid the ground for the publication in 1716 of *Onania; or, The Heinous Sin of Self-Pollution*. Its author, still not conclusively identified, published it anonymously to give it greater authority, with startling success: it ran to sixty English editions in ninety years and pursued a career in other languages.[27]

Onania borrowed most of its arguments from previous authors but nevertheless gathered together some of the stereotypes of the next quarter-millennium of pointless paranoia, going beyond Woodward in turning the spotlight on female as well as male self-abuse. It artfully linked spurious medical concerns to Christian morality and biblical citation, via the sin of Onan described in Genesis 38.8–10. Rather like the sin of Sodom, Onan's misdemeanour was not as exact a fit to later circumstances as moralists claimed – particularly since it had no clear relevance to women. Despite its popularity, *Onania* was outclassed by the international authority of the similarly titled work *L'Onanisme* (1760), respectably emerging in French from a Latin original of 1759 and bearing the authorial prestige of the leading Swiss Protestant physician Samuel Tissot, though in fact Tissot only improved on *Onania* by creating a text that read more like a work of Enlightenment medicine. Among translations into perhaps fourteen other languages, *L'Onanisme* was paid the compliment of drastically abridged English versions in John Wesley's prolific republication of books of advice and Christian literature for his expanding Methodist congregations.[28]

Amid all this continent-wide obsession with masturbation as a threat to human health and morals, it is startling to find the practice turned into a recreational group pursuit within men's clubs in eighteenth-century Protestant Scotland. A century and more previously, Scotland had pioneered the all-male societies of Freemasonry, rich in myth-making and carefully bounded masculine socializing. The 'Beggar's Benison' founded in Fife in 1732 with satellites in Edinburgh and Glasgow represents a bizarre turn in the Masonic ethos. These societies determinedly concentrated group efforts on enthusiastic and onanistic contemplation of females hired for the spectacle, compiling wearisomely innuendo-laden

To the ſerious READER.

I Never yet ſaw any thing wrote on this ſubject, which a modeſt Perſon could well bear to read. The well known Engliſh Treatiſe, entitled, Onania, is a moſt fulſome and ſhocking performance. And the French tract, lately tranſlated, is if poſſible, more immodeſt and fulſome ſtill. Some parts of it moſt of the London ſtreet-walkers, would be aſhamed to read aloud. So groſs, ſo indelicate, ſo more than beaſtly, is his manner of treating this moſt delicate ſubject!

What was uſeful in his treatiſe, you have in this Extract, and what was wanting in that, is here ſupplied: and how neceſſary is a tract of this Kind? For thouſands both of men and women groan under bodily diſorders, whereof this ſin is the cauſe; and they never ſuſpected it. Such are many, I had almoſt ſaid, moſt of the diſorders of the nervous kind. But till the Cauſe of them is removed, the Effect of it muſt remain. And thouſands *make ſhipwreck of the faith*, and are again weak and *faint in their mind*, from the very ſame cauſe, which is equally deſtructive to the ſoul and body. If this has been *your* caſe, ariſe, ſhake yourſelf from the duſt: the grace of God is ſufficient for you! Give not place to the devil a moment longer! From this inſtant, eſcape for your life! And *when thou art converted, ſtrengthen thy brethren!* Labour to help them in particular, who are ſtill in that fatal *ſnare of the devil*, ſtill *taken captive at his will.*

23. John Wesley, prefacing his pamphlet *Thoughts on the Sin of Onan* (1767), was an unctuous salesman in disparaging both *Onania* and Tissot's *L'Onanisme*, whose texts he had extensively plagiarized.

minute books and the like for their programmatically heterosexual though inescapably homosocial activities. Members of the Beggar's Benison included ministers of the Church of Scotland and at least one future bishop of the early Victorian Scottish Episcopal Church, David Low. It is astonishing that any archives or artefacts from these organizations survived the club's eventual disbanding on the eve of the Victorian era in 1836, but they have.[29]

The sudden male preoccupation with a primordial human habit in the eighteenth century is yet another symptom of the age of individual choice, for few pursuits are more shaped by individual decision than masturbation.

It must have been encouraged by the general development of greater privacy in the design of northern European housing, and the value on personal privacy that sprang out of that: many more sexual activities could now take place in private than would have been the case for earlier generations.[30] Society's inability to control masturbation unnerved the self-confident *philosophe* or the moralizing clergyman just as much as did the self-assertion of women or the public emergence of homosexuality. At the end of the century, the lifelong bachelor Immanuel Kant accompanied his exposition of Enlightenment with extended intemperate remarks about masturbation: he loaded 'self-abuse' with preconceptions shaped more by personal dread than by logic, condemning it as worse than self-murder, that is, suicide. It was the ultimate enemy of the mature government of the self that Kant proclaimed as Enlightenment. This was in the context of his affirmation that any sexual act is of itself automatically debasing: 'a stance almost religious in its dourness', in the splendid phrase of one modern commentator on the German Enlightenment and society.[31]

THE CHANCE TO CHOOSE: EVANGELICALISM

European Protestant religion meanwhile was striving against dourness in a series of religious movements emphasizing human passions as much as did the Enlightenment. These twin phenomena may seem unrelated, or even opposed, since the religious fervour of what came to be known as 'Evangelicalism' sprang out of the Augustinian theology of Martin Luther, who had reaffirmed Christian pessimism about humanity in sharp contrast to Kant's praise of humanity coming of age in the Enlightenment. Nevertheless, many religious leaders were in fact keenly interested in the scientific advances that accompanied Enlightenment thought, notably the founder of Methodism, John Wesley. Wesley's championing of a doctrine of 'Christian perfection' crafted out of Reformation Protestantism was an emphatic rejection of the conclusions that John Calvin had drawn from Augustine on salvation, putting Wesley bitterly at odds with fellow Evangelical leaders who self-consciously championed Calvin's predestinarianism.[32]

The new-found freedoms of choice encouraged people to choose, shape and even re-invent their religion, pouring new life into Churches of the Reformation just at the moment when Protestant powers were beginning to create overseas empires that spread the Word across the world. What is remarkable is the interconnection of the various movements, which all took their immediate and their long-term origins from Protestant Germany, still recovering in the long aftermath of its seventeenth-century trauma in the Thirty Years War (1618–48). As we have noted in Chapter 14, from the 1670s a movement that came to be known (at first abusively by its opponents) as 'Pietism' affected first the Lutheran and later the Reformed Protestant Churches, and it was appreciatively noted by the serious-minded in England. Pietism sought to bring a new individual and emotional commitment to enrich the parish systems inherited from the medieval Western Church and make up for much devotional variety that Protestants had lost in the Reformation.

Out of Pietism came the peculiar construction of an episcopally led 'Moravian Church' conjured up out of the remnants of the *Unitas Fratrum* ('Unity of Brothers'), an ecclesiastical shadow persisting from religious crises in the fifteenth-century kingdom of Bohemia. The Moravians' refounding and presiding Bishop was Count Nikolaus Ludwig von Zinzendorf, an eccentric and charismatic aristocrat who was closely acquainted with some of the chief movers of Pietist Lutheranism, but who took his own path beyond them. From 1722 von Zinzendorf gathered a motley array of the religiously dissatisfied or persecuted from central Europe, first on his own extensive estates in the rural southern borders of Saxony and then in further communities reminiscent of some of the radical groupings of the Reformation such as the Hutterites.

The Moravians were thus not a nationality but a newly crafted religious identity. They had an importance out of all proportion to their always relatively small numbers, because they were the first Protestant Church to commit itself to world mission with consistent passion. People who had already undergone one exile to join the Moravian family zestfully threw themselves into fresh overseas exiles to share the joy they experienced in their own reconstructed lives. Unlike the missionary outreach of Counter-Reformation religious Orders or Jesuits, they were primarily laypeople, often quite humble and uneducated folk, seeking to earn a living by their craft skills on missions that reached out to people equally disadvantaged.[33]

The Moravians spread their work to the Atlantic Isles, ruled after 1714 by the German Lutheran George I (also Elector of Hanover); they met with a warm reception, which included the unprecedented ecumenical gesture of formal recognition by the British Parliament in 1749.

There they became one of many influences on the brothers John and Charles Wesley. The Wesleys were priests of the Church of England; despite being sacramentalist 'High Churchmen' in theological outlook, they felt compelled to leave the security of church buildings in order to preach more widely (even in the open air) a 'religion of the heart'. It was styled 'Evangelical' because it preached a gospel message of sin acknowledged, repented and cancelled in reconciliation to God through Christ's sacrifice on the Cross. Evangelicalism took to itself and emphasized the universal application of the models of individual conversion provided by the stories of Paul of Tarsus and Augustine of Hippo: a profound alteration of personal identity in a new relationship with God.

Thousands of converts mushroomed beyond the existing religious structures of Britain, creating mass 'revivals' which the tidy mind of John Wesley sought to channel into an organization, fuelled by Charles Wesley's prolific and compelling output of hymns for crowds to learn and sing. The resulting structure did not call itself a Church but a 'Connexion', reflecting the Wesleys' embarrassed efforts to show loyalty to the Church of their birth. Increasingly, nevertheless, their Connexion did look like a Church, particularly when it crossed the Atlantic away from its parent Church of England. Its congregations took to themselves the name that had begun as a satirical nickname for the Wesleys and their pious friends at Oxford University, 'Methodists'. That had been an allusion to the 'methodical' nature of the daily life that the young Oxford men had shared, something that the Reformation had rendered problematic because of its 'popish' overtones. It illuminates one reason for Methodism's success: it was answering a sense in Protestantism that there was something missing, which thoughtful Protestants might have conceded was rather effectively supplied within Counter-Reformation Catholicism.

Not all Evangelical preachers followed the Wesleyan Methodist Connexion out of the established Church; they managed to bring their work of revival to various parishes where they had a foothold, creating a lasting Evangelical identity within the Church itself. In the anglophone colonies of north America, the same sense of revival and renewal moved across the various denominational Churches of the first settlers, which were finding it hard to cope with the rapid expansion of immigration and social change. The resulting 'Great Awakening' was a religion of enthusiasm suitable for the relentlessly enthusiastic European advance westward into the heartland of the continent. It spread through drama-filled 'revival' gatherings held outdoors in settings that as yet had no buildings big enough to contain the crowds; the pattern had been set a century earlier in Presbyterian Scotland and in colonial-style Scots Presbyterian settlements in Gaelic northern Ireland.[34]

It is worth setting out these interconnected developments in some detail because they have shaped worldwide Protestantism ever since, providing the context for Western Christianity's successive and current entanglements with sexuality. Evangelicalism is recognizably part of the same newly forming world of choice that produced such phenomena as the emergence of homosexual identity and the drive for personal privacy in society. Evangelical rhetoric makes a great deal of play with the idea of choice: a personal decision to turn to Christ and accept him as one's personal Saviour. To make a choice was powerfully to assert individual self: a life-changing source of comfort for those who had already experienced their lives changed by economic or political revolutions, losing touch with previous familiar settings and often feeling little sense of agency in the process. The European parish systems of medieval and Reformation religion, static and formed for the use of older economies and communities, were often effectively absent from newly industrializing societies. The mobile ministry of Evangelicals could provide a new model for being a Christian.

The effect might lead to public explosions of extreme emotion. There are famous accounts of the open-air preaching of John Wesley and others among the coalmines on the edge of the city of Bristol at Kingswood, an area effectively outside the medieval parish system of the city and its surrounds: whole families shrieked, wept and rolled on the ground in their sense of transformation, and their delight that someone – not just their Saviour, but the Revd John Wesley – cared about them. Such behaviour was liable to break out repeatedly in Methodist revivals throughout the century, provoking in the increasingly institutionalized Wesleyan leadership a mixture of alarm, embarrassment and delighted wonder at God's power.[35] Wesley's answer was to establish an annual 'Conference' of his Connexional preachers, meeting under his own direction in various cities and towns through the kingdom. Conference exercised tight central control on these preachers, whose ministry was purposefully itinerant, and who were encouraged to be celibate to make that easier – the whole organization was remarkably like a Protestant version of the Society of Jesus.[36]

The awful warning as to where uncontrolled emotional release might go was the crisis that hit the Moravians in the late 1740s in the middle of their transatlantic expansion.[37] This was the Moravian 'Sifting Time' – an uninformative label hiding a very considerable trauma that the Church in its denominational history long sought to obscure. Moravian community life and worship were centred on joyful celebration; equally important was their free use of medieval mystical themes that re-emerged in Lutheranism during the seventeenth century, despite the fact that Luther himself had largely rejected them. Moravian concentration on the wounds of Christ produced a great deal of cringe-making reference to his 'side-hole', pierced on the cross by the Roman soldier's spear, but it was a different New Testament theme, the bridal union of Christ and his Church, that fatally excited the rapidly rising emotional temperature.

Many activists in the *Unitas Fratrum* were very young to be placed in positions of leadership. Among them was Count von Zinzendorf's son Christian Renatus, just out of his teens when made a presbyter in the Church, together with von Zinzendorf's son-in-law Johannes von Watteville, regarded by many as the major actor in the disaster. Not for the first time in Christian history, many believers framed their perception of Christ's forgiveness of sins as an absolute gift that included sins still to be committed – an 'antinomianism' (freedom from moral law) which was a dangerously logical extension of Martin Luther's rejection of good works in salvation. They experienced union with Christ not merely through the joys of marriage, but in extramarital sex as well – their stripping-away of gender in mystical joy further extended to same-sex kisses and embraces. Young people plunged with delight into this proof of their freely given salvation.

This was a repeat of the mystical promiscuity of Swiss radicals in the 1520s, and it has not proved the last time that new groups of Christians have improvised ethical codes encouraged by leaders with more charisma than self-discipline, threatening institutional and personal collapse. In this case, von Zinzendorf himself belatedly perceived where his own enthusiasms had led his movement. In 1749 those who could be identified as motivators in holy promiscuity were swiftly sidelined, including young Christian Renatus and von Watteville. Moravian hymns were purged of language from the Sifting Time; all talk of bridal mysticism ended, and the side-hole of Christ ceased to be a subject of mawkishly pious reflection. The Passion and wounds of Christ did remain at the heart of Moravian devotion, however; after all, these were themes that might equally resonate in Methodist, Pietist or Catholic Counter-Reformation religious practice. Moravians carefully reinvented themselves as relatively low-temperature Protestants, and negotiated a tactfully communal form of new leadership that managed not to appear ungrateful to their aristocratic founder while setting aside a good deal of what was new and distinctive in what he had set up.

The most striking proof of the centrality of choice in Evangelical Protestantism was the way in which it took root amid those who might have been thought the least likely to believe its message of freely given love: millions of Africans forcibly seized from their homeland and transported by Europeans across the Atlantic to work as slaves for the benefit of international, white-led economies. Conditions were at their worst in the sugar production of the British West Indies, whose plantation economy, based on fragile white control of a large and bitterly resentful enslaved African population, was only sustainable by brutal arbitrary punishment, including humiliating forced nakedness while working, and casual rape. Sexual brutality towards Africans became a means for European Christians systematically to dehumanize them.[38]

Eventually the grotesque mismatch of this system with Evangelical aims to transform the everyday lives of Christians became too obvious to ignore. Morgan Godwyn, a Church of England priest who had worked in plantation societies in Virginia and Barbados, precociously set out an attempt to square the circle as early as a pamphlet of 1680: he argued that conversion and education in English would encourage enslaved Africans or indigenous people to obey their masters 'in their present state [of slavery]', as it allegedly did among the 'papists' in the Iberian empires; not to do so would be 'a manifest apostasy from the Christian faith'. His last known work goes further: his sermon preached in Westminster Abbey around 1685 (and repeated thereafter elsewhere) shows a man getting increasingly furious at the moral disaster into which the slave trade was leading his country.[39]

Nevertheless it was not Church of England but Moravian missionaries who first made much effort to convert enslaved peoples to Christianity in the British West Indies and America. Moravians avoided hostility from slave-owners by resolutely avoiding politics, which meant a careful official silence about growing calls in Britain itself for the abolition of the slave trade and of slavery itself (below, Chapter 17). Yet regardless of what they thought about slavery Evangelicals could hardly long postpone bringing Christianity to the enslaved, hungry as they were for souls to save. That meant offering a choice to turn to Christ to people who had been deprived of any vestige of choice in their lives: it was an enticing incentive.[40]

Once the principle had been established that enslaved human beings were entitled to be baptized and to worship as Christians, despite objections from many plantation-owners, Christian marriage must follow: Morgan Godwyn had already pointed that out in his first pamphlet of 1680 in the course of his general argument for recognizing the humanity of enslaved people. Church weddings had been legal for slaves in canon law for centuries, though the British Parliament in Lord Hardwicke's landmark Marriage Act of 1753 nervously tried to restrict those rights. Yet, even when enslaved people were allowed to marry, social, political and ethical Christian codes clashed, and Churches might fight shy of resolving the dilemma. North Carolina Baptists confronted with such a case in 1790 faint-heartedly (or compassionately) resolved that 'it shall not break fellowship with us if Sam should git another wife', Sam's master having removed the first wife and forcibly married her elsewhere. Another Baptist Church in Virginia could not decide whether such masters should be censured: a question 'thought by a majority to be so difficult, that no answer could be given it'.[41]

There was a deep illogicality as well as an irony here: the transatlantic slave trade broke up polygamous bonds among Africans, at best replaced them with monogamy in an enslaved context, and then frequently destroyed that. Christian logic did also mean that exceptional African men in America might move towards the only profession that white Christians could recognize for them: clerical ministry, first in separate Churches established beyond white prejudice, but then, tentatively, after the 1790s, within historic Church denominations as well. Evangelical choice thus did bear fruit for African American dignity and self-worth. Indeed, in their Sunday worship it afforded worshippers as well as ministers the chance to wear decent and carefully chosen clothes, to affirm the God-given human dignity that their masters had deliberately violated in the nakedness of slavery.[42]

The only alternative logically for those opposing such recognition was to deny that enslaved Africans were part of created humanity, which is what some American Evangelical defenders of slavery did. They creatively distorted an exegetical suggestion from the English Methodist biblical scholar (and fervent abolitionist) Adam Clarke in 1810 that the 'serpent' (*nachash*) of Genesis 3.1–4 who tempted Eve in the Garden of Eden was in fact 'a creature of the ape or ouran-outan kind'. The *Nachash* then became a 'Negro' in the hands of American commentators. Hence Satan's part in the Fall of humanity justified enslaving African Americans for all time, as well as identifying them with the image of the Great Seducer: source of much subsequent white paranoia and brutality. The consequent supposedly biblical 'theology' became a useful prop for the Confederacy of the South in the American Civil War of 1861–5, and has not entirely disappeared in American racist circles even now; it provides a warning about the irresponsible use of biblical exegesis.[43]

The Evangelical Revival and Great Awakening brought another form of potential liberation: for women. They allowed women new opportunities of self-expression and achievement, as so often when new religious movements grow and improvise, but – equally characteristically – as new institutions settled down into masculine patterns those opportunities were curtailed. The Moravian 'Sifting Time' was an unsurprising example. Count von Zinzendorf had travelled down some surprisingly radical theological pathways: he rejected the Virgin Birth or any notion of Mary's Immaculate Conception, and emphasized the role of the Holy Spirit as Mother, picking up a Christian theme last prominent in third- or fourth-century Syria. He parted company with Reformation Protestantism and Augustine of Hippo sufficiently to reject the idea of original sin, including Eve's part in the Fall, which led him to allow women into the Moravian presbyterate. Much of this went missing when the Church was remodelled after the Sifting Time, the chief casualty predictably being female ordination.[44]

The Methodist movement shows the same general profile from opportunity to exclusion. John Wesley's own personal relationships with women were tumultuous, starting with the fiasco of his venture as a Church of England chaplain to the new British colony of Georgia in 1737, sent home in disgrace after he had irresponsibly mixed pastoral care with female emotional entanglements. In 1748 his brother Charles (fearing further scandal over a social mismatch) sabotaged John's plans to marry Grace Murray, a Methodist society housekeeper and John's companion on a preaching tour in Ireland. John's impulsive rebound-marriage to a well-off widow, Mary Vazeille, proved a bad mistake, and ended in separation.[45] He channelled later passions into several apparently chaste intense friendships with female followers; the positive aspect of his preoccupations was that he listened to women and sympathized with their wish for active roles in Methodist mission more than most of his male contemporaries.

The house journal Wesley founded for the Connexion in 1778, the *Arminian Magazine* (later *Methodist Magazine*), gave almost equal space to biographical or autobiographical writings from women as from men, and in 1782, with remarkable risk-taking, it published a quarter-century-old correspondence about one of the relationships that had caused Wesley's wife particular grief, Wesley defiantly commenting on the importance of the letters' spiritual content.[46] Wesley's capricious editorial control in the *Magazine* is symptomatic. Early Methodism was indeed 'a movement of women, who formed a clear majority of society members almost everywhere Methodism took root', but it remained publicly run by men.[47]

Wesley's emotional impulses held the key to the exceptions. He was not generally in favour of women becoming preachers but encouraged Methodist women to lead small bible-study and devotional groups ('classes') and spread the gospel in informal ways. Mrs Sarah Crosby, one of the younger female recipients of his passions (and, like him, separated from her spouse), regularly exchanged letters with him and won his cautious approval for a public preaching ministry, against his original High Church instincts. It likewise began against her inclinations. Normally she expected around thirty people in her classes, but, on 8 February 1761, she found that nearly two hundred had turned up. Wesley, whom she hastened to consult, was prepared to accept her testimony about a series of crowded meetings that 'My soul was much comforted in speaking to the people, as my Lord has removed all my scruples respecting the propriety of my acting thus publicly.' His personal authorization to her to preach expanded in 1771 to Conference allowing other women to preach. Sarah recorded in her diary that, in the twelve months to December 1777, she had ridden 960 miles, preached at 220 public meetings and held around 600 private meetings, and that she had written 116 letters of spiritual advice. She became one of the most famous Methodist preachers in Britain and was Wesley's colleague on some of his preaching tours.[48]

Immediately after the death of the great man in 1791, male prudence took over. At the *Methodist Magazine*, the publication of letters from women dried up and female autobiography was carefully edited to emphasize wifely dutifulness and esteem for male preachers. In 1803, the last year of Sarah Crosby's life, the Wesleyan Methodist Conference officially put a stop to women preaching in the Connexion. Many of the Methodist denominational offshoots established in frustration at the Wesleyan

Conference's general conservatism did re-establish the preaching of women, which proved a major attraction to new converts, but amid these rebel denominations of Methodism – Methodist New Connexion, Bible Christians, Primitive Methodists and many others – exactly the same pattern prevailed during the nineteenth century: steady exclusion of women from preaching or authority.[49]

In the background to this was the memory of things not easily discussed in pious circles: the mid-eighteenth-century crisis of world Evangelicalism that had included the Moravians' 'Sifting Time', John Wesley's marital misadventures and – in that same period 1748–50 – the still greater misadventure of the Welsh evangelist Howell Harris, a charismatic preacher much influenced by the Moravians. Harris fell deeply in adulterous love with a married woman, Mrs Sidney Griffith: she became his companion on his preaching tours and acquired prophetic powers, including the celestial intelligence that Divine Providence would soon free them of their respective spouses. Harris defiantly proclaimed that 'God is on my side, and all the opposition to me is against the Lord', but the opposition included John Wesley and Wesley's mesmeric Calvinist preaching counterpart George Whitefield. The Welshman found his ministry severely curtailed.

Evangelical embarrassments continued. In 1780, Christian advocacy of polygyny made one of its periodic historic appearances in a publication by Dr Martin Madan, an Evangelical whose prominent London ministry hovered between Methodism, Calvinist Evangelicalism and the Church of England. Madan's book sparked public horror, including an interestingly forward-looking critique from the leading Evangelical clergyman Thomas Haweis that the masculine privilege in Madan's advocacy of polygyny demeaned women. Even after Wesley's death, the Wesleyan Connexion had to cope with the public-relations disaster of the popular female itinerant preacher Jane Davison, who in 1794 was unmasked as a man when one of her/his young lady devotees became pregnant.[50]

Georgian satirists naturally had a field day with all this, and, in the manner of William Hogarth's bitingly grotesque satirical cartoon *Credulity, Superstition and Fanaticism*, created a collage of Evangelical irrationality and general sexual licence that was grossly exaggerated, but carried with it a powerful message that Evangelical revival betrayed everything that decorous Enlightenment Protestantism stood for. In the wider world around embattled Evangelicals, there were even more profound reasons to pull up the drawbridge against anything new. In the 1790s, a global crisis was unleashed in France, bringing fundamental

24. William Hogarth's print *Credulity, Superstition and Fanaticism* (1762) is often described as an attack on Methodism, but it satirizes all irrational religion; it is set in a parish church with three-decker pulpit, whose occupant is revealed as tonsured and so a secret Papist using the rhetoric of Protestant fanaticism. At the front of the besotted congregation Mary Toft, 'The Imposteress Rabbit Breeder', gives birth to her leporine brood.

and irreversible transformation to the institutions of Western Christendom. The trauma has made it easy for Christians over subsequent centuries to view those changes as a fundamental challenge to the whole Christian enterprise.

16

Revolution and Catholicism Rebuilt (1789–1914)

During the eighteenth century, the Enlightenment seemed the ally of princes and even of popes. The Society of Jesus until its dissolution in 1773 was at the centre of scientific discussion and curiosity about the natural world, just as was the Royal Society in Protestant London. As an 'Enlightened Despot' the Holy Roman Emperor Joseph II attempted large-scale dissolutions of monasteries in his dominions, but his thoroughly rational Enlightenment plans included redeploying confiscated assets for Catholic reform from a Religious Fund under his control, with such measures as endowing new parishes to meet modern needs. The Emperor was taken aback by the popular fury that he met, particularly in the Catholic Netherlands, where full-scale popular revolt broke out in 1789, derailing his schemes.[1]

Yet we do not remember 1789 for this triumphant defence of Catholic Christendom and monasticism in the Low Countries. The Revolution that sprang out of the bankruptcy of the French monarchy became seized by the rhetoric of the most anti-Christian version of Enlightenment in Europe, provoked by hatred of a Church that, despite considerable internal tensions, had seemed one of the most powerful and successful versions of Catholicism on the continent after its victory over French Protestantism in the seventeenth century: it was distinguished by its proud 'Gallican' independence of Rome under its 'Most Christian' kings. The last of them, Louis XVI, took his name like so many of his predecessors from that King Clovis who in the fifth century turned the Christianity of Francia away from a possible Arian future towards Catholicism (above, Chapter 11).[2] It was only to be expected that the destruction of the Bourbon monarchy and the religious system in which it was enmeshed radically altered European attitudes to sexuality and the family – though not always with the revolutionary effects that we might expect. This chapter explores the resulting complications.

THE FRENCH REVOLUTION: A BID TO CRUSH CHRISTENDOM

In view of events over the following two decades, it was ironic that the crumbling of royal power in 1789 was provoked by the French clergy's traditionalist insistence on recalling the States General, the kingdom's medieval representative body, to tackle France's financial crisis. As the remaking of the regime moved into a parliamentary monarchy, its inaugural Constituent Assembly pressured the King into accepting a complete reorganization of the French Church, including an extension to all faiths of a royal measure which in 1787, before the Revolution, had tentatively opened toleration for the Reformed Protestant Church. Monasteries were dissolved, Church wealth confiscated for the State, an oath of loyalty to the Civil Constitution required of all clergy. Soon it became apparent that the Pope was bitterly opposed to the measures; as provisions for a Constitutional Church unfolded during 1791, the Church became fatally divided as to whether to accept the new order, while the King was increasingly identified with conservatives opposing the very Church of which he was now nominal head. The Legislative Assembly's declaration of war on the Habsburg monarchy (the family of Queen Marie Antoinette) in 1792 turned division into a chasm. That September, the Paris prisons witnessed the mass murder of people arrested on suspicion of treachery; furious frenzy knows no tidy boundaries, but among those slaughtered were three anti-Constitutional bishops and over two hundred priests. It was the beginning of the Terror.

Amid all this, on 20 September 1792 the Legislative Assembly ended its work by enacting a new penal code, overturning centuries of Catholic shaping of the law in the cause of Enlightenment. It legalized divorce; marriage had already been declared once more to be a civil contract. It said nothing about sodomy, in a striking example of the principle gathering strength in eighteenth-century Europe that it was not the task of state legislation to interfere in private life. That legal silence on homosexuality remained characteristic of countries deriving their law from the changes in France, in comparison with the persistence of a much more punitive attitude in anglophone societies.[3] The context was that those now dominating the regime were abandoning even the Constitutional Church for a busily manufactured religion of

Reason, Law and Liberty, with liturgical ceremonies to match, even in Paris's Cathedral of Notre-Dame. Underlying it was the plan for a system of universal state education that would create an informed citizen body, overturning the patchwork of educational provision largely controlled by the old Church.[4]

The pace of events brought the elimination of the King, executed on 21 January 1793, systematic execution of those defined as enemies of the new Republic, and a savage war against regions of France itself that had risen to defend traditional Catholic faith. Amid the slaughter, in October 1794 a revolutionary calendar was decreed as a centrepiece of de-Christianizing the everyday life of France, eliminating every Christian festival (and even Sundays) by its determinedly decimal construction of weeks around ten months with new seasonal names. Clergy, whether for or against the Constitutional Church, were hunted down for imprisonment or exile, and the only reliable safe course for them was to marry. The Revolution showed itself vigorously enthusiastic for marriage generally, and to return the clergy to the married state represented a gleeful extra blow against the old Church. As in the sixteenth-century European Reformations, many French priests discovered a vocation for matrimony; exactly how many will never be certain. When something of the old Catholic framework returned a decade later, more than three thousand, including around a thousand monks and supplemented by nearly three hundred nuns, sought papal absolution; probably many more chose not to reveal what they had done in bewildering times.[5]

That turn away from de-Christianization in the first decade of the nineteenth century was the work of Napoleon Bonaparte, the most successful general to emerge from the Revolution. He extended its conquests but turned them to new ends to suit himself and consolidate power won both on the battlefield and in the fractious Republic. In 1799 he headed a *coup d'état* against the increasingly dysfunctional regime of the Directory and then thrust aside his fellow conspirators. Successive plebiscites, only partially rigged, gave overwhelming majorities to his assumption first of a Republican title of First Consul in 1802 and then, in 1804, Emperor of the French. Almost his first act on seizing power had been a symbolic step to reconciliation with the shattered Catholic Church: providing a decent funeral for Pope Pius VI, who had died exiled in France as a prisoner of the Revolution in 1799.

Napoleon's own religion was a collage of random pieties and Enlightenment clichés, but, in any case, it took second place to his sense of political realities. It happened that most of the Revolution's most lasting conquests were in the Catholic parts of the continent, especially the Catholic Low Countries, southern Germany and Italy. Napoleon realized what could be gained from ending internal warfare in France against Catholic traditionalism, and how much lost if the Republic persisted in anti-Catholic brutality elsewhere in Europe. There was an all-embracing deal to be done, not with the troubled Constitutional Church of France but with a new Pope – Pius VII – a serious-minded Benedictine monk-bishop reputed to have Enlightenment sympathies, though also cousin to the late Pius VI. Very soon after Pius's election in Venice in 1800, Napoleon, fresh from an unexpectedly shattering victory over the Austrian Habsburgs at Marengo in northern Italy, declared that he intended 'that the Roman Catholic and Christian religion be preserved in its entirety, that it be exercised publicly . . .'.[6] It was a bold move that risked alienating the strong anti-clericalism in his army while failing to impress conservatives with bitter recent memories of the Revolution, but Napoleon persisted, his goal a new version of the Concordat agreed back in 1516 between Pope Leo X and the French monarchy.

The Concordat signed after protracted negotiations in 1802 solved the problem of France's rival Churches by demanding resignations from all existing bishops and reordering the diocesan structure. In place of the old Church's now dispersed wealth, the State would pay clergy salaries, guarantee public worship and recognize Catholicism as France's leading faith. The Pope gained new power in the Church, but so did its bishops, senior clergy toughened by their experience of leadership during some of the most testing conditions in the Church's history. The effectiveness of the bishops was in marked contrast with the general quality of parish clergy, decimated and demoralized by the Revolution and, for the time being, inadequate in numbers and resources for training. The protracted process of new recruitment tended to focus on rural areas that had fought to save Catholicism, anticipating phenomena that have remained noticeable in the West over the last two centuries: a contrast between religious practice in city and country, an identification of the Church with rural conservatism and, in a Catholic context, parish priests with an increasingly fierce loyalty to the Pope, who might protect lower clergy against arbitrary episcopal authority.[7]

The nature of Napoleon's deal with Pius VII meant that Gallicanism in the French Church was obsolete. Just at the moment that might have seemed the nadir of papal power and prestige, the Concordat set a pattern of reasserting central papal control that has persisted in the Roman Catholic Church to the present day. A further consequence of Napoleon's conquests in central and northern Europe was the formal dissolution of the Holy Roman Empire in 1806, but three years earlier he had also ended the mixed temporal and spiritual rule of the various imperial prince-bishops and other clerical territorial rulers. Now the chief alternative sources of authority to the Pope within the Western Latin Church had all been eliminated. The Catholic impulse to centralize the Church on the Papacy had long borne the name of 'ultramontanism', deriving its image of being 'beyond the mountains' from the perspective of people in northern Europe, caught up in medieval papal conflicts with the Holy Roman Empire. Besides the opposing French Gallicans, those hostile to Roman centralization had been known as 'Cisalpines' ('from this side of the Alps'), but now the power of Gallicanism and Cisalpinism atrophied. Nineteenth-century ultramontanism was so old as to seem new: it revived the medieval ambitions of Gregory VII and Innocent III.

The Concordat set patterns widely repeated in Catholic Europe and beyond over the next century, far beyond Napoleon's immediate priorities or intentions. In effect, it created modern Catholicism, nesting uncomfortably but unignorably inside a European society whose political structures and wider social patterns also reflected the Enlightenment and Revolution, often in anti-clerical forms hostile to Church power. In France, in particular, national politics continued as late as the 1960s in patterns set by the Revolution and the Concordat, with political labels 'Right' and 'Left' (created by the layout of the French Legislative Assembly chamber during the Revolution) signifying primarily rightist clerical politics nostalgic for sacred monarchy, set against, on the Left, Republicanism with anti-clericalism as a defining ethos. The ideological fissure spread across the nation and, eventually, across the continent.

One of the lasting achievements of the Napoleonic era, besides its new deal with the Church, was launched soon after Napoleon first came to power and completed in 1804: a wholesale reconstruction of France's legal system. It was part of a wider enterprise that included a final goodbye to the Revolutionary calendar, reforms to education and the introduction of metric measurement. Appropriately for a newly minted Emperor, this 'Civil Code of the French', or *Code Napoléon*, derived its principles from Roman law. Like so much of Napoleonic government, it marked a decisive break with the multiple jurisdictions and legal structures of Western Christendom, while also curbing the radicalism of the French Revolution; it is significant that the restored French Bourbon monarchy of 1815 only felt the need to make relatively minor modifications to it. The Code had an effect on world legal systems even greater than the Concordat.

The whole tendency of the *Code Napoléon* was to draw far more tightly a masculine framework for law. Women lost rights that the Revolution had granted them, legal personhood in court actions and the control of their property. That reflected not simply the ever-growing Enlightenment tendency to define and separate male and female roles, but the appearance in the Revolutionary wars of a new social phenomenon: the citizen army. Armies before 1789 had been composed of hired mercenaries or subjects seized by arbitrary impressment: the Revolution was defended by male citizens of France, just like the earlier successful revolution of 1776–83 in the British Crown's North American thirteen colonies. Of the three components of the eleventh-century social trope, *oratores, bellatores, laboratores*, the Revolution removed not only the caste who pray, but the caste who fight, leaving simply a citizen people.

The medieval image of the knight, 'the Armed Man', was of an elite figure, symbolized by the medieval convention of portraying elite laymen on their tombs wearing armour. Now male honour was democratized, in a new blend of manliness and patriotism. This was perfectly expressed in the constitution agreed in 1804 for the newly independent Caribbean state of Haiti, formerly France's slave-economy colony of Saint-Domingue, which had fought for its independence with support from the French National Convention: a Haitian citizen was 'a good father, a good son, a good husband, and above all a good soldier'. Napoleon's legal code was constructed in the same fashion, including provision for dutiful wives to support their husbands and provide children for the next generation of soldiers. It was symptomatic that the right to vote, so characteristic of post-Revolutionary society, was reserved for males.[8]

This was not a social formation to which the Church was going to raise many objections. In many ways the Code's modification of the Revolution's social reforms met traditional priorities for married layfolk more than did Western canon law, with its inconvenient interest in Paul's statement of a mutual 'marital debt' in 1 Corinthians 7. In its return to Roman law, the *Code Napoléon* went further than the Church towards Graeco-Roman patriarchy, requiring parental consent to marriage for those under twenty-five and prohibiting legal actions on disputed paternity for children born in wedlock: such children were automatically to be presumed the child of the husband, while a child born out of wedlock was the child of nobody.[9] Yet the Catholic Church could only welcome new restrictions on divorce, which in 1792 had been made possible by mutual consent. The Code removed incompatibility as a ground for divorce, and in 1816 the Bourbon Restoration government prohibited divorce altogether; its return in 1884 was dependent on an assertively Republican and anti-clerical regime.[10]

AN ULTRAMONTANE CHURCH

It was symptomatic of the new ultramontanism in the Church that when Pius VII restored the Society of Jesus in 1814, the Society's gratitude to the renewed Papacy made it a bastion of conservative Vatican Catholicism. The sense of creative theological exploration, intellectual flexibility and discreetly independent initiative that had characterized the Society before its dissolution faded away, and only returned amid the wider changes of Catholicism in the 1960s. Nineteenth- and twentieth-century layfolk would experience this in the confessional, where the moral counsel and penances that clergy handed out to penitents were modelled on what was said in official manuals of penitential advice. The most influential was from a Jesuit source, the widely plagiarized manual of a nineteenth-century French moral theologian, Jean-Pierre Gury SJ. Following a steady development in penitential manuals over the previous century, Gury's work showed a particular rigidity and punitive precision in what it had to say about sexual pleasure, even in marriage. It does not raise the spirits to hear what one of Gury's Jesuit admirers said about his own discussion of moral theology, as he extended the genre of manuals from Latin into vernacular languages: manuals 'are not intended for edification, nor do they hold up a high ideal of Christian perfection for the imitation of the faithful. They deal with what is of obligation under pain of sin; they are books of moral pathology.'[11]

Just as in the Counter-Reformation, such tightening of personal discipline was dependent on lay willingness to accept it; that rested on the remarkable turnaround in papal fortunes and prestige. Just as important as the political transformations was a wholly unanticipated side-effect of Napoleon's boldest move of self-assertion; in 1804 he crowned himself as Emperor, having invited Pius VII to travel to Paris to participate in a carefully balanced pageant of medieval liturgy and imperial sovereignty based on the assent of the people. The Pope's journey north provoked extraordinary public excitement and reverence, not so surprising in Italy but in France far beyond expectations, even on the streets of the capital. Pius was revealed as an international popular celebrity, which was confirmed when, seven years later, relations with Napoleon broke down and he suffered arrest and exile like his predecessor. His tribulations, near-fatal illness in prison and then triumphant restoration to Rome as Napoleon's power collapsed only affirmed what the Paris coronation began in shaping the charisma of the modern Papacy.[12]

Alongside a revival of Catholicism in the parishes, the regime allowed a minimal restoration of male monastic life, but it considered that it had much less to fear from female religious Orders, particularly those that could take up the educational and charitable functions so prominent up to the Revolution. In fact, a remarkable number of new Orders were now founded for the same purposes, and Napoleon's regime had too much else to think about to do much to stop them. These Orders took advantage of a relaxation in the Church's rules on female religious from before the Revolution. In 1749, Pope Benedict XIV had arbitrated in a local row in Bavaria between the Bishop of Augsburg and a group of religious women in the diocese: as the 'Institute of the Blessed Virgin Mary', they were still obstinately carrying on the work of Mary Ward, the would-be founder of a female equivalent of the Society of Jesus a century before (above, Chapter 14). Rather surprisingly, the Pope ruled against the Bishop and allowed his opponents a continuing existence as an 'Institute': effectively he recognized them as more than just a group of pious laywomen. In the post-Revolutionary era, women gleefully seized on this breach in the Council of Trent's decree of female enclosure for their own purposes.[13]

The Concordat was not designed to give women a greater active share in the life of the Church, but the vacuum was there to be filled – and not merely by nuns. The nineteenth century witnessed a remarkable re-enchantment of the world that the Enlightenment had sought to govern by reason; this reflected priorities among devout laywomen. The French Revolution was not the first time that women had guarded Christian practice through difficult times through observances they cherished (above, Chapters 10 and 14). Women kept the Church going through the worst phases of Revolutionary de-Christianization; they sustained their faith through their loyalty to Catholic customs that pre-Revolutionary clergy had often despised but did not now have the power to discourage – the cult of saints and pilgrimages, for instance. Such practices had a rich future at the dawn of the nineteenth century.

In Catholic Europe after 1815, where secular political authority took its cue from the *Code Napoléon* and emphasized the superiority and agency of a man as *paterfamilias*, it proved to be the Church that gave more space for women to seize initiatives for themselves. In that frequent paradox of Western Christianity since the Reformation, as for instance in British Methodism, French Catholicism became an organization run by (clerical) men for the benefit of women. The institutional component of female Catholic life was led by a quite astonishing proliferation of convents and female Orders, a process heralded in pre-Revolutionary France but now spreading elsewhere, as both Enlightenment and Revolution cut a swathe through comfortably funded male monasteries.

Belgium, for instance, was a new country on the European map from 1830, forged in a national revolt based on Catholic resentment of the Protestant Dutch monarchy imposed on the former Habsburg Netherlands in the international peace settlement of Vienna in 1815. Belgium became a laboratory for the new shapes of European Catholicism. Between 1780 and 1860, the proportion of Belgian women religious to men reversed, from 40/60 to 60/40, and latterly, in a decided rebuff to what the Council of Trent had decreed, only 10 per cent of Belgian nuns were in contemplative Orders: the vast majority devoted themselves to working out in the world in teaching, health care and help for the poor.[14]

In nineteenth-century Ireland, as in Belgium, Catholicism became the prime vehicle of national identity against external rule, and statistics for nuns compared with clergy are equally striking. There were a mere 120 nuns in the whole island in 1800, but 8,000 in 1900 – nuns outnumbered priests and male religious in the Irish Church two to one, with the numbers still rising.[15] That growth had a worldwide effect because of the remarkable scale of Irish emigration across the anglophone world, especially to the United States and Australia. A persistent feature of Irish migration, unique amid the various streams of nineteenth-century European migrants overseas, was the high proportion of women participating; that helped to spread Irish patterns of convent life across the globe. In the rapidly growing Catholic population of the United States (of course not all Irish in origin), more than two hundred women's Orders were operating by the early twentieth century, and nuns then outnumbered priests four to one. A common feature of convent life in all these situations was a rhetoric of female subservience to male clerical authority combined with a sturdy independence of action in testing circumstances, often of dire social deprivation that demanded heroic initiative. One might call it a manifestation of Catholic feminism, though the rapid rise in numbers of nuns in relation to monks and other male clergy can be strikingly paralleled in the Orthodox Church in tsarist Russia in the same period.[16]

Nuns were at least under formal obedience to Church authorities, but the same conformity was not so easily demanded of laywomen, particularly the leading laywoman of them all, the Virgin Mary. Since the French Revolution, Our Lady has greatly increased the frequency of her visits to both Europe and other heartlands of Catholic faith such as Latin America, and she has generally made a point of singling out the powerless as recipients of her appearances: children and women without worldly resources or much education, characteristically amid crises of politics or rapid social transformation. The classic template came in Mary's three appearances to Catherine Labouré, a newly professed young nun of Paris in 1830, during the political turmoil that swept away the Bourbon monarchy in France in favour of the more liberal Orléanist Pretender Louis Philippe. Mary gave the nun the pattern for a medal to be struck showing her image trampling the snakes of original sin in the world (Plate 30). Within twelve years, a hundred million copies of the medal were providing powerful help to Catholics in personal or physical distress: more comfort than an Orléanist monarchy which many Catholics regarded as a distressing usurpation of the Bourbon monarchy and compromise with the French Revolution.[17]

The Church hierarchy was often less than enthusiastic about such female drama. When a visionary cult became too successful to ignore, like that of Bernadette Soubirous and other village women and girls around Lourdes in 1858, clergy put some effort into disciplining the often-folkloric narrative of the original events and downplaying the wilder elements.[18] Sometimes senior clergy showed themselves downright unsympathetic to such appearances, as at Marpingen in Germany in 1876, which the German bishops would probably have quashed as a devotion had they not been tangled in a separate contest with the Protestant government of the new German Empire for the rights and freedom of Catholicism (the *Kulturkampf*). That has often subsequently been the case, notably at Međugorje in what is now Bosnia-Herzegovina; after Mary's initial appearances to six children in 1981, supportive Franciscans clashed bitterly with the sceptical diocesan bishop, and tensions have not altogether subsided in nearly a half-century.[19]

Our Lady has not generally been shy of expressing opinions on current affairs, commonly expressing a negative view of regimes under which she and the Catholic faithful find themselves. Her appearances actually multiplied in the later twentieth century, correlating with declining church attendance in the West, and the coming of social norms that traditional-minded Catholics find difficult (below, Chapter 19). That means that her critique has usually borne a rightward political slant; yet she was equally critical of godless Nazism in some German appearances in the 1930s and 1940s. Some of her nineteenth-century manifestations had actually encouraged local insurrection against existing Catholic monarchies, such as that of the priest Miguel Hidalgo y Costilla against Spanish government in Mexico in 1810, and in various Catholic regions during the Europe-wide upheavals in 1848–9.[20]

By contrast, in one famous appearance in Ireland at Knock in 1879, Mary and her fellow visitants did remain completely silent. It was a wise decision in countryside torn with discontents, including tensions between Catholic laity and clergy, but which, crucially, was also experiencing a more profound linguistic contest between dying Irish Gaelic and the English then rapidly being adopted even in rural Catholic Ireland. One modern analyst acutely sees Mary in her worldwide appearances as playing the starring role of an 'alternative modernity'.[21] That captures an essential feature of post-Revolutionary Marian devotion: it was one of the first movements of popular Christianity to be able to take advantage of the rapid advance of transport and communications from the early nineteenth century to the present day, onwards from steam railways, cheap print and the electric telegraph. The Marian message could spread with unprecedented speed, and, as a result, individual visions have acquired a variety of international meanings, often far from the political and social context in which they originated.[22]

Around the medal envisioned by Catherine Labouré in 1830, and so successfully marketed over the next decades, was inscribed 'O Mary, *conceived without sin*, pray for us who turn to you for help', putting into words the symbolism of the snake of sin on which Mary trampled. That proposition, the Immaculate Conception of Mary, free from all stain of original sin, became a theme of many of the nineteenth-century Marian appearances, and the sense of a tide of the Spirit running through the faithful propelled Pope Pius IX into making a decision on the doctrine, after some seven hundred years of often heated disagreement. It had been first mooted by English monks in the springtide of Marian devotion in the twelfth century, but first Cistercians and then the Dominican Order of friars set their faces against its acceptance; Thomas Aquinas, a Dominican authority not to be ignored, maintained that it undermined the mission of her Son to save all sinful humanity. Franciscans contrariwise became the doctrine's greatest supporters; popes hedged their bets. Even the impulse to strengthen devotion to Mary against Protestant negativity in the Reformation had not been enough to overcome Dominican opposition to the doctrine and present a united Catholic front on the issue during the sixteenth century.[23]

There the case had rested, but the upsurge of Marian devotion of which Labouré was a centrepiece moved the theological goalposts. Pope Gregory XVI, an austere Camaldolese monk conservative in every way, hesitated; his successor Pius IX gave warm heed to the popular clamour. In 1854, in a fashion almost unprecedented, the Pope gave maximum publicity and papal authority to his definition of the Immaculate Conception. Protestants had their worst fears confirmed: Catholic doubts were stilled by a tragic atrocity in 1857, when Archbishop Sibour of Paris, despite his own personal reservations about the Immaculate Conception, suspended a priest who attacked the doctrine from the pulpit. In an unbalanced rage, the priest stabbed his Archbishop to death in a public procession.[24] Meanwhile, Our Lady more than once lent repeated authority to the doctrine. In her appearance at Lourdes in 1858, Soubirous heard her say 'I am the Immaculate Conception', which sounds syntactically illogical until one realizes that the child had probably frequently seen the phrase 'The Immaculate Conception' captioning Marian devotional cards and the like, and considered that her vision was simply introducing herself by name (see Plates 30 and 31). Our Lady of Marpingen gently corrected the misapprehension in German a decade later by announcing, grammatically, 'I am the Immaculately Conceived.'[25]

The belated triumph of the Immaculate Conception in 1854 was linked to another startling innovation in Catholic doctrine concerned with conception and pregnancy: an absolutist position on abortion, formally stated in the course of Pius IX's bull of 1869 entitled *Apostolicae sedis*, tidying up the Church's system of spiritual punishments. This took a stance which, so far, the Vatican has not modified, that abortions at any stage of pregnancy merit excommunication. The argument is dependent on asserting that the moment of conception represents the moment when an individual soul enters its body. Previously that had always been a minority position in the Church. The majority view was based on Graeco-Roman teaching on biology, backed up by selective biblical citation.

Galen and Aristotle agreed that a good rule of thumb was that the soul entered the body after forty days of pregnancy for a male child and eighty days for a female – a differentiation caused by the fact that the female sex was colder and moister, thus taking longer to take form in the womb. The Western Church took this up. Western Christians supplemented scientific authority with the consideration that it was not appropriate for ensoulment to accompany the original sin that was inevitably part of conception; Aquinas added his authority to this view that 'ensoulment' was not simultaneous with conception. Armed with such mitigations, the faithful were capable of coming up with some remarkable devotional by-products, such as one theme in early Irish hagiographical texts that some male saints were instrumental in securing miraculous abortions for pregnant nuns.[26]

The view that triumphed in Pius IX's bull of 1869 crucially dropped previous references to 'the ensouled foetus' in official pronouncements on abortion, and thus extended condemnation to all abortions. It could point to one or two biblical texts for justification, notably Psalm 51.5 and Job 3.3, and to some early theologians in support. They included Latin and Greek theological giants, Tertullian and Gregory of Nyssa; Martin Luther (who took a low view of Aristotle generally) could have been added to the roster, along with John Calvin, were it not for other considerations.[27] In general the convergence of moral rigour in Reformation and Counter-Reformation had encouraged absolutists on abortion, but the matter had remained controversial. In 1588, Pope Sixtus V made an unprecedented papal affirmation that ensoulment began at conception, in a bull on abortion which was part of his general campaign of harsher laws on sexual deviation. His successor Gregory XIV swiftly repealed its provisions, less than three years later.[28]

Why the radical shift in 1869? In the background was the general sidelining of Graeco-Roman medicine in the Enlightenment, but that still left a high level of ignorance about the biology of reproduction in early nineteenth-century medicine that was only gradually corrected, let alone providing guidance for the Church. The discovery of the female ovum was made in 1827, but it was only in the 1870s that the joint action in generation by the male spermatozoon and the ovum was convincingly demonstrated.[29] Rather, the main impulse was theological. It was based precisely on the doctrine of original sin that had previously made the Western Church hesitate about identifying ensoulment with conception. Now the doctrine of the Immaculate Conception, as defined in 1854, demanded that the uniqueness of Mary's conception should be the exception to an otherwise universal rule; that was precisely what Thomas Aquinas had denied. Subsequent rulings by the official Church only tightened up on medical exceptions to the ban on abortions, eventually even including ectopic pregnancies life-threatening to the mother. In the early twentieth century this stance was strengthened in reaction not merely to an opposite tendency to liberalization in Protestant thought, but to the legalization of abortion in Communist Russia, amid many other undeniable horrors. The Catholic insistence on the right to life, of which opposition to abortion was now a centrepiece, chimed with many emphases in Western liberalism when so much else in official Catholic teaching did not.[30]

The bull of 1869 and the proclamation of the Immaculate Conception in 1854 were parts of a greater pattern. Pius IX's personal popularity and more than three decades as Pope, the longest reign in Catholic history, combined in encouraging him to affirm more and more dogma that the Church had before left indeterminate. He needed to produce a coherent response to the legacy of the Revolution: not merely its destruction of ancient authority but its creation of government based on Enlightenment principles, paying at least lip-service to popular consent and choice. The Revolutionary idea of a nation became the chief motor of politics in nineteenth-century Europe, where often no comparable political unit, common culture or mass consciousness had previously existed. For many a 'liberal', nationalism became an emotional replacement for the Christian religion. It might imitate the French example, but many lands overrun by French Revolutionary or Napoleonic armies gained a full sense of national unity in outraged reaction. On that basis, Belgium, Italy and Germany all built up national identities during the nineteenth century, in the process also overturning what remained of ancient political structures. Their rhetoric of national resistance in turn provided a model for the twentieth-century struggles of non-European colonial peoples against the rule of those same nation-states.

Could a Catholic also be a liberal or a nationalist? In the first years of his papal reign, Pius had shown sympathy with some aspects of liberal changes and aspirations, but he was horrified by the continent-wide upheavals of 1848–9; among much else, a republic was declared in the Papacy's 1,110-year-old endowment of territories in central Italy, and the Pope had to flee Rome. He became more bitter still when the royal House of Savoy reinvented itself as a monarchy for all Italy and pursued its goal through military conquest, not least of those same Papal States. In his 'Syllabus of Errors' of 1864 the Pope compiled a ragbag of denunciations from recent papal statements which famously culminated in condemning the error that the Pope 'can and ought to reconcile himself with progress, liberalism and modern civilization'.[31]

The Syllabus made some sense in the context of Catholic southern Europe and Latin America amid continuing anti-clerical onslaughts on the Church; yet, for many conscientious French and German Catholics seeking reconciliation with liberal principles, it was disastrous. It made no sense in European Protestant countries (as for instance in Britain, which had politically emancipated Catholics in 1829) or in the United States, where the freedom of Roman Catholicism was dependent on liberal extension of freedoms regardless of religion. It also meant that the Papacy was not going to show much sympathy to the proliferating movements of socialism in Europe and America: socialism was an aggregation of explorations of how to turn the French Revolution's slogan of 'liberty, equality and fraternity' into a much more radical egalitarianism than liberalism generally offered.

Pius IX's ideological war on liberalism led him into some dubious moral decisions, one of which was his blanket hostility to that characteristic feature of post-Revolutionary Europe, the reintroduction of civil marriage. Protestant Britain, which was far from sharing the Revolutionary heritage, introduced civil marriage in England and Wales in 1836, to accommodate the significant proportion of its population who were not part of its established Churches: Nonconformist and Methodist Protestants, but also Roman Catholics, none of whom wished to sully their marriages with a ceremony in the parish church. Pius simply denounced civil marriage as adultery, raising a host of historical and practical questions, not least when the devoutly Catholic Habsburg Emperor instituted civil marriage in his dominions in 1868.[32]

Worst of all was the Pope's moral obtuseness about what in other circumstances he would have denounced as an attack on the family: the effective kidnap of a Jewish boy, Edgardo Mortara. In 1858, Mortara was born to Jewish parents in Bologna in the Papal States, a sickly baby: the teenage nurse summoned to the apparently dying child took it on herself to give him an emergency baptism as a Christian. Six years later the Roman Inquisition learned of the case and forcibly seized Edgardo from his parents, took him to Rome and gave him a Catholic education, which took him into the priesthood; he lived until 1940, loudly defending Pope Pius IX in the interest of converting Jews to Christianity. Mortara's abduction nevertheless caused outrage at the time on either side of the Atlantic: there were protests from devout and thoughtful Catholics as exalted as the French Emperor Napoleon III (nephew of the great Napoleon). The Pope was unmoved, and liberals noted his intransigence.[33]

The new mood in Rome included official rehabilitation of Thomas Aquinas as the guide theologian for Roman Catholicism after fluctuations in his posthumous fortunes and much neglect in Enlightenment Catholicism. In the Counter-Reformation, the Society of Jesus and Aquinas's own Dominican Order had both structured their teaching around his works, and now they set aside centuries of rivalry in jointly championing Thomism once more. As 'neo-Thomism', the teaching of Aquinas was given explicit backing by Pope Leo XIII in 1879. Thereafter, for nearly a century, it remained the vital force in Catholic theological training and reflection, despite the inconvenience of Aquinas's reflections on ensoulment in relation to the Immaculate Conception. Contrary intellectual exploration, including attempts to examine the history of the Church or to explore some of the complications of biblical textual history exposed by Protestant scholarship, faced rigorous repression and elimination from any Catholic educational institution. At the beginning of the twentieth century, Pope Pius X denounced all such research as 'Modernism', a term whose vagueness suggested a sinister foe like early Christian coinages such as 'encratism' or 'messalianism', conveniently applied to anyone whom the authorities did not like.[34]

This vigorous if selectively ultramontane affirmation of tradition had as its centrepiece the first Vatican Council of worldwide bishops in 1869–70. In characteristic post-Revolutionary papal style, it resolved matters that had remained previously too difficult for consensus, chiefly the decision (which the Council of Trent had avoided) to spell out the Pope's divine authority, as successor to Christ's commission of sacred power to the Apostle Peter. This decree, *Pastor Aeternus*, affirmed that in carefully defined circumstances, the Pope could make pronouncements on doctrine that were infallible and could not be altered (the first being the doctrine of the Immaculate Conception). The vote on *Pastor Aeternus*, from which agonized doubters absented themselves rather than oppose the Holy Father, took place in a city on the brink of being seized by the Italian army; French troops sent by the Emperor Napoleon III to guard the Pope's ancient possession of Rome from Italy had suddenly been withdrawn following the Emperor's disastrously declared war on Prussia.[35]

The aged Pope Pius was left governing the tiny enclave of the Vatican, a living symbol for the devout of the Church's suffering at the hands of the Enlightenment and Revolution. His death eight years later carried equal symbolism, because he wished to be buried elsewhere in his former city. The burial was postponed for three years and was then distressingly disrupted by hostile rioters; anti-clerical liberals nearly threw the coffin in the Tiber. The public neuralgia continued within the nation at the heart of a now global Catholicism, while Catholics made their pilgrimage to Rome in huge numbers to show their reverent solidarity with Pius and his successors: 'Peter in Chains' within the Vatican walls (Plate 32).

The sense of siege and confrontation persisted in official Roman Catholicism for another century. The structures of the Church were themselves a bulwark against outside interference: two celibate gender silos of priests and nuns together with the copulating lay family, whose husband and wife were encouraged to procreate as much as they could, and who were hectored from the pulpit or in the confessional if they did not. They were also increasingly the Church's main source of finance through their giving, after so much wealth had disappeared over the previous century – not least from the loss of the Papal States, previously a direct source of revenue for the Vatican. The clergy were trained in institutions that increasingly recruited boys on the verge of puberty to 'minor seminaries', and then kept their education and general development in a wholly single-sex environment through the seminary until they were released into pastoral ministry in their twenties. It is surprising that any of them were capable of ministering effectively to the majority female congregations in front of them.[36]

Amid the Church hierarchy's increasing pastoral attention to their lay flocks who were their chief source of financial support, at the beginning of the twentieth century Pope Pius X introduced a liturgical change with a corollary that further affected – and indeed celebrated – the Catholic family. Intervening in a long-standing debate in the Church about how often laypeople should receive the Eucharistic elements of bread and wine when attending Mass, he recommended as frequent reception as possible. In 1907 he further decreed that the minimum age for a first communion should be lowered from twelve or fourteen years to seven. Now this 'First Communion' became a new piece of charming theatre for young children dressed in appropriately innocent finery, with their putatively adoring parents looking on. This innovation in Catholic folk-culture liturgically affirmed family life in the local parish church: it is a fixture now, though so comparatively recent in origin.[37]

The Roman Catholic Church as it had evolved by the beginning of the twentieth century might be considered the unwanted but spectacularly successful child of the French Revolution. For all its rhetoric of tradition and its campaign against Modernism, it was a new creation, rebuilt out of the trauma and lack of leadership of 1800. It followed newly constricted doctrinal paths backed by the restored prestige and authority of its celibate clergy, against the backdrop of vigorous numerical growth across the world aided by all the possibilities of communication that technological advance offered. Memories of both the Enlightenment and Revolution combined with the Papacy's new self-confidence in its teaching role to determine how it would face a host of fresh challenges to Christian life and belief. Not all have concerned sex, but many do. During the same period the rival heirs of medieval Western Christianity, Protestants of all varieties, produced their own solutions to these same questions, equally played out on a global stage.

17
Global Western Christianity (1800–1914)

By 1900, European political and economic power straddled the globe, based on the continent's sudden and dramatic concentration of industrial power and wealth, in which Industrial Revolutions in Protestant England and Scotland led the way. Around 1800, average incomes in coastal China were much the same as those of western Europeans or those living on the east coast of north America; a century later, the Chinese were disadvantaged by a factor of around ten to one. A fall in infant mortality, combined with rising living standards, began first in eighteenth-century England and propelled the surplus populations of western Europeans across the world in ever-greater numbers: to what was now the United States of America, but also to settle elsewhere in the Americas and in Australasia. In other places, European power was expressed not in migration but in the seizing of territory, or in the sheer power of European financial institutions alongside the older empires of Asia.[1]

European Christian mission was not far behind, though often relating uneasily to the aims and strategies of imperial power and presenting a huge regional variety of action. Eastwards from Europe, its advance was across Asia from the Russian Empire, reaching as far as the Pacific and promoting Orthodox Christianity as the instrument of tsarist government. Roman Catholicism maintained its presence where the Counter-Reformation had sent it, even though the Catholic monarchies of Iberia were forced to recognize the independence of nearly all their Latin American territories during the nineteenth century. France's continuing overseas expansion was mainly into Africa and Indochina, where even anti-clerical Republican regimes allowed the Catholic Church more favour and freedom than at home, seeing it as a useful agent of French culture and language.

Yet the chief flavour of nineteenth-century worldwide Christian expansion was Protestant, and, within that, anglophone. Understanding it means taking notice of the tangled religious history of what in the sixteenth century had been Reformations on the margins of Europe in England and Scotland, kingdoms of the second or third rank in continental terms. The English, numerically dominant in the Atlantic archipelago, began overseas ventures in the seventeenth century at the same time as they united the three Atlantic kingdoms under a single monarch (in fact the current King of Scotland, James VI, in 1603). The resulting Protestant polity sought to enfold its never completely integrated peoples under a new name as 'British', and then it redeployed the usage of 'British Empire' from a primarily Irish reference to its steadily expanding territories across the globe.[2] Mid-eighteenth-century wars with France delivered north America to the British Empire and swayed a struggle for the Indian subcontinent in Britain's favour. The loss of thirteen British north American colonies to independence as a new entity, the United States, was a major British humiliation, but in fact it laid the basis for a new world power that carried anglophone culture even further.

The missionary energy that emerged at the end of the eighteenth century perpetuated this complicated story of two contrasting established Protestant Churches in the Atlantic Isles: the Presbyterian Church of Scotland and the episcopally governed Church of England ('and Ireland', after institutional assimilation in 1801). How to name those national bodies in different circumstances? 'Presbyterian' was an easy enough label to export for Scots, but the Church of England found it more difficult, as became apparent when its congregations in the former thirteen colonies had to sever their allegiance to the British Crown in 1783. Forming a new ecclesiastical identity, they developed the awkward title of 'The Protestant Episcopal Church of the United States of America'. Over the next century, a more convenient general usage evolved across the world for similar Churches, from an English word hardly ever used before: 'Anglicanism'. The resulting 'Anglican Communion' of linked episcopal Churches has no central head apart from a personal focus of esteem and tradition in the Archbishop of Canterbury.[3]

Alongside Presbyterians and Anglicans truculently marched the separate denominations of English Protestantism that made it uniquely varied in European religious formations: 'Dissenters' (now more commonly styled 'Nonconformists' or 'Free Churches') and Methodists, along with the increasingly distinctive developments of these Churches in the USA. All British Churches were profoundly affected by the Evangelical Revival and Great Awakenings, and in general Evangelicalism was the launching power for world anglophone mission. Around 1830, Evangelical religion probably involved more than 60 per cent of British Protestants, registering a high level of excitement that such events as the French Revolution were heralds of the Last Days; this possibility increased enthusiasm for overseas mission still further.[4] Entangled with this global vision was a more particular cause that, after some hesitation, the majority of British Evangelicals and some of their American counterparts made distinctively their own: an agitation to end the transatlantic commerce in enslaved people forced to work in plantations.

ABOLISHING SLAVERY, AND OTHER GOOD CAUSES

The abolition of slavery was not originally an Evangelical cause, for the good reason that the Bible, both Old and New Testaments, unmistakably accepts the institution of slavery as part of the fabric of the created and fallen world.[5] Christians did often consider that slavery was not a desirable condition – particularly for oneself – and to free slaves was an act of Christian charity. That is not at all the same as flying in the face of biblical assumptions and condemning the existence of slavery as intrinsically evil. The first Christians corporately to make that leap of the imagination and re-examine the biblical text in the light of prior conviction were those who already sought authority not in the Bible but in the light of God planted within themselves: Quakers. After seven decades of quiet argument, in 1758 the Friends used their dominance in the colony of Pennsylvania to produce an official condemnation of all slavery: a first in any Christian polity. From there, through a chain of personal friendships involving the indomitable Anthony Benezet, a Pennsylvanian Quaker from a refugee Huguenot family, the cause spread to various British Evangelicals. They ventured on the same thought-experiment as the Quakers to reconstruct biblical morality in an entirely new light and came to embrace the fight against slavery as a compelling cause for reform.[6]

The long-drawn-out but eventually successful campaign for abolition in Britain has usually been told as a male story of clergy and politicians bringing about parliamentary change. Yet the abolition first of the trade in 1807, and of the institution in 1833, could not have succeeded against the overwhelming economic interest of the British landowning class were it not for decades of agitation by whole families of Evangelicals, with mothers and sisters at the forefront. They applied the standard expectations of Evangelical conversion – a total change of heart after hearing the message – to this new moral cause. They were up against formidable entrenched interests; it would have been well-nigh impossible for anyone in the British elite not to have some direct or indirect entanglement in the trade that became the backbone of British imperial wealth, as became apparent from the very wide range of those benefiting from generous government financial compensation after 1833.[7]

There were highs and lows in anti-slavery activism, with the 1790s and the 1830s being key moments; in between, women were instrumental in keeping the issue alive. While the cause involved Evangelicals across denominations, the most radical voices were generally from the wing of 'rational Dissent', especially Quakers and prosperous and highly educated Unitarian Dissenting congregations, formed from earlier Independent or Presbyterian Churches after they had rejected belief in the Trinity.[8] In the 1790s, radical abolitionists invented an activist strategy adroitly linking consumer choice with the Evangelical family: popular economic boycotts of sugar products which constituted the main products of plantation slavery. The idea was weaponized by what has been called 'the most widely distributed pamphlet of the eighteenth century'. This publishing phenomenon was written in 1791 by the otherwise obscure radical William Fox, in collaboration with an equally radical Baptist Martha Gurney (the only woman publisher involved in the campaign, but central to it): *An Address to the People of Great Britain, on the Propriety of Refraining from the Use of West India Sugar and Rum*. It was enthusiastically promoted by the archetypal captain of industry of the period, the famous Staffordshire potter and Unitarian Josiah Wedgwood, who had his own hugely successful line in anti-slavery ceramics.[9]

The boycott was literally a family affair, though the master of the house was inclined to be less involved in organizing it than the mistress. Proud parents noted their sons and daughters enthusiastically taking up the cause despite children's love of sweet things; we might also notice beneficial mitigation of the growing European-wide epidemic of tooth decay, the sugar plantation workers' quiet revenge for their exploitation.

This was Evangelical personal self-discipline applied to politics, no doubt in a fine balance between parental prompting and a genuine childhood pleasure in an individual achievement (though occasionally, perhaps, in the form of self-assertion against parental control in the direction of anorexia). The boycott was in any case the perfect way to enrol the next generation in the fight, and a flood of anti-slavery literature for children swelled mightily, not to mention the likes of anti-slavery picture-puzzles. This was perhaps the first time that Christians had recruited children for a specific role in a moral campaign. Evangelicals could note the good results, which might make them warm to Enlightenment themes on childhood innocence that mitigated the more natural Evangelical emphasis on original sin inherited from Augustine of Hippo. It all added to nineteenth-century Europe's idealization of the loving companionate family.

Nevertheless, the male leaders of anti-slavery campaigning were commonly less than grateful for what they regarded as an offence to God-given hierarchy. Not long before final parliamentary success, the aged Evangelical William Wilberforce in 1826 expressed his severe reservations on the matter:

> for ladies to meet, to publish, to go from house to house stirring up petitions – these appear to me proceedings unsuited to the female character as delineated in Scripture. And though we should limit the interference of our ladies to the cause of justice and humanity, I fear its tendency would be to mix them in all the multiform warfare of political life.[10]

Wilberforce and other male abolitionists who echoed him were absolutely correct in their foreboding; they were witnessing the birth of what has been termed 'first-wave feminism', the beginning of profound and permanent change in Western culture, in parallel to the feminism of Catholic Europe (above, Chapter 16). If they quoted misogynist scripture, it was adroitly countered by female campaigners who used to feminine advantage all the current commonplaces of separate gender spheres: were not women more open to the voice of God and Christian morality than men, and should they not therefore preach fearlessly? English Dissent and Methodism – and their American denominational equivalents – had already given women guidance in how to push the boundaries of male assumptions about female initiative within institutions. Rhetorical constructs of society for public consumption were always capable of being manipulated within the complexities of private reality.[11]

Some abolitionist men, such as the prominent north American campaigner against slavery William Lloyd Garrison, did draw the conclusion that women had earned their place in politics on an equal basis with men. Yet most stayed with Wilberforce, as became painfully apparent in 1840, when the World Anti-Slavery convention convening in London proposed that women should not occupy the platform, nor even the main hall; a fierce row on the first day did not sway the organizers, and women were left as spectators in the gallery. American delegates to the London Convention, outraged, organized their own Convention on Women's Rights in Seneca Falls, New York, in 1848; it included both female and male delegates, mostly Quakers, and called for women's full legal equality with men. The veteran English Quaker campaigner Anne Knight also found the London Convention a galvanizing moment towards her wider conclusion about gender equality: she was even drawn into the revolutionary upheavals in Paris in 1848, where the appeal for women's rights fell on equally deaf male ears. In 1851, back in Britain, Knight (now in her mid-sixties) founded the first organization to campaign for women's suffrage, the Sheffield Female Political Association, confronting the British House of Lords with a petition on the subject. Among other pioneering consumer gambits were her branded

25. Anne Knight, photographed by Victor Franck, *c.*1855, brandishes a placard reading 'By tortured millions, By the Divine Redeemer, Enfranchise Humanity, Bid the Outraged World, BE FREE'.

envelope labels in a scheme of bright colours to be displayed on campaigning letters.[12]

The campaign against slavery provided the cue, the righteous anger and, perhaps crucially, a successful result: in the end, not merely the British legislation against slavery but a hard-fought military victory against the slave-holding Confederate cause in the American Civil War of the 1860s. From the 1820s there blossomed a variety of campaigns in both Britain and the worldwide Anglosphere that particularly concerned women. They appealed to as wide a constituency as possible by framing themselves as struggles for family welfare in the face of male misbehaviour: the purity and restraint of women against the unruly passions of men. Especially in the USA, the activity was at first closely linked with high-temperature Evangelical enthusiasm, drawing on a renewed wave of revival from the 1790s that later came to be termed 'the Second Great Awakening'. Often such revivals might seem to reverse the general trend of Western Christianity towards dominance by women, since church membership after many revivals revealed a rather higher minority percentage of men than was usually the case. It might be more realistic to view such a result as chastened menfolk paying more attention to the fervent exhortations of their wives and daughters, at least for a while.[13]

The 1820s thus saw the founding of various themed pressure groups that supplemented the traditional Evangelical call to conversion by spelling out that the next steps after conversion must be very specific lifestyle changes. The war on drunkenness – temperance or 'total abstention' – became the flagship of family-centred protest, with greater extrovert élan in revivalist America than in Britain. In 1873, ladies of Hillsboro (Ohio) were so enthused by their temperance meeting that they marched together to a local saloon to pray and sing hymns, which cast a damper on the convivial atmosphere; similar actions led to the majority of saloon proprietors in town ceasing to sell liquor. The resulting sensation led to the creation of the Women's Christian Temperance Union in 1874: the largest female-led organization the USA had ever known, and in close touch with its British equivalent. Such activism became not just cross-confessional but interfaith, as Catholic and Jewish women formed parallel institutions. Amid highly coloured personal testimony and exhortation to fight against alcohol, fidelity to the biblical message was not always absolute. The Gospel story of Jesus's miracle at

19. John's Gospel features the special relationship between Jesus and the 'Beloved Disciple': a charged theme, here sculpted by Master Heinrich of Konstanz, *c.*1285.

20. David and Jonathan, depicted in Christian art relatively infrequently, appear at St Mark's Episcopal Church in the genteel Edinburgh watering-place of Portobello. Glass commemorates George Frederick Paterson, d. 1890, young bachelor laird of Castle Huntly, Longforgan (Perthshire); the gift of his mother.

21. '*Sacra Conversazione*' (the Holy Family informally grouped) here includes Joseph, Mary Magdalen and infant John the Baptist; painting by Marco Palmezzano *c.*1494.

22. A formidable St Anne teaches her daughter Mary from an even more formidable book, with grandson Jesus also featuring: South Netherlandish sculpture, *c.*1500–25.

23. Joseph, newly promoted to Protector of Spain (1679), is transformed into an Inka Prince with his stepson Jesus by an artist of the Cuzco School (*c.*1700).

24. The Wittenberg Town Church altarpiece by Lukas Cranach father and son (1547–8) memorializes the late Martin Luther preaching Christ crucified (and dressed in windblown loincloth, a common late medieval and Lutheran artistic motif). The attentive congregation highlights the preacher's own wife, Katharina von Bora, and family: the clerical family sacralised.

25. Thomas Cranmer's *Book of Common Prayer* (1549) stipulated holy communion following a wedding. English church chancel areas, now reserved for communions and therefore mostly wedding communions, were demarcated by redeployed rood screens and even new screens. Vowchurch screen (Herefordshire, 1613) depicts naked though decorously half-length carvings of the archetypal married couple Adam and Eve.

26. Lot's wife, disobediently looking back at Sodom's destruction or drowning in fire ('*Summertio Sodome*'), is turned into a pillar of salt (Genesis 19.26), in this case a saline statue: mosaic, Monreale Cathedral, Sicily (late 12th century).

27. Our Lady and her infant Son rescue a youthful participant in same-sex activity from burning at the stake in Avignon, 1320: the older participant has already vanished in the flames (mid-14th-century MS illustrated by Simone Martini).

28. A generously bearded St Uncumber/Wilgefortis is crucified: sculpture of 1646 in her chapel, St Martin's parish church, Velzeke (Belgium).

29. Mary (Charles) Hamilton is pilloried in four West Country Market towns for marrying Mary Price in the role of a man: the local parson supervises this flogging with discreet enthusiasm. Cruickshank's frontispiece to the 1813 edition of Henry Fielding's sensationalist *The Surprising Adventures of a Female Husband* (1746).

30, 31 &32. *Top left*: engraving of the 'miraculous medal' envisaged by Catherine Labouré, 1830, already captioned '*Immaculée Conception*'. *Top right*: a late 19th-century Italian postcard depicts Our Lady announcing to Bernadette Soubirous at Lourdes in 1858 that '*Je suis l'Immaculée Conception*' (speaking French, rather than the original reported pronouncement in Occitan). *Below*: Pope Pius IX, here informally posed in old age in 1877, defined the Dogma of the Immaculate Conception in 1854.

33. Cardinal Raymond Burke, prominent Catholic traditionalist, here pictured during a pilgrimage affirming the Tridentine Latin Mass (2017), remarked in an interview in 2015 that 'the radical feminism which has assaulted the Church and society since the 1960s has left men very marginalized.'

34 & 35. Gene Robinson at his consecration as Bishop of the Episcopalian Diocese of New Hampshire, 2003 (*left*), and Joshua Phelps of Westboro Baptist Church (Topeka, Kansas) demonstrating outside (*right*).

36. Pope Francis ecumenically visited the Anglican Ugandan martyrs' shrine at Namugongo, Kampala, in 2015. Behind him (in Canterbury cap) stands Anglican Archbishop Stanley Ntagali, strong supporter of Ugandan legislation reintroducing the death penalty for homosexual offences. The Pope's public remarks avoided the subject.

37. Tammy Faye Messner (formerly Bakker) speaking at Gay Pride, Boston, 2002.

the Wedding in Cana inconveniently puts a premium on superior-quality wine to make the party go with a swing; temperance preachers needed a good deal of exegetical wriggling to explain that this wine was not alcohol as known and hated by campaigners.[14]

Temperance led the way, yet social evils had a habit of being interlinked, and one of the most salient was urban prostitution. The general move in the sixteenth century against officially regulated brothels had done little to suppress the sex trade in major cities; it was a particularly notorious feature of eighteenth-century London, complete with meticulously maintained published directories for the discriminating client.[15] Further dramatic urban growth in nineteenth-century Europe, coupled with the huge expansion in standing armies (and navies in the case of Britain's maritime empire), encouraged a return to official management of prostitution, as in the medieval West. Napoleonic France led the way in 1802, but during the century more or less every European urban society established regulatory systems, even the Ottoman Empire; likewise, the Russian Empire built up regulation from 1843, mostly for its urbanizing European territories. Supervision in Russia included the stipulation (patchily enforced) that brothels should not be situated near churches or synagogues. Just as in the medieval Bishop of Winchester's 'Stews' in Southwark, Russian customers were not to be accommodated on Orthodox holy days or before the Sunday liturgy; moreover, brothels should not ornament their facilities with loyal portraits of the Tsar or imperial family, defenders of the Orthodox faith.[16]

In this era of masculine self-assertion, there was no greater gulf between male and female outlooks than on prostitution. As early as the 1830s, respectable American ladies would ostentatiously gather as a group outside town brothels and note down the names of the clients, which they would then publish in a magazine designed for the purpose.[17] No one was more forceful than the English Evangelical Josephine Butler, daughter of a reform-minded Whig MP, and married to a scholarly Anglican clergyman. She applied her father's hatred of slavery in the Empire to slavery at home. Her fury targeted parliamentary legislation of the 1860s, the Contagious Diseases Acts, that ordered the compulsory medical regulation of prostitutes in the interest of their male clients' health (the concern being fighting efficiency among Britain's soldiers and sailors). Often local police singled out poverty-stricken women for bullying and humiliation regardless of any evidence of prostitution, just because they could. It was the gender double standard at its worst.

Butler reminisced about hearing a woman's cry outside her comfortable Oxford home: 'a woman aspiring to heaven and dragged back to hell – and my heart was pierced with pain. I longed to leap from the window, and flee with her to some place of refuge.' Instead, she concentrated on more systematic and effective campaigns against male indifference to the impossible situation of women who ended up selling their bodies. Shocked males deplored a well-brought-up married lady speaking on public platforms about venereal disease: 'That dreadful woman, Mrs Butler', fumed one leading Oxford High Churchman, Canon Henry Liddon. Yet she won; in 1886, Parliament repealed the Contagious Diseases Acts. Her triumph was in line with a clear development in transatlantic Protestantism: female activism begun by radical dissenting groups moved into the ultra-respectable mainstream and was now shaping the narrative of all society. By the late twentieth century, the dreadful Mrs Butler had gained a commemorative feast day in the Church of England's liturgy.[18]

Temperance and prostitution were the supernova causes in a galaxy of fights against such expressions of hyper-masculinity as duelling, gambling, tobacco-smoking or the eating of meat. They were all summed up in a phrase that on both sides of the Atlantic in the 1870s became a common shorthand for moral campaigning movements: 'Social Purity', really a euphemism for sexual purity. In this cause, the US Women's Christian Temperance Union used its considerable political influence to diversify its concerns. At the end of the two-decade reign of its Methodist President Frances Willard in 1898, twenty-five of its fifty-nine departments had campaigning briefs other than temperance; naturally they included votes for women, in the cause of pushing for legislation on alcohol.[19]

It is significant that the WCTU also sought to limit Catholic immigration, a clear threat to the purity of Protestant America. The tone of such campaigning organizations was white, female, Protestant, middle class. They did not spare either men or social elites in seeking to hold all Americans to a common standard of sexual behaviour, and were determined to educate the next generation in principles to reflect that standard; public censorship of literature and entertainment was high on their list of priorities, merging into temperance campaigns. Their Christian values became American family values. In all this, they were in uneasy alliance with the increasingly powerful and well-organized medical profession, the uneasiness in large part because doctors were almost exclusively male, and might not share their moral preoccupations. In one important respect doctors yielded to Social Purity activists, in leaving public sex education to Protestant organizations led by women. It was an aspect of women's duties to their families, and male clergy were as generally inclined as doctors to make a grateful escape from the obligation.[20]

The cautious alliance of the Social Purity movement with the new medical establishment reflected a respect for the remarkable advances in medical science from the mid-nineteenth century that made diagnosis, treatment and surgery less threatening to human life than they had ever been. Western humans simply knew more about the physical realities of reproduction than in any previous generation, but, as so often in rapid advances of knowledge, there was overconfidence about the implications. One considerable wrong turn was to take too seriously the intellectual respectability of the 'science' of eugenics: the proposition that it was possible to breed high achievement through bloodlines, which just happened to favour members of the white social elite. The arguments were fostered from within what appeared to be a textbook case to prove the point: the extended clan of British intellectuals that included Charles Darwin. Darwin's polymathic cousin Francis Galton's major publication in 1869, *Hereditary Genius*, set the standard for constructing what looked like scientific arguments, effectively inventing intelligence tests and allied statistical tools, which other scientists much expanded into the twentieth century.[21]

Galton had developed his family Quakerism into a general secularist hostility to Church institutions, but that did not greatly concern Social Purity activists in Britain or America. They placed their own construction on an approach to genetics that fitted neatly with their concern to promote Christian families with standards set by white Protestantism; in the USA the movement was suffused with the idea of America's special place in a divine Providence of Protestant flavour.[22] The norms of the American heterosexual family entered the twentieth century further reinforced by work on genetics by an American enthusiast for racial segregation who, like Galton, came from a devout Quaker family: H. H. Goddard. His bestseller of 1912, *The Kallikak Family*, advocated preventing some families from breeding, to cut short their hereditary degeneracy and feeble-mindedness. The family tree of the 'Kallikaks' at the heart of the book was actually Goddard's own invention.[23]

Later, Goddard did adjust his findings to deal with criticism even from some enthusiasts for eugenics, but that gave little pause to those favouring selective sterilization on eugenic grounds for humans classed as 'feeble-minded'. Early Christian proponents of scientific contraception did not distance themselves. Mrs Margaret Sanger (an Episcopalian convert from Roman Catholicism) was the founder in 1921 of what became Planned Parenthood, and she was also an advocate of 'birth control' targeting the American poor, among whom she discerned the socially 'unfit': 'human weeds which threaten the blooming of the finest flowers of American civilization'. British legislation on 'Mental Deficiency', enthusiastically sponsored by Winston Churchill from within the government in 1912, was in the end modified to avoid legalizing sterilization, concentrating instead on physically isolating in institutions those caught within its definitions.[24] By contrast, various programmes in states of the USA have, overall, resulted in around 80,000 sterilizations. The example of the United States inspired Nazi legislation in imitation during the 1930s, and although that tainted association might be considered to have thoroughly discredited the whole eugenics programme, officially sponsored sterilization programmes persisted in the USA and Canada into the twenty-first century.[25]

The broad spectrum within the Protestant alliance that composed Social Purity did not map onto future Christian cultural divisions across the world. By the end of the nineteenth century, the female Social Purity movement in the USA and its expanding efforts to provide moral education for an entire society was dominated by the liberal or low-temperature Protestant mainstream of American religion: Presbyterian, Congregationalist or Unitarian, Methodist, Episcopalian. The rhetoric of Social Purity nevertheless still united it with the shaggier parts of the American Protestant ecclesiastical family such as the Southern Baptists, or the new manifestation of Protestant revivalist energy that emerged around 1900 in the form of Pentecostalism (below, Chapter 18). The rhetoric has subsequently survived much longer within conservative forms of Protestantism than among liberals. Lurking in the background in the USA was the defeat of the slave-holding Confederacy in the Civil War of 1861–5, which left many Southern Evangelicals unreconciled to the idea of equality for African Americans; that racist ethos had actually been the *raison d'être* for the Southern Baptist Convention separating from abolitionist Baptists in the North in 1845.[26]

Protestant identity would in the end splinter into two contrasting directions for world Christianity, but in 1914 the present-day divisions between liberal and conservative theologies were not yet at all fixed, let alone the global political consequences that have flowed from them. An important stage in the process was a series of very widely distributed short British and American essays published in twelve volumes between 1910 and 1915, *The Fundamentals*. They articulated increasing unease among some Evangelicals about nineteenth-century Protestant explorations of the Bible, and set out a series of points to be defended. These five main principles were 'verbal inerrancy' (that is, no possibility of the Bible being mistaken in its literal meaning); the divinity of Jesus Christ; his Virgin Birth; the affirmation that Jesus died on the cross in the place of sinful humanity (a theory technically known as penal substitution); and the proposition that Christ was physically resurrected to return again in the flesh.[27]

In 1919 the World's Christian Fundamentals Association was founded, expanding through its use of mass rallies from a mainly Baptist base, with Pentecostalism a growing component, to affect most Protestant Churches. It was then not at all obvious that within a century matters of sex and gender would be the chief battleground on which Fundamentalists would take their stand, in alliance with other varieties of conservative Christians. Yet already the expansion of anglophone Protestantism through formal and informal imperialism had turned its theological debate on sex into a global conversation.

VICTORIAN VALUES AND IMPERIAL CULTURES

As nineteenth-century Britain built up an increasingly vast empire on the back of generally successful achievements by its army and navy, so it evolved a masculine ethos similar to that of the citizen armies of mainland Europe in the Revolutionary and Napoleonic eras. There were important differences: this was a patriotism of deference, shaped by British pride in its constitutional monarchy and attendant aristocracy, both of which had been strengthened after previous humiliations in the American War of Independence by their epic achievements contributing to Napoleon's defeat. All that was framed from 1837 by the long reign of Queen Victoria, who by 1901 had managed to outlive any previous ruler in the Atlantic Isles, and who learned over time how to play the role of grandmotherly figurehead for her subjects worldwide. British territorial reach continued to expand into the 1920s (its largest nominal extent came with its acquisition of a League of Nations' mandate over the former Ottoman territories of Palestine in 1923). By that time its real power was beginning to cede to that of the United States, but in the intervening century the imperial achievements of a modestly sized north Atlantic archipelago were impressive, even considering its temporary industrial and technological advantages.

Out of Britain's relatively small population, there needed to be a means of selecting and training enough men to govern and administer a dauntingly varied spread of formal territories, as well as to staff the organization of the informal British empire beyond. This required an educational revolution to transform Hanoverian England's miscellaneous and often ramshackle provision of schools. Certainly, Victorians sought to spread popular literacy generally throughout the United Kingdom, which they did mostly through often acrimoniously competing efforts from Britain's various religious denominations; but, within that wider programme, they created a leadership cadre on the basis of a class-stratified and hierarchical society. This was achieved through a system of 'public schools' – an English rather than Scots or Irish phenomenon. The name was misleading, since these schools were the reverse of public, being aimed at the landed elite and the large number of middle-class parents anxious to model their families on elite patterns of behaviour. Schools which in the medieval and Tudor period had been founded to provide opportunities for boys of exceptional talent from a humble background, such as Eton or Winchester Colleges, were now hijacked for an imperial governing class.

By 1900 there were around 150 members of the 'Headmasters' Conference' of public schools. Reflecting the ethos of the English landed gentry and nobility, they were predominantly Anglican (and indeed largely low-temperature Evangelical), with some outliers from what had been a parallel world of upper-class Roman Catholic recusancy, and there were even a handful of public schools that were Methodist. For around a decade of a boy's life from about the age of seven, he was taken away from his family and boarded with his peers in an inward-looking, single-sex world that emphasized physical fitness, team sport and participation in the Officer Training Corps, alongside frequent chapel attendance and a Classical academic curriculum that provided a reference framework of imperial experience from the Roman Empire. In the mordant words of one eminent modern historian who endured it all, '[t]he English upper classes traditionally made up for the

26. English Roman Catholic public schools readily reflected the general educational ethos of military maleness created by their Anglican equivalents. Here the Downside Officer Training Corps (created 1909) poses with sundry monks of the Benedictine Abbey and a field gun.

comfort of their background and the privileges of their station by ten years of misery at boarding-school.'[28] The British Empire has long gone, but the public school system survives into the twenty-first century, not as yet doing much to question its reason for a continued existence.

The ideal products of Victorian public schools were obedient but resourceful officers in the armed forces, or colonial administrators programmed to endure lonely leadership amid alien cultures. Socialization even with female siblings, let alone any other variety of female, was not on the syllabus. Instead, the inevitable consequences of an all-male adolescent environment lent a peculiar anxiety to British elite attitudes to masturbation and homosexuality, particularly because of the widespread conviction that (in the words of an old Etonian and noted cricketer, who returned to Eton as Headmaster) 'animal desires [are] far stronger in the male than in the female, at least in England'.[29]

A Classical school curriculum brought public schools the usual problems in dealing with literary references to ancient Mediterranean sexual mores, and additionally there were some difficulties in handling the Christian message itself. The New Testament was little help in instilling martial manliness, and even the Saviour himself needed careful treatment by theologians who were worried that Victorian Christianity had less appeal to men than to women. Jesus's sacrifice, nailed helpless on the cross, needed to be reframed as a specialized ideal of what the prolific writer on morality and church affairs Charles Kingsley termed 'true manhood'; the scholar and preacher F. D. Maurice complained of the widespread perception that the Sermon on the Mount had a 'passive or feminine character'.[30] The Hebrew Bible was a good deal more promising, but amid its descriptions of military heroes and armed mayhem well up to the standards of British imperial warfare lurked the obstinate problem of David and Jonathan. In most respects they could be seen as the perfect archetype for a Captain and Vice-Captain of Games, but rarely were they found in the myriad stained-glass windows that the Victorians commissioned for British church buildings, and their appearance always suggests an interesting agenda to investigate (Plate 20).[31]

It is notable that a standard multi-volume and multi-author English biblical commentary edited by the Bishop of Gloucester and Bristol in the 1880s showed a rare openness to interfaith dialogue in dealing with this problematic Old Testament couple. Canon Spence, the commentator on 1 Samuel, reached gratefully for a quotation by one of his commentary colleagues Dean Payne Smith from the liberal German rabbi and biblical scholar Ludwig Philippson (whose parallel Hebrew/German edition of the Hebrew Bible was later much esteemed by Sigmund Freud):

> We may indeed wonder at the delicacy of feeling and the gentleness of the sentiments which these two men in those old rough times entertained for one another. No ancient writer has set before us so noble an example of a heartfelt, unselfish, and thoroughly human state of feeling, and none has described friendship with such entire truth in all its relations, and with such complete and profound knowledge of the human heart.

This was a neat means of providing a descriptive framework for the intimate male friendships that characterized the nineteenth-century West, without descending to the 'beastliness' that was the constant lurking foe in the Victorian public school.[32]

There was one real Victorian religious sub-culture within a sub-culture that burrowed further into the themes Rabbi Philippson was evading: a homosexual identity within a new creation of Anglicanism, Anglo-Catholicism.[33] Anglo-Catholicism as an alternative to the Evangelical emphasis on the Protestant and Reformation identity of the Church of

England emerged in the 1830s among academics and students in Oxford University, hence it was frequently known as 'the Oxford Movement'. Their promotion of a Catholic and sacramental view of Anglicanism in a series of 'Tracts' produced an alternative name: 'Tractarianism'. The self-absorbed single-sex culture of university life in Oxford inevitably drew in leading personalities of homosexual orientation, notably the Vicar of the University Church, John Henry Newman.

Newman was the most prominent among several Tractarians eventually to decide that the logic of their theological views pushed them to convert to Roman Catholicism. His stellar career thereafter as a spiritual and theological writer and eventually Cardinal of the Roman Church has led to much obfuscation on his obvious sexual inclinations, which, while almost certainly sublimated, led to his insistence on imitating various medieval same-sex couples in demanding burial in the grave of his most intimate friend and fellow convert, the priest Ambrose St John. Less conventional had been Newman's grief-stricken insistence at St John's death in 1875 on spending the night on the bed beside the corpse.[34]

Newman and St John were by no means the last Anglo-Catholics to arrive in Rome with that sort of emotional baggage. The Oxford undergraduate Gerard Manley Hopkins was affected for life by one encounter over a few days with Digby Dolben, an Etonian Catholic convert and son of a Northamptonshire squire. Dolben drowned before traits possibly charming in a teenager could become irritating in adult years (though his homoerotic verse might have improved). Hopkins's grief and loneliness add intensity to his quite extraordinary poetic output, sensuously exploring the glory of God's created universe against the background of his Catholic faith, yet always on the edge of desperation. The Society of Jesus showed remarkable forbearance with his self-destructive awkwardness and wilfully Anglican interpretation of his Jesuit vocation.[35]

Plenty more Anglo-Catholics stayed within the Anglican fold, and the movement spread through the global Communion, increasingly at odds with the previously dominant Evangelicalism. One particular aspect of its reassertion of Catholic values within Anglicanism obviously attracted gay men: its emphasis on the superiority over marriage of a celibate vocation to the priesthood. At the same time, Anglicanism was developing 'theological colleges' to provide professional training for its clergy. These were increasingly identified in a party fashion as 'High', 'Low'

(Evangelical) or 'Broad' – resolutely non-party, a party in itself; prospective ordinands could embark on the road to their clerical career selecting training in a congenial same-sex atmosphere, theologically and perhaps in more general terms. The result was that Anglican ordination provided the only profession in Victorian England apart from the officer class in the armed forces where lifelong abstention from marriage did not seem too questionable.

Simultaneously Anglo-Catholics revived the monastic life. The first male effort at Benedictinism by the flamboyant Joseph Lyne ('Father Ignatius') was doomed mainly through the homosexual scandal surrounding it, but Orders of nuns with social and teaching vocations like those of the contemporary Catholic Church gained more public acceptance. Evangelicals nevertheless deplored their alarming adoption of Counter-Reformation nuns' habits. One sour comment compared two women, both distinguished in relieving army medical incompetence in the Crimean War: 'Miss [Florence] Nightingale and Miss [Lydia] Sellon [Mother Superior of the Sisters of Mercy] stand out as the representatives of the true and false method of our nineteenth-century work for unmarried women.'[36]

Another borrowing from Rome that Anglo-Catholic clergy reintroduced was individual auricular confession. Many a Victorian *paterfamilias* feared for the moral welfare of impressionable daughters and wives in this intimate setting, but the seal of the confessional was probably much more significant in bringing some sort of self-awareness to confused homosexual males, as they talked through personal confusions to a trusted authority-figure, confident that what they said would not be repeated. Among the parishes to which Anglo-Catholicism spread, a significant proportion were in deprived urban areas. Their large congregations would probably be as predominantly female as elsewhere, but they could easily shelter an inner homosocial coterie of men and boys who assisted at increasingly dramatic and beautiful liturgy directed by an often-charismatic parish priest, probably with a public-school background: it was an unusual institutional reaching-out over Victorian class barriers, and Eros is a great leveller. Such circles fostered a 'camp' theatrical style: conversation and socializing that drew with ironic wit on a more general homosexual sub-culture, daring the observer or participant to identify what it was all about. Anglo-Catholic ecclesiastical style and liturgy was (and is) a natural setting for it all.[37]

Amid a nostalgic portrait of Oxford in the 1920s, the novelist Evelyn

Waugh made a brutal summary of what was already an established theme, in ventriloquized advice to an undergraduate: 'Beware the Anglo-Catholics: they're all sodomites with unpleasant accents.' That was a breezily incomplete account of a major world religious movement with many other facets. The Roman Catholic convert Waugh will have been aware that, a century before, English elite culture had still been broadly hostile to Roman Catholicism, and would in Reformation fashion have categorized Catholics alongside Anglo-Catholics as sexually suspect; indeed Anglo-Catholicism was widely regarded as sinister precisely because it appeared to be a Catholic subversion of English Protestantism from within. Such was the opinion of the aggressively manly and uxorious spokesman of 'Broad Church' Anglicanism Charles Kingsley, who sneered at the 'fastidious, maundering, die-away effeminacy, which is mistaken for purity and refinement' among both Roman and Anglo-Catholics – Kingsley had a particular dislike for John Henry Newman.[38]

All this was against the background of the peculiarly punitive public attitudes of imperial Britain towards male homosexuality. The Westminster Parliament (whose two Houses were for obvious reasons largely a collection of former public schoolboys) made successive moves to update the archaic law on buggery from 1534. The changes might seem liberalizing, since the first in 1861 abolished the death penalty and replaced it with terms of imprisonment.[39] Various questions of interpretation of what buggery might be – between men? involving animals? – led to further refinements, the most famous and consequential of which was an amendment to the Criminal Law Amendment Act of 1885 proposed by (the Etonian) Henry Labouchère. It created a crime of 'gross indecency': a catch-all term for any male same-sex act in public or private. Arrest and punishment rates did not for the moment greatly increase, but the self-inflicted downfall of the extrovert genius Oscar Wilde ten years later was the beginning of nearly a century of official harassment and imprisonment of British gay men that did not cease with the partial decriminalization of male homosexuality in 1967. Various attempts by moral campaigners to get legislators interested in action against lesbians never came to anything: males were the real worry for males.[40]

There is a striking contrast between UK law and legal provisions on male homosexuality in the rest of Europe modelled on the *Code Napoléon*; yet one exception to that general rule had grave consequences. Prussia was, like the United Kingdom, a Protestant and expansionist state with a monarchical, aristocratic and military ethos:

its Hohenzollern monarchy became closely bound into Queen Victoria's extensive maternal network in Europe, and the newly minted German Empire of 1871 led by Prussia played a jealous though frustratingly belated game of catch-up with British colonial success wherever that still remained possible. The existing Prussian legal code was the basis of a new Imperial lawcode created for all Germany in 1871; Paragraph 175 of the Imperial Code was (against the advice of medical experts in Prussia) actually a recriminalization of male homosexuality, vaguely justified with reference to public opinion. It had dire repercussions in the Nazi years, and in both post-war West and East Germany it was only abolished at the end of the 1960s. That did not stop a vigorous and unusually public gay culture continuing to develop in the German Empire, echoed in urban settings throughout the continent as far east as St Petersburg and Moscow, adjusting itself to the local variants of attempted suppression.[41]

Labouchère's amendment on homosexuality in the 1885 Act was all the more consequential because it was copied in penal codes created throughout the British Empire. In many parts of the world, especially in Africa and South East Asia, its punitive provisions are one of the most lasting legacies of British colonialism, even more so than Victorian legislative prohibitions on abortion. They infuse much highly coloured rhetoric against homosexuality in African Christianity to the present day. Yet Western colonialism had an even wider and more profound effect on sexual attitudes throughout the world. From the mid-eighteenth century, three Muslim great powers that in previous centuries had seemed daunting to Westerners successively fell into decay: first Moghul power in India gave way piecemeal to British rule, and later the Persian and Ottoman empires experienced growing vulnerability to European pressure, including tsarist Russia's huge expansion east and south.

Muslim reverses continued despite strenuous efforts, particularly by the Ottoman Sultan, to learn from Western modes of government and military success. The trauma for Islamic society was considerable: with the exception of Reconquista Spain in the Middle Ages, the Muslim world had never previously needed to think about the experience of losing political power. Now it was having to react in a very varied set of regional settings, the common factor across them being a likely progression to seeing Muslim political degeneration as only one symptom of social degeneration from former Islamic greatness. Perhaps the West had lessons to teach there too. Among such reactions, therefore, were various appropriations of Western sexual attitudes previously uncharacteristic of Islam.[42]

When considering how to formulate truth and use knowledge, Classical Islamic society had embraced paradox and ambiguity amid a playfulness with language in Arabic or Farsi, and it was generally content with probability rather than seeking absolutes. Muslims noted negativity in the Qur'an towards such matters as figural representation in art, same-sex relations and alcohol, and they then commonly found a place for them all in everyday life. In the ninth century CE, the majority decision in Islam was against a rigorist school of theology in rejecting the idea of eternal punishment, so that hellfire was much less available than in Christianity to scourge deviant sexual behaviour; the overriding criterion in an individual's fate in the afterlife was one's fidelity to Islam. Within that general framework, Islamic societies preserved Graeco-Roman sexual mores while Christianity transformed them: a range of sexual acts were normal and healthy, while any ungovernable emotion of love was dangerous to personal well-being.

Now in the colonial era, the anglophone missionary movement represented a particularly propositional form of Protestant theology, centred on generally literal expositions of God's biblical word. Westerners confronted Islam with a new insistence on clarity and certainty that included a much more rigid set of moral values about sexual acts, within a set of binary definitions and added prohibitions that characterized both Enlightenment and Victorian Protestant society. The effect on nineteenth-century Islamic society has been lasting. Just as nineteenth-century Roman Catholicism was moulded by its apparent antagonist the French Revolution, so has modern Islam been restructured by Western imperialism. Modern reform movements within Islam from the eighteenth century have only encouraged this: Wahhabite reform in Arabia demolished centuries of Islamic complexity with a thoroughness reminiscent of the Protestant Reformation, and so its later sexual puritanism was predictable. The Deobandi reform in the nineteenth-century Raj had a similar character, effectively adopting Victorian prudery and family values despite its goal of defending Islam in India from Western ideas.[43]

In reaction to Muslim perception of Western Christian models of family and sex, many Islamic societies have therefore discarded much ambiguity and pluralism in their traditions. The past has been censored or rewritten. New editions of ancient Arabic literary works have come to omit verse that might be considered raunchily erotic, especially the abundant poetry of same-sex relationships. Islamic societies have found it extremely difficult to discuss in public matters that were once part of everyday Muslim life, but which are now defined by the Western term 'homosexuality' invented by Károly Mária Kertbeny and treated as alien imports from the West. Legal texts have added sections on masturbation or sodomy that would not previously have been considered necessary discussion. There has not only been subtraction, but innovation in the name of invented tradition: before the twentieth century, Islamic sources reveal hardly any evidence for executing males for mutual and consensual sexual activity.

Such were some unanticipated outcomes from the playing fields of Eton. The same Western self-confidence was present wherever Anglophone Protestant missions were allowed to flourish. In China, where the massive Protestant missionary effort was new in the nineteenth century yet also very conscious of three previous centuries of Catholic presence, the new arrivals often shared their predecessors' sense of outrage against local customs: for instance, noting in disgust local same-sex activity that they could equally well have seen at home. They placed it alongside other customs that they regarded as the cultural femininity of Chinese males: the pigtail, or the pious avoidance of meat by Chinese Buddhists. Assumptions about gender marched alongside Western theological assumptions across the Reformation divide: once more Protestantism was echoing the Jesuit Matteo Ricci, who had vigorously critiqued Buddhist vegetarian practice in both men and women. Protestant missionaries consciously or unconsciously repeated his arguments, emphasized how vegetarianism feminized male practitioners and regarded it as a triumph of evangelism when a convert gingerly took to the consumption of meat. In Protestant terms, such conversion was also a rejection of the popish custom of fasting.[44]

The binary gendering of nineteenth-century Western culture did mean that the mission field reflected Protestant first-wave feminism as well as the masculinism of both government and Church. From mid-century, female energies that had begun expressing themselves in anti-slavery and temperance organizations were turned towards the already flourishing worldwide missionary enterprise, both sides of the Atlantic. In the British Empire, the missionary growth burst out of its original Evangelical context to involve Anglo-Catholics as well; as early as the 1860s even the new Orders of Anglican nuns. In the USA, the missionary movement soon outgrew the impressive achievements of the Women's Christian Temperance Union, with missionary societies reaching memberships of around 3 million by the 1920s, supporting around twice as many women as there were male missionaries.[45]

Those involved, both male and female, had become very conscious that, in most of the cultures to whom mission was addressed, it was impossible for men to have any useful contact with women in households. Female missionaries in India made much of the concept of *zenana*, the segregated space for women in both Hindu and Muslim contexts, to which their femininity held the key; it became a more general metaphor for a special female missionary role beyond the formal existence of *zenana*.[46] *Woman's Work for Woman* was the title of the monthly magazine of the main US Presbyterian missionary organization from the 1870s; it stood as a programme for the whole movement, which broadened in its self-understanding and aims as the work expanded, away from simple evangelism towards medical skills, childcare, education and a broadening concept of women's rights. The overwhelming majority of female missionaries through the period were single, and so not constrained by families in patriarchal mode: they could justifiably claim to be more free than men to listen to the experiences of those women to whom they sought to minister, and they had the capacity to acquire multiple skills after appropriate training that formed them into as much of a profession as the male clergyman.

All this was so successful that after the 1920s a half-century of separate female leadership was subsumed in mixed missionary societies. In one sense that was a statement of equality between the sexes, but it was also an end to the separate female world of control and initiative which possessed its own distinctive agenda.[47] Nevertheless, by that time, female missionary efforts had created institutions that carved out a permanent place for women to co-operate and express themselves in ways that cut across male institutions. The Mothers' Union, one of the most large-scale and effective, was created for Anglicans in 1876 by Mary Sumner, the wife of an Anglican bishop. Notably it was one of the very few voluntary organizations in the Anglican Communion not to take on the colours of one theological 'party'. Its ideology of motherhood and family sounds conservative (Queen Victoria graciously agreed to be its patron in 1897), but in fact such assumptions sheltered a remarkable degree of flexibility and freedom of thought, rather as the profession of papal loyalty had done for the old Society of Jesus. The leadership was female and international; discussions among members led some of them to become among the earliest Anglican advocates of the ordination of women.[48]

In some circumstances, the Mothers' Union might wield formidable social power, such as the occasion in 1953 when the British Governor of Uganda was startled to receive an angry delegation from distinguished members of the colony's MU after he exiled the Kabaka (King) of Buganda for political reasons. They denounced his action as a threat to all Christian marriage in the Kingdom of Buganda, since the Kabaka's coronation was a marriage to the Kingdom, sealed by the bestowing of a ring by the Anglican Bishop.[49] This was a directly Christian intervention in Ugandan politics, but, over the previous century and a half, the self-assertion of women in Western society had a wider effect in the cultures to which the missionaries travelled. In India, the rhetoric and intentions of the Deobandi movement (and other revivalist moves in Islam) were emphatically conservative and in opposition to 'Western' institutions of the British Raj, but their effectiveness involved a necessary adjustment in their own approach to the Muslim faithful. In defence against Western encroachment, they gave women an unprecedented degree of agency. To begin with, it was expressed in a literature of men writing for women, but that was in itself a novelty, reaching out to an audience now broadly assumed to be literate or wishing to be, and to have a rational grasp of how to make the most of women's admittedly highly bounded place in society. In the twentieth century, such hitherto unexpressed thoughts went on to be the basis of an Islamic feminism.[50]

POLYGAMIES AND MORE

One new cultural conversation left Western Christianity somewhat on the back foot. During the nineteenth century, it moved into a position of power in relation to polygamous (nearly all polygynous) societies in different settings in the world, especially in Africa and among indigenous peoples in north America, but also in Asia. This was the first time for nearly a millennium that Western Christians had needed to spend much time thinking or making decisions about polygamy, after the Latin Church had spent much energy eliminating it from northern Europe and had turned back the Islamic and Jewish cultures of Iberia. Such had been the effect of imposing monogamy that after the eleventh century, as we have observed, European Jews had abandoned polygyny in defensive reaction to the Christian culture round them. Otherwise, sixteenth- and seventeenth-century Iberian missions in colonial America imposed monogamous family groupings on indigenous societies wherever they had the chance to restructure them in a Western Catholic mould, without much discussion – certainly not with those who were the objects of their social engineering.[51] At the same time, Martin Luther's musings on polygamy subsided into oblivion, and those who, like Bernardino Ochino and Martin Madan, had raised the subject at least as a discussion point were soon shown it was unwise to do so (above, Chapters 14 and 15). Now, Christian assertion of monogamy would once more face contemporary realities.

In some parts of the world, Western powers did not have formal control over cultures and polities practising polygyny, and, in such circumstances, Churches were in the position of the Church of the East under Sasanian or Muslim rule more than a millennium before; all they could do was to police their own communities as best they could and assert monogamy as an ideal for Christian identity, against considerable alternative social pressures. Such was the case in imperial and early Republican China, where, just as in early medieval Europe, Christian Churches faced a legally established social institution of concubinage, only abolished by the Republic in 1929. Some missionaries took a lenient view: in the 1920s, Bishop Frederick Graves of Shanghai emphasized that he was not going to insist on a man ending his relationship with a woman who under Chinese law was a concubine, but 'innocent of wrongdoing'; all three parties in the relationship would suffer. It was enough that the Church should postpone the man's baptism till either the wife or the concubine died. In a masterly piece of analogous pragmatism, his contemporaries as Anglican bishops in China generally allowed baptism to the women involved, since the Lambeth Conference of worldwide Anglicanism in its pronouncements on polygamy had said nothing specific prohibiting the baptism of family members of polygynous men.[52]

In Ethiopia, Africa retained one ancient indigenous Christian culture, whose Christian monarchy rode out Western colonialism throughout the nineteenth century, crushing an invading Italian army at Adwa in 1896. Over the centuries the Ethiopian Orthodox Church had come to an uneasy understanding with polygamy. This marital custom was general in African cultures to the south but, more importantly, it reflected the peculiarly strong identification of Ethiopian Christianity with Judaism that steadily grew between the twelfth and seventeenth centuries. Ethiopian Christians reached back to the Hebrew Bible and adopted Jewish customs that the rest of Christianity had dispensed with, including circumcision and abstention from pork: likewise, polygyny.

King Solomon was a role model for Christian kings of Ethiopia (from the thirteenth century the dynasty claimed Solomonic lineage), and that included his impressive array of wives. The habitual royal enthusiasm for multiple marriage was one of several long-term bones of contention between Ethiopian monarchy and clergy. The foundational compilation of local Christian literature, the medieval *Kebra Nagast* ('Book of the Glory of Kings', actually regarded as part of the canon of Scripture in Ethiopia), proclaims Ethiopian royal descent from Solomon and the Queen of Sheba, while tartly pointing out that 'after Christ, it was given to live with one woman under the law of marriage'. Monarchs ignored this pronouncement, as did very many of their subjects. Ethiopia's compromise remains that lay polygynists reverently refrain from becoming communicants, and instead centre their devotion on a rigorous programme of fasting.[53]

In Africa beyond the Sahara, marriage was a universal institution, but also very remote from the nuclear family systems of nineteenth-century Europe. Kin had a greater value in a marriage than an individual spouse, and this meant that genuine polygamy was more of a reality than in other cultural regions, giving women a greater agency than in polygynous systems elsewhere. From 1800 the African continent was an open mission field for Western Catholics and Protestants, contending with a dynamic Islam expanding southward across the Sahara. In the central belt of the continent the two world faiths were in direct competition, and Islam's practice of polygyny gave it an advantage in appealing to potential converts. Both there and in the south, where Christianity had little competition in missionary effort, this was an urgent issue for monogamous European missionaries. Since in Africa as elsewhere polygyny was a practice favoured by wealthy elites, it actually increased in reaction to the greater circulation of wealth that initially resulted from colonial contacts.[54]

As missionaries tried to eliminate polygamy, dire social consequences emerged for individuals in polygamous societies cut off from traditional support: abandoned women and children. Social misery was not the only consideration. The more thoughtful missionaries were faced with the dilemma that they were promoting divorce among polygamous couples, against a background of the Church of England's own fierce resistance to Parliament's widening of divorce in the Mother Country. The same tragedies and perplexities affected missions to First Nations people in Canada, where the Churches worked closely with the secular government to eliminate a custom that was the bedrock of indigenous societies.[55]

One of the first Christian leaders to point out the tragic social effects of attacking local marriage customs was the outspoken and independent-minded John William Colenso, Anglican Bishop of Natal from 1853. It was one of several topics on which Colenso's idiosyncratic 'Broad Churchmanship' was ostracized in what was now emerging as a worldwide Anglican Communion; his vigorous if – by modern standards – naïve critical analysis of the Bible text, encouraged by shrewd comments from his Zulu diocesan flock, offended Evangelicals and Anglo-Catholics alike. In 1862, Colenso published an open 94-page 'letter' to the Archbishop of Canterbury, not his first treatment of the subject. He made clear his own principled disapproval of polygyny; nevertheless, deploying his usual rigorous logic and an unnerving grasp of history, he concluded that to enforce the putting away of wives on men seeking Christian baptism would be 'unwarranted by the Scriptures, unsanctioned by apostolic example or authority, condemned by common reason and sense of right, and altogether unjustifiable'. Colenso had the temerity to cite an array of other missionaries across the denominational spectrum who agreed with him, not to mention pronouncements from the likes of John Calvin.[56]

Bishop Robert Gray of Cape Town, a High Churchman determined to establish a proper apostolic authority in southern African Anglicanism, already had Colenso in his sights for questioning the literal truth of the Book of Genesis. In 1863, Gray was instrumental in getting Colenso sacked. Colenso, supported by a large proportion of his diocese, refused to go quietly, and one of the main motives behind the first Lambeth Conference of 'Anglican' Bishops in 1867, the first collective action of worldwide Anglicanism, was to discipline him. Polygamy has troubled Lambeth Conferences ever since. The 1888 meeting sought to outlaw it among African Christians, with the concurrence of the one native African bishop present at the Conference, the Yoruba-born Samuel Ajayi Crowther, who stressed the injustice of polygyny for women.[57]

Yet a mark of Anglican failure to hold that line in the face of African Anglican expansion is that exactly a century later, in 1988, a further

Lambeth Conference resolution affirmed that men in polygamous marriages could be baptized and received into the Church. At no stage was much attention paid to what African women might have to say on the subject. Between 1988 and 1998, Lambeth resolutions went on to make the world safer for heterosexual polygynous African men, while making it considerably more unsafe for gay people of either sex.[58] The problem did not just affect the Anglican Communion; the question of polygyny in Africa became inextricably tangled with the aspirations of Africans to make Christianity authentically African in self-understanding and leadership.

In 1917, the Nigerian Methodist Church expelled sixty-five of its Yoruba ministers for practising polygyny. Yorubaland, birthplace of Bishop Crowther, was a cultural frontier where the contest between Islam, Christianity and traditional religion encouraged people to probe religious conundrums for themselves, and the Yoruba were not inclined to submit meekly to the external exercise of power. The expelled Methodist ministers went on to found their own 'United African Methodist Church', and the acceptance of polygyny was one of its marks of identity.[59] The extraordinarily long-lasting and widespread effect in West Africa of the indigenous Liberian prophet William Wadé Harris (1865–1929) was thanks to his embrace of African cultural forms around a quite conventionally Western Protestant theological package. Among those forms were local clothing for a prophet and the liturgical calabash gourd-rattle, but also polygamy, which Harris probably practised himself, and which he cautiously commended in phrasing uncannily resonant of a Pauline epistle, though a little more good-natured: 'If you marry two women, that is awkward, but do it if you cannot do otherwise . . . If you can marry ten women, do it, but follow the rules of God.'[60]

One nineteenth-century eruption of polygamy within a white Western culture was remarkable but has had an inconclusive and divisive history. Early in the century Joseph Smith, an imaginative young man growing up in a humble family in rural New York State, created a distinctive offshoot of Protestantism: the Church of Latter-Day Saints (or 'Mormons', from the name of the sacred book that Smith constructed, by revelation, as he claimed). The first major home-grown American variant of Christian religion, the 'LDS' quickly numbered a devoted following, who were prepared to brave hostility from their peers and native Americans alike in establishing a divine empire beyond US frontiers as settlers streamed westward. Just before his death at the hands of angry unbelieving vigilantes in 1844, Joseph Smith had a supplementary revelation that the LDS must introduce polygamy, a revelation posthumously released to the public in 1852. It had startled even his senior lieutenants, particularly the man who took Smith's work forward after his violent end, Brigham Young.

Smith stands in a long line of charismatic self-taught prophets who use their exceptional imaginative abilities to serve as cultural sponges for events around them, to create their own new reality. The context of his revolutionary pronouncement on marital relations was the extraordinary proliferation of American social experiments in utopian communities during his youth; they might be considered as a luxuriant outgrowth of early socialism, but equally they often expressed an apocalyptic excitement which puts them among the products of the Evangelical 'Second Great Awakening'. Amid the freedom afforded by the vast territories of north America, one aspect of such utopian experimentation was to explore alternatives to the conventional patterns of Western Christian marriage.

In this spirit, and in disgust at the hypocrisy of slave-holding Protestant Christianity, the wealthy Scots emigrant Frances Wright created a utopian anti-slavery community in Tennessee in the 1820s, where the races not only mixed but placed no boundaries on their voluntary sexual activity, in contrast to the sexual coercion of the plantations. In 1848, four years before Brigham Young announced the late Joseph Smith's revelation, an even larger commune at Oneida, New York State, constituted itself in a regulated system of swapping heterosexual partners: 'complex marriages'.[61] Smith was positioning the future of his growing community amid all this, with the aim of creating true polygamy for this life and the next: some of the first plural Mormon marriages involved a woman with multiple husbands. Brigham Young, in his later systematic application of the Smith revelation, turned away from polygamy to what might be termed traditional polygyny, an institution that bore all the hallmarks of nineteenth-century male assertiveness. Multiple wives were expected to demonstrate the wifely obedience to a husband that was the ideal in wider monogamous society: all of them.[62]

The implementation of polygynous marriage had mixed results for the Mormons' craving to extend their mission. For the time being, it abruptly ended what had at first been promising growth in a now scandalized and amused monogamous Europe.[63] Yet in societies that already practised polygyny, local reaction could be very different. A notable example is among the Maori in Aotearoa (the pair of major islands that Europeans have called New Zealand). Maori had both a lively curiosity about the British culture that was encroaching on their lands from the 1820s, and an exceptional ability to position themselves in relation to it; they took to Christianity with enthusiasm. Yet, by the 1860s, the increasing settler population and the untrustworthiness of the colonial administration led to bitterness and open war, a particular blow to the progress of Anglicanism that was so closely associated with the government. The Maori filled the religious vacuum with their own syntheses of Christian practice and traditional religion, but additionally many of them became enthusiastic for the LDS, whose young American missionaries were treated as unwelcome outsiders by the British, and who made clear their affirmation of Maori polygyny. It was a lasting cultural alliance, though increasingly strained by the Western racial character of Mormon belief.[64]

Mainstream Mormonism in the USA reluctantly brought polygyny to an end under threat of federal legal action threatening its property assets; in 1890 the Church formally laid aside the practice as a prelude to gaining full statehood for its home territory of Utah. In practice, the LDS leadership went on clandestinely sanctioning plural marriage until further political pressure on the newly established State of Utah produced a more thoroughgoing prohibition in 1904. Beyond the now monogamous LDS Church with its base in Salt Lake City, polygyny still has its Mormon strongholds in Idaho, Arizona and Montana, with the largest number in Utah itself where there are well in excess of ten thousand people in polygynous families. Meanwhile, the worldwide missionary movement looking to Salt Lake City presents the most conventional imaginable version of a mid-twentieth-century monogamous family as the norm for Mormon life. Indeed, the fascination of LDS with family genealogy, in the interests of retrieving ancestors for enrolling in heaven, is perhaps one of the most American features of the Church.[65]

The United States spread westward as a land empire after its independence from Britain; meanwhile Russia had also extended its imperial territory landward to the coasts of eastern Asia, and, for a century down to 1867, over the Bering Sea into Alaska. Popular Russian Orthodox Christianity continued to build on its tradition of self-assertion beyond the bureaucratic religion of the Tsars, and it was often inspired by new recruits to the identity of the Holy Fool in rebrandings of faith that could be as radical as anything embraced by the LDS. One peculiar eruption of enthusiasm in particular took a branch of Russian Christianity in the opposite direction to the Mormon theme of procreation, embracing practices that the mainstream Church of the Mediterranean had hesitantly repudiated in the third century CE (above, Chapter 7). In the late eighteenth century, a self-taught peasant prophet, Kondratii Selivanov, emerged in western Russia from an earlier dissident Orthodox group characterized by penitential flagellation. Outdoing their rigorism and extending the Orthodox tradition of negativity about sex, he founded a sect devoted to eliminating sexual lust from the human race through very specific and literal forms of self-mutilation.

Selivanov based his teachings on particular proof-texts crafted out of his own misreadings of the Bible in Russian. He read a command of God to the Israelites as *plotites'* ('castrate yourselves') rather than *plodites'* (be fruitful), and he rendered *Iskupitel'* ('Redeemer') as *Oskopitel'* ('Castrator') where the New Testament speaks of Jesus. As a result, to achieve purity his male followers, the *Skoptsy* ('castrated ones'), cut off their genitals, and women their breasts. The tsarist authorities were no less horrified or baffled than their Soviet successors after the 1917 Revolution, but persecution and punishment were not going to have much effect on people who had punished themselves so drastically; reports of them persist even after the Second World War.[66] By then, the Christian matrices of *Skoptsy* and Mormons alike were drastically different from the societies that had unwillingly fostered them, but, in the globalism of the modern age, their respective adherents might actually encounter one another in a fashion that would once have been inconceivable. We must now introduce them and all the other abundant fruits of eighteenth- and nineteenth-century religion into the modern world.

18

A Century of Contraception (1900–)

The first half of the twentieth century witnessed two world wars generated by European powers, though they spread outwards to devastate much more of the planet; only the Americas largely escaped direct damage, an incidental prompt to the rise of the United States as the world's only surviving superpower by 2000. In no more than a half-century from the end of the Second World War in 1945, both the short-lived and the longer-established European colonial empires were dismantled, culminating after 1991 in the collapse of the Soviet Union. With that seven-decade experiment in atheism dismantled, the emerging Russian Federation lost many satellite territories and much of its tsarist inheritance of conquests; it was much reduced not merely in territorial extent but in real global influence.

The Russian Communist collapse did mean the end of marginalization and persecution for the Russian Orthodox Church, with consequences that are still unfolding (below, Chapter 19), but otherwise the twentieth century finally put an end to that medieval construction called Christendom. Hereditary monarchy, which still ruled the great majority of Europeans and much of the world in 1900, suffered major collateral damage in the world wars and revolutions, and none of the surviving European monarchies now represent great powers. Western Christendom, once an integrated society shaped and bounded by the decisions of the Church, was already disrupted by the sixteenth-century Reformation and sorely wounded by the French Revolution; it is now represented by little more than the ecclesiastical institutions and splendid buildings that it created. In the Europe of the twenty-first century, from Ireland to Scandinavia to Russia to the Balkans and Iberia, active Christian practice has become a minority pastime, with Roman Catholicism and Orthodoxy following a pattern of drastic numerical decline first seen by mainstream Protestantism.

For Christianity worldwide, these developments represent not extinction but transformation. They are shaped partly by the demography of the modern world; the same period that has seen a revolution in artificial contraception has witnessed world human population numbers rocketing from a sudden take-off in the early nineteenth century, thanks largely to steep declines in infant mortality. The catastrophic toll of premature death caused by twentieth-century wars has had little long-term effect. It has been estimated that between the time of the late Roman Republic and the accession of Queen Victoria, human numbers quadrupled; from that base around 1837, they have risen sevenfold, and the current population of humans has risen well past 7 billion. Crucially, for the interaction of world cultures, human population has radically shifted in distribution. Some societies, chiefly Europe and its east Asian counterpart Japan, but also more unexpected places like Thailand and Lebanon, have begun moving away from dynamic population growth into demographic deceleration, producing striking reverses across continents. If Japan's population in 1950 was about twice that of Nigeria, the ratio has now turned into something like one to nine in Nigeria's favour.[1]

We are all familiar with the strains on the planet's resources and climate that these changes have caused, worsened by our two centuries of prodigal over-reliance on fossil fuels. Social strains are also apparent. Ageing populations are less prone to interpersonal violence, a nexus that is connected to the fact that across the world, these societies also generally enjoy greater financial and personal security. Violence has been particularly disruptive in many regions with rapidly expanding and therefore predominantly young human populations, leading to the mass movement of peoples that encourages angry rhetoric about migration among politicians looking for votes. Lurking alongside their opportunism is the uncomfortable contrary fact that the areas of twentieth-century power in Europe, north America and Japan still consume far more economic resources than the rest of the world, which they are reluctant to share more equally. What passes for theological and ethical reflection in many Christian quarters is an exercise in ignoring the reality of these present imbalances that disfigure divine creation, usually through strident repetition of old certainties, not least about how to speak about sex and gender.

Amid these cross-cultural tensions and anxieties, Christians remain the world's most numerous adherents of any religion, with around twice as many followers as their nearest competitor, Islam. Moreover, one survey of world religions made after the final phases of disintegration of the European empires revealed the most movement around Christian practice, mostly in Christianity's favour: the estimate was that in one year in the 1990s worldwide, around 25 million people chose a new faith, 18 million of them converts to Christianity and 7 million moving from Christianity to other beliefs. Africa has confounded those who predicted that the end of Christian colonial empires would also bring the death of African Christianity: instead, around 1985, African Christian numbers exceeded the total of African Muslims for the first time. Equally unexpected has been the resurgence of Chinese Christianity, demonized in 1949 by the victorious Communist regime as symbolizing nineteenth- and early twentieth-century humiliations of China by Europeans; the expulsion of all missionaries followed. As systematic Communist ideology leached away from the government system in the 1980s, an extraordinary variety of now indigenous Christian practice emerged out of repression, and its vitality remains a difficult challenge for the Chinese authorities.[2]

THE RISE OF PENTECOSTALISM

Most of this energy worldwide is associated with a bewildering variety of Pentecostal Christianities, which sprouted into institutional form in the USA in the first decade of the twentieth century but were hardly noticed by the world at large until the 1950s.[3] Pentecostalism emphasizes the work and power of the Holy Spirit: the Third Person of the Trinity, but the Cinderella of the Triune Unity since the early days of the Church. Institutional Christianity has often experienced the Spirit as associated with unpredictability and inexpressible ecstasy beyond the control of authority, and has sought to place its activity firmly within such manageable contexts as the ordination of (male) clergy. The fact that radicals in the Reformation rediscovered the wildness and often the femininity of the Spirit in the sixteenth and seventeenth centuries only underlined the point.

Pentecostal Churches are like the Church of the Latter-Day Saints in being a product of nineteenth- and twentieth-century globalism. They may seem more closely bound to the Christian mainstream than the LDS, and indeed their re-encounter with the Holy Spirit has affected both Catholicism and Protestantism in a 'Charismatic' movement that rooted itself in these older ecclesial formations. Yet Pentecostalism has commonalities with the LDS; both movements have origins in the eighteenth- and nineteenth-century Great Awakenings of American Evangelicalism, and both add their own distinctive features – in the case of Pentecostals, the practice of 'speaking in tongues' only comprehensible through interpretation that the Holy Spirit prompts. It is described in two passages of the Book of Acts (2.1–13 and 10.44–48), first when fifty days ('Pentecost') after Christ's resurrection, in the presence of Jew and Gentile alike, Christian leaders filled with the Spirit spoke words understood by everyone hearing them as the praise of God. There could be no better symbol of modern globalism, which has provided gifts of rapid communication, translation and travel not available to the first disciples in Jerusalem.

After unmistakably discouraging comment from Paul of Tarsus, ecstatic utterance in tongues did not feature much in Christianity anywhere up to the early nineteenth century, when it reappeared without warning in the Church of Scotland. Equally with little precedent, some sections of the early Pentecostal movement evolved a distinctive theology of baptism in the name of Jesus (based on the second of those passages in Acts, 10.48); this inadvertently revived a form of Christian sub-Trinitarian theology chased out of the mainstream Christian Churches in the second and third centuries CE. Termed 'modalist Monarchianism' in the forbidding jargon of Church historians, 'Oneness' or 'Jesus-Only' Pentecostal belief now infuses the joyful faith of around a quarter of Pentecostalism's vast constituency worldwide.[4]

It is hardly surprising that in the early years of Pentecostalism, Evangelicals generally detested Pentecostals as much as they had once despised Quakers. After all, the essence of Evangelicalism is an affirmation of the clarity and comprehensibility of the Word of God in Scripture, rather than the wordless sighs of the Spirit of God (once praised in passing by Paul of Tarsus himself, Rom. 8.26). Cerebral Fundamentalism like this is a particularly awkward fit for the Pentecostal outlook. An opposite problem was the closeness of much Pentecostal belief to some of the theological innovations made by nineteenth-century Evangelical Protestantism – like quarrelsome siblings, they could bicker over the finer points of for instance 'Spirit Baptism' or 'Dispensationalism' – terms that would generally provoke blank looks in other parts of the Christian family. Moreover, the extrovert style of Pentecostal revivalism was irritatingly familiar to Evangelicals, while the Pentecostal penchant for giving women dramatic leadership roles was embarrassingly reminiscent of female freedoms that most wings of Evangelicalism spent the nineteenth century closing down (above, Chapter 15).[5]

Nevertheless, the widening global success of Pentecostalism could not fail to impress Evangelicals. One important commonality was their shared growing suspicion of liberal Protestantism, particularly when it centred itself on a 'Social Gospel' of justice and political action that seemed to them a dangerous distraction to the task of evangelism. A crucial moment came in 1943 when a major component of the Pentecostal Movement in the USA, the Assemblies of God, agreed to join the National Association of Evangelicals.[6] It was a time when American Evangelicalism seemed especially vulnerable and in need of allies. In the inter-war period, it had suffered dual blows on the national scene, first in widespread ridicule after a set-piece confrontation over the teaching of Charles Darwin's theory of evolution in the school curricula in Tennessee and Oklahoma, and then in the abject failure of its attempt to impose compliance with Prohibition on the nation's drinkers. The favourite cause of 'first-wave feminism' met its match in the repeal of Prohibition in 1933 by the Democrat President Franklin D. Roosevelt and a Congress dominated by (overwhelmingly male) Democrats.

The Pentecostal–Evangelical pact grew in strength after 1943. It meant that theological education for both parties fell into conservative patterns set by the Evangelicals, who were generally better financed. Styles of worship evolved in similar ways. The burgeoning Christianity of Africa found Pentecostalism's celebratory and spontaneous forms of worship more congenial than older European liturgies whether Protestant or Catholic; so did the emerging indigenous Christianities of Asia from India to Korea. Celebration of God's love was often the only celebration that desperately poor people could count on. In much of this still rapidly growing new Christianity, one would often be hard put to label any single congregation as specifically Pentecostal, Charismatic or Evangelical, yet over the last half-century they are likely to display one common characteristic: an angry alarm at what the liberal West is saying and doing about sex and sexual expression. That has stemmed from one of the greatest and most rapid revolutions in human behaviour in recorded history.

CONDOMS, SHEATHS AND PILLS

The most fundamental change in the experience of human sexuality over the last century and a half has been the development of reliable methods of contraception. A new mid-nineteenth-century para-reproductive technology, supplanting centuries of rudimentary contraceptive devices, was based on a boom in Brazilian rubber production. Contraceptive methods radically diversified during the twentieth century, with a crucial extension from mechanical into medical means in the late 1950s.[7] Now contraceptives are readily available to anyone throughout most of the world. The result is that most sexual encounters in the developed world today are non-reproductive – heterosexual as well as homosexual, within marriage as outside it. Mutual pleasure, or maybe pleasure for one partner at least, has trumped procreation, which would not please either Pythagoreans or Clement of Alexandria. Such mutuality may recall Paul of Tarsus's notion of the 'marital debt', but contraception knows no marital boundaries.

Mainstream Protestantism worldwide has largely accepted this development as unavoidable and not necessarily sinful; successively modified official statements moved from blanket condemnation to cautious acceptance, a process that unfolded remarkably quickly in the first half of the twentieth century. The classic, and indeed puzzlingly precocious, example is the Anglican Communion, through the statements of successive Lambeth Conferences between 1908 and 1930. In 1908, the bishops assembled at Lambeth Palace predictably recorded their alarm at 'the growing practice of the artificial restriction of the family, and earnestly call[ed] upon all Christian people to discountenance the use of all artificial means of restriction as demoralising to character and hostile to national welfare.' Speaker after speaker condemned contraception as unnatural, not to mention a danger to health, rather as if it had been a form of masturbation. There was also a good deal of favourable reference to eugenics in the speeches, for instance in warnings of the diminishing birth rate of British 'superior stocks'.[8]

Twelve years later in 1920, the next Conference still spoke in similar terms of 'the grave dangers – physical, moral and religious' of contraception, and with a reminiscence of the ancient 'Alexandrian rule' pronounced the primary purpose for marriage as 'the continuation of the race through the gift and heritage of children'. Yet the bishops could hardly avoid noticing how opinions in the medical profession were shifting, or that campaigners for birth control were gaining confidence and national attention. In the following year, no less a figure than King George V's personal physician, Bernard Lord Dawson, President of the Royal College of Physicians, bluntly warned the Anglican Church Congress in Birmingham that 'birth control is here to stay'. His exalted status was probably only one factor in the Church leadership listening to him: what may be the key to the bishops' growing change of stance was the fact that Dawson's informed opinions were part of a conversation among former public schoolboys who moved in the same social world.[9]

As a result, a great change in attitudes appeared in 1930, when the Lambeth Conference acknowledged in cautious Anglican-speak that there would be occasions when 'a clearly felt moral obligation to limit or avoid parenthood', and 'a morally sound reason for avoiding complete abstinence' would justify contraception in the light of Christian principles. The decision to use contraceptives should thus be up to the consciences of individual couples. More importantly, a majority among the bishops no longer considered birth control sinful by its nature. Some even argued that there was no real moral difference between sexual abstinence and artificial contraception, since both set out deliberately to prevent conception.[10]

All through this discussion, eugenics remained significant; it was the chosen emphasis of the Church's self-appointed expert on birth control, Theodore Woods, the Bishop of Winchester, who noted the alarming decline in birth rate among the middle and upper classes and considered that the lesser orders needed encouraging to limit their families so that the British population would be rebalanced towards the leaders of society and Empire. That argument swayed many doubters, though other speakers did say more about individual morality, and also equity for women.[11] The Anglican Communion had by whatever route become the first major Church grouping in the world to accept contraception as legitimate. The triumph of contraception in Anglicanism was sealed at the Lambeth Conference of 1958, where over three hundred bishops from forty-six countries unanimously decided that family planning was a 'right and important factor in Christian family life' – and it seems that where Anglicans lead, the world follows: in 2012 the United Nations declared access to family planning a universal human right.[12]

Opposition to this momentous step had been still loud in the Lambeth debates in 1930. Anglo-Catholics were split, the final direction of the

Conference being set from among their ranks by the moral theologian and later Bishop of Oxford Kenneth Kirk, while others in opposition echoed nineteenth-century Roman Catholic moral theology, chief among them being the veteran Anglo-Catholic leader and monk, Bishop Charles Gore of Oxford. Gore was an exceptionally clear-sighted theologian, austerely ready to call a spade a spade. He was prepared to spell out the inescapable link between contraception and homosexual sex: 'what we used to call unnatural vice ... appears to be very prevalent now.' He insisted in classic Alexandrian fashion that there must be a connection between sex and reproduction: to separate sexual pleasure from procreation 'justifies the philosophy of homosexuality'. Gore was of course perfectly correct, and prophetic of later developments in liberal Protestantism, as we will see.[13]

In the short term, Anglican leaders mid-century sought to stem a social tide beyond the moral limits that they had now set. Geoffrey Fisher (Archbishop of Canterbury from 1945 until 1961) and his wife, Rosamond (worldwide Central President of the Mothers' Union, 1944–53) were prominent in ecumenical Christian moves to limit the sale of contraceptives in vending machines, and the model by-law that they created for such a prohibition was taken up by an astonishing 90 per cent of British local authorities in the early 1950s. The gilt was taken off this achievement by the brutal reality that retail sales of contraceptives continued steadily to rise in the United Kingdom: a statistical tribute to the quiet pressure of public opinion. The whole picture would in any case soon be transformed by the introduction of oral contraceptives (first launched in the USA and UK in 1957 and given a mass roll-out in 1961): that changed the premises of any realistic theological debate.[14]

Rome was hardly likely to sign up to a Protestant U-turn of this magnitude. Instead, on 31 December 1930, in full awareness of the new Lambeth resolutions and similar statements from both Protestant Churches and liberal rabbis in the USA, Pope Pius XI issued the decree *Casti Connubii*, 'On Chaste Wedlock', prohibiting Catholics from using any form of artificial birth control – and condemning eugenic laws that forced sterilization. This created a new gulf within Western Christianity, at least at an official level. The ecumenical and interfaith American Social Hygiene Association, the largest moral education programme in the USA, had deliberately kept away from the birth control issue because of the widening disagreement, but its most prominent Catholic member, the priest John Montgomery Cooper, now felt compelled to resign, while pointedly maintaining that most of his Catholic colleagues approved of the ASHA's work.[15] Pope Pius XII in public statements of the 1940s uninhibitedly termed 'frustrating the marriage act' by artificial contraception 'criminal abuse' and 'a deed which is shameful and intrinsically vicious'; his words echoed in pastoral pronouncements throughout the Catholic world.[16]

More unexpected was the reaffirmation of *Casti Connubii* four decades later by Pope Paul VI, in the wake of the second Vatican Council (1962–65). Pope Paul had taken over the presidency of the Council on the death of his ebullient predecessor John XXIII in June 1963; he had been a loyal collaborator in Pope John's astonishing turn away from the arid certainties of the Church hierarchy in the aftermath of Vatican I and the fight against Modernism (above, Chapter 16). Yet during the 1964 sessions of the Council, Pope Paul announced without warning that it would not discuss birth control, as he awaited the findings of a 'Pontifical Commission' of experts on natural law to examine the issue. Its members included laypeople, even women, very much in the general spirit that had come to characterize Vatican II. In 1968, they were at last about to make public their findings; they had concluded that there was no good argument for banning contraceptive devices.[17]

The Pope was alarmed. He enlarged the commission and changed the criteria for those entitled to vote, hoping for a different outcome: instead, it was reinforced. So, finally, he ignored the commission's work and instead accepted a conservative minority recommendation reaffirming *Casti Connubii*. Just to emphasize how much the spirit of 1930 lived on, this minority report specifically pointed to the Anglican Communion's reverse of direction on birth control, and observed that for the Catholic Church to follow suit would imply that the Holy Spirit was active outside the Roman obedience.[18] On this basis, Paul VI issued his own statement in 1968: the encyclical *Humanae Vitae* ('Of Human Life'), which gave no place for artificial contraception in a Catholic family. To his astonishment and dismay, the case was not closed when Rome had spoken.

What the Pope had not appreciated was that Catholic laity had already been quietly thinking for themselves on this issue, and indeed had re-evaluated their Catholicism on the basis of their conclusions. A sensitive analysis of opinion among American Catholics in the 1960s speaks of a new sense among them of 'moral autonomy – a process nearly always connected to agonizing over contraception'.[19] There were open and angry protests both lay and clerical all over the Catholic world, and, worse still, demographics soon revealed that millions of Catholic laity were paying no attention to the papal ban – as emphatic a rejection as the earlier reaction to Anglican efforts to limit the sale of contraceptives. Paul VI never really recovered from the shock and took no initiatives of significance in the remaining decade of his pontificate.[20] It was the first time that the Catholic faithful – and Catholic families in particular – had so consistently scorned a major papal pronouncement intended to structure intimate parts of their lives, but it has not been the last sexual topic on which Catholic laypeople have parted company with the authority of the Church as presented to them.

NEW VOICES FOR CHRISTIAN WOMEN

Entangled with the story of a reproductive revolution is the ongoing readjustment of gender relations and definitions between women, men and others; they offer an alternative story to a great many assumptions about these matters that have shaped three thousand years of Judaism and Christianity. The new feminism of the modern age might not have taken the shape that it has done were it not for the invention of the contraceptive pill in the mid-twentieth century, yet the expenditure of time and scientific funding on that success may have become a desirable priority precisely because gender relations in Western society were already changing.[21] Once more, the underlying patterns of demography are also important: during the first decades of the twentieth century, female excess mortality disappeared from Europe, and patterns of life expectancy tipped in favour of women over men. Partly this must have been the result of reducing serious infections, especially around childbirth, but there is also no doubt that earlier generations in Christian Europe had exercised discrimination in feeding and nurturing boys over girls. That is still the case in some other parts of the world and suggests a further complex causal relationship between the changing position of women and the biological realities of their new advantage in survival.[22]

There was a low base to work from in Western social attitudes at the beginning of the twentieth century. That was exemplified in the case brought in the Westminster Court of Appeal in 1914, that for the purposes of admission as a solicitor to the Law Society of England and Wales, a woman was not a person, owing to the inherent 'disability' of the female sex; for the moment that decision remained the law in Great Britain.[23] In contemporary Irish Roman Catholicism, one classic history of the heroic pioneering days in early Celtic monasticism was unintentionally revealing. It back-projected present-day reality onto what was for the Jesuit historian-author Dr Ryan the problematic phenomenon of Celtic double monasteries: 'Women religious in their turn could relieve the monks of services for which the normal male is supremely ill-fitted, such as the making of vestments and clothes, care of altar linen, and general attention to cleanliness and beauty within the church.'[24]

In various cultural settings across the anglophone world, efforts of imagination began to move on from such predictable opinions. Consistent with its ability to listen to such promptings more attentively than other British institutions, the early twentieth-century Church of England took some remarkable initiatives. The Bishop of Lincoln, Edward Hicks, headed the Church League for Women's Suffrage before the First World War – an organization interestingly inspired by the Anglo-Catholic exploration of the Incarnation in the writings of Bishop Gore. When the Westminster Parliament and the Church set up a brand-new legislative 'National Assembly of the Church of England' in 1920, the Assembly achieved equal suffrage nine years before Parliament.[25] Among its deliberations over its first decade was an initiative from that same Bishop Hicks to remove an ancient peculiarity of the Anglican wedding service, in which a woman swore to 'obey' her husband. In Roman Catholic and Orthodox marriage liturgies, the marriage vows had never been unequal like this (despite the common patriarchal assumptions of all Churches); it was a late medieval northern European idiosyncrasy fossilized by Cranmer's Prayer Book and imitated by English Dissent. By the early twentieth century, the obedience clause was sufficiently annoying to many clergy and people to be quietly omitted, and when the Church of England untidily acquired alternative liturgies in 1928, the change was made permanent, to widespread public approval.[26]

Forty of the elected lay members at the first meeting of the Church Assembly in 1920 were female, and from their ranks, members of what had been the Church League for Women's Suffrage (now 'League of the Church Militant') straight away raised the question of the ordination of women. We have seen something of the prehistory of this in the Quakers and Methodists, and after those initiatives, first-wave feminism had produced some ordinations of women to pastoral charges, first in American liberal Protestant Churches (from 1815) and then in England (1917). Nineteenth-century Germany and then England had instituted Orders of Deaconesses, though had generally firmly discouraged any exploration of their clerical character that might draw on early Church practice (above, Chapters 6 and 7).[27] Now a major section of the Western Church was being asked to rethink the question.

Against predictable fierce clerical opposition, it was remarkable enough for an Archbishops' Commission on the Ministry of Women rather lamely to conclude in 1932 that although they were not able to come up with any good reasons why women should not be ordained priest, 'there are no practical reasons to justify it.' Anglican women did not allow the question to rest, and in the emergency of the Second World War in 1944, there was indeed a practical reason: Bishop Ronald Hall of Hong Kong and South China ordained a deaconess, Li Tim-Oi, as priest, since otherwise no one was free to administer the sacraments in Hong Kong. This assertion of reality was too much for Anglican leaders in Britain; under pressure, Miss Li honourably withdrew from active ministry until much later when times had changed. She will have had the consolation meanwhile of knowing that around 1970 similar circumstances had provoked a similar provision in the Catholic Church of Communist-era Czechoslovakia, although the sacerdotal actions of those women were quite limited, and their story remains obscure.[28]

In contrasting cultural settings, twentieth-century women took matters into their own hands. A minor English symptom was the ministry of Mrs Mabel Barltrop (aka 'Octavia', daughter of God). Widow of an Anglican clergyman, in bereavement she became fascinated by the sensational proclamations of the early nineteenth-century Joanna Southcott, a prophet with an enthusiastic following parallel to Methodism, with various Victorian successors in prophecy – the designation 'Octavia' placed Barltrop as the eighth prophet on from Southcott. Her home in Bedford became the new Garden of Eden, and her never very numerous followers, predominantly female, persisted throughout the twentieth century in a gentle postal ministry of healing across the world. Their Bedford properties still offer a comfortable Edwardian welcome to Christ in his prospective Second Coming.[29]

A more tragic later career was that of the prophetess Alice Lenshina, in what is now Zambia. In 1953, Lenshina experienced death and resurrection; her initially low-key ministry had an electrifying effect in building up a movement from the region's Presbyterians and Roman

Catholics, gathering her flock on the basis of her new message from Jesus. Her followers were eventually bloodily dispersed by the new Zambian state and its Presbyterian first President, Kenneth Kaunda, in the 'Lumpa War' of 1964. Lenshina was hardly unique as a female prophet in African Independent Churches, and she was not the last to lead her followers into fatal violence; the truly horrifying fiery end to the prophetic ministry of the formerly Catholic Keledonia Mwerinde in 2000 is one of the worst tragedies of Uganda's troubled religious history.[30]

Early Pentecostalism was particularly fertile in fostering women's ministry. Most prominent on the international scene, perhaps the first Pentecostal to make an impression on the wider public was the redoubtable Canadian Mrs Aimee Semple McPherson, who in 1927 set up the 'Finished Work' International Church of the Foursquare Gospel, in which eventually 40 per cent of the pastorate was female. She chalked up a number of evangelistic firsts, including the first Christian radio station and the first sermon preached by a woman on the radio, not to mention her ministry of scattering Christian leaflets from an aeroplane, and she was probably the first preacher of any gender to enter the worship arena on a motorbike. McPherson was also honourably prominent in combating racism and the commerce in drugs. Colourful sensation ranging between a shrewd awareness of showbiz and some dubious personal episodes characterized her public career, and indeed also her eventual death from a prescription drug overdose.[31]

Evangelicals took note of such successes and promoted an extraordinary evangelistic phenomenon in the inter-war period: dramatic public testimony by prepubescent and adolescent girls, who provided a Fundamentalist riposte to the popular image of the hedonistic young 'Flapper'. This was, after all, the period in which the child star Shirley Temple burst onto cinematic screens, and an analogous pioneer was Uldine Utley, a protégée of Mrs McPherson, who for a decade or so from 1923 enjoyed as much name recognition as some of the most celebrated contemporary evangelists. Her career as a Fundamentalist preacher was as sadly meteoric as many equally well-known starlets of Hollywood, effectively over at twenty-four before six more decades of obscurity fighting recurrent mental illness. Pentecostals consciously turned against the promotion of girl evangelists just before the Second World War, and in north America at least, a familiar pattern of gender institutionalization emerged. The proportion of women in the ministry of the Church of the Nazarene declined from 20 per cent in 1908 to 1 per cent in 1989, and in the Church of God in Christ, from 32 per cent in 1925 to 15 per cent in 1992. Worldwide in Pentecostalism, the picture remains a good deal more varied.[32]

Inevitably, these twentieth-century stories of world Christianity as they project into our own time leave undecided an overall view of their consequences or any sense of finality. They intersect with a set of new ethical and moral directions that gathered strength from the 1960s: the period within living memory, during which Christian Churches, particularly in the West, have had to face a dramatic set of transformations in the way that humans behave – generally in reactive mode against developments that few Christian leaders anticipated or discussed. It is hardly surprising that theological reflection in Christianity has hardly begun to take coherent forms, confronted by it all. Nevertheless, we must finally turn to survey what can be made of such reactions so far, both positive and negative. The starting point will be some public excitements in the United Kingdom, a global imperial power in decline, in the wake of the Second World War.

19
Choices and *Lady Chatterley* (1950–)

> Sexual intercourse began
> In nineteen sixty-three
> (which was rather late for me) –
> Between the end of the Chatterley ban
> And the Beatles' first LP.
>
> Philip Larkin, *Annus Mirabilis*

An elegiac verse from the patron saint of university librarians rather accurately dates the emergence of the permissive 'Sixties', more a state of mind than an exact decade – a change of social mood which mass media spread across the world, enfolding in itself the concept of a youth culture entitled to challenge the assumptions and mores of a previous generation, not least on matters of sex and gender. D. H. Lawrence's *Lady Chatterley's Lover* may now seem a pretentiously overheated celebration of integrating mind and body in human love, but it was then notorious: after its first private publication in 1928, the unexpurgated text of the novel had never been legally available in Britain. The prosecution of Penguin Books in 1960 for publishing an obscene book was a deliberately symbolic case, quietly arranged between the UK Director of Public Prosecutions and the publisher in order to test the boundaries of the recent Obscene Publications Act (1959). A policeman called at Penguin's London offices by prior arrangement to collect a proof copy that counted as publication and therefore the basis of the court action. Among the expert witnesses lined up to defend it were prominent Anglican clergy, including an Anglican monk. Penguin's acquittal ensured handsome sales across the world.[1]

AWAKENINGS OLD AND NEW

It is in this era, from 1951 onwards to be precise, that I must abandon any spurious claim to historical objectivity, having become a participant observer in events. What Philip Larkin's verse does not capture is how unexpected the subsequent social and religious changes seemed at the beginning of the 1960s. In the USA, the 1950s have been viewed as another Protestant 'Great Awakening', with Church membership increasing from 50 per cent of the population in 1940 to almost 70 per cent in 1960: actual church attendance peaked at around half the American population in 1955. The two decades after the Second World War seemed peculiarly promising for mainstream Protestantism worldwide. It was possible to see the destruction of Nazism as a victory for the values of liberty and democracy much prized by anglophone Protestant societies – so long as one did not leave too much space on the moral high ground for Soviet Russia's part in Hitler's defeat. Certainly, the Universal Declaration of Human Rights that accompanied the foundation of the United Nations in the late 1940s emerged from the same circle of liberal Protestants who had been active in developing ecumenical ties between Churches over the previous half-century.[2]

The Atlantic Isles shadowed this north American profile in general ecclesiastical optimism. In 1959 the Anglican Bishop of Woolwich, John Robinson (soon to be notorious for disturbing British theological certainties) could assure his confirmation candidates that they were 'at a time when great things are afoot' in the Church: 'I believe that in England we may be at a turning of the tide. Indeed, in Cambridge, where I have recently come from, I am convinced that the tide has turned.'[3] In the Republic of Ireland, now fully independent of the United Kingdom, a different cultural history underlay the unrivalled hegemony of the Roman Catholic Church in the 1950s. It was personified by the formidable figure of Archbishop John McQuaid in Dublin, assiduously courted by successive Irish governments and by President de Valera himself. The Republic, sheltered by neutrality in the Second World War, had changed little after Independence in its Edwardian rural poverty. Over thirty years from the break with the British Empire, its Protestant population had plummeted, the lost Protestant Ascendancy visually symbolized across the Irish landscape by ruined gentry houses and derelict Church of Ireland parish churches. Outside the Protestant remnant, McQuaid and his lieutenants ruthlessly maintained Catholic family and clerical life in the image of Vatican I, and made sure that the Censorship of Publications Board protected the whole population from sexual filth.[4]

Success bred ecclesiastical self-confidence, yet in the case of mainstream Protestantism, that meant a continuing openness to what might need modification in moral pronouncements. In the United Kingdom, there was general public surprise in the 1950s that influential clergy of the Church of England (and rather more hesitantly, the Church of Scotland) would consider the decriminalization of homosexuality. Behind the scenes in the 1930s, Cosmo Gordon Lang, the Archbishop of Canterbury, had been involved in thoughtful correspondence about the wider implications of the decision on contraception at the 1930 Lambeth Conference, and after the hiatus of the Second World War, others felt impelled to revive the subject.[5] Derrick Sherwin Bailey was a genial and scholarly Anglican clergyman who had the independence of mind to produce a general survey of *Homosexuality and the Western Christian Tradition*, in a monograph of 1955 still worth reading; he carried his scholarship into public action in further publications and on the Church of England Moral Welfare Council.

As a result, Bailey's was an influential voice when a series of gay sex scandals involving the prosecution of prominent people embarrassed the Conservative government into setting up a committee of enquiry chaired by Lord Wolfenden to investigate the laws on prostitution and homosexuality. It recommended a limited decriminalization. Even Archbishop Geoffrey Fisher – ever the public-school headmaster, after his years at Repton School – was cautiously in favour, though he would personally have preferred extending the criminal law to cover heterosexual adultery (on that subject, his staff at Lambeth Palace saved him from public ridicule by quietly intercepting his letter intended for *The Times*). Tory fears meant that legislation on Wolfenden's recommendations was postponed into the time of a reform-minded Labour government in 1967; Scotland had to wait till 1980.[6]

By 1967, the mood of the 'Swinging Sixties' obscured how much the Church of England had been involved in the background of the law partially decriminalizing male homosexuality. Nevertheless, the then Archbishop of Canterbury Michael Ramsey robustly supported the Bill in the House of Lords, riding out criticism because of his Anglo-Catholic theological conviction that the law of the State had no business interfering in private morality, which should be the concern of the Church alone.

He was one of a generation of liberal Anglo-Catholics who had already been infuriated by the secular Parliament interfering with reform of Anglican liturgy in 1927–8. Now in answering a private letter from one outraged opponent of changing the law, he tartly commented: 'It seems to me that an enlightened Christian morality does require that we avoid suggesting that sexual sins are necessarily more terrible than others because Christ does not suggest this.'[7]

In north American mainstream Protestantism, there was a similar mood. The National Council of Churches hearkened to changing medical and psychiatric opinion in the 1950s when it sought to reduce a quarter of a millennium of Western panic about masturbation. This emphasis on the necessity of drawing on supposedly objective medical expertise did raise the question of what special authority Christians would be bringing to such questions; Protestant liberals did their best. They reconsidered sexual activity among young people by applying criteria of reason and love, part of what was soon to be termed 'the New Morality' – a term first given publicity in 1959 and taken up on both sides of the Atlantic: its first exponent, the Episcopalian priest Joseph Fletcher, pursued the theme in his book *Situation Ethics* (1966). A five-day conference at Green Lake, Wisconsin, in 1961 on 'Church and the Family' managed to push its agenda beyond the relatively uncontroversial discussion of sexual intercourse in marriage into sexual

27. The Quaker campaigner Mary Steichen Calderone displays useful pamphlets on sexual matters, 1969.

and 'New Morality' matters generally: the Quaker Mary Steichen Calderone, a former Director of Planned Parenthood, in a speech that left a lasting impact, inter alia afforded various male delegates their first viewing of selected female hygiene products.[8]

None of this was calculated to impress conservative Christians, and in the 1970s the already fragile nexus between liberal and conservative Protestants withered away. A century of mainstream Protestant dominance in American sex education was coming to an end; as gradually became apparent, so was the expansion of American churchgoing. One factor might be that liberal Protestants, mindful and approving of artificial contraception, were now planning smaller families than their conservative neighbours. Around the anglophone world, in a considerable irony, the family unit that had triumphed in the Protestant Reformation against centuries of celibate ascendancy now steadily undermined churchgoing.

The rhetoric of the twentieth-century family emphasized affectionate companionship – 'Love and marriage go together like a horse and carriage', in the words of a popular song of my early boyhood – and that family was smaller than in the past, inviting the prospect of a new intimacy. First the radio and then the television became fixtures to gather family members together in the evening, and on Sundays, the leisure day from work, they might all enjoy going out somewhere together in the newly acquired family car. From the eighteenth century, anglophone parents (possibly with a sense of relief at having some time to themselves) had sent their children off to Sunday School, one of the chief success stories of the Evangelical Revival. From the late 1960s, they stopped doing so. British statistics tell the tale: in 1900, 55% of British children attended Sunday School, 24% in 1960, 9% in 1980, and 4% in 2000. Traditional Christian literacy, handed down the generations across the UK by such means, began to erode, and the habit of churchgoing along with it.[9]

Such consequences were not immediately apparent, and Protestantism's general mood of optimism and hospitality to a variety of changes in the Christian message seemed to be paralleled in Catholicism in the wake of the second Vatican Council, which generated unprecedented ecumenical warmth between Western Churches. This was particularly perceptible in Dutch Catholicism, right up to its leading figure, Cardinal Bernardus Alfrink, who attended the Council following a recent joyful swerve away from his previous conservatism. The Dutch clergy proposed changes to canon law easing the way for those who entered 'mixed' or cross-confessional marriages, already becoming more frequent in the Netherlands as traditional confessional 'silos' in Dutch society broke down. They also voted overwhelmingly for an end to eight centuries of compulsory clerical celibacy. Pope Paul VI had been loyal to the agenda rather surprisingly set by progressives at the second Vatican Council with the encouragement of Pope John XXIII – liturgy in the vernacular, affirmation of lay ministry in the Church, openness to other Christian bodies and, indeed, to the world in general. But on issues of gender, family and sexuality, Paul VI found the limits of his progressive instincts: a year before his disastrous decision on artificial contraception, he reaffirmed the celibacy rule for the priesthood, and discouraged any further debate on the issue.

The angry reaction to this among many clergy anticipated the more general fury and disappointment at *Humanae Vitae*. Worldwide, priests renounced their public ministry to marry; in the West, numbers offering themselves for ordination began an inexorable decline. Among Catholics in many parts of Africa, where marriage was considered de rigueur for everyone regardless of clerical status, the reaction was simply to carry on as usual and to look benevolently on Catholic priests who cherished their spouses and offspring: a pattern with a precedent in many parts of medieval Europe (above, Chapters 12 and 13). In Africa, significantly, vocations to the priesthood continued to flourish.[10]

Through the 1970s and beyond, Western Churches contended with successive fallouts from the contraceptive revolution and the 'New Morality': first mainly in renewed campaigns for female ordination and then for acceptance of openly gay people and their relationships within Church membership. What had been a rather hesitant growth in Protestant Churches ordaining women broke a notable barrier in one of Europe's most liberal countries when the established Lutheran Church of Sweden began such ordinations in 1960 – now more than half the Swedish Church's priests are women – and after that, anglophone Presbyterianism in various settings. The Anglican Communion followed, with Hong Kong defiantly resuming the practice in 1971; British Methodists adopted female ordination without too much fuss in 1974, having already postponed the move in order to facilitate reunion schemes with the Church of England that ultimately failed. The dramatic Anglican

28. St Peter's Seminary, Cardross (Argyll and Bute) was planned for clergy training in the glory-days of the Scottish Catholic Church in the 1950s, and eventually designed in a self-confident Brutalist architectural idiom. *Concrete Quarterly* commented in 1967 that 'the timber-lined bedrooms are comparable with those of a comfortable hotel, and better designed than most.' The collapse in numbers entering the priesthood rapidly rendered it redundant; it closed in 1980 and is now a poignant ruin.

sequence came not in the UK but in the USA and Canada, unilateral moves causing great unease in Lambeth Palace. The Church of England became an ecclesial battleground, postponing the ordination even of women deacons till 1987, and waiting till 1994 to ordain female priests. It then took twenty more years of argument and political manoeuvre in the Church's General Synod to see the first consecration of a woman as bishop in England.

One of the reasons for that long-drawn-out result was the divisive effect of this issue on the theological parties that had emerged worldwide in the nineteenth-century Anglican Communion. Both Evangelicals and Anglo-Catholics now fissured between traditionalists and those sympathetic to change, and that has endured into subsequent fights, notably around attitudes to homosexuality. There has never been an exact transference: it is notable that a few female Evangelical bishops still fail to notice that the same theological arguments propelling them to consecration to the episcopate apply just as much to accepting homosexual relationships on equal terms, while the same inconsistency is perceptible among some gay Anglo-Catholics who still deplore the ordination of women while gratefully accepting the liberalization that has helped them organize their lives as they would wish. Indeed, for obvious historical reasons, conservative Anglo-Catholics have never been as convincing or full-throated opponents of gay equality as conservative Evangelicals, despite usually voting in the same direction when Church legislative bodies have proposed change.

Campaigns for gay rights were the logical fulfilment of Bishop Charles Gore's prophecy on contraception (above, Chapter 18), though not a result he would have sought. The first impulse of gay Christians in the West, like African Americans in eighteenth-century north America or African Independent Churches in subsequent centuries, was to found their own Church communities, free of condescension or worse from the existing Churches. So, in 1968, Troy Perry, a former Pentecostal pastor, gathered a little congregation, at first in his own home in Huntington Park, a low-income suburb of Los Angeles. Perry chose to call his congregation the 'Metropolitan Community Church' (MCC). The carefully neutral description additionally reflected a consistent characteristic of the emerging gay liberation movement: as with self-assertions of identity throughout Western history, it was easier to make one's own choice amid the relative anonymity of an urban setting.

The MCC ethos remained Bible-based in a Pentecostal fashion, though from the beginning a diverse sacramental flavour was mixed in by Perry's insistence on the centrality of a weekly Eucharist. He performed the first public same-sex wedding of the modern age in 1969, and after many difficulties in finding a place to worship, the congregation gained its first permanent building in 1971 – the victim of arson within two years. Conservative Evangelical hostility was predictable and vocal, often wildly misrepresenting the reality of the MCC. Interestingly it echoed the anger that Evangelicals had expressed towards Pentecostalism in general at the beginning of the century, and for a similar reason: the MCC looked too infuriatingly similar to Evangelical revivalism for comfort, so much of the vitriol was directed to alerting those who might have been tempted by its devotional style to the moral dangers that the community offered. Evangelicals had some reason for their alarm: the MCC grew at a rate that Evangelicals or Pentecostalists could only envy, having within five years of its foundation achieved 40 congregations with 13,000 members. Over the following half-century MCC congregations have emerged in hundreds of different contexts, still largely urban, across at least thirty-seven different countries.[11]

Just as in the days of slavery in America, other gay Christians were determined to make their presence felt within existing denominations. Roman Catholics, inspired by Vatican II, were pioneers, with pastoral counselling groups founded by clergy that turned into more public witness and campaign organizations: Dignity from 1969 in the USA and, in the UK, Quest from 1973. Hardly surprisingly the Quakers were early pioneers as well, in the UK founding the Friends' Homosexual Fellowship that same year. The next logical step was to try for a more ecumenical approach, witnessed by the creation of the Gay Christian Movement in 1976. The name was significantly male-centred, and the early ethos of GCM was predominantly Anglo-Catholic or liberal Anglican. In an organization notable for strongly fought internal debate, it took nearly a decade for a renaming as the Lesbian and Gay Christian Movement. Since 2017 the recognition of further complexities in queer identities have brought a name that is a more inclusive as well as theological proclamation: OneBodyOneFaith.[12]

A TIME FOR JUDGING

Church institutions everywhere found it difficult to formulate a coherent reaction to these sudden incursions of lesbian and gay activism within Christianity; they could not be ignored or simply othered, as might at first have seemed possible in response to the sudden eruption of secular gay anger against public repression that famously produced a week of rioting against the New York police around the Stonewall gay bar in 1969. In England, many gay Anglo-Catholics were particularly disconcerted by an eruption of Christian lesbian and gay openness that paid little respect to their carefully bounded historic sub-culture (unsympathetically summed up by one informed observer as 'gin, lace and backbiting').[13] The dilemma was wider than that: one phenomenon of the 1980s was the embarrassment of gay Anglican bishops when their silence about their sexuality was challenged as hypocrisy by those who were no longer silent. Was it a Christian act to 'out' them without their consent? The tabloid press was gleeful. The problem of double standards has continued to challenge numerous conservative gay politicians and clergy in the public eye across the world.[14]

A decade or more of indecision among Western Churches as gay equality was asserted more in Western society generally, as well as in the Church, was terminated by a new brutal reality. From 1981 reports made clear the emergence across the world of a sexually transmitted disease as devastating in its effects as syphilis had been in the sixteenth century, but more rapid in its transmission thanks to the global interlinking of modern society: Acquired Immunodeficiency Syndrome (AIDS). From the early 1980s till now, AIDS may have brought premature death to more than 30 million people, and a greater number are currently living with the virus that causes it, Human Immunodeficiency Virus (HIV).

It gradually became apparent as this new medical terminology was hastily forced into precision that the origins of the pandemic appeared to have been in Africa, but by 1981 HIV and consequent deaths were already widely dispersed, and in the United States one of the worst affected categories were sexually active gay men. The virus had capitalized on a gay culture that had revelled in its new sexual freedom and acted accordingly, so that infection was sexually transmitted via bodily fluids. Young, healthy males were prominent among those dying, at first with little hope of survival. Grief was mixed with terror of the unknown, and commentators who had hated the permissive society and the 'New Morality' exhibited a good deal of *Schadenfreude* masquerading as old morality. A widespread conservative reaction was that AIDS was God's wrath on homosexuality; it was not explained why God did not seem so wrathful against lesbians, who turned out to be among those least affected by the epidemic, while he was instead showing a great deal of wrath towards male and female Africans generally, despite the mushroom growth of Christianity in sub-Saharan Africa.

With few allies or interest in major medical funding to begin with, the gay male community in the West first turned to self-help, and its existing links with liberal Protestantism did begin to furnish some of its sources of support. Then AIDS, like syphilis in Renaissance Europe, proved itself an equal-opportunities killer, no respecter of hierarchy or political or religious conviction, and embarrassing revelations of where the virus had spread did unlock official funding for medical research and official campaigns for prevention. Medical services rallied across the world, including those provided by Churches of all descriptions. Yet one major source of negativity came from the central institutions of the Catholic Church in Rome. On the eve of the crisis, in 1978, Cardinal Karol Wojtyła had been elected as Pope John Paul II, taking the papal name of his tragically short-lived predecessor.

Wojtyła was the first non-Italian Pope since the sixteenth century, and a compelling personality able to charm the world as his predecessor Pius IX had done 150 years before. His life and ministry had encompassed heroic survival against first Nazi and then Communist repression of the Catholic Church, and his religious leadership in hastening the fall of repressive Communist regimes in eastern Europe, especially in his native Poland, remains inspiring. Nevertheless, his adamantine consistency against tyranny, founded on a flinty Counter-Reformation understanding of his Catholic faith, was less adept at handling the complexities of Western democratic societies.

In his own impressive self-control and commitment to celibacy, John Paul found little understanding of pluralism in sexual or family life. Such a leader could not have been worse suited to formulating Catholic pastoral responses to the AIDS crisis in the 1980s. It had become apparent that rubber contraceptives played a vital role in preventing infection (the salvation of a condom industry facing apparently unstoppable competition from contraceptive medicine). John Paul's reaction was that the only permissible preventive mechanism available to faithful Catholics was sexual abstinence: logical indeed in his theological framework, but woodenly unrealistic in dealing with real human beings.

In a conference for medical professionals on AIDS at the Vatican in 1989, the Pope's keynote address referred to 'morally illicit' means of preventing the disease; he meant condoms. His justification was not from Scripture or tradition, but – in a classic Catholic fashion – from natural law. Habitually he used the resonant phrase 'a culture of death' to define artificial contraception, along with abortion. Catholic Africans who listened to the Vatican hierarchy experienced their own culture of death. In Uganda, for instance, they were faced with the Pope's diplomatic representative, the Apostolic Nuncio Archbishop Christophe Pierre reiterating that the use of condoms was sinful, to the fury of the country's Vice-President who, as a medical doctor, was promoting condoms in the face of the continuing epidemic.

Structures of employment in parts of Africa dependent on the earnings of migrant workers make it particularly likely that men away from their wives for months on end will turn to the services of prostitutes; in such circumstances, condoms are essential to prevent the spread of HIV/AIDS. Any Catholic across the world involved in work for HIV and AIDS sufferers who has faced reality and advises individuals to use condoms if abstinence is beyond them has done so at her or his own risk. Often the contrary message from official Catholic sources has been that condoms do not actually work – demonstrated by 'serious scientific studies', according to Cardinal Alfonso López Trujillo speaking in 2003 for the Vatican's Council for the Family. There was a particular irony in Cardinal Trujillo taking a high moral line on sex, as was already becoming apparent.[15]

During the three decades of John Paul II's papacy, an old story emerged from the shadows into public discussion, to have a catastrophic effect on the Catholic Church worldwide: abuse, sexual, physical and emotional, of a variety of vulnerable people, children among them, in Church settings. There was nothing new about the abuse, which had been particularly encouraged by the well-intended restructurings of papal Catholicism in the Counter-Reformation (above, Chapter 14): the novelty was that, with the crumbling of old structures of deference, victims came forward expecting to be listened to, and that there were many listeners. These did not generally include Pope John Paul II, who did not exhibit the capacity to join up the growing cacophony of individual cases into a coherent narrative that needed a coherent solution. A major problem was his anti-Communism. Understandable though that was in view of his past struggles, it disposed him to see any liberal or left-wing agenda through the same prism, including 'Liberation Theologians' inspired to social and political action by the memory of the second Vatican Council. By contrast, any conservative who was loud enough in hostility to 'Marxism' was likely to win the Pope's sympathy.

Among these was that same Cardinal Trujillo, a major agent in remodelling the South American episcopate in John Paul II's mould, and deeply involved in campaigns to curb Liberation Theology throughout the continent, extending (without papal condemnation) to brutalizing and assassination. Trujillo was close to far-right politicians and paramilitaries in his native Colombia until his sudden move to Rome to head the Council for the Family in 1990. In that position, he was as fervent in denouncing abortion and homosexuality as he was in condemning artificial contraception; simultaneously, he conducted an energetic sex life with a series of young men. Trujillo's is simply one of the most prominent among many similar stories: the more sexually active a senior Vatican cleric was with males, the louder was likely to be their theological condemnation of same-sex activity. Across the Catholic world, the outwardly celibate, claustrophobically single-sex world of the clergy had become a haven for gay men terrified of their sexuality: a ready-made alibi with the bonus of traditional prestige. In the absence of any moral code to make sense of their contradictions, their activities were liable to be full of self-hatred and devoid of anything resembling a moral compass.[16]

Trujillo's story is put in the shade by Pope John Paul's protégé, the priest Marcial Maciel Degollado, who had grown up while Mexico was riven by violent confrontation between an anti-clerical government and defiant popular Catholicism; he was the founder of the militantly proselytizing and fervently orthodox Legion of Christ, which spread far beyond his native country. Persistent accusations of Maciel's sexual abuse, ranging from paedophilia to adult sexual assault to the fathering of children, were ignored in Rome up to the very end of John Paul II's long pontificate. Not so under his successor Benedict XVI, who as Cardinal Josef Ratzinger and Prefect of the Congregation for the Doctrine of the Faith (the former Roman Inquisition) had done his best to rein in Pope John Paul's wilder theological impulses. In May 2006 a statement about Maciel was issued on behalf of Benedict's own successor as Prefect, that the Church had decided 'taking account of the advanced age of the Reverend Maciel and his delicate health – to renounce any canonical process and to invite the Father to a reserved life of prayer and penance, renouncing every public ministry'. That was the extent of any action against Maciel before his death in 2008.[17]

At last the Vatican was showing signs of taking the abuse problem seriously, but the damage had been done, and Benedict's sense of its daunting scale was one factor in his unanticipated resignation in 2013. The wider world was losing its patience. The crisis was larger than sexual abuse; it was a general abuse of clerical power and prestige by damaged or frightened personalities among the clergy, particularly in covering up abuse where it was unearthed. Certain states founded on their Catholic identity, such as the Canadian province of Quebec or the Kingdom of Belgium, saw church attendance plummet, but nowhere has the reaction been more extreme than in the Irish Republic. The tipping point came in the 1990s when certain prominent priests, notably the extrovert Bishop of Galway Eamonn Casey, were revealed as having clandestine female partners and children. Back in Archbishop McQuaid's days, 'everyone knew . . . and at the same time they managed not to know' about ecclesiastical misuse of power; now the revelations poured out in increasing detail.[18] Particularly devastating was the *Final Report of the Commission of Investigation into the Mother and Baby Homes* published by the Irish government in 2020, which included details of archaeological work on the site of a sewage tank containing the remains of illegitimate babies from a Catholic-run children's home in Tuam.

On cherished shibboleths in the Vatican I construction of a Catholic family, the Irish population and its representatives in the Dáil (Parliament) now repeatedly exercised their right of rejection, despite strong attempts from the Church authorities to influence the votes. In 1993 male homosexual practice ceased to be illegal; in 1995 a referendum approved divorce (a result which was now backed by all the Republic's political leaders); in 2015, Ireland became the first country in the world to introduce equal marriage for same-sex couples by popular vote; and in 2018 a decisive two-to-one referendum vote led to an end on the ban on abortion. Already in 2011, the Republic had pointedly closed its embassy in the Vatican, while Archbishop McQuaid's posthumous reaction to an openly gay man becoming Taoiseach (Prime Minister) in 2017 is not recorded. In 1973–4, 91 per cent of Irish Catholics, the overwhelming majority of the Republic's population, had been recorded as attending Mass weekly; that had fallen to 66 per cent by 1997, and in the later subsequent rejection of the Church, led by major towns in the Republic, by 2016 a third of the inhabitants of Dublin and Galway City identified as non-Catholic.[19]

It soon became apparent that sexual abuse was an ecumenical matter. The scandal attached to Roman Catholicism had merely opened up a wider story of concealment and evasion across the world. Two English Anglican cases are instructive, since they respectively concern leaders at its two theological extremes, with a comparable amount of delay in revealing the whole story. Among Anglo-Catholics, Peter Ball (educated at Lancing College) was a charismatic figure, a monk and co-founder of a new monastic community, who brought genuine religious inspiration to many and rose to be Bishop of Gloucester. He was also a devious sexual abuser who targeted serious-minded and sometimes emotionally vulnerable young men as participants in his fantasies. Ball was able to draw not merely on the venerable Anglo-Catholic sub-culture of homosexuality but also to play on 'New Morality' and gay liberation themes; in my personal archive is a letter from his rural retreat in disgrace, attempting (unsuccessfully) to enlist my sympathy by playing on the persecuted gay man topos. Ball was eventually tried and imprisoned for his crimes, but that retribution was postponed for many years by inaction at the highest levels of the Church, some of it admittedly through concern not to be accused of anti-gay prejudice.[20]

At the other end of the Anglican theological scale, gay conservative Evangelicals historically have had nowhere emotionally to run to, facing an irreconcilable clash between their sexual orientation and their biblical literalism. Unlike Anglo-Catholics, until recently they have had no supportive sub-culture (the group 'Living Out' does now offer a network for those willing to live in permanent sexual abstention). For some, that has predictably led to internal moral anarchy. Conservative Evangelicalism in the UK is still also remarkably entangled with the English public school system, not least thanks to the institution of evangelistic summer camps aimed at public schoolboys – not public schoolgirls, whose presence was tolerated mainly to do the washing-up. The camps were founded in the 1940s by the lifelong bachelor clergyman Eric J. H. Nash and hence informally known from his nickname as 'Bash Camps'. Nash had discerned God's call to evangelize private schools more distinguished than his own alma mater Maidenhead College. Bash Camps have been unashamedly aimed at capturing the British elite. They were peculiarly influential after the Second World War in breeding future bishops of the Church of England, pulling conservative Evangelicalism out of its long Anglican marginalization into a position of power. Hence the difficulties of coping with a deeply damaging abuse scandal at their heart.[21]

The (so far, incomplete) nemesis of Bash Camps was John Smyth, as charismatic as Peter Ball but in a completely different mould as a successful Evangelical lawyer: the conservative Methodist Mrs Mary Whitehouse was among his clients when her moral campaigns reached the law courts. An extrovert family man with easy access to certain public schools, Smyth rose to be chairman of the Iwerne Trust (the sponsor of the 'Bash Camps'), as well as a trustee of the closely related Scripture Union. Once in contact with schoolboys, he would select some for grooming and work out his own moral chaos on them, particularly through repeated sessions of flagellation, which in some cases he continued into their life after schooldays. Gradually evidence of Smyth's crimes began to emerge; he was nevertheless not reported to the police, but simply forced to step back from his positions of responsibility, and in 1984 he emigrated to southern Africa. There his pattern of offending continued, including the unexplained death of a young man in Zimbabwe. He himself died in South Africa before he could face trial. At the time of writing, Anglican conservative Evangelical leaders have failed to face up adequately to what happened, nor have they fully addressed the implications of other analogous behaviour in the same circle. One response has been a rebranding exercise, in which the Iwerne Trust has become the Titus Trust.[22]

WEAPONIZING SEX FOR POLITICS

From the 1960s onwards, the United Kingdom has proved a failure for those trying to hold back the permissive society. Fundamentalism in its original sense has long been a lost cause, but conservative Evangelicals have done their best. Prominent among their campaigning organizations in the 1970s was the Nationwide Festival of Light, which staged rallies and the like defending the patriarchal family as the only means of saving the United Kingdom from moral decay. The NFOL's Director,

Raymond Johnston, stood in the private school and Oxbridge Evangelical tradition; he unhesitatingly proclaimed the Western nuclear family ('mum, dad and kids') to be 'the Christian norm', despite the difficulty of matching it up to the impressionistic depictions of Christian families that may be extracted from the New Testament. Johnson fulminated against abortion, but, following a significant trend in conservative Evangelicalism generally, he was much more equivocal on artificial contraception.[23]

Standing alongside NFOL was the National Viewers' and Listeners' Association (NVLA), strongly female in membership and run by Mrs Mary Whitehouse, a schoolteacher armed with handbag and hat in personification of the monochrome 1950s. She concentrated her fury more selectively on the liberal subversion of society in the programme output of the BBC. Mrs Whitehouse came from the same provincial Wesleyan Methodist background as the long-serving Tory Prime Minister Margaret Thatcher: Mrs Thatcher did find it expedient to play on their commonalities when she wished to stress what was, in reality, a manufactured image of herself as an ordinary housewife. Mrs Thatcher might have suggested her agreement with the social anxieties that fuelled NFOL or NVLA activism, and both ladies were outraged at what they saw as the elitist liberalism of the Church of England hierarchy, but Mrs Thatcher was much more subtle in her vague deployment of such phrases as 'common sense' or 'Victorian values'. Until the early 1990s, the vagueness paid electoral dividends for her and her party, where a more explicit alignment would have put off many British voters.[24]

By contrast with Mrs Thatcher, neither the NFOL nor all Mrs Whitehouse's skills at self-promotion in the NVLA achieved much. Their problem was their base in Evangelicalism; it was too narrow a springboard for populist action given the erosion of churchgoing in the UK. In overheated debates on sexuality in the Church of England General Synod in 1987, John Taylor, the Bishop of St Albans, argued that 'the Church would gain popularity by taking a firmer line against homosexuality.'[25] This betrayed the myopia of a traditionalist Evangelical bishop: homophobia might be a crowd-pleaser in some parts of the diminishing constituency of churchgoers, but it soon became evident that it was worse than useless with most of the British public. Conservative moral campaigning in western Europe generally was now primarily part of intra-Church politics: a pale echo of some much more effective deployments of conservative outrage at sexual change in the

USA, which in turn were part of global conservative movements that are still unfolding.

Throughout the modern world, the most easily heard tone in religion (not just in Christianity) is one of angry conservatism. Why? The anger centres on a profound shift in gender roles traditionally given a religious significance and validated by religious traditions. It embodies the hurt of men at cultural changes that have handed a share of power to women and made room for a variety of sexual and gender identities. That threatens to marginalize heterosexual men and deprive them of dignity, hegemony or even much usefulness – not merely those who already enjoy male privilege, but those who in traditional cultural systems would expect to inherit it. Sociologists of religion have observed that the most extreme forms of conservatism found in modern world religions, conservatisms which in a borrowing from Christianity have been termed 'fundamentalism', attract 'literate but jobless, unmarried male youths marginalized and disenfranchised by the juggernaut of modernity' – those whom modernity has created, only to fail to offer them any worthwhile purpose.[26]

In the now ubiquitous para-world of social media and virtual 'influencing', this variety of impressionable young man may be co-opted into toxic misogyny, with homophobia as a side-dish. It is not surprising that male homosexuality should be a major threat to insecure male egos. Lesbianism has not proved so salient in conservative anger: men, including male theologians, have historically never been much interested in what women do with other women, apart from out of prurience. The same themes emerge in religious settings as apparently contrasting as the fundamentalist Islam of the Taliban in Afghanistan, the Orthodox Christianity of nationalist Russians, or those who take seriously the 'Make America Great Again' rhetoric that has seized so much of the American Republican Party. Within Christianity, those caught up in such furies often make common cause with historical foes, so that the propaganda machine of ex-KGB President Putin, with its rhetoric of Russian Orthodox traditionalism, can use social media to link up with formerly anti-Soviet MAGA activists, or reach out to conservative Catholics in Europe and the USA. A bon mot on conservative Evangelicalism by a veteran historian of American Protestantism applies to all of them: a fundamentalist is 'an evangelical who is angry about something'.[27]

In this ecumenism of the right, anger, fear and hatred of an imagined Other combine to forge a common creed bridging theological divides that once seemed truly fundamental, such as the often-murderous disputes about the Eucharist or the Trinity in the sixteenth-century Reformation. For this uniting purpose, issues of sexuality have proved hugely useful, both as a way of papering over theological cracks within conservative ranks within Churches, but also on the wider political stage. The Anglican Communion furnishes one of the most notorious cases inside Christianity: its internal disagreements are often simplistically presented as between a compromised and compromising liberal affluent West and a global alliance of developing countries devoted to defending old certainties.

As always in Anglicanism, that narrative has complications. Much of the rhetoric and financial muscle backing conservative self-assertions come from Western Evangelicals who fear that they have lost the cultural battle in the USA, Europe and anglophone ex-British Dominions, and therefore direct their resources elsewhere where there might be a greater chance of success. Moreover, by no means all of the 'Global South' conforms to the conservative stereotype. South African Anglicans are more sensitive to Western concerns because of their history of the liberation struggle against theologically justified Reformed Protestant apartheid; they have taken a progressive line on both women's ordination and homosexuality, particularly in passionate statements from the late Archbishop Desmond Tutu, a militant saint, who emphasized that the acceptance of the moral integrity of same-sex relationships is 'a matter of ordinary justice'.[28]

Prominent in Anglican global conservatism is the diocese of Sydney, heir to most of the historic endowments from early Anglican hegemony in colonial Australia, and since the 1930s under the control of a steadily more idiosyncratic conservative Evangelicalism.[29] From the 1970s, in reaction to an increasingly visible local gay culture and the growing movement for the ordination of women, the Sydney hierarchy took a strong stance against both, which – not without justification – they saw as related phenomena, challenging their masculinist version of Christianity. 'Sydney Anglicanism' has made its own cultural accommodation with some of the distinctive stereotypes of traditional Australian masculinity, which historians of gender have analysed as ranging from the 'Lone Hand' of the Outback, happiest relaxing in an all-male drinking and gambling ambience, to the 'Domestic Man', an abstemious and churchgoing *paterfamilias*. In many historical settings, male clergy have been uncertain as to how to negotiate the feminine aspects of the clerical role in nurturing pastoral sensitivity and thoughtfulness. In Sydney they have been eager to balance them with bluff Australian manliness; that is backed up with an emphasis on male headship in family and Church not found elsewhere in Australian Evangelical Anglicanism, and with a particularly aggressive stance against male homosexuality.[30]

This combination has been available for export wherever traditional male roles look threatened. Sydney is central to a worldwide campaigning network throughout Anglicanism that has made no secret of its aim to supplant Lambeth Palace at the centre of the Anglican Communion, in order to promote a tailored version of 'traditional values'. The campaign against homosexuality was galvanized by the choice of an openly partnered gay man as Bishop in the US Episcopal Church in 2003. Gene Robinson's consecration for New Hampshire followed his open election by the diocese and took place in the largest venue available in the state, a university ice-hockey stadium (Plates 34 and 35). Following a slew of hate mail, both Robinson and his partner wore bullet-proof vests during the ceremony, as did Frank Griswold the Presiding Bishop of the Church: not a normal liturgical provision in the Anglican Communion.[31]

In 2007, five provinces of the Communion took further joint action. They agreed to boycott the forthcoming Lambeth Conference and laid the foundations for an alternative, in an organization known as Global Anglican Future Conference (GAFCON). Four of the provinces were large Churches in central and east Africa, the other a small province in southern south America; others showed interest, including various conservative splinter groups formed in opposition to the progress of gay rights and women's ministry in the US Episcopal and Canadian Anglican Churches. GAFCON has grown since, but it faces the recurrent difficulty of schisms based on principle; participants are liable to carry on splitting on principle. This is the value of homosexuality as an issue: women's ordination divides GAFCON members, with some provinces ordaining women despite bitter criticism from others, but everyone can agree on condemning homosexuality, with the added advantage that it plays well on the frontiers of African Christianity and Islam.

A favourite argument of African Anglicans denouncing Western attitudes to sexuality is that African Christians are ridiculed or worse by African Muslims because of their association with Churches that condone homosexuality. There is some truth in this; it has been one consideration in the Egyptian Coptic Church's official reaffirmation of a firmly traditionalist line on same-sex relations. Despite gay people

29. Outside the Anglican Lambeth Conference debate on homosexuality in August 1998, Emmanuel Chukwuma, Bishop of Enugu (Nigeria) (*right*), made a spontaneous and apparently unsuccessful attempt to exorcise homosexuality out of the Revd Richard Kirker (*left*), General Secretary of the Lesbian and Gay Christian Movement.

among the Coptic faithful urging change, the leadership is aware of the fragile position of Copts in a majority-Muslim Egyptian society.[32] Yet the competition between African Christians and African Muslims as to who can be most hostile to homosexuality irresistibly recalls competitive Protestant and Catholic punitive action against witchcraft in the European Reformation (above, Chapter 14).

Less frequently articulated is the history of serious sectarian violence within African Christianity itself. The East African Evangelical Revival that, from the 1930s, spread through the region and into central Africa, brought with it conflict and destruction of property affecting Roman Catholics, Anglicans and Protestant breakaway Churches; that was in the background of the Rwanda genocide of 1994.[33] In Uganda, violence in the Revival interacted with much older tensions between the hegemonic Anglicanism of Buganda and disadvantaged Roman Catholics, and it was exacerbated in the 1970s by President Idi Amin's murderous campaigns to promote Uganda's Muslim minority over the Anglicans.[34]

Any crusade against homosexuality in Uganda therefore acts as a scapegoating force to transcend this legacy of hatreds, particularly because it handily coincides there with a proud local narrative of martyrdom: the story of forty-five royal pages in Buganda, both Anglican and Roman Catholic. Over two years in the 1880s the victims were burned alive by Mwanga the then Kabaka of Buganda, apparently because, among other acts of defiance, they had refused to yield to his sexual demands – an aspect of the atrocity that has been increasingly emphasized in recent years, whatever its original part in Mwanga's brutality. That complex of considerations lies behind Uganda's move in 2023 to criminalize homosexuality up to imprisonment and even execution, to the baffled horror of Westerners who are not aware of the backstory (see Plate 36).[35]

Sex has for more than half a century had an even more important instrumental role in promoting right-wing secular politics, particularly in the United States. Here it has become the most salient issue for identity in the Republican Party, gathering together conservative Evangelicals and ultra-right Catholics. The process began in the 1960s and represents a paradox. The Democrats started out as the party of the white supremacist South after the Civil War of 1861–5: the Republicans were the party of President Lincoln, who oversaw the South's defeat. In terms of historic Evangelical Protestant campaign issues, the Democrat record was ambiguous: the populist Democrat and sometime Presidential candidate William Jennings Bryan was the leading counsel against the teaching of Darwinian evolution in the Scopes 'Monkey Trial' of 1925 (above, Chapter 18), dying just after the end of proceedings. On the other hand, in the 1930s the Democrats were responsible for bringing down the nationwide experiment in Prohibition, that cause which Evangelicals had latterly made their own; and then in the 1960s successive Democrat presidents and Congress majorities formulated the Civil Rights legislation dismantling the apparatus of racial segregation across the nation.

Two religious issues began pulling the Republicans and conservative Evangelicals together: one was the banning of school prayer in America's public schools in 1962, a result of the courts trying to enforce the principle of the American constitutional separation of Church and State, and then the *Roe* v. *Wade* judgment of the Supreme Court in 1973, effectively legalizing abortion. The latter, a deliberate test case like the *Lady Chatterley* prosecution in the UK a decade before, was not as straightforward as it has been remembered: 'Jane Roe' was a lesbian and mother of three who never actually had an abortion, and for much of her remaining rather troubled life she became involved in anti-abortion campaigning.[36] *Roe* v. *Wade* might have been more permanently secure if Congress and the Democratic Party had taken more seriously a constitutional amendment proposed by the redoubtable Democrat Congresswoman Bella Abzug to bar states from restrictive legislation on abortion; instead the Supreme Court judgment remained to stand by itself.

At the time of the *Roe* v. *Wade* verdict, its future significance was not entirely clear. Abortion had been widely available and legal in the early days of the USA, and its steady criminalization in the 1860s and 1870s had been thanks to pressure not from American Catholics (then a minority widely subject to discrimination) but from physicians.[37] Thereafter opposition to abortion had not been strong among conservative Evangelicals, who saw campaigning against abortion as something that Roman Catholics did, and therefore suspect. In 1970, abortion was legal only in Oregon and California, but other states were liberalizing their laws; in that year, 90 per cent of Texas Baptists thought the law too restrictive in their state and 70 per cent of Baptist pastors supported abortion 'to protect the mental or physical health of the mother'. The formidable and popular Republican First Lady Betty Ford roundly declared her support for *Roe* v. *Wade* in 1975. Only gradually did the Republican Right complete its jigsaw of support among conservative Christians.[38]

In a considerable irony, the turning point was the Presidency of the Democrat Jimmy Carter (1977–81), who was a devout and 'born-again' Southern Baptist, but who came from that minority of Southern Evangelical Christians who had enthusiastically embraced Civil Rights. On various issues, such as his openness to Christian ecumenism and his lukewarmness towards 'faith schools' that countered the perceived liberalism of public education, Carter alienated conservatives, but in no respect more than the tone of the national 'White House Conference on the Family' that the President belatedly convened in 1980. It was an attempt to shore up his vote among Christian conservatives, particularly Catholics, but Carter's progressive Christian moral instincts defeated his electoral pragmatism. The tone set from the top was of liberal Protestantism in its post-Sixties mode: the organizers pluralized the Conference's title to 'on Families' and made thoughtful statements about gay relationships. Just as offensive to Southern conservatives, though more difficult to express publicly, was the presence on the Advisory Committee of such Civil Rights icons as the Revd Jesse Jackson and Coretta Scott King, the widow of Martin Luther King.[39]

Even before the Conference had begun, angry Evangelical leaders met in 1979 and stumbled across a resonant title for an organization to do something about their wrath: the 'Moral Majority'. By the end of Carter's turbulent period in office, he had lost the conservative Evangelical constituency. In 1980 they voted for Ronald Reagan and the Republican Party, and have done so ever since, regardless of the religious affiliations (or lack of them) of successive Republican Presidents. They even made common cause with the old enemy Catholics, opposition to abortion and all, for the 'Moral Majority' was designed to include them both. The Evangelical leader Francis Schaeffer godfathered this strategy, though he still cautioned in 1982 that 'we must never forget that this is only a passing co-belligerency and not an alliance.' The Evangelical televangelist-turned-politician Pat Robertson had declared in the year of Reagan's election: 'We have enough votes to run the country . . . and when the people say, "We've had enough" we are going to take over.'[40] That was premature: no Republican President has allowed his term in office to be dominated by the legislative programme of the Religious Right on family policy generally, and particularly not on measures against abortion until the turn of the century.

Nevertheless, in the 1980s conservatives successfully kidnapped the theme of 'family values', once the common concern of progressive and conservative American Protestants. They added to it the new themes of extreme hostility to both abortion and homosexual practice that cemented the alliance with conservative Roman Catholics; that also did something to paper over the fundamental theological differences of Evangelicals and Pentecostalists (above, Chapter 18). A gradual social shift in post-AIDS America towards acceptance of public gay identity blunted the electoral advantage of Religious Right rhetoric on homosexuality, leaving the abortion issue to do most of the heavy polemical lifting, until in the twenty-first century the increasing public visibility of trans and non-binary people provided a new issue for Republican-dominated state legislatures to turn into restrictive and discriminatory legislation. It remains to be seen whether the Republican-dominated Supreme Court's decision in 2023 to reverse the effect of *Roe* v. *Wade* will fuel a long-term defeat for conservative Evangelicalism similar to the routing of Prohibition in the 1930s. Certainly American churchgoing is now belatedly following European patterns of decline, as many in the generation coming to adulthood decide that their parents' religious practice and moral outlook are not for them.

The influence of conservative Christianity in American politics is baffling to western Europeans, who overwhelmingly disapprove of their own politicians making a public fuss of their personal religious convictions. The picture is much more mixed in eastern Europe, and it is now utterly different in post-Soviet Russia, scene of one of the most cynical contemporary appropriations of the weaponizing of sex. In the background is the twentieth-century story of Orthodox Europe north of Greece. From 1917 to 1918, and then still more widely from the late 1940s, those regions were under the rule of Communist regimes that were part of the Soviet Empire (Communist Yugoslavia excepted). Communist hostility to the Church incorporated various measures of State control long familiar in Orthodox lands: the Orthodox have never forgotten that they treated first Byzantine emperors and then Russian emperors as sacral figures in God's purposes, just like King David in ancient Israel. The Ottoman and Soviet periods of alien dominance did not expunge this deep-rooted assumption, however much they tested it. What confrontations there were between Church and State in eastern Europe after 1945 mostly featured the Catholic Church and Reformed Protestantism, which were both in the Western Christian tradition and therefore possessed a more robust tradition of political resistance than Orthodoxy.

With the collapse of the Soviet Empire in 1989–91, Orthodox hierarchies were left with dilemmas about their new relationships with the successor-states: particularly between the Patriarch of the Russian Orthodox Church and the Russian Federation. Churchmen were grateful for restored opportunities for charitable work in society or to provide education from kindergarten to university level, all of which had been eliminated in the Soviet era. The Moscow Patriarchate luxuriated in the new place of honour (and wealth) awarded it in post-Soviet Russia. It has been remarked that as the Soviet Union finally disintegrated in 1991, it left the Russian Orthodox Church as 'arguably the most "Soviet" of all institutions' remaining in Russia.[41] One remarkable symptom was that the FSB, the Russian intelligence service that had rather seamlessly succeeded the Soviet KGB, lovingly restored a Moscow parish church for its own use. In 2002 the Church of the Holy Wisdom was reconsecrated with full Orthodox pomp by no less a figure than Patriarch Aleksii, who amid the festivities presented the FSB's Director, Nikolai Patrushev, with an icon of his name-saint Nikolai.[42]

In 1999 President Boris Yeltsin nominated as his successor a little-known St Petersburg politician and former KGB officer, Vladimir Putin. It was a decade before Putin decided to weaponize sex as part of his consolidation of power, reversing a direction set by Yeltsin's regime. Yeltsin had repealed Stalin's criminalization of male homosexuality in 1993 as part of dismantling Soviet-era legislation, and gay activism had become increasingly visible in public, at least in Moscow or St Petersburg. Increasingly, conservative–nationalist political groups seized on this issue in their anger at the Western humiliation of the Soviet Union and the chaos of post-Soviet Russia. A debate on sex in the Duma (Parliament) in 2002 was nevertheless significant for what it failed to achieve: a restoration of Stalin's law on male homosexuality, not to mention a ban on lesbianism and even fines for masturbation, all decisively voted down.[43]

At this stage President Putin showed little support for such moves, evidently cautious about openly repudiating the assumptions about human rights that governed social change in the European Union and the West generally. Conservatives nevertheless learned from their defeat. They would have to be more precise in their campaigns for what they increasingly called 'traditional sexuality', a new coinage to describe a new idea. This meant turning the focus on homosexuality. Official support came in the wake of the world economic crisis of 2008–9, which had ended the domestic economic growth that had made Putin popular despite the obvious corruption of his regime. Twenty eleven brought a sudden surge in new legislation across the Russian Federation banning 'gay propaganda' aimed at minors. It is not clear how far Putin orchestrated this, but at the end of the year, he suffered a personal humiliation when attending a wrestling match in Moscow at which he was mocked by the spectators (of course, overwhelmingly male). That was a particular trauma for a leader whose public propaganda already cultivated his bare-chested macho outdoor image, though in the West that might have been labelled as rather camp.[44]

In 2012, Putin quietly backed one of his associated Duma politicians, Elena Mizulina, in drawing up blanket legislation against 'non-traditional sexual relations'. Its passage was surrounded by much denunciation of paedophilia, silently eliding that with homosexuality in general, and adding strident concerns that sexual deviancy had a part in contemporary Russia's striking demographic decline. These were themes that many conservative Western politicians had repeatedly used sixty years earlier as various countries dismantled their penal legislation on homosexuality. Altogether the new Russian moral panic was more reminiscent of the punitive atmosphere of Victorian England than anything 'traditionally' Russian. In fact, Westerners visiting Muscovy in the seventeenth century had remarked in surprise on the degree of open toleration for both male and female same-sex behaviour; they noted that Muscovites even lacked a respectable penalty like execution for it.[45]

The underlying Russian nationalist ideology of the present day is really that of the Napoleonic citizen army, strongly associated with masculinist hegemony and the gender binaries of nineteenth-century western Europe (above, Chapter 16). That is a natural consequence of the astonishing sacrifices of the Red Army in the defeat of Adolf Hitler, but it is a product of Western history and not at all specifically Russian or Orthodox. Because of this international character, it chimes with similar populist movements elsewhere across the world, and the twin polemics against homosexuality and trans visibility are the themes most likely to appeal to the repressive instincts of dictators and would-be dictators. There can be no more striking instances of personal self-assertion than affirming a gay, trans or non-binary identity for oneself, and the authoritarian temperament detests other people making their own personal choices in anything.

From the mid-2010s, Putin's government has been closely in step with the Russian Orthodox Church's denunciations of Western decadence, particularly in Patriarch Kirill I's fulminations very soon after Mizulina's proposals became law: it was in counterpoint to the legal recognition of equal marriage spreading in many parts of the West. Patriarch Kirill was simultaneously bidding to replace the Ecumenical Patriarch Bartholomew of Constantinople (Istanbul) as the effective head of worldwide Orthodoxy. Personal and ecclesiastical ambition blended with Kirill's fury at the Ecumenical Patriarch's willingness to help Ukrainian Orthodoxy assert itself against the Moscow Patriarchate in the newly independent Ukrainian Republic. The dynamic continued, as both Church and State weaponized their resentment at Ukraine's growing estrangement from Russia and its popular overthrow of a pro-Russian President in 2014 to seek alignment with the West. Russian military intervention in eastern Ukraine followed that same year, and led, in

February 2022, to Putin's botched invasion of the whole country. By now, the construction of a Russian ideological crusade against the decadent West was fully formed. Within a month of the invasion, in March 2022, Patriarch Kirill was preaching that Putin's invasion and the Russian army were saving the Russian-occupied Donbas region from 'gay parades': clearly a sacred task, though gay parades were not notably part of Ukrainian President Zelensky's declared military strategy.[46]

In the background were Putin's often successful efforts to link up with and encourage far-right nationalist groups in the West who agreed with him that the West had become decadent, particularly on sexual matters. A major figure in this has been Hilarion Alfeyev, an articulate theologian and bishop whose personal knowledge of the West began with his doctoral studies in Oxford. Appointed in 2003 to an Orthodox episcopal charge in Vienna, Alfeyev made it his business to link up with conservative Catholics; central to his overtures was the call to make common cause against the new Western sexual freedoms. It was an adroit theme to adopt: right-wing Catholic hostility to Pope Francis is international, including many members of the Catholic episcopate in the USA appointed during the papacies of John Paul II and Benedict XVI who share their former patrons' discreet distaste for the reforming work of the second Vatican Council. Such Catholics were increasingly angry at Pope Francis's piecemeal reversal of the policies of his predecessors (see Plate 33). In 2022 Alfeyev was sent from his foreign relations post in the Moscow Patriarchate headquarters back to central Europe, to Budapest. Many at the time interpreted this move as a snub and minor exile; nevertheless, it coincided with the explicit turn to Moscow and against Ukraine by Hungary's authoritarian nationalist Prime Minister, Victor Orbán. Orbán's recent years in power have likewise witnessed legislation eroding LGBTQ+ rights and ending the legal recognition of transgender people.

Patriarch Kirill and Putin have managed to divide the whole Orthodox world, and they cannot be regarded as its spokesmen. Yet they do have a rhetorical advantage in raising the question of sexuality to a place it has never held before in Orthodox theology. In the long years of marginalization, first by the Ottomans and then by the Soviets, Orthodox contact with two centuries of social change in Western Christianity was partial and limited, and there was little incentive to rethink a theology of sexual ethics in step with the Western Enlightenment. In Greece, since the nineteenth century Orthodoxy has had far more contact with the West than elsewhere; Western powers helped to carve the modern state out of Ottoman lands and its Orthodox Church was restructured with the aid of an imported German-Danish monarchy. Yet when the Greek Republic in 2015 extended registered civil partnership to same-sex couples (so far uniquely in an Orthodox country), the Greek Church hierarchy passionately denounced the move in terms little different from anything Moscow might say.[47]

The Orthodox world in general has seen the rise of a conservatism that has been labelled 'rigorism', to stand alongside Protestant fundamentalism or the ultra-conservative Catholic movement crystallized in opposition to Pope Francis. After our survey of Eastern Christianity in earlier centuries, we might echo the observation of a contemporary Orthodox commentator in Greece: 'In its struggle to remain true to the Byzantine worldview at any cost, the Eastern Church has opted to remain more Byzantine than truly Orthodox, if Orthodoxy signifies constant growth, self-critical development, and continuous expansion in space and time.'[48]

Much in this present chapter has been sombre. It is easy to despair of both world and Church in the early twenty-first century, particularly if one looks for a Christian message affirming hope and redemption. Yet, as so often in Christian history, light may come through sudden unexpected reversals. A heartening story is that of the sometime evangelist Tammy Faye Bakker, later Messner, née LaValley: a kind of redemption after falling very low. In 1961, Tammy Faye married a fellow Pentecostalist, Jim Bakker, and started on a public career in a classic conservative Christian mode. Their evangelism was structured on a variation of Pentecostalism often styled the 'Prosperity Gospel', which proclaims that prayer is the route to success and wealth, citing Christ's promise in Mark 11.23–24 that 'whatever you ask in prayer, believe that you have received it, and it will be yours'. Tammy Faye predictably emphasized how traditional, stable nuclear heterosexual families were now under threat from the New Morality, although in a pattern remarkably frequent among her fellow women campaigners on the Christian Right, her own family background had in fact been disrupted and unhappy. Likewise, her husband later claimed that he had suffered sexual abuse in his youth behind a conventional Pentecostal facade.[49]

From 1965 the Bakkers built up a phenomenally successful TV evangelistic show, *PTL* (*Praise the Lord*, or *People That Love*), in step with the growth of American religious and political conservatism. In the echo chamber of the Religious Right, though carefully avoiding endorsing a particular political party unlike some of their competitors, they enjoyed regular viewing figures of 12 million by 1986. By then behind the scenes all was unravelling: both Bakkers were suffering addictions seeking to counter severe stress, and their lives were becoming chaotic. Sexual abuse accusations against Jim Bakker in 1987 were followed by revelations that he had embezzled vast sums from the contributions of the devout, funding the pair's lavish lifestyle. This is a not unfamiliar progression in popular evangelism, but there was a twist. While Jim went to prison, Tammy Faye persevered in developing an unexpected and individual strand in their TV show that she herself had pioneered.

In 1985, to widespread Evangelical astonishment and disapproval, Tammy Faye staged an interview on *PTL* with Steve Pieters, a minister of the Metropolitan Community Church – by satellite, since he was by then in an advanced stage of AIDS and too sick to come to the *PTL* studio. It was an emotional and ideologically chaotic occasion, but out of it emerged Tammy Faye's tearful acceptance of Pieters on screen as a fellow Christian, at a time when AIDS sufferers were often seen as alien threats to American society. After the Bakkers' final disgrace and divorce, she persisted, co-hosting a TV talk show with a gay actor and becoming a regular and welcome fixture at public gay events (Plate 37). 'When we lost everything, it was the gay people that came to my rescue, and I will always love them for that,' she told *Larry King Live* in 2006. A year later she was dead of cancer, mourned by the leading US gay magazine *The Advocate* as 'one of the few Christian conservatives to openly support us'.[50]

Tammy Faye Bakker's version of a conversion narrative represents one possible outcome of seventy years of bitterness and confrontation on sexual matters: a story of judgement suspended and transformed by personal experience. It may be juxtaposed with recent words of challenge and comfort to fellow Jesuits from a Catholic priest well-placed to have a perspective on recent decades of world history: 'do our contemporaries not fear that Christians and indeed believers of all faiths are just this, an uncontained movement of reaction and resentment, furious at the freedoms and liberations of the modern age? . . . the gospel is no spectre of retribution. It is flesh and bones.'[51]

20
A Story Without an Ending

This is not the first of my books to lack a conclusion, since its story is in no sense over. Christianity continues to be the chameleon faith it always has been, like all successful world religions: remarkable in its ability to take root in new situations and reinvent itself for new times. An aspect of that, as we have repeatedly noticed, is the capacity of theologians and clergy to retrofit theology onto new realities. That is not necessarily an unhealthy process, as long as it does not pretend that the result has always been there, pristine and unchallengeable in authority. To read the history of three thousand years of Christians and their predecessors talking about sex, men, women, children, marriage, is to realize just how complicated and varied the conversation has been – how much Christian teaching has changed and adapted to the circumstances in which it finds itself.

We have fought our way past numerous misunderstandings of the past, and noted creations of new circumstances based on those misunderstandings. We have noted the way in which metaphors intended to help people understand mystery may expand into creating new realities. As they do, Christians have often ceased to hear voices from their past that suggest older complexities: in particular, past versions of the Church that were less dominated by male clerical stories. Fundamental to any reassessment is the replacement of male circumcision by baptism for all believers as the mark of Christian identity in the earliest generation of Christianity's existence. Yet despite that, we have witnessed the marginalization of female ministry in the early centuries of the Church, as well as the ways in which unauthorized forms of female leadership can emerge in times of acute change or ecclesiastical disarray, only to be forced once more into the margins as conditions become more settled. In the last three centuries, these regressive patterns have begun to become less insistent; female activism – for instance in opposition to the slave trade, or in efforts to curb male excess such as the Temperance Movement – left permanent results impossible to ignore. Women have gained political voices, even in Church hierarchies: no longer so reliant on occasional historical accidents, such as the vagaries of dynastic marriage that once gave Byzantine empresses the chance to sway the Iconoclastic Controversy. When the configurations of Church politics shift irretrievably, it is possible to write history as Elisabeth Schüssler Fiorenza has done, 'In Memory of Her', and see a picture of the past reshaped for everyone.

Many errors in understanding sex and Christianity have clustered round the complexities in the nature of marriage, not least the frequent assertions that there is something called 'traditional marriage' that needs defending against all competitors. This 'traditional marriage' tends to be the sort of modern companionate and carefully limited nuclear family that suits many people at the present day, but it has very little precedent in the history of the Church. Love and marriage have not always gone together like a horse and carriage. In fact, if one hearkened to Pythagorean philosophers, or to the Christian theologians captained by Jerome of Stridon who parroted what Pythagoreans had said, to love one's wife too much is to commit adultery (above, Chapter 7).

It can never be too often emphasized that through most of recorded Christian history, and in the societies that preceded Christianity, marriage was a contract between two men: the fathers of the bride and groom respectively. Paul of Tarsus introduced a Christian complication into this by speaking in one of his letters to the Corinthians of the mutuality and sexual equality of a couple in marriage: that emphasis has continued to thrust itself into subsequent Christian discussions of marriage, though as a result it has frequently been written out of the theological picture. Here medieval Western canon lawyers deserve salutation for their efforts to ensure that at least the Western Church remembered what Paul had said (above, Chapter 13). My observation of the discussion of sexual morality during six decades of ecclesiastical life and politics has been that self-styled traditionalists rarely know enough about the tradition that they proclaim; conservatives do not fully admit to themselves or to others what it is they are trying to conserve, and why they are trying to conserve it.

It is important when demolishing myths from the past not to create new ones to justify the present. That was the quixotic aim of John Boswell, a creative and original historian who nevertheless suggested that his work revealed a past where the Church tolerated gay people and indeed created a liturgy of gay marriage. It was largely illusory, and later historians have seen the need gently to correct him (above, Chapter 8). The work of Michel Foucault was equally misleading, shot through with monocausal explanation of social and ideological change through repression, regulation and definition, plus an excessive francophone preoccupation with Catholic sacramental confession. Foucault gave minimal credit to the obstinate ability of human beings to think for themselves, to struggle towards what they want in unpromising circumstances, and on occasion to succeed; that potential has been one of the recurrent themes of this book.

It was likewise a natural impulse to find a history to accompany the new roles for women that emerged in the nineteenth and twentieth centuries; the resulting body of pseudo-history has not stood up to scholarly investigation. Some late Victorian folklore enthusiasts, and then the archaeologist moonlighting as an anthropologist, Margaret Murray, spoke of a barely Christianized medieval Europe, in which pre-Christian religion lived on in full force as witchcraft. Romantic ideas of an ancient surviving religion of 'the Great Goddess' and the like leached into popular and still enjoyable literature for adults and children. As recently as the 1940s the corpus was enriched by the creation of an entire new religion of witchcraft in the romantic English imaginations of Gerald Gardner and his wife Donna. Virtually all the historical evidence for witchcraft cults or Wicca has been courteously dismantled: the chief demolition expert, Ronald Hutton, reminds us to distinguish between 'surviving paganism' and 'a pagan survival', such as the English custom of lighting bonfires at Midsummer.[1]

One also needs to appreciate and celebrate the perennial human capacity to hold contradictory ideas at the same time to useful effect. We have entertainingly watched late medieval and Reformation English bishops (or their officials) solemnly tell a lie in the interests of eliminating particular instances of manorial serfdom: not just to lie, but to give a positive value to illegitimacy, something that they would have regarded in other circumstances in a punitive light (above, Chapter 14). At the present day, similar elastic thinking is helping many Evangelicals and Pentecostalists to move towards affirming LGBTQ+ identities when otherwise they might be emotionally floundering.[2]

Christian theology is not just a matter of opening the Bible and reeling off a text or learning Church dogma. It is dependent on countless echoes of the past, back to Greeks, Jews, even Hindus or Buddhists. The consequence is that contrary to many assertions over the last two centuries, a sustained journey through Christian history reveals that there is no such thing as a Christian theology of sex. There are multiple Christian theologies of sex, many of which have over two millennia been downright contradictions of each other. That shows no sign of changing. All those centuries of chatter and fuss and argument were also accompanied by laughter and love, despite (sometimes even because of) the Church. If sex is definitely a problem, it is also great fun. It seems implausible that any creator God worthy of the name can always disapprove of fun. It is also possible that with that in mind, Christian theology may newly extend itself to discussing topics that male theologians have usually found too embarrassing to discuss. A pioneer in that regard has been the former Archbishop of Canterbury, Rowan Williams. In 1989, in the course of a lecture sponsored by the then Lesbian and Gay Christian Movement, he had this to say on a topic and on a bodily part rarely featured in classical Christian discourse:

> the question . . . is also raised for some kinds of moralist by the existence of the clitoris in women; something whose function is joy. If the creator were quite so instrumentalist in 'his' attitude to sexuality, these hints of prodigality and redundancy in the way the whole thing works might cause us to worry about whether he was, after all, in full rational control of it. But if God made us for joy . . . ?[3]

Between 1700 and the present day, we have seen major social developments challenge the various narratives of society, ethics and morality that Christian Churches created over previous centuries: so far, Christianity whether Western or Eastern has had at best only partial success in dealing constructively with these novelties. First in the eighteenth century came a general privatization of life-choices, including sexual relationships. Modern homosexual identity and feminism were assertions of individual discernment without automatic reference to the commands of external authorities about the most fundamental aspects of personality. That is a rather Protestant thing to do, and Protestants did gradually come to terms with many feminist choices. Yet it took another 250 years for either Protestants or Catholics to move beyond anything other than repression or condemnation of same-sex relationships. Equally, Christianity has yet to say much that is distinctive or constructive about the remarkably swift recent rise to public visibility of trans and non-binary identities for humans, a further move in personal discernment. All these represent sexual and gender identities that either did not exist in public consciousness before the late seventeenth century, or only existed in a negative image. Christians are barely in the middle of assimilating them into any useful conversation about morality.

How might Christians do that? The Bible has not proved adequate to providing answers on questions of sex and gender, given the silences on now significant matters in the recorded discourses of Jesus. That is not an insurmountable problem: in the past, Christians have found more than one problem of ethics where the Bible is not adequate as the only point of moral reference. The institution of slavery has been one of those matters, leading to a major Christian turnaround in the eighteenth and nineteenth centuries from acceptance to blanket rejection. Another moral question once of equal importance is the taking of interest on money, usury. C. S. Lewis in that classic of popular evangelism *Mere Christianity* was only one of the most well-known modern commentators to point out the consensus between Greek philosophers, the Hebrew Bible and medieval interpreters of them that usury was a very wicked thing, and how that has subsequently changed.

Reformation Protestants as well as Counter-Reformation Catholics puzzled over the problem of usury, since they were trying to be faithful to the Bible, but they also lived at a time when the levying of interest was increasingly basic to the way their society functioned. The end-result of their ingenious musings is that one finds it difficult to imagine the modern world functioning without the levying of interest in economic transactions: as Lewis brutally expressed it, 'three great civilisations had agreed . . . in condemning the very thing on which we have based our own life.'[4] The relevance of that to present-day discussion of sexuality is expressed in an exasperated comment from one of those conscientious Catholic scholars who in 1968 watched Paul VI reject their efforts in his Pontifical Commission on artificial contraception: official Catholicism would only shift its attitude on birth control

> when the official Church realizes that just as the meaning of money is not what it was in the thirteenth century, so with low mortality and a world population approaching 6 billion, the meaning of human reproduction is not what it was then, or even as late as the nineteenth century.[5]

Professor Burch was calling the Church back to the way that it has normally considered matters of sexual morality: not so much by Scripture but by natural law illuminated by history. The classic discussions of natural law were pre-Christian, because their terms were set out in Greek philosophy, particularly that of Aristotle, but Christians decided that judicious use of them provided the best framework for understanding the created universe. Aristotle's categories and structures looked increasingly frayed after progress in medical understanding began in the sixteenth century through new discoveries from scientists (then known as natural philosophers): the English natural philosopher William Harvey's demonstration of the circulation of the blood was only one such new understanding about the mechanics of the human body. Nevertheless, the increasing tide of such modifications could still be seen as in line with Aristotle, and in nineteenth-century Roman Catholicism they gained a new authority through the privileging of Aristotelian Thomism in Catholic theology (above, Chapter 16).

Thus historically, the Church in both East and West has not generally tackled matters of sexual morality through biblical proof-texting, but through deploying natural law. As late as the 1970s, that was as true for Anglicans as it was for Catholics. These natural law arguments were not at root especially profound: there were men and there were women, and their bodily parts were designed to fit together in sexual congress. Any other use of them was literally 'disordered', a favourite phrase of Catholic moral discourse about same-sex activity in the time of John Paul II and Benedict XVI. The foray of Churches beyond Rome into weaponizing verses of the Bible in the last decades to address arguments about sexuality has not produced helpful results or clarity. It has revealed among other things what a blunt instrument the Bible can be when faced with categories of sex and gender that receive no meaningful coverage in scriptural pronouncements.[6]

It would be helpful in present disagreements if Christians returned to discussing moral questions through a more flexible and creative exploration of natural law, fortified in the enterprise by what has become apparent about human behaviour and biology over the last century. If, for instance, it becomes clear that some people are predominantly sexually attracted by nature to people of their own sex, then the terms of argument through natural law will have moved on. A further vital element in any reconstructed version of natural law will be a more comprehensive understanding of historical process, something that was largely lacking from any previous natural law discussion. This book is an attempt to contribute to that reframing.

Fitting the Bible in a properly historical fashion into a renewed and more adequate understanding of natural law is not to jettison the Bible's meaning or authority, but to enrich it. The Infancy Narratives of Matthew's and Luke's Gospels, for instance, are not history in the conventional modern sense, but they are admirably prophetic descriptions of what has happened in Christian history. A child in south-west Asia whose birth fell outside the conventional family patterns of his day took on a cosmic significance that has brought him allegiance worldwide. Those who worshipped at the manger ranged from illiterate teenagers in marginal occupations to scholars of ancient wisdom; between them they have confounded the efforts of the rulers of this world to destroy him or co-opt him – just as the Infancy Narratives say. That is a two-millennium-long tale beyond attendant sheep, camels or courtiers in the palace of King Herod. Birth is women's business, not men's, and in the next two millennia we may be liberated to listen to women's accounts of the Incarnation more than we have been able to amid the din of male theological voices.

Does it matter that marriage has not previously been available as a loving commitment to people of the same sex? The variety of what Christian marriage *has* meant in the past is remarkable, squeezed into a mere two thousand years. Such a timespan is like an evening gone even in human experience; one would not expect it to reveal all Christianity's potential riches. Interestingly, after a pronouncement from Pope Francis in December 2023 (*Fiducia Supplicans*) and similar moves in the Church of England, same-sex couples throughout much of Western Christianity are now in much the same position as heterosexual married couples were in the second-century Church: following a civil ceremony formalizing their relationship, they can come along to their worship community and receive a blessing.[7] Elsewhere in the Protestant and Anglican Christian world, matters have moved along further to equal marriage; elsewhere, again, they have not.

There is more variety to come in marriage, sex and the family. We can end our long journey by returning to a saying of Jesus himself: from Mark's Gospel, reframed by Matthew and Luke. It is a playful riposte to those in Jesus's generation seeking to tie him down into the legalities and traditions in past Jewish marriage practice. When Sadducees sought a simple response from him to a complicated scenario they sketched out about marriages in the afterlife, Jesus blindsided them:

> Is not this why you are wrong, that you know neither the scriptures nor the power of God? For when they rise from the dead, they neither marry nor are given in marriage, but are like angels in heaven.[8]

We may sympathize with the Lord's implication that marriages in this life have a tendency to be less than angelic. But it remains the duty of historians to describe and analyse them, along with much else – while we can leave angels to work out their own arrangements.

Further Reading

After a book that has cited more than eight hundred primary and secondary sources, this is designed to provide a summary of general introductory reading or classic works in English in the various sections of the book. Detailed reading on particular topics is cited in the endnotes relating to the main text, including works in languages other than English, and is not necessarily repeated here.

GENERAL

A remarkable classic survey of the background is V. L. Bullough, *Sexual Variance in Society and History* (2nd edn, Chicago, 1980), and there is now more briefly S. Kingsley Kent, *Gender: A world history* (Oxford, 2021). On same-sex activity and homosexual identity, one should acknowledge pioneering work from Michel Foucault, particularly the four volumes of his *History of Sexuality*, tr. R. Hurley (London, 1978–2021), and also from John Boswell (especially *Christianity, Social Tolerance and Homosexuality: Gay people in western Europe from the beginning of the Christian era to the fourteenth century*, Chicago, 1980), and from Alan Bray (especially *The Friend*, Chicago and London, 2006). It has to be said that in each case, their work was affected and somewhat distorted by their relationship to Roman Catholicism. Foucault's rejection of conventional childhood French Catholicism left him still over-extending the significance of sacramental confession or its equivalents as an explanatory mechanism. The Catholic conversions of Boswell and Bray from Episcopalianism/Anglicanism encouraged both of them in an agenda to find a gay past that might provide an accepted place for homosexuality in present-day Catholic practice. All three nevertheless creatively explored matters that others had ignored.

J. Barton, *The Word: On the translation of the Bible* (London, 2022) guides those who wish to understand methodological issues in the whole library of books that shape Christian practice and belief. The complexity and instability of the Greek New Testament, not readily appreciated in the Bibles that one normally reads, becomes apparent through the systematic parallel texts of K. Aland (ed.), *Synopsis of the Four Gospels, Greek–English edition of the Synopsis Quattuor Evangeliorum* (9th edn, Stuttgart, 1989), derived from the German original of 1964, K. Aland (ed.), *Synopsis quattuor Evangeliorum, locis parallelis Evangeliorum apocryphorum et patrum adhibitis*.

I have already tried to provide an overview of the Christian story in D. MacCulloch, *A History of Christianity: The first three thousand years* (London, 2009); now classic and enjoyable accounts of particular aspects of that history are E. Duffy, *Saints and Sinners: A history of the Popes* (3rd edn, New Haven, Conn. and London, 2006) and J. A. McGuckin, *The Eastern Orthodox Church: A new history* (New Haven, Conn. and London, 2020). On Catholic/Orthodox attitudes to Christianity and sex, see J. Keenan, *A History of Catholic Theological Ethics* (New York, 2022) and T. Arentzen, A. M. Purpura and A. Papanikolaou (eds), *Orthodox Tradition and Human Sexuality* (New York, 2022). H. King, *Immaculate Forms: Uncovering the history of women's bodies* (London, 2024) opens up long-term perspectives on matters long on the edge of scholarly vision for historians. For one very important actor in the story, Mary the Mother of God, one should never neglect the engrossing M. Warner, *Alone of All Her Sex: The myth and cult of the Virgin Mary* (London, 1976), now complemented by M. Rubin, *Mother of God: A history of the Virgin Mary* (London, 2009).

ORIGINS IN PRE-CHRISTIAN CULTURE, THE HEBREW BIBLE AND NEW TESTAMENT

J. Barton, *A History of the Bible: The book and its faiths* (London, 2019) is a reliable way into the field, and a cheerfully informal but well-informed consideration of biblical discussion of sex is M. Coogan, *What the Bible Really Says about Sex* (New York and Boston, Mass., 2010). A fine collection of essays by specialists of both Jewish and Christian backgrounds introduces many different aspects of the Hebrew Bible/Old

Testament from a range of perspectives, some more radical than others: J. Barton (ed.), *The Hebrew Bible: A critical companion* (Princeton, NJ and Oxford, 2016). B. Dunning (ed.), *The Oxford Handbook of New Testament, Gender and Sexuality* (Oxford, 2019) marshals a great range of sensible and up-to-date scholarship. Provocative and learned on the ancient matrix of the Judaeo-Christian tradition is F. Stavrakopoulou, *God: An anatomy* (London, 2021), leading on to M. Goodman, *Rome and Jerusalem: The clash of ancient civilisations* (London, 2006) and C. A. Williams, *Roman Homosexuality: Ideologies of masculinity in Classical antiquity* (New York and Oxford, 1999). K. E. Børresen (ed.), *The Image of God: Gender models in Judaeo-Christian tradition* (Minneapolis, Minn., 1995) gathers essays that are an excellent forensic historical analysis of the contortions of Jewish and Christian thinkers around one of the chief focuses of such problems, the passage on the creation of humanity at Gen. 1.26–27, and an important and tightly argued monograph treatment of intellectual origins is K. L. Gaca, *The Making of Fornication: Eros, ethics and political reform in Greek philosophy and early Christianity* (Berkeley, Calif., 2003). A classic work of iconoclasm is E. Schüssler Fiorenza, *In Memory of Her: A feminist theological reconstruction of Christian origins* (New York, 1983). Indispensable for understanding our scraps of knowledge about the first Christians is W. A. Meeks, *The First Urban Christians: The social world of the Apostle Paul* (New Haven, Conn. and London, 1983).

EARLY CHRISTIANITY AND LATE ANTIQUITY

It will have become apparent to the observant reader that I am unenthusiastic about the historical aspect of Michel Foucault's oeuvre in general, and on sexuality in particular. There is much sensible historical material in vols. 2 to 4 of his *History of Sexuality*, but most of it has been better explored by others, most notably in the sparkling P. Brown, *The Body and Society: Men, women and sexual renunciation in early Christianity* (new edn, New York, 2008). An enjoyable introduction is K. Cooper, *Band of Angels: The forgotten world of early Christian women* (London, 2013); taking no prisoners is R. S. Kraemer, *Unreliable Witnesses: Religion, gender and history in the Greco-Roman Mediterranean* (Oxford, 2010). Impressively thorough is P. Reynolds, *Marriage in the Western*

Church: The Christianization of marriage during the patristic and early medieval periods (Leiden and New York, 1994). Among a range of distinguished biographies of the chief figure in Western theology, P. Brown, *Augustine of Hippo: A biography* (London, 1969) still holds its own, though the most recent substantial study is R. Lane Fox, *Augustine: Conversions and confessions* (London, 2015). Another key personality is illuminated by the accessible and learned P. Sarris, *Justinian: Emperor, soldier, saint* (London, 2024). Fine guides to the transition from antiquity from two scholars who allow the reader to appreciate the importance of gender are J. Herrin, *The Formation of Christendom* (with new intro., Princeton, NJ, 2022) and A. Cameron, *The Mediterranean World in Late Antiquity, 395–700* (rev. edn, London, 2015).

THE MEDIEVAL WORLD AND THE REFORMATION

On Islam and Eastern Christianity, a good English rendering of the Qur'an is M. A. S. Abdel Haleem (ed.), *The Qur'an: A new translation* (Oxford, 2004), and an exemplary monograph is L. E. Weitz, *Between Christ and Caliph: Law, marriage and Christian community in early Islam* (Philadelphia, Pa., 2018). Sumptuously illustrated and pleasurably well-informed is C. Baumer, *The Church of the East: An illustrated history of Assyrian Christianity* (London and New York, 2006).

The medieval West is well introduced by K. Harvey, *The Fires of Lust: Sex in the Middle Ages* (London, 2021) and R. Mazo Karras, *Sexuality in Medieval Europe: Doing unto others* (2nd edn, New York, 2012). Magisterial overviews beyond them are E. van Houts, *Married Life in the Middle Ages, 900–1300* (Oxford, 2019) and J. Brundage, *Law, Sex and Christian Society in Medieval Europe* (Chicago, 1987). The early medieval picture in the Atlantic Isles is enjoyably clarified by J. Blair, *The Church in Anglo-Saxon Society* (Oxford, 2005) and by C. Harrington's monograph *Women in a Celtic Church: Ireland 450–1150* (Oxford, 2002). R. Meens, *Penance in Medieval Europe, 600–1200* (Cambridge, 2014) is a fine clarification of a highly important strand in Western Christianity. R. I. Moore, *The Formation of a Persecuting Society: Power and deviance in Western Europe, 950–1250* (Oxford, 1987) is at the centre of a literature of lively controversy. A fascinating first anglophone in-depth study of medieval northern Orthodoxy is E. Levin,

Sex and Society in the World of the Orthodox Slavs 900–1700 (Ithaca, NY, 2018). A. Ivanov, *Holy Fools in Byzantium and Beyond* (Oxford, 2006) is an engaging and surprising survey.

On the Reformation, I provide an overview of sex and gender in D. MacCulloch, *Reformation: Europe's house divided* (London, 2003), chs. 15 and 16. A great Jesuit scholar provides a sympathetic but objective study in J. O'Malley, *The First Jesuits* (Cambridge, Mass., 1993). R. Hutton, *The Witch: A history of fear, from ancient times to the present* (New Haven, Conn. and London, 2017) puts the paranoia of Reformation and Counter-Reformation in the widest of contexts. Highly important and well-informed in gathering together recent reshapings of our understanding of European same-sex phenomena is N. Malcolm, *Forbidden Desire in Early Modern Europe: Male–male sexual relations, 1400–1750* (Oxford, 2024). Po-chia Hsia (ed.), *A Companion to Early Modern Catholic Global Missions* (Leiden and Boston, Mass., 2018) is a good guide to a sprawling subject.

THE ENLIGHTENMENT AND THE MODERN WORLD

R. Robertson, *The Enlightenment: The pursuit of happiness, 1680–1790* (London, 2020), provides a substantial and reliable introduction. The emerging world power of eighteenth-century Great Britain is well served by F. Dabhoiwala, *The Origins of Sex: A history of the first sexual revolution* (London, 2012) and W. Gibson and J. Begiato, *Sex and the Church in the Long Eighteenth Century: Religion, Enlightenment and the sexual revolution* (London and New York, 2017). H. D. Rack, *Reasonable Enthusiast: John Wesley and the rise of Methodism* (3rd edn, London, 2002) is an affectionately acerbic portrait of a hugely influential figure, warts and all, by a Methodist insider. D. Andress, *The French Revolution and the People* (London, 2004) is one way into a vast subject. On north America, an engrossing general analysis is P. Bonomi, *Under the Cope of Heaven: Religion, society and politics in colonial America* (Oxford, 2003), and more briefly but over a greater chronological range, A. Braude, *Sisters and Saints: Women and American religion* (Oxford, 2008).

The continuing vitality of Marian devotion in the modern world can be sampled in R. Harris, *Lourdes: Body and spirit in the secular age*

(London, 1999), followed by C. Maunder, *Our Lady of the Nations: Apparitions of Mary in 20th-century Europe* (Oxford, 2016). A sobering theme is presented in C. Kidd, *The Forging of Races: Race and scripture in the Protestant Atlantic world, 1600–2000* (Cambridge, 2006). A now classic guide to the UK is J. Weeks, *Sex, Politics, and Society: The regulations of sexuality since 1800* (3rd edn, London, 2012), and an equally keen eye on a British subject with much wider implications is H. Cook, *The Long Sexual Revolution: English women, sex, and contraception 1800–1975* (Oxford, 2004).

A. Anderson, *An Introduction to Pentecostalism* (Cambridge, 2004) sets out a still-fluid worldwide story up to its publication date. Likewise reliable in their coverage to their publication dates are the very substantial works of A. Hastings, *The Church in Africa 1450–1950* (Oxford, 1994) and of B. Sundkler and C. Steed, *A History of the Church in Africa* (Cambridge, 2000). H. McLeod, *The Religious Crisis of the 1960s* (Oxford, 2007) examines the cultural shift which has fuelled the last sixty years. As events unfold, it is difficult to provide reading that has kept pace, but J. Micklethwait and A. Wooldridge, *God is Back: How the global revival of faith is changing the world* (London, 2009) represents one unbuttoned attempt to make sense of what has happened; another sobering analysis is M. Northcott, *An Angel Directs the Storm: Apocalyptic religion and American empire* (London, 2004).

On modern Roman Catholicism, a good introduction is N. Atkin and F. Tallett, *Priests, Prelates and People: A history of European Catholicism since 1750* (London, 2003). One unfolding modern development in Catholicism can be sampled in A. T. Hennelly (ed.), *Liberation Theology: A documentary history* (Maryknoll, NY, 1990). Regrettably well-informed, though also over-egged and gossipy, is F. Martel, tr. S. Whiteside, *In the Closet of the Vatican: Power, homosexuality, hypocrisy* (London, 2019). It can be balanced or supplemented by J. Cornwell, *Church, Interrupted: Havoc and Hope: The tender revolt of Pope Francis* (San Francisco, 2021) and Pope Francis's conversation with Austen Ivereigh, *Let Us Dream: The path to a better future* (London, 2020). Anglicanism's world debates are unflinchingly analysed by S. Bates, *A Church at War: Anglicans and homosexuality* (London and New York, 2004) and W. L. Sachs, *Homosexuality and the Crisis of Anglicanism* (Cambridge, 2009). For the all-important theme of religious extremism, see the essays in J. D. G. Dunn (ed.), *Fundamentalisms: Threats and ideologies in the modern world* (London, 2015), and for a fine historical survey, G. M. Marsden, *Understanding Fundamentalism and Evangelicalism* (Grand Rapids, Mich., 1991).

For major reshapings in modern society, a foundational text is J. Butler, *Gender Trouble: Feminism and the subversion of identity* (New York and London, 1990), and more recent, passionately expressed accounts are S. Faye, *The Transgender Issue: An argument for justice* (London, 2021) and (with a Christian perspective) S. G. Chappell, *Trans Figured: On being a transgender person in a cisgender world* (London, 2024). M. Coren, *Reclaiming Faith: Inclusion, grace, and tolerance* (Toronto, 2019) collects his essays suggesting some ways forward for Christian Churches placed in so many new situations.

Abbreviations Used in the Notes

Arentzen et al. (eds), *Orthodox Tradition and Human Sexuality*	T. Arentzen, A. M. Purpura and A. Papanikolaou (eds), *Orthodox Tradition and Human Sexuality* (New York, 2022)
Ariès and Béjin (eds), *Western Sexuality*	P. Ariès and A. Béjin (eds), tr. A. Forster, *Western Sexuality: Practice and precept in past and present times* (Oxford, 1985)
Barton, *History of the Bible*	J. Barton, *A History of the Bible: The book and its faiths* (London, 2019)
Barton, *The Word*	J. Barton, *The Word: On the translation of the Bible* (London, 2022)
Børresen (ed.), *Image of God*	K. E. Børresen (ed.), *The Image of God: Gender models in Judaeo-Christian tradition* (Minneapolis, Minn., 1995)
Boswell, *Christianity, Social Tolerance and Homosexuality*	J. Boswell, *Christianity, Social Tolerance and Homosexuality: Gay people in western Europe from the beginning of the Christian era to the fourteenth century* (Chicago, 1980)
Brown, *Body and Society*	P. Brown, *The Body and Society: Men, women and sexual renunciation in early Christianity* (new edn, New York, 2008)
Bullough, *Sexual Variance in Society and History*	V. L. Bullough, *Sexual Variance in Society and History* (2nd edn, Chicago, 1980)
CH	*Church History*
CWE	*Collected Works of Erasmus*, various editors (Toronto)

Dunn, *Unity and Diversity in the New Testament*	J. Dunn, *Unity and Diversity in the New Testament: An inquiry into the character of early Christianity* (London, 1977)
Fiorenza, *In Memory of Her*	E. Schüssler Fiorenza, *In Memory of Her: A feminist theological reconstruction of Christian origins* (New York, 1983)
Foucault, *History of Sexuality*	M. Foucault, tr. R. Hurley, *The History of Sexuality*, vol. 1: *The Will to Knowledge* (1976: English edn London, 1978); 2: *The Use of Pleasure* (1984: English edn London, 1987); 3: *The Care of the Self* (1984: English edn London, 1990); 4: *Confessions of the Flesh* (2018: English edn London, 2021)
Gaca, *Making of Fornication*	K. L. Gaca, *The Making of Fornication: Eros, ethics and political reform in Greek philosophy and early Christianity* (Berkeley, Calif., 2003)
Gathercole (ed.), *Apocryphal Gospels*	S. Gathercole (ed.), *The Apocryphal Gospels* (Oxford, 2021)
Goodman, *Rome and Jerusalem*	M. Goodman, *Rome and Jerusalem: The clash of ancient civilisations* (London, 2006)
Harrington, *Women in a Celtic Church*	C. Harrington, *Women in a Celtic Church: Ireland 450–1150* (Oxford, 2002)
Harvey, *Fires of Lust*	K. Harvey, *The Fires of Lust: Sex in the Middle Ages* (London, 2021)
HJ	*Historical Journal*
van Houts, *Married Life in the Middle Ages*	E. van Houts, *Married Life in the Middle Ages, 900–1300* (Oxford, 2019)
Hunter, *Jovinianist Controversy*	D. G. Hunter, *Marriage, Celibacy, and Heresy in Ancient Christianity: The Jovinianist Controversy* (Oxford, 2007)
JEH	*Journal of Ecclesiastical History*
JOH	*Journal of Homosexuality*

Karras, *Sexuality in Medieval Europe*	R. Mazo Karras, *Sexuality in Medieval Europe: Doing unto others* (2nd edn, New York, 2012)
Kraemer, *Unreliable Witnesses*	R. S. Kraemer, *Unreliable Witnesses: Religion, gender and history in the Greco-Roman Mediterranean* (Oxford, 2010)
Kraemer and D'Angelo (eds), *Women and Christian Origins*	R. S. Kraemer and M. R. D'Angelo (eds), *Women and Christian Origins* (Oxford, 1999)
Levin, *Sex and Society in the World of the Orthodox Slavs*	E. Levin, *Sex and Society in the World of the Orthodox Slavs 900–1700* (Ithaca, NY, 2018)
MacCulloch, *Christianity*	D. MacCulloch, *A History of Christianity: The first three thousand years* (London, 2009); US edition *Christianity: The first three thousand years* (New York, 2010)
MacCulloch, *Reformation*	D. MacCulloch, *Reformation: Europe's house divided* (London, 2003)
PP	*Past and Present*
Reynolds, *Marriage in the Western Church*	P. Reynolds, *Marriage in the Western Church: The Christianization of marriage during the patristic and early medieval periods* (Leiden and New York, 1994)
SCJ	*Sixteenth Century Journal*
Stevenson (ed.), rev. Frend, *Creeds, Councils and Controversies*	J. Stevenson (ed.), rev. W. H. C. Frend, *Creeds, Councils and Controversies: Documents illustrating the history of the Church* AD *337–461* (London, 1989)
Stevenson (ed.), rev. Frend, *New Eusebius*	J. Stevenson (ed.), rev. W. H. C. Frend, *A New Eusebius: Documents illustrating the history of the Church to* AD *337* (London, 1987)
Swanson (ed.), *Church and Mary*	R. N. Swanson (ed.), *The Church and Mary*, Studies in Church History 39 (Woodbridge, 2004)

Swanson (ed.), *Gender and Christian Religion*	R. N. Swanson (ed.), *Gender and Christian Religion*, Studies in Church History 34 (Woodbridge, 1998)
TRHS	*Transactions of the Royal Historical Society*
Weitz, *Between Christ and Caliph*	L. E. Weitz, *Between Christ and Caliph: Law, marriage and Christian community in early Islam* (Philadelphia, Pa., 2018)

Biblical Abbreviations Used in the Text and Notes

SELECTED BOOKS OF THE HEBREW SCRIPTURE/ HEBREW BIBLE/TANAKH/OLD TESTAMENT

Deut.	Deuteronomy
Exod.	Exodus
Ezek.	Ezekiel
Gen.	Genesis
Isa.	Isaiah
Jer.	Jeremiah
Judg.	Judges
Lev.	Leviticus
Prov.	Proverbs
Ps. (pl. Pss)	Psalms
1 Sam.	1 Samuel
2 Sam.	2 Samuel
Zech.	Zechariah

SELECTED BOOKS OF THE CHRISTIAN NEW TESTAMENT

Acts	Acts of the Apostles
Col.	Colossians
1 Cor.	1 Corinthians
2 Cor.	2 Corinthians
Eph.	Ephesians
Gal.	Galatians
Heb.	Hebrews
John	John (Gospel)
1 John	1 John (Epistle)

2 John	2 John (Epistle)
3 John	3 John (Epistle)
Matt.	Matthew
1 Pet.	1 Peter
Phil.	Philippians
Rev.	Revelation
Rom.	Romans
1 Thess.	1 Thessalonians
2 Thess.	2 Thessalonians
1 Tim.	1 Timothy
2 Tim.	2 Timothy

Notes

CONVENTIONS USED IN THE TEXT

1. See a helpful treatment of this matter in Barton, *The Word*, 153–7.
2. A sensible discussion of the issue, including frank recognition of the awkwardness of the chronological boundary involved, can be found in Kraemer, *Unreliable Witnesses*, 26; cf. ibid., 179–80, 196, for illustrations of why a distinction becomes an aid to understanding historical issues.

1. SETTING OUT

1. L. Crompton (ed. and intro.), 'Jeremy Bentham's essay on "Paederasty"', *JOH* 3 (1978), 383–405, at 384–5 (citing University College London, Bentham Papers Box 72 f. 188d); cf. the continuation of Crompton's edition, *JOH* 4 (1978), 91–107, at 106. Bentham wrote a good deal on what we would call homosexuality, this essay being written around 1785, though none of it was published in his lifetime. I was amused by a coincidence of title with my own thoughts in the useful C. D. Shanafelt, *Uncommon Sense: Jeremy Bentham, queer aesthetics, and the politics of taste* (Charlottesville, Va., 2021).
2. The doors of a handsome cupboard in a concourse area of UCL used to open to reveal Bentham's seated skeleton and wax substitute head (the actual skull latterly more securely housed elsewhere following a student prank), furnishing a decorous conversation-piece. The relocation of these relics in 2020 to the new UCL Student Union, in a more secure though less retiring display-case, has not been without controversy.
3. L. L. Patton, *Who Owns Religion? Scholars and their publics in the late twentieth century* (Chicago, 2019), 247.
4. Quoted in the review by E. C. Stoykovich of S. Bhattacharya, *Archiving the British Raj: History of the archival policy of the Government of India, with selected documents, 1858–1947* (2019), *Archives* 55/2 (2020), 61–2.
5. The exception to this rule might be the sixteenth-century Reformation: see below, Ch. 14.

6. Boswell, *Christianity, Social Tolerance and Homosexuality*, 7.
7. I discuss this curious and distinctively Christian initiative in MacCulloch, *Christianity*, 158.
8. 'Inter-Testamental literature' was also an unsatisfactory term for the pedantic reason that at either extreme some of the texts respectively predated the end of the 'Old Testament' and postdated parts of the New Testament.
9. Barton, *The Word*, 1 (the opening sentence of his study) and 86. A summary introduction to the questions that Barton treats for the Hebrew Bible is C. McCarthy, 'Textual criticism and biblical translation', in J. Barton (ed.), *The Hebrew Bible: A critical companion* (Princeton, NJ and Oxford, 2016), 532–56. For a dazzlingly intricate exposition of ancient attitudes to translating sacred text, culminating in the work of paraphrase by the fifth-century CE poet Nonnus, see S. Goldhill, *The Christian Invention of Time: Temporality and the literature of late antiquity* (Cambridge, 2022), ch. 11.
10. Mark 5.41. Interestingly, the rewritings of this episode in the slightly later Gospels of Matthew and Luke (Matt. 9.18–26, Luke 8.40–56) dispense with the Aramaic phrase.
11. A fine treatment of this is T. M. Law, *When God Spoke Greek: The Septuagint and the making of the Christian Bible* (Oxford, 2013).
12. Matt. 6.9–15; Luke 11.1–4; see also Mark 11.25–26. Both the latter are abbreviated compared with the full version in Matthew. For further discussion, see MacCulloch, *Christianity*, 89. Barton, *The Word*, provides examples of irretrievably damaged texts from both the Hebrew Bible and New Testament in ch. 9.
13. P. M. Joyce, *Ezekiel: A commentary* (New York and London, 2007), 49, and see accompanying discussion 44–9: on Ezekiel see also Law, *When God Spoke Greek*, 53–4, 136. For a significant example of unstable text from the Hebrew Bible at 1 Sam. 20.41 about David and Jonathan, bearing on an important aspect of sexuality, see below, Ch. 3, p. 514.
14. F. Stavrakopoulou, *God: An anatomy* (London, 2021), 160–61.
15. B. Cummings (ed.), *The Book of Common Prayer: The texts of 1549, 1559, and 1662* (Oxford, 2011), 217, 229, 750–51.
16. We await the full publication of work by the research team led by Ed Oxford and Kathy Baldock; their arguments so far can be sampled at https://www.forgeonline.org/blog/2019/3/8/what-about-romans-124-27 (visited 10 Jan. 2023). For a concise summary of the question, C. Richie, 'An argument against the use of the word "homosexual" in English translations of the Bible', *Heythrop Journal* 51 (2010), 723–9, and for a crisp round-up of the wider background, R. K. Gnuse, 'Seven gay texts: biblical passages used to condemn homosexuality', *Biblical Theology Bulletin* 45 (2015), 68–87.
17. One careful and sensible summary discussion is S. Palmer, 'Recovering female authors of the Bible', *Studia Antiqua* 15 (2016), 13–26. Particularly important is her point (pp. 25–6) that likely female biblical compositions

appear to be in formal poetry, which would be an easier medium in composing, memorizing and performance for those likely to lack the technology of literacy. An imaginative approach to viewing the composition of New Testament texts is C. Moss, *God's Ghostwriters: Enslaved Christians and the making of the Bible* (Boston, Mass., 2024).

18. Summary analysis of the Song of Songs/Solomon is usefully provided in J. Barton and J. Muddiman (eds), *The Oxford Bible Commentary* (Oxford, 2001), 429–33, and see also below, Ch. 3, for further comment. For 'defiling the hands', and its reference to the Divine Name, see Barton, *The Word*, 281–2. For God's instruction to women to teach the professional craft of lamenting, including the performance of songs of lamentation, see e.g. Jer. 9. 17–20. English Protestant commentators in the seventeenth century already recognized women's distinctive biblical role in singing (and radicals saw it as a contemporary precedent): S. Apetrei, *The Reformation of the Heart: Gender and radical theology in the English Revolution* (Oxford, 2024), 154–64.
19. Fiorenza makes this point about her choice of title in Fiorenza, *In Memory of Her*, xiii. For Jesus's pronouncement she used the translation of the New American Standard Bible (1960), v. 9 of Mark 14.3–9 (with parallels at Matt. 26.6–13; Luke 7.36–50; John 12.3–8, where the woman is identified with Mary of Bethany). In subsequent discussion (ibid., 60–61) Fiorenza sums up suggestions that some New Testament writings may involve women's writing, for instance Adolf von Harnack's proposal that Hebrews might have been by Paul's colleagues Priscilla and Aquila; she comments that this does not affect their general androcentricity.
20. Barton, *The Word*, 146.
21. This is likely, as observed above, to include the Magnificat. The famous description of male deployment of women 'to think with', originally coined by the anthropologist Claude Lévi-Strauss, was popularized for historians by Peter Brown: e.g. Brown, *Body and Society*, 153. For cautionary remarks about his use of the concept, see Kraemer, *Unreliable Witnesses*, 128n.
22. For a balanced analysis of how to assess the evidential significance of legislation in relation to late Roman and Byzantine society, see R. S. Bagnall, 'Women, law, and social realities in late antiquity: a review article', *Bulletin of the American Society of Papyrologists* 32 (1995), 65–86, at 80–86: reviewing J. Beaucamp, *Le statut de la femme à Byzance (4e–7e siècle)* (2 vols, Paris, 1990, 1992).
23. C. L. Meyers, 'Was ancient Israel a patriarchal society?', *Journal of Biblical Literature* 133 (2014), 8–27, at 26–7.
24. For one example of a sensitive probing into such a case, see C. Marsh, '*The Woman to the Plow; and the Man to the Hen-Roost*: wives, husbands and best-selling ballads in 17th-century England', *TRHS* 6th ser. 28 (2018), 65–88. Marsh is building on the excellent earlier work of T. Watt, *Cheap Print and Popular Piety 1550–1640* (Cambridge, 1991).

25. Bullough, *Sexual Variance in Society and History*, 677: Prof. Bullough would have penned these words around 1975.
26. R. Beachy, 'The German invention of homosexuality', *Journal of Modern History* 82 (2010), 801–38, esp. 804: an enjoyable demolition by an accomplished historian of Michel Foucault's undeservedly influential account of the 19th-century 'invention' of homosexuality.
27. For a useful recent analysis of the still unstable state of our language for discussion, see M. Thelwall, T. J. Devonport, M. Makita, K. Russell and L. Ferguson, 'Academic LGBTQ+ terminology 1900–2021: increasing variety, increasing inclusivity?', *JOH* 70 pt xi (2023), 2514–38.
28. *Times Literary Supplement*, Letters to the Editor 18 and 26 July 2019 between John Lauritsen, Hal Jensen and Hugh Ryan, author of *When Brooklyn was Queer* (London, 2019), and I cite the quotation from Dr Ryan.
29. E. H. Brown, *Work! A Queer History of Modeling* (Durham, NC, 2019), 9, part of a good discussion of the discursive uses of the term 'queer' in her 'Introduction'; she further cites and echoes C. J. Cohen, 'Punks, bulldaggers, and welfare queens: the radical potential of queer politics?', *GLQ: A Journal of Lesbian and Gay Studies* 3 (1997), 437–65. For a measured critique of the bounds of queer theory from inside the scholarly gates, see the review essay by W. Stockton, 'Shakespeare and queer theory', *Shakespeare Quarterly* 63 (2012), 224–35.
30. J. Wallach Scott, *Gender and the Politics of History* (New York, 1988), 'Introduction', 2. See also her fine discussion in J. W. Scott, 'Gender: a useful category of historical analysis', *American Historical Review* 91 (1986), 1053–75.
31. These conundrums are discussed with clarity and concision by Arianne Shahvisi, *London Review of Books*, 8 Sept. 2022, 7–8, reviewing G. Rippon, *The Gendered Brain: The new neuroscience that shatters the myth of the female brain* (London, 2019) and S. Moalem, *The Better Half: On the genetic superiority of women* (London, 2021). For passionate presentations of the issues by trans people, see S. Faye, *The Transgender Issue: An argument for justice* (London, 2021), and S. G. Chappell, *Trans Figured: On being a transgender person in a cisgender world* (London, 2024). A classic discussion is J. Butler, *Gender Trouble: Feminism and the subversion of identity* (New York and London, 1990); see her usefully complicating proposition, ibid., 7: 'gender is not to culture as sex is to nature; gender is also the discursive/cultural means by which "sexed nature" or "a natural sex" is produced as "prediscursive", prior to culture, a politically neutral surface *on which* culture acts.'
32. For an incisive analysis of how gender-aware historiography has transformed our understanding of Byzantine Christian history over half a century, see the introduction by Judith Herrin, 'An octogenarian welcome', to S. Tougher (ed.), *The Palgrave Handbook of Gender in Byzantium* (London, forthcoming).

33. Heb. 2.7, quoting the Septuagint version of Ps. 8.5, which in the Hebrew speaks of God making humanity 'little less than God' (or 'the gods'); clearly the Alexandria Jewish-Greek translators of the psalm found this a difficult idea. Many translations evasively try to harmonize the two. For contextual comment on the entangled history of these two complex texts, see S. Gillingham, *Psalms Through the Centuries: A reception history* (3 vols, Oxford, 2007–2022), ii, 72–82, and H. W. Attridge, ed. H. Koester, *The Epistle to the Hebrews: A commentary on the Epistle to the Hebrews* (Philadelphia, Pa., 1989), 69–77.
34. Jubilees 15.27: H. F. D. Sparks (ed.), *The Apocryphal Old Testament* (Oxford, 1984), 56. I am grateful to John Barton for pointing this out to me.
35. T. Martin, 'The development of winged angels in early Christian art', *Espacio, Tiempo y Forma VII: Historia del Arte* 14 (2001), 11–29, at 17, 22–3; further discussed in Ch. 8 below.
36. J. Milton, *Paradise Lost* 1.423–428; and cf. ibid., 8.620–629. I am indebted to Sophie Grace Chappell for pointing me to these references. Milton's considerable interest in angels, albeit structured by Protestant selectivity from the tradition, is thoroughly explored in F. G. Mohamed, *In the Anteroom of Divinity: The Reformation of the angels from Colet to Milton* (Toronto, 2008), chs. 4–6.
37. P. Marshall and A. Walsham (eds), *Angels in the Early Modern World* (Cambridge, 2006), 28. On Counter-Reformation devotion to angels, see M. Friedrich, tr. J. N. Dillon, *The Jesuits: A history* (Princeton, NJ and Oxford, 2022), 161–3. For comment on modern angels' apparently female gender in some US contexts, see P. Rackin, 'Historical difference/sexual difference', in J. R. Brink (ed.), *Privileging Gender in Early Modern England* (Sixteenth Century Essays & Studies 23, 1993), 37–63, at 47.
38. S. Brock, 'The Holy Spirit as feminine in early Syriac literature', in J. Soskice (ed.), *After Eve* (London, 1990), 73–88.
39. For a return in the radical Reformation to an emphasis on a female *Sophia* principle in divinity, via Paracelsus, Jakob Boehme and John Pordage, see Apetrei, *The Reformation of the Heart*, 37–9.
40. K. E. Børresen, 'God's image. Is Woman excluded? Medieval interpretation of Gen. 1.27 and I Cor. 11.7', in Børresen (ed.), *Image of God*, 210–35, at 210.
41. Kallistos Ware, foreword to collected essays in *The Wheel* 13/14 (2018), 9–10; subsequently much quoted, e.g. in Arentzen et al. (eds), *Orthodox Tradition and Human Sexuality*, 3 and 128.

2. GREEKS AND JEWS

1. R. Beaton, *The Greeks: A global history* (London, 2021), 1. What follows is well-summarized in ibid., chs. 2 and 3.

2. A fascinating rediscovery of evidence about such ties in times of crisis between Anatolian Teos and its founding Greek city of Abdera has recently been elucidated in M. Adak and P. Thonemann, *Teos and Abdera: Two cities in peace and war* (Oxford, 2022).
3. A. Uchitel, 'The earliest tyrants: from Luwian *Tarwanis* to Greek Τύραννος', in G. Herman and I. Shatzman (eds), *Greeks between East and West: Essays in Greek literature and history in memory of David Asheri* (Jerusalem, 2007), 13–30, which makes the point that the Greeks had misunderstood the political significance of the title, simply finding an exotic word useful to describe a power that they could not otherwise define. I am indebted to Michael Harazin for this reference.
4. W. D. Desmond, *The Greek Praise of Poverty: Origins of ancient Cynicism* (Notre Dame, Ind., 2006), esp. 6–7, 60–61, 144.
5. C. H. Kahn, *Pythagoras and the Pythagoreans: A brief history* (Indianapolis, Ind. and Cambridge, 2001), 6–10.
6. H. N. Fowler and W. R. M. Lamb (eds), *Plato, with an English Translation I: Euthyphro; Apology; Crito; Phaedo; Phaedrus* (London and Cambridge, Mass., 1953), 132–3 [*Apology*, 38a]. A good treatment of Socrates' trial and death is E. Wilson, *The Death of Socrates: Hero, villain, chatterbox, saint* (London, 2007).
7. M. Schofield, *Plato: Political philosophy* (Oxford, 2006), esp. 40–42, 88–9.
8. Beaton, *The Greeks*, 97.
9. R. G. Bury (ed.), *Plato, with an English Translation VII: Timaeus; Critias; Cleitophon; Menexenus; Epistles* (London and Cambridge, Mass., 1961), 50–53, 176–9 [*Timaeus* XXVIIIa–XXIXd; LXVIIIe–LXIXc].
10. Good summary discussion of the *Timaeus* and its effects is to be found in R. Radford Ruether, '*Imago Dei*: Christian tradition and feminist hermeneutics', in Børresen (ed.), *Image of God*, 267–91, at 272–3.
11. Effective pictures of Alexander are P. Cartledge, *Alexander the Great: The hunt for a new past* (Basingstoke and Oxford, 2004); C. Mossé, *Alexander: Destiny and myth* (Edinburgh, 2004).
12. H. Maehler, 'Alexandria, the Mouseion, and cultural identity', in A. Hirst and M. Silk (eds), *Alexandria: Real and imagined* (Aldershot, 2004), 1–14.
13. The pioneer was the Prussian historian J. G. Droysen: see good summary discussion on his thesis on the relationship between Christianity and the Hellenistic world in P. Cartledge, 'Introduction', in P. Cartledge, P. Garnsey and E. S. Gruen (eds), *Hellenistic Constructs: Essays in culture, history and historiography* (Berkeley, Calif., 1997), 1–19, at 2–6.
14. Cartledge, *Alexander the Great*, 215–27.
15. This thesis has been contested in recent years, without being decisively controverted: see Cartledge, 'Introduction', 6–10.
16. For a useful discussion of the contrasts in the two accounts, see P. A. Bird, 'Sexual differentiation and divine image in the Genesis Creation Texts', in Børresen (ed.), *Image of God*, 5–28.

17. I will be making some sweeping general claims in this summary history of Israel that readers may find unacceptably iconoclastic, though others will find it conservative. I set out the argument with greater detail and reference to the background literature in MacCulloch, *Christianity*, ch. 2.
18. H. Jagersma, tr. J. Bowden, *A History of Israel in the Old Testament Period* (London, 1982), 37–9.
19. See my comments on usage in 'Conventions Used in the Text', above. I deal at greater length with the Hebrew evolution of the divine names in MacCulloch, *Christianity*, 53–5. Still valuable is the pioneering A. Alt, 'The God of the Fathers', repr. in Alt, *Essays on Old Testament History and Religion* (Oxford, 1966), 3–65. On the later use of *Adonai*, see Barton, *The Word*, 153–7.
20. Hosea 13.8–9; Ps. 91.4.
21. Gen. 49.25–26, and see the discussion in F. Stavrakopoulou, *God: An anatomy* (London, 2021), 148–53, 267, 321–2.
22. A debate in recent years as to whether David had an historical existence or was a mere literary construct has been resolved in his favour. See my summary of the arguments, 'Nobody's perfect', *London Review of Books*, 27 Sept. 2018, 19–20, reviewing Y. Garfinkel, S. Ganor and M. G. Hasel, *In the Footsteps of King David: Revelations from an ancient biblical city* (London, 2018).
23. Barton, *History of the Bible*, ch. 2, demonstrates how the monarchical narratives relate to the other strands of narrative in the Hebrew Bible. For a crisply minimalist account of historicity in its historical books, see F. Stavrakopoulou, 'The historical framework: biblical and scholarly portrayals of the past', in J. Barton (ed.), *The Hebrew Bible: A critical companion* (Princeton, NJ and Oxford, 2016), 24–53.
24. Barton, *History of the Bible*, ch. 4.
25. Hosea 1.2–3, 9.1–9.
26. J. Davidson, 'I told you so!', *London Review of Books*, 2 Dec. 2004, 12–18 at 15, reviewing M. Wood, *The Road to Delphi: The life and afterlife of oracles* (London, 2004). For commentary on Ezek. 23, see P. Joyce, *Ezekiel: A commentary* (New York and London, 2007), 161–4.
27. Gaca, *Making of Fornication*, 133–4; F. Dal Bo, 'Sexualities and il/licit relationships in late ancient Jewish literatures', in N. Koltun-Fromm and G. Kessler (eds), *A Companion to Late Ancient Jews and Judaism: Third Century BCE–Seventh Century CE* (Hoboken, NJ, 2020), 307–32, at 310.
28. An accessible and realistic account of Cyrus is M. Waters, *King of the World: The life of Cyrus the Great* (Oxford, 2022).
29. A useful overview is K. Kenny, *Diaspora: A very short introduction* (Oxford, 2013); see especially ch. 1.
30. For unsuccessful efforts at restoration with the governor Zerubbabel as candidate, see Haggai 2.6–7, 21–24 and Zech. 6.9–15.
31. S. G. Rosenberg, 'The Jewish temple at Elephantine', *Near Eastern Archaeology* 67 (2004), 4–13, also discussing temples in Judah that could rival the Jerusalem Temple.

32. A. Doig, *Liturgy and Architecture from the Early Church to the Middle Ages* (Aldershot, 2008), 2, 11–12; Goodman, *Rome and Jerusalem*, 283–5. See also C. K. Barrett (ed.), *The New Testament Background: Selected documents* (rev. edn, London, 1987), 53–5.
33. For substantial analysis of the various likely origins, together with consideration of the subsequent use of each psalm in Christianity and Judaism, see S. Gillingham, *Psalms Through the Centuries: A reception history* (3 vols, Oxford, 2007–2022).
34. Stavrakopoulou, *God: An anatomy*, 149, 152.
35. The chronological priority of the *Instruction* is naturally upsetting to those who do not wish to acknowledge the borrowings of biblical text from other traditions. For a careful demonstration of its priority, see e.g. P. Overland, 'Structure in *The Wisdom of Amenemope* and Proverbs', in J. E. Coleson and V. H. Matthews (eds), '*Go to the Land I Will Show You': Studies in honor of Dwight W. Young* (Winona Lake, Ind., 1996), 275–91.
36. E. W. Heaton, *The Hebrew Kingdoms* (Oxford, 1968), 165.
37. Fiorenza, *In Memory of Her*, 132, 134. For a friendly critique, see E. A. Clark, 'The lady vanishes: dilemmas of a feminist historian after the "linguistic turn"', *CH* 67 (1998), 1–31, at 24–6, but see also supportive analysis in M. R. D'Angelo, '(Re)Presentations of women in the Gospel of Matthew and Luke–Acts', in Kraemer and D'Angelo (eds), *Women and Christian Origins*, 171–97, at 176–7.
38. Patriarchal and primeval covenants are outlined after Gen. 2.15–17 at Gen. 9.8–17 (with Noah), and Gen. 15.18 and Gen. 17 (with Abraham). For summary discussion of the development of Covenant theology, see H. Ringgren, tr. D. Green, *Israelite Religion* (London, 1966), 15–16, 115–20, 192–200, 302–6.
39. The complexities behind these statements are helpfully set out in Barton, *History of the Bible*, ch. 2, and see also ibid., 222.

3. HELLENISM MEETS JUDAISM

1. Barton, *History of the Bible*, ch. 9.
2. Gen. 3.8–19; Gen. 18.20–33; Exod. 33.23.
3. H. C. Porter, 'The nose of wax: Scripture and the Spirit from Erasmus to Milton', *TRHS* 5th ser. 14 (1964), 155–74, entertainingly analyses the problems for everyone involved in those Reformation debates. A different image for the same malleability of Scripture, 'a shipman's hose', is liable to be misunderstood today: it does not refer to a sailor's nether garments, but the flexible hosepipe then chiefly to be found on board ships.
4. Goodman, *Rome and Jerusalem*, 59–63, 311, 315.
5. Ibid., 164–5.

6. J. König, *Athletics and Literature in the Roman Empire* (Cambridge, 2005), esp. 25–6, chs. 2 and 5.
7. Healthy warnings against the unconsidered use of the term 'patriarchy' for such societies are provided in C. L. Meyers, 'Was ancient Israel a patriarchal society?', *Journal of Biblical Literature* 133 (2014), 8–27, and see discussion above, Ch. 1.
8. A useful placing of the condemnation in its Judaic cultural context is J. Huehnergard and H. Liebowitz, 'The biblical prohibition against tattooing', *Vetus Testamentum* 63 (2013), 59–77.
9. F. Stavrakopoulou, *God: An anatomy* (London, 2021), 128–36.
10. A. Hultgård, 'God and image of woman in early Jewish religion', in Børresen (ed.), *Image of God*, 29–49, especially 42–4.
11. F. Dal Bo, 'Sexualities and il/licit relationships in late ancient Jewish literatures', in N. Koltun-Fromm and G. Kessler (eds), *A Companion to Late Ancient Jews and Judaism: Third Century BCE–Seventh Century CE* (Hoboken, NJ, 2020), 310.
12. J. R. Branham, 'Bloody women and bloody spaces: menses and the Eucharist in late antiquity and the early Middle Ages', *Harvard Divinity Bulletin* 30 (2002), 15–22, at 16–17.
13. Bullough, *Sexual Variance in Society and History*, 106.
14. R. Beaton, *The Greeks: A global history* (London, 2021), 37; see comments in R. S. Bagnall, 'Women, law, and social realities in late antiquity: a review article', *Bulletin of the American Society of Papyrologists* 32 (1995), 77, Fiorenza, *In Memory of Her*, 88–9, and useful refinements in Karen J. Torjesen, 'In praise of noble women: gender and honor in ascetic texts', *Semeia* 57 (1992), 41–64.
15. H. King, *Hippocrates Now: The 'father of medicine' in the internet age* (London, 2019), 19–42.
16. For a fine analysis of the extraordinary persistence of the theory of humours in the Christian West down to the seventeenth century, see H. Hackett, *The Elizabethan Mind: Searching for the self in an age of uncertainty* (New Haven, Conn. and London, 2022), esp. 21–46.
17. Amid a vast literature on these subjects, the following are helpful ways in: Brown, *Body and Society*, 10–13; S. Kingsley Kent, *Gender: A world history* (Oxford, 2021), 14–16; Karras, *Sexuality in Medieval Europe*, 66–7. H. King, 'Women and doctors in Ancient Greece', and R. Flemming, 'Galen's generation of seeds', in N. Hopwood, R. Flemming and L. Kassell (eds), *Reproduction: Antiquity to the present day* (Cambridge, 2018), 39–52, 95–108, drill down further.
18. Among the *Birkot haShachar*, blessings recited at the beginning of the day: W. A. Meeks, 'The image of the androgyne: some uses of a symbol in earliest Christianity', *History of Religions* 13 (1974), 165–208, at 167–8.
19. Foucault, *History of Sexuality* 2, 44–52, 61–91.

20. P. Veyne, 'Homosexuality in ancient Rome', in Ariès and Béjin (eds), *Western Sexuality*, 26–35, at 30–31. Cf. revulsion against oral sex in writings of the respected analyst of dreams Artemidorus of Daldis in the 2nd century CE: Foucault, *History of Sexuality* 3, 23–4.
21. For comment on the persistence over time in the Mediterranean and Middle Eastern world, see D. M. Halperin, *How to Do the History of Homosexuality* (Chicago, 2002), 139–40, and for examples of it in particular periods and settings, see M. Rocke, *Forbidden Friendships: Homosexuality and male culture in Renaissance Florence* (New York and Oxford, 1996); G. Ruggiero, *The Boundaries of Eros: Sex crime and sexuality in Renaissance Venice* (New York and Oxford, 1985), ch. 6; N. Malcolm, 'Forbidden love in Istanbul: patterns of male–male sexual relations in the early-modern Mediterranean world', *PP* 257 (2022), 55–88.
22. Foucault, *History of Sexuality* 2, 58, 259 n. 16, quoting Aristotle, *History of Animals* VII.1.582A; Foucault does not seem to have grasped the full significance of Aristotle's casual justification of the sexual hierarchy.
23. The classic study is still K. J. Dover, *Greek Homosexuality* (London, 1978). It is constructively critiqued, along with entertaining swipes at Michel Foucault's use of it, in J. Davidson, 'Dover, Foucault and Greek homosexuality: penetration and the truth of sex', *PP* 170 (2001), 3–51; see also J. Davidson, *The Greeks and Greek Love: A radical reappraisal of homosexuality in ancient Greece* (London, 2007). For comments on the phenomenon in art and sculpture, see Beaton, *The Greeks*, 95–6, 125–6. On Roman same-sex activity, see Veyne, 'Homosexuality in ancient Rome', 26–30, and for a fine overall survey of Graeco-Roman literary sources, C. A. Williams, *Roman Homosexuality: Ideologies of masculinity in Classical antiquity* (New York and Oxford, 1999).
24. Halperin, *How to Do the History of Homosexuality*, 27–35, 72.
25. On the reality of the 'Theban Band', P. Cartledge, *Thebes: The forgotten city of Ancient Greece* (London, 2020), 190–92, 229. Foucault, *History of Sexuality* 2, 195, rounds up examples of Greek authors trying to account for the anomaly of the apparent equality in the Achilles/Patroklos relationship. On lesbianism in Graeco-Roman thought, Halperin, *How to Do the History of Homosexuality*, 50–51.
26. For examples of more clearly focused recent discussion, see J. Joosten, 'A new interpretation of Leviticus 18.22 (par. 20.13) and its ethical implications', *Journal of Theological Studies* 71 (2020), 1–10; J. Töyräänvuori, 'Homosexuality, the Holiness Code, and ritual pollution: a case of mistaken identity', *Journal for the Study of the Old Testament* 45 (2020), 236–67.
27. Dal Bo, 'Sexualities and il/licit relationships in late ancient Jewish literatures', 311. See also Gaca, *Making of Fornication*, 123–6. For the unusual nature of Judaic attitudes to same-sex activity, see G. J. Wenham, 'The Old Testament attitude to homosexuality', *Expository Times* 102/12 (1991), 359–63, esp. at 360: a scholarly microstudy all the more

impressive for its author's evident theological reservations about modern homosexuality.

28. R. K. Gnuse, 'Seven gay texts: biblical passages used to condemn homosexuality', *Biblical Theology Bulletin* 45 (2015), 68–87, at 72. Attempts by commentators to argue that the conduct of the men of Sodom did not include the intention of sexual assault seem feeble in the extreme.
29. Bullough, *Sexual Variance in Society and History*, 83–5, 181–2; Dal Bo, 'Sexualities and il/licit relationships in late ancient Jewish literatures', 312. On the Maccabees and gymnastics, see Goodman, *Rome and Jerusalem*, 293.
30. To quote Frederic Gardiner's embarrassment mixed with scholarly honesty in an influential Victorian Protestant reference work, C. J. Ellicott (ed.), *An Old Testament Commentary for English Readers by Various Writers* (5 vols, London, 1882–84), ii, 382: 'The LXX. translators here are quite unintelligible in their rendering, which represents David as weeping "until a (or the) great consummation."' The one surviving *Vetus Latina* reading of the text to follow the Septuagint is Léon, Biblioteca de la Real Colegiata de San Isidoro MS 91, Codex Gothicus Legionensis, cited in C. Vercellone, *Variae Lectiones Vulgatae Latinae Bibliorum editionis* (Rome, 1864), ii, 276, s.v. Liber I Regum Cap. XX.
31. I am much indebted to my colleagues John Barton, Alison Salvesen and David Parker for our enjoyable conversations around these intricacies. The most exhaustive and clear-sighted treatment of the question, B. L. Gerig, *Jonathan and David: A love story*, is alas not yet in print, but can be read at http://epistle.us/hbarticles/jondavealovestory.pdf as a complete text.
32. The case for the literary construction of the relationship is well made in J. Baden, *The Historical David: The real life of an invented hero* (New York, 2013), 70–76.
33. An engagingly combative response to the general consensus on the Song, arguing for the texts consciously originating in spirituality, but also expanding on their radical opposition to the misogyny and denunciations of the prophets, is E. Kingsmill, *The Song of Songs and the Eros of God: A study in biblical intertextuality* (Oxford, 2009). For a summary account of its reception in Christianity, see S. D. Moore, 'The Song of Songs in the history of sexuality', *CH* 69 (2000), 328–49.
34. D. Boyarin, 'Gender', in M. C. Taylor (ed.), *Critical Terms for Religious Studies* (Chicago, 1998), 117–35, at 118–21; Meeks, 'The image of the androgyne: some uses of a symbol in earliest Christianity', 165–208, at 176–7.
35. On the role of Philo and the new significance of *porneia*, see Gaca, *Making of Fornication*, ch. 7. Overall, her monograph is a sustained and effective refutation of the notion promoted by Michel Foucault that little changed in sexual principles between Classical society and Christian constructions of sex. At ibid., 239, she draws attention to Foucault's summary argument in interviews on the 'Genealogy of Ethics', appended to H. L. Dreyfus and

P. Rabinow (eds), *Michel Foucault: Beyond structuralism and hermeneutics* (2nd edn, Chicago, 1983), 226–51. A further perceptive critique of Foucault's blind spots is J. Zachhuber, 'Sexuality and the Christian self: Michel Foucault's reading of the Church Fathers', *Toronto Journal of Theology* 36/2 (2020), 170–82, which bluntly concludes that it is, 'in a strictly scholarly sense, outdated'.

36. The availability of polygyny is suggested for around 85% of historic world societies in J. Henrich, R. Boyd and P. J. Richerson, 'The puzzle of monogamous marriage', *Philosophical Transactions of the Royal Society B: Biological Sciences* 367 (2012), 657–69, at 657. That seems over-precise but is indicative.

37. R. S. Kraemer, 'Jewish women and women's Judaism(s) at the beginning of Christianity', in Kraemer and D'Angelo (eds), *Women and Christian Origins*, 50–79, at 53–60. For detailed studies of Babatha's papers and those of a contemporary close female neighbour, see A. E. Hanson, 'The widow Babatha and the poor orphan boy', in R. Katzoff and D. Schaps (eds), *Law in the Documents of the Judean Desert* (Leiden and Boston, Mass., 2005), 85–103, and K. Czajkowski, *Localized Law: The Babatha and Salome Komaise Archives*, Oxford Studies in Roman Society and Law (Oxford, 2017).

38. Van Houts, *Married Life in the Middle Ages*, 47; Karras, *Sexuality in Medieval Europe*, 62–3.

39. Veyne, 'Homosexuality in ancient Rome', 308–9; P. Coleman, ed. M. Langford, *Christian Attitudes to Marriage* (London, 2004), 23.

40. The standard study is T. Whitmarsh, *Narrative and Identity in the ancient Greek Novel: Returning romance* (Cambridge, 2011).

41. F. J. Beltrán Tapia and M. Szołtysek, '"Missing girls" in historical Europe: reopening the debate', *The History of the Family* 27 (2022), 619–57, and G. Hanlon, *Death Control in the West, 1500–1800: Sex ratios at baptism in Italy, France and England* (London and New York 2022). For general background on the situation in the ancient Mediterranean, E. Eyben, 'Family planning in Graeco-Roman antiquity', *Ancient Society* 11/12 (1980–81), 5–82, and for a sad case of a pregnant widow in Roman Alexandria in 8 BCE being given legal permission to expose her infant when it was born if she wished, Hanson, 'The widow Babatha and the poor orphan boy', 97.

42. J. Evans Grubbs, *Women and the Law in the Roman Empire: A sourcebook on marriage, divorce and widowhood* (London, 2002), 136–43.

43. K. Hopkins, 'Brother–sister marriage in Roman Egypt', *Comparative Studies in Society and History* 22 (1980), 303–54.

44. Evans Grubbs, *Women and the Law in the Roman Empire*, 141–3.

45. Hopkins, 'Brother–sister marriage in Roman Egypt', 353; Evans Grubbs, *Women and the Law in the Roman Empire*, 141–3. By contrast, early Syrian Christian authors including Tatian and Bardaisan were vociferous

in denouncing close-kin marriage in their own cultural region: S. Minov, *Memory and Identity in the Syriac Cave of Treasures: Rewriting the Bible in Sasanian Iran*, Jerusalem Studies in Religion and Culture 26 (Leiden, 2021), 165–6. When a Christian emperor attacked a close-kin marriage practice in 475, he elided Egyptian and Jewish customs in condemning a particular form of levirate marriage, a brother marrying the still-virgin wife of his dead brother, as a practice of the 'Egyptians': Evans Grubbs, *Women and the Law in the Roman Empire*, 165n.

46. J. F. Strange, 'Recent discoveries at Sepphoris and their relevance for biblical research', *Neotestamentica* 34 (2000), 125–41.

4. JESUS THE CHRIST

1. For examples of earlier Jeshuas, see M. Goldstein, *Jesus in the Jewish Tradition* (London, 1950), 73–7. In the second century CE, the son of Babatha (discussed in Ch. 2 above) was called Jeshua: K. Czajkowski, *Localized Law: The Babatha and Salome Komaise Archives*, Oxford Studies in Roman Society and Law (Oxford, 2017), 8.
2. John Barton points out to me an example of the scrupulous scholarship of the King James Bible, where Heb. 4.8 does call Joshua 'Jesus' (translating *Jesous* in the Greek text), and a marginal note explains that it refers to Joshua.
3. R. A. Burridge, *What are the Gospels? A Comparison with Graeco-Roman Biography* (Cambridge, 1992), 217.
4. This insouciant summary of a textual problem that has occupied some of the sharpest minds of Western scholarship without conclusive result should be enriched by embarking on the subject via Barton, *History of the Bible*, 188–211.
5. L. L. Patton, *Who Owns Religion? Scholars and Their Publics in the Late Twentieth Century* (Chicago, 2019), 194–5, 198–9, and F. Reilly, 'Jane Schaberg, Raymond E. Brown, and the problem of the illegitimacy of Jesus', *Journal of Feminist Studies in Religion* 21/1 (2005), 57–80, at 60: in reference to J. Schaberg, *The Illegitimacy of Jesus: A feminist theological interpretation of the Infancy Narratives* (rev. edn, 2006). I make more detailed comment in MacCulloch, *Christianity*, 77–82, and see G. Vermes, *The Nativity: History and legend* (London, 2006).
6. The genealogies are Matt. 1.1–17; Luke 3.23–38. A guide through early Christian genealogical thickets, though treating them less astringently than here, is R. Bauckham, *Jude and the Relatives of Jesus in the Early Church* (Edinburgh, 1990), 355–64. For medieval Western attempts to fill the genealogical gap with an ancestry for Jesus via Mary, see D. Skinner, 'The Marian anthem in late medieval England', in Swanson (ed.), *Church and Mary*, 168–80, at 173–5.
7. Micah 5.2; John 7.40–43.

8. Mark 6.3; cf. Matt. 13.55 and Luke 4.22; John 6.42. For careful discussion, see G. Lüdemann, tr. J. Bowden, *Virgin Birth? The Real Story of Mary and Her Son Jesus* (London, 1998), 49–60.
9. Vermes, *Nativity*, 147–9. R. E. Brown, *The Birth of the Messiah: A commentary on the Infancy Narratives of Matthew and Luke* (New York and London, 1977), 349–55, concurs that the Lukan canticles are likely to be earlier compositions, but offers some alternative settings in early Jewish Christianity; that possibility is still compatible with a Maccabean origin. It is clear that the Magnificat, whatever its real date and authorship, is modelled on the Song of Hannah, 1 Sam. 2.1–10; this contains similar themes of the overthrow of the powerful, but is actually more consistently focused on its theme of miraculous birth than is the Magnificat.
10. Schaberg, *The Illegitimacy of Jesus*, esp. 95–101, 117–19, 127–44.
11. Goldstein, *Jesus in the Jewish Tradition*, 32–9; on the Pantera gravestone, see A. Deissmann, *Light from the Ancient East: The New Testament illustrated by recently discovered texts of the Graeco-Roman world* (London, 1911), 68–9. Schaberg, *The Illegitimacy of Jesus*, 169–78, makes a good case for arguing that the development of Jewish polemic on Jesus's birth is an outcrop of reading the Infancy Narratives and cannot be dated before 200 CE at the earliest. For discussions of the main embodiment of that polemic, the *Toledot Yeshu*, see the essays in P. Schäfer, M. Meerson and Y. Deutsch (eds), *Toledot Yeshu ('The Life Story of Jesus') Revisited: A Princeton conference* (Tübingen, 2011).
12. There are Christian translations of the Hebrew Bible/Old Testament that without comment replace 'young woman' with 'virgin' in Isaiah 7.14, to square it with Matt. 1.23: they include the New International Version, the 21st Century King James Version, the American Standard Version and the Amplified Bible.
13. Schaberg, *The Illegitimacy of Jesus*, 68–73. Vermes, *Nativity*, 77, points out that the great Lukan scholar Joseph Fitzmyer opined that when Luke's account 'is read in and for itself – without the overtones of the Matthean annunciation to Joseph – every detail of it could be understood of a child born to Mary in the usual human way': J. A. Fitzmyer, 'The virginal conception of Jesus in the New Testament', *Theological Studies* 34 (1973), 541–75, at 567. Pressure from Roman Catholic colleagues led him to abandon this position. For a useful schematic diagram plausibly illustrating how the biblical material on Jesus's birth builds up, see Lüdemann, *Virgin Birth?*, 139.
14. Gen. 1.2; Ps. 33.6; Ps. 104.30.
15. Reilly, 'Jane Schaberg, Raymond E. Brown, and the problem of the illegitimacy of Jesus', 73n, comments on a remarkably unbuttoned article on this theme published by Brown around the time of Schaberg's publication: R. E. Brown, 'The genealogy of Jesus Christ', *Worship* 60 (1986). For 'Tamar', a charming poem on the subject by another distinguished biblical

scholar, Michael Goulder, beginning 'Exceedingly odd is the means by which God / Has provided our path to the heavenly shore . . .', see Goulder in *The Reader* 98/4 (Winter 2004), 20, or as originally printed in his Oxford Speaker's Lectures, M. D. Goulder, *Midrash and Lection in Matthew* (London, 1974), 232.

16. Brown, *Birth of the Messiah*, 530.
17. H. D. F. Sparks (ed.), *The Apocryphal Old Testament* (Oxford, 1984), 809–10.
18. R. Betancourt, *Byzantine Intersectionality: Sexuality, gender and race in the Middle Ages* (Princeton, NJ, 2020), 32–5. For arguments for the Christmas dating of Proklos's sermons, and his discussion of Mary's ear and of rival theories, see N. Constas, *Proclus of Constantinople and the Cult of the Virgin in Late Antiquity: Homilies 1–5, texts and translations* (Leiden and Boston, Mass., 2003), ch. 5.
19. I say more about this in MacCulloch, *Christianity*, 769–70; for the stories in the *Infancy Gospel of Thomas*, probably of second-century dates, see Gathercole (ed.), *Apocryphal Gospels*, 31–42.
20. Hunter, *Jovinianist Controversy*, 179–86. See also I. M. Resnick, 'Marriage in medieval culture: consent theory and the case of Joseph and Mary', *CH* 69 (2000), 350–71, at 354. For other early Christian views on what Mary's virginity signified (and what it did not), see J. Kelto Lillis, 'No hymen required: reconstructing Origen's view on Mary's virginity', *CH* 89 (2020), 249–267, and Kelto Lillis, 'Paradox *in partu*: verifying virginity in the *Protevangelium of James*', *Journal of Early Christian Studies* 24 (2016), 1–28. She there provides further discussion of Tertullian's remark (ibid., 22–4).
21. Gal. 1.19, and cf. his mention of 'the brothers of the Lord', 1 Cor. 9.5. M. Miller, 'Greek kinship terminology', *Journal of Hellenic Studies* 73 (1953), 46–52.
22. For more extended comment on the person and message of Jesus, see MacCulloch, *Christianity*, 82–96, and for a thoughtful overview, Dunn, *Unity and Diversity in the New Testament*, chs. 1–6.
23. Mark 10.29–30; cf. Matt. 19.29–30; Luke 18.29–30.
24. Mark 3.31–35; Matt. 12.46–50; Luke 8.19–21. Interestingly, the sisters are only present in some early MSS of Mark, and are excised in Matt. and Luke, who only have 'brothers'.
25. For an introduction to the content and thought of 'Q', Dunn, *Unity and Diversity in the New Testament*, 35–6, 70–74, 219–21, 283–8. For further careful exploration of this material, see A.-J. Levine, 'Women in the Q Communit(ies) and traditions', in Kraemer and D'Angelo (eds), *Women and Christian Origins*, 150–70, and for a fine overview of the whole subject, E. A. Clark, 'Antifamilial tendencies in ancient Christianity', *Journal of the History of Sexuality* 5 (1995), 356–80.
26. A Syro-Phoenician or Canaanite woman had her daughter healed by Jesus: Mark 7.24–30 and Matt. 15.21–28. Exchanges between Jesus and a

Samaritan woman and their aftermath: John 4.4–42. For concise and pertinent reflections on these, see M. R. D'Angelo, 'Talking back to Jesus', *Reflections: Journal of the Yale Divinity School* (Spring 2011), 35–7.

27. Luke 24.13–35, an elaborate expansion of Mark 16.12–13, which likewise does not gender the two post-Resurrection witnesses.

28. I am grateful to Glyn Redworth for guiding me to the original of this bon mot, often lazily cited by historians from secondary sources: 'con que Cristo avía tenido su Juan, y él tenía su Jorge' features in a report to the Habsburg Archduke Albert about the Privy Council meeting, by Gondomar, Spanish Ambassador to England, 12 Oct. 1617: Duke of Alva et al. (eds), *Correspondencia Oficial de Don Diego Sarmiento de Acuña conde de Gondomar*, being the first 4 volumes of *Documentos inéditos para la historia de España* (Madrid, 1936–1945), i, 101–2. For a no-nonsense view of King James's sexuality, with wider historiographical implications, see M. B. Young, 'James VI and I: time for a reconsideration?', *Journal of British Studies* 51 (2012), 540–67. For other examples of the Jesus–John motif, F. Dabhoiwala, *The Origins of Sex: A history of the first sexual revolution* (London, 2012), 129–30, and N. Malcolm, *Forbidden Desire in Early Modern Europe: Male–male sexual relations, 1400–1750* (Oxford, 2024), 190, 192.

29. M. R. D'Angelo, '(Re)Presentations of women in the Gospel of Matthew and Luke–Acts', in Kraemer and D'Angelo (eds), *Women and Christian Origins*, 171–97, at 189, points to the interesting variant on this Lucan saying in the apocryphal Gospel of Thomas, logion 79, which turns it towards an endorsement of celibacy for women; is Luke deliberately avoiding such a thought, or is Thomas introducing it?

30. J. Barr, ''Abbā isn't "Daddy"', *Journal of Theological Studies* 39 (1988), 28–47; his targets were chiefly assertions by the distinguished New Testament scholar Joachim Jeremias, e.g. J. Jeremias, *New Testament Theology* (London, 1971), 67. See also critical comment on *'abbā* in G. Vermes, *Jesus and the World of Judaism* (London, 1983), 41–3. I must record my repentance for following Jeremias's argument in MacCulloch, *Christianity*, 81–2, but his idea has precedents: for a mid-seventeenth-century discussion of 'Daddy' from the English radical mystic Walter Cradock, see S. Apetrei, *The Reformation of the Heart: Gender and radical theology in the English Revolution* (Oxford, 2024), 124–5.

31. The two versions of the Lord's Prayer are Matthew 6.9–14, Luke 11.2–4; for commentary, Jeremias, *New Testament Theology*, 193–203. The Greek *patēr* goes into Latin identically as *pater*, and hence the name for the Lord's Prayer still widely used in the formerly Latin West, derived from its two opening words 'Our Father' – the 'Paternoster'.

32. For discussion of contrasting iconographies of this scene in Western and Eastern Christianity, see below, Ch. 12, pp. 279–80.

33. Genesis 2.24 is quoted and discussed in Mark 10.2–12 and in modified form in Matthew 19.3–12; cf. Luke 16.18.

34. Matt. 22.2–12 (the parallel in Luke does not make this a wedding feast), 25.1–13; Luke 12.35–38.
35. On Qumran and polygyny, F. Dal Bo, 'Sexualities and il/licit relationships in late ancient Jewish literatures', in N. Koltun-Fromm and G. Kessler (eds), *A Companion to Late Ancient Jews and Judaism: Third Century BCE–Seventh Century CE* (Hoboken, NJ, 2020), 312.
36. W. R. G. Loader, *The Dead Sea Scrolls on Sexuality: Attitudes towards sexuality in sectarian and related literature at Qumran* (Grand Rapids, Mich., 2009), and W. R. G. Loader, *Sexuality and Gender: Collected essays* (Tübingen, 2021), 195–240, esp. on polygyny, 208–9, 228, 237–8. Loader is healthily resistant to seeing a single 'Qumran' attitude to sexual matters, rather than a developing conversation within the texts. For some of the debate, cf. M. Goodman, *A History of Judaism* (London, 2017), 146–58, with G. Vermes, *Scrolls, Scriptures and Early Christianity* (London and New York, 2005), esp. 18–30. On the lack of good evidence of direct links between the Scrolls and early Christianity, G. J. Brooke, *The Dead Sea Scrolls and the New Testament: Essays in mutual illumination* (London, 2005), esp. xviii, 8–10, 13, 19–26, 261–71. For samples from the Qumran literature, see C. K. Barrett (ed.), *The New Testament Background: Selected documents* (rev. edn, London, 1987), 218–51.
37. Cf. Matt. 19.9 with Mark 10.11–12 and Luke 16.18.
38. 1 Cor. 7.10–11, 15, and esp. see below, Ch. 5, pp. 89–92.
39. On the dead burying their dead, see Matt. 8.21–22, expanded in Luke 9. 59–60. On the imminent return of Jesus, Paul's rare citation of 'the word of the Lord' in 1 Thess. 4.15. His citation of the sounding 'trumpet' in the following v. 16, echoed in 1 Cor. 15.52, suggests that this element was part of the Lord's word.
40. K. Maas, 'Lex, Rex and sex: the bigamy of Philipp of Hesse and the Lutheran recourse to natural law', in E. Gebarowski-Shafer, A. Null and A. Ryrie (eds), *Contesting Orthodoxies in the History of Christianity: Essays in honour of Diarmaid MacCulloch* (Woodbridge, 2021), 56–76, at 61–2, has a useful collection of citations. For the enterprising effort of Methodios of Olympus to present polygyny as a past phase in God's plan for history, see below, Ch. 8, pp. 156–7.
41. Augustine, *Reply to Faustus* 22.47: translation from *Nicene and Post-Nicene Fathers*, ed. P. Schaff et al., series 1, iv (1887), 289. Augustine used the same argument in his almost contemporary and highly influential tracts on marriage and virginity: see below, Ch. 9.
42. We can lay aside a forged text, 'The Secret Gospel of Mark', probably created by the maverick biblical scholar Morton Smith in the 1950s, which included a text that could be construed as describing a sexual encounter between Jesus and a 'young man' who seems to be Mark. For the text and sensible summary debunking of it, see Gathercole (ed.), *Apocryphal Gospels*, 403–7.

43. C. K. Barrett, *The Gospel according to St John: An introduction with commentary and notes on the Greek text* (2nd edn, London, 1978), 592, amid helpful crisp commentary on this passage. For further informed speculation on the doodles: F. Stavrakopoulou, *God: An anatomy* (London, 2021), 304–5.

5. PAUL AND THE FIRST CHRISTIAN ASSEMBLIES

1. Scholarly consensus is that the genuine letters of Paul are Galatians, 1 and 2 Thessalonians, 1 and 2 Corinthians, Romans, Philippians and Philemon. There is some dispute about 2 Thessalonians, which contrasts with 1 Thessalonians in its assessment of the end-time.
2. Pseudonymous Paul or texts doubtfully attributed to him consist of letters conventionally addressed to the Colossians, the Ephesians (rather less certainly), 1 and 2 Timothy and Titus. For summary discussion of all this, see M. M. Mitchell, 'The emergence of the written record', and H. Gamble, 'Marcion and the "The Canon"', in M. M. Mitchell and F. M. Young (eds), *The Cambridge History of Christianity 1: Origins to Constantine* (Cambridge, 2006), 175–94, at 181–4; 195–213, at 208–9: in more detail, the various essays in J. D. G. Dunn (ed.), *The Cambridge Companion to St Paul* (Cambridge, 2003).
3. I discuss the impact and thought of Paul in MacCulloch, *Christianity*, 97–105, at greater length than is possible in these paragraphs.
4. For Jesus's baptism by John, see Matt. 3.13–17; Mark 1.9–11; Luke 3.21–22. For a variety of statements about Jesus's superiority to John, mostly placed in the mouth of John himself, see Matt. 3.11–14; Mark 1.7–8; Luke 3.16–17; John 1.6–8, 1.35–37, 3.25–30, 4.1–2.
5. A fine discussion of this is W. A. Meeks, 'The image of the androgyne: some uses of a symbol in earliest Christianity', *History of Religions* 13 (1974), 165–208, at 180–82.
6. See in particular Paul's discussion of himself in 2 Cor. 10.10; 11.21–30; 12. 5–10, and for useful comment, Kraemer, *Unreliable Witnesses*, 270.
7. L. Fatum, 'Image of God and glory of man: women in the Pauline congregations', in Børresen (ed.), *Image of God*, 50–133, at 51, 82 n.3.
8. One should point out the bizarre apparent exception to Paul's general rejection of circumcision in Acts 16.3, where he is said to have had his assistant Timothy (son of a Jewish mother and Greek father) circumcised in order to ease mission to Jews resident in southern Anatolia. The suspicion arises that the author of Acts or his source has made this up, perhaps by extrapolation from Paul's remarks about becoming a Jew to Jews and a Gentile to Gentiles, 1 Cor. 9.20–21. For useful discussion, including the scepticism of previous commentators about Acts 16.3, see Kraemer, *Unreliable Witnesses*, 198–9.
9. Fiorenza, *In Memory of Her*, 47.

10. U. E. Eisen, *Women Officeholders in Early Christianity: Epigraphical and literary studies* (Collegeville, Minn., 2000), esp. on Junias, 47–8, 54, 56. For a thorough treatment of these problems, see M. Y. MacDonald, 'Reading real women through the undisputed letters of Paul', and E. Castelli, 'Paul on women and gender', in Kraemer and D'Angelo (eds), *Women and Christian Origins*, 199–235. See also (including other examples of early tampering with biblical texts to downplay the role of women) Fiorenza, *In Memory of Her*, 52–3, 246–7.
11. Fatum, 'Image of God and glory of man: women in the Pauline congregations', 50–133, at 53, 58–9, emphasizes that modern feminist privileging of Gal. 3.28 over 1 Cor. 11.2–16 is no more accurate than previous patriarchal readings in the other direction.
12. On the nature of the Corinthian community, see W. A. Meeks, *The First Urban Christians: The social world of the Apostle Paul* (New Haven, Conn. and London, 1983), esp. 70–71, 117–21.
13. M. Black and H. H. Rowley (eds), *Peake's Commentary on the Bible* (London, 1962), 963.
14. 1 Cor. 7.2, 9; Clement quoted in Eusebius, *Church History, Life of Constantine the Great, and Oration in praise of Constantine* (*Nicene and Post-Nicene Fathers*, ed. P. Schaff et al., new ser. I, 1890), 162 [3.30], with commentary there. It is possible that Clement was indulging in eisegesis on 1 Cor. 9.5: 'Do we not have the right to be accompanied by a sister as wife, as the other apostles and the brothers of the Lord and Cephas [Peter]?'
15. P. Kalaitzidis, 'Civil marriage and civil union from an ecclesial perspective: the case of the Orthodox Church of Greece', in Arentzen et al. (eds), *Orthodox Tradition and Human Sexuality*, 105–43, at 117, 138 n. 49.
16. J. Meyendorff, 'Christian marriage in Byzantium: the canonical and liturgical tradition', *Dumbarton Oaks Papers* 44 (1990), 99–107, at 104.
17. For useful summary discussion on the marital debt and on ancient medicine, see Ariès and Béjin (eds), *Western Sexuality*, 117–19.
18. MacDonald, 'Reading real women through the undisputed letters of Paul', 212; J. P. Hallett, 'Women's lives in the ancient Mediterranean', in Kraemer and D'Angelo (eds), *Women and Christian Origins*, 13–34, at 18.
19. For summary discussion, see Kraemer, *Unreliable Witnesses*, 35–6. It will be apparent that neither of these Pauline passages gives any justification for the anachronistic speculation that the 'thorn' in Paul's flesh was a consciousness of his own homosexuality. That reflects modern binary sexual preoccupations that have no relevance to Paul's construction of same-sex relations as being a matter of activity rather than innate predisposition, except putatively by divine punishment for the deliberately idolatrous: hardly part of Paul's self-image.
20. J. T. McNeill and F. L. Battles (eds), *Calvin: Institutes of the Christian religion* (2 vols, Library of Christian Classics xx, xxi, 1960), ii, 1577: index of biblical references s.v. Rom. 1.

6. FROM JEWISH SECT TO CHRISTIAN CHURCHES

1. For a careful and undogmatic account of the evidence for Peter's death in Rome, see J. Toynbee and J. Ward-Perkins, *The Shrine of St Peter and the Vatican Excavations* (London, 1956), 127–8, 133, 155–61.
2. A recent treatment of the complexities is J. Carleton Paget, '"Jewish Christianity" in antiquity: meaningless category or heuristic irritant?', in E. Gebarowski-Shafer, A. Null and A. Ryrie (eds), *Contesting Orthodoxies in the History of Christianity: Essays in honour of Diarmaid MacCulloch* (Woodbridge, 2021), 7–24. For careful presentation of what we can learn of Jewish and Hellenistic Christianity from the New Testament, see Dunn, *Unity and Diversity in the New Testament*, 235–308.
3. M. Goodman, *A History of Judaism* (London, 2017), 289–300. It is interesting to note (ibid., 297, 299) that Hellenistic Judaism in the Mediterranean took a turn towards the use of Latin in the imperial period, just like much of Mediterranean Christianity.
4. C. Harline, *Sunday: A history of the First Day from Babylonia to the Superbowl* (New York, 2007), 4–6. For fine summaries on Jewish reconstruction after the destruction of the Temple, Goodman, *Rome and Jerusalem*, 463–511; and Goodman, *History of Judaism*, 229–88.
5. Pliny's puzzled correspondence with the Emperor Trajan may be enjoyed in Stevenson (ed.), rev. Frend, *New Eusebius*, 18–21.
6. K. Hopkins, 'Christian number and its implications', *Journal of Early Christian Studies* 6 (1998), 185–226, at 185, 202. To reinforce Hopkins's rigorous minimalism, see P. Heather, *Christendom: The triumph of a religion* (London, 2022), 20–25, and his pertinent criticism (590–91, n. 30) of the ill-conceived arguments in R. Stark, *The Rise of Christianity: A sociologist reconsiders history* (Princeton, NJ, 1996) (arguments to which Hopkins is generous).
7. For summary thoughts on sightings of gnosticism within Christianity in the period of the creation of the New Testament, see Dunn, *Unity and Diversity in the New Testament*, 275–88.
8. On Ignatios and 'Catholic', writing to the Christians of Smyrna, W. R. Schoedel, *Ignatius of Antioch: A commentary on the letters of Ignatius of Antioch* (Philadelphia, Pa., 1985), 238, 243–4. Dunn, *Unity and Diversity in the New Testament*, 341–68, is a useful introduction to the latest 'Catholic' layer in the New Testament texts.
9. Brown, *Body and Society*, xl; at xxxix, he describes second-century Christianity as 'an army of generals'.
10. The best social analysis is that of W. A. Meeks, *The First Urban Christians: The social world of the Apostle Paul* (New Haven, Conn. and London, 1983).
11. A pitiless but well-informed analysis of this phenomenon is B. D. Ehrman, *Forgery and Counterforgery: The use of literary deceit in early Christian polemics* (Oxford, 2012).

12. For an explicit rejection of the use of the marriage metaphor among seventeenth-century English mystical radicals, seeing it as inadequate to describe the intimacy of Christian union with Christ, see S. Apetrei, *The Reformation of the Heart: Gender and radical theology in the English Revolution* (Oxford, 2024), 115–18.
13. Eph. 5.21–6.9; Col. 3.18–4.1; 1 Pet. 2.13–3.7. 1 Peter is indebted in several respects to Ephesians. For summary discussion of the Pastorals and their content, see A. J. Hultgren in J. D. G. Dunn (ed.), *The Cambridge Companion to St Paul* (Cambridge, 2003), 141–55, and for more extended treatment of differences between 'authentic' Paul and the Pastorals, see D. R. MacDonald, *The Legend and the Apostle: The battle for Paul in story and canon* (Philadelphia, Pa., 1983).
14. Eph. 6.1–4; cf. Deut. 5.16, significantly deprived of its reference to the Promised Land.
15. 2 Tim. 3.14–15; for Lois and Eunice, see 2 Tim. 1.5.
16. Compare 1 Tim. 5.11–16 with 1 Cor. 7.39–40; see useful comment in M. Y. MacDonald, 'Rereading Paul: Early interpreters of Paul on women and gender', in Kraemer and D'Angelo (eds), *Women and Christian Origins*, 236–55, at 248.
17. C. Methuen, '"For pagans laugh to hear women teach": gender stereotypes in the *Didascalia Apostolorum*', in Swanson (ed.), *Gender and Christian Religion*, 23–35, at 31. The metaphor is an interesting reflection of the increasing assumption that Christians should worship in separate, purpose-built churches.
18. U. E. Eisen, *Women Officeholders in Early Christianity: Epigraphical and literary studies* (Collegeville, Minn., 2000), 143–5. Notably this inscription from Rome is in Greek, emphasizing the nature of the Christian community in Rome as still one remove from traditional Roman society.
19. Brown, *Body and Society*, 144–5.
20. J. A. Harrill, *Slaves in the New Testament: Literary, social and moral dimensions* (Minneapolis, Minn., 2006), 6–16, 177–8. A traditional story has Onesimus stealing money from Philemon, then running away from his master to meet Paul, for reasons unknown (cf. ibid., 6–7). This has no basis in the text and probably arose from a desire to make sense of the letter's peculiar content. The survival of that tradition unchallenged in much modern scholarship is remarkable.
21. Foucault, *History of Sexuality* 3, 172, notes the Stoic philosopher Musonius (1st century CE) as wishing to prohibit a household master's sexual activity with his servants, even if the slave is not married; that does imply a view in Roman society beyond the letter of the law that a married slave couple in a household could exist, and were entitled to a certain respect.
22. Brown, *Body and Society*, 58–9: see Ignatios, *Letter to Polycarp* 4.3.
23. Titus 2.5.
24. 1 Tim. 3.7.

25. Gathercole (ed.), *Apocryphal Gospels*, 301: the culminating thought of a post-Resurrection conversation from the fourth century entitled *The Questions of Bartholomew.* On the generally highly negative early Christian discussion of remarriage, as well as on divorce, see Harrington, *Women in a Celtic Church*, 156, and J. P. Arendzen, 'Ante-Nicene interpretations of the sayings on divorce', *Journal of Theological Studies* 20 (1919), 230–41.
26. For discussion of New Testament apocalyptic, putting Revelation in its biblical contexts, see Dunn, *Unity and Diversity in the New Testament*, 325–40.
27. Gathercole (ed.), *Apocryphal Gospels*, 56 [log. 42]; cf. Luke 10.25–37.
28. M. Franzmann, 'A complete history of early Christianity: taking the "heretics" seriously', *Journal of Religious History* 29 (2005), 117–28, at 120, quoting Epiphanios, *Panarion* 26.4–5.
29. Gathercole (ed.), *Apocryphal Gospels*, 176–7. Elsewhere (*Panarion* 49.1.2) Epiphanios also claims that the Montanist prophet he calls Quintilla or Priscilla announced that she was inseminated by Christ. One therefore suspects a certain personal excitement in his use of the theme, though if there is any truth in his report, it may be an early example of the sexualized language of mysticism: J. Lössl, 'A clash between *Paideia* and *Pneuma*? Ecstatic women prophets and theological education in the second-century Church', in C. Methuen, A. Ryrie and A. Spicer (eds), *Inspiration and Institution in Christian History*, Studies in Church History 57 (Cambridge, 2021), 32–53, at 48.
30. A moderate (though widely criticized) exposition of gnostic opposition to authority and sympathy to female potential is E. Pagels, *The Gnostic Gospels* (New York, 1979), especially 48–69.
31. Gathercole (ed.), *Apocryphal Gospels*, xxi, with a variety of examples of form and substance in gnosticism at 53, 60, 70, 170–80, 303, 301, 313–14. For useful comparisons between gnostic and other Christian texts on the theme of gender elision, see K. Vogt, '"Becoming male": a gnostic and early Christian metaphor', in Børresen (ed.), *Image of God*, 170–86.
32. A remark quoted from a letter of Robin Scroggs in W. A. Meeks, 'The image of the androgyne: some uses of a symbol in earliest Christianity', *History of Religions* 13 (1974), 165–208, at 203 n. 53.
33. Franzmann, 'A complete history of early Christianity', 124, quoting Tertullian, 'The Prescription against Heretics', cap. 41. For further examples of prominent gnostic women, mostly viewed through polemical Catholic Christian prisms, see A. McGuire, 'Women, gender, and gnosis in gnostic texts and traditions', in Kraemer and D'Angelo (eds), *Women and Christian Origins*, 257–99.
34. Gathercole (ed.), *Apocryphal Gospels*, 70 (logion 114, the final logion in the collection).
35. C. Tuckett, *The Gospel of Mary* (Oxford, 2007), 101 [*Gospel of Mary* 18. 11–15] and see esp. 52–4, 201–3; E. Pagels and K. L. King, *Reading Judas: The Gospel of Judas and the shaping of Christianity* (New York, 2007),

35–73. For varying scholarly opinions about the various Marys involved in this and other texts, see F. S. Jones (ed.), *Which Mary? The Marys of early Christian tradition* (Atlanta, Ga., 2002).

36. Gathercole (ed.), *Apocryphal Gospels*, 368 (*Coptic Gospel of Philip,* logion 32, and see logia 55–6); for 'The Gospel of Jesus' Wife', ibid., 408–9 (and cf. R. Harris, *Selling Hitler: The story of the Hitler Diaries*, London, 1986). For commentary, see M. R. D'Angelo, 'Reconstructing "real" women in Gospel literature: the case of Mary Magdalene', in Kraemer and D'Angelo (eds), *Women and Christian Origins*, 105–28, at 119–20.

37. Methuen, '"For pagans laugh to hear women teach"', 30.

38. J. Wijngaards, *Women Deacons in the Early Church: Historical texts and contemporary debates* (New York, 2002), 4–5, 68–75, 80–83.

39. For this argument, see F. Cardman, 'Women, ministry, and Church order in early Christianity', in Kraemer and D'Angelo (eds), *Women and Christian Origins*, 300–329, at 311–12. For an effective counter-argument, J. Shaw, 'Women, gender and ecclesiastical history', *JEH* 55 (2004), 102–17, at 104–5.

40. Stevenson (ed.), rev. Frend, *New Eusebius*, 11–12.

41. W. Tabbernee, *Fake Prophecy and Polluted Sacraments: Ecclesiastical and imperial reactions to Montanism* (Leiden and Boston, Mass., 2007).

42. G. Salmon in W. Smith and H. Wace (eds), *Dictionary of Christian Biography* (4 vols, London, 1877–87), iii, 941, s.v. Montanus.

43. R. Knox, *Enthusiasm: A chapter in the history of religion with special reference to the XVII and XVIII centuries* (Oxford, 1950), 20. Mgr Knox would probably not have been gratified by the anticipation of his remarks (with added anti-Romanism) by the great Latitudinarian Anglican Bishop Edward Stillingfleet in 1675: Apetrei, *The Reformation of the Heart*, 193–4.

44. T. V. Buttery, 'The *Spintriae* as an historical source', *Numismatic Chronicle* 7th ser. 13 (1973), 52–63, explores a series of bizarre and pornographic bronze tokens now termed *Spintriae*, and makes the interesting suggestion that Suetonius invented the Emperor Tiberius' notorious sexual antics on Capri in an effort to account for these puzzling objects; so they are a testimony to Antonine prudery rather than to first-century excess.

45. For the comic novelist Apuleius' hostile anecdote about an instance of Christians using erotic magic, see A. Wypustek, 'Un aspect ignoré des persécutions des chrétiens dans l'Antiquité: les accusations de magie érotique imputées aux chrétiens aux II et III siècles', *Jahrbuch für Antike und Christentum* 42 (1999), 50–71, at 58. Cf. J. A. Hanson (ed.), *Apuleius: Metamorphoses* (2 vols, Cambridge, Mass. and London, 1989), ii, 179–85 [IX.29–31].

7. VIRGINS, CELIBATES, ASCETICS

1. For entertaining accounts of Carmelite fabulations, see A. Jotischky, *The Carmelites and Antiquity: Mendicants and their pasts in the Middle Ages* (Oxford, 2002), esp. ch. 1, and R. Copsey, 'Simon Stock and the scapular vision', *JEH* 50 (1999), 652–83.
2. For a forceful statement of scepticism, following an informed change of mind on the genuineness of the account, see Kraemer, *Unreliable Witnesses*, ch. 3, which particularly engages with the opposite argument in J. E. Taylor, *Jewish Women Philosophers of First-Century Alexandria: Philo's 'Therapeutae' reconsidered* (Oxford, 2003). Kraemer also notes the influence of *On the Contemplative Life* on Georg Conrad Beissel, founder (1732) of the celibate Ephrata Cloister in Lancaster County, Pennsylvania: Kraemer, *Unreliable Witnesses*, 62. On that remarkable radical Protestant revival of celibate life, J. Bach, 'The Ephrata community in the Atlantic world', in P. Lockley (ed.), *Protestant Communalism in the Trans-Atlantic World, 1650–1850* (London, 2016), 39–66.
3. Luke, the putative author of Acts, was after all also the author of one of the Gospels' Infancy Narratives; of all four Evangelists, he is the one most interested in renouncing worldly goods.
4. J. M. Gundry-Wolf, 'Celibate pneumatics and social power: on the motivations for sexual asceticism in Corinth', *Union Seminary Quarterly Review* 48 (1994), 105–26, and summary discussion in Dunn, *Unity and Diversity in the New Testament*, 275–83.
5. For a sympathetic study of him, see E. J. Hunt, *Christianity in the Second Century: The case of Tatian* (London, 2003).
6. Hunter, *Jovinianist Controversy*, 102; Gaca, *Making of Fornication*, 101–2.
7. Luke 20.36 is discussed in S. Brock, 'Early Syrian asceticism', *Numen* 20 (1973), 1–19, at 6–7. Compare Luke 20.34–36 with parallels in Mark 12. 24–25 and Matt. 22.29–30.
8. Quoted in Brown, *Body and Society*, 67.
9. Justin Martyr, *First Apology* 29.2: J. Cleveland Coxe, J. Donaldson and A. Roberts (eds), *The Ante-Nicene Fathers: Translations of the writings of the fathers down to A.D. 325* (10 vols, rev. edn, Grand Rapids, Mich., 1985–87), i, 454.
10. Eusebius, *Church History, Life of Constantine the Great, and Oration in Praise of Constantine* 6.8: P. Schaff (ed.), *A Select Library of the Nicene and Post-Nicene Fathers of the Christian Church: Second series* (14 vols, rev. edn, Grand Rapids, Mich., 1988–91), i, 616–17.
11. Gaca, *Making of Fornication*, 65–6, 223–46; for the observation on Sappho, ibid., 237.
12. Hunter, *Jovinianist Controversy*, 227, quoting a fragment of Tatian's *On Perfection*.

13. Brown, *Body and Society*, 100–101, is one of the few summary discussions of this priority.
14. M. E. Doerfler, 'Translating Eve: death and female identity in a funerary hymn ascribed to Ephrem', *Journal of Theological Studies* 73 (2022), 167–94.
15. For up-to-date summary discussion of these 'super-crafts', J. Belich, *The World the Plague Made: The Black Death and the rise of Europe* (Princeton, NJ and Oxford, 2022), 15–19.
16. E. A. Judge, 'The earliest use of *monachos* for "monk" (P. Coll. Youtie 77) and the origins of monasticism', *Jahrbuch für Antike und Christentum* 20 (1977), 72–89, at 73–4. For a realistic introduction to Pachomian monasticism, J. E. Goehring, 'Withdrawing from the desert: Pachomius and the development of village monasticism in Upper Egypt', *Harvard Theological Review* 89 (1996), 267–85.
17. On Diogenes and masturbation, H. Cherniss (ed.), *Plutarch's Moralia* (17 vols, London and Cambridge, Mass., 1927–2004), xiii pt. II, 501 [*On Stoic Self-contradictions* 21].
18. See the accessible translation in Gathercole (ed.), *Apocryphal Gospels*, 3–21.
19. Brown, *Body and Society*, 273–4. Salome's vaginal investigation is likely to be misunderstood by modern readers familiar with the idea popularized in late Roman medicine that women possessed a hymen that needed breaking to end their virginity, but see J. Kelto Lillis, 'Paradox *in partu*: verifying virginity in the *Protevangelium of James*', *Journal of Early Christian Studies* 24 (2016), 1–28.
20. Hunter, *Jovinianist Controversy*, 177.
21. Ode 19, qu. ibid., 175.
22. Hunter, *Jovinianist Controversy*, 173 and n. 7.
23. The theme is found in the hugely popular, possibly ninth-century hymn *Ave Maris Stella* ('Hail Mary Star of the Sea'), v. 2: *Sumens illud 'Ave' / Gabrielis ore, / funda nos in pace, / mutans Evae nomen.*
24. On all this, see Kraemer, *Unreliable Witnesses*, ch. 4. See also Brown, *Body and Society*, 153–9. A further careful and illuminating discussion of Thecla is K. Cooper, *Band of Angels: The forgotten world of early Christian women* (London, 2013), 77–104.
25. The confrontation of the two works is effectively demonstrated in D. R. MacDonald, *The Legend and the Apostle: The battle for Paul in story and canon* (Philadelphia, Pa., 1983).
26. Kraemer, *Unreliable Witnesses*, 244 and n. 5, extends her general hermeneutic of suspicion to the authenticity of Perpetua's account, while acknowledging that scholarly opinion on this is divided. At ibid., 123–4, she emphasizes that modern suggestions that the *Acts of Paul and Thecla* were written by a woman or for women lack plausibility; among those concurring on this is A. Cameron, 'Virginity as metaphor', in A. Cameron (ed.), *History as Text: The writing of ancient history* (London, 1989), 184–205, at 193–4.

27. The best general account is B. Shaw, 'The passion of Perpetua', *PP* 138 (1993), 3–51. The exact chronology he suggests is not entirely secure, since it is dependent on a supposed Empire-wide persecution by the Emperor Septimius Severus that is probably a fourth-century fiction. A date for the text at the beginning of the third century is not in doubt.
28. Hunter, *Jovinianist Controversy*, 114–15, 121–2, 281; Harrington, *Women in a Celtic Church*, 40; E. Cameron, *Interpreting Christian History: The challenge of the Churches' past* (Malden, Mass. and Oxford, 2005), 65; Harvey, *Fires of Lust*, 14.
29. Chadwick's phrase was that the text 'merely consists of the scribblings of an intelligent but nasty-minded adolescent of somewhat pornographic tendencies' – J. E. L. Oulton and H. Chadwick (eds), *Alexandrian Christianity: Selected translations of Clement and Origen*, Library of Christian Classics, ii (London, 1954), 25.
30. An interesting reappraisal of Epiphanes forms ch. 10 of Gaca, *Making of Fornication*. See also R. M. Price, 'Celibacy and free love in early Christianity', *Theology and Sexuality* 12 (2006), 121–41.
31. Theophilus, *Ad Autolycum* 2.28, qu. in Hunter, *Jovinianist Controversy*, 100.
32. S. de Beauvoir, tr. C. Borde and S. Malovany-Chevallier, *The Second Sex* (London, 2011), 107, 191.
33. F. Forrester Church, 'Sex and salvation in Tertullian', *Harvard Theological Review* 68 (1975), 83–101, at 83–7. The phrases quoted in slightly altered form from ibid., 86 and 87, are respectively from Tertullian, *De Jeiunio* ['On Fasting'] 3.2 ('salutem gula vendidit') and *De Testimonio animae* ['On the witness of the soul'] 3.2 ('exinde totum genus de suo semine infectum suae etiam damnationis traducem fecit').
34. P. F. Beatrice with A. Kamesar (tr. and ed.), *The Transmission of Sin: Augustine and the pre-Augustinian sources* (Oxford, 2013), present an intellectual ancestry for 'traducianism' up to Augustine, deriving it from 'encratite' circles in second-century Egypt via early North African theologians, but not directly through Tertullian, as has been commonly asserted since Augustine's own time. The strong point of their argument (see especially ibid., ch. 13) is that, while Tertullian does make remarks such as that just quoted, he is also an opponent of infant baptism, which would seem to be a logical consequence of the doctrine, to cleanse infants of the taint of inherited sin. The thesis has remained controversial since Beatrice's first publication in Italian in 1978; in any case, there is no doubt of the North African matrix for Augustine's use of the idea.
35. Church, 'Sex and salvation in Tertullian', 95, quoting Tertullian, *Ad Uxorem* ii, 8.7–9.
36. Ibid., quoting Tertullian, *Adversus Marcionem* 1.29.5: 'si nuptiae non erunt, sanctitas nulla est.'

37. Hunter, *Jovinianist Controversy*, 118, quoting Tertullian, *De exhortatione castitatis* 9.4: 'Nec immerito, quia et ipsae ex eo constant quod est stuprum.'
38. Church, 'Sex and salvation in Tertullian', 97n.
39. Brown, *Body and Society*, 132.
40. Gaca, *Making of Fornication*, 268.
41. Gaca, ibid., emphasizes the pre-Christian Jewish tradition on these lines, especially via Philo, rather than Christianity having a direct inheritance from Greek philosophy. That is clearly true of Clement; not so much for others.
42. Gaca, *Making of Fornication*, 95, 251–4; the quotation at 251 is from Clement, *Stromateis* 3.24.1–2. Gaca points out (ibid., 115) that although the Stoic philosopher Seneca expounded the procreationist rule, he was completely out of line with most of his fellow Stoics in that respect; it sat far more logically with Pythagorean thought than with Stoicism, and it is unhelpful to see procreationism as primarily Stoic, as is sometimes asserted. On Clement, Philo and Pythagoras, see D. Runia, 'Why does Clement of Alexandria call Philo "The Pythagorean"?', *Vigiliae Christianae* 49 (1995), 1–22.
43. Bullough, *Sexual Variance in Society and History*, 185.
44. Hunter, *Jovinianist Controversy*, 125–6.
45. H. Chadwick (ed.), *The Sentences of Sextus: A contribution to the history of early Christian Ethics* (Cambridge, 1959), 38–9 (no. 231).
46. On Philo's version, see Gaca, *Making of Fornication*, 205. Runia, 'Why does Clement of Alexandria call Philo "The Pythagorean"?', 14, points to Henry Chadwick's conclusion that the editors of Sextus were operating in the same intellectual milieu as Clement of Alexandria.
47. Vincent of Beauvais (d.?1264), *Speculum Doctrinale* 10.45, cited in Boswell, *Christianity, Social Tolerance and Homosexuality*, 164: 'Adulter est in sua uxore ardentior amator. In aliena quippe uxore omnis amor turpis est, et in sua nimius. Sapiens iudicio debet amare coniugem, non affectu.' On Jerome and the works of Sextus, see Runia, 'Why does Clement of Alexandria call Philo "The Pythagorean"?', 14.
48. An excellent discussion is J. Branham, 'Bloody women and bloody spaces: menses and the eucharist in late antiquity and the early Middle Ages', *Harvard Divinity Bulletin* 30 (2002), 15–22, with useful supplementary observations in V. A. Karras, 'Female deacons in the Byzantine Church', *CH* 73 (2004), 272–316, at 295, 312. S. J. D. Cohen, 'Menstruants and the sacred in Judaism and Christianity', in S. B. Pomeroy (ed.), *Women's History and Ancient History* (Chapel Hill, NC, 1991), 273–99, provides useful comparisons with the different rhythm of change in Jewish practice.
49. On Bishop Dionysios, Cohen, 'Menstruants and the sacred in Judaism and Christianity', 288. Branham, 'Bloody women and bloody spaces', 20, rounds

up a few mentions between Gregory the Great in the late sixth century (see below, Ch. 11) and Jonas, Bishop of Orléans, in the ninth century. For the position in medieval Orthodox Russia, see Levin, *Sex and Society in the World of the Orthodox Slavs*, 169–70.

50. For arguments against the 'special appeal for women' thesis, see J. M. Lieu, 'What did women do for the early Church?', in P. D. Clarke and C. Methuen (eds), *The Church on its Past*, Studies in Church History 49 (Woodbridge, 2013), 261–81, and Kraemer, *Unreliable Witnesses*, 182–4.
51. G. Corrington Streete, 'Women as sources of redemption and knowledge in early Christian traditions', in Kraemer and D'Angelo (eds), *Women and Christian Origins*, 330–53, at 349.

8. SUDDENLY IN POWER

1. For the invention of this word by the extraordinarily creative scholarship of the Anglo-Saxons, see below, Ch. 11, p. 230.
2. A brilliant treatment of these themes of powerlessness transforming into power is A. Cameron, *Christianity and the Rhetoric of Empire: The development of Christian discourse* (Berkeley, Calif., 1991), esp. ch. 1.
3. The key texts relating to the Diocletian and Galerius persecution and Constantine's campaigns and policies are conveniently gathered in Stevenson (ed.), rev. Frend, *New Eusebius*, 271–318; the quotation is at 318. I provide context and summary discussion in MacCulloch, *Christianity*, 172–6, 189–200.
4. On Damasus's claim, H. Inglebert, *Les Romains chrétiens face à l'histoire de Rome: Histoire, christianisme et romanités en Occident dans l'Antiquité tardive (IIIe–Ve siècles)* (Paris, 1996), 197–9. The first known reference to the Bishop of Rome as 'Papa' is to Bishop Marcellinus (296–304): V. Fiocchi Nicolai, F. Bisconti and D. Mazzoleni, *The Christian Catacombs of Rome: History, decoration, inscriptions* (Regensburg, 1999), 165.
5. G. D. Dunn, 'The validity of marriage in cases of captivity: the letter of Innocent I to Probus', *Ephemerides Theologicae Lovanienses* 83 (2007), 107–19, esp. 114–15, and for the general background, Reynolds, *Marriage in the Western Church*, 145–7.
6. Brown, *Body and Society*, 207. On branding, D. Daube, 'The marriage of Justinian and Theodora: legal and theological reflections', *Catholic University Law Review* 16 (1967), 380–99, at 399 and n.
7. On the constitution of 326, C. Humfress, '"Cherchez la femme!" Heresy and law in late antiquity', in R. McKitterick, C. Methuen and A. Spicer (eds), *The Church and the Law*, Studies in Church History 56 (Cambridge, 2020), 36–59, at 46. A fine summary of the question is K.-L. Noethlichs, 'Éthique chrétienne dans la législation de Constantin le Grand?', in S. Crogriez-Pétrequin and P. Jaillette (with O. Huck), *Le Code Théodosien: Diversité des approches et nouvelles perspectives* (Rome, 2009), 225–37.

8. E. Eyben, 'Family planning in Graeco-Roman antiquity', *Ancient Society* 11/12 (1980–81), 5–82, at 29–31: Constantine had merely tried to restrict the practice.
9. Weitz, *Between Christ and Caliph*, 204.
10. R. Beaton, *The Greeks: A global history* (London, 2021), 263.
11. Boswell, *Christianity, Social Tolerance and Homosexuality*, 137–50, describes this strand of hostile comment, which mostly derives its denunciation from the *Epistle of Barnabas*, probably composed in the early second century, rehashing several misunderstandings in ancient natural philosophy about animal physiology.
12. L. Crompton, *Homosexuality and Civilization* (Cambridge, Mass., 2022), 133–5; for the lasting effect of the text, R. M. Frakes, 'Reading the *Collatio Legum Mosaicarum* (or *Lex Dei*) in the Middle Ages', *Studies in Late Antiquity* 6 (2022), 35–53.
13. Brown, *Body and Society*, 438.
14. Boswell, *Christianity, Social Tolerance and Homosexuality*, 131–2, 160–61, 347. On Peter Damian, see below, Ch. 12.
15. Ibid., 361–2, from Chrysostom's Commentary on Romans.
16. Bullough, *Sexual Variance in Society and History*, 333.
17. Their fate (which much excited Edward Gibbon in *Decline and Fall of the Roman Empire*) is detailed in E. Jeffreys, M. Jeffreys and R. Scott (tr. and eds), *The Chronicle of John Malalas* (Leiden and Boston, Mass., 1986), 253 [Bk. 18.18].
18. Bullough, *Sexual Variance in Society and History*, 333–5; see also P. Stephenson, *New Rome: The Empire in the East* (London, 2022), 200–201, and P. Sarris, *Justinian: Emperor, Soldier, Saint* (London, 2024), 121–2, 281, 365. For an excellent overview, see D. Stathakopoulos, 'Crime and punishment: the plague in the Byzantine Empire, 541–749', in L. K. Little (ed.), *Plague and the End of Antiquity: The pandemic of 541–750* (Cambridge, 2007), 99–118.
19. The Vestal Virgins were not necessarily virgins, did not have a lifelong vocation and were part of a very different set of religious assumptions: M. Beard, 'The sexual status of vestal virgins', *Journal of Roman Studies* 70 (1980), 12–27. For Ambrose of Milan's anticipation of this revisionism, see P. G. Walsh (ed.), *Augustine: De Bono Coniugali; De Sancta Virginitate* (Oxford, 2001), xii, 20 n. 41.
20. On the early community at Ligugé, see L.-J. Bord, *Histoire de l'abbaye Saint-Martin de Ligugé 361–2001* (Paris, 2005), ch. 2.
21. For summary discussion of stylitism and other heroic asceticisms, see MacCulloch, *Christianity*, 206–9.
22. Brown, *Body and Society*, liv, and previous discussion, li–liv; at ibid., 213n, he cautions that the text may not be directly by Athanasios. For Richard Reitzenstein's suggestion in 1914 that it may be modelled on a *Life of Pythagoras*, see E. A. Clark, 'The lady vanishes: dilemmas of a feminist historian

after the "linguistic turn"', *CH* 67 (1998), 1–31, at 21–2. None of that is relevant to its impact in antiquity. For the text, see T. Vivian and A. N. Athanassakis with R. A. Greer (eds), *The Life of Antony by Athanasios of Alexandria* (Kalamazoo, Mich., 2003).

23. On Martin's posthumous importance, see MacCulloch, *Christianity*, 312–15, 320, 323–5.
24. C. Stewart, *'Working the Earth of the Heart': The messalian controversy in history, texts and language to* AD *431* (Oxford, 1991), esp. 2–4, 12–24. Strategic official use of the term 'messalianism' persisted: for a Syriac context, see P. Wood, 'The chorepiscopoi and controversies over orthopraxy in sixth-century Mesopotamia', *JEH* 63 (2012), 446–57, esp. 454–6. For further remarks about the unavoidable structural tensions between asceticism and episcopal authority, see D. MacCulloch, *Silence: A Christian history* (London, 2013), 69–71.
25. That celebrated phrase is the title of a book by the distinguished Anglican spiritual writer A. M. Allchin: *The Silent Rebellion: Anglican religious communities, 1845–1900* (London, 1958).
26. C. T. Schroeder, *Children and Family in Late Antique Egyptian Monasticism* (Cambridge, 2021), 197–8; the curious name Patermutus ('the silent father') might nevertheless suggest an exemplary fiction, or at least a pseudonym. The troubling story of Abraham and Isaac is Gen. 22.1–19.
27. J. Herrin, *The Formation of Christendom* (with new intro., Princeton, NJ, 2022), 50.
28. For summary discussion, see A. Cameron, 'Virginity as metaphor', in A. Cameron (ed.), *History as Text: The writing of ancient history* (London, 1989), 184–205.
29. K. Cooper, *The Virgin and the Bride: Idealized womanhood in late antiquity* (Cambridge, Mass., 1996), 68–74 and ch. 5; see also the fine narrative in A. Cain, *The Letters of Jerome: Asceticism, biblical exegesis, and the construction of Christian authority in late antiquity* (Oxford, 2009), ch. 4.
30. D. Brakke, 'Ethiopian demons: male sexuality, the black-skinned other, and the monastic self', *Journal of the History of Sexuality* 10 (2001), 501–35.
31. J. F. Keenan, *A History of Catholic Theological Ethics* (New York, 2022), 61, 103–5, though Keenan does note a possible but not certain earlier exception in the writings of Clement of Alexandria. On the problem of temptation aroused by young monks, see Brown, *Body and Society*, 230, 246–8; D. Krueger, 'Between monks: tales of monastic companionship in early Byzantium', *Journal of the History of Sexuality* 20 (2011), 28–61.
32. Brakke, 'Ethiopian demons', 524–6. The story of Pachon forms part of the widely read 5th-century *Lausiac History* of Palladius of Galatia, written for a courtier of the Emperor Theodosius.
33. For excellent background commentary on these themes, Brown, *Body and Society*, 217–40. A. Tilby, *The Seven Deadly Sins: Their origin in the spiritual*

teaching of Evagrius the Hermit (London, 2009), 63, observes that Evagrius makes gluttony the primary evil thought; one can understand how that would be a prime concern in the eremitical life.

34. C. Rapp, *Brother-making in Late Antiquity and Byzantium: Monks, laymen and Christian ritual* (Oxford, 2016), 48, 55, 66, 77.
35. For representative comment from Boswell on these lines, see J. Boswell, *The Marriage of Likeness: Same-sex unions in pre-modern Europe* (London, 1996), 186–7. I myself chaired and subsequently edited for publication the lecture that Boswell gave in London in 1982 first revealing his findings to a fascinated audience of the then Gay Christian Movement: published as *Rediscovering Gay History: Archetypes of gay love in Christian history*, Michael Harding Memorial Lecture, 1982.
36. The crux of her critique may be followed in Rapp, *Brother-making in Late Antiquity and Byzantium*, 72–6: note in particular Boswell's efforts to find a parallel to the imposition of crowns on a couple in marriage, which were not a success.
37. Rapp, *Brother-making in Late Antiquity and Byzantium*, 70–71.
38. Ibid., 91, 94–5.
39. Ibid., 50–53, 76, 123, 256–61.
40. For an exhaustive discussion of the original character and later understanding of the 'angels' or 'Sons of God' in Gen. 6.1–5, see C. Westermann, tr. J. J. Scullion, *Genesis 1–11: A commentary* (London, 1984), 371–83, from the German original of 1974.
41. T. Martin, 'The development of winged angels in early Christian art', *Espacio, Tiempo y Forma VII: Historia del Arte* 14 (2001), 11–29.
42. Brown, *Body and Society*, 329–34.
43. Ibid., 87.
44. G. Sfameni Gasparro, 'Image of God and sexual differentiation in the tradition of *Enkrateia*', in Børresen (ed.), *Image of God*, 134–69, at 146–7: chief critic was Jerome's former close friend turned bitter opponent, Rufinus of Aquileia. On the sequence of thought on this subject from Philo through to the fourth century, see D. Casey, 'The spiritual valency of gender in Byzantine society', in B. Neil and L. Garland (eds), *Questions of Gender in Byzantine Society* (Farnham, 2013), 167–81, at 170–71.
45. On Gregory and procreation before the Fall, H. Boersma, *Embodiment and Virtue in Gregory of Nyssa: An anagogical approach* (Oxford, 2013), 103. See also ibid., 15–20, 46–9, 71, 105–16, 126, 135, 143–4, 215, 245, 248.
46. A compelling reinterpretation of the theology of Maximos is E. Brown Dewhurst, 'Beyond the borders of society: sex and gender as tropos in Maximus the Confessor's theology and its relevance to contemporary ethics', *Theology and Sexuality* 28 (2022), 25–51.
47. S. Tougher, *The Eunuch in Byzantine History and Society* (London and New York, 2008), 68–9.

48. M. E. Stewart, *Masculinity, Identity and Power Politics in the Age of Justinian: A study of Procopius* (Amsterdam, 2020), 132–3.
49. K. Ringrose, *The Perfect Servant: Eunuchs and the social construction of gender in Byzantium* (Chicago, 2003), 9–12, 16, 26, 29, 126–8; S. Tougher, 'Bearding Byzantium: masculinity, eunuchs and the Byzantine life course', in Neil and Garland (eds), *Questions of Gender in Byzantine Society*, 153–66.
50. Tougher, *The Eunuch in Byzantine History and Society*, ch. 6.
51. J. Herrin, *Ravenna: Capital of Empire, crucible of Europe* (London, 2020), 166–7.
52. Foucault, *History of Sexuality* 4, 163. Foucault notes, ibid., 158, that this work (his *On the Integrity of Virginity*) used to be attributed to Basil's contemporary namesake and Gregory of Nyssa's brother, Basil of Caesarea 'the Great'; this was perhaps to avoid the complication of Basil of Ancyra's hesitant embrace of Nicene orthodoxy.
53. M. Feldman, *The Castrato: Reflections on natures and kinds* (Oakland, Calif., 2015), 3, 9, 29–30, 287 n.97. See below, Ch. 14.
54. B. Ward, *The Desert of the Heart: Daily readings with the Desert Fathers* (London, 1988), 46 (my italics).
55. J. Anson, 'The female transvestite in early monasticism: the origin and development of a motif', *Viator* 5 (1974), 1–32; D. Brakke, 'The lady appears: materializations of "woman" in early monastic literature', *Journal of Medieval and Early Modèrn Studies* 33 (2003), 387–402.
56. L. L. Coon, *Sacred Fictions: Holy women and hagiography in late antiquity* (Philadelphia, Pa., 1997), 84–94. For a startling outbreak of interest in Mary of Egypt in mid-17th-century English radical mystical circles, where wild naked female prophets were considered a good idea, see S. Apetrei, *The Reformation of the Heart: Gender and radical theology in the English Revolution* (Oxford, 2024), 95–6.
57. Mark 14.3–9; Matt. 26.6–13; Luke 7.36–50; John 12.1–8, where the woman becomes yet another Mary, the sister of Martha and Lazarus. For Elisabeth Schüssler Fiorenza's use of this passage, see above, Ch. 1, pp. 12–13.
58. W. Harmless, *Desert Christians: An introduction to the literature of early monasticism* (Oxford, 2004), 24, 443, and cf. 420–21.
59. E. Castelli, 'Virginity and its meaning for women's sexuality in early Christianity', *Journal of Feminist Studies in Religion* 2 (1986), 61–88, at 74–5, alongside other contemporary examples.
60. Amma Sarah, *Sayings*, Sarah 4, 230; cited in Brown Dewhurst, 'Beyond the borders of society', 34.
61. Brown, *Body and Society*, 262n.
62. On Tertullian and Cyprian, see Harrington, *Women in a Celtic Church*, 137. For a good account of Methodios's argument, see Foucault, *History of Sexuality* 4, 122–34; see also E. A. Clark, 'Antifamilial tendencies in ancient Christianity', *Journal of the History of Sexuality* 5 (1995), 356–80, at 364.

63. A. Roberts et al. (ed.), *Ante-Nicene Christian Library: Translations of the writings of the Fathers down to A.D. 325* (24 vols, 1867–85), xiv, 74–5 [Discourse VIII.8].
64. Harrington, *Women in a Celtic Church*, 137, citing Jerome, *Epistola* 22, ch. 25 (*Patrologia Latina* 22, 411). On Jerome to Eustochium (*Epistula* 22), N. Henry, 'The Song of Songs and the liturgy of the *velatio* in the 4th century: from literary metaphor to liturgical reality', in R. N. Swanson (ed.), *Continuity and Change in Christian Worship*, Studies in Church History 35 (Woodbridge, 1999), 18–28, at 18.
65. D. Hunter, 'The Virgin, the Bride, and the Church: reading Psalm 45 in Ambrose, Jerome and Augustine', *CH* 69 (2000), 281–303, at 285, and Hunter, *Jovinianist Controversy*, 70–71.
66. For summary remarks on Ambrose and his political acumen, see MacCulloch, *Christianity*, 299–301.
67. Hunter, *Jovinianist Controversy*, 197–202, and see below, Ch. 9. On Ambrose's new theology of the hymen, see J. Kelto Lillis, 'No hymen required: reconstructing Origen's view on Mary's virginity', *CH* 89 (2020), 249–67, at 260–63, and background discussion in H. King, *Immaculate Forms: Uncovering the history of women's bodies* (London, 2024), ch. 3.
68. Brown, *Body and Society*, 351–6, 363.
69. Henry, 'The Song of Songs and the liturgy of the *velatio* in the 4th century', stresses the liturgical role of the Song in her introduction to the earliest surviving text. Hunter, *Jovinianist Controversy*, 229, observes that the ceremony was a useful way of strengthening episcopal authority: Ambrose needed such support in the turbulent ecclesiastical politics of his city. See also Brown, *Body and Society*, 356–7.
70. Brown, *Body and Society*, 263–4.
71. K. Cooper, *Band of Angels: The forgotten world of early Christian women* (London, 2013), 225–53, is a succinct discussion of the two extremes in female asceticism.
72. Cain, *The Letters of Jerome*, chs. 1 and 2. For a balanced judgement on a brilliant but unlikeable man, summing up a clear-eyed biography, see J. N. D. Kelly, *Jerome: His life, writings and controversies* (London, 1975), 333–6.
73. On Jerome and scholarship, see MacCulloch, *Christianity*, 294–6, and M. H. Williams, *The Monk and the Book: Jerome and the making of Christian scholarship* (London, 2006), 1–5, 131, 167–9, 200.
74. MacCulloch, *Christianity*, 193–5: note especially the travel diary of the Spanish nun Egeria, from the 380s.
75. A comprehensive survey is S. J. Davis, *The Cult of St Thecla: A tradition of women's piety in late antiquity* (Oxford, 2001). See also the study of the main 5th-century rewrite of her career, S. Fitzgerald Johnson, *The Life and Miracles of Thekla: A literary study* (Cambridge, Mass. and London, 2006).

76. S. Matitashvili, 'Female asceticism in late antique Georgian literature: the origins of the *Vita of St Nino*', *Vigiliae Christianae* 75 (2021), 253–77.
77. For the course of the dispute Stevenson (ed.), rev. Frend, *Creeds, Councils and Controversies*, 332–68; the quotation is from ibid., 353.
78. Documents detailing the messy events at Ephesus in 431 are set out in Stevenson (ed.), rev. Frend, *Creeds, Councils and Controversies*, 300–313.
79. J. Herrin, *Unrivalled Influence: Women and Empire in Byzantium* (Princeton, NJ, 2013), 52–4.
80. L. M. Peltomaa, *The Image of the Virgin Mary in the Akathistos Hymn* (Leiden and Boston, Mass., 2001), esp. ch. 6. It is called *akathistos*, 'unseated', as it is given the honour of being the one part of the liturgy for which all must stand.
81. N. Constas, *Proclus of Constantinople and the Cult of the Virgin in Late Antiquity: Homilies 1–5, Texts and Translations* (Leiden and Boston, Mass., 2003), esp. ch. 4.
82. A careful account of all this is A. Cameron, 'The cult of the Virgin in late antiquity: religious development and myth-making', in Swanson (ed.), *Church and Mary*, 1–21. It is only fair to point out the different emphasis in S. J. Shoemaker, *Mary in Early Christian Faith and Devotion* (New Haven, Conn., 2016), which points to material from before the Nestorian controversy which Shoemaker sees as evidence of popular devotion. This does involve dating certain key texts as early as possible, and he does admit (ibid., 96) that, after the *Protevangelium* and some possible gnostic interest, the tally of 3rd-century references is 'disappointingly meagre'. For some detailed criticisms of Shoemaker, see R. Price in *Journal of Theological Studies* 68 (2017), 363–5.
83. J. Baun, 'Discussing Mary's humanity in medieval Byzantium', in Swanson (ed.), *Church and Mary*, 63–72, at 65; Cameron, 'The cult of the Virgin in late antiquity', 6–7, and Kraemer, *Unreliable Witnesses*, 247, are both sceptical that there is any factual content in Epiphanios's claims about these so-called 'Collyridians'.
84. For summary discussion of Sergius and Bacchus, see MacCulloch, *Christianity*, 237–8, 270–71. Predictably, though not inappropriately, John Boswell took a great interest in Sergius and Bacchus: see Boswell, *The Marriage of Likeness*, 146–8, 151–4, and index refs., s.v. Serge and Bacchus. He prints a translation of the entire text of their martyr-narrative, perhaps 5th century (see ibid., 147n), at ibid., 375–90; for the women's clothing, and their defiant reaction, ibid., 379.

9. MARRIAGE: SURVIVAL AND VARIETY

1. Hunter, *Jovinianist Controversy*, 1–9.
2. Ibid., 25–30, 43–50.

3. Ibid., chs. 5, 6. For the Reformation revisiting of this controversy, see below, Ch. 14.
4. J. Barr, 'The Vulgate Genesis and Jerome's attitude to women', *Studia Patristica: Proceedings of the 1979 International Patristic Congress in Oxford* 18/2 (1982), 268–73.
5. M. Turner, *The Wife of Bath: A biography* (Princeton, NJ, 2022), 15, 18, 49, 80–82, 106.
6. 'Qui enim semel venit ad nuptias, semel docuit esse nubendum': *Patrologia Latina* 23, col. 282 [*Adversus Jovinianum* 1.40].
7. E. A. Clark, 'Antifamilial tendencies in ancient Christianity', *Journal of the History of Sexuality* 5 (1995), 356–80, at 177.
8. I have repunctuated the text in J. Barr, 'The influence of St Jerome on medieval attitudes to women', in J. Soskice (ed.), *After Eve* (London, 1990), 89–102, at 97, translating 'Quid angustiarum habeant nuptiae, didicisti in ipsis nuptiis . . . Egessisti acescentes et morbidos cibos: relevasti aestuantem stomachum. Quid vis rursum ingerere, quod tibi noxium fuit? *Canis revertens ad vomitum* . . . An vereris, ne proles Furiana deficiat, et ex te parens tuus non habeat pusionem, qui reptet in pectore, et cervicem ejus stercore liniat?': *Patrologia Latina* 22, col. 0551 [Jerome, *Epistula* 54 'Ad Furiam de viduitate servanda']. C. Connolly, *Enemies of Promise* (2nd edn, London, 1948), 116: 'There is no more sombre enemy of good art than the pram in the hall.'
9. Reynolds, *Marriage in the Western Church*, 342–3. See also M. Resnick, 'Marriage in medieval culture: consent theory and the case of Joseph and Mary', *CH* 69 (2000), 350–71, esp. on Jerome, 354.
10. For incisive comment on the problems surrounding Joseph's role even in the Gospel texts, see D. C. Allison, 'Divorce, celibacy and Joseph (Matthew 1. 18–25 and 19.1–12', *Journal for the Study of the New Testament* 49 (1993), 3–10, and P. Shepherd, 'The canonical and non-canonical nativity/infancy narratives: some theological issues', https://modernchurch.org.uk/nativity (accessed 23 Aug. 2022).
11. See the Introduction to the edition by P. G. Walsh (ed.), *Augustine: De Bono Coniugali; De Sancta Virginitate* (Oxford, 2001); my account owes a great deal to his analysis of these texts.
12. A. G. Soble, 'Correcting some misconceptions about St Augustine's sex life', *Journal of the History of Sexuality* 11 (2002), 545–69, effectively cuts down to size absurd promotions of a 'gay' Augustine, while still busily trying to deny the possibility of any physical same-sex relationship.
13. Hunter, *Jovinianist Controversy*, 269–84, usefully explores how Jerome is as much if not more in Augustine's sights than Jovinian.
14. H. Bettenson and D. Knowles (eds), *Augustine: Concerning the City of God against the Pagans* (London, 1967), 579 [XIV.17].
15. I have in the past expressed that view, and it is vigorously expressed in the work of that major modern Catholic commentator on theological ethics John Mahoney SJ: J. Mahoney, *The Making of Moral Theology: A study of*

the Roman Catholic tradition (Oxford, 1987), ch. 2. The reader may perceive in my present account a slightly more sympathetic perspective on Augustine.

16. M. I. Bogan (ed.), *St. Augustine: The Retractations*, The Fathers of the Church 60 (Washington, DC, 1968), 247 [*Retractationes* 83].
17. Reynolds, *Marriage in the Western Church*, 55 [Preamble to Justinian's Novel 22].
18. M. Perisanidi, 'Was there a marital debt in Byzantium?', *JEH* 68 (2017), 510–28, at 514–16. Dr Perisanidi's article seems to draw a conclusion precisely opposite to what her data warrant: a misrepresentation of both East and West on sex.
19. J. Meyendorff, 'Christian marriage in Byzantium: the canonical and liturgical tradition', *Dumbarton Oaks Papers* 44 (1990), 99–107, at 102–3, 106; Levin, *Sex and Society in the World of the Orthodox Slavs*, 108–11, 181. For discussion of Western theologies of annulment and prohibited degrees, see below, Ch. 12.
20. Mahoney, *Making of Moral Theology*, 9–10.
21. Bettenson and Knowles (eds), *Augustine: Concerning the City of God*, 304–15 [VIII.5–15]; quotation at 313 [VIII.10].
22. The quotation is from R. S. Pine-Coffin (ed.), *Saint Augustine: Confessions* (London, 1961), 233 [X, 29]. H. Chadwick, *Augustine of Hippo: A life* (Oxford, 2009), 145–62, provides a fine summary of the Pelagian controversy.
23. For a note on the origins of 'traducianism', see above, Ch. 7, n. 34.
24. A helpful guide is T. H. Irwin, 'Splendid vices: Augustine for and against pagan virtues', *Medieval Philosophy and Theology* 8 (1999), 105–27. Irwin points out, ibid., 106, that Augustine himself never used the famous phrase 'splendid vices' to describe pagan 'virtues'.
25. See in particular J. Lössl, 'Julian of Aeclanum on pain', *Journal of Early Christian Studies* 10 (2002), 203–43, on which I base much of the following account.
26. G. Bonner, *Saint Augustine of Hippo: Life and controversies* (2nd edn, Norwich, 1963), 378, points to a catalogue of such phrases in O. Rottmanner, *Der Augustinismus. Eine dogmengeschichtliche Studie* (Munich, 1892), 8. For a sample of Augustine's argument, see Stevenson (ed.), rev. Frend, *Creeds, Councils and Controversies*, 238–9.
27. Recently there has been a movement among both patristic and Reformation scholars, some with admirably ecumenical motives, to assert the importance of *theōsis* ('deification') in Latin Western theology, alongside its characteristic use in the East. Its place in the theology of Augustine is explored in D. Meconi, *The One Christ: St Augustine's theology of deification* (Washington, DC, 2013). No one is saying that Westerners have not been capable of deploying the idea, but it cannot be seen as a general organizing principle of Western theology as it is among the Orthodox. For

succinct remarks on this, see A. Louth in *JEH* 71 (2020), 835–7, reviewing J. Ortiz (ed.), *Deification in the Latin Patristic Tradition* (Washington, DC, 2019).

28. Hunter, *Jovinianist Controversy*, 268, instances such arguments in two tracts, *De Castitate* (which may be the work of the interesting Pelagian known as the 'Sicilian Anonymous'), and the *Opus imperfectum in Matthaeum*. For a 4th-century link back to similar 2nd- and 3rd-century negativity on marriage, see discussion of the Egyptian biblical commentator Hierakas in Brown, *Body and Society*, 244–5.
29. Perisanidi, 'Was there a marital debt in Byzantium?', 521–2; Brown, *Body and Society*, 253–4.
30. A good introduction to the early history of syneisactism is D. Elliott, *Spiritual Marriage: Sexual abstinence in medieval wedlock* (Princeton, NJ, 1983), chs. 1–2.
31. E. A. Clark, 'John Chrysostom and the *subintroductae*', *CH* 46 (1977), 171–85, at 172–3; cf. useful summary discussion in Harrington, *Women in a Celtic Church*, 255–7.
32. Jerome, *Epistola* 22, ch. 14 (*Patrologia Latina* 22, 403). For other choice snippets from this letter, see above, Ch. 8, n. 64.
33. Clark, 'John Chrysostom and the *subintroductae*', 180–82.
34. K. Cooper, *Band of Angels: The forgotten world of early Christian women* (London, 2013), 247.
35. Melania has recently been well-served by two studies: E. A. Clark, *Melania the Younger: From Rome to Jerusalem* (Oxford, 2021) and C. M. Chin and C. T. Schroeder (eds), *Melania: Early Christianity through the life of one family* (Oakland, Calif., 2021).
36. The texts are presented in A. P. Alwis, *Celibate Marriages in Late Antique and Byzantine Hagiography: The Lives of Saints Julian and Basilissa, Andronikos and Athanasia, and Galaktion and Episteme* (London, 2011), 157–308. For other examples from the Latin West, see Elliott, *Spiritual Marriage*, 63–73.
37. Elliott, *Spiritual Marriage*, 61–2.
38. M. Clayton and J. Mullins (ed. and tr.), *Old English Lives of Saints: Aelfric* (3 vols, Cambridge, Mass., 2019), i, xix and 123–5; iii, 207–61.
39. J. F. Keenan, *A History of Catholic Theological Ethics* (New York, 2022), 60; and for the Pastoral Epistles, see above, Ch. 6.
40. C. A. Frazee, 'The origins of clerical celibacy in the Western Church', *CH* 57 (1988), 108–26, at 114. The Canons of Nicaea are presented in Stevenson (ed.), rev. Frend, *New Eusebius*, 338–44.
41. Brown, *Body and Society*, 256.
42. B. Schimmelpfennig, '*Ex fornicatione nati:* studies on the position of priests' sons from the twelfth to the fourteenth century', *Studies in Medieval and Renaissance History* NS 2 (1979), 3–50, at 6.
43. Eustathius: Hunter, *Jovinianist Controversy*, 133.

44. Brown, *Body and Society*, 357.
45. For Synesius and his contemporary bishop in Ephesus, Brown, *Body and Society*, 292–3, and good summary discussion in Harrington, *Women in a Celtic Church*, 44–7.
46. On successive synodal pronouncements in Spain in 589, 590 and 633, Schimmelpfennig, '*Ex fornicatione nati*', 13; K. Dark, 'Stones of the saints? Inscribed stones, monasticism and the evangelisation of western and northern Britain in the fifth and sixth centuries', *JEH* 72 (2021), 239–58, at 245 (respectively Llansadwrn in Anglesey and Llantrisant).
47. D. L. d'Avray, *Papal Jurisprudence, 385–1234: Social origins and medieval reception of canon law* (Cambridge, 2022), 263, in his useful Appendix A of legislative and pastoral statements of Leo I; cf. ibid., ch. 10.
48. B. Brennan, '"Episcopae": bishops' wives viewed in sixth-century Gaul', *CH* 54 (1985), 311–23, and at 322 for S. Prassede. For a reasonably tentative statement of an opposite view, U. E. Eisen, *Women Officeholders in Early Christianity: Epigraphical and literary studies* (Collegeville, Minn., 2000), 199–205. For the *diaconissa* usage in the West, for instance at the Synod of Tours in Gaul in 567, J. Wijngaards, *Women Deacons in the Early Church: Historical texts and contemporary debates* (New York, 2002), 112–13, 202 n. 21.
49. Wijngaards, *Women Deacons in the Early Church*, 5–6, 95–8.
50. On Olympias, ibid., 3–5, and Brown, *Body and Society*, 148, 263, 265, 279, 282–4, 318. See also J. Herrin, *Ravenna: Capital of Empire, crucible of Europe* (London, 2020), 213, for the 6th-century presence of 'the place of the deaconesses' (*in sanctas diaconissas*) as a familiar landmark in this meeting-place of Eastern and Western Christianity.
51. Brennan, '"Episcopae"', 322. Confusingly, the Council *In Trullo* is also often called the Quinisext ('Fifth and Sixth') Council, since it is seen as providing the canons of legislation not undertaken by the previous Fifth and Sixth Oecumenical (that is, General) Councils.
52. A fine account is A. Sterk, *Renouncing the World Yet Leading the Church: The monk-bishop in late antiquity* (Cambridge, Mass. and London, 2004).
53. C. Baumer, *The Church of the East: An illustrated history of Assyrian Christianity* (London and New York, 2006), ch. 5.
54. Ibid., 61–2, 78–80.
55. Weitz, *Between Christ and Caliph*, 206.
56. S. Minov, *Memory and Identity in the Syriac Cave of Treasures: Rewriting the Bible in Sasanian Iran*, Jerusalem Studies in Religion and Culture 26 (Leiden, 2021). Minov demonstrates that the work was written in a Syrian milieu that was Miaphysite rather than Dyophysite, but, by attributing itself to the universally revered Syrian figure of Ephrem, it consciously positioned itself to appeal across the theological divide in Syriac Christianity (ibid., 40–44, 294–9).

57. Ibid., 223–47. It is notable that these magi are already the conventional number of three, a number not specified in the New Testament account of them (Matt. 2.1–12).
58. Ibid., 163–77.
59. Weitz, *Between Christ and Caliph*, 149; for what follows, ibid., 174–8.
60. Ibid., 179, citing S. Brock, 'Regulations for an association of artisans from the late Sasanian or early Arab period', in P. Rousseau and M. Papoutsakis (eds), *Transformations of Late Antiquity: Essays for Peter Brown* (Farnham, 2009), 51–62.

10. EASTERN CHRISTIANITY: ENTER ISLAM

1. M. D. Baer, *The Ottomans: Khans, Caesars and Caliphs* (London, 2021), 79.
2. M. A. S. Abdel Haleem (tr. and ed.), *The Qur'an: A new translation* (Oxford, 2004), 68 [*The Feast* 5.5]; cf. also ibid., 9 [*The Cow* 2.62], where Jews, Christians and the now obscure local monotheists 'the Sabians' are approvingly described alongside Muslims as 'those who believe in God and the Last Day and do good' and so 'will have their rewards with the Lord'.
3. C. Ibrahim, *Women and Gender in the Qur'an* (Oxford, 2020), 23–4, commenting on *The Byzantines* 30.21 [Abdel Haleem (tr. and ed.), *The Qur'an*, 258].
4. Ibrahim, *Women and Gender in the Qur'an*, 31–2, 46–8, 65, 74, 77, 81–2, 85, 98–109, 115–20, 134–5, 147–9. J. Pelikan, *Mary Through the Centuries: Her place in the history of culture* (New Haven, Conn. and London, 1996), ch. 5.
5. Bullough, *Sexual Variance in Society and History*, ch. 9, esp. 205.
6. Abdel Haleem (tr. and ed.), *The Qur'an*, 75–6 [*The Feast* 5.82], and 119 [*Repentance* 9.31, 34]. Some of the complications are entertainingly set out in E. Campbell, 'A heaven of wine: Muslim–Christian encounters at monasteries in the early Islamic Middle East', unpublished Ph.D. dissertation, University of Washington (2009), and for summary discussion on this and on the Sufi mysticism of Islam, see MacCulloch, *Christianity*, 263, 488.
7. C. Baumer, *The Church of the East: An illustrated history of Assyrian Christianity* (London and New York, 2006), 97, 181.
8. For the redating of the battle from the traditional date of 732, see J. Herrin, *The Formation of Christendom* (with new intro., Princeton, NJ, 2022), 137.
9. Abdel Haleem (tr. and ed.), *The Qur'an*, 29 [*The Cow* 2.256].
10. Ibid., 381 [*Prohibition* 66.12].
11. R. G. Hoyland, *Seeing Islam as Others Saw It: A survey and evaluation of Christian, Jewish and Zoroastrian writings on early Islam* (Piscataway, NJ,

2019), 144–5: a letter to the rebellious Bishop Simeon of Rewardashir. Hoyland does point out that the letter should be seen in the context of rival Christian attempts to curry favour with the new Muslim rulers.

12. Weitz, *Between Christ and Caliph*, 74–5, 219; Baumer, *Church of the East*, 174–6.
13. Weitz, *Between Christ and Caliph*, 51, 201, and cf. ibid., 4, 50–51, 66, 214–19. On the changing profile of Judaism under Islam, P. I. Lieberman, *The Fate of the Jews in the Early Islamic Near East: Tracing the demographic shift from West to East* (Cambridge, 2022), esp. ch. 3 and 278–82, and A. Chrysostomides, 'Creating a theology of icons in Umayyad Palestine: John of Damascus's "Three treatises on the divine images"', *JEH* 72 (2021), 1–17, at 17.
14. Those prurient enough to seek it out may do so at Weitz, *Between Christ and Caliph*, 188, and cf. ibid., 186.
15. Ibid., 42 (slightly adapted), and cf. ibid. 41–3, 53–6, 63–5.
16. For a different and exactly contemporary approach to the problem of maintaining Christian identity in the face of Umayyad dominance, based instead on baptism, Eucharist and making the sign of the Cross as 'rites of maintenance', see B. Hansen, 'Making Christians in the Umayyad Levant: Anastasius of Sinai and Christian rites of maintenance', in F. Knight, C. Methuen and A. Spicer (eds), *The Churches and Rites of Passage*, Studies in Church History 59 (Cambridge, 2023), 98–118.
17. Church of England, *Living in Love and Faith: Christian teaching and learning about identity, sexuality, relationships and marriage* (London, 2020).
18. On burial, V. Fiocchi Nicolai, F. Bisconti and D. Mazzoleni, *The Christian Catacombs of Rome: History, decoration, inscriptions* (Regensburg, 1999), and H. Geake, 'The control of burial practice in Anglo-Saxon England', in M. Carver (ed.), *The Cross Goes North: Processes of conversion in northern Europe, AD 300–1300* (York, 2003), 259–69, at 264–7. There was early controversy about whether young children should be admitted for baptism: N. Orme, *Medieval Children* (New Haven, Conn. and London, 2001), 22–3.
19. P. Kalaitzidis, 'Civil marriage and civil union from an ecclesial perspective: the case of the Orthodox Church of Greece', in Arentzen et al. (eds), *Orthodox Tradition and Human Sexuality*, 105–43, at 116–17 (citing Ignatios, *Letter to Polycarp* 5.2). Reynolds, *Marriage in the Western Church*, 368–9, notes the fairly conclusive refutation by Korbinian Ritzer of arguments that various theological reflections on marriage by Tertullian in the 3rd century concern contemporary liturgical practice.
20. Foucault, *History of Sexuality 3*, 72–6, notes this development, but also that evidence for any public involvement of the traditional religious hierarchies in marriage is purely from great cities, not from the countryside.
21. Kalaitzidis, 'Civil marriage and civil union from an ecclesial perspective', 138 n. 49; J. Meyendorff, 'Christian marriage in Byzantium: the

canonical and liturgical tradition', *Dumbarton Oaks Papers* 44 (1990), 99–107, at 104.

22. Chrysostom: Brown, *Body and Society*, 313; Gregory: Meyendorff, 'Christian marriage in Byzantium', 104. Jerome: Letter to Nepotian, *Epistula* 52.16: 'praedicator continentiae nuptias ne conciliet'. K. Stevenson, 'The origins of nuptial blessing', *Heythrop Journal* 21 (1980), 412–16, at 414–15, interprets this phrase as telling clergy to 'keep well away from marriages', which is probably pushing the meaning too far.
23. Kalaitzidis, 'Civil marriage and civil union from an ecclesial perspective', 118, and see also P. L'Huillier, 'Novella 89 of Leo the Wise on marriage: an insight into its theoretical and practical impact', *Greek Orthodox Theological Review* 32 (1987), 153–62, at 156.
24. Stevenson, 'The origins of nuptial blessing', 415–16.
25. See D. Hunter, 'Sexuality, marriage and the family', in A. Casiday and F. W. Norris (eds), *The Cambridge History of Christianity 2: Constantine to c.600* (Cambridge, 2007), 585–600, at 592.
26. L'Huillier, 'Novella 89 of Leo the Wise on marriage', 155.
27. A recent study of Pseudo-Dionysios does not see him as a non-Chalcedonian, noting his general avoidance of Christological debate: C. M. Stang, *Apophasis and Pseudonymity in Dionysius the Areopagite: 'No longer I'* (Oxford, 2012), 93–4, 97–98, 101. Whatever the conclusion, the pseudonymous author was as much respected among Chalcedonians, indeed eventually including Western Latins, as among the Oriental Orthodox.
28. Kalaitzidis, 'Civil marriage and civil union from an ecclesial perspective', 121.
29. Ibid., 118; L'Huillier, 'Novella 89 of Leo the Wise on marriage', 158.
30. Kalaitzidis, 'Civil marriage and civil union from an ecclesial perspective', 119.
31. Herrin, *Formation of Christendom*, 430–31.
32. On Leo's motivation, see J. Herrin, *Byzantium: The surprising life of a medieval empire* (London, 2007), 106–9.
33. R. Cholij, *Theodore the Stoudite: The ordering of holiness* (Oxford, 1996), 15n.
34. L. Brubaker and J. Haldon (eds), *Byzantium in the Iconoclast Era (ca. 680–850): The sources, an annotated survey* (Aldershot, 2001), 30–36; M. Piccirillo, *The Mosaics of Jordan* (Amman, 1993), 41–2.
35. The argument is expressed with characteristic elegance in P. Brown, 'A Dark Age crisis: aspects of the iconoclastic controversy', in Brown, *Society and the Holy in Late Antiquity* (London, 1982), 251–301, esp. at 258–64, 272–4, 282–3; also J. Herrin, *Unrivalled Influence: Women and Empire in Byzantium* (Princeton, NJ, 2013), ch. 3.
36. A point made by Kallistos Ware, 'Eastern Christianity', in R. Harries and H. Mayr-Harting (eds), *Christianity: Two thousand years* (Oxford, 2001), 65–95, at 251 n. 20.
37. Chrysostomides, 'Creating a theology of icons in Umayyad Palestine', 1–17, at 12.

38. Herrin, *Unrivalled Influence*, 63–4.
39. D. F. Wright, 'From "God-Bearer" to "Mother of God" in the late Fathers', in Swanson (ed.), *Church and Mary*, 22–30, at 24–26.
40. M. B. Cunningham, 'The meeting of the old and the new: the typology of Mary the *Theotokos* in Byzantine homilies and hymns', in Swanson (ed.), *Church and Mary*, 52–62, at 53, 61–2.
41. A. Cameron, 'The cult of the Virgin in late antiquity: religious development and myth-making', in Swanson (ed.), *Church and Mary*, 1–21, at 3.
42. L'Huillier, 'Novella 89 of Leo the Wise on marriage', 156. For comment on the future significance of Roman/Byzantine polemic in the Bulgarian dispute, see H. Chadwick, *East and West: The making of a rift in the Church, from apostolic times until the Council of Florence* (Oxford, 2003), 188–91.
43. S. Franklin, *Writing, Society and Culture in Early Rus, c. 950–1300* (Cambridge, 2002), ch. 2.
44. For a more extended account of what follows, see MacCulloch, *Christianity*, 503–10.
45. The apostrophe reflects pronunciation in Russian, Belarussian and Ukrainian. The derivation of the name is still the subject of inconclusive controversy.
46. For what follows, see Levin, *Sex and Society in the World of the Orthodox Slavs*, ch. 1.
47. Ibid., 14.
48. Ibid., 73–4, 172: Levin admits ruefully to having (along with other scholars) mistaken the *na koně* phrase as a reference to bestiality.
49. Ibid., 161.
50. Ibid., 83–5.
51. On this engaging subject, see A. Ivanov, *Holy Fools in Byzantium and Beyond* (Oxford, 2006).

11. THE LATIN WEST: A LANDSCAPE OF MONASTERIES

1. M. Lambert, *Christians and Pagans: The conversion of Britain from Alban to Bede* (New Haven, Conn. and London, 2010), 11–12: the three British bishops at Arles are associated with slightly garbled place names, two easily resolvable into Londinium (London) and Eboracum (York); the third, from 'Colonia Londinensium', could have been from Lincoln (Lindum) or Colchester (Camulodunum).
2. A fine summary introduction to this period is provided by W. Löhr and K. Schäferdiek in A. Casiday and F. W. Norris (eds), *The Cambridge History of Christianity 2: Constantine to c.600* (Cambridge, 2007), 9–69. They describe the new polities without resorting to the word 'barbarian', another unhelpful traditional label that is a barrier to historical understanding.

3. R. Fletcher, *The Conversion of Europe: From paganism to Christianity 371–1386 AD* (London, 1997), 104–5.
4. A good discussion of the relationship and its legal ramifications is M. Innes, 'Land, freedom and the making of the medieval West', *TRHS* 6th ser. 16 (2006), 39–74.
5. C. H. Lawrence, 'St Benedict and his Rule', *History* 67 (1982), 185–94. A reliable version, though without editorial annotations, is P. Barry (tr.), *Saint Benedict's Rule: A new translation for today* (Ampleforth, 1997).
6. On the survival of British Christianity and its relationship to what came next, J. Blair, *The Church in Anglo-Saxon Society* (Oxford, 2005), 10–34, or the longer recent account in Lambert, *Christians and Pagans*. For my own summary remarks on what follows on Patrick and the mission to Ireland, see D. MacCulloch, 'Who kicked them out?', *London Review of Books*, 1 Aug. 2019, 23–4.
7. Key texts are presented with useful commentary (wobbling on the question of Patrick's childhood home) in Stevenson (ed.), rev. Frend, *Creeds, Councils and Controversies*, 378–84.
8. A good summary introduction to what follows is to be found in Fletcher, *Conversion of Europe*, 87–92.
9. For examples beyond Ireland, Harrington, *Women in a Celtic Church*, 101–3, 119, 126, 130.
10. P. Ó Riain, 'Irish saints' cults and ecclesiastical families', in A. Thacker and R. Sharpe (eds), *Local Saints and Churches in the Early Medieval West* (Oxford, 2002), 291–302.
11. Harrington, *Women in a Celtic Church*, 122–30, 191, 247–9.
12. Ibid., 247–8, 258. Saint Brendan appears to have lived in the 6th century, though that does not have much bearing on his supposed contemporaneity with St Scothíne.
13. Ibid., 280–81.
14. Luke 8.2: A. Tilby, *The Seven Deadly Sins: Their origin in the spiritual teaching of Evagrius the Hermit* (London, 2009), esp. 19. Cassian had added an eighth deadly sin, *accedia* or spiritual torpor, which the sevenfold system amalgamated with general sloth. *Accedia* has much the character of depression, which may be why spiritual advisors recognized that it was not always a sinful state.
15. For a summary of the early history of confession, see J. Mahoney, *The Making of Moral Theology: A study of the Roman Catholic tradition* (Oxford, 1987), 2–5.
16. The priority between Ireland and Wales is uncertain; they were part of the same religious culture in the 6th century, to which era the earliest penitentials belong, but archaeology provides a clearer picture of the background in Ireland than it does in Wales. The best discussion of these early materials is R. Meens, *Penance in Medieval Europe, 600–1200* (Cambridge, 2014), ch. 3. For the relevant texts, see J. T. McNeill and H. M. Gamer (eds), *Medieval*

Handbooks of Penance: A translation of the principal 'libri poenitentiales' *and selections from related documents* (New York, 1938), chs. 1 and 2.

17. Mahoney, *Making of Moral Theology*, 15–16; Meens, *Penance in Medieval Europe*, 113–18.
18. A point made by P. Heather, *Christendom: The triumph of a religion* (London, 2022), 271. Mahoney, *Making of Moral Theology*, 6, points particularly to the continent-wide impact of the 6th-century Irish monk Columbanus (not to be confused with Columba or Colmcille of Iona), and it is discussed at length in Meens, *Penance in Medieval Europe*, ch. 4.
19. McNeill and Gamer (eds), *Medieval Handbooks of Penance*: 'The Penitential of Cummean', 101–5, 112–14.
20. For the high evidential value of penitentials in medieval and early modern Slavic Orthodoxy, see Levin, *Sex and Society in the World of the Orthodox Slavs*, esp. 11–12, 25–33, 78.
21. For crisp combined praise and sharp castigation of the system and its long-term effects, see Mahoney, *Making of Moral Theology*, ch. 1.
22. J. Richards, *Consul of God: The life and times of Gregory the Great* (London, 1980), 240–42.
23. Ibid., 238–41: Richards, ibid., 239, points out in favour of the story that we know that Gregory sought to buy English enslaved youths in 595, though evidently they did not accompany Augustine to Kent. Cf. B. Colgrave and R. A. B. Mynors (eds), *Bede's Ecclesiastical History of the English People* (Oxford, 2022), 132–5 [II.1]. The extension of the misquotation to '*Not* Angels, but *Anglicans*' in W. C. Sellar and R. J. Yeatman, *1066 and All That* (London, 1975 edn), 14, is clearly a Good Thing.
24. See the argument of M. W. Herren and S. A. Brown, *Christ in Celtic Christianity: Britain and Ireland from the fifth to the tenth century* (Woodbridge, 2002), 96–7; but note W. H. C. Frend's criticism of their main thesis that the Irish and other Christians in Britain or England took their theology directly from Pelagianism, and pointing out the link to John Cassian, *JEH* 55 (2004), 140.
25. Blair, *The Church in Anglo-Saxon Society*, 39–40.
26. P. Hayward, 'Gregory the Great as "Apostle of the English"', *JEH* 55 (2004), 19–57.
27. L. Blackmore, I. Blair and S. M. Hirst (eds), *The Prittlewell Princely Burial: Excavations at Priory Crescent, Southend-on-Sea, Essex, 2003* (London, 2019), esp. 344–8.
28. Richards, *Consul of God*, 240: my modification of the translation.
29. R. Meens, 'Ritual purity and Gregory the Great', in R. N. Swanson (ed.), *Unity and Diversity in the Church*, Studies in Church History 32 (Oxford, 1997), 31–43, esp. 35–7. Cf. Colgrave and Mynors (eds), *Bede's Ecclesiastical History*, 78–103 [I.27].
30. Blair, *The Church in Anglo-Saxon Society*, 170–74, 230–34; Blair points out the contrary and contrasting fashion in the same period for quite austerely

equipped burials for women who were clearly of equally exalted status. For a detailed study of one 7th-century female burial that highlights its multiform spiritual resonances, see H. Hamerow, 'A Conversion-period burial in an ancient landscape: a high-status female grave near the Rollright Stones, Oxfordshire/Warwickshire', in A. Langlands and R. Lavelle (eds), *The Land of the English Kin: Studies in Wessex and Anglo-Saxon England in honour of Professor Barbara Yorke* (Leiden and Boston, Mass., 2020), 231–44. We are still absorbing the significance of an extraordinary high-status Christian female burial discovered at Harpole (Northamptonshire) in 2020.

31. B. Yorke, 'The adaptation of the Anglo-Saxon royal courts to Christianity', in M. Carver (ed.), *The Cross Goes North: Processes of conversion in northern Europe, AD 300–1300* (York, 2003), 243–57.

32. For a summary account of Æthelthryth, emphasizing the difficulty of separating out subsequent projections on to her story, and for her sisters/half-sisters, S. Wragg, *Anglo-Saxon Queens, 650–850: Speculum Reginae* (London and New York, 2022), 92–8, 222–43. John Blair has generously given me a foretaste of the chapter dealing with multiple implications of Æthelthryth's miraculously preserved body when disinterred in 695, from his forthcoming study of the 'unquiet dead' in Anglo-Saxon England. The Latinization of these already picturesque Anglo-Saxon royal names affords us for instance the Totally Memorable Sexburga.

33. J. Blair, 'A saint for every minster? Local cults in Anglo-Saxon England', in Thacker and Sharpe (eds), *Local Saints and Churches in the Early Medieval West*, 455–94, especially its handlist of saints. For background, see B. Yorke, *Nunneries and the Anglo-Saxon Royal Houses* (London, 2003), esp. 17–18, 26–35, 118, 153–4; Wragg, *Anglo-Saxon Queens*, ch. 1.

34. For examples, Blair, *The Church in Anglo-Saxon Society*, 361. A nuanced study of the complications is S. Foot, *Monastic Life in Anglo-Saxon England, c.600–900* (Cambridge, 2006).

35. Bede to Bishop Ecgberht of York, 734: tr. by C. Grocock and I. N. Wood (eds), *Abbots of Wearmouth and Jarrow: Bede's Homily i.13 on Benedict Biscop, Bede's History of the abbots of Wearmouth and Jarrow, the anonymous Life of Ceolfrith, Bede's Letter to Ecgbert, Bishop of York* (Oxford, 2013), 147–9. For the background, see Blair, *The Church in Anglo-Saxon Society*, 42, 81–91, 100–108.

36. Colgrave and Mynors (eds), *Bede's Ecclesiastical History*, 420–27 [IV.25]. I am grateful to John Blair for reminding me of Coldingham.

37. A fine summary of the evidence is Blair, *The Church in Anglo-Saxon Society*, 291–323.

38. J. Bately (ed.), *The Old English Orosius* (Early English Text Society, supplementary ser. 6, 1980), esp. p. 27, l. 15; for a discussion of authorship and dating, ibid., lxxiii–xcii. For summary comment on Alfred as active in literature, see J. Nelson, 'England and the continent in the ninth century: IV. Bodies and minds', *TRHS* 6th series 15 (2005), 1–28, at 25–6.

39. S. Foot, *Aethelstan: The first King of England* (New Haven, Conn. and London, 2011), esp. on the Church, 94–126, and on the British dimension, 212–26.
40. J. Nightingale, 'Oswald, Fleury and continental reform', in S. Brooks, K. Cubitt and N. Brooks (eds), *St Oswald of Worcester: Life and influence* (London, 1998), 23–45, at 24.
41. Foot, *Aethelstan*, 109.
42. Harrington, *Women in a Celtic Church*, 3, 205 contrasts this change with the evidence for continuity in Irish female monastic life. Katy Cubitt makes the point to me that a deliberate marginalization of female religious is already perceptible in the ecclesiastical canons issued by Theodore of Tarsus as Archbishop of Canterbury (668–90). I am grateful to her for an advance view of her so far unpublished paper 'The lady vanishes: imposing order in Theodore's Penitential in seventh-century England'.
43. K. Weikert, 'Ely Cathedral and the afterlife of Ealdorman Byrhtnoth', in Langlands and Lavelle (eds), *The Land of the English Kin*, 556–81.
44. M. Clayton, *The Cult of the Virgin Mary in Anglo-Saxon England* (Cambridge, 1990); on the centrality of Winchester to the 10th-century cult, ibid., 89.
45. See a suggestive essay on the political background by C. Leyser, 'From maternal kin to Jesus as mother: royal genealogy and Marian devotion in the 9th-century West', in C. Leyser and L. Smith (eds), *Motherhood, Religion and Society in Medieval Europe, 400–1400: Essays presented to Henrietta Leyser* (Farnham and Burlington, Vt., 2011), 21–39.
46. R. Sowerby, *Angels in Early Medieval England* (Oxford, 2016), 34–42.
47. Ibid., 35; the quotations are from a royal charter of 966 to New Minster. The composite biblical account of the expulsion of rebel angels is founded on pre-Exilic passages in Isa. 14.12–17 and Ezek. 28.11–19.
48. Blair, *The Church in Anglo-Saxon Society*, 361–2; see also J. Barrow, *The Clergy in the Medieval World: Secular clerics, their families and careers in north-western Europe, c.800–c.1200* (Cambridge, 2015), 345.
49. Blair, *The Church in Anglo-Saxon Society*, 351, rightly stresses the incompleteness of English reform, but M. Gretsch, *The Intellectual Foundations of the English Benedictine Reform* (Cambridge, 1999), lays out its continent-wide implications, well summed up at 425–7.
50. P. Fouracre, 'The long shadow of the Merovingians', in J. Story (ed.), *Charlemagne: Empire and society* (Manchester, 2005), 5–21.
51. Indispensable in following the consequences is H. Chadwick, *East and West: The making of a rift in the Church, from apostolic times until the Council of Florence* (Oxford, 2003), chs. 14–30.
52. S. Coupland, 'Charlemagne's coinage', in Story (ed.), *Charlemagne*, 211–29, at 223–7.
53. H. Mayr-Harting, 'The early Middle Ages', in R. Harries and H. Mayr-Harting (eds), *Christianity: Two thousand years* (Oxford, 2001), 44–64, at

51–5, and see J. LeClercq, tr. C. Misrahi, *The Love of Learning and the Desire for God: A study in monastic culture* (New York, 1982), ch. 3.

54. R. McKitterick, 'The Carolingian Renaissance of culture and learning', in Story (ed.), *Charlemagne*, 151–66.
55. S. G. Bruce, *Silence and Sign Language in Medieval Monasticism: The Cluniac tradition c. 900–1200* (Cambridge, 2007), 38.
56. For monks as angels among the Cluniacs from the 10th century onwards, see ibid., 3, 20–23, 65–6, 74–6, and for an interesting case study against the wider background, K. Tanton, 'A monastic angelology in stone: the sculpted angels at Conques', *Journal of Medieval History* 49 (2023), 467–94. For the Western encounter with Pseudo-Dionysios, see P. Rorem, 'The early Latin Dionysius: Eriugena and Hugh of St Victor', in S. Coakley and J. M. Stang (eds), *Re-thinking Dionysius the Areopagite* (Chichester, 2009), 71–84.
57. See above, Ch. 8, especially on Cassian's distasteful story of Patermutus and his son, and C. T. Schroeder, *Children and Family in Late Antique Egyptian Monasticism* (Cambridge, 2021), esp. chs. 1 and 3.
58. M. de Jong, *In Samuel's Image: Child oblation in the early medieval West* (Leiden and New York, 1996), ch. 1, and, for Basil's comment, ibid., 19.
59. Ibid., 288.
60. 'Mass', a distinctively Western Christian word, derives from *missa*, a late Latin form of the word *missio*, a 'sending' – in the liturgy of the Roman Mass current until the 20th century, the priest enigmatically dismissed the people with the curious phrase *ite missa est*, 'Go, it is the sending'.
61. De Jong, *In Samuel's Image*, esp. ch. 8; Barrow, *Clergy in the Medieval World*, 344–5.
62. C. N. L. Brooke, 'Priest, deacon and layman, from St Peter Damian to St Francis', in W. J. Sheils and D. Wood (eds), *The Ministry: Clerical and lay*, Studies in Church History 26 (Oxford, 1989), 65–86, at 69–71.
63. The classic plan is anticipated in the famous though probably at the time theoretical 9th-century 'Plan of St Gall': A. Doig, *Liturgy and Architecture from the Early Church to the Middle Ages* (Aldershot, 2008), 143–6.
64. Bruce, *Silence and Sign Language in Medieval Monasticism*, 65, 121–2. Besides that excellent study, see also various signage lists in D. Sherlock, *Monastic Sign Language in Medieval England* (Ipswich, 2016).
65. J. M. Smith, 'Gender and ideology in the early Middle Ages', in Swanson (ed.), *Gender and Christian Religion*, 51–73, at 60–61; Mahoney, *Making of Moral Theology*, 14–15.
66. The development of the system is summarized in Heather, *Christendom*, 431–7, and for England, see Blair, *The Church in Anglo-Saxon Society*, ch. 8.
67. C. M. Eska (ed.), *Cáin Lánamna: An Old Irish tract on marriage and divorce law* (Leiden and Boston, Mass., 2010), 20–23. Eska dates the texts she has edited to the early 8th century.
68. Reynolds, *Marriage in the Western Church*, 99–100.

69. Ibid., 38–40. One complicating irrelevance to the discussion of northern European marriage can be dismissed: the idea of an institution of *Friedelehe* or quasi-marriage, women contracting marriage on their own without family or property arrangements. This is already queried in R. Karras, 'Concubinage and slavery in the Viking age', *Scandinavian Studies* 62 (1990), 141–62, at 156, and is briskly dismissed in E. T. Dailey, *Queens, Consorts, Concubines: Gregory of Tours and women of the Merovingian elite* (Leiden and Boston, Mass., 2015), 112 n. 40.
70. Dailey, *Queens, Consorts, Concubines*, 102–17; that discussion effectively counters the thesis still propounded in secondary literature that the Merovingians practised formal polygyny in marriage. On 'resource polygyny', van Houts, *Married Life in the Middle Ages*, 204–10.
71. Eska (ed.), *Cáin Lánamna*, 14n.
72. Harrington, *Women in a Celtic Church*, 133.
73. Karras, 'Concubinage and slavery in the Viking age', 142; further overall discussion, including the suggestion that Scandinavian polygyny triggered a shortage of available women leading to the early Viking raids, in B. Raffield, N. Price and M. Collard, 'Polygyny, concubinage, and the social lives of women in Viking-age Scandinavia', *Viking and Medieval Scandinavia* 13 (2017), 165–209.
74. Raffield, Price and Collard, 'Polygyny, concubinage, and the social lives of women in Viking-age Scandinavia', 177.
75. Karras, 'Concubinage and slavery in the Viking age', 145.
76. J. M. Jochens, 'The Church and sexuality in medieval Iceland', *Journal of Medieval History* 6 (1980), 377–92.
77. Eska (ed.), *Cáin Lánamna*, 23 and n: quoting the text entitled *Bretha Crólige*.

12. GREGORY VII AND A FIRST SEXUAL REVOLUTION

1. S. G. Bruce, *Silence and Sign Language in Medieval Monasticism: The Cluniac tradition c. 900–1200* (Cambridge, 2007), 79.
2. Comment and useful presentation of documents on penitential pilgrimage in D. Webb, *Pilgrims and Pilgrimage in the Medieval West* (London, 2001), 14–16, 34–9, ch. 2. On pilgrimage by wealthy serfs with official permission (for a substantial fee), ibid., 161.
3. L. A. Craig, *Wandering Women and Holy Matrons: Women as pilgrims in the later Middle Ages* (Leiden and Boston, Mass., 2009), 261–2.
4. M.-L. Ehrenschwendtner, 'Virtual pilgrimages? Enclosure and the practice of piety at St Katherine's Convent, Augsburg', *JEH* 50 (2009), 45–73, referring to Villingen at 67–8.
5. The evidence for gradual escalation is judiciously presented in C. Morris, *The Sepulchre of Christ and the Medieval West from the Beginning to 1600*

(Oxford, 2005), 134–46. Hākim's vandalism should not be attributed as much to Islam as to insanity, which eventually resulted in his murder by outraged fellow-Muslims after he had proclaimed himself *Allāh*: P. Jenkins, *The Lost History of Christianity: The thousand-year golden age of the Church in the Middle East, Africa and Asia* (New York, 2008), 109.

6. On Glaber, Adémar and the millennium, see D. F. Callahan, 'Ademar of Chabannes, millennial fears and the development of Western anti-Judaism', *JEH* 46 (1995), 19–35.
7. K. G. Cushing, *Reform and the Papacy in the Eleventh Century: Spirituality and social change* (Manchester, 2005), 39–40, 47–9.
8. For the significance of Norman victories in Sicily, see P. E. Chevedden, 'The Islamic view and the Christian view of the Crusades: a new synthesis', *History* 93 (2008), 181–200, esp. 184–6, 192–4.
9. Bernard, *De laude novae militiae*, qu. by C. Tyerman, *God's War: A new history of the Crusades* (London, 2006), 28.
10. Z. Karabell, *People of the Book: The forgotten history of Islam and the West* (London, 2007), 93–4, 100–101; for a summary description of the massacre, Tyerman, *God's War*, 157–61.
11. Tyerman, *God's War*, 247.
12. Elsewhere the theme is to be found in apocalyptic texts in Matthew's Gospel, Matt. 13.41, 13.49, echoed at Matt. 26.53. A precocious early exception to the iconographical rule is the 6th-century mosaic depiction of Christ as a soldier in the Archbishop's Chapel in Ravenna, on a border of Eastern and Western Christendom: illus. in P. Stephenson, *New Rome: The Empire in the East* (Cambridge, Mass., 2022), 122.
13. D. Denny, 'A Romanesque fresco in Auxerre Cathedral', *Gesta* 25 (1986), 197–202, provides a robust case for dating and context.
14. I. Moilanen, 'The concept of the three orders of society and social mobility in eleventh-century England', *English Historical Review* 131 (2016), 1,331–52.
15. On criticism of the *raison d'être* of the military Orders, Tyerman, *God's War*, 255–6; on the Templars' fall, ibid., 838–43, and for the refocusing of the Teutonic Knights, ibid., 674–712. For arguments that the Templars were indeed guilty of some of the blasphemies attributed to them, see J. Riley-Smith, 'Were the Templars guilty?', in S. J. Ridyard (ed.), *The Medieval Crusade* (Woodbridge and Rochester, NY, 2004), 107–24.
16. C. Wright, *The Maze and the Warrior: Symbols in architecture, theology and music* (Cambridge, Mass. and London, 2001), ch. 7.
17. For a thoughtful discussion of the often toxic obsession with the Templars, in relation to Rosslyn Chapel (Lothian), see L. Swarbrick, 'Doubt and surety: using my own authoritative voice', *Scottish Historical Review* 102 (2023), 327–31.
18. For more extended remarks on these papalist forgeries and the whole context of medieval forgery, see MacCulloch, *Christianity*, 351–2.

19. H. Chadwick, *East and West: The making of a rift in the Church, from apostolic times until the Council of Florence* (Oxford, 2003), 206–18.
20. Cushing, *Reform and the Papacy*, 78–9.
21. R. W. Southern, *Western Society and the Church in the Middle Ages* (London, 1970), 100–105.
22. On Christian universities' institutional debt to Islam, G. Makdisi, *The Rise of Colleges: Institutions of learning in Islam and the West* (Edinburgh, 1981), esp. 285–91. On translation, R. Swanson, *The Twelfth-Century Renaissance* (Manchester, 1999), 41–2, 50–54, 127, 131, 134.
23. On the contrast between monastic and university approaches to doctrine and theology, see J. LeClercq, tr. C. Misrahi, *The Love of Learning and the Desire for God: A study in monastic culture* (New York, 1982), esp. 1–7. On the impact of Aristotle and the difficulties of incorporating him in theology, see M. Haren, *Medieval Thought: The Western intellectual tradition from antiquity to the thirteenth century* (2nd edn, Basingstoke, 1992), chs. 5–6.
24. A point made by Southern, *Western Society and the Church in the Middle Ages*, 131–2. Elucidation of the complex formation of 'Gratian' is thanks to A. Winroth, *The Making of Gratian's Decretum* (Cambridge, 2000), esp. ch. 6 and 193–6. For background comment, see Swanson, *Twelfth-Century Renaissance*, 70–77.
25. The Encyclical *Vehementer Nos* (1906), qu. in G. O'Collins and M. Farrugia, *Catholicism: The story of Catholic Christianity* (Oxford, 2003), 307n. For 'Gratian' and the distinction between 'two classes of Christians', see ibid., 307, quoting *Decretum*, 2.12.1.
26. D. L. d'Avray, *Papal Jurisprudence, 385–1234: Social origins and medieval reception of canon law* (Cambridge, 2022), 171–2, 175–8.
27. H. Parish, *Clerical Celibacy in the West, c.1100–1700* (Cambridge, 2010), 90–93, 95–7; L. Wertheimer, 'Children of disorder: clerical parentage, illegitimacy, and reform in the Middle Ages', *Journal of the History of Sexuality* 15 (2006), 382–407, repr. in S. Hunt (ed.), *Christianity* (Farnham and Burlington, Vt., 2010), 191–217, esp. ibid., 202 on Bourges and its proposal to ban marriage to clerical children. For a 16th-century English Catholic proposal that Archbishop Cranmer's children should be declared serfs of the Church, by which time it seemed ludicrously antiquarian, see D. MacCulloch, *Thomas Cranmer: A life* (New Haven, Conn. and London, rev. edn 2016), 577.
28. On this relabelling, van Houts, *Married Life in the Middle Ages*, 221. G. Macy, 'The doctrine of transubstantiation in the Middle Ages', *JEH* 45 (1994), 11–41, usefully reminds us of the medieval latitude of understanding in the doctrine of transubstantiation.
29. A. Gransden, 'The cult of St Mary at *Beodericisworth* and then in Bury St Edmunds Abbey', *JEH* 55 (2004), 627–53, at 644–5.
30. H. Mayr-Harting, 'The idea of the Assumption of Mary in the West, 800–1200', in Swanson (ed.), *Church and Mary*, 86–111, at 103–4.

31. On Bernard, see B. Sella, 'Northern Italian confraternities and the Immaculate Conception in the fourteenth century', *JEH* 49 (1998), 599–619, at 601–2.
32. Cushing, *Reform and the Papacy*, 122, and L. Melve, 'The public debate on clerical marriage in the late 11th century', *JEH* 61 (2010), 688–706, at 689. For Damian's complicated emotions about a popular and charismatic clergy couple whom he had long known, see van Houts, *Married Life in the Middle Ages*, 174–5. Boswell, *Christianity, Social Tolerance and Homosexuality*, 210–13, is probably correct in arguing that Damian's diatribes against same-sex activity were for the moment less successful in gaining attention than his other obsessions.
33. M. Resnick, 'Marriage in medieval culture: consent theory and the case of Joseph and Mary', *CH* 69 (2000), 350–71, at 357.
34. Harrington, *Women in a Celtic Church*, 258–9; Parish, *Clerical Celibacy in the West*, 83, 97–8, 101–2, 108–10. Parish enlarges on the rhetorical connection to the Great Schism in H. Parish, 'A Church "without stain or wrinkle": the reception and application of Donatist arguments in debates on priestly purity', in C. Methuen, A. Ryrie and A. Spicer (eds), *Inspiration and Institution in Christian History*, Studies in Church History 57 (Cambridge, 2021), 96–119, esp. 102–3.
35. Andrew of Strumi, *Vita sancti Arialdi* c. 6, qu. in D. Elliott, *Spiritual Marriage: Sexual abstinence in medieval wedlock* (Princeton, NJ, 1983), 101. R. I. Moore, *The War on Heresy: Faith and power in medieval Europe* (London, 2012), 77, accounts for the *Pataria* name as sneeringly referring to the humblest of clothworkers.
36. Cushing, *Reform and the Papacy*, 74–6, 102–5; quotation, slightly edited, from the thoughtful study by P. Nagy, 'Collective emotions, history writing and change: the case of the *Pataria* (Milan, eleventh century)', *Emotions: Culture, History, Society* 2 (2018), 132–52, at 146. For a slightly earlier case of a Peace Movement event getting out of control and descending into violence, at Bourges in 1038, see T. Head, 'Andrew of Fleury and the Peace League of Bourges', *Historical Reflections/Réflexions Historiques* 14 (1987), 513–29.
37. B. Schimmelpfennig, '*Ex fornicatione nati:* studies on the position of priests' sons from the twelfth to the fourteenth century', *Studies in Medieval and Renaissance History* NS 2 (1979), 3–50, at 14–28.
38. Parish, *Clerical Celibacy in the West*, 107–8, 121–3, 125–6.
39. B. Gordon, 'Switzerland', in A. Pettegree (ed.), *The Early Reformation in Europe* (Cambridge, 1992), 70–93, at 73n.
40. The Sigüenza example is quoted by Peter Linehan in *JEH* 70 (2019), 867–9, reviewing A. García y García (ed.), *Synodicum Hispanum XII: Osma, Sigüenza, Tortosa y Valencia* (Madrid, 2014). Summary discussion in Harvey, *Fires of Lust*, 94–5, and on Catalan priestly concubinage whose discussion has much wider reference, see M. Armstrong-Partida, *Defiant*

Priests: Domestic unions, violence, and clerical masculinity in 14th-century Catalunya (Ithaca, NY and London, 2017).

41. Van Houts, *Married Life in the Middle Ages*, 188–9, discussing *Nos uxorati sumus*; Melve, 'The public debate on clerical marriage in the late 11th century', is an excellent overall study of the tract. See also Parish, *Clerical Celibacy in the West*, 89, 118–19.
42. R. I. Moore, *The First European Revolution c.970–1215* (Oxford, 2000), 72.
43. Van Houts, *Married Life in the Middle Ages*, 6–7; R. I. Moore, 'Duby's eleventh century', *History* 69 (1984), 36–49, at 41–2; on Peter Damian's espousement of Burchard's system, Moore, *War on Heresy*, 117.
44. J. Brundage, *Law, Sex and Christian Society in Medieval Europe* (Chicago, 1987), 141, 193–4, 437.
45. Elliott, *Spiritual Marriage*, 141.
46. Van Houts, *Married Life in the Middle Ages*, 44–5, 224–5, 235–6; R. Koopmans, 'The conclusion of Christina of Markyate's *Vita*', *JEH* 51 (2000), 663–98; K. A.-M. Bugyis, 'The author of the Life of Christina of Markyate: the case for Robert de Gorron (d. 1166)', *JEH* 68 (2017), 719–46.
47. Harvey, *Fires of Lust*, 75–6.
48. On consummation, see D. L. d'Avray, *Medieval Marriage: Symbolism and society* (Oxford, 2005), ch. 4, summarized at 200–201. For continuing celibate or 'spiritual' marriage in Western society, see Karras, *Sexuality in Medieval Europe*, 48–9, together with the comprehensive study by Elliott, *Spiritual Marriage*. A classic extreme statement of the evolved position is the opinion of Pope Paul VI, expressed in his encyclical *Humanae Vitae* (1968): 'The Church . . . teaches that each and every marriage act . . . must remain open to the transmission of life . . . That teaching . . . is founded upon the inseparable connection, willed by God and unable to be broken by man on his own initiative, between the two meanings of the conjugal act: the unitive meaning and the procreative meaning.' For the consequences of that statement, see below, Ch. 18.
49. Harvey, *Fires of Lust*, 52, and Resnick, 'Marriage in medieval culture: consent theory and the case of Joseph and Mary', 359–62, though he also notes how a definition involving sexual intercourse might strengthen rights of landed inheritance.
50. M. Perisanidi, 'Was there a marital debt in Byzantium?', *JEH* 68 (2017), 510–28, although her evidence indicates a conclusion precisely the opposite from the conclusion that she draws.
51. Levin, *Sex and Society in the World of the Orthodox Slavs*, 60–66, 88, 162.
52. Brundage, *Law, Sex and Christian Society in Medieval Europe*, 201–3, summarizes the developments around annulment.
53. See the discussion in J. M. Smith, 'Gender and ideology in the early Middle Ages', in Swanson (ed.), *Gender and Christian Religion*, 51–73, esp. 63–5.
54. Van Houts, *Married Life in the Middle Ages*, 7, 257.

55. Ibid., 9, 63–83.
56. J. Herrin, *The Formation of Christendom* (with new intro., Princeton, NJ, 2022), 466.
57. Van Houts, *Married Life in the Middle Ages*, 64–6.
58. For an excellent discussion of porches, far more general in application than the book's title implies, see H. F. Lunnon, *East Anglian Church Porches and their Medieval Context* (Woodbridge, 2020). See my comments on weddings and porches in reviewing her book: *JEH* 72 (2021), 410–11; and for further useful comment on the late medieval decline in the significance of ceremony at the church door, C. Peters, 'Gender, sacrament and ritual: the making and meaning of marriage in late medieval and early modern England', *PP* 169 (2000), 63–96, at 80–81. S. McSheffrey, *Marriage, Sex and Civic Culture in Late Medieval London* (Philadelphia, Pa., 2006), 42–4, emphasizes that marriage within the church building had become the norm in London by then.
59. G. Bonner, *Saint Augustine of Hippo: Life and controversies* (2nd edn, Norwich, 1963), 386–7, provides an analysis of which texts may with confidence be attributed to Augustine. J. Barrow, *The Clergy in the Medieval World: Secular clerics, their families and careers in north-western Europe, c.800–c.1200* (Cambridge, 2015), 100–144, summarizes the 11th–12th-century development of the Augustinian movement.
60. On some of the complexities of this story of largely unfulfilled hopes at Fontevraud and among the Gilbertines, see J. M. B. Porter, 'Fontevrault looks back to her founder: reform and the attempts to canonise Robert of Arbrissel', in R. N. Swanson (ed.), *The Church Retrospective*, Studies in Church History 33 (Woodbridge, 1997), 361–78; K. Sykes, '"Canonici albi et moniales": perceptions of the 12th-century double house', *JEH* 60 (2009), 233–45, and K. Sykes, *Inventing Sempringham: Gilbert of Sempringham and the origins of the role of the Master* (Münster, 2011); B. Golding, 'Keeping nuns in order: enforcement of the rules in 13th-century Sempringham', *JEH* 59 (2008), 657–79, esp. at 658.
61. M. de Jong, *In Samuel's Image: Child oblation in the early medieval West* (Leiden and New York, 1996), 293–302.
62. E. J. Wells, 'A "Matter" of popular piety or divine discipline? Reflections on lay devotion and the cathedral in medieval England', in M. Kirby (ed.), *The Lay Experience of the Medieval Cathedral* (London, 2023), 11–26, at 14–15.
63. Reginald of Durham, *Libellus de admirandis beati Cutberti virtutibus quae novellis patratae sunt temporibus* (London, 1835), 151–4 [ch. 74]: 'vade . . . quam citius, et lacissam illam, quae ecclesiae meae limina progrediendo foedavit, sub festinatione projiciendo expelle.' I am indebted for this wonderfully dreadful tale to R. Bartlett, *Why Can the Dead Do Such Great Things? Saints and worshippers from the martyrs to the Reformation* (Princeton, NJ, 2013), 262–3. This was part of a contemporary pattern at

Durham: V. Tudor, 'The misogyny of St Cuthbert', *Archaeologia Aeliana* 5th ser. 12 (1984), 157–67.

64. J. Hawkes, 'Approaching the Cross: the sculpted High Crosses of Anglo-Saxon England', in P. Turner and J. Hawkes, *The Rood in Medieval Britain and Ireland c.800–c.1500* (Woodbridge, 2020), 15–30, at 25–6.

13. WESTERN CHRISTENDOM ESTABLISHED

1. Helpful in understanding the role of the fourth Lateran Council in these developments is E. Freeman, 'The fourth Lateran Council of 1215, the prohibition against new religious Orders, and religious women', *Journal of Medieval Religious Cultures* 44 (2018), 1–23.
2. A fine exposition of the importance of fraternal preaching is D. L. d'Avray, *Medieval Marriage: Symbolism and society* (Oxford, 2005), ch. 1.
3. R. Swanson, *The Twelfth-Century Renaissance* (Manchester, 1999), 116–17.
4. The phrase titles the classic study by R. I. Moore, *The Formation of a Persecuting Society: Authority and deviance in Western Europe, 950–1250* (2nd edn, Oxford, 2006).
5. On the development of persecution of heretics, ibid., 13–18. Moore, ibid., 13, incorrectly states that Christian burning of heretics had a precedent in a Christian emperor's burning of Priscillian in 4th-century Gaul, and on occasion I have carelessly echoed this. In fact, Priscillian suffered (a distinctly preferable) execution by sword, for practising magic.
6. For 7th-century Byzantine burnings, and the isolated later case of the burning of the Bogomil Basil, J. Hamilton and B. Hamilton (eds and trs), *Christian Dualist Heresies in the Byzantine world, c. 650–c. 1450* (Manchester and New York, 1998), 13, 175–80. For the introduction of burning at the stake to the Orthodox Church of Moscow, G. H. Williams, 'Protestants in the Ukraine during the period of the Polish-Lithuanian Commonwealth', *Harvard Ukrainian Studies* 2 i (1978), 41–72, at 50.
7. On Jude and allied New Testament texts, see above, Ch. 6, p. 109.
8. R. Abels and E. Harrison, 'The participation of women in Languedocian Catharism', *Mediaeval Studies* 41 (1979), 215–51. J. Arnold, 'Heresy and gender in the Middle Ages', in J. Bennett and R. Mazo Karras (eds), *The Oxford Book of Women and Gender in Medieval Europe* (Oxford, 2013), 496–510, at 505, does point out a qualified female exception to this general rule, late in the trajectory of Cathar activity, Arnauda de Lamothe, but effectively she had been forced by persecution to become an itinerant nun.
9. C. Tyerman, *God's War: A new history of the Crusades* (London, 2006), 563–605, provides a succinct account of the Albigensian Crusade.
10. E. Le Roy Ladurie, tr. B. Bray, *Montaillou: Cathars and Catholics in a French village 1294–1324* (London, 1978), 179. For examples from elsewhere, see Harvey, *Fires of Lust*, 156–7.

11. B. Hamilton, 'Cathar links with the Balkans and Byzantium', in A. Sennis (ed.), *Cathars in Question* (Woodbridge, 2016), 131–50, presents the evidence for the contacts. On the *Book of Two Principles*, D. d'Avray, 'The Cathars from non-Catholic sources', also in Sennis (ed.), *Cathars in Question*, 177–85, at 178–80.
12. R. I. Moore, *The War on Heresy: Faith and power in medieval Europe* (London, 2012), 238–40.
13. S. Hamilton, 'The Virgin Mary in Cathar thought', *JEH* 56 (2005), 24–49, esp. 24–8.
14. For lively discussion of the Moore thesis culminating in his *War on Heresy*, see essays in M. Frassetto (ed.), *Heresy and the Persecuting Society in the Middle Ages: Essays on the work of R. I. Moore* (Leiden, 2006), Sennis (ed.), *Cathars in Question*, and J.-L. Biget, S. Caucanas, M. Fournié and D. le Blévec (eds), *Le 'Catharisme' en questions* (Fanjeaux, 2020).
15. Moore, *War on Heresy*, 175–9; see also the account of Lambert in W. Simons, *Cities of Ladies: Beguine communities in the medieval Low Countries, 1200–1565* (Philadelphia, Pa., 2001), 24–35, which effectively disposes of the idea that he was the founder of the later Beguine movement.
16. On the concrete evidence for Valdes's career, P. Biller, 'Goodbye to Waldensianism?', *PP* 192 (2006), 3–34, at 13–14.
17. D. Elliott, *Spiritual Marriage: Sexual abstinence in medieval wedlock* (Princeton, NJ, 1983), 127–30, 140–42, 155–6.
18. Simons, *Cities of Ladies*, 22–4.
19. See especially Moore, *War on Heresy*, 136–9, 182, 283–4, 330.
20. Ibid., 215–19.
21. Ibid., 215–19, 277, 286, 314–17; Hamilton, 'Cathar links with the Balkans and Byzantium', 136–8.
22. For summary discussion of the ill-fated 'Spiritual Franciscans' and the followers of Gerardo Segarelli, see MacCulloch, *Christianity*, 410–11.
23. J.-L. Biget, 'Retour sur le "concile de Saint-Félix"', in Biget, et al. (eds), *Le 'Catharisme' en questions*, 81–110. For arguments nevertheless for its authenticity, see Hamilton, 'Cathar links with the Balkans and Byzantium', 140–43.
24. On English heresy, Moore, *War on Heresy*, 7–8; depressingly meticulous accounts are E. M. Rose, *The Murder of William of Norwich: The origins of the blood libel in medieval Europe* (Oxford, 2015) and R. R. Mundill, *England's Jewish Solution: Experiment and expulsion, 1262–1290* (Cambridge, 1998). For the wider and continuing story of the blood libel, see R. Po-chia Hsia, *The Myth of Ritual Murder: Jews and magic in Reformation Germany* (New Haven, Conn. and London, 1988).
25. For my own reminiscence of an example of one of these paintings in the Museo de Arte Antica in Lisbon, from an anonymous 16th-century Portuguese master, see MacCulloch, *Christianity*, 554–5. For a modern American example of this devotion to the Circumcision as one of the Sorrows of

Joseph, see the website of the National Sanctuary of our Sorrowful Mother, run by Servite Friars in Portland, Oregon, in St Joseph's Grove: https://thegrotto.org/septenary-of-st-joseph/ (accessed 27 Aug. 2023).

26. M. Barber, 'Lepers, Jews and Moslems: the plot to overthrow Christendom in 1321', *History* 66 (1981), 1–18.

27. M. D. Jordan, *The Invention of Sodomy in Christian Theology* (Chicago, 1997), 29. G. W. Olsen, *Of Sodomites, Effeminates, Hermaphrodites and Androgynes: Sodomy in the age of Peter Damian* (Toronto, 2011), 35–6, points out that Damian did not actually invent the word *sodomia*, an apparent coinage of the 9th-century Hincmar of Rheims.

28. J. Noonan, *Contraception: A history of its treatment by the Catholic theologians and canonists* (Cambridge, Mass., 1958), 172–3.

29. Boswell, *Christianity, Social Tolerance and Homosexuality*, 281–2, and see discussion of sodomitical 'othering' in Karras, *Sexuality in Medieval Europe*, 132–3.

30. M. Goodich, *The Unmentionable Vice: Homosexuality in the later medieval period* (Santa Barbara, Calif. and Oxford, 1979), 42–3. John Boswell is at his least reliable in his characteristic anxiety to minimize and chronologically postpone official Christian persecution in this period (cf. Boswell, *Christianity, Social Tolerance and Homosexuality*, 288–93); he is explicitly followed in that by Moore, *Formation of a Persecuting Society*, 92–8, 146–7. For balancing comment and background, see also H. Puff, 'Same-sex possibilities', in Bennett and Karras (eds), *Oxford Book of Women and Gender in Medieval Europe*, 379–95, and for the spread of punitive legislation into secular legal systems, Harvey, *Fires of Lust*, 126–8, and N. Malcolm, *Forbidden Desire in Early Modern Europe: Male–male sexual relations, 1400–1750* (Oxford, 2024), 129–40.

31. Bonaventure, *Opera Omnia* (9 vols, Florence, 1882–1902), ix, 122–3, Sermon XXII, *In nativitate Domini*: the wiping-out of sodomites both male and female, says Bonaventure, was the seventh of twelve miracles God worked at the time of Christ's birth. For the story's early and continuing connections to the friars, N. Bériou, *L'avènement des maîtres de la Parole: la prédication à Paris au XIIIe siècle* (2 vols, Paris, 1998), i, 333–5; R. W. Granger (ed. and tr.), *Jacobus de Voragine, The Golden Legend: Readings on the saints* (Princeton, NJ, 2012), 41 (6. *The Birth of our Lord Jesus Christ*). My discussions with David d'Avray and Robin Ward on this topic have been most helpful.

32. S. Powell (ed.), *John Mirk's Festial*, Early English Text Society 334, 335 (2 vols, Oxford, 2010, 2011), i, 25 (no. 6, *Nativity of Christ*, ll. 79–92); ii, 284; cf. also notes ibid., ii, 313 (to no. 16. *Sexagesima*, ll. 102–7).

33. On Bernardino, Malcolm, *Forbidden Desire in Early Modern Europe*, 115, 192. For the legend's casual deployment by the idiosyncratically 'sex-positive' mystic Agnes Blannbekin, see U. Wiethaus (ed. and tr.), *Agnes Blannbekin, Viennese Beguine: Life and revelations* (Cambridge, 2002), 8 and text

sections 193–4, and for its intellectual ancestry before the very popular late 15th-century catechism by the German Franciscan Observant, Dietrich Kolde (running to forty editions in two centuries), B.-U. Hergemöller, tr. J. Phillips, *Sodom and Gomorrah: On the everyday reality and persecution of homosexuals in the Middle Ages* (London, 2001), 146–59.

34. Levin, *Sex and Society in the World of the Orthodox Slavs*, 197–203; Karras, *Sexuality in Medieval Europe*, 135.
35. Levin, *Sex and Society in the World of the Orthodox Slavs*, 204.
36. M. Camille, 'The pose of the queer: Dante's gaze, Brunetto Latini's body', in G. Burger and S. F. Kruger (eds), *Queering the Middle Ages* (Minneapolis, Minn., 2001), 57–86, at 76–8. On the tomb and John XXII's erection of various chapels in Avignon Cathedral, see L.-H. Labande, 'Cathédrale Notre-Dame-des-Doms', in *Congrès archéologique de France: LXXVIe session tenue à Avignon en 1909 par la Société française pour la conservation des monuments historiques* (1910), i, 7–16.
37. This is a logical confusion perceptible in Peter Damian: Olsen, *Of Sodomites, Effeminates, Hermaphrodites and Androgynes*, 322–3 and ch. 9.
38. MacCulloch, *Christianity*, 471–3.
39. On Dunstan's copy of *Ars Amatoria*, see letter by D. Ganz in *Times Literary Supplement*, 18 May 2007, 17; the MS is now Bodleian Library Oxford MS Auct.F.4.32. T. J. Garbáty, '*Pamphilus, de Amore*: an introduction and translation', *Chaucer Review* 2 (1967), 108–34. For later medieval examples, see C. Harris, *Obscene Pedagogies: Transgressive talk and sexual education in late medieval Britain* (Ithaca, NY, 2018).
40. C. Morris, *The Discovery of the Individual, 1050–1200* (London, 1972); helpful discussion of the problem in Swanson, *Twelfth-Century Renaissance*, 139–51.
41. Abelard on sex, quoting from his *Ethics* by van Houts, *Married Life in the Middle Ages*, 190. On Abelard and the ordination of women, G. Macy, 'Heloise, Abelard and the ordination of abbesses', *JEH* 57 (2006), 16–32.
42. Bullough, *Sexual Variance in Society and History*, 224–39 and K. El-Rouayheb, *Before Homosexuality in the Arab-Islamic world, 1500–1800* (Chicago and London, 2005), esp. Introduction; T. Carmi (ed. and tr.), *The Penguin Book of Hebrew Verse* (London, 1981), 298, 313, 325–6, 344–5, 361–3; Boswell, *Christianity, Social Tolerance and Homosexuality*, 233–4.
43. Boswell, *Christianity, Social Tolerance and Homosexuality*, 235–66; for Abelard's *planctus* over Jonathan, ibid., 238.
44. On Baldric's verse, Boswell, *Christianity, Social Tolerance and Homosexuality*, 244–7. I am indebted to Helen King for pointing me to the Ovidian reference.
45. M. de Jong, *In Samuel's Image: Child oblation in the early medieval West* (Leiden and New York, 1996), 297.
46. J. LeClercq, tr. C. Misrahi, *The Love of Learning and the Desire for God: A study in monastic culture* (New York, 1982), 84–6. On the lack of female

commentary, see S. D. Moore, 'The Song of Songs in the history of sexuality', *CH* 69 (2000), 328–49, at 331–2n.

47. A fine study, with particular reference to Aelred of Rievaulx and Bernard of Clairvaux, is J. P. Haseldine, 'Monastic friendship in action in the twelfth century', in A. Classen and M. Sandidge (eds), *Friendship in the Middle Ages and Early Modern Age: Explorations of a fundamental ethical discourse* (Berlin and New York, 2010), 349–94.

48. Aelred, *Speculum Caritatis* 1.112, qu. in Karras, *Sexuality in Medieval Europe*, 144.

49. 'Solus ego patior quod solent pariter pati qui si diligent, cum se amittunt': D. Sabersky, 'Affectum, confessus sum, et non negavi: reflections on the expression of affect in the 26th sermon on the Song of Songs of Bernard of Clairvaux', in E. R. Elder (ed.), *The Joy of Learning and the Love of God: Studies in honor of Jean Leclercq* (Kalamazoo, Mich., 1995), 187–216, at 201, 214 n. 85.

50. S. Düll, A. Luttrell and M. Keen, 'Faithful Unto Death: The tomb slab of Sir William Neville and Sir John Clanvowe, Constantinople 1391', *Antiquaries Journal* 71 (1991), 174–90; discussion of other examples of joint tombs in Puff, 'Same-sex possibilities', 382, and A. Bray, *The Friend* (Chicago and London, 2006), ch. 1, with later examples in chs. 6 and 7. For background on sworn brotherhood, see C. Rapp, *Brother-making in Late Antiquity and Byzantium: Monks, laymen and Christian ritual* (Oxford, 2016), 21–5.

51. Macy, 'Heloise, Abelard and the ordination of abbesses', 28–30; see also his extended argument in G. Macy, *The Hidden History of Women's Ordination: Female clergy in the medieval West* (New York and Oxford, 2008).

52. John ap Rice to Thomas Cromwell, 23 Aug. 1535: National Archives, Kew, SP 1/95 f.148. I have modernized spellings but not altered the words.

53. G. Chaucer, General Prologue to *The Canterbury Tales*, ll.124–6 (modernized spellings).

54. G. Warnock (ed.), *Revelations of Divine Love recorded by Julian Anchoress at Norwich . . . 1373 . . .* (London, 1901), 3 (1st Revelation, Ch. 2); 10 (1st Revelation, Ch. 5).

55. On Adelheid (also known as Uchthilt von Frowenberg/Frabenberg), see M. Rubin, 'Epilogue', in M. Dzon and T. M. Kenney (eds), *The Christ Child in Medieval Culture: Alpha es et O!* (Toronto, 2012), 293–7, at 296, and J. Carroll, 'Subversive obedience: images of spiritual reform by and for fifteenth-century nuns', in T. Martin (ed.), *Reassessing the Roles of Women as 'Makers' of Medieval Art and Architecture* (2 vols, Leiden, 2012), ii, 705–38, at 726–8.

56. E.g. Wiethaus (ed. and tr.), *Agnes Blannbekin, Viennese Beguine*, 36–7 (chs. 37–8).

57. G. Parsons, *The Cult of Saint Catherine of Siena: A study in civil religion* (Aldershot and Burlington, Vt., 2008), 17–18, 37–8.

58. R. I. Moore, *The First European Revolution c.970–1215* (Oxford, 2000), 33.
59. D. C. Coleman, *The Economy of England 1450–1750* (Oxford, 1977), 20; the definitive study of the city's parish church provision is J. Schofield et al., 'Saxon and medieval parish churches in the City of London', *Transactions of the London and Middlesex Archaeological Society* 45 (1994), 23–146.
60. R. Gilchrist, *Medieval Life: Archaeology and the life course* (Woodbridge, 2012), 71–2, 101–3.
61. J. Rossiaud, 'Prostitution, sex and society in French towns in the fifteenth century', in Ariès and Béjin (eds), *Western Sexuality*, 76–94, at 83–6. For a study of a similar male group culture among the 15th- and 16th-century English legal profession concentrated in the capital city, see A. McVitty, 'Homosociality, sexual misconduct and gendered violence in England's pre-modern legal profession', *PP* 261 (2023), 86–117.
62. G. Ruggiero, *The Boundaries of Eros: Sex crime and sexuality in Renaissance Venice* (New York and Oxford, 1985), 89–108, 156.
63. Ibid., ch. 6; B. Krekić, 'Abominandum crimen: punishment of homosexuals in Renaissance Dubrovnik', *Viator* 18 (1987), 337–46.
64. C. L. Polecritti, *Preaching Peace in Renaissance Italy: Bernardino of Siena and his audience* (Washington, DC, 2000), 52–3; on 'florentzen', Karras, *Sexuality in Medieval Europe*, 138.
65. M. J. Rocke, *Forbidden Friendships: Homosexuality and male culture in Renaissance Florence* (New York and Oxford, 1996), 115, and see also 88, 94–7, 100–108, 112–32; Malcolm, *Forbidden Desire in Early Modern Europe*, 170–71. Also useful is M. J. Rocke, 'Sodomites in fifteenth-century Tuscany: the views of Bernardino of Siena', *JOH* 16 (1988), 7–32.
66. S. Evangelisti, *Nuns: A history of convent life, 1450–1700* (Oxford and New York, 2007), 5. For an interesting analysis of the implications of archaeology from the most prominent nunnery in Lisbon, see L. U. Afonso, M. V. Gomes and R. V. Gomes, 'Chinese pornography in a Portuguese nunnery: on a transitional period blue and white porcelain bowl recovered from the Santana Convent (Lisbon)', *Antiquaries Journal* 103 (2023), 315–32.
67. This is the overall theme of Malcolm, *Forbidden Desire in Early Modern Europe*. N. Malcolm, 'Forbidden love in Istanbul: patterns of male–male sexual relations in the early-modern Mediterranean world', *PP* 257 (2022), 55–88, at 79–81, sums up his critique of contrasting main arguments in A. Bray, *Homosexuality in Renaissance England* (London, 1982).
68. Karras, *Sexuality in Medieval Europe*, 69. R. Mazo Karras, *Common Women: Prostitution and sexuality in medieval England* (Oxford, 1996), 8–12, usefully discusses the terminology of prostitution over a range of activities.
69. J. Brundage, *Law, Sex and Christian Society in Medieval Europe* (Chicago, 1987), 106, quoting Augustine, *De Ordine* 2.4.12 [*PL* 32, 1000]: 'aufer meretrices de rebus humanis, turbaueris omnia libidinibus; constitue matronarum

loco, labe ac dedecore dehonestaueris'; on Ptolemy's amplification, which he wrongly attributed to Augustine himself (*De regimini principum ad Regem Cypri*, 4.14.6), see Karras, *Sexuality in Medieval Europe*, 106, 188.

70. P. G. Walsh (ed.), *Augustine: De Bono Coniugali; De Sancta Virginitate* (Oxford, 2001), 25–6 [11–12].
71. Karras, *Common Women*, 90, 132–3.
72. On municipal brothels, see Harvey, *Fires of Lust*, 167–9, and Karras, *Common Women*, 35–43. On the Notre Dame confrontation, J. W. Baldwin, *The Language of Sex: Five voices from Northern France around 1200* (Chicago, 1994), 81–2. E. Wurtzel, 'Passionate encounters, public healing: medieval urban bathhouses in northern France', *French Historical Studies* 46 (2023), 331–60.
73. Harvey, *Fires of Lust*, 166–7; Karras, *Common Women*, 34–5.
74. See for instance on the Franciscans B. Roest, *Order and Disorder: The Poor Clares between foundation and reform* (Leiden, 2013), esp. Chs. 1 and 2, and on the Dominicans M.-L. Ehrenschwendtner, 'Virtual pilgrimages? Enclosure and the practice of piety at St Katherine's Convent, Augsburg', *JEH* 50 (2009), 45–73, at 57, 61.
75. E. Makowski, *Canon Law and Cloistered Women: Periculoso and its commentators* (Washington, DC, 1997), is a fine study of the results and limitations of the bull.
76. Simons, *Cities of Ladies*, 6–10. My account of the Beguines is taken from this exemplary monograph unless otherwise stated.
77. Ibid., 143, and on the origins of the name 'Beguine', ibid., 121–3.
78. D'Avray, *Medieval Marriage*, ch. 1, 204.
79. Ibid., 69–70 and nn. I am grateful to Prof. d'Avray for our discussions on medieval marriage: he makes the point to me that discussion of sex for pleasure was more rigorist and negative in medieval Latin writings that the laity would never read than the message that they heard from the pulpit.
80. Text tr. by T. Berkeley, in *Aelred of Rievaulx 1. Treatises; Pastoral Prayer*, Cistercian Fathers Series 2 (Kalamazoo, Mich., 1971), 3–39, and for the remembrance of Yvo, ibid., 3–4n.
81. M. Rubin, *Mother of God: A history of the Virgin Mary* (London, 2009), 228–36, 252–5, 301–2; on the very late medieval case of Regensburg, see A. F. Creasman, 'The Virgin Mary against the Jews: anti-Jewish polemic in the pilgrimage to the Schöne Maria of Regensburg, 1519–25', *SCJ* 33 (2002), 963–79, and below, Ch. 14, p. 330.
82. For a good overview of Our Lady of Pity, R. Marks, *Image and Devotion in Late Medieval England* (Stroud, 2004), ch. 6.
83. D. Spivey Ellington, *From Sacred Body to Angelic Soul: Understanding Mary in late medieval and early modern Europe* (Washington, DC, 2001), 193. For a sprightly discussion of medieval views on swooning in both Our Lady and Mary Magdalen, see N. Booth, *Swoon: A poetics of passing out* (Manchester, 2021), ch. 1.

84. For such themes of dramas riskily playing around with Mary's sexual reputation, see Harvey, *Fires of Lust*, 224–5.
85. Rubin, *Mother of God*, 323–7; M. Rubin, 'Europe remade: purity and danger in late medieval Europe', *TRHS* 6th ser. 11 (2001), 101–24, at 113–14. On Joseph as a name, R. Bireley, *The Refashioning of Catholicism, 1450–1700* (Basingstoke, 1999), 113, and for his Counter-Reformation career, C. Villaseñor Black, 'Love and marriage in the Spanish Empire: depictions of holy matrimony and gender discourses in the 17th century', *SCJ* 32 (2001), 637–67, esp. 637, 645.
86. N. Orme, 'Church and chapel in medieval England', *TRHS* 6th ser. 6 (1996), 75–102, at 89–91.
87. Marks, *Image and Devotion in Late Medieval England*, 148–53. In my own University of Oxford in the twentieth century, female Anglican and Catholic scholars were impressed by Anne's commitment to teaching and named a college for women after her.
88. K. L. Jansen, *The Making of the Magdalen: Preaching and popular devotion in the later Middle Ages* (Princeton, NJ, 2001), ch. 1.
89. Karras, *Common Women*, 120–27; on Mary Magdalen's iconography, J. Dillenberger, *Style and Content in Christian Art* (London, 1965), 72, 83–4, 92–5, 145–6.
90. On Loreto, see A. Vauchez, 'Saints and pilgrimages, new and old', in M. Rubin and W. Simons (eds), *The Cambridge History of Christianity 4: Christianity in western Europe c.1100–c.1500* (Cambridge, 2009), 324–39, at 338.
91. Qu. by d'Avray, *Medieval Marriage*, 70. For background comment, suggesting a reaction to Catharism in such pronouncements, see Karras, *Sexuality in Medieval Europe*, 48, 72.
92. N. Orme, *Medieval Children* (New Haven, Conn. and London, 2001), 9. A thorough refutation of Stone's approach, as exemplified in L. Stone, *The Family, Sex, and Marriage in England* (New York, 1977), is S. Ozment, *Ancestors: The loving family in old Europe* (Cambridge, Mass., 2001).
93. Rubin, 'Europe remade: purity and danger in late medieval Europe', 106.

14. THE SECOND REVOLUTION: THE REFORMATION CHASM

1. I give an account of such an episode from the English Province of the Order, surprisingly and ironically launching Thomas Cromwell's career promoting Boston indulgences rivalling the Augustinians' own salesmanship, in D. MacCulloch, *Thomas Cromwell: A life* (London, 2018), 31–4, 40–42. It is important to distinguish the Austin Friars from the earlier monastic formation of the Augustinian Canons Regular. They both esteemed Augustine of Hippo, but not each other.

2. A good discussion for one region is R. Rex, 'The friars in the English Reformation', in P. Marshall and A. Ryrie (eds), *The Beginnings of English Protestantism* (Cambridge, 2002), 38–59.
3. An original account of this quite extraordinary turnaround in Luther's career is A. Pettegree, *Brand Luther: How an unheralded monk turned his small town into a center of publishing, made himself the most famous man in Europe – and started the Protestant Reformation* (New York, 2015).
4. O. Chadwick, *The Early Reformation on the Continent* (Oxford, 2001), 165, 168–70, and S. Evangelisti, *Nuns: A history of convent life, 1450–1700* (Oxford and New York, 2007), 39. The extensive work of Henrike Lähnemann has delightfully revealed the life of Cistercian nunneries in the Lutheran society of northern Germany, surviving to the present day; it can be sampled in H. Lähnemann, 'From devotional aids to antiquarian objects: the Prayer Books of Medingen', in E. Stead (ed.), *Reading Books and Prints as Cultural Objects* (Cham, 2018), 33–56.
5. The lazy and inadequate description of Reformed Protestants as 'Calvinists' after John Calvin is to be avoided, and I use it here only when unavoidable.
6. On the intricate conundrum of Erasmus's name, see discussion by Percy Allen: P. S. Allen, H. M. Allen and H. W. Garrod (eds), *Opus Epistolarum Des. Erasmi Roterodami* . . . (12 vols, Oxford, 1906–58), i, 73n.
7. R. J. Schoeck, *Erasmus of Europe: The making of a humanist 1467–1500* (Edinburgh, 1990), is a reliable account of Erasmus's early years, except that it is too indulgent to this master of self-concealment, and shies away from the reality of Erasmus's relationship with Servatius Roger. Such nervousness did not distort earlier sensible if not always sympathetic comment: Allen, Allen and Garrod (eds), *Opus Epistolarum Des. Erasmi Roterodami*, i, app. III, 584–6; J. Huizinga, tr. F. Hopman and B. Flower, *Erasmus of Rotterdam; with a Selection from the Letters of Erasmus* (London, 1952), 10–12; G. Nuttall, writing in *JEH* 26 (1975), 403, briskly reviewing R. A. B. Mynors (tr.), and D. F. S. Thomson and W. K. Ferguson (eds), *The Correspondence of Erasmus: Letters 1 to 141: 1484 to 1500* (*CWE*, i).
8. A sprightly and clear-sighted discussion of this is B. Cummings, 'Gay Erasmus', *Renaissance Quarterly* 77 (2024), 789–840; we await Prof. Cummings's full biography of Erasmus.
9. D. MacCulloch, *Thomas Cranmer: A life* (New Haven, Conn. and London, rev. edn, 2016), 34–5, 37, 67, 98–9, 291. The Polish future reformer Johannes à Lasco (Jan Łaski) was one of Erasmus's charming young men with brains, who bought Erasmus's library in reversion, effectively to provide him with a pension: B. Hall, *John à Lasco 1499–1560: A Pole in Reformation England*, Friends of Dr Williams's Library 25 (London, 1971), 13–14.
10. Allen, Allen and Garrod (eds), *Opus Epistolarum Des. Erasmi Roterodami*, iii, 376, no. 858, l. 561; writing to Paul Volz. Cf. a similar, more extended

passage in a letter to Servatius Roger in 1514, ibid., i, 567–8, no. 296, ll. 70–88.

11. For the complicated history of this work, see *CWE*, xxv/xxvi: *Literary and Educational Writings*, ed. J. K. Sowards (1985), 528–9, and for one version of the text, ibid., 129–45.
12. *CWE*, xxv/xxvi: *Literary and Educational Writings*, 130, 137.
13. See his response to Clichthove in *CWE*, lxxxiii: *Controversies*, ed. G. Bedouelle (1998), 115–48, and for an earlier response to a critic, *CWE*, lxxi: *Controversies*, ed. J. K. Sowards (1993), 85–96.
14. On Zwingli's marriage and problems with celibacy, see B. Gordon, *God's Armed Prophet: Zwingli* (New Haven, Conn. and London, 2021), 42–3, 68–70. There is understandable Protestant eagerness to claim the first clerical marriage. The citing of Kaspar Adler from Augsburg in 1516 or Paul Speratus from Salzburg in 1517 looks like simple historical confusions with other dates in their careers, but Jakob Knade of Gdańsk and Toruń in 1518 seems more plausible: M. E. Plummer, *From Priest's Whore to Pastor's Wife: Clerical marriage and the process of reform in the early German Reformation* (Abingdon and New York, 2012), 52n.
15. Gordon, *God's Armed Prophet*, 28.
16. Luther to Spalatin, 6 Dec. 1525: *D. Martin Luthers Werke* (Weimar, 1883–) [*Weimarer Ausgabe* BR3], *Briefwechsel*, iii (1933), no. 952, pp. 634–5. 'Ego quoque, cum diuinauero diem, qua has acceperis, mox ea nocte simili opere meam amabo in tui memoriam et tibi par pari referam.' Earlier editions omitted this sentence.
17. *D. Martin Luthers Werke* [*Weimarer Ausgabe* TR 1], *Tischreden 1531–46*, i (1912), no. 55, p. 19: 'Viri habent lata pectora et parva femora, ideo habent sapientiam. Mulieres habent angusta pectora et lata femora. Mulier debet *oikouros*; id creatio indicat, habent enim latum podicem et femora, *das sie sollen still sizen*.' The comment was recorded by Luther's associate Veit Dietrich sometime in 1531.
18. J. Dempsey Douglass, 'The image of God in women as seen in Luther and Calvin', in Børresen (ed.), *Image of God*, 236–66, at 246–7; J. Calvin, *Commentary on the Epistles of Paul the Apostle to the Corinthians* (tr. and ed. J. Pringle, 2 vols, Calvin Translation Society, 1848–9), i, 230–35 [on 1 Cor. 7. 6–8]; J. Calvin, *Commentaries on the Four Last Books of Moses . . . in the Form of a Harmony* (tr. and ed. C. W. Bingham, 4 vols, Calvin Translation Society, 1852–5), iii, 84, 95–6 [on Deut. 24.5; Lev. 20.18].
19. W. Breul, 'Celibacy – marriage – unmarriage: the controversy over celibacy and clerical marriage in the early Reformation', in D. M. Luebke and M. Lindemann (eds), *Mixed Matches: Transgressive unions in Germany from the Reformation to the Enlightenment* (New York and Oxford, 2014), 31–44.
20. Plummer, *From Priest's Whore to Pastor's Wife*, the conclusions of which are usefully summarized in M. E. Plummer, '"Partner in his calamities": pastors' wives, married nuns and the experience of clerical marriage in the

early German Reformation', *Gender and History* 20 (2008), 207–27. A fine summary study of von Bora is J. C. Smith, 'Katharina von Bora through five centuries: a historiography', *SCJ* 30 (1999), 745–73.

21. H. Selderhuis, *Marriage and Divorce in the Thought of Martin Bucer* (Kirksville, Mo., 1999), 116–28, esp. 125; on Oecolampadius, Plummer, '"Partner in his calamities"', 217.
22. Chadwick, *Early Reformation on the Continent*, 147.
23. D. MacCulloch, *Tudor Church Militant: Edward VI and the Protestant Reformation* (London, 1999), 77, 128, 186–7; for background, E. J. Carlson, *Marriage and the English Reformation* (Oxford and Cambridge, Mass., 1994), 50–66. On Tillotson, J. Gregory, 'Gender and the clerical profession in England, 1660–1850', in Swanson (ed.), *Gender and Christian Religion*, 235–71, at 258: to add to the comedy, Tillotson had married a niece of that nemesis of the episcopal Church of England, Oliver Cromwell.
24. I record my childhood pleasure at visits to the family of the resident successor to the last Copinger-Hill, playing in Buxhall Rectory attics.
25. G. Murdock, *Calvinism on the Frontier 1600–1660: International Calvinism and the Reformed Church in Hungary and Transylvania* (Oxford, 2000), 231. I have myself observed this elevated ministerial status in rural Transylvanian villages in the 2000s – and it was a pastor of the Reformed Church, László Tőkés, who triggered the Romanian revolution of 1989 against the regime of Nicolae Ceauşescu.
26. P. Benedict, *Christ's Churches Purely Reformed: A social history of Calvinism* (New Haven, Conn. and London, 2002), 436.
27. H. Chadwick, *East and West: The making of a rift in the Church, from apostolic times until the Council of Florence* (Oxford, 2003), 12.
28. MacCulloch, *Tudor Church Militant*, 145, on the mid-Tudor Catholic propagandist Miles Huggarde. On Chrysostom and syneisactism, above, Ch.9, pp. 181–2.
29. R. Rex, *The Theology of John Fisher* (Cambridge, 1990), ch. 4.
30. Luther, *Address to the German Nobility* 75: *Weimarer Ausgabe*, vi, no. 447, p. 18, and n. For an illustration of a copy of Michael Ostendorfer's 1520 print of the Regensburg pilgrimage, with an added hostile MS comment of 1523 by Albrecht Dürer, S. Michalski, *The Reformation and the Visual Arts: The Protestant image question in western and eastern Europe* (London, 1993), pl. 3. See also above, Ch. 13, pp. 311–12.
31. Matt. 12: G. E. Corrie (ed.), *Sermons by Hugh Latimer ...* (Parker Society, 1844), 383; Luke 2.41–51: G. E. Corrie (ed.), *Sermons and Remains of Latimer ...* (Parker Society, 1845), 158.
32. J. Ayre (ed.), *The Works of John Jewel, Bishop of Salisbury* (Parker Society, 2 vols. in 4, 1845–50), vol. 3, 578. Calvin's commentary on Luke quoted in W. J. Bouwsma, *Calvin: A sixteenth century portrait* (New York and Oxford, 1988), 123, 267.

33. Ezek. 44.2; Isa. 7.14.
34. L.-E. Halkin, *Erasmus: A critical biography* (Oxford, 1993), 225: cf. *Modus Orandi Deum: Opera Omnia Desiderii Erasmi Roterodami* (9 vols, Amsterdam, 1969–), i, 146–7.
35. I expand on these themes in D. MacCulloch, 'Mary and sixteenth-century Protestants', in Swanson (ed.), *Church and Mary*, 191–217, repr. in D. MacCulloch, *All Things Made New: Writings on the Reformation* (London, 2016), 32–54.
36. K. Maas, 'Lex, Rex and sex: the bigamy of Philipp of Hesse and the Lutheran recourse to natural law', in E. Gebarowski-Shafer, A. Null and A. Ryrie (eds), *Contesting Orthodoxies in the History of Christianity: Essays in honour of Diarmaid MacCulloch* (Woodbridge, 2021), 56–76, at 59–60. I follow Maas's excellent account below.
37. Ibid., 70.
38. Ibid., 64–71.
39. C. S. Mackay (ed. and tr.), *False Prophets and Preachers: Henry Gresbeck's account of the Anabaptist Kingdom of Münster* (University Park, Pa., 2016), 4, 31–2, 110–20, 122–31, 135–6, 213–15, 256. Gresbeck's is the only eyewitness narrative of events, and in most respects is to be preferred to other primary sources.
40. D. Spivey Ellington, *From Sacred Body to Angelic Soul: Understanding Mary in late medieval and early modern Europe* (Washington, DC, 2001), 184–5.
41. P. McNair, 'Ochino's apology: three gods or three wives?', *History* 60 (1975), 353–73.
42. A. Jelsma, 'A "Messiah for women": religious commotion in the north-east of Switzerland, 1525–1526', in W. J. Sheils and D. Wood (eds), *Women in the Church*, Studies in Church History 27 (Woodbridge, 1990), 295–306, at 302.
43. W. Harrison, 'The role of women in Anabaptist thought and practice: the Hutterite experience of the 16th and 17th centuries', *SCJ* 23 (1992), 49–70, at 54.
44. Ibid., 57–8.
45. M. Todd, *The Culture of Protestantism in Early Modern Scotland* (New Haven, Conn. and London, 2002), 267–8.
46. Selderhuis, *Marriage and Divorce in the Thought of Martin Bucer*; C. Euler, 'Heinrich Bullinger, marriage, and the English Reformation: *The Christen state of Matrimonye* in England, 1540–53', *SCJ* 34 (2003), 367–94, where she cautions that some of the several English versions of this originally German work silently and prudently left out the section on divorce.
47. I discuss such cases in MacCulloch, *Reformation*, 655–6.
48. B. Cottret, tr. M. W. McDonald, *Calvin: A biography* (Grand Rapids, Mich. and Edinburgh, 2000), 184.
49. For the failed divorce provisions, see G. Bray (ed.), *Tudor Church Reform: The Henrician Canons of 1535 and the Reformatio Legum Ecclesiasticarum*,

Church of England Record Society 9 (Woodbridge and Rochester, NY, 2000), 264–79, and Introduction, xli–lxxvi. On Milton, Bullough, *Sexual Variance in Society and History*, 465.

50. For 'especial liturgy', see H. Barrow, *A Brief Discoverie of the False Church*, in L. H. Carlson (ed.), *The Writings of Henry Barrow 1587–90* (London, 1962), 453. For examples of wedding practice by this group of Separatist martyrs, see L. H. Carlson (ed.), *The Writings of John Greenwood and Henry Barrow 1591–1593* (London, 1970), 338; L. H. Carlson (ed.), *The Writings of John Greenwood 1587–1590* (London, 1962), 24–5.

51. P. Bonomi, *Under the Cope of Heaven: Religion, society and politics in Colonial America* (Oxford, 2003), 69.

52. See the useful summary account of Lutheran practice in S. C. Karant-Nunn, *The Reformation of Ritual: An interpretation of early modern Germany* (London and New York, 1997), 13–42.

53. C. Harline, *Sunday: A history of the first day from Babylonia to the Super-Bowl* (New York, 2007), 82–3; Todd, *Culture of Protestantism in Early Modern Scotland*, 73–4, 267–75.

54. For a preliminary discussion of this, D. MacCulloch, 'Roods, screens and weddings', *JEH* 63 (2022), 368–81. The post-Reformation English screens have often been taken as evidence of Catholic religious sympathy, but their only architectural parallel is in the parish churches of the Dutch Reformed Church: J. Kroesen, 'Accommodating Calvinism: the appropriation of medieval interiors for Protestant worship in the Netherlands after the Reformation', in J. Harasimowicz (ed.), *Protestantischer Kirchenbau der frühen Neuzeit in Europa: Grundlagen und neue Forschungskonzepte* (Regensburg, 2015), 81–98, esp. 86.

55. J. Wickham Legg, *Ecclesiological Essays* (London, 1905), 200–205, collects some near-contemporary Catholic examples of Cranmer's theme, presumably from some common earlier source. I am indebted to Robin Ward for this reference.

56. R. Heber and C. P. Eden (eds), *The whole works of the Right Rev. Jeremy Taylor . . .* (12 vols, London, 1847–54), v, 224. Cf. Taylor's allusion to a Greek infant enticed off a dangerous precipice by 'his mother's pap': ibid., v, 216–17; on the 'fontinels', ibid., ii, 75, and see rather acerbic commentary in R. Askew, *Muskets and Altars: Jeremy Taylor and the last of the Anglicans* (London, 1997), 57–9.

57. H. J. Schroeder (ed. and tr.), *Canons and Decrees of the Council of Trent* (London, 1941), 182 [Canon 10 on the Sacrament of Matrimony, 1563].

58. R. Bellarmine, tr. by R. Haydock, *An ample declaration of the Christian doctrine: composed in Italian by the renowned Cardinal: Card. Bellarmine* ('Roan', 1604?), 257–8; for other Catholic examples, Spivey Ellington, *From Sacred Body to Angelic Soul*, 168. Heber and Eden (eds), *The whole works of the Right Rev. Jeremy Taylor*, v, 212 (my italics).

59. Summary discussion of the various unions up to Brest in MacCulloch, *Christianity*, 275–7, 533–6; and for the influence on Trent of the previous agreement with the Armenians on the sacraments at the Council of Florence (1439), J. W. O'Malley, *Trent: What happened at the Council* (Cambridge, Mass. and London, 2013), 119.
60. For the tangled jurisdictional situation in the Church of the East, see C. Baumer, *The Church of the East: An illustrated history of Assyrian Christianity* (London and New York, 2006), 248–9. For Pope Pius IV's invitations in 1561 to Orthodox and Oriental Orthodox patriarchs and attempts to reach the Metropolitan of Moscow, O'Malley, *Trent*, 169; for Trent's discussions of the vernacular in relation to the Glagolitic Rite of central European Orthodoxy, see F. J. Thomson, 'The legacy of SS Cyril and Methodios in the Counter-Reformation', in E. Konstantinou (ed.), *Methodios und Kyrillos in ihrer europäischen Dimension* (Frankfurt-am-Main and Oxford, 2005), 85–247, at 102–53.
61. Schroeder (ed. and tr.), *Canons and Decrees of the Council of Trent*, 182 [Canon 9 on the Sacrament of Matrimony, 1563]; 148, 150 [Doctrine of the Mass, ch. 8; Canon 9, 1562]. J. W. O'Malley, *Four Cultures of the West* (Cambridge, Mass., 2004), 113–14, comments usefully on the muted tones of these decrees, though he does not discuss their eastwards dimension.
62. J. R. Farr, *Authority and Sexuality in Early Modern Burgundy* (New York and Oxford, 1995), 73–4; for the earlier execution of a priest and nun in Rome by the ultra-rigorist Sixtus V in 1590, J. Christopoulos, *Abortion in Early Modern Italy* (Cambridge, Mass., 2021), 137. On a contrasting slow pace of change in central Europe, R. Pörtner, *The Counter-Reformation in Central Europe: Styria 1580–1630* (Oxford, 2001), 4, 97–9, 182, 188.
63. P. Caraman, *Ignatius Loyola: A biography of the founder of the Jesuits* (New York, 1990), provides details not otherwise referenced below.
64. For further comment, see MacCulloch, *Christianity*, 661–2; on prostitute rescue work embarrassment, O. Hufton, 'Altruism and reciprocity: the early Jesuits and their female patrons', *Renaissance Studies* 15 (2001), 328–53, at 333.
65. Hufton, 'Altruism and reciprocity', 336, 340–41. The surviving son of this marriage, inheriting his father's title of Duke of Parma, played a crucial role in the Counter-Reformation in the Netherlands as Governor of the Habsburg possessions for twenty-one years.
66. J. W. O'Malley, *The First Jesuits* (Cambridge, Mass., 1993), 306–7.
67. On the Society and Protestantism, ibid., 274–5, 278; on education, ibid., ch. 6.
68. Caraman, *Ignatius Loyola*, 135–7; Hufton, 'Altruism and reciprocity', 337.
69. A good account of Ward is provided by P. Harriss, 'Mary Ward in her own writings', *Recusant History* 30 (2010), 229–39; I am also indebted to my conversations about Ward with Gemma Simmonds. On Stackpole and

Limerick, see B. McShane, 'Negotiating religious change and conflict: female religious communities in early modern Ireland, *c.*1530–*c.*1641', *British Catholic History* 33 (2017), 357–82, at 370.

70. Q. Mazzonis, *Spirituality, Gender, and the Self in Renaissance Italy: Angela Merici and the Company of St Ursula (1474–1540)* (Washington, DC, 2007).
71. See commentary and text of one late medieval version of the legend in K. A. Winstead (ed.), *Chaste Passions: Medieval English virgin martyr legends* (Ithaca, NY and London, 2000), 164–8.
72. For an introduction to the Ursulines, see Evangelisti, *Nuns*, chs. 6 and 7.
73. O. Hufton, 'The widow's mite and other strategies: funding the Catholic Reformation', *TRHS* 6th ser. 8 (1998), 117–37, at 134–6.
74. On the Daughters of Charity, founded by Louise de Marillac and the priest Vincent de Paul, see Evangelisti, *Nuns*, 224–30. For further examples of similar work also involving Canada, see E. Rapley, *The Dévotes: Women and Church in seventeenth century France* (Montreal, 1990), esp. chs. 4, 5.
75. K. Liebreich, *Fallen Order: A history* (London, 2004), from which the outline of this story is taken.
76. Ibid., 75.
77. Ibid., 8, 78, 213–14. The Piarists were of course not unique as a religious Order in which sexual abuse took place; what was exceptional was the way in which they were so quickly and thoroughly subverted by abusers. For a study of cases of abuse and sexual misdemeanour in the pre-1773 Society of Jesus across the world, see U. L. Lehner, *Inszenierte Keuschheit: Sexualdelikte in der Gesellschaft Jesu im 17. und 18. Jahrhundert* (Berlin and Boston, Mass., 2024).
78. B. B. Warfield, *Calvin and Augustine* (Philadelphia, Pa., 1956), 332.
79. R. Bireley, *The Refashioning of Catholicism, 1450–1700* (Basingstoke, 1999), 77; Melanchthon's thought on the subject is well summarized in J. Estes, 'The role of godly magistrates in the Church: Melanchthon as Luther's interpreter and collaborator', *CH* 67 (1998), 463–83.
80. S. Lipscomb, *The Voices of Nîmes: Women, sex, and marriage in Reformation Languedoc* (Oxford, 2019), 113–14.
81. W. Gibson and J. Begiato, *Sex and the Church in the Long Eighteenth Century: Religion, Enlightenment and the sexual revolution* (London and New York, 2017), 20–21; they note that the later Catholic English translation by Bishop Richard Challoner did not share Dodwell's sexual prissiness.
82. A. D. Wright, *The Counter-Reformation: Catholic Europe and the non-Christian world* (Aldershot, 2005), 49–50, and D. d'Avray, 'A document on bigamy from the Congregation of the Council and the problem of continuity before and after the Council of Trent', *Zeitschrift für Kirchengeschichte* 131 (2020), 43–71, at 43. D'Avray points out that because French Church courts were worried about a different issue, pre-existing clandestine marriages blocking the possibility of a valid second marriage,

they unostentatiously decided to implement *Tametsi* as if the monarchy had accepted it.

83. C. Villaseñor Black, 'Love and marriage in the Spanish Empire: depictions of holy matrimony and gender discourses in the 17th century', *SCJ* 32 (2001), 637–67, at 662–3.
84. J. M. Ferraro, *Marriage Wars in Late Renaissance Venice* (Oxford, 2001), 28–9, 155–60.
85. W. G. Naphy, *Sex Crimes from Renaissance to Enlightenment* (Stroud, 2002), 21–3; S. Burghartz, *Zeiten der Reinheit: Orte der Unzucht. Ehe und Sexualität in Basel während der frühen Neuzeit* (Paderborn, 1999), 152–63, 287–8, 298; H. Kamen, *The Phoenix and the Flame: Catalonia and the Counter-Reformation* (New Haven, Conn. and London, 1993), 281–7.
86. M. Ingram, *Church Courts, Sex and Marriage in England, 1570–1642* (Cambridge, 1987), esp. chs. 11, 12.
87. Naphy, *Sex Crimes*, 42–3; K. M. Brown, 'In search of the godly magistrate in Reformation Scotland', *JEH*, 40 (1989), 553–81, at 568–9; Farr, *Authority and Sexuality in Early Modern Burgundy*, 74.
88. Ingram, *Church Courts, Sex and Marriage*, 335; cf. K. Thomas, 'The Puritans and adultery: the Act of 1650 reconsidered', in D. Pennington and K. Thomas, *Puritans and Revolutionaries: Essays in 17th-century history presented to Christopher Hill* (Oxford, 1978), 257–82, and D. Hirst, 'The failure of godly rule in the English Republic', *PP* 132 (1991), 33–66.
89. My journalistic exposé of this story is D. MacCulloch, 'Bondmen under the Tudors', in C. Cross, D. Loades and J. J. Scarisbrick (eds), *Law and Government under the Tudors: Essays Presented to Sir Geoffrey Elton on His Retirement* (Cambridge, 1988), 91–109. The salience of the diocese of Norwich suggests that the lawyer originating the process was a Norfolk man: Norfolk wiles many a man beguiles.
90. Todd, *Culture of Protestantism in Early Modern Scotland*, ch. 3.
91. W. Coster, *Family and Kinship in England 1450–1800* (Harlow, 2001), 24–5; on France, J.-L. Flandrin, 'Sex in married life in the early Middle Ages: the Church's teaching and behavioural reality', in Ariès and Béjin (eds), *Western Sexuality*, 114–29, at 123–4. For a bizarrely extreme exception to the general Counter-Reformation pattern in parts of Austria, depending on legal marriage peculiarities and lasting till modern times, see C. Sumnall, 'The social and legal reception of illegitimate births in the Gurk Valley, Austria, 1868–1945', in R. McKitterick, C. Methuen and A. Spicer (eds), *The Church and the Law*, Studies in Church History 56 (Cambridge, 2020), 362–82.
92. O'Malley, *Trent*, 122.
93. J. Arrizabalaga, J. Henderson and R. K. French, *The Great Pox: The French Disease in Renaissance Europe* (New Haven, Conn. and London, 1997), chs. 7, 8. On St Job associated with syphilis sufferers as early as 1499, see ibid., 22.

94. N. Orme, 'The Reformation and the red light', *History Today* 37 (March 1987), 36–41; on Spain, M. Friedrich, tr. J. N. Dillon, *The Jesuits: A history* (Princeton, NJ and Oxford, 2022), 188.
95. For a more positive view of bathhouses, E. Wurtzel, 'Passionate encounters, public healing: medieval urban bathhouses in northern France', *French Historical Studies* 46 (2023), 331–60.
96. T. de Bèze, ed. A. Machard, *Juvenilia* (Paris, 1879), editor's introduction and 234–37, '*De sua in Candidam et Audebertum benevolentia*'.
97. N. Malcolm, *Forbidden Desire in Early Modern Europe: Male–male sexual relations, 1400–1750* (Oxford, 2024), 155–6, and C. S. Denton, 'Sanitizing philosophical love: the French Enlightenment confronts Greek pederasty', *French Historical Studies* 45 (2022), 1–17, at 9–10.
98. N. S. Davidson, 'Sodomy in early modern Venice', in T. Betteridge (ed.), *Sodomy in Early Modern Europe* (Manchester, 2002), 65–81, at 71–4; Malcolm, *Forbidden Desire in Early Modern Europe*, 156–8.
99. P. Yin, 'Matteo Ricci's legacy for comparative theology', *Modern Theology* 38 (2022), 548–67, and J. Spence, *The Memory Palace of Matteo Ricci* (New York and London, 1985), 201–31; see also H. Yang, 'Matteo Ricci and Michel Foucault's readings of Epictetus: a quest of "zhi" (知 knowing) and "xing" (行 application)', *Christianity & Literature* 68 (2018), 36–54.
100. For useful summary discussion of Chinese sexual mores, L. U. Afonso, M. V. Gomes and R. V. Gomes, 'Chinese pornography in a Portuguese nunnery: on a transitional period blue and white porcelain bowl recovered from the Santana Convent (Lisbon)', *Antiquaries Journal* 103 (2023), 315–32, at 317–26.
101. N. Matar, *Turks, Moors and Englishmen in the Age of Discovery* (New York, 1999), ch. 4.
102. For some examples from the Protestant point of view, Malcolm, *Forbidden Desire in Early Modern Europe*, 86–87, 183.
103. MacCulloch, *Thomas Cromwell*, 241, 245. The date of the legislation is often inaccurately given as 1533: the legislation passed in 1534 New Style.
104. A. Delvigne, *Mémoires de Martin Antoine del Rio . . . 1576–78* (3 vols, Brussels, 1869–71), iii, 212–15: I am grateful to Jan Machielsen for this reference.
105. Spanish statistics from M. R. Boes, 'On trial for sodomy in early modern Germany', in Betteridge (ed.), *Sodomy in Early Modern Europe*, 27–45, at 27, and M. E. Perry, 'The "nefarious sin" in early modern Seville', in K. Gerard and G. Hekma (eds), *The Pursuit of Sodomy: Male homosexuality in Renaissance and Enlightenment Europe* (Binghamton, NY, 1989), 67–89. On Sixtus V, Christopoulos, *Abortion in Early Modern Italy*, 137.
106. Spence, *Memory Palace of Matteo Ricci*, 227.
107. K. Heyam, *Before We were Trans: A new history of gender* (London, 2022), 206–7.
108. Malcolm, *Forbidden Desire in Early Modern Europe*, 327–8.

109. M. Feldman, *The Castrato: Reflections on natures and kinds* (Oakland, Calif., 2015), 81–5 (the recorded singer was Alessandro Moreschi): see ibid., esp. Preface and ch. 1, and K. Crawford, 'Privilege, possibility, and perversion: rethinking the study of early modern sexuality', *Journal of Modern History* 78 (2006), 412–33, at 418.
110. A useful little overview of the subject is still G. Scarre, *Witchcraft and Magic in 16th and 17th century Europe* (Basingstoke, 1987); for a global treatment, R. Hutton, *The Witch: A history of fear, from ancient times to the present* (New Haven, Conn. and London, 2017).
111. On Sprenger and the rosary, Spivey Ellington, *From Sacred Body to Angelic Soul*, 34 and n., 257. There is at last a reliable full English translation of the *Malleus*: C. S. Mackay, *The Hammer of Witches: A complete translation of the Malleus Maleficarum* (Cambridge, 2009).
112. For the vulnerable position of widows, see A. Rowlands, 'Witchcraft and old women in early modern Germany', *PP* 173 (2001), 50–89, esp. 65, 70, 78; see also M. Gaskill, *Crime and Mentalities in Early Modern England* (Cambridge, 2000), 48–66, at 78.
113. C. Larner, *Enemies of God: The witch-hunt in Scotland* (London, 1981), esp. 63, 107.
114. A. Bray, *Homosexuality in Renaissance England* (London, 1981), 21.
115. R. Godbeer, *Escaping Salem: The other witch hunt of 1692* (New York and Oxford, 2005). For the prelude in Springfield, Massachusetts, in 1651–52 to the Salem events, much more complex in its outcomes, see M. Gaskill, *The Ruin of All Witches: Life and death in the New World* (London, 2021).
116. The available sources on eastern witchcraft are now plentiful. See N. Davies, *God's Playground: A history of Poland. 1: The origins to 1795* (Oxford, 1981), 196–7; Hutton, *The Witch*, ch. 3; B. Ankarloo and G. Henningsen (eds), *Early Modern Witchcraft: Centres and peripheries* (Oxford, 1989), chs. 8–10; G. Klaniczay and E. Póc (eds), *Witchcraft and Demonology in Hungary and Transylvania* (Basingstoke and Cham, 2017).
117. J. Kelly, 'Did women have a Renaissance?', repr. from R. Bridenthal and C. Koonz (eds), *Becoming Visible: Women in European history* (Boston, Mass., 1977), in L. Hutson (ed.), *Feminism and Renaissance Studies* (Oxford, 1999), 21–47.
118. P. Matheson, *The Imaginative World of the Reformation* (Edinburgh, 2000), 133.
119. Bireley, *The Refashioning of Catholicism*, 37.
120. On the established Dutch Reformed Church, see Benedict, *Christ's Churches Purely Reformed*, 200. On Friesland, discussion by James D. Tracy, reviewing W. Bergsma, *Tussen Gideonsbende en publieke kerk: een studie over gereformeerd Protestantisme in Friesland, 1580–1610* (Hilversum, 1999), *SCJ* 32 (2001), 893.
121. P. Crawford, *Women and Religion in England, 1500–1720* (London and New York, 1993), 143, and B. Curtis Clark and J. Cruickshank, 'Converting

Mrs Crouch: women, wonders and the formation of English Methodism, 1738–1741', *JEH* 652 (2014), 66–83, at 67; for later figures, C. Field, 'Adam and Eve: gender in the English Free Church constituency', *JEH* 44 (1993), 63–79, esp. 67–71.

122. Bonomi, *Under the Cope of Heaven*, 111–15.
123. S. Apetrei, *The Reformation of the Heart: Gender and radical theology in the English Revolution* (Oxford, 2024), examines the prehistory of female preaching and theological radicalism that went on to take shape in the Society of Friends. On Hassard (and her second husband, minister at Bristol St Ewen's), see ibid., 13–14; on Ainsworth (and those troubled by his interpretation), ibid., 29, 154; on the appointment of women as deaconesses or 'widows' in a Yarmouth gathered congregation, and other examples, ibid., 104, 115.
124. C. G. Pestana, 'The Quaker executions as myth and history', *Journal of American History* 80 (1993), 441–69.
125. On restructuring the Quakers, K. Peters, '"Women's speaking justified": women and discipline in the early Quaker movement, 1652–1656', in Swanson (ed.), *Gender and Christian Religion*, 205–34, and B. Adams, 'The "Durty Spirit" at Hertford: a falling out of Friends', *JEH* 52 (2001), 647–75; on Dr Johnson, Gregory, 'Gender and the clerical profession in England, 1660–1850', 240, and, on 18th-century female Quaker ministers, S. Wright, 'Quakerism and its implications for Quaker women: the women itinerant ministers of York Meeting, 1780–1840', in Sheils and Wood (eds), *Women in the Church*, 403–14.
126. Matheson, *Imaginative World*, 130.
127. S. Apetrei, 'Masculine virgins: celibacy and gender in later Stuart London', in S. Apetrei and H. Smith (eds), *Religion and Women in Britain, c.1660–1760* (London and New York, 2016), 41–59, at 43–5. I have modernized the Defoe quotation.
128. Bonomi, *Under the Cope of Heaven*, 113.
129. Gregory, 'Gender and the clerical profession in England, 1660–1850', 243–4; Apetrei, 'Masculine virgins', 52.
130. O. Hufton, 'Women in history: early modern Europe', *PP* 101 (1983), 125–40, at 136–7.

15. ENLIGHTENMENT AND CHOICE

1. F. Dabhoiwala, 'Lust and liberty', *PP* 207 (2010), 89–179, at 92–4. This is the background theme of his important study *The Origins of Sex: A history of the first sexual revolution* (London, 2012). See also R. B. Shoemaker, 'The decline of public insult in London 1660–1800', *PP* 169 (2000), 97–130, at 128, and for parallel developments in 18th-century Scotland, S. J. Brown, '"No more standing the Session": gender and the end of corporate

discipline in the Church of Scotland, *c.*1890–*c.*1930', in Swanson (ed.), *Gender and Christian Religion*, 447–60, at 451.

2. An overview is G. L. Freeze, 'Russian Orthodoxy: Church, people and politics in imperial Russia', in D. Lieven and R. G. Suny (eds), *The Cambridge History of Russia* (3 vols, Cambridge, 2006), ii, 284–305.
3. T. Isaacs, 'The Anglican hierarchy and the reformation of manners 1688–1738', *JEH* 33 (1982), 391–411; on Parliament, W. Gibson and J. Begiato, *Sex and the Church in the Long Eighteenth Century: Religion, Enlightenment and the sexual revolution* (London and New York, 2017), 33–4, 98.
4. I. Kant, 'An Answer to the Question, "What is Enlightenment?"' (1784), qu. by R. Robertson, *The Enlightenment: The pursuit of happiness, 1680–1790* (London, 2020), 30; see more generally ibid., ch. 1.
5. Summary discussion of these origins in MacCulloch, *Christianity*, 769–80.
6. S. D. Snobelen, '"The true frame of nature": Isaac Newton, heresy and the Reformation of Natural Philosophy', in J. Brooke and I. Maclean (eds), *Heterodoxy in Early Modern Science and Religion* (Oxford, 2005), 223–62.
7. The cause célèbre is enjoyably dissected in K. Harvey, *The Imposteress Rabbit Breeder: Mary Toft and eighteenth-century England* (Oxford, 2020).
8. MacCulloch, *Reformation*, 112–14, 185.
9. I provide an overview of these events in ibid., chs. 7, 8, 12 and 17. On the end of royal toleration for the Huguenots, see the vivid microstudy by C. Chappell Lougee, *Facing the Revocation: Huguenot families, faith and the King's will* (New York and Oxford, 2017), and for a brilliant exposition of the world of scepticism with Amsterdam at its centre, J. I. Israel, *Radical Enlightenment: Philosophy and the making of modernity 1650–1750* (Oxford, 2001).
10. N. Keene, '"A two-edged sword": biblical criticism and the New Testament canon in early modern England', in A. Hessayon and N. Keene (eds), *Scripture and Scholarship in Early Modern England* (Aldershot, 2006), 94–115, at 104–6, 109. On Laodiceans, see Col. 4.16. To minimize the embarrassment of this text, most Bibles translate the reference as referring to a letter *from* the Laodiceans, though that does not really solve the canonical problem: see comment in E. Schweizer, tr. A. Chester, *The Letter to the Colossians: A commentary* (London, 1982), 242 and n. 18.
11. A. Cunningham and O. P. Grell, *The Four Horsemen of the Apocalypse: Religion, war, famine and death in Reformation Europe* (Cambridge, 2000), 243–6.
12. P. Withington, 'Intoxicants and the invention of "consumption"', *Economic History Review* 73 (2020), 384–408.
13. J. de Vries, *The Industrious Revolution: Consumer behaviour and the household economy, 1650 to the present* (Cambridge, 2008), esp. 40–58. A brilliant portrait of the effect on the 17th-century Netherlands is S. Schama, *The Embarrassment of Riches: An interpretation of Dutch culture in the*

Golden Age (London, 1987), esp. ch. 5, and for an equally vigorous treatment, F. Trentmann, *Empire of Things: How we became a world of consumers, from the fifteenth century to the twenty-first* (London, 2016), esp. ch. 1. For a significant microstudy of the spreading effect of mass consumption, H. Bovenkerk and C. Fertig, 'Consumer revolution in north-western Germany: material culture, global goods, and proto-industry in rural households in the seventeenth to nineteenth centuries', *Economic History Review* 76 (2022), 551–74.

14. Qu. by D. Outram, *The Enlightenment* (2nd edn, Cambridge, 2005), 77; ibid., ch. 6, forms a useful critique of the Enlightenment on gender.
15. For some summary comment, see S. Kingsley Kent, *Gender: A world history* (Oxford, 2021), 83–4, and T. Hitchcock, *English Sexualities, 1700–1800* (Basingstoke, 1997), ch. 4, but, for extended treatment, see H. King, *The One-Sex Body on Trial: The Classical and early modern evidence* (Farnham, 2013), pt 1.
16. S. D. Amussen, 'The gendering of popular culture in early modern England', in T. Harris (ed.), *Popular Culture in England, c.1500–1800* (New York, 1995), 48–68, at 66.
17. T. van der Meer, 'Sodomy and its discontents: discourse, desire, and the rise of a same-sex proto-something in the early modern Dutch Republic', *Historical Reflections/Réflexions Historiques* 33 (2007), 41–68. For the same transition in 18th-century France from legal authorities considering acts to envisaging a 'breed' of homosexuals, see P. Ariès, 'Thoughts on the history of homosexuality', in Ariès and Béjin (eds), *Western Sexuality*, 62–75, at 72n.
18. N. Malcolm, 'Forbidden love in Istanbul: patterns of male–male sexual relations in the early-modern Mediterranean world', *PP* 257 (2022), 55–88, at 79–81. For further instances contrasting with the Mediterranean pattern before the late 17th century, see L. Mott, 'Love's labours lost: five letters from an early seventeenth-century Portuguese sodomite', in K. Gerard and G. Hekma (eds), *The Pursuit of Sodomy: Male homosexuality in Renaissance and Enlightenment Europe* (Binghamton, NY, 1989), 91–101, and M. R. Boes, 'On trial for sodomy in early modern Germany', in T. Betteridge (ed.), *Sodomy in Early Modern Europe* (Manchester, 2002), 27–45, esp. at 33.
19. P. Laslett, *Family Life and Illicit Love in Earlier Generations* (rev. edn, Cambridge, 1980), ch. 1.
20. R. Norton, *Mother Clap's Molly House: The gay subculture in England 1700–1830* (London, 1992); T. van der Meer, 'The persecutions of sodomites in early eighteenth-century Amsterdam: changing perceptions of sodomy', in Gerard and Hekma (eds), *Pursuit of Sodomy*, 263–309; Hitchcock, *English Sexualities*, ch. 5.
21. W. G. Naphy, *Sex Crimes from Renaissance to Enlightenment* (Stroud, 2002), 98–100, 106, 130, 165–70; Hitchcock, *English Sexualities*, ch. 6.

For robust scepticism on Randolph Trumbach's exposition of this idea, see N. Malcolm, *Forbidden Desire in Early Modern Europe: Male–male sexual relations, 1400–1750* (Oxford, 2024), 349–52.

22. H. Skoda, 'St Wilgefortis and her/their beard: the devotions of unhappy wives and non-binary people', *History Workshop* 95 (2023), 51–74. Harvey, *Fires of Lust*, 184–5, discusses isolated medieval cases, one of which, that of the southern English trans person John Rykener, has been the subject of a study whose methodology forms a classic warning against reckless over-interpretation: J. Goldberg, 'John Rykener, Richard II and the governance of London', *Leeds Studies in English* 45 (2014), 49–70.
23. J. Manion, *Female Husbands: A trans history* (Cambridge, 2020); F. Easton, 'Gender's two bodies: women warriors, female husbands and plebeian life', *PP* 180 (2003), 131–74. On the growth of pornography, K. Harvey, 'The century of sex? Gender, bodies and sexuality in the long 18th century', *HJ* 45 (2002), 899–915, esp. 900.
24. On Bentham see above, p. 3. C. S. Denton, 'Sanitizing philosophical love: the French Enlightenment confronts Greek Pederasty', *French Historical Studies* 45 (2022), 1–17.
25. T. Laqueur, *Solitary Sex: A cultural history of masturbation* (New York, 2003), ch. 3, is an enjoyable overview. See also J. Noonan, *Contraception: A history of its treatment by the Catholic theologians and canonists* (Cambridge, Mass., 1958), 172–3, and J. F. Keenan, *A History of Catholic Theological Ethics* (New York, 2022), 61, 103–5. For Henry VIII's unprecedented enquiries on monastic masturbation in 1535, D. MacCulloch, *Thomas Cromwell: A life* (London, 2018), 305–6. On Russia, Levin, *Sex and Society in the World of the Orthodox Slavs*, 188, 259–60.
26. The most careful treatment of origins is M. Stolberg, 'Self-pollution, moral reform, and the venereal trade: notes on the sources and historical context of *Onania* (1716)', *Journal of the History of Sexuality* 9 (2000), 37–61. Although Laqueur, *Solitary Sex*, 178–9, deals with Beverland, he ignores the important preliminary contribution of the tract of 1676 noticed by Stolberg, and of Woodward, on whom see Gibson and Begiato, *Sex and the Church in the Long Eighteenth Century*, 34–5.
27. On *Onania*, Laqueur, *Solitary Sex*, 13–16, 25–37, 84–5, 179, 224, 232, 249, 256–61, 272, 324–6; for dating *Onania* and cautionary remarks on the uncertainty of authorship, see Stolberg, 'Self-pollution, moral reform, and the venereal trade'.
28. Laqueur, *Solitary Sex*, 37–44; J. G. Donat, 'The Rev. John Wesley's extractions from Dr Tissot: a Methodist *Imprimatur*', *History of Science* 39 (2001), 285–98.
29. D. Stevenson, *The Beggar's Benison: Sex clubs of Enlightenment Scotland and their rituals* (East Linton, 2001). Stevenson also pitilessly pioneered our proper understanding of Masonic history in Stevenson, *The Origins of Freemasonry: Scotland's century, 1590–1710* (Cambridge, 1988), essential

basis for the wider picture presented in J. Dickie, *The Craft: How Freemasons made the modern world* (London, 2020).

30. A connection between sexual activity and domestic architecture early made by Bullough, *Sexual Variance in Society and History*, 540.
31. I. V. Hull, *Sexuality, State and Civil Society in Germany, 1700–1815* (Ithaca, NY and London, 1996), 306. See also Laqueur, *Solitary Sex*, 57–60.
32. H. D. Rack, *Reasonable Enthusiast: John Wesley and the rise of Methodism* (3rd edn, London, 2002), 198–202, 282–91, 333–4, 450–60.
33. A masterly gathering of the interconnections is W. R. Ward, *The Protestant Evangelical Awakening* (Cambridge, 1992). I summarize the development of Pietism and the Moravians in MacCulloch, *Christianity*, 738–47.
34. For the origins of colonial American revivalism in open-air Scots and Ulster Scots Eucharists, see L. E. Schmidt, *Holy Fairs: Scottish communions and American revivals in the early modern period* (Princeton, NJ, 1989).
35. Rack, *Reasonable Enthusiast*, 192–8; C. M. Norris, '"A blessed and glorious work of God . . . attended with some irregularity": managing Methodist revivals, *c.*1740–1800', in C. Methuen, A. Ryrie and A. Spicer (eds), *Inspiration and Institution in Christian History*, Studies in Church History 57 (Cambridge, 2021), 210–32.
36. On Wesley and celibacy, Gibson and Begiato, *Sex and the Church in the Long Eighteenth Century*, 177–9.
37. The first full-length scholarly investigation is P. Peucker, *A Time of Sifting: Mystical marriage and the crisis of Moravian piety in the eighteenth century* (University Park, Pa., 2021), which informs the following account.
38. The chilling casualness of this system revealed in the diaries of one plantation manager, Thomas Thistlewood, can be sampled in T. Burnard, *Mastery, Tyranny and Desire: Thomas Thistlewood and his slaves in the Anglo-Jamaican world* (Chapel Hill, NC, 2004); see also the analysis of K. Morgan, 'Slave women and reproduction in Jamaica, *c.* 1776–1834', *History* 91 (2006), 231–53.
39. M. Godwyn, *The Negro's & Indians Advocate, Suing for their Admission into the Church: or A persuasive to the instructing and baptizing of the Negro's and Indians in our plantations* . . . (London, 1680); M. Godwyn, *Trade preferr'd before religion and Christ made to give place to Mammon represented in a sermon relating to the plantations* . . . (London, 1685). For subsequent Church of England agonizings around slavery and missionary outreach, J. Cox, *The British Missionary Enterprise since 1700* (New York and London, 2008), 22–44.
40. J. C. S. Mason, *The Moravian Church and the Missionary Awakening in England, 1760–1800* (London, 2001), esp. 125–42, 179–92; for summary discussion, P. Bonomi, *Under the Cope of Heaven: Religion, society and politics in Colonial America* (Oxford, 2003), 119–27.
41. A. Braude, *Sisters and Saints: Women and American religion* (Oxford, 2008), 18–19.

42. C. Harline, *Sunday: A history of the first day from Babylonia to the Super Bowl* (New York, 2006), 323–4.
43. H. R. Davis, 'The Negro a beast: *Nachash* theology and the nineteenth-century re-making of Negro origins', unpublished Ph.D. dissertation, Saint Louis University (2012); cf. A. Clarke, *The Holy Bible: Containing the Old and New Testaments* (4 vols, London, 1810), i, 115. For alternative 'Hamitic' theories about blacks and slavery, see MacCulloch, *Christianity*, 867–8.
44. Peucker, *A Time of Sifting*, 6, 38–9, 148–52. A. J. Freeman, *An Ecumenical Theology of the Heart: The theology of Count Nicholas Ludwig von Zinzendorf* (Bethlehem, Pa., 1998) is informative if one reads past its ecumenical intentions and interest in Carl Jung.
45. Gibson and Begiato, *Sex and the Church in the Long Eighteenth Century*, 152–5.
46. M. Jones, 'From "The State of my Soul" to "Exalted Piety": women's voices in the *Arminian/Methodist Magazine*, 1778–1821', in Swanson (ed.), *Gender and Christian Religion*, 273–86.
47. D. Hempton, *Methodism: Empire of the Spirit* (New Haven, Conn. and London, 2005), 30–31, 144–6.
48. P. Chilcote, 'John Wesley and the women preachers of early Methodism', unpublished Ph.D. dissertation, Duke University (1984), 151–2, 194–5, 220.
49. Jones, 'From "The State of my Soul" to "Exalted Piety"', 280–86; on later Methodist masculinist retrenchment, D. Shorney, '"Women may preach but men must govern": gender roles in the growth and development of the Bible Christian denomination', in Swanson (ed.), *Gender and Christian Religion*, 309–22, esp. 319–21.
50. On Davison and Madan, Gibson and Begiato, *Sex and the Church in the Long Eighteenth Century*, 146–7, 251–6. On Harris, G. Tudur, *Howell Harris: From conversion to separation, 1735–1750* (Cardiff, 2000), from whom the quotation is taken, ibid., 229.

16. REVOLUTION AND CATHOLICISM REBUILT

1. D. Beales, *Prosperity and Plunder: European Catholic monasteries in the age of revolution, 1650–1815* (Cambridge, 2003), 210–28. On the Jesuits, Enlightenment and the 18th-century Papacy, see O. Chadwick, *The Popes and European Revolution* (Oxford, 1981), esp. chs. 5 and 6.
2. A masterly short survey of what follows, where not otherwise referenced, is J. McManners, *The French Revolution and the Church* (London, 1969). A recent detailed and vigorous overview is J. Israel, *Revolutionary Ideas: An intellectual history of the French Revolution from The Rights of Man to Robespierre* (Princeton, NJ, 2014).
3. R. Beachy, 'The German invention of homosexuality', *Journal of Modern History* 82 (2010), 801–38, at 807, draws attention to this profound shift

as dating from 1792, rather than to later enactments of the *Code Napoléon* (below).

4. J. I. Israel, *Radical Enlightenment: Philosophy and the making of modernity 1650–1750* (Oxford, 2001), ch. 14.
5. McManners, *The French Revolution and the Church*, 112–17. For the continuing uncertainties of married versus celibate clergy during the Napoleonic era, see A. Caiani, *To Kidnap a Pope: Napoleon and Pius VII* (New Haven, Conn. and London, 2021), 107–8, 279.
6. Qu. by Caiani, *To Kidnap a Pope*, 58.
7. On these long-term effects of the Concordat, see N. Atkin and F. Tallett, *Priests, Prelates and People: A history of European Catholicism since 1750* (London, 2003), 72–7.
8. S. Kingsley Kent, *Gender: A world history* (Oxford, 2021), 86–94; for the same developments in anglophone culture, J. Begiato, 'Between poise and power: embodied manliness in 18th- and 19th-century British culture', *TRHS* 6th ser. 26 (2016), 125–47.
9. N. B. Milanich, *Paternity: The elusive quest for the father* (Cambridge, Mass., 2019), 13–16. The provision on illegitimacy is an interesting parallel with the principle of English common law that had provided a convenient legal fiction for the freeing of serfs: above, Ch. 14, pp. 353–4.
10. Bullough, *Sexual Variance in Society and History*, 564–5.
11. J. F. Keenan, *A History of Catholic Theological Ethics* (New York, 2022), 109–10, 250–52; M. Friedrich, tr. J. N. Dillon, *The Jesuits: A history* (Princeton, NJ and Oxford, 2022), 640–45. The quotation is from Thomas Slater, SJ: T. Slater, *A Manual of Moral Theology for English-speaking Countries* (2 vols, New York, 1906), i, 6.
12. Caiani, *To Kidnap a Pope*, is a reliable account; on Pius VII travelling to Paris in 1804, see ibid., 120–28.
13. M. P. Magray, *The Transforming Power of the Nuns: Women, religion and cultural change in Ireland, 1750–1900* (Oxford, 1998), 7–9.
14. V. Viaene, 'The second sex and the First Estate: the Sisters of St-André between the Bishop of Tournai and Rome, 1850–1886', *JEH* 59 (2008), 447–74, at 449.
15. Magray, *The Transforming Power of the Nuns*, 9.
16. A. Braude, *Sisters and Saints: Women and American religion* (Oxford, 2008), 71–6; S. Connolly, *On Every Tide: The making and remaking of the Irish world* (London, 2022), 24–5, 65–7, 81–5, 90. For parallel developments in 19th-century Russian Orthodoxy, see S. Dixon, 'The Russian Orthodox Church in imperial Russia 1721–1917', in M. Angold (ed.), *The Cambridge History of Christianity 5: Eastern Christianity* (Cambridge, 2006), 325–47, at 339–40.
17. J. Garnett, 'The nineteenth century', in R. Harries and H. Mayr-Harting (eds), *Christianity: Two thousand years* (Oxford, 2001), 192–217, at

199–201; S. J. Boss, 'The Immaculate Heart of Mary: visions for the modern world', in Swanson (ed.), *Church and Mary*, 319–48, at 330–33.

18. T. Taylor, '"So many extraordinary things to tell": letters from Lourdes, 1858', *JEH* 46 (1995), 457–81, at 464, 472–7. An indispensable analysis is R. Harris, *Lourdes: Body and spirit in the secular age* (London, 1999).
19. D. Blackbourn, *Marpingen: Apparitions of the Virgin Mary in Bismarckian Germany* (Oxford, 1993), esp. 278–81, 400–401, 405. An excellent objective guide to Marian appearances after 1900 is C. Maunder, *Our Lady of the Nations: Apparitions of Mary in 20th-century Europe* (Oxford, 2016), which deals with Medjugorje in ch. 13.
20. On Marian devotional cults and the Nazis, Maunder, *Our Lady of the Nations*, ch. 9.
21. R. A. Orsi, in A.-K. Hermkens, W. Jansen and C. Nortermans (eds), *Moved by Mary: The power of pilgrimage in the modern world* (Farnham, 2009), ch. 13, 'Abundant history: Marian apparitions as alternative modernity'. E. Hynes, *Knock: The Virgin's apparition in nineteenth-century Ireland* (Cork, 2008), is a fine contextual account.
22. On that theme in relation to Medjugorje, taking the cult far from its sometime and unfortunate associations with Catholic and anti-Muslim Croat nationalism, Maunder, *Our Lady of the Nations*, 165–70.
23. P. Preston, 'Cardinal Cajetan and Fra Ambrosius Catharinus in the controversy over the Immaculate Conception of the Virgin in Italy, 1515–51', in Swanson (ed.), *Church and Mary*, 181–90; Catharinus, a Dominican, stood out against the general Dominican line and they never forgave him for his treachery.
24. O. Chadwick, *A History of the Popes 1830–1914* (Oxford, 1998), 119–22.
25. Blackbourn, *Marpingen*, 408, n. 36 highlights the contrast. I owe the insight on Soubirous to Chris Maunder.
26. Harrington, *Women in a Celtic Church*, 237. J. Christopoulos, *Abortion in Early Modern Italy* (Cambridge, Mass., 2021), 8–10; J. T. Noonan, 'Abortion and the Catholic Church: a summary history', *Natural Law Forum* 12 (1967), 85–131, at 101 and n. 75, makes the connection between Aquinas's views on ensoulment and his objections to the doctrine of the Immaculate Conception.
27. D. A. Jones, *The Soul of the Embryo: An enquiry into the status of the human embryo* (London, 2004), ch. 1, 100–102, 141–50. Cf. Ps. 51.5: 'Behold, I was brought forth in iniquity, and in sin did my mother conceive me'; Job 3.3: 'Let the day perish wherein I was born, and the night which said "A man-child is conceived."'
28. Christopoulos, *Abortion in Early Modern Italy*, 2–3, 10, 127–49.
29. F. Vienne, 'Eggs and sperm as germ cells', in N. Hopwood, R. Flemming and L. Kassell (eds), *Reproduction: Antiquity to the present day* (Cambridge, 2018), 413–26.

30. Noonan, 'Abortion and the Catholic Church: a summary history', 114–18.
31. Chadwick, *History of the Popes 1830–1914*, 174–6.
32. Ibid., 233–4, 247–9.
33. After conservative Catholic controversy stirred by D. Kertzer, *The Kidnapping of Edgardo Mortara* (London, 1997), see now the further reflections by Kertzer, 'The enduring controversy over the Mortara case', and P. Turner, 'Considering the baptism of Edgardo Mortara in the context of Catholic teachings and rituals then and now', *Studies in Jewish–Christian Relations* 14 (2019), 1–9, 10–19.
34. A good overview of neo-Thomism is B. McGinn, *Thomas Aquinas's Summa Theologiae* (Princeton, NJ, 2004), ch. 5; on 'Modernism', Chadwick, *History of the Popes 1830–1914*, 346–59.
35. On the events outlined here, Chadwick, *History of the Popes 1830–1914*, chs. 5–6.
36. The latter days of this seminary system are astringently described in J. Cornwell, *The Dark Box: A secret history of confession* (London, 2014), pts. 2 and 3.
37. E. Duffy, *Saints and Sinners: A history of the Popes* (3rd edn, New Haven, Conn. and London, 2006), 322–3.

17. GLOBAL WESTERN CHRISTIANITY

1. P. Morland, *The Human Tide: How population shaped the modern world* (London, 2019), 22, 41–5.
2. For the Irish Protestant role in applying the term 'British Empire' to a genuinely overseas Empire, cf. J. Redmond, 'Religion, civility and the "British" of Ireland in the 1641 Irish rebellion', *Irish Historical Studies* 45 (2021), 1–21, and D. MacCulloch, 'Forging Reformation: a cautionary tale', in MacCulloch, *All Things Made New: Writings on the Reformation* (London, 2016), 321–58, at 339, 343.
3. The 'Protestant' part of the American title did not suit the US Episcopal Church in less Reformation mood in later years, and was effectively dropped in 1964. For a little more discussion of the evolution of the 'Anglican' label, see MacCulloch, *All Things Made New*, 219, 252, 359.
4. R. Brown, 'Victorian Anglican Evangelicalism: the radical legacy of Edward Irving', *JEH* 58 (2007), 675–704, esp. 675, 680–81.
5. J. A. Harrill, *Slaves in the New Testament: Literary, social and moral dimensions* (Minneapolis, Minn., 2006) sets out the arguments.
6. I set out the background in more detail in MacCulloch, *Christianity*, 866–73.
7. For British society's involvement in the institution, particularly revealed by the massive national compensation scheme for investors after the abolition

of 1833, see e.g. C. Hall, 'Troubling memories: nineteenth-century histories of the slave trade and slavery', *TRHS* 6th ser. 21 (2011), 147–69.

8. On the distinctive contribution of 'rational Dissent', see E. J. Clapp, 'Introduction', in E. J. Clapp and J. Roy Jeffrey (eds), *Women, Dissent and Anti-Slavery in Britain and America, 1790–1865* (Oxford, 2011), 1–19, esp. 15.
9. K. Gleadle and R. Hanley, 'Children against slavery: juvenile agency and the sugar boycotts in Britain', *TRHS* 6th ser. 30 (2020), 97–118. The quotation on Fox is from T. Whelan, 'Martha Gurney and the Anti-Slave Trade movement, 1788–94', in Clapp and Jeffrey (eds), *Women, Dissent and Anti-Slavery*, 57. See also J. Barrell and T. Whelan (eds), *The Complete Writings of William Fox: Abolitionist, Tory, and friend to the French Revolution* (Nottingham, 2011), which sorts out much confusion between its subject and other activists with the same name. On Wedgwood, see T. Hunt, *The Radical Potter: Josiah Wedgwood and the transformation of Britain* (London, 2021).
10. Wilberforce to Thomas Babington, qu. by Clapp, 'Introduction', in Clapp and Jeffrey (eds), *Women, Dissent and Anti-Slavery*, 1–19, at 1.
11. A subtle and realistic analysis is A. Vickery, 'From golden age to separate spheres? A review of the categories and chronology of English women's history', *HJ* 36 (1993), 383–414.
12. S. Kingsley Kent, *Gender: A world history* (Oxford, 2021), 96–8; L. Delap, *Feminisms: A global history* (Chicago, 2020), 141–44.
13. A. Braude, *Sisters and Saints: Women and American religion* (Oxford, 2008), 34–6.
14. Ibid., 69–70, 78. On Evangelical squirming about the miracle of Cana, see P. J. Gomes, *The Good Book: Reading the Bible with mind and heart* (New York, 1996), 78–83.
15. H. Rubenhold, *The Covent Garden Ladies: Pimp General Jack and the extraordinary story of Harris's List* (Stroud, 2005).
16. S. Hearne, *Policing Prostitution: Regulating the lower classes in late imperial Russia* (Oxford, 2021), 1, 4, 11, 159–61.
17. Braude, *Sisters and Saints*, 37.
18. H. Mathers, 'The evangelical spirituality of a Victorian feminist: Josephine Butler, 1828–1906', *JEH* 52 (2001), 282–312, at 299, 302.
19. Braude, *Sisters and Saints*, 78–81.
20. K. L. Slominski, *Teaching Moral Sex: A history of religion and sex education in the United States* (New York, 2021), 1–7, 23–4, 37, 52–3; see also the useful review article, M. A. Kibler, 'Gender, politics, and mass culture', *Gender and History* 12 (2000), 477–81.
21. A. Rutherford, *Control: The dark history and troubling present of eugenics* (London, 2022), 39–52. On the extraordinarily long-term intellectual entanglement of Dalton with the Darwin and Huxley dynasties, see A. Bashford, *An Intimate History of Evolution: The story of the Huxley Family* (London, 2022), esp. 349–51.
22. Slominski, *Teaching Moral Sex*, 23.

23. Rutherford, *Control*, 69–71, 93–6.
24. On Sanger, Rutherford, *Control*, 72, and on British legislation, ibid., 78–90.
25. On the US programmes, ibid., 65–6, 74, 146–7, 153–4.
26. S. E. Ahlstrom, *A Religious History of the American People* (2nd edn, New Haven, Conn. and London, 2004), 664–65.
27. J. D. G. Dunn (ed.), *Fundamentalisms: Threats and ideologies in the modern world* (London, 2015), esp. 9–26.
28. M. Howard, *Captain Professor: A life in war and peace* (London, 2006), 25 (Sir Michael's public school was the programmatically military Wellington College).
29. The Revd the Hon. E. Lyttelton, *The Training of the Young in Laws of Sex* (London, 1900), 10 ('the young' being exclusively teenage boys: cf. remarks at ibid., 63). The nexus between masturbation and homosexuality in public schools is discussed in T. Laqueur, *Solitary Sex: A cultural history of masturbation* (New York, 2003), 258–60.
30. S. Gill, 'How muscular was Victorian Christianity? Thomas Hughes and the cult of Christian manliness reconsidered', in Swanson (ed.), *Gender and Christian Religion*, 421–30, at 423, 427. M. Girouard, *The Return to Camelot: Chivalry and the English gentleman* (New Haven, Conn. and London, 1981), ch. 11, gives a good overview of the medieval chivalric contribution to the public-school ethos, including its homoerotic aspect.
31. For further discussion of the David and Jonathan theme in Victorian England, D. Janes, *Visions of Queer Martyrdom from John Henry Newman to Derek Jarman* (Chicago, 2019), 154–81.
32. L. Philippson, quoted by Canon H. D. M. Spence via Dean R. Payne Smith in C. J. Ellicott (ed.), *An Old Testament Commentary for English Readers by Various Writers* (5 vols, London, 1882–83), ii, 382. On 'beastliness', see J. Richards, *Happiest Days: The public school in English fiction* (Manchester, 1988), esp. chs. 2, 8.
33. I treat this phenomenon at greater length in D. MacCulloch, *Silence: A Christian history* (London, 2013), 184–90.
34. See the careful but incisive analysis against a background of much countervailing noise in J. Cornwell, *Newman's Unquiet Grave: The reluctant saint* (London and New York, 2010), esp. 205. For an analysis of Newman denialism, S. Skinner, 'History *versus* hagiography: the reception of Turner's *Newman*', *JEH* 61 (2010), 764–81; and see further exchange between E. Duffy and Skinner, *JEH* 63 (2012), 534–67. On same-sex graves, see above, Ch. 13, p. 298.
35. A carefully sympathetic study of Hopkins is R. B. Martin, *Gerard Manley Hopkins: A very private life* (London, 1991), esp. 80–110, 159–64.
36. On Father Ignatius, see Janes, *Visions of Queer Martyrdom*, 67–96, with the quotation from an anonymous reviewer in the *Living Age* 83 (1864), ibid., 70.

37. Camp Anglo-Catholicism is well analysed by M. Stringer, 'Of gin and lace: sexuality, liturgy and identity among Anglo-Catholics in the mid-twentieth century', *Theology and Sexuality* 7 (2000), 35–54, though he is unfortunately unaware of the wider chronological context provided by the classic analysis of D. Hilliard, 'UnEnglish and unmanly: Anglo-Catholicism and homosexuality', *Victorian Studies* 25 (1982), 181–210. Less sprightly, though austerely perceptive, is W. S. F. Pickering, *Anglo-Catholicism: A study in religious ambiguity* (London and New York, 1989), 184–206.
38. For Kingsley, writing at a particularly heightened moment of English anti-Romanism in 1851, see Hilliard, 'UnEnglish and unmanly', 188. E. Waugh, *Brideshead Revisited* (London, 1967), 30. For Reformation 'effeminacy', see above, Ch. 14, p. 328.
39. There had been no executions for buggery since 1835, although around 200 formal records of a death sentence were made thereafter until 1861: L. Crompton, '*Don Leon*, Byron and homosexual law reform', *JOH* 8 (1983), 53–72, at 68. Recent claims to the contrary by Naomi Wolf were based on her misunderstanding of English law, leading to a withdrawal of the original edition of her book: N. Wolf, *Outrages: Sex, censorship and the criminalisation of love* (London, 2019).
40. J. Weeks, *Sex, Politics, and Society: The regulations of sexuality since 1800* (3rd edn, London, 2012), 122–33.
41. R. Beachy, 'The German invention of homosexuality', *Journal of Modern History* 82 (2010), 801–38, esp. 803, 806–7, 823–5, 836–7; on the wider European scene, see G. Robb, *Strangers: Homosexual love in the 19th century* (London, 2003), and O. Petri, *Places of Tenderness and Heat: The queer milieu of fin-de-siècle St Petersburg* (Oxford, 2023).
42. On the following paragraphs where not otherwise referenced, see T. Bauer, tr. H. Biesterfelt and T. Tunstall, *A Culture of Ambiguity: An alternative history of Islam* (New York, 2021), ch. 7: his use of Foucault adds little to his fascinating analysis.
43. J. Jones, 'Islam at home: religion, piety and private space in Muslim India and Victorian Britain, *c.*1850–1905', in J. Doran, C. Methuen and A. Walsham (eds), *Religion and the Household*, Studies in Church History 50 (Woodbridge, 2014), 378–404.
44. E. Reinders, *Borrowed Gods and Foreign Bodies: Christian missionaries imagine Chinese religion* (Berkeley, Calif., 2004), 57–61, ch. 10; on Ricci and homosexuality, see above, Ch. 14, p. 358.
45. E. E. Prevost, *The Communion of Women: Missions and gender in colonial Africa and the British metropole* (Oxford, 2010), 2–4, usefully rounds up institutional growth in the UK. On Anglican nuns in Hawaii and elsewhere from 1864, see S. S. Maughan. 'Sisters and brothers abroad: gender, race, Empire and Anglican missionary reformism in Hawai'i and the Pacific, 1858–75', in F. Knight, C. Methuen and A. Spicer (eds), *The Churches and*

Rites of Passage, Studies in Church History 59 (Cambridge, 2023), 328–44. On the USA, Braude, *Sisters and Saints*, 80–84.

46. E. Prevost, 'Married to the mission field: gender, Christianity, and professionalization in Britain and colonial Africa, 1865–1914', *Journal of British Studies* 47 (2008), 796–826, at 801, 804–7.

47. F. J. Heuser, '*Woman's Work for Woman*, cultural change, and the foreign missionary movement', *Journal of Presbyterian History* 75 (1997), 119–30.

48. C. Moyse, *A History of the Mothers' Union: Women, Anglicanism and globalisation, 1876–2008* (Woodbridge, 2009). Prevost, *The Communion of Women*, is largely a study of the extraordinary impact of the Mothers' Union in west Africa.

49. D. R. Peterson, 'Culture and chronology in African history', *HJ* 50 (2007), 483–97, at 495–6.

50. Jones, 'Islam at home', 394–401.

51. M. Friedrich, tr. J. N. Dillon, *The Jesuits: A history* (Princeton, NJ and Oxford, 2022), 515, 524.

52. T. Yung, '"Does God mind?": reshaping Chinese Christian rites of passage, *c.*1877–1940', in Knight, Methuen and Spicer (eds), *The Churches and Rites of Passage*, 359–82, at 379–80.

53. A. Hastings, *The Church in Africa 1450–1950* (Oxford, 1994), 10–12, 27–8; D. Crummey, 'Church and nation: the Ethiopian Orthodox *Täwahedo* Church (from the thirteenth to the twentieth century)', in M. Angold (ed.), *The Cambridge History of Christianity 5: Eastern Christianity* (Cambridge, 2006), 457–87, at 460.

54. T. W. Jones, 'The missionaries' position: polygamy and divorce in the Anglican Communion, 1888–1988', *Journal of Religious History* 35 (2011), 393–408, at 395.

55. S. C. Carter, *The Importance of Being Monogamous: Marriage and nation building in western Canada to 1915* (Athabasca, 2008), esp. chs. 6 and 7. On Africa, Jones, 'The missionaries' position', 396–7; see also useful earlier framing of discussion in F. K. Ekechi, 'African polygamy and Western Christian ethnocentrism', *Journal of African Studies* 3 (1976), 329–49.

56. J. W. Colenso, *A letter to his Grace the Archbishop of Canterbury upon the Question of the Proper Treatment of Cases of Polygamy as found already existing in Converts from Heathenism* (Cambridge and London, 1862), 2, 22, 37. See also J. W. Colenso, *Remarks upon the proper Treatment of Polygamy* ... (Pietermaritzburg, 1855), printed together with an angry anonymous rebuttal of his arguments.

57. P. R. McKenzie, *Inter-religious Encounters in West Africa: Samuel Ajayi Crowther's attitude to African traditional religion and Islam*, Leicester Studies in Religion 1 (Leicester, 1976), 37, 84–5. One eminent (and male) Nigerian historian accuses Crowther of pronouncing 'irrationally' on polygamy at Lambeth and misleading his fellow bishops: E. A. Ayandele, *The*

Missionary Impact on Modern Nigeria 1842–1914: A political and social analysis (London, 1966), 206.

58. On Lambeth tergiversations to 1988, see Jones, 'The missionaries' position', 400–408. On the recent history of Anglicanism and homosexuality, see below, Ch. 19.
59. B. Sundkler and C. Steed, *A History of the Church in Africa* (Cambridge, 2000), 232. On Yoruba religious culture, see J. D. Y. Peel, *Religious Encounter and the Making of the Yoruba* (Bloomington, Ind., 2000), esp. 121–2, 213–14, 275–7, 286–9, 295–8.
60. The 'last will and testament' of Harris, 1928: Sundkler and Steed, *History of the Church in Africa*, 201. On Harris, see also Hastings, *Church in Africa 1450–1950*, 443–7.
61. F. Dabhoiwala, *The Origins of Sex: A history of the first sexual revolution* (London, 2012), 126–7. S. M. S. Pearsall, *Polygamy: An early American history* (New Haven, Conn., 2019) goes some way to putting Mormon (LDS) polygamy in both its 19th-century and its more long-term American context.
62. P. Lindholm (ed.), *Latter-day Dissent: At the crossroads of intellectual inquiry and ecclesiastical authority* (Salt Lake City, Utah, 2011), 41–2.
63. On the ending of early Mormon mission in Great Britain in ridicule and fiasco after the announcement of polygamy in 1853, see O. Chadwick, *The Victorian Church* (2 vols, London, 1966–71), i, 436–9.
64. D. Hilliard, 'Australasia and the Pacific', in A. Hastings (ed.), *A World History of Christianity* (Grand Rapids, Mich., 1999), 508–35, at 517–18, and G. Colvin, 'A Maori Mormon testimony', in G. Colvin and J. Brooks (eds), *Decolonizing Mormonism: Approaching a postcolonial Zion* (Salt Lake City, Utah, 2018), 27–46, at 32. For background on the early Anglican alliance with the Maori and its gradual disintegration, see L. S. Rickard, *Tamihana the Kingmaker* (Wellington and Auckland, 1963).
65. M. Ruthven, *The Divine Supermarket: Travels in search of the soul of America* (2nd edn, New York and London, 2012), 125–9; D. M. Quinn, 'LDS Church authority and new plural marriages, 1890–1904', *Dialogue: A journal of Mormon thought* 18 (1985), 9–105, and for context on that study, Lindholm (ed.), *Latter-day Dissent*, 110–11.
66. A. Sinyavsky, tr. J. Turnbull and N. Formozov, *Ivan the Fool: Russian folk belief: a cultural history* (Moscow, 2007), 367–81.

18. A CENTURY OF CONTRACEPTION

1. Excellent overview in P. Morland, *The Human Tide: How population shaped the modern world* (London, 2019), esp. 11–16, 142, 263, 282.
2. Useful summary discussion by L. Sanneh, 'Religion's return', *Times Literary Supplement*, 13 Oct. 2006, 13–14.

3. For a summary drawing-together of the strands in the making of Pentecostalism, MacCulloch, *Christianity*, 910–14. G. Wacker, 'Travail of a broken family: Evangelical responses to Pentecostalism in America, 1906–1916', *JEH* 47 (1996), 505–28, at 528, observes the belated recognition of Pentecostal strength in mid-20th-century America.
4. A. Anderson, *An Introduction to Pentecostalism* (Cambridge, 2004), 47–51.
5. Early conflicts are described with verve by Wacker, 'Travail of a broken family'.
6. Anderson, *Introduction to Pentecostalism*, 247–50.
7. Two good and complementary accounts of modern developments relating to Britain, both with wider implications, are J. Borge, *Protective Practices: A history of the London Rubber Company* (Montreal and Kingston, 2020), with an account of the prehistory at 15–17, and C. L. Jones, *The Business of Birth Control: Contraception and commerce in Britain before the sexual revolution* (Manchester, 2020).
8. P. Sedgwick, 'The Lambeth Conferences on contraception, 1908–68', *Theology* 123 (2020), 95–103, discusses successive resolutions at 96–7. Fine background discussion is T. W. Jones, *Sexual Politics in the Church of England, 1857–1957* (Oxford, 2012), ch. 5.
9. Jones, *The Business of Birth Control*, 106, and further on Dawson, Borge, *Protective Practices*, 71. He had attended St Paul's School, founded 1509.
10. Sedgwick, 'Lambeth Conferences on contraception, 1908–68', 98.
11. A. Moeller, 'Eugenics and the approval of birth control at the 1930 Lambeth Conference', *JEH* 75 (2024), 96–115.
12. Borge, *Protective Practices*, 105, 220.
13. Jones, *Sexual Politics in the Church of England*, 159–60. On the importance of Bishop Kirk in the 1930 decisions, Sedgwick, 'Lambeth Conferences on contraception, 1908–68', 97–98, 101.
14. Borge, *Protective Practices*, 129, 137. On the Fishers and the by-laws, Jones, *The Business of Birth Control*, 192–5, 198.
15. K. L. Slominski, *Teaching Moral Sex: A history of religion and sex education in the United States* (New York, 2021), 14, 141, 151, 153.
16. The quotation is via an anglophone pamphlet on the subject by a prominent clerical popularizer couched in the form of a pastoral correspondence, F. J. Ripley, *Letters to Molly* (Dublin, 1946), 8; I am grateful to David Hilliard for drawing my attention to this.
17. On the background, M. J. Wilde, *Vatican II: A sociological analysis of religious change* (Princeton, NJ, 2007), 116–25; R. McClory, *Turning Point: The inside story of the Papal Birth Control Commission, and how Humanae Vitae changed the life of Patty Crowley and the future of the Church* (New York, 1995), esp. chs. 11, 14.
18. See the minority report text at 'B. The Value and Dignity of the Church's Teaching Authority': http://www.bostonleadershipbuilders.com/ochurch/

birth-control-minority.htm (accessed 27 Nov. 2023; I am grateful to Judith Maltby for pointing me to this source).

19. L. W. Tentler, *Catholics and Contraception: An American history* (Ithaca, NY, 2018), 231.
20. N. Atkin and F. Tallett, *Priests, Prelates and People: A history of European Catholicism since 1750* (London, 2003), 297–8.
21. A point made by Morland, *Human Tide*, 9–10.
22. F. J. Beltrán Tapia and M. Szołtysek, '"Missing girls" in historical Europe: reopening the debate', *The History of the Family* 27 (2022), 619–57. For the earlier European picture, see G. Hanlon, *Death Control in the West, 1500–1800: Sex ratios at baptism in Italy, France and England* (London and New York 2022), and for a survey of the implications of the contraceptive revolution in one society, see H. Cook, *The Long Sexual Revolution: English women, sex, and contraception 1800–1975* (Oxford, 2004).
23. *Bebb* v. *The Law Society* [1914]; there is an extensive literature around this case, among which a good contextual study is R. Auchmuty, 'Whatever happened to Miss Bebb? *Bebb* v. *The Law Society* and women's legal history', *Legal Studies* 31 (2011), 199–230.
24. J. Ryan, *Irish Monasticism: Origins and early development* (Dublin and Cork, 1931), 142.
25. R. Saunders, '"A great and holy war": religious routes to women's suffrage, 1909–14', *English Historical Review* 134 (2019), 1,471–502; Jones, *Sexual Politics in the Church of England*, 79–88.
26. T. W. Jones, 'Love, honour and obey? Romance, subordination and marital subjectivity in interwar Britain', in A. Harris and T. W. Jones (eds), *Love and Romance in Britain, 1915–1970* (London, 2014), 124–43.
27. On 19th-century American initiatives, see A. Braude, *Sisters and Saints: Women and American religion* (Oxford, 2008), 98. E. Kaye, 'A turning-point in the ministry of women: the ordination of the first woman to the Christian ministry in England in September 1917', in W. J. Sheils and D. Wood (eds), *Women in the Church*, Studies in Church History 27 (Woodbridge, 1990), 505–12. On deaconesses, H. Blackmore (ed.), *The Beginning of Women's Ministry: The revival of the deaconess in the 19th-century Church of England*, Church of England Record Society 14 (Woodbridge, 2007).
28. Jones, *Sexual Politics in the Church of England*, 103–6. On Czechoslovakia: M. T. Winter, *Out of the Depths: The story of Ludmila Javorova, ordained Roman Catholic priest* (New York, 2001).
29. The tale is told with empathetic analysis in J. Shaw, *Octavia, Daughter of God: The story of a female messiah and her followers* (London, 2011).
30. On Lenshina, B. Sundkler and C. Steed, *A History of the Church in Africa* (Cambridge, 2000), 790, 974. For Mwerinde and the Marian Movement, E. K. Twesigye, *Religion, Politics and Cults in East Africa: God's warriors and Mary's saints* (New York, 2010), esp. chs. 1, 6–7.

31. Anderson, *Introduction to Pentecostalism*, 56–7.
32. Braude, *Sisters and Saints*, 100. On Utley, T. A. Robinson, *Preacher Girl: Uldine Utley and the industry of revival* (Waco, Tex., 2016), and for the wider phenomenon, T. A. Robinson and L. D. Ruff, *Out of the Mouths of Babes: Girl evangelists in the Flapper era* (New York and Oxford, 2012).

19. CHOICES AND *LADY CHATTERLEY*

1. On the pre-arrangement, see remarks of Jonathan Sumption in reviewing I. Bing, *The Ten Legal Cases that made Modern Britain* (London, 2022), *Times Literary Supplement*, 2 Sept. 2022, 10. On Anglican involvement, M. Roodhouse, 'Lady Chatterley and the monk: Anglican radicals and the Lady Chatterley trial of 1960', *JEH* 59 (2008), 475–500.
2. J. Nurser, *For All Peoples and All Nations: Christian Churches and human rights* (Geneva, 2005).
3. With rueful honesty, Bishop Robinson quoted these enthusiastic remarks in a new preface to a second edition of his collected essays (first published in 1960), *On Being the Church in the World* (London, 1969), 9. On the USA, R. T. Handy, *A History of the Churches in the United States and Canada* (Oxford, 1976), 396.
4. L. Fuller, 'Catholicism in 20th-century Ireland: from "an atmosphere steeped in the faith" to *à la carte* Catholicism', *Journal of Religion in Europe* 5 (2012), 484–513, at 485–8. A vivid account of that period and what happened next is F. O'Toole, *We Don't Know Ourselves: A personal history of Ireland since 1958* (London, 2021).
5. M. Chapman, 'Enjoying what comes naturally: the Church of England and sexuality in the 1930s', in C. Cubitt, C. Methuen and A. Spicer (eds), *The Church, Hypocrisy and Dissimulation*, Studies in Church History 60 (Cambridge, 2024), 453–76.
6. M. Grimley, 'Law, morality and secularisation: the Church of England and the Wolfenden Report, 1954–1967', *JEH* 60 (2009), 725–41 (on Fisher, see 727–38); J. Meek, 'Scottish Churches, morality and homosexual law reform', *JEH* 66 (2015), 596–613. On Bailey's summary essay in J. Tudor Rees and H. V. Usill (eds), *They Stand Apart: A critical survey of the problem of homosexuality* (London, 1955), 36–63, see the cautious remarks of Judge J. Tudor Rees in the Introduction, p. ix; the clergyman's contribution was the least paranoid contribution to the collection, which is a remarkable and sobering period piece. For further useful background, see L. Sefton-Minns and M. H. Johnson, 'Attitudes to male homosexuality within the British Medical Association in the 1950s', *JOH* 71 (2024), 545–73.
7. Ramsey to Suzanne Goodhew, then wife of the Conservative MP for St Albans, 30 June 1965: M. Barber and S. Taylor with G. Sewell (eds), *From the Reformation to the Permissive Society: A miscellany in celebration of*

the 400th Anniversary of Lambeth Palace Library, Church of England Record Society 18 (Woodbridge, 2010), 678.

8. K. L. Slominski, *Teaching Moral Sex: A history of religion and sex education in the United States* (New York, 2021), 164–5, 171–4, 178–86, 194, 212.
9. G. Parsons, 'How the times they were a-changing: exploring the context of religious transformation in the 1960s', in J. Wolffe (ed.), *Religion in History: Conflict, conversion and coexistence* (Manchester, 2004), 161–89, at 164, and H. McLeod, *The Religious Crisis of the 1960s* (Oxford, 2007), 169–75.
10. McLeod, *Religious Crisis of the 1960s*, 92–9.
11. A. Stell, 'Panic of proximity: antigay evangelical discourse on the Metropolitan Community Churches in the 1970s', *Theology and Sexuality*, forthcoming. An early account of the MCC's development, written from within the heartland of conservative Evangelicalism and so itself now an historical primary source of interest, is R. M. Enroth and G. E. Jamison, *The Gay Church* (Grand Rapids, Mich., 1974).
12. A well-informed account by Sean Gill of the movement's origins and history is S. Gill (ed.), *The Lesbian and Gay Christian Movement: campaigning for justice, truth and love* (London, 1998), 2–109. In necessary disclosure, I was involved in the early stages of GCM's development.
13. This mordant coinage of the Anglo-Catholic socialist priest Fr Kenneth Leech began differently ordered, as 'lace, gin and backbiting', in Leech's letter to the *Catholic Standard* (Nov. 1975), 3, then reported in the *Church Times*, 12 Dec. 1975. Popular usage gave it the more punchy formulation; see K. Leech, 'Beyond gin and lace: homosexuality and the Anglo-Catholic subculture', in *Speaking Love's Name: Homosexuality: some Catholic and socialist reflections*, Jubilee Group Pamphlets (London, 1988), 16–27, at 16. Matthew Bemand-Qureshi helped me excavate this intellectual genealogy.
14. See W. Whyte, 'OutRage! Hypocrisy, episcopacy, and homosexuality in England, 1968–1995', in K. Cubitt (ed.), *The Church and Hypocrisy*, Studies in Church History 60 (forthcoming).
15. J. Cornwell, *The Pope in Winter: The dark face of John Paul II's papacy* (London, 2004), 234–46.
16. F. Martel, *In the Closet of the Vatican: Power, homosexuality, hypocrisy* (London, 2019), 279–97, and 82, 123. For a summary discussion of the whole problem against a long-term background, see J. Cornwell, *The Dark Box: A secret history of confession* (London, 2014), ch. 10.
17. Vatican Press Office statement, 19 May 2006: clumsily translated from the Italian http://nationalcatholicreporter.org/update/maciel_communique.pdf (accessed 19 Dec. 2023).
18. A phrase of the novelist John Banville, reviewing O'Toole, *We Don't Know Ourselves*, *Times Literary Supplement*, 17 Dec. 2021, 3–4.
19. Fuller, 'Catholicism in 20th-century Ireland', 497, 504, 507; C. Gribben, *The Rise and Fall of Christian Ireland* (Oxford, 2021), 205–6.

20. While there is as yet no monograph on the Ball affair, a devastating account of his activities is provided by Dame Moira Gibb's independent report, 'An abuse of faith', commissioned by the Church of England: churchofengland.org/sites/default/files/2017-11/the-independent-peter-ball-review.pdf (accessed 11 Jan. 2024).
21. A scathing newspaper article on the Bash Camp atmosphere from a female Evangelical insider and first-hand witness is A. Atkins, 'Inside the sexual apartheid of John Smyth's summer camps', *Daily Telegraph*, 3 Feb. 2017.
22. Currently the best way of following the story is the Independent Report, J. Pickles and G. Woods, *Review into the Abuse by John Smyth of Pupils and Former Pupils of Winchester College* (Winchester, 2021), commissioned by the College and published with admirable honesty on the internet: https://www.winchestercollege.org/assets/files/uploads/john-smyth-review-winchester-college-jan-2022-final.pdf (accessed 2 Dec. 2023).
23. A sympathetic analysis of Johnston is A. Atherstone, 'Christian family, Christian nation: Raymond Johnston and Nationwide Festival of Light in defence of the family', in J. Doran, C. Methuen and A. Walsham (eds), *Religion and the Household*, Studies in Church History 50 (Woodbridge, 2014), 456–68. On the failure of Fundamentalism in 20th-century UK, M. M. Ruotsila, 'The last embers of British fundamentalism', *JEH* 74 (2023), 349–69.
24. J. Prestidge, 'Housewives having a go: Margaret Thatcher, Mary Whitehouse and the appeal of the right wing woman in late twentieth-century Britain', *Women's History Review* 28 (2019), 277–96.
25. J. Weeks, *Sex, Politics, and Society: The regulations of sexuality since 1800* (3rd edn, London, 2012), 378.
26. B. A. Brasher, *Encyclopedia of Fundamentalism* (New York and London, 2001), 18, and cf. ibid., xvii, 16–17, 292–3. For a series of essays exploring commonalities in Fundamentalism, see J. D. G. Dunn (ed.), *Fundamentalisms: Threats and ideologies in the modern world* (London, 2015).
27. G. M. Marsden, *Understanding Fundamentalism and Evangelicalism* (Grand Rapids, Mich., 1991), 1: a description opportunistically adopted by the veteran Evangelical politician Jerry Falwell.
28. S. Bates, *A Church at War: Anglicans and homosexuality* (London, 2004), 129–30; see also ibid., 136–7.
29. For background, I. Breward, *A History of the Churches in Australasia* (Oxford, 2001), 253–4, 303–7; C. McGillion, *The Chosen Ones: The politics of salvation in the Anglican Church* (Sydney, 2005) and M. Porter, *Sydney Anglicans and the Threat to World Anglicanism: The Sydney experiment* (London, 2016).
30. D. Hilliard, 'Gender roles, homosexuality, and the Anglican Church in Sydney', in Swanson (ed.), *Gender and Christian Religion*, 509–23.
31. Bates, *A Church at War*, 206–7.

32. A. Krawchuk, 'Homophobia in Orthodox contexts: socio-political variables and theological strategies for change', in Arentzen et al. (eds), *Orthodox Tradition and Human Sexuality*, 172–91, at 174, 186.
33. J. Bruner and D. C. Kirkpatrick, 'Intra-Christian violence and the problematization of the World Christian paradigm', *JEH* 74 (2023), 370–97, at 389–97.
34. For the Ugandan background, E. K. Twesigye, *Religion, Politics and Cults in East Africa: God's warriors and Mary's saints* (New York, 2010), 2–3, 22–44, 74–83, 91–129. Twesigye is entertaining in his impatience with Victorian missionary rivalries.
35. Useful background in K. Koschorke, F. Ludwig and M. Delgado (eds), *A History of Christianity in Asia, Africa, and Latin America 1450–1990: A documentary sourcebook* (Grand Rapids, Mich. and Cambridge, 2007), 201–4.
36. J. Prager, *The Family Roe: An American story* (New York, 2021), chs. 3–4.
37. Ibid., 33–4; R. Todd Peters, *Trust Women: A progressive Christian argument for reproductive justice* (Boston, Mass., 2018), 102–12.
38. On Betty Ford, L. P. Ribuffo, 'Family policy past as prologue: Jimmy Carter, the White House Conference on Families, and the mobilization of the New Christian Right', *Review of Policy Research* 23 (2006), 311–37, at 319. See background commentary by D. Friedell, reviewing Prager, *The Family Roe*, in *London Review of Books*, 23 June 2022, 13–18, at 13.
39. Ribuffo, 'Family policy past as prologue', 320–25.
40. R. Freedman, 'The religious Right and the Carter administration', *HJ* 48 (2005), 231–60, esp. 231 (quotation), 236–8. On Schaeffer, see E. S. Johnson, *This is Our Message: Women's leadership in the new Christian Right* (New York, 2019), 86–7.
41. M. Bourdeaux and A. Popescu, 'The Orthodox Church and Communism', in M. Angold (ed.), *The Cambridge History of Christianity 5: Eastern Christianity* (Cambridge, 2006), 558–79, at 575.
42. C. Andrew and V. Mitrokhin, *The Mitrokhin Archive II: The KGB and the World* (London, 2005), 490–91, and Pls 23 and 24.
43. D. Healey, *Russian Homophobia from Stalin to Sochi* (London, 2018), 7–8, ch. 6.
44. Ibid., 6–15.
45. Levin, *Sex and Society in the World of the Orthodox Slavs*, 203–5.
46. Krawchuk, 'Homophobia in Orthodox contexts', 179, 189 n. 21; see also P. Elie, 'The Pope, the Patriarchs and the battle to save Ukraine', *New Yorker*, 12 March 2022.
47. E. Tsalampouni, 'Biblical and same-sex traditions: a difficult hermeneutical path', in Arentzen et al. (eds), *Orthodox Tradition and Human Sexuality*, 79–101, at 79 and 93 n. 1. In the same volume, see also P. Kalaitzidis, 'Civil marriage and civil union from an ecclesial perspective: the case of the Orthodox Church of Greece', 105–43, and B. E. Rich,

'Something new under the sun: sexualities, same-sex relationships, and Orthodoxy', 46–65, at 56.

48. H. Ventis, 'The antinomic eschatological transfiguration of Christian eros and sexuality', in Arentzen et al. (eds), *Orthodox Tradition and Human Sexuality*, 265–80, at 276.
49. Johnson, *This is Our Message*, 47, 70, 96–118.
50. Ibid., 110–20.
51. From the homily of Fr Arturo Sosa, SJ, current Father General of the Society of Jesus, preaching at Campion Hall, Oxford, 13 April 2023.

20. A STORY WITHOUT AN ENDING

1. R. Hutton, *Queens of the Wild: Pagan goddesses in Christian Europe, an investigation* (New Haven, Conn. and London, 2022), 30, 33; the book's demolition of 'pagan' archetypes extends to the much-romanticized 'Green Man' as a gender bonus. On the modern origins of witchcraft, Wicca, etc., see the affectionate analysis in R. Hutton, *The Triumph of the Moon: A history of modern pagan witchcraft* (Oxford, 1999), esp. chs. 11 and 12.
2. For examples, see the absorbing analyses of S. Thumma, 'Negotiating a religious identity: the case of the gay Evangelical', *Sociological Analysis* 52 (1991), 333–47, and T. Wijaya Mulya, 'On being LGBT-affirming Pentecostals: exploring affirming resources from within Indonesian Pentecostal Churches', *Theology and Sexuality* 29 (2023), 34–51.
3. R. Williams, 'The body's grace', Michael Harding Memorial Lecture, London, 1989, in a text perhaps now difficult of access but conveniently reprinted in C. C. Hefling (ed.), *Our Selves, Our Souls and Bodies: Sexuality and the household of God* (Cambridge, Mass., 1996), 58–68, at 66. I am grateful to Helen King for reminding me of it.
4. C. S. Lewis, *Mere Christianity* (London, 1952), 67. For further crisp and sceptical discussion of Christian attitudes to usury, see E. Kerridge, *Usury, Interest and the English Reformation* (Aldershot, 2002), ch. 1.
5. Thomas K. Burch (1934–2022), academic demographer, Canadian participant in the Pontifical Commission on birth control, 1964–6, was reviewing R. McClory, *Turning Point: The inside story of the Papal Birth Control Commission, and how Humanae Vitae changed the life of Patty Crowley and the future of the Church* (New York, 1995), in *Population and Development Review* 21 (1995), 882–5.
6. In this I have been much helped by discussion with Professor Mark Chapman, whose major book on modern Anglican theology and homosexuality we await. Meanwhile a crisp distillation of his arguments is to be found at https://viamedia.news/2022/05/04/its-not-just-about-the-bible/ (accessed 13 Dec. 2023).

7. The document, specifically a response to formal *dubia* (dissenting statements) raised by certain conservative cardinals, may be accessed in English at https://press.vatican.va/content/salastampa/it/bollettino/pubblico/2023/12/18/0901/01963.html#en (accessed 19 Dec. 2023). For the 2nd-century Church, see above, Ch. 10, pp. 200–201.
8. Mark 12.24–25, with parallels in Matt. 22.29–30; Luke 20.34–36; see also above, Ch. 7, p. 115.

Index of Biblical References

Books listed in alphabetical order from the Hebrew Bible/Scripture/Tanakh or Old Testament, New Testament and Apocrypha. The 150 Psalms are numbered after the Hebrew number pattern.

General Index

All dates are CE unless stated as BCE. Monarchs are gathered under their principal territory, Archbishops of Canterbury under Canterbury, Oecumenical Patriarchs under Constantinople, Patriarchs of the Church of the East under Church of the East and Popes under Rome, Bishops of. Biblical, legendary and mythological figures are not generally identified by date. Monarchs and Popes have (where possible or appropriate) their birth-date followed by the date of their accession to the throne, followed by their date of death. Members of European nobility are indexed under their surnames. Those who have been declared saints by one or other Christian Church are indexed either under their first names or their surnames, not at 'Saint'.